Lecture Notes in Computer Sci
Edited by G. Goos, J. Hartmanis, and J. va

T0250662

Springer
Berlin
Heidelberg
New York
Barcelona
Hong Kong
London
Milan
Paris
Tokyo

Agostino Cortesi (Ed.)

Verification, Model Checking, and Abstract Interpretation

Third International Workshop, VMCAI 2002
Venice, Italy, January 21-22, 2002
Revised Papers

Springer

Series Editors

Gerhard Goos, Karlsruhe University, Germany
Juris Hartmanis, Cornell University, NY, USA
Jan van Leeuwen, Utrecht University, The Netherlands

Volume Editor

Agostino Cortesi
Università Ca' Foscari di Venezia
Dipartimento di Informatica
Via Torino 155, 30170 Mestre-Venezia, Italy
E-mail: cortesi@dsi.unive.it

Cataloging-in-Publication Data applied for

Die Deutsche Bibliothek - CIP-Einheitsaufnahme

Verification, model checking, and abstract interpretation : third international workshop ; revised papers / VMCAI 2002, Venice, Italy, January 21 - 22, 2002. Agostino Cortesi (ed.). - Berlin ; Heidelberg ; New York ; Barcelona ; Hong Kong ; London ; Milan ; Paris ; Tokyo : Springer, 2002
(Lecture notes in computer science ; Vol. 2294)
ISBN 3-540-43631-6

CR Subject Classification (1998): F.3.1-2, D.3.1, D.2.4

ISSN 0302-9743
ISBN 3-540-43631-6 Springer-Verlag Berlin Heidelberg New York

This work is subject to copyright. All rights are reserved, whether the whole or part of the material is concerned, specifically the rights of translation, reprinting, re-use of illustrations, recitation, broadcasting, reproduction on microfilms or in any other way, and storage in data banks. Duplication of this publication or parts thereof is permitted only under the provisions of the German Copyright Law of September 9, 1965, in its current version, and permission for use must always be obtained from Springer-Verlag. Violations are liable for prosecution under the German Copyright Law.

Springer-Verlag Berlin Heidelberg New York
a member of BertelsmannSpringer Science+Business Media GmbH

http://www.springer.de

© Springer-Verlag Berlin Heidelberg 2002
Printed in Germany

Typesetting: Camera-ready by author, data conversion by Boller Mediendesign
Printed on acid-free paper SPIN 10722206 06/3142 5 4 3 2 1 0

Preface

This volume contains the revised version of papers presented at VMCAI 2002, the Third International Workshop on Verification, Model Checking, and Abstract Interpretation, Venice (Italy), January 21-22, 2002.

The main goal of the workshop was to give an overview of the main directions decisive for the growth and cross-fertilization of major research activities in program analysis and verification.

The VMCAI series was started in 1997 with the aim of gathering researchers interested in investigating similarities and differences among these three research methodologies, that may be summarized as follows:

- program verification aims at proving that programs meet their specifications, i.e., that the actual program behavior corresponds to the desired one.
- model checking is a specific approach to the verification of temporal properties of reactive and concurrent systems, which has been very successful in the area of finite-state programs.
- abstract interpretation is a method for designing and comparing semantics of program, expressing various types of program properties; in particular, it has been successfully used to infer run-time program properties that can be valuable in optimizing programs.

The program committee selected 22 papers out of 41 submissions on the basis of at least 3 reviews. The principal selection criteria were relevance, quality, and clarity. The resulting volume offers the reader an interesting perspective of the current research trends in the area. In particular, the papers contribute to the following topics: Security and Protocols, Timed Systems and Games, Static Analysis, Optimizations, Types and Verification, and Temporal Logics and Systems.

The quality of the papers, the interesting discussions at the workshop, and the friendly atmosphere enjoyed by all participants in Venice, encouraged us in the project of making VMCAI an annual privileged forum for researchers in the area.

Special thanks are due to the institutions that sponsored the event: the Computer Science Department of the University Ca' Foscari, the European Association for Programming Languages and Systems (EAPLS), the MIUR Project "Interpretazione Astratta, Type Systems e Analisi Control-Flow" and the MIUR Project "Metodi Formali per la Sicurezza - MEFISTO". We are especially grateful to C. Braghin for her helpful support in organizing the workshop.

March 2002 Agostino Cortesi

Program Committee Chair

Agostino Cortesi	Univ. Ca' Foscari - Venezia (Italy)

Program Committee

Annalisa Bossi	Univ. Ca' Foscari
Dennis Dams	Bell Labs and TU Eindhoven
Javier Esparza	TU Munchen
Chris Hankin	Imperial College
Joxan Jaffar	NU Singapore
Thomas Jensen	Irisa Rennes
Cosimo Laneve	Univ. di Bologna
Baudouin Le Charlier	UC Louvain La Neuve
Michael Leuschel	Univ. of Southampton
Giorgio Levi	Univ. di Pisa
Torben Mogensen	DIKU, Copenhagen
Supratik Mukhopadhyay	Univ. of Pennsylvania
Thomas Reps	Univ. of Wisconsin
Hanne Riis Nielson	TU of Denmark
David Schmidt	Kansas State University
Pascal Van Hentenryck	Brown University

Additional Referees

Busi Nadia
Charatonik Witold
Thao Dang
Di Pierro Alessandra
Elphick Daniel
Faella Marco
Ferrari Gianluigi
Giacobazzi Roberto
Godefroid Patrice
Gori Roberta
Hansen Michael R.
Hansen Rene Rydhof
Khoo Siau-Cheng
La Torre Salvatore
Levi Francesca
Levin Vladimir
Lovengreen Hans Henrik
Maggiolo Schettini Andrea
Maier Patrick
Martinelli Fabio
Murano Aniello
Namjoshi Kedar
Ngan Chin Wei
Pinna Michele
Ravi Kavita
Roychoudhury Abhik
Sacerdoti Coen Claudio
Scozzari Francesca
Sharygina Natasha
Sokolsky Oleg
Spoto Fausto
Steffen Martin
Sun Hongyan
Taguchi Kenji
Thiagarajan P.S.
Tronci Enrico
Varea Mauricio
Voicu Razvan
Xiaoqun Du
Zavattaro Gianluigi

Table of Contents

Security and Protocols

Combining Abstract Interpretation and Model Checking for Analysing Security Properties of Java Bytecode 1
Cinzia Bernardeschi, Nicoletta De Francesco

Proofs Methods for Bisimulation Based Information Flow Security 16
Riccardo Focardi, Carla Piazza, Sabina Rossi

A Formal Correspondence between Offensive and Defensive JavaCard Virtual Machines 32
Gilles Barthe, Guillaume Dufay, Line Jakubiec, Simão Melo de Sousa

Analyzing Cryptographic Protocols in a Reactive Framework 46
R.K. Shyamasundar

Timed Systems and Games

An Abstract Schema for Equivalence-Checking Games 65
Li Tan

Synchronous Closing of Timed SDL Systems for Model Checking 79
Natalia Sidorova, Martin Steffen

Automata-Theoretic Decision of Timed Games 94
Marco Faella, Salvatore La Torre, Aniello Murano

Static Analysis

Compositional Termination Analysis of Symbolic Forward Analysis 109
Witold Charatonik, Supratik Mukhopadhyay, Andreas Podelski

Combining Norms to Prove Termination 126
Samir Genaim, Michael Codish, John Gallagher, Vitaly Lagoon

Static Monotonicity Analysis for λ-definable Functions over Lattices 139
Andrzej S. Murawski, Kwangkeun Yi

A Refinement of the Escape Property 154
Patricia M. Hill, Fausto Spoto

Optimizations

Storage Size Reduction by In-place Mapping of Arrays 167
Remko Tronçon, Maurice Bruynooghe, Gerda Janssens, Francky Catthoor

Verifying BDD Algorithms through Monadic Interpretation 182
Sava Krstić, John Matthews

Improving the Encoding of LTL Model Checking into SAT 196
Alessandro Cimatti, Marco Pistore, Marco Roveri, Roberto Sebastiani

Types and Verification

Automatic Verification of Probabilistic Free Choice 208
Lenore Zuck, Amir Pnueli, Yonit Kesten

An Experiment in Type Inference and Verification by Abstract Interpretation 225
Roberta Gori, Giorgio Levi

Weak Muller Acceptance Conditions for Tree Automata 240
Salvatore La Torre, Aniello Murano, Margherita Napoli

A Fully Abstract Model for Higher-Order Mobile Ambients 255
Mario Coppo, Mariangiola Dezani-Ciancaglini

Temporal Logics and Systems

A Simulation Preorder for Abstraction of Reactive Systems 272
Ferucio Laurenţiu Ţiplea, Aurora Ţiplea

Approximating ATL* in ATL 289
Aidan Harding, Mark Ryan, Pierre-Yves Schobbens

Model Checking Modal Transition Systems Using Kripke Structures 302
Michael Huth

Parameterized Verification of a Cache Coherence Protocol: Safety and Liveness 317
Kai Baukus, Yassine Lakhnech, Karsten Stahl

Author Index 331

Combining Abstract Interpretation and Model Checking for Analysing Security Properties of Java Bytecode

Cinzia Bernardeschi and Nicoletta De Francesco

Dipartimento di Ingegneria della Informazione
Università di Pisa, Via Diotsalvi 2, 56126 Pisa, Italy
{cinzia, nico}@iet.unipi.it

Abstract. We present an approach enabling end-users to prove security properties of the Java bytecode by statically analysing the code itself, thus eliminating the run time check for the access permission. The approach is based on the combination of two well-known techniques: abstract interpretation and model checking. By means of an operational abstract semantics of the bytecode, we built a finite transition system embodying security informations and abstracting from actual values. Then we model check it against some formulae expressing security properties. We use the SMV model checker. A main point of the paper is the definition of the properties that the abstract semantics must satisfy to ensure the absence of security leakages.

1 Introduction and Motivation

Java Virtual Machine Language (referred to hereafter as JVML) [12] is becoming a widely used medium for distributing platform-independent programs. In multilevel secure systems, the problem of the disclosure of sensitive information of programs written in JVML is particularly important. One of the main motivations is avoiding the damages produced by malicious programs which try to broadcast secret information. Mobile Java bytecode is checked by the Virtual Machine for safety properties: a bytecode Verifier enforces static constraints on Java bytecode to rule out type errors, access control violation, object initialisation failure and other dynamic errors. Moreover, to protect end-users from hostile programs, Java security model assigns access privileges to code and provides a customisable "sandbox" in which Java bytecode runs. At run-time a Java bytecode can do anything within the boundaries of its sandbox, but it can not take any action outside those boundaries.

This paper presents an approach enabling end-users to prove security properties of the Java bytecode by statically analysing the code itself, thus eliminating the run time check for the access permission. The approach is based on the combination of two well-known techniques: abstract interpretation and model checking. *Abstract interpretation* [7] is a method for analyzing programs by collecting approximate information about their run-time behavior. It is based on

A. Cortesi (Ed.): VMCAI 2002, LNCS 2294, pp. 1–15, 2002.
© Springer-Verlag Berlin Heidelberg 2002

a non-standard semantics, that is a semantic definition in which simpler (abstract) domains replace the standard (concrete) ones, and the operations are interpreted on the new domains. Using this approach different analyses can be systematically defined. In particular we refer to abstract interpretation based on operational semantics [7,15]. *Model checking* [6] is an automatic technique for verifying finite state systems. This is accomplished by checking whether a structure, representing the system, satisfies a temporal logic formula describing the expected behavior. The approach combining abstract interpretation and model checking has been defined in [16,17].

In [4] we defined an abstract interpretation based method to check *secure information flow* of a subset of JVML. The secure information flow property [9,1,18,3] requires that information at a given security level does not flow to lower levels. A program, in which every variable is assigned a security level, has secure information flow if, when the program terminates, the value of each variable does not depend on the initial value of the variables with higher security level. Let us suppose that variable `y` has security level higher than that of variable `x`. Examples of violation of secure information flow in high level languages are: `x:=y` and `if y=0 then x:=1 else x:=0`. In the first case, there is an *explicit* information flow from `y` to `x`, while, in the second case there is an *implicit* information flow: in both cases, observing the final value of `x` reveals information on the value of the higher security variable `y`. In [4] a concrete operational semantics of the language is defined, able to keep information flow during execution. The basic ideas on which the semantics is based are: i) values carry a security level which changes dynamically, depending on how the values are manipulated, and ii) implicit flows are modeled by an environment under which the instructions are executed; the environment, at every step of the computation, records the security level of the open implicit flows. Then an abstract operational semantics is defined, which disregards the numerical part of the values, and operates only on their security levels. By examining the final states of the abstract semantics it is possible to check secure information flow.

Other security leakages may occur when high level information is revealed not only by the value of the variables, but by the behavior of the program [10,19]. These leakages are also known as *covert channels*. Consider the program `while (y > 0) do skip`, where `y` is an high variable. It loops indefinitely when `y` is greater than zero. Thus high level information can be leaked by examining the termination behavior of the program. Another leakage is when high level information affects the number of instructions executed during the computations. For example, information on the initial value of the high security variable `y` can be leaked by observing the number of instructions executed by the program `if y=0 then { x:=1; skip } else x:=1` .

Covert channels do not concern the input-output behavior of the program, but its dynamic behavior. They can be checked only by examining the intermediate states of the computations. In the present paper we define an approach to check security of programs, and in particular covert channels, which combines abstract interpretation with model checking: once built the abstract semantics of the program, we inspect it for the security properties. In such a way we fully exploit the information embodied in the abstract semantics, which, being operational, shows (the abstraction of) all possible execution paths of the program. The main point of the paper is the definition of the properties that the abstract semantics must satisfy to ensure the absence of covert channels. The properties are then expressed as temporal logic formualae, and checked by using the SMV model checker [11].

The paper is organised as follows: Section 2 presents the language and the security model. Section 3 defines the concrete and abstract semantics. Section 4 introduces the program security properties and our method. Section 5 concludes the work.

2 The Language and the Security Model

Given a set A, $A^\star$ denotes the set of finite sequences of elements of A; λ indicates the empty sequence; if w is a finite sequence, $\sharp w$ denotes the length of w, i.e. the number of elements of w; $\cdot$ denotes both the concatenation of a value to a sequence and the standard concatenation operation between sequences. Finally, if $i \in \{1, \ldots, \sharp w\}$, with $w[i]$ we denote the *i-th* element of w. We represent stacks by sequences, with the convention that, if w is a nonempty stack, $w[1]$ is the top element.

Our language is the subset of JVML called JVML0 in [20]. It has an operand *stack*, a *memory* containing the local variables, simple arithmetic instructions and conditional/unconditional jumps. The instructions are reported in Fig. 1, where x ranges over a set *var* of *local variables* and `op` over a set of binary arithmetic operations (`add, sub, ..`). Note that the language supports subroutine calls via the `jsr` and `ret` instructions.

`op`	pop two operands off the stack, perform the operation, and push the result onto the stack
`pop`	discard the top value from the stack
`push` k	push the constant k onto the stack
`load` x	push the value of the variable x onto the stack
`store` x	pop off the stack and store the value into variable x
`if` j	pop off the stack and jump to j if non-zero
`goto` j	jump to j
`jsr` j	at address p, jump to address j and push return address $p+1$ onto the operand stack
`ret` x	jump to the address stored in x
`halt`	stop

Fig. 1. Instruction set

A program is a sequence c of instructions, numbered starting from address 1; $\forall i \in \{1, \cdots, \sharp c\}$, $c[i]$ is the instruction at address i. In the following, we denote by $Var(c)$ the variable names occurring in c. We assume that a program is always executed starting from the instruction $c[1]$ and with an empty operand stack. Moreover, we assume that programs respect the following static constraints, checked the Java bytecode Verifier: no stack overflow and underflow occur, and executions will not jump to undefined addresses.

We give the standard semantics of the language in terms of a Kripke structure [6]. A Kripke structure $K = (Q, Q^0, AP, L, \rightarrow)$ is a 5-tuple where:

Q is a set of states;
$Q^0 \subseteq Q$ is a set of initial states;
AP is a finite set of atomic propositions;
$L : Q \rightarrow 2^{AP}$ is a function that labels each state with the set of atomic propositions true in that state;
$\rightarrow \subseteq Q \times Q$ is a total transition relation on Q which gives the possible transitions between states.

The semantics uses the domain $\mathcal{V}^\epsilon$ of constant values, ranged over by $v, v', ..$ and $\mathcal{A}^\epsilon$ of addresses, ranged over by $i, j, ...$ $\mathcal{V}^\epsilon \cup \mathcal{A}^\epsilon$ is ranged over by $k, k', ...$ For each $X \subseteq var$, $\mathcal{M}^\epsilon_X = X \rightarrow (\mathcal{V}^\epsilon \cup \mathcal{A}^\epsilon)$ is the domain of memories defined on X, ranged over by $m, m', \ldots$. $\mathcal{S}^\epsilon = (\mathcal{V}^\epsilon \cup \mathcal{A}^\epsilon)^\star$ is the domain of stacks, ranged over by $s, s', \ldots$. In the following, $\mathcal{M}^\epsilon = \cup_{X \subseteq var} \mathcal{M}^\epsilon_X$ and, given $m \in \mathcal{M}^\epsilon_X$ and $Y \subseteq X$, $m\!\downarrow_Y$ is the restriction of m to Y.

The domain of the states of the standard semantics is $\mathcal{Q}^\epsilon = \mathcal{A}^\epsilon \times \mathcal{M}^\epsilon \times \mathcal{S}^\epsilon$. A state is given by the value of three variables, PC, MEM and $STACK$, where PC is the program counter, MEM is the memory, and $STACK$ is the operand stack. Each state is labeled by an atomic proposition for each variable, expressing its value. We denote by $\langle i, m, s\rangle$ the state labeled by $PC = i, MEM = m, STACK = s$.

Given a program c and a memory $m_0 \in \mathcal{M}^\epsilon$, the standard semantics of the program is the structure $(\mathcal{Q}^\epsilon, \langle 1, m_0, \lambda\rangle, AP, L, \longrightarrow^\epsilon)$, where $\longrightarrow^\epsilon$ is defined in Fig. 2. The notation $m[k \;/\; x]$ is used in the figure to indicate the memory m' which agrees with m for all variables, except for x, for which it is $m'(x) = k$. Since the program is deterministic, the corresponding structure has only one, possibly infinite, path. We call *final* a state such that $PC = i$ with $c[i] =$ `halt`. Note that self loops on these states are necessary to respect the totality of the transition relation.

We now recall the notion of control flow graph of a program, containing the control flow information among the instructions of the program, and the notion of postdomination and immediate postdomination in directed graphs [2].

Definition 1 (control flow graph). *Given a program c, the* control flow graph *of the program is the directed graph (V, E), where $V = \{1, .., \sharp c + 1\}$ is the set of nodes; and $E \subseteq V \times V$ contains the edge (i, j) if and only if (a) the instruction at address j can be immediately executed after that at address i; or (b) $c[i] =$* `halt` *and $j = \sharp c + 1$. The node $\sharp c + 1$ is the final node of the graph and does not correspond to any instruction.*

$$c[i] = \texttt{op}: \quad \langle i, m, k_1 \cdot k_2 \cdot s\rangle \longrightarrow^{\epsilon} \langle i+1, m, (k_1\ op\ k_2) \cdot s\rangle$$

$$c[i] = \texttt{pop}: \quad \langle i, m, k_1 \cdot s\rangle \longrightarrow^{\epsilon} \langle i+1, m, s\rangle$$

$$c[i] = \texttt{push}\ k: \quad \langle i, m, s\rangle \longrightarrow^{\epsilon} \langle i+1, m, k \cdot s\rangle$$

$$c[i] = \texttt{load}\ x: \quad \langle i, m, s\rangle \longrightarrow^{\epsilon} \langle i+1, m, m(x) \cdot s\rangle$$

$$c[i] = \texttt{store}\ x: \quad \langle i, m, k \cdot s\rangle \longrightarrow^{\epsilon} \langle i+1, m[k\ /\ x], s\rangle$$

$$c[i] = \texttt{goto}\ j: \quad \langle i, m, s\rangle \longrightarrow^{\epsilon} \langle j, m, s\rangle$$

$$c[i] = \texttt{if}\ j: \quad \langle i, m, 0 \cdot s\rangle \longrightarrow^{\epsilon} \langle i+1, m, s\rangle$$

$$c[i] = \texttt{if}\ j: \quad \langle i, m, (k \neq 0) \cdot s\rangle \longrightarrow^{\epsilon} \langle j, m, s\rangle$$

$$c[i] = \texttt{jsr}\ j: \quad \langle i, m, s\rangle \longrightarrow^{\epsilon} \langle j, m, (i+1) \cdot s\rangle$$

$$c[i] = \texttt{ret}\ x: \quad \langle i, m, s\rangle \longrightarrow^{\epsilon} \langle m(x), m, s\rangle$$

$$c[i] = \texttt{halt}: \quad \langle i, m, s\rangle \longrightarrow^{\epsilon} \langle i, m, s\rangle$$

Fig. 2. Standard semantics

Definition 2 (postdomination). *Let i and j be nodes of the control flow graph of a program. We say that node j* postdominates *i, denoted by j pd i, if $j \neq i$ and j is on every path from i to the final node. We say that node j* immediately postdominates *i, denoted by $j =$ipd(i), if j pd i and there is no node r such that j pd r pd i.*

3 Abstract Interpretation

This section presents an instrumented concrete operational semantics of the language, embodying annotations on the information flow, and then an abstraction of this semantics, concentrating only on the information flow aspects and ignoring actual values. We assume a set $\mathcal{L} = \{l, h\}$ of security levels, ordered by $l \subset h$, and with $\sqcup$ we denote the upper bound between levels. We consider annotated programs, where each variable is associated with a security level. A program P is a triple $\langle c, H, L\rangle$ where c is a sequence of instructions, and and H and L are the high and low variables of P, respectively, with $H \cup L = Var(c)$.

The semantics handles values enriched with a security level. During the execution of a program, the security level of a value indicates the least upper bound of the security levels of the explicit and implicit information flows, on which the value depends. Moreover, the semantics executes instructions under a *security environment*, which is a security level. At each moment during the execution, the security environment represents the least upper bound of the security levels of the open implicit flows.

We now introduce the domains of the concrete semantics. $\mathcal{V} = (\mathcal{V}^\epsilon \times \mathcal{L})$ is the domain of concrete values. Concrete values are pairs (v, σ), where $v \in \mathcal{V}^\epsilon$ and $\sigma \in \mathcal{L}$. Low (high) values are those with the form (v, l) (resp. (v, h)). The concrete domain of addresses is $\mathcal{A} = (\mathcal{A}^\epsilon \times \mathcal{L})$. Note that also addresses need to be annotated, since the decision on the address to jump to, can be made depending on high information. For each $x \in var$, $\mathcal{M}_X = X \to (\mathcal{V} \cup \mathcal{A})$ is the domain of concrete memories, ranged over by $M, M', \cdots$ and $\mathcal{S} = (\mathcal{V} \cup \mathcal{A})^\star$ are the concrete operand stacks, ranged over by $S, S', \cdots$. The domain of concrete states is $\mathcal{Q} = \mathcal{L} \times \mathcal{A}^\epsilon \times \mathcal{M} \times \mathcal{S} \times (\mathcal{A}^\epsilon \cup \{0\})$. Each state is a configuration the state variables $\langle ENV, PC, MEM, STACK,\ IPD\rangle$, where ENV is the environment and contains a security level, PC, MEM and $STACK$ are the program counter, the memory and the operand stack, respectively, and IPD is a flag used to handle high implicit flow, as explained below. The transition relation $\longrightarrow$ on the concrete states is shown in Fig. 3.

$$\frac{i = i'}{\langle \sigma, i, M, S, i' \rangle \longrightarrow \langle l, i, M, S, 0 \rangle}$$

$i \neq i'$

$c[i] = \texttt{op}, S = (k_1, \tau_1) \cdot (k_2, \tau_2) \cdot S'$:	$\langle \sigma, i, M, S, i' \rangle \longrightarrow \langle \sigma, i+1, M, (k_1\ op\ k_2, \tau_1 \sqcup \tau_2) \cdot S', i' \rangle$
$c[i] = \texttt{pop}, S = (k, \tau) \cdot S'$:	$\langle \sigma, i, M, S, i' \rangle \longrightarrow \langle \sigma, i+1, M, S', i' \rangle$
$c[i] = \texttt{push}\ k$:	$\langle \sigma, i, M, S, i' \rangle \longrightarrow \langle \sigma, i+1, M, (k, \sigma) \cdot S, i' \rangle$
$c[i] = \texttt{load}\ x, M(x) = (k, \tau)$:	$\langle \sigma, i, M, S, i' \rangle \longrightarrow \langle \sigma, i+1, M, (k, \sigma \sqcup \tau) \cdot S, i' \rangle$
$c[i] = \texttt{store}\ x, S = (k, \tau) \cdot S'$:	$\langle \sigma, i, M, S, i' \rangle \longrightarrow \langle \sigma, i+1, M[(k, \tau)/x], S', i' \rangle$
$c[i] = \texttt{goto}\ j$:	$\langle \sigma, i, M, S, i' \rangle \longrightarrow \langle \sigma, j, M, S, i' \rangle$
$c[i] = \texttt{if}\ j, S = (k \neq 0, \tau) \cdot S'$:	$\langle \sigma, i, M, S, i' \rangle \longrightarrow ((\sigma = l) \wedge (\tau = h))?$ $\langle h, j, up_M(M, i), up_S(S), ipd(i) \rangle : \langle \sigma \sqcup \tau, i+1, M, S, i' \rangle$
$c[i] = \texttt{if}\ j, S = (0, \tau) \cdot S'$:	$\langle \sigma, i, M, S, i' \rangle \longrightarrow ((\sigma = l) \wedge (\tau = h))?$ $\langle h, i+1, up_M(M, i), up_S(S), ipd(i) \rangle : \langle \sigma \sqcup \tau, i+1, M, S, i' \rangle$
$c[i] = \texttt{jsr}\ j$:	$\langle \sigma, i, M, S, i' \rangle \longrightarrow \langle \sigma, j, M, (i+1, \sigma) \cdot S, i' \rangle$
$c[i] = \texttt{ret}\ x, M(x) = (j, \tau)$:	$\langle \sigma, i, M, S, i' \rangle \longrightarrow ((\sigma = l) \wedge (\tau = h))?$ $\langle h, j, up_M(M, i), up_S(S), ipd(i) \rangle : \langle \sigma \sqcup \tau, j, M, S, i' \rangle$
$c[i] = \texttt{halt}$:	$\langle \sigma, i, M, S, i' \rangle \longrightarrow \langle \sigma, i, M, S, i' \rangle$

Fig. 3. Concrete semantics

To keep the security level of a value equal to the security level of the information on which it depends, the semantics modifies the security level of each value pushed onto the operand stack according to the present environment. For example, the execution of `load x` assigns to the value pushed onto the stack the least upper bound between the security level of $M(x)$ and the environment. Note that `jsr` associates the return address pushed onto the stack with the security level of the present environment.

An implicit flow is entered with an `if` or a `ret` instruction. We use the notion of immediate postdomination to control implicit flows. Given an `if` (`ret`) instruction at address i, $ipd(i)$ is the first instruction not affected by the implicit flow, since it represents the point in which the different branches join. Consider an `if` instruction at address i. If this instruction is executed under the low security environment and the value on top of the operand stack is high, then the environment is upgraded to h and $ipd(i)$ is recorded in IPD. Moreover the security level is upgraded of each value held by a variable assigned by a `store` instruction in at least one of the two branches. More precisely, let $W = \{x|c[j] = \texttt{store}\ x$ and j belongs to a path of the control flow graph starting at i and ending at $ipd(i)$, excluding $ipd(i)\}$. For each $x \in W$, if $M(x) = (k, \sigma)$, then $up_M(M, i)(x) = (k, h)$. The contents of the variables not in W is not changed. Upgrading the memory in this way takes into account the fact that a variable may be modified in one branch and not in the other one. Similarly, the security level of each value present in the operand stack is upgraded to h by applying the function up_S. We upgrade the operand stack on entering an implicit flow to take into account the fact that the stack may be manipulated in different ways by the two branches. When the instruction $c[ipd(i)]$ is executed, i.e. when $PC = IPD$, the environment is downgraded and IPD is reset to 0 (corresponding to no instruction). The `ret` x instruction is handled similarly, taking into account the security level of the address stored in x. Note that having only two security levels simplifies the semantics. In fact, if we consider whatever number of levels, IPD would be a stack of addresses, instead of a single address. In our case, a high `if` that depends on another high `if` is already in a high region and the region terminates at the ipd of the outermost `if`. For the same reason, the upgrading of environment, memory and stack, and the modification of IPD is performed only when an `if` (`ret` x) instruction is executed in the low environment, and with a high value on the top of the stack (resp. a high address stored in x).

Given a program $P = \langle c, H, L\rangle$ and a memory $M_0 \in \mathcal{M}$, the concrete semantics of P is the structure with $\langle l, 1, M_0, \lambda, 0\rangle$ as the initial state: it consists of the low environment, the address of the first instruction, the given memory, the empty operand stack and the IPD flag equal to 0.

If we ignore information on security, then the concrete semantics is isomorphic to the standard semantics of the language. The concrete semantics has an only extra case (case $i = i'$ in Fig. 3) concerning the handling of IPD. It is applied when $PC = IPD$ and has the effect of downgrading the environment and resetting IPD. Given a memory $m \in \mathcal{M}_X^\epsilon$ and a concrete memory $M \in \mathcal{M}_X$, we say that they are *consistent* ($M \leftrightarrow m$) if $\forall x \in X : M(x) = (m(x), \tau)$, for some τ. Given a stack $s \in \mathcal{S}^\epsilon$ and a concrete stack $S \in \mathcal{S}$, we say that they are *consistent* ($S \leftrightarrow s$) if $\sharp s = \sharp S$ and $\forall i \in \{1, .., \sharp S\}$, $S[i] = (s[i], \tau)$, for some τ.

Theorem 1 (standard and concrete semantics consistency). *Given a program $P = \langle c, H, L\rangle$, let $M_0 \in \mathcal{M}_{Var(c)}$ and $m_0 \in \mathcal{M}^\epsilon$ such that $M_0 \leftrightarrow m_0$.*

$\langle l, 1, M_0, \lambda, 0\rangle \overset{*}{\longrightarrow} \langle \tau, i, M, S, j\rangle$ *if and only if* $\langle 1, m_0, \lambda\rangle \overset{*}{\longrightarrow}^{\epsilon} \langle i, m, s\rangle$ *with* $M \leftrightarrow m$ *and* $S \leftrightarrow s$.

The purpose of abstract interpretation (or abstract semantics) [7,8] is to correctly approximate the concrete semantics of all executions in a finite way. We now present an abstract operational semantics which is an abstraction of the concrete semantics: concrete values are abstracted by keeping only their security level and disregarding their numerical part. Addresses maintain their identity. All other structures are abstracted consequently.

The domain of values $\mathcal{V} = \mathcal{V}^{\epsilon} \times \mathcal{L}$ is abstracted in the following way: $(\mathcal{V}^{\epsilon})^{\natural} = \{\odot\}$ and $\mathcal{L}^{\natural} = \mathcal{L}$. Thus $\mathcal{V}^{\natural} = \{\odot\} \times \mathcal{L}^{\natural}$ which is isomorphic to $\mathcal{L}$. For every concrete value $(k, \sigma) \in \mathcal{V}$, its abstraction is given by $\alpha_{\mathcal{V}}((k, \sigma)) = (\odot, \sigma) = \sigma$. The domain of addresses $\mathcal{A} = \mathcal{A}^{\epsilon} \times \mathcal{L}$ is abstracted in the following way: $(\mathcal{A}^{\epsilon})^{\natural} = \mathcal{A}^{\epsilon}$ and thus $\mathcal{A}^{\natural} = \mathcal{A} \times \mathcal{L}^{\natural}$ and $\alpha_{\mathcal{A}}((j, \sigma)) = (j, \sigma)$. The abstract memories $\mathcal{M}^{\natural}_X : X \to (\mathcal{V}^{\natural} \cup \mathcal{A}^{\natural})$ are the functions from variable identifiers to abstract values and addresses. The abstraction function on memories $\alpha_{\mathcal{M}} : \mathcal{M}_X \to \mathcal{M}^{\natural}_X$ assigns the abstraction of $M(x)$ to $M^{\natural}(x)$, for each $x \in X$. The domain of stacks $\mathcal{S}^{\natural}$ is defined analogously. The abstract states, $\mathcal{Q}^{\natural}$, contains the abstractions of the components of $\mathcal{Q}$: $\alpha_{\mathcal{Q}} : \mathcal{Q} \to \mathcal{Q}^{\natural}$ is defined as $\alpha_{\mathcal{Q}}(\langle \sigma, i, M, S, j\rangle) = \langle \sigma, i, \alpha_{\mathcal{M}}(M), \alpha_{\mathcal{S}}(S), j\rangle$.

The abstract semantics is defined by the same rules of the concrete semantics, used on the abstract domains. The transition relation of the abstract semantics is denoted by $\longrightarrow^{\natural}$. Note that, for `if` instructions both alternative branches are executed, since every value is abstracted to "$\odot$". Moreover, since addresses maintain their identity, also all possible return points are explored. Given $P = \langle c, H, L\rangle$ we denote by $A(P)$ the abstract transition system defined by the abstract rules and starting from the state $\langle l, 1, M^{\natural}_0, \lambda, 0\rangle$ where $M^{\natural}_0 \in \mathcal{M}_{var(c)}$ is such that $\forall x \in L : M^{\natural}(x) = l$ and $\forall x \in H : M^{\natural}_0(x) = h$. The following theorem states that the abstract semantics mimics all possible concrete executions: the abstraction of every path of a concrete semantics is a path of the abstract one.

Theorem 2 (correctness of the abstract semantics). *Given two concrete states* $Q, Q' \in \mathcal{Q}$, $Q \longrightarrow Q'$ *implies* $\alpha_{\mathcal{Q}}(Q) \longrightarrow^{\natural} \alpha_{\mathcal{Q}}(Q')$.

Note that the abstract semantics is finite. In fact, since security levels, environments and abstract values are finite, then abstract memories are finite too. Abstract operand stacks are finite because we assume stack boundedness.

4 Model Checking the Abstract Semantics

In this section we define some security properties guaranteeing the absence of different security leakages and we show how it is possible to prove them for a program P by model checking the abstract semantics of P for a set of logic formulae.

In the following, we assume a program $P = \langle c, H, L\rangle$. The following property states that the final value of each low variable does not depend on the initial value of the high variables.

Definition 3 (secure information flow). *P satisfies the secure information flow property (SIF) if for each pair of memories* $m_1, m_2 \in \mathcal{M}^{\epsilon}_{Var(c)}$, *with* $m_1 \downarrow_L = m_2 \downarrow_L$,
if $\langle 1, m_1, \lambda \rangle \xrightarrow{*}{}^{\epsilon} \langle i_1, m'_1, s_1 \rangle$ *and* $\langle 1, m_2, \lambda \rangle \xrightarrow{*}{}^{\epsilon} \langle i_2, m'_2, s_2 \rangle$ *with* $c[i_1] = c[i_2] =$ `halt`,
then $m'_1 \downarrow_L = m'_2 \downarrow_L$.

The second property we consider concerns the timing flows due to termination observation [10,19]: it is not possible to leak high information by observing the termination of the program.

Definition 4 (termination agreement). *P satisfies the termination agreement property (TERM) if for each pair of memories* $m_1, m_2 \in \mathcal{M}^{\epsilon}_{Var(c)}$, *with* $m_1 \downarrow_L = m_2 \downarrow_L$,
if $\langle 1, m_1, \lambda \rangle \xrightarrow{*}{}^{\epsilon} \langle i_1, m'_1, s_1 \rangle$ *with* $c[i_1] =$ `halt`, *then* $\langle 1, m_2, \lambda \rangle \xrightarrow{*}{}^{\epsilon} \langle i_2, m'_2, s_2 \rangle$ *with* $c[i_2] =$ `halt`.

The third property concerns timing channels where the number of instructions executed in a computation may reveal information on the value of the high variables.

Definition 5 (timing agreement). *We say that P satisfies the timing agreement property (TIME) if for each pair of memories* $m_1, m_2 \in \mathcal{M}^{\epsilon}_{Var(c)}$, *with* $m_1 \downarrow_L = m_2 \downarrow_L$,
if $\langle 1, m_1, \lambda \rangle \xrightarrow{*}{}^{\epsilon} \langle i_1, m'_1, s_1 \rangle$ *with* $c[i_1] =$ `halt`, *and* $\langle 1, m_2, \lambda \rangle \xrightarrow{*}{}^{\epsilon} \langle i_2, m'_2, s_2 \rangle$ *with* $c[i_2] =$ `halt`, *then the two computations have the same length.*

The following theorems relate the abstract semantics with the above properties.

Theorem 3. *P satisfies SIF if for each state of* $A(P)$ *such that* $c[PC] =$ `halt`, *then* $\forall x \in L, MEM[x] = l$ *or* $MEM[x] = (i, l)$ *for some* i.

Theorem 4. *P satisfies TERM if every state of* $A(P)$ *such that* $ENV = h$ *does not belong to a cycle.*

Theorem 5. *P satisfies TIME if:*

all paths in $A(P)$ *starting from a state satisfying* $STACK[1] = h$ *and* $PC = i$ *where* $c[i] =$ `if` *and ending with a state satisfying* $PC = ipd(i)$ *have the same length.*
all paths in $A(P)$ *starting from a state satisfying* $PC = i$ *and* $MEM[x] = (j, h)$ *where* $c[i] =$ `ret` x *and ending with a state satisfying* $PC = ipd(i)$ *have the same length.*

Theorem 3 states that to check SIF it suffices to examine the final states of the abstract semantics, and, in particular, to check that in these states the low variables hold low values and the stack contains only low values. Theorem 4 says that $TERM$ can be controlled by checking that no instruction is executed more than once under a high environment. Theorem 5 states that, to ensure $TIME$, the branches starting from an `if` instruction at address i with an high condition (the value on top of the stack is h) must have the same length until $ipd(i)$ is reached. A similar condition is stated for `ret` instructions with high return address.

The proof of the above theorems is based on a set of properties of the concrete semantics that we now briefly show. We need some definitions. Two concrete values $(k_1, \sigma_1), (k_2, \sigma_2) \in (\mathcal{V} \cup \mathcal{A})$ are low equivalent ($(k_1, \sigma_1) \sim^{\mathcal{V}} (k_2, \sigma_2)$) if and only if if either they are equal or $\sigma_1 = \sigma_2 = h$. Two concrete memories $M, M' \in \mathcal{M}_X$ are low equivalent ($M \sim^{\mathcal{M}} M'$) if and only if for each $x \in X, M(x) \sim^{\mathcal{V}} M'(x)$. To define low equivalence of operand stacks, we represent them in a canonical form. Each $S \in \mathcal{S}$ is uniquely representable in canonical form as $S = u \cdot w$, where w contains only high values and the bottom element of u is a low value. Two concrete operand stacks $S = u \cdot w$ and $S' = u' \cdot w'$ are low equivalent ($S \sim^{\mathcal{S}} S'$) if and only if
$\sharp u = \sharp u'$ and $\forall i \in \{1, .., \sharp u\} : u[i] \sim^{\mathcal{V}} u'[i]$.

Two operand stacks are low equivalent if and only if the u parts of their canonical representation have the same length and hold low equivalent values in the same positions.

The following lemma states that, if the environment is low, two concrete transitions starting from the same instruction and low equivalent memories and operand stacks, maintain low equivalence of memories and stacks. Moreover, after the transitions, the environments are equal. Finally, if the environment is still low, then also the contents of the program counter is the same and IPD. Instead, if the environment becomes high, then $ipd(i)$ is stored into IPD.

Lemma 1. *Let* $M_1 \sim^{\mathcal{M}} M_2$ *and* $S_1 \sim^{\mathcal{S}} S_2$.
$\langle l, i, M_1, S_1, 0\rangle \rightarrow \langle \tau, i_1, M_1', S_1', j\rangle$ *implies* $\langle l, i, M_2, S_2, 0\rangle \rightarrow \langle \tau, i_2, M_2', S_2', j\rangle$ *with* $M_1' \sim^{\mathcal{M}} M_2'$, $S_1' \sim^{\mathcal{S}} S_2'$, *and,*
if $\tau = l$, *then* $i_1 = i_2$ *and* $j = 0$; *if* $\tau = h$, *then* $j = ipd(i)$

The following lemma states that, in each transition executed under the high security environment, the memory and the operand stack before and after the transition are low equivalent to each other. Moreover, the environment is downgraded only when the instruction at address IPD is executed, and in this case IPD is reset to 0.

Lemma 2. $\langle h, i, M, S, j\rangle \rightarrow \langle \tau, i', M', S', j'\rangle$ *implies* $M \sim^{\mathcal{M}} M', S \sim^{\mathcal{S}} S'$ *and,* *if* $\tau = l$, *then* $i' = j$ *and* $j' = 0$.

The proofs of the Theorems 3, 4 and 5 is based on the following informal reasoning. Consider two standard computations starting from memories that agree on the value of low variables. Consider the corresponding concrete computations, existing by Theorem 1. By Lemma 1, until the environment is low, the two computations perform the same instructions, keep low quivalence of memories and operand stacks, and maintain the same environment and $IPD = 0$. By the same lemma, if one of them upgrades the environment, also the other one do. While executing in the high environment, low equivalence of memory and stacks is maintained by Lemma 2. The proof then follows by considering the abstract computations corresponding to the concrete ones, existing by Theorem 2, and the conditions expressed by the theorems.

4.1 Implementation in SMV

We have used the SMV tool [11] to implement our method. SMV is a tool for checking finite state systems against specifications in the temporal logic CTL [6]. The specifications are assertions on the state variables and on the paths of the system. Using the SMV model checker, the three conditions above can be written as follows:

$$\begin{aligned}\varphi_{SIF} = \wedge_{x \in L} AG((PC = i) \wedge c[i] = \texttt{halt})\\ \rightarrow ((MEM[x] = l) \vee (MEM[x] = (j, l)));\end{aligned}$$

$$\varphi_{TERM} = AG(((PC = i) \wedge (ENV = h)) \rightarrow AG(PC! = i));$$

$$\begin{aligned}\varphi_{TIME} = \; & AG(((PC = i) \wedge (STACK[1] = h) \wedge ((c[i] = \texttt{if}))\\ & \rightarrow \vee_{r=1,..n} X^r(PC = ipd(i))\\ & \wedge AG(((PC = i) \wedge (MEM[x] = (j, h) \wedge (c[i] = \texttt{ret}\ x))\\ & \rightarrow \vee_{r=1,..n} X^r(PC = ipd(i))\end{aligned}$$

where $n = \sharp c$ and $X^r = X ... X$ r times.

We recall that in CTL a state Q satisfies $A\ \phi$ if ϕ is true in all paths starting from Q; Q satisfies $G\ \phi$ if ϕ is true in all states reachable from Q; Q satisfies $X\ \phi$ if ϕ is true in all states reachable from Q by only one transition. The three formulae are the translation in the logic of SMV of the conditions expressed by Theorems 3, 4 and 5. In φ_{TIME}, to check that the lengths of the paths from a state to another one are all equal, we use the sequences of the X operator with length $\leq \sharp c$: the formula is true if $r \leq \sharp c$ exists such that $X^r(PC = ipd(i))$ is true; in this case all paths have length r.

4.2 Examples

Consider programs with $L = \{\texttt{x}\}$ and $H = \{\texttt{y}\}$. Fig. 4 shows a non-secure implicit flow. It corresponds to the program: `if y=0 then x:=1 else x:=0`. Fig. 4(c) shows the abstract structure of the program. $A(P)$ does not satisfy φ_{SIF} nor φ_{TIME}, while φ_{TERM} is satisfied. Fig. 4(b) shows a concrete computation violating SIF.

```
1 load y
2 if 5
3 push 1
4 goto 6
5 push 0
6 store x
7 halt
```

(*a*)

$\langle ENV, PC, [MEM(x)\ MEM(y)], STACK, IPD\rangle$

$\langle l, 1, [(5,l)(1,h)], \lambda, 0\rangle$
$\downarrow_{\texttt{load}}$
$\langle l, 2, [(5,l)(1,h)], (1,h), 0\rangle$
$\downarrow_{\texttt{if}_{\texttt{true}}}$
$\langle h, 5, [(5,l)(1,h)], \lambda, 6\rangle$
$\downarrow_{\texttt{push}}$
$\langle h, 6, [(5,l)(1,h)], (0,h), 6\rangle$
$\downarrow_{\texttt{ipd}}$
$\langle l, 6, [(5,l)(1,h)], (0,h), 0\rangle$
$\downarrow_{\texttt{store}}$
$\langle l, 7, [(0,h)(1,h)], \lambda, 0\rangle$
$\downarrow_{\texttt{halt}}$ $\uparrow$

(*b*)

$\langle l, 1, [(l)(h)], \lambda, 0\rangle$
$\downarrow_{\texttt{load}}$
$\langle l, 2, [(l)(h)], (h), 0\rangle$
$\swarrow_{\texttt{if}_{\texttt{true}}}$ $\searrow_{\texttt{if}_{\texttt{false}}}$
$\langle h, 5, [(l)(h)], \lambda, 6\rangle$ $\langle h, 3, [(l)(h)], \lambda, 6\rangle$
$\downarrow_{\texttt{push}}$
$\downarrow_{\texttt{push}}$ $\langle h, 4, [(l)(h)], h, 6\rangle$
$\downarrow_{\texttt{goto}}$
$\langle h, 6, [(l)(h)], (h), 6\rangle$
$\downarrow_{\texttt{ipd}}$
$\langle l, 6, [(l)(h)], (h), 0\rangle$
$\downarrow_{\texttt{store}}$
$\langle l, 7, [(h)(h)], \lambda, 0\rangle$
$\downarrow_{\texttt{halt}}$ $\uparrow$

(*c*)

Fig. 4. A program not satisfying *SIF*

The program in Fig. 5 is an example of violation of termination agreement. This program terminates depending on the value non-zero or zero of the high security level variable `y`. It corresponds to the high level program: `while (y) do skip`. Fig. 5(b) shows the abstract semantics of the program. Note that it satisfies φ_{SIF}, but not φ_{TERM}: there is a cycle including states with $ENV = h$.

Fig. 6 shows an example of not secure program due to to a timing channel. The number of steps of the program depends on the value of the high security level variable `y`. When the program terminates the low variable `x` always holds `1`. Fig. 6 (b) shows the abstract semantics of the program. It satisfies φ_{SIF} and φ_{TERM}, but it does not satisfy φ_{TIME}.

5 Conclusions

The work [5] presents an approach, based on abstract interpretation and model checking, enabling a smart card issuer to verify that a new applet securely interacts with already downloaded applets. The work concentrates on applet interfaces, therefore the security levels correspond to the possible interactions among applets. Covert channels are not handled and in general the formulae are not general but specific for the particular applet to be verified.

An alternative approach to check secure information flow in assembly code may be developed by defining a typing system for this purpose. Typing systems have been defined for high level languages for example in [19,14]. Typing systems for assembly code have been defined, for example, in [13,20,21], but they check safety and do not handle secure information flow. An advantage of our approach with respect to those based on typing is that it is semantics based and thus keeps information on the dynamic behavior of programs, allowing to check more precisely the desired properties. A further advantage is flexibility: different security properties can be checked on the abstract semantics by expressing them as temporal logic formulae. For example, the condition that a low variable never holds a high value during the computations can be expressed by the formula: $\wedge_{x \in L} AG(MEM[x] = l)$. This condition, that ensures secure information flow, corresponds to that checked by the typing approaches and it is stronger than that expressed in Theorem 3.

$$\langle ENV, PC, [MEM(y)], STACK, IPD \rangle$$

$$\langle l, 1, [(h)], \lambda, 0 \rangle$$
$$\downarrow \text{load}$$
$$\langle l, 2, [(h)], (h), 0 \rangle$$

1 load y $\nearrow$ if$_{\text{false}}$ $\searrow$ if$_{\text{true}}$ $\leftarrow$
2 if 1 $\langle h, 1, [(h)], \lambda, 3 \rangle$ |
3 halt $\downarrow$ load |
                                          $\langle h, 2, [(h)], h, 3 \rangle$ |
(a) $\nearrow$ if$_{\text{false}}$ $\searrow$ if$_{\text{true}}$ |
$\langle h, 3, [(h)], \lambda, 3 \rangle$
$\downarrow$ ipd
$\langle l, 3, [(h)], \lambda, 0 \rangle$
$\downarrow$ halt $\uparrow$
                               (b)

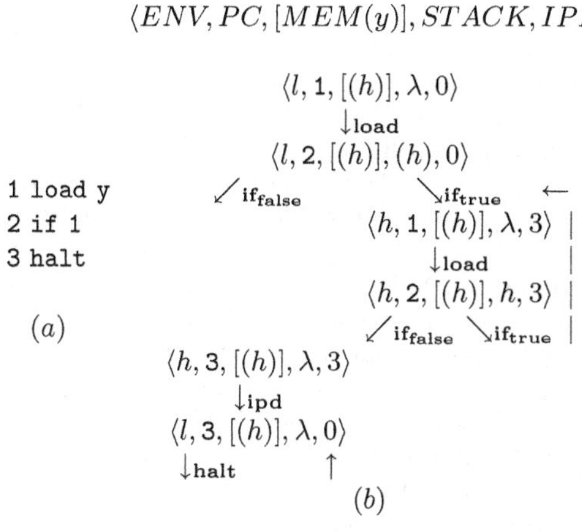

Fig. 5. A program not satisfying $TERM$

References

1. G. R. Andrews, R. P. Reitman. An axiomatic approach to information flow in programs. ACM Transactions on programming languages and systems, 2(1), 1980, pp. 56-76.

$$\langle ENV, PC, [MEM(x)\ MEM(y)], STACK, IPD \rangle$$

$$\langle l, 1, [(l)(h)], \lambda, 0 \rangle$$
$$\downarrow \text{load}$$
$$\langle l, 2, [(l)(h)], (h), 0 \rangle$$

1	load y
2	if 5
3	push 0
4	pop
5	push 1
6	store x
7	halt

(a)

$\nearrow \text{if}_{\text{false}}$ $\downarrow \text{if}_{\text{true}}$

$\langle h, 3, [(l)(h)], \lambda, 5 \rangle$

$\downarrow \text{push}$

$\langle h, 4, [(l)(h)], h, 5 \rangle$

$\searrow \text{pop}$

$$\langle h, 5, [(l)(h)], \lambda, 5 \rangle$$
$$\downarrow \text{ipd}$$
$$\langle l, 5, [(l)(h)], \lambda, 0 \rangle$$
$$\downarrow \text{push}$$
$$\langle l, 6, [(l)(h)], l, 0 \rangle$$
$$\downarrow \text{store}$$
$$\langle l, 7, [(l)(h)], \lambda, 0 \rangle$$
$$\downarrow \text{halt} \qquad \uparrow$$

(b)

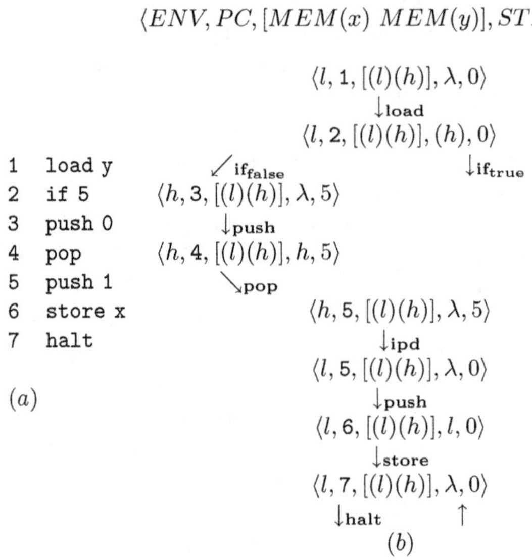

Fig. 6. A program not satisfying $TIME$

2. T. Ball. What's in a region? Or computing control dependence regions in near-linear time for reducible control flow. ACM Letters on Programming languages and Systems, Vol. 2, N. 1-4, 1993, pp. 1-16.
3. R. Barbuti, C. Bernardeschi, N. De Francesco. Abstract Interpretation of Operational Semantics for Secure Information Flow. To appear on Information Processing Letters.
4. R. Barbuti, C. Bernardeschi, N. De Francesco. Checking Security of Java Bytecode by Abstract Interpretation. Proceedings of the Special Track on Security at the ACM Symposium on Applied Computing (SAC2002), March 10-14, Spain 2002, (to appear).
5. P. Bieber, J. Cazin, P. Girard, J-L. Lanet, V.Wiels, G. Zanon. Checking Secure Interactions of Smart Card Applets. Proceedings of ESORICS 2000.
6. E.M. Clarke, E.A. Emerson, A.P. Sistla. Automatic verification of finite-state concurrent systems using temporal logic specifications. *ACM Transactions on programming Languages and Systems*, vol. 8, n. 2, 1986, 244-263.
7. P. Cousot, R. Cousot. Abstract interpretation frameworks. Journal of Logic and Computation, 2, 1992, pp. 511-547.
8. P. Cousot, R. Cousot. Inductive Definitions,Semantics and Abstract interpretations. *Proc. 19th ACM Symposium on Principles of programming languages*, POPL'92, 1992, pp. 83-94.
9. D. E. Denning, P. J. Denning. Certification of programs for secure information flow. Communications of the ACM, 20(7), 1977, pp. 504-513.
10. B.W. Lampson. A note on the confinement problem. Communications of the ACM, Vol. 16, n. 10, 1973, pp. 613-615.
11. K.L. McMillan. The SMV language. Cadence Berkeley Labs, Cadence Design Systems, Berkeley, March 1999.

12. Lindholm T., F. Yellin. The java virtual machine specification. Addison-Wesley, 1996.
13. G. Morrisett, D. Walker, K. Crary, N. Glew. From System F to Typed Assembly Language. ACM Transactions on Programming Languages and Systems, Vol. 21, N. 3, 1999, pp. 527-568.
14. A. Sabelfeld, D. Sands. The impact of synchronization on secure information flow in concurrent programs. Proceedings Andrei Ershov 4th International Conference on Perspective of System Informatics, Novosibirsk, LNCS, Springer-Verlag, July 2001.
15. D. A. Schmidt. Abstract interpretation of small-step semantics. Proceedings 5th LOMAPS Workshop on Analysis and Verification of Multiple-Agent Languages, M. Dam and F. Orava, eds. Springer, 1996.
16. D. A. Schmidt, B. Steffen. Program analysis as model checking of abstract interpretations. Proc. 5th Static Analysis Symposium, G. Levi. ed., Pisa, September, 1998. Springer LNCS 1503.
17. D. A. Schmidt. Data-flow analysis is model checking of abstract interpretations. Proc. 25th ACM Symp. Principles of Programming Languages, San Diego, 1998.
18. D. Volpano, G. Smith, C. Irvine. A sound type system for secure flow analysis. Journal of Computer Security, 4(3), 1996, pp. 167-187.
19. D. Volpano, G. Smith. Eliminating covert flows with minimum typing. Proceedings 10th IEEE Computer Security Security Foundation Workshop, June 1997, pp. 156-168.
20. R. Stata, M. Abadi. A type system for java bytecode subroutine. ACM Transactions on Programming Languages and Systems, Vol. 21, n. 1, 1999, pp. 90-137.
21. Z. Xu, B. P. Miller, T. Reps. Safety Checking of Machine Code. Proceedings ACM SIGPLAN Conference on Programming Language Design and Implementation, Vancouver, Canada, 2000, pp. 70-82.

Proofs Methods for Bisimulation Based Information Flow Security*

Riccardo Focardi, Carla Piazza, and Sabina Rossi

Dipartimento di Informatica, Università Ca' Foscari di Venezia
{focardi,piazza,srossi}@dsi.unive.it

Abstract. *Persistent_BNDC* (*P_BNDC*, for short) is a security property for processes in dynamic contexts, i.e., contexts that can be reconfigured at runtime. We study how to efficiently decide if a process is *P_BNDC*. We exploit a characterization of *P_BNDC* through a suitable notion of *Weak Bisimulation up to high level actions*. In the case of finite-state processes, we study two methods for computing the largest weak bisimulation up to high level actions: (1) via *Characteristic Formulae* and Model Checking for μ-calculus and (2) via *Closure up to a set of actions* and *Strong Bisimulation*. This second method seems to be particularly appealing: it can be performed using already existing tools at a low time complexity.

1 Introduction

Systems are becoming more and more complex, and the security community has to face this by considering, e.g., issues like process mobility among different architectures and systems. A mobile process moving on the network can be influenced and reconfigured by the environments it crosses, possibly leading to new security breaches. A program executing in a "secure way" inside one environment could find itself in a different setting (with different malicious attackers) at runtime, e.g., if the process decides to migrate during its execution.

Persistent_BNDC (*P_BNDC*, for short) [11, 12], is a security property based on the idea of Non-Interference [13] (formalized as *BNDC* [10]), which is suitable to analyze processes in dynamic environments. The basic idea is to require that every state which is reachable by the system still satisfies a basic Non-Interference property. If this holds, we are assured that even if the system migrates during its execution no malicious attacker will be able to compromise it, as every possible reachable state is guaranteed to be secure. This extension of *BNDC* leads to some interesting results, as it can be equivalently defined as a *Weak Bisimulation up to high level actions*. This result, allowing to avoid both the universal quantification over all the possible attackers, present in *BNDC*, and the universal quantification over all possible reachable states, required by the definition of *P_BNDC*, naturally suggests the effective computability of *P_BNDC*.

* Partially supported by the MURST projects "Interpretazione astratta, type systems e analisi control-flow" and "Modelli formali per la sicurezza" and the EU Contract IST-2001-32617 "Models and Types for Security in Mobile Distributed Systems".

A. Cortesi (Ed.): VMCAI 2002, LNCS 2294, pp. 16–31, 2002.
© Springer-Verlag Berlin Heidelberg 2002

In this paper we consider the specific problem of automatically checking *P_BNDC*. In particular, we describe two methods for determining whether a system is *P_BNDC*. The first method is based on the derivation of *Characteristic Formulae* [21, 24] in the language of modal μ-calculus [16]. The characteristic formulae can be automatically verified using model checkers for μ-calculus, such as NCSU Concurrency Workbench [4]. The second method is in the spirit of [24]: it is based on the computation of a sort of transitive closure (*Closure up to high level actions*) of the system and on the verification of a *Strong Bisimulation*. This allows us to use existing tools as a large number of algorithms for computing the largest strong bisimulation between two processes have been proposed [22, 2, 17, 7] and are integrated in model checkers, such as NCSU Concurrency Workbench, XEVE [1], FDR2 [23]. In particular, this second approach improves on the polynomial time complexity of the Compositional Security Checker CoSeC presented in [9], since only one bisimulation test is necessary.

The paper is organized as follows. In Section 2 we recall the *Security Process Algebra* (SPA, for short) and the notions of Strong and Weak bisimulation. In Section 3 we introduce the *P_BNDC* property and we recall its characterization in terms of weak bisimulation up to high level actions. In Section 4 we propose two methods to prove the weak bisimulation up high level actions and we demonstrate some complexity results. Finally, in Section 5 we draw some conclusions.

2 Preliminaries

The *Security Process Algebra* (SPA, for short) [10] is a slight extension of Milner's CCS [20], where the set of visible actions is partitioned into high level actions and low level ones in order to specify multilevel systems. SPA syntax is based on the same elements as CCS that is: a set $\mathcal{L}$ of *visible* actions such that $\mathcal{L} = I \cup O$ where $I = \{a, b, \ldots\}$ is a set of *input* actions and $O = \{\bar{a}, \bar{b}, \ldots\}$ is a set of *output* actions; a special action τ which models internal computations, i.e., not visible outside the system; a complementation function $\bar{\cdot} : \mathcal{L} \to \mathcal{L}$, such that $\bar{\bar{a}} = a$, for all $a \in \mathcal{L}$, and $\bar{\tau} = \tau$; $Act = \mathcal{L} \cup \{\tau\}$ is the set of all *actions*. The set of visible actions is partitioned into two sets, Act_H and Act_L, of high and low level actions such that $\overline{Act_H} = Act_H$ and $\overline{Act_L} = Act_L$, and $Act_H \cup Act_L = \mathcal{L}$ and $Act_H \cap Act_L = \emptyset$. The syntax of SPA *agents* (or *processes*) is defined as follows:

$$E ::= \mathbf{0} \mid a.E \mid E + E \mid E|E \mid E \setminus v \mid E[f] \mid Z$$

where $a \in Act$, $v \subseteq \mathcal{L}$, $f : Act \to Act$ is such that $f(\bar{\alpha}) = \overline{f(\alpha)}$ and $f(\tau) = \tau$, and Z is a constant that must be associated with a definition $Z \stackrel{\text{def}}{=} E$.

Intuitively, $\mathbf{0}$ is the empty process that does nothing; $a.E$ is a process that can perform an action a and then behaves as E; $E_1 + E_2$ represents the non deterministic choice between the two processes E_1 and E_2; $E_1|E_2$ is the parallel composition of E_1 and E_2, where executions are interleaved, possibly synchronized on complementary input/output actions, producing an internal action τ;

$$\text{Prefix}\quad \frac{}{a.E \xrightarrow{a} E}$$

$$\text{Sum}\quad \frac{E_1 \xrightarrow{a} E_1'}{E_1 + E_2 \xrightarrow{a} E_1'} \qquad \frac{E_2 \xrightarrow{a} E_2'}{E_1 + E_2 \xrightarrow{a} E_2'}$$

$$\text{Parallel}\quad \frac{E_1 \xrightarrow{a} E_1'}{E_1|E_2 \xrightarrow{a} E_1'|E_2} \qquad \frac{E_2 \xrightarrow{a} E_2'}{E_1|E_2 \xrightarrow{a} E_1|E_2'} \qquad \frac{E_1 \xrightarrow{a} E_1' \; E_2 \xrightarrow{\bar{a}} E_2'}{E_1|E_2 \xrightarrow{\tau} E_1'|E_2'} \; a \in \mathcal{L}$$

$$\text{Restriction}\quad \frac{E \xrightarrow{a} E'}{E \setminus v \xrightarrow{a} E' \setminus v} \; \text{if } a \notin v$$

$$\text{Relabelling}\quad \frac{E \xrightarrow{a} E'}{E[f] \xrightarrow{f(a)} E'[f]}$$

$$\text{Constant}\quad \frac{E \xrightarrow{a} E'}{A \xrightarrow{a} E'} \; \text{if } A \stackrel{\text{def}}{=} E$$

Fig. 1. The operational rules for SPA

$E \setminus v$ is a process E prevented from performing actions in v[1]; $E[f]$ is the process E whose actions are renamed *via* the relabelling function f.

The operational semantics of SPA agents is given in terms of *Labelled Transition Systems.* A *Labelled Transition System* (LTS) is a triple $(S, A, \rightarrow)$ where S is a set of states, A is a set of labels (actions), $\rightarrow \subseteq S \times A \times S$ is a set of labelled transitions. The notation $(S_1, a, S_2) \in \rightarrow$ (or equivalently $S_1 \xrightarrow{a} S_2$) means that the system can move from the state S_1 to the state S_2 through the action a. The operational semantics of SPA is the LTS $(\mathcal{E}, Act, \rightarrow)$, where the states are the terms of the algebra and the transition relation $\rightarrow \subseteq \mathcal{E} \times Act \times \mathcal{E}$ is defined by structural induction as the least relation generated by the axioms and inference rules reported in Fig. 1. The operational semantics for an agent E is the subpart of the SPA LTS reachable from the initial state E and we refer to it as $LTS(E) = (S_E, Act, \rightarrow)$, where S_E is the set of processes reachable from E. A process E is said to be *finite-state* if S_E is finite.

The concept of *observation equivalence* between two processes is based on the idea that two systems have the same semantics if and only if they cannot be distinguished by an external observer. This is obtained by defining an equivalence relation over $\mathcal{E}$, equating two processes when they are indistinguishable. In the following, we report the definitions of two observation equivalences called *strong bisimulation* and *weak bisimulation* [20].

[1] In CCS the operator $\setminus$ requires that the actions of $E \setminus v$ do not belong to $v \cup \bar{v}$.

Definition 1 (Strong Bisimulation). *A binary relation* $\mathcal{R} \subseteq \mathcal{E} \times \mathcal{E}$ *over agents is a* strong bisimulation *if* $(E, F) \in \mathcal{R}$ *implies, for all* $a \in Act$,

- *if* $E \xrightarrow{a} E'$, *then there exists* F' *such that* $F \xrightarrow{a} F'$ *and* $(E', F') \in \mathcal{R}$;
- *if* $F \xrightarrow{a} F'$, *then there exists* E' *such that* $E \xrightarrow{a} E'$ *and* $(E', F') \in \mathcal{R}$.

Two agents $E, F \in \mathcal{E}$ *are* strongly bisimilar, *denoted by* $E \sim F$, *if there exists a strong bisimulation* $\mathcal{R}$ *containing the pair* (E, F).

A weak bisimulation is a bisimulation which does not care about internal τ actions. So, when F simulates an action of E, it can also execute some τ actions before or after that action. We will use the following auxiliary notations. If $t = a_1 \cdots a_n \in Act^*$ and $E \xrightarrow{a_1} \cdots \xrightarrow{a_n} E'$, then we write $E \xrightarrow{t} E'$. We also write $E \stackrel{t}{\Longrightarrow} E'$ if $E(\xrightarrow{\tau})^* \xrightarrow{a_1} (\xrightarrow{\tau})^* \cdots (\xrightarrow{\tau})^* \xrightarrow{a_n} (\xrightarrow{\tau})^* E'$ where $(\xrightarrow{\tau})^*$ denotes a (possibly empty) sequence of τ labelled transitions. If $t \in Act^*$, then $\hat{t} \in \mathcal{L}^*$ is the sequence gained by deleting all occurrences of τ from t. Hence, $E \stackrel{\hat{a}}{\Longrightarrow} E'$ stands for $E \stackrel{a}{\Longrightarrow} E'$ if $a \in \mathcal{L}$, and for $E(\xrightarrow{\tau})^* E'$ if $a = \tau$.

Definition 2 (Weak Bisimulation). *A binary relation* $\mathcal{R} \subseteq \mathcal{E} \times \mathcal{E}$ *over agents is a* weak bisimulation *if* $(E, F) \in \mathcal{R}$ *implies, for all* $a \in Act$,

- *if* $E \xrightarrow{a} E'$, *then there exists* F' *such that* $F \stackrel{\hat{a}}{\Longrightarrow} F'$ *and* $(E', F') \in \mathcal{R}$;
- *if* $F \xrightarrow{a} F'$, *then there exists* E' *such that* $E \stackrel{\hat{a}}{\Longrightarrow} E'$ *and* $(E', F') \in \mathcal{R}$.

Two agents $E, F \in \mathcal{E}$ *are* weakly bisimilar, *denoted by* $E \approx F$, *if there exists a weak bisimulation* $\mathcal{R}$ *containing the pair* (E, F).

In [20] it is proved that $\sim$ is the largest strong bisimulation, $\approx$ is the largest weak bisimulation and they are equivalence relations.

3 Security Properties

We recall the *Persistent_BNDC* (*P_BNDC*, for short) security property and its characterization in terms of weak bisimulation up to high level actions [11, 12].

We first give the definition of *Bisimulation-based Non Deducibility on Compositions* (*BNDC*, for short) [8, 10]. The *BNDC* security property aims at guaranteeing that no information flow from the high to the low level is possible, even in the presence of malicious processes. The main motivation is to protect a system also from internal attacks, which could be performed by the so called *Trojan Horse* programs. Property *BNDC* is based on the idea of checking the system against all high level potential interactions, representing every possible high level malicious program. In particular, a system E is *BNDC* if for every high level process Π a low level user cannot distinguish E from $(E|\Pi) \setminus Act_H$, i.e., if Π cannot interfere [13] with the low level execution of the system E.

Definition 3 (BNDC). *Let* $E \in \mathcal{E}$.

$$E \in BNDC \text{ iff } \forall\, \Pi \in \mathcal{E}_H,\ E \setminus Act_H \approx (E|\Pi) \setminus Act_H.$$

In [11, 12] it is shown that the *BNDC* property is not strong enough to analyse systems in dynamic execution environments. For example, if code mobility is allowed, a program could migrate to a different host in the middle of its computation. In this setting we have to guarantee that every reachable state of the process is secure. Another interesting example is the execution of an applet on a Java Card, where an attacker could try to bring the card in an unstable (insecure) state by powering off the card in the middle of applet computation.

To deal with these situations, in [11, 12] it has been introduced the security property named *P_BNDC*.

Definition 4 (Persistent_BNDC). *Let* $E \in \mathcal{E}$.

$$\begin{aligned} E \in P\_BNDC \ \textit{ iff } \ \forall\, E' \textit{ reachable from } E \textit{ and } \forall\, \Pi \in \mathcal{E}_H, \\ E' \setminus Act_H \approx (E'|\Pi) \setminus Act_H., \ \textit{i.e.,} \ \ E' \in BNDC. \end{aligned}$$

Example 1. Consider the process $E_1 = l.h.j.\mathbf{0} + l.(\tau.j.\mathbf{0} + \tau.\mathbf{0})$ where $l, j \in Act_L$ and $h \in Act_H$. E_1 can be proved to be *BNDC*. Indeed, the causality between h and j in the first branch of the process is "hidden" by the second branch $l.(\tau.j.\mathbf{0} + \tau.\mathbf{0})$, which may simulate all the possible interactions with a high level process. Suppose now that E_1 is moved in the middle of a computation. This might happen when it find itself in the state $h.j.\mathbf{0}$ (after the first l is executed). Now it is clear that this process is not secure, as a direct causality between h and j is present. In particular $h.j.\mathbf{0}$ is not *BNDC* and this gives evidence that E_1 is not *P_BNDC*. The process may be "repaired" as follows: $E_2 = l.(h.j.\mathbf{0}+\tau.j.\mathbf{0}+\tau.\mathbf{0})+l.(\tau.j.\mathbf{0}+\tau.\mathbf{0})$. It may be proved that E_2 is *P_BNDC*. Note that, from this example it follows that *P_BNDC* $\subset$ *BNDC*.

In [12] it has been proven that property *P_BNDC* is equivalent to the security property *SBSNNI* [9, 10] which is automatically checkable over finite state processes. However, this property still requires a universal quantification over all the possible reachable states from the initial process. In [11, 12] it has been shown that this can be avoided, by including the idea of "being secure in every state" inside the bisimulation equivalence notion. This is done by defining an equivalence notion which just focus on observable actions not belonging to Act_H. More in detail, it is defined an observation equivalence, named *weak bisimulation up to* Act_H, where actions from Act_H are allowed to be ignored, i.e., they are allowed to be matched by zero or more τ actions. To do this, it is used a transition relation which does not take care of both internal and high level actions.

We use the following notations. For an action $a \in Act$, we write $(\stackrel{a}{\to})^{\{0,1\}}$ to denote a sequence of zero or one a actions. The expression $E \stackrel{\hat{a}}{\Longrightarrow}_{\setminus Act_H} E'$ is a shorthand for $E \stackrel{\hat{a}}{\Longrightarrow} E'$ if $a \notin Act_H$, and for $E(\stackrel{\tau}{\longrightarrow})^*(\stackrel{a}{\longrightarrow})^{\{0,1\}}(\stackrel{\tau}{\longrightarrow})^*E'$ if $a \in Act_H$. Notice that the relation $\stackrel{\hat{a}}{\Longrightarrow}_{\setminus Act_H}$ is a generalization of the relation $\stackrel{\hat{a}}{\Longrightarrow}$ used in the definition of weak bisimulation [20]. In fact, if $Act_H = \emptyset$, then for all $a \in Act$, $E \stackrel{\hat{a}}{\Longrightarrow}_{\setminus Act_H} E'$ coincides with $E \stackrel{\hat{a}}{\Longrightarrow} E'$.

Definition 5 (Weak Bisimulation up to Act_H). *A binary relation $\mathcal{R} \subseteq \mathcal{E} \times \mathcal{E}$ over agents is a* weak bisimulation up to Act_H *if $(E, F) \in \mathcal{R}$ implies, for all $a \in Act$,*

- *if $E \xrightarrow{a} E'$, then there exists F' such that $F \stackrel{\hat{a}}{\Longrightarrow}_{\setminus Act_H} F'$ and $(E', F') \in \mathcal{R}$;*
- *if $F \xrightarrow{a} F'$, then there exists E' such that $E \stackrel{\hat{a}}{\Longrightarrow}_{\setminus Act_H} E'$ and $(E', F') \in \mathcal{R}$.*

Two agents $E, F \in \mathcal{E}$ are weakly bisimilar up to Act_H, *written $E \approx_{\setminus Act_H} F$, if $(E, F) \in \mathcal{R}$ for some weak bisimulation $\mathcal{R}$ up to Act_H.*

The relation $\approx_{\setminus Act_H}$ is the largest weak bisimulation up to Act_H and it is an equivalence relation. In [12] it is proven that *P_BNDC* can be characterized in terms of $\approx_{\setminus Act_H}$ as follows. We will exploit this result for verifying *P_BNDC*.

Theorem 1. *Let $E \in \mathcal{E}$. Then, $E \in P\_BNDC$ iff $E \approx_{\setminus Act_H} E \setminus Act_H$.*

4 Checking *P_BNDC*

In this section we present two methods to determine whether $E \approx_{\setminus Act_H} E \setminus Act_H$, in the case that E is a finite-state process. In particular, we tackle the problem of proving $E \approx_{\setminus Act_H} F$, when E and F are finite-state processes. The first method we propose consists in defining from a given process E a modal μ-calculus formula $\phi^{\approx_{\setminus Act_H}}(E)$ such that F satisfies $\phi^{\approx_{\setminus Act_H}}(E)$ if and only if $E \approx_{\setminus Act_H} F$. The second method consists in deriving from the LTS's of E and F two transformed LTS's that are strongly bisimilar if and only if $E \approx_{\setminus Act_H} F$.

4.1 Characteristic Formulae

The modal μ-calculus [16] is a small, yet expressive process logic. We consider modal μ-calculus formulae constructed according to the following grammar:

$$\phi ::= \mathbf{true} \mid \mathbf{false} \mid \phi_1 \wedge \phi_2 \mid \phi_1 \vee \phi_2 \mid \langle a \rangle \phi \mid [a]\phi \mid X \mid \mu X.\phi \mid \nu X.\phi$$

where X ranges over an infinite set of variables and a over a set of actions Act. The *fixpoint operators* μX and νX bind the respective variable X and we adopt the usual notion of closed formula. For a finite set M of formulae, we write $\bigwedge M$ and $\bigvee M$ for the conjunction and disjunction of the formulae in M.

Modal μ-calculus formulae are interpreted over processes, which are modelled by LTS's. Let E be a process and $LTS(E) = (S_E, Act_H, \rightarrow)$. The subset of states that satisfy a formula ϕ, denoted by $M_E(\phi)(\rho)$, is intuitively defined in Fig. 2. We use the notion of *environment* that is a partial mapping $\rho : Var \nrightarrow 2^{S_E}$ which interprets at least the free variables of ϕ by subsets of S_E. For a set $x \subseteq S_E$ and a variable X, we write $\rho[X \mapsto x]$ for the environment that maps X to x and that is defined on a variable $Y \neq X$ iff ρ is defined on Y and maps Y then to $\rho(Y)$.

Intuitively, **true** and **false** hold for all resp. no states and $\wedge$ and $\vee$ are interpreted by conjunction and disjunction, $\langle a \rangle \phi$ holds for a state $E' \in S_E$ if there is a state E'' reachable from E' with an action a which satisfies ϕ, and $[a]\phi$

$$\begin{aligned}
M_E(\mathbf{true})(\rho) &= S_E\\
M_E(\mathbf{false})(\rho) &= \emptyset\\
M_E(\phi_1 \wedge \phi_2)(\rho) &= M_E(\phi_1)(\rho) \cap M_E(\phi_2)(\rho)\\
M_E(\phi_1 \vee \phi_2)(\rho) &= M_E(\phi_1)(\rho) \cup M_E(\phi_2)(\rho)\\
M_E(\langle a\rangle\phi)(\rho) &= \{E' \mid \exists E'' : E' \xrightarrow{a} E'' \ \wedge\ E' \in M_E(\phi)(\rho)\}\\
M_E([a]\phi)(\rho) &= \{E' \mid \forall E'' : E' \xrightarrow{a} E'' \ \Rightarrow\ E'' \in M_E(\phi)(\rho)\}\\
M_E(X)(\rho) &= \rho(X)\\
M_E(\mu X.\phi)(\rho) &= \bigcap\{x \subseteq S_E \mid M_E(\phi)(\rho[X \mapsto x]) \subseteq x\}\\
M_E(\nu X.\phi)(\rho) &= \bigcup\{x \subseteq S_e \mid M_E(\phi)(\rho[X \mapsto x]) \supseteq x\}
\end{aligned}$$

Fig. 2. Semantics of modal mu-calculus

holds for E' if all states E'' reachable from E' with an action a satisfy ϕ. The interpretation of a variable X is as prescribed by the environment. The formula $\mu X.\phi$, called *least fixpoint formula*, is interpreted by the smallest subset x of S_E that recurs when ϕ is interpreted with the substitution of x for X. Similarly, $\nu X.\phi$, called *greatest fixpoint formula*, is interpreted by the largest such set. Existence of such sets follow from the well-known Knaster-Tarski fixpoint theorem. As the meaning of a closed formula ϕ does not depend on the environment, we sometimes write $M_E(\phi)$ for $M_E(\phi)(\rho)$ where ρ is an arbitrary environment.

The set of processes *satisfying* a closed formula ϕ is $Proc(\phi) = \{F \mid F \in M_F(\phi)\}$. We also refer to (closed) *equation systems* of modal μ-calculus formulae,

$$Eqn : X_1 = \phi_1, \ldots, X_n = \phi_n$$

where $X_1, \ldots, X_n$ are mutually distinct variables and $\phi_1, \ldots, \phi_n$ are modal μ-calculus formulae having at most $X_1, \ldots, X_n$ as free variables.

An environment $\rho : \{X_1, \ldots, X_n\} \rightarrow 2^{S_E}$ is a *solution* of an equation system Eqn, if $\rho(X_i) = M_E(\phi_i)(\rho)$. The fact that solutions always exist, is again a consequence of the Knaster-Tarski fixpoint theorem. In fact the set of environments that are candidates for solutions, $Env_E = \{\rho \mid \rho : \{X_1, \ldots, X_n\} \rightarrow 2^{S_E}\}$, together with the lifting $\sqsubseteq$ of the inclusion order on 2^{S_E}, defined by $\rho \sqsubseteq \rho'$ iff $\rho(X_i) \subseteq \rho'(X_i)$ for $i \in [1..n]$ forms a complete lattice. Now, we can define the *equation functional* $Func_E^{Eqn} : Env_E \rightarrow Env_E$ by $Func_E^{Eqn}(\rho)(X_i) = M_E(\phi_i)(\rho)$ for $i \in [1..n]$, the fixpoints of which are just the solutions of Eqn. $Func_E^{Eqn}$ is monotonic as $M_E(\phi_i)$ is monotonic. In particular, there is the largest solution $\nu Func_E^{Eqn}$ of Eqn (with respect to $\sqsubseteq$), which we denote by $M_E(Eqn)$. This definition interprets equation systems on the states of a given process E. We lift this to processes by agreeing that a process satisfies an equation system Eqn, if its initial state is in the largest solution of the first equation. Thus the set of processes satisfying the system Eqn is $Proc(Eqn) = \{F \mid F \in M_F(Eqn)(X_1)\}$.

The relation $\approx_{\setminus Act_H} \subseteq \mathcal{E} \times \mathcal{E}$ can be characterized as the greatest fixpoint $\nu Func_{\approx_{\setminus Act_H}}$ of the monotonic functional $Func_{\approx_{\setminus Act_H}}$ on the complete lattice of relations $\mathcal{R} \subseteq \mathcal{E} \times \mathcal{E}$ ordered by set inclusion, where $(E, F) \in Func_{\approx_{\setminus Act_H}}(\mathcal{R})$ if and only if points (1) and (2) of Definition 5 hold. Thus a relation $\mathcal{R}$ is a weak bisimulation up to Act_H if and only if $\mathcal{R} \subseteq Func_{\approx_{\setminus Act_H}}(\mathcal{R})$, i.e., $\mathcal{R}$ is a *post-fixpoint* of $Func_{\approx_{\setminus Act_H}}$. By the Knaster-Tarski fixpoint theorem, $\nu Func_{\approx_{\setminus Act_H}}$ is the union of all post-fixpoints of $Func_{\approx_{\setminus Act_H}}$, i.e., it is the largest weak bisimulation up to Act_H. If we restrict to the complete lattice of relations $\mathcal{R} \subseteq S_E \times S_F$ we obtain a monotonic functional $Func^{(E,F)}_{\approx_{\setminus Act_H}}$ whose greatest fixpoint is exactly $\nu Func_{\approx_{\setminus Act_H}} \cap (S_E \times S_F)$, and this is enough to determine if $E \approx_{\setminus Act_H} F$.

Let E be a finite-state process, $E_1, \ldots, E_n$ its $|S_E| = n$ states, and $E_1 = E$ its initial state. We construct a *characteristic equation system* [21]

$$Eqn_{\approx_{\setminus Act_H}} : X_{E_1} = \phi^{\approx_{\setminus Act_H}}_{E_1}, \ldots, X_{E_n} = \phi^{\approx_{\setminus Act_H}}_{E_n}$$

consisting of one equation for each state $E_1, \ldots, E_n \in S_E$. We define the formulae $\phi^{\approx_{\setminus Act_H}}_{E_i}$ such that the largest solution $M_F(Eqn_{\approx_{\setminus Act_H}})$ of $Eqn_{\approx_{\setminus Act_H}}$ on an arbitrary process F associates the variables $X_{E'}$ just with the states F' of F which are weakly bisimilar up to Act_H to E'. Theorem 2 is in the spirit of [21] and shows the exact form of such formulae. We use these notations:

$$\langle\langle a\rangle\rangle_{\setminus Act_H}\phi \stackrel{\text{def}}{=} \begin{cases} \langle\langle\tau\rangle\rangle\phi & \text{if } a = \tau \\ \langle\langle a\rangle\rangle\phi & \text{if } a \notin Act_H \text{ and } a \neq \tau \\ \langle\langle a\rangle\rangle\phi \vee \langle\langle\tau\rangle\rangle\phi & \text{if } a \in Act_H \text{ and } a \neq \tau \end{cases}$$

where $\langle\langle\tau\rangle\rangle\phi \stackrel{\text{def}}{=} \mu X.\phi \vee \langle\tau\rangle X$ and $\langle\langle a\rangle\rangle\phi \stackrel{\text{def}}{=} \langle\langle\tau\rangle\rangle\langle a\rangle\langle\langle\tau\rangle\rangle\phi$. Notice that $\langle\langle a\rangle\rangle_{\setminus Act_H}$, $\langle\langle\tau\rangle\rangle$ and $\langle\langle a\rangle\rangle$ correspond to $\stackrel{a}{\Longrightarrow}_{\setminus Act_H}$, $\stackrel{\hat{\tau}}{\Rightarrow}$ and $\stackrel{a}{\Rightarrow}$, respectively, since

$$\begin{aligned} M_E(\langle\langle a\rangle\rangle_{\setminus Act_H}\phi)(\rho) &= \{E' \mid \exists E'' \;:\; E' \stackrel{\hat{a}}{\Longrightarrow}_{\setminus Act_H} E'' \wedge E'' \in M_E(\phi)(\rho)\}, \\ M_E(\langle\langle\tau\rangle\rangle\phi)(\rho) &= \{E' \mid \exists E'' \;:\; E' \stackrel{\hat{\tau}}{\Longrightarrow} E'' \wedge E'' \in M_E(\phi)(\rho)\}, \\ M_E(\langle\langle a\rangle\rangle\phi)(\rho) &= \{E' \mid \exists E'' \;:\; E' \stackrel{a}{\Longrightarrow} E'' \wedge E'' \in M_E(\phi)(\rho)\}. \end{aligned}$$

Theorem 2. *$M_F(Eqn_{\approx_{\setminus Act_H}})(X_{E'}) = \{F' \in S_F \mid E' \approx_{\setminus Act_H} F'\}$ when*

$$\begin{aligned} \phi^{\approx_{\setminus Act_H}}_{E'} \stackrel{\text{def}}{=} &\bigwedge\{\bigwedge\{\langle\langle\hat{a}\rangle\rangle_{\setminus Act_H} X_{E''} \mid E' \stackrel{a}{\rightarrow} E''\} \mid a \in Act\} \wedge \\ &\bigwedge\{[a]\bigvee\{X_{E''} \mid E' \stackrel{\hat{a}}{\Longrightarrow}_{\setminus Act_H} E''\} \mid a \in Act\}. \end{aligned}$$

Example 2. Consider the process E_1 of Example 1. For every state E' reachable from E', let $\psi_{E'}$ denote $\phi^{\approx_{\setminus Act_H}}_{E'}$. Then

$$\begin{aligned} \psi_{E_1} &= \langle\langle l\rangle\rangle_{\setminus Act_H} X_{h.j.\mathbf{0}} \wedge \langle\langle l\rangle\rangle_{\setminus Act_H} X_{\tau.j.\mathbf{0}+\tau.\mathbf{0}} \wedge \\ &\quad [l](X_{h.j.\mathbf{0}} \vee X_{\tau.j.\mathbf{0}+\tau.\mathbf{0}} \vee X_{j.\mathbf{0}} \vee X_{\mathbf{0}}) \wedge [\tau]X_{E_1} \wedge [h]X_{E_1} \\ \psi_{\tau.j.\mathbf{0}+\tau.\mathbf{0}} &= \langle\langle\tau\rangle\rangle_{\setminus Act_H} X_{j.\mathbf{0}} \wedge \langle\langle\tau\rangle\rangle_{\setminus Act_H} X_{\mathbf{0}} \wedge \\ &\quad [\tau](X_{\tau.j.\mathbf{0}+\tau.\mathbf{0}} \vee X_{\tau.j.\mathbf{0}} \vee X_{j.\mathbf{0}} \vee X_{\tau.\mathbf{0}} \vee X_{\mathbf{0}}) \wedge \\ &\quad [h](X_{\tau.j.\mathbf{0}+\tau.\mathbf{0}} \vee X_{\tau.j.\mathbf{0}} \vee X_{j.\mathbf{0}} \vee X_{\tau.\mathbf{0}} \vee X_{\mathbf{0}}) \\ \psi_{\tau.j.\mathbf{0}} &= \langle\langle\tau\rangle\rangle_{\setminus Act_H} X_{j.\mathbf{0}} \wedge [\tau](X_{\tau.j.\mathbf{0}} \vee X_{j.\mathbf{0}}) \wedge [h](X_{\tau.j.\mathbf{0}} \vee X_{j.\mathbf{0}}) \\ \psi_{h.j.\mathbf{0}} &= \langle\langle h\rangle\rangle_{\setminus Act_H} X_{j.\mathbf{0}} \wedge [\tau]X_{h.j.\mathbf{0}} \wedge [h](X_{h.j.\mathbf{0}} \vee X_{j.\mathbf{0}}) \\ \psi_{j.\mathbf{0}} &= \langle\langle j\rangle\rangle_{\setminus Act_H} X_{\mathbf{0}} \wedge [h]X_{j.\mathbf{0}} \wedge [\tau]X_{j.\mathbf{0}} \wedge [j]X_{\mathbf{0}} \\ \psi_{\tau.\mathbf{0}} &= \langle\langle\tau\rangle\rangle_{\setminus Act_H} X_{\mathbf{0}} \wedge [\tau](X_{\tau.\mathbf{0}} \vee X_{\mathbf{0}}) \wedge [h](X_{\tau.\mathbf{0}} \vee X_{\mathbf{0}}) \\ \psi_{\mathbf{0}} &= [h]X_{\mathbf{0}} \wedge [\tau]X_{\mathbf{0}} \end{aligned}$$

Corollary 1. *$Proc(Eqn_{\approx_{\setminus Act_H}}) = \{F \mid E \approx_{\setminus Act_H} F\}$.*

This result holds for all processes F as $Eqn_{\approx_{\setminus Act_H}}$ does not depend on F.

Characteristic formulae, i.e., *single* formulae characterizing processes can be constructed by applying simple semantics-preserving transformation rules on equation systems as described in [21]. These rules are similar to the ones used by A. Mader in [19] as a mean of solving Boolean equation systems (with alternation) by Gauss elimination. Hence, since for any equation system Eqn there is a formula ϕ such that $Proc(Eqn) = Proc(\phi)$, we obtain that:

Theorem 3. *For all finite-state processes E there is a modal μ-calculus formulae $\phi^{\approx_{\setminus Act_H}}(E)$ such that $Proc(\phi^{\approx_{\setminus Act_H}}(E)) = \{F \mid E \approx_{\setminus Act_H} F\}$.*

Using this method we can for instance exploit the model checker NCSU Concurrency Workbench ([4]) to check whether $E \approx_{\setminus Act_H} F$. Unfortunately, in the μ-calculus formula we obtain for a process E there are both μ and ν operators (see [21]). In the worst case the number of μ and ν alternations in $\phi^{\approx_{\setminus Act_H}}(E)$ is $2|S_E|+1$ (when $LST(E)$ has a unique strongly connected component) and in that case the complexity of model checking $\phi^{\approx_{\setminus Act_H}}(E)$ on $LTS(F)$ is $O(|S_F|^{(2|S_E|+1)/2})$ (see [18, 3]).

4.2 Strong Bisimulation

We show now how to reduce the problem of testing whether two processes are weakly bisimilar up to Act_H to a strong bisimulation problem. The next property follows from the definition of $\stackrel{\hat{a}}{\Longrightarrow}_{\setminus Act_H}$.

Proposition 1. *A binary relation $\mathcal{R} \subseteq \mathcal{E} \times \mathcal{E}$ over agents is a* weak bisimulation up to Act_H *if and only if $(E, F) \in \mathcal{R}$ implies, for all $a \in Act$*

- *if $E \stackrel{\hat{a}}{\Longrightarrow}_{\setminus Act_H} E'$, there is $F' \in \mathcal{E}$ such that $F \stackrel{\hat{a}}{\Longrightarrow}_{\setminus Act_H} F'$ and $(E', F') \in \mathcal{R}$;*
- *if $F \stackrel{\hat{a}}{\Longrightarrow}_{\setminus Act_H} F'$, there is $E' \in \mathcal{E}$ such that $E \stackrel{\hat{a}}{\Longrightarrow}_{\setminus Act_H} E'$ and $(E', F') \in \mathcal{R}$.*

Proof. ($\Rightarrow$). We prove that if $\mathcal{R} \subseteq \mathcal{E} \times \mathcal{E}$ is a weak bisimulation up to Act_H, and $(E, F) \in \mathcal{R}$, then, for all $a \in Act$ we have

- if $E \stackrel{\hat{a}}{\Longrightarrow}_{\setminus Act_H} E'$, there is $F' \in \mathcal{E}$ such that $F \stackrel{\hat{a}}{\Longrightarrow}_{\setminus Act_H} F'$ and $(E', F') \in \mathcal{R}$;
- if $F \stackrel{\hat{a}}{\Longrightarrow}_{\setminus Act_H} F'$, there is $E' \in \mathcal{E}$ such that $E \stackrel{\hat{a}}{\Longrightarrow}_{\setminus Act_H} E'$ and $(E', F') \in \mathcal{R}$.

We distinguish three cases.

Case 1. $a = \tau$. In this case $E \stackrel{\hat{a}}{\Longrightarrow}_{\setminus Act_H} E'$ coincides with $E(\stackrel{\tau}{\rightarrow})^* E'$. The proof follows by induction on the number of τ actions in $E(\stackrel{\tau}{\rightarrow})^* E'$. The base case arises when zero τ actions are performed and it is trivial. For the induction step, let $E \stackrel{\tau}{\rightarrow} E''(\stackrel{\tau}{\rightarrow})^* E'$. Since, $(E, F) \in \mathcal{R}$, by Definition 5 there exists $F'' \in \mathcal{E}$ such that $F \stackrel{\hat{\tau}}{\Longrightarrow}_{\setminus Act_H} F''$, i.e., $F(\stackrel{\tau}{\rightarrow})^* F''$ and $(E'', F'') \in \mathcal{R}$. By the induction hypothesis, there exists $F' \in \mathcal{E}$ such that $F'' \stackrel{\hat{\tau}}{\Longrightarrow}_{\setminus Act_H} F'$, i.e., $F''(\stackrel{\tau}{\rightarrow})^* F'$ and $(E', F') \in \mathcal{R}$. This proves the thesis since $F(\stackrel{\tau}{\rightarrow})^* F''(\stackrel{\tau}{\rightarrow})^* F'$, i.e., $F \stackrel{\hat{\tau}}{\Longrightarrow}_{\setminus Act_H} F'$.

Case 2. $a \in \mathcal{L}$ and $a \notin Act_H$. In this case we have that $E \stackrel{\hat{a}}{\Longrightarrow}_{\backslash Act_H} E'$ coincides with $E(\stackrel{\tau}{\rightarrow})^* E'' \stackrel{a}{\rightarrow} E'''(\stackrel{\tau}{\rightarrow})^* E'$. By Case 1 above, there exists $\bar{F}'' \in \mathcal{E}$ such that $F(\stackrel{\tau}{\rightarrow})^* \bar{F}''$ and $(E'', \bar{F}'') \in \mathcal{R}$. By Definition 5 there exists $\bar{F}''' \in \mathcal{E}$ such that $\bar{F}'' \stackrel{\hat{a}}{\Longrightarrow}_{\backslash Act_H} \bar{F}'''$, i.e., $\bar{F}''(\stackrel{\tau}{\rightarrow})^* F'' \stackrel{a}{\rightarrow} F'''(\stackrel{\tau}{\rightarrow})^* \bar{F}'''$ and $(E''', \bar{F}''') \in \mathcal{R}$. Again, by Case 1 above, there exists $F' \in \mathcal{E}$ such that $\bar{F}'''(\stackrel{\tau}{\rightarrow})^* F'$ and $(E', F') \in \mathcal{R}$. This proves the thesis since $F(\stackrel{\tau}{\rightarrow})^* F'' \stackrel{a}{\rightarrow} F'''(\stackrel{\tau}{\rightarrow})^* F'$, i.e., $F \stackrel{\hat{a}}{\Longrightarrow}_{\backslash Act_H} F'$.

Case 3. $a \in Act_H$. In this case $E \stackrel{\hat{a}}{\Longrightarrow}_{\backslash Act_H} E'$ coincides either with $E(\stackrel{\tau}{\rightarrow})^* E'$ or with $E(\stackrel{\tau}{\rightarrow})^* E'' \stackrel{a}{\rightarrow} E'''(\stackrel{\tau}{\rightarrow})^* E'$. The proof follows by Case 1 and Case 2 above.

($\Leftarrow$). It is easy to prove that if $\mathcal{R} \subseteq \mathcal{E} \times \mathcal{E}$ is a binary relation over agents such that for all $(E, F) \in \mathcal{R}$, $a \in Act$ it holds

- if $E \stackrel{\hat{a}}{\Longrightarrow}_{\backslash Act_H} E'$, there is $F' \in \mathcal{E}$ such that $F \stackrel{\hat{a}}{\Longrightarrow}_{\backslash Act_H} F'$ and $(E', F') \in \mathcal{R}$;
- if $F \stackrel{\hat{a}}{\Longrightarrow}_{\backslash Act_H} F'$, there is $E' \in \mathcal{E}$ such that $E \stackrel{\hat{a}}{\Longrightarrow}_{\backslash Act_H} E'$ and $(E', F') \in \mathcal{R}$;

then $\mathcal{R}$ is a weak bisimulation up to Act_H. In particular, this follows from the fact that, by the definition of $\stackrel{\hat{a}}{\Longrightarrow}_{\backslash Act_H}$, $E \stackrel{a}{\rightarrow} E'$ implies $E \stackrel{\hat{a}}{\Longrightarrow}_{\backslash Act_H} E'$ for each $E, E' \in \mathcal{E}$ and $a \in Act$. ∎

A direct consequence of this theorem is that two systems E and F are weakly bisimilar up to Act_H if and only if they are strongly bisimilar when in place of the transition relation $\stackrel{a}{\rightarrow}$ we consider the set of labelled transitions $\stackrel{\hat{a}}{\Longrightarrow}_{\backslash Act_H}$.

We can exploit this fact to determine whether $E \approx_{\backslash Act_H} F$ by: (i) translating the two labelled transition systems $LTS(E)$ and $LTS(F)$, into $LTS^H(E)$ and $LTS^H(F)$; (ii) computing the largest strong bisimulation $\sim$ between $LTS^H(E)$ and $LTS^H(F)$. More formally we define:

Definition 6 (Closure up to Act_H). *Let $E \in \mathcal{E}$ with $LTS(E) = (S_E, Act, \rightarrow)$. The closure up to Act_H of E is the labelled transition system $LTS^H(E) = (S_E, Act, \hookrightarrow)$, where $\stackrel{a}{\hookrightarrow}$ is defined as $\stackrel{\hat{a}}{\Longrightarrow}_{\backslash Act_H}$, i.e.:*

$$E' \stackrel{a}{\hookrightarrow} E'' = \begin{cases} E'(\stackrel{\tau}{\rightarrow})^* E'' & \text{if } a = \tau \\ E'(\stackrel{\tau}{\rightarrow})^* F' \stackrel{a}{\rightarrow} F''(\stackrel{\tau}{\rightarrow})^* E'' & \text{if } a \notin Act_H \\ E'(\stackrel{\tau}{\rightarrow})^* F' \stackrel{a}{\rightarrow} F''(\stackrel{\tau}{\rightarrow})^* E'' \text{ or } E'(\stackrel{\tau}{\rightarrow})^* E'' & \text{if } a \in Act_H \end{cases}$$

Let us denote with E^H a process whose operational semantics is given by the transformed transition system $LTS^H(E)$, i.e., $LTS(E^H) = LTS^H(E)$. The next result is an immediate consequence of Proposition 1.

Corollary 2. *Let $E, F \in \mathcal{E}$. Then, $E \approx_{\backslash Act_H} F$ iff $E^H \sim F^H$.*

Now, our first problem is to compute $LTS^H(E)$ from $LTS(E)$, using Definition 6. This can be immediately obtained with the following algorithm:

Algorithm 1 Let $E \in \mathcal{E}$ with $LTS(E) = (S_E, Act, \rightarrow)$. The *closure up to Act_H* of E, $LTS^H(E) = (S_E, Act, \hookrightarrow)$, is computed as follows:

1. calculate $\stackrel{\tau}{\hookrightarrow}$ as $(\stackrel{\tau}{\rightarrow})^*$, i.e., as the reflexive and transitive closure of $\stackrel{\tau}{\rightarrow}$;
2. calculate $\stackrel{a}{\hookrightarrow}$ as the composition $\stackrel{\tau}{\hookrightarrow} \circ \stackrel{a}{\rightarrow} \circ \stackrel{\tau}{\hookrightarrow}$;
3. if $a \in Act_H$ then add $E \stackrel{a}{\hookrightarrow} F$, every time $E \stackrel{\tau}{\hookrightarrow} F$.

Correctness of algorithm above is trivially obtained by observing that (by Definition 6): $\stackrel{\tau}{\hookrightarrow}$ is equivalent to $(\stackrel{\tau}{\rightarrow})^*$; $\stackrel{a}{\hookrightarrow}$ with $a \in \mathcal{L} \setminus Act_H$ is equivalent to $(\stackrel{\tau}{\rightarrow})^* \circ \stackrel{a}{\rightarrow} \circ (\stackrel{\tau}{\rightarrow})^*$, i.e., to $\stackrel{\tau}{\hookrightarrow} \circ \stackrel{a}{\rightarrow} \circ \stackrel{\tau}{\hookrightarrow}$; $\stackrel{a}{\hookrightarrow}$ with $a \in Act_H$ is equivalent to the union of $(\stackrel{\tau}{\rightarrow})^* \circ \stackrel{a}{\rightarrow} \circ (\stackrel{\tau}{\rightarrow})^*$ (calculated in step 2 above) and $(\stackrel{\tau}{\rightarrow})^*$ (calculated in step 3 above). As far as time and space complexities are concerned, we notice that they depend on the algorithms used for computing the reflexive and transitive closure and the composition of relations. We start by fixing some notations. Let $n = |S_E|$ be the number of states in $LTS(E)$, for each $a \in Act$, let m_a be the number of $\stackrel{a}{\rightarrow}$ transitions in $LTS(E)$, and $m = \sum_{a \in Act} m_a$. Similarly, let $\hat{m}_a$ be the number of $\stackrel{a}{\hookrightarrow}$ transitions in $LTS^H(E)$, and $\hat{m} = \sum_{a \in Act} \hat{m}_a$.

The next theorem shows that $E \approx_{\setminus Act_H} F$ can be checked in polynomial time with respect to the number of states of the system.

Theorem 4. *Algorithm 1 can be executed in time $O(n\hat{m}_\tau + n^w)$ and space $O(n^2)$, where w denotes the exponent in the running time of the matrix multiplication algorithm used.*[2] *If $\hat{m} \leq n$, then it is possible to work in time $O(n\hat{m})$ and space $O(n)$.*

Proof. First of all we have to determine the transitive closure of $\stackrel{\tau}{\rightarrow}$. The algorithm proposed in [14] computes the transitive closure of a graph represented with adjacency-lists in time $O(m_\tau + ne)$, where e is the number of edges in the transitive closure of the graph of the strongly connected components. Since $m_\tau, e \leq \hat{m}_\tau$, an upper bound to the cost of the computation of $(\stackrel{\tau}{\rightarrow})^*$ is $O(n\hat{m}_\tau)$.

Let us consider the computation of the composition $(\stackrel{\tau}{\rightarrow})^* \circ \stackrel{a}{\rightarrow} \circ (\stackrel{\tau}{\rightarrow})^*$. Given two transition relations $\rightarrow_1$ and $\rightarrow_2$ on a set of n nodes, the problem of determining the composition $\rightarrow_1 \circ \rightarrow_2$ is known to be equivalent to the $n \times n$ Boolean matrix multiplication problem (see [6]). In particular, if A_i is the adjacency-matrix defined by $\rightarrow_i$, for $i = 1, 2$, then the adjacency-matrix of $\rightarrow_1 \circ \rightarrow_2$ is the matrix $A_1 \cdot A_2$. Hence, in our case, we have to: (i) determine the adjacency-matrixes $A_{\tau *}$ and A_a associated to $(\stackrel{\tau}{\rightarrow})^*$ and $\stackrel{a}{\rightarrow}$ respectively; (ii) compute the product $(A_{\tau *} \cdot A_a) \cdot A_{\tau *}$; (iii) rebuild the adjacency-list representation (in the computation of the strong bisimulation it is important to use the adjacency-list representation). Starting from the adjacency-list representations of $(\stackrel{\tau}{\rightarrow})^*$ and $\stackrel{a}{\rightarrow}$ in time $O(n^2)$ we obtain their adjacency-matrix representations $A_{\tau *}$ and A_a. The matrix product $(A_{\tau *} \cdot A_a) \cdot A_{\tau *}$ can be determined in time $O(n^{2.376})$ using twice the algorithm in [5]. Then, again in time $O(n^2)$, we rebuild the adjacency-list representation. So, the global cost of the computation of $(\stackrel{\tau}{\rightarrow})^* \circ \stackrel{a}{\rightarrow} \circ (\stackrel{\tau}{\rightarrow})^*$ is $O(n^{2.376})$. We have to perform this step once for each $a \in \mathcal{L}$, assuming that $|\mathcal{L}|$ is

[2] In the algorithm in [5], which is at the moment the fastest in literature, we have that $w = 2.376$.

a constant wrt. n. Notice that we could work using only 2 matrix multiplications, instead of $2|\mathcal{L}|$ matrix multiplications, but in this case we would have to use matrixes in which each element is an array of length $\mathcal{L}$ of bits, hence also in this way it is not possible to drop the assumption that $|\mathcal{L}|$ is a constant wrt. n.

Hence, we have described a procedure which maps E into $LTS^H(E)$ in time $O(n\hat{m}_\tau + n^w)$ and space $O(n^2)$, where w is the exponent in the running time of the matrix multiplication algorithm used ($w = 2.376$ using [5]).

In the procedure just described we use the adjacency-matrix representation to compute $\xrightarrow{a} \circ (\xrightarrow{\tau})^*$. If we know that $\hat{m} \leq n$, then using the adjacency-list representation and a naïve algorithm (two iterations of the naïve algorithm for the transitive closure [6]) we can perform this step in time $O(n\hat{m})$. Thus, when $\hat{m} \leq n$, we determine $LTS^H(E)$ in time $O(n\hat{m})$ and space $O(n + \hat{m}) = O(n)$. ■

The theorem above is applicable to the general case $E \approx_{\setminus Act_H} F$. However, since in our case $F = E \setminus Act_H$, we can interleave the computation of $LTS^H(E)$ and $LTS^H(E \setminus Act_H)$, lowering the constant involved in the time complexity. To do so, we need the notion of Act_H-Completion defined as follows:

Definition 7 (Act_H-Completion). *Let $E \in \mathcal{E}$ with $LTS(E) = (S_E, Act, \rightarrow)$. The Act_H-Completion of E, $LTS_{\mathcal{C}}(E) = (S_E, Act, \hookrightarrow)$, is defined as follows: we have $E \overset{a}{\hookrightarrow} E'$ every time $E \xrightarrow{a} E'$. Moreover, every time $E \xrightarrow{\tau} E'$ we have $E \overset{a}{\hookrightarrow} E'$ for all $a \in Act_H$.*

Intuitively, the Act_H-completion extends a given LTS by adding an edge $\overset{a}{\hookrightarrow}$, with $a \in Act_H$, each time that there is an edge $\xrightarrow{\tau}$ in the original LTS.

Let us denote with $E^\emptyset$ a process whose operational semantics is given by the closure up to $\emptyset$ of $LTS(E)$. Note that this amounts to saying that $LTS(E^\emptyset) = (S_E, Act, \overset{\hat{a}}{\Longrightarrow})$. In fact, recall that if $Act_H = \emptyset$, then $E \overset{\hat{a}}{\Longrightarrow}_{\setminus Act_H} E'$ coincides with $E \overset{\hat{a}}{\Longrightarrow} E'$ for all $a \in Act$. The following holds:

Proposition 2. *Let $E \in \mathcal{E}$ be a process.*

(i) $LTS^H(E) = LTS_{\mathcal{C}}(E^\emptyset)$
(ii) $LTS^H(E \setminus Act_H) = LTS_{\mathcal{C}}(E^\emptyset \setminus Act_H)$

Proof. The first equation follows immediately from the definitions and states that the Act_H-Completion of $E^\emptyset$ is the closure up to high level actions of E.

We prove the second equation. By definition, $LTS^H(E \setminus Act_H)$ is the LTS obtained by substituting $\xrightarrow{a}$ with $\overset{\hat{a}}{\Longrightarrow}$ in $LTS(E \setminus Act_H)$, as $E \setminus Act_H$ cannot execute high level actions. Thus, if E' is a state in $LTS^H(E \setminus Act_H)$, then E' is also a state in $LTS(E \setminus Act_H)$, i.e., there is a path from E to E' which does not involve actions of Act_H. This implies that E' is a state of $LTS(E^\emptyset \setminus Act_H)$, and hence it belongs also to $LTS_{\mathcal{C}}(E^\emptyset \setminus Act_H)$. Similarly we can prove that if E' is a state in $LTS_{\mathcal{C}}(E^\emptyset \setminus Act_H)$, then E' is a state in $LTS^H(E \setminus Act_H)$.

Now, we prove that $E' \overset{a}{\hookrightarrow} E''$ in $LTS^H(E \setminus Act_H)$ if and only if $E' \overset{a}{\hookrightarrow} E''$ in $LTS_{\mathcal{C}}(E^\emptyset \setminus Act_H)$. We distinguish three cases.

Case 1. $a = \tau$. Since operation $\backslash Act_H$ has no effects on τ transitions in both cases the τ transitions are exactly those in the transitive closure $(\stackrel{\tau}{\rightarrow})^*$ of E.

Case 2. $a \in \mathcal{L}$ and $a \notin Act_H$. Again, since operation $\backslash Act_H$ has no effects on the a transitions in both cases the a transitions are exactly the transitions in $(\stackrel{\tau}{\rightarrow})^* \circ \stackrel{a}{\rightarrow} \circ (\stackrel{\tau}{\rightarrow})^*$ computed on E.

Case 3. $a \in Act_H$. The a transitions which are in $LTS^H(E \setminus Act_H)$ are exactly the transitions in $(\stackrel{\tau}{\rightarrow})^*$ computed on E and also the a transitions which are in $LTS_{\mathcal{C}}(E^{\emptyset} \setminus Act_H)$ are exactly the transitions in $(\stackrel{\tau}{\rightarrow})^*$ computed on E. ∎

Hence we can determine $LTS^H(E)$ and $LTS^H(E \setminus Act_H)$ as follows:

Algorithm 2 Let $E \in \mathcal{E}$. We calculate $LTS^H(E)$ and $LTS^H(E \setminus Act_H)$ through the following steps:

1. compute $E^{\emptyset}$;
2. compute and give as output $LTS_{\mathcal{C}}(E^{\emptyset})$;
3. compute $E^{\emptyset} \setminus Act_H$;
4. compute and give as output $LTS_{\mathcal{C}}(E^{\emptyset} \setminus Act_H)$.

The correctness of the algorithm is given by Proposition 2 which proves that $LTS_{\mathcal{C}}(E^{\emptyset}) = LTS^H(E)$ (step 2 above) and $LTS_{\mathcal{C}}(E^{\emptyset} \setminus Act_H) = LTS^H(E \setminus Act_H)$ (step 4 above). The time and space complexity of the algorithm are the ones in Theorem 4, since steps 2, 3, and 4 can be performed using three visits.

Once we have the LTS's $LTS^H(E)$ and $LTS^H(E \setminus Act_H)$ there are many algorithms which can be used to decide whether $E^H \sim (E \setminus Act_H)^H$ (e.g., [22, 15, 17, 2, 7]). Some of these algorithms are integrated in model checkers [1, 4, 23]. The worst case time complexity of the algorithms in [22, 7] to decide $E^H \sim (E \setminus Act_H)^H$ is $O(\hat{m} \log n)$, assuming that the LTS's are represented using adjacency-lists. Using these complexity results together with Theorem 4 we obtain that:

Corollary 3. *It is possible to decide* $E \approx_{\setminus Act_H} E \setminus Act_H$ *in time* $O(n\hat{m}_\tau + n^w + \hat{m} \log n)$ *and space* $O(n^2)$*, where* w *denotes the exponent in the running time of the matrix multiplication algorithm used. If* $\hat{m} \leq n$*, then it is possible to work in time* $O(n\hat{m})$ *and space* $O(n)$.

Notice that using this approach in many practical cases there are a large number of states which occur both in $LTS^H(E)$ and in $LTS^H(E \setminus Act_H)$. We can avoid to replicate these states, share them among the two LTS's, and test whether the two roots are bisimilar. In particular, this can be done in the following way: after the computation of $E^{\emptyset}$, using a backward visit, mark all the nodes of $E^{\emptyset}$ which do not reach a transition whose label is in Act_H; while computing $LTS_{\mathcal{C}}(E^{\emptyset} \setminus Act_H)$ with a breath-first visit consider that if E' is a marked node, then E' is also a node in $LTS_{\mathcal{C}}(E^{\emptyset})$, hence share E' with $LTS_{\mathcal{C}}(E^{\emptyset})$ and do not call the breath-first visit on E'. In this way we lower again the constants involved in the effective time and space complexities: if we mark n' nodes, then in steps 3. and 4. of Algorithm 2 we have to visit only $n - n'$ nodes, and the total space required to store the nodes is $2n - n'$ instead of $2n$.

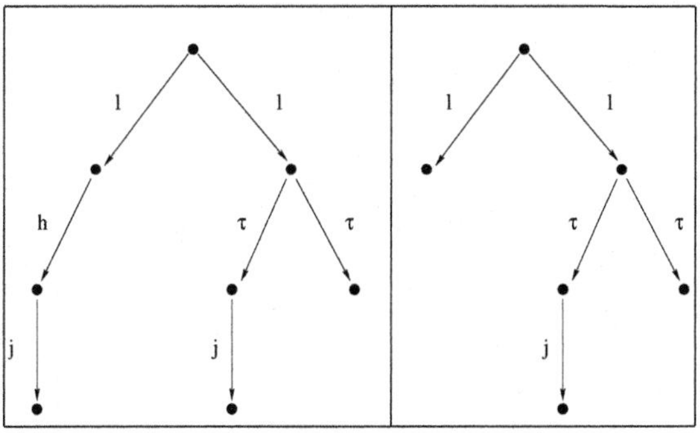

Fig. 3. The labelled transition systems of E_1 and $E_1 \setminus Act_H$.

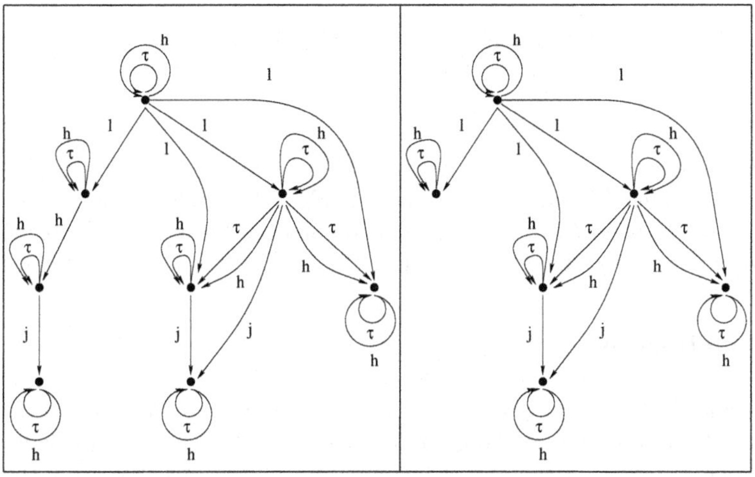

Fig. 4. The labelled transition systems $LTS^H(E_1)$ and $LTS^H(E_1 \setminus Act_H)$.

Example 3. Consider again process $E_1 = l.h.j.\mathbf{0} + l.(\tau.j.\mathbf{0} + \tau.\mathbf{0})$ of Example 1. In Fig. 3 we show $LTS(E_1)$ and $LTS(E_1 \setminus Act_H)$. By performing the closure up to Act_H (Algorithm 1) we obtain the transformed labelled transition systems $LTS^H(E_1)$ and $LTS^H(E_1 \setminus Act_H)$ reported in Fig. 4. In particular, the first step just adds the τ-loops in every state; the second one, adds two transitions labelled with l corresponding to $l.\tau$ and one transition labelled with j corresponding to $\tau.j$; finally, step 3 adds a h-labelled transition every time there is a τ transition. The two transformed transition systems are not strongly bisimilar: the leftmost node after l in $LTS^H(E_1)$ is not bisimilar to any node in $LTS^H(E_1 \setminus Act_H)$, since in $LTS^H(E_1 \setminus Act_H)$ all the nodes are either "sink-nodes" (which only executes τ and h loops) or they have at least one outgoing edge with label j or l. Indeed, that node in $LTS^H(E_1)$ may execute only h and τ actions and could thus be simulated only by sink-nodes in $LTS^H(E_1 \setminus Act_H)$. However, differently

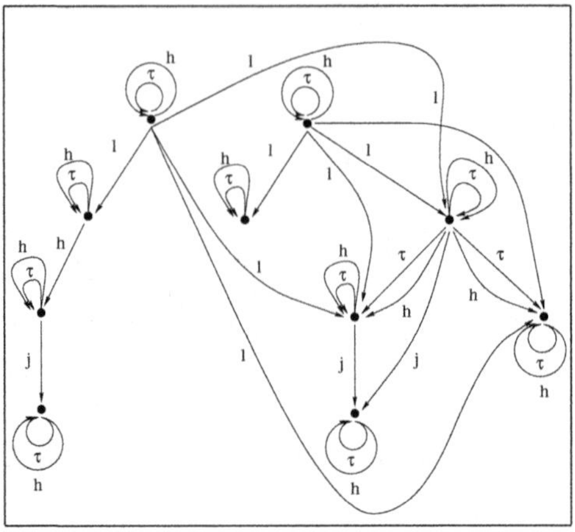

Fig. 5. The labelled transition systems $LTS^H(E_1)$ and $LTS^H(E_1 \setminus Act_H)$ with sharing.

from sink-nodes, after one h, it is also able to execute a j. This proves that $E_1^H \not\approx (E_1 \setminus Act_H)^H$, thus, by Corollary 2, $E_1 \notin P\_BNDC$. In Fig. 5 we show again $LTS^H(E_1)$ and $LTS^H(E_1 \setminus Act_H)$, now sharing the common states, i.e., we avoid to repeat the states (and the sub-LTS's) which do not reach an action h.

5 Conclusions

We consider the security property *P_BNDC* and we present two methods to prove it. While the first method exploit model checkers for the μ-calculus, the second one is based on the use of bisimulation algorithms. We show that this second approach can perform the *P_BNDC*-check in polynomial time with respect to the number of states of the system and improves on the polynomial time complexity of the Compositional Security Checker CoSeC presented in [9].

References

[1] A. Bouali. XEVE, an ESTEREL verification environment. In A. J. Hu and M. Y. Vardi, editors, *Proc. of Int. Conference on Computer Aided Verification (CAV'98)*, volume 1427 of *LNCS*, pages 500–504. Springer, 1998.

[2] A. Bouali and R. de Simone. Symbolic bisimulation minimization. In G. von Bochmann and D. K. Probst, editors, *Proc. of Int. Conference on Computer Aided Verification (CAV'92)*, volume 663 of *LNCS*, pages 96–108. Springer, 1992.

[3] E. M. Clarke, O. Grumberg, and D. A. Peled. *Model checking.* The MIT Press, 1999.

[4] R. Cleaveland and S. Sims. The NCSU concurrency workbench. In R. Alur and T. Henzinger, editors, *Proc. of Int. Conference on Computer Aided Verification (CAV'96)*, volume 1102 of *LNCS*, pages 394–397. Springer, 1996.

[5] D. Coppersmith and S. Winograd. Matrix multiplication via arithmetic progression. In *Proc. of the 19th Symposium on Theory of Computing*, pages 1–6, 1987.
[6] T. H. Cormen, C. E. Leiserson, and R. L. Rivest. *Introduction to Algorithms*. The MIT Press, 1990.
[7] A. Dovier, C. Piazza, and A. Policriti. A fast bisimulation algorithm. In G. Berry, H. Comon, and A. Finkel, editors, *Proc. of Int. Conference on Computer Aided Verification (CAV'01)*, volume 2102 of *LNCS*, pages 79–90. Springer, 2001.
[8] R. Focardi and R. Gorrieri. A Classification of Security Properties for Process Algebras. *Journal of Computer Security*, 3(1):5–33, 1994/1995.
[9] R. Focardi and R. Gorrieri. The Compositional Security Checker: A Tool for the Verification if Information Flow Security Properties. *IEEE Transactions on Software Engineering*, 23(9):550–571, 1997.
[10] R. Focardi and R. Gorrieri. Classification of Security Properties (Part I: Information Flow). In R. Focardi and R. Gorrieri, editors, *Foundations of Security Analysis and Design*, volume 2171 of *LNCS*. Springer, 2001.
[11] R. Focardi and S. Rossi. A Security Property for Processes in Dynamic Contexts. In *Proc. of Workshop on Issues in the Theory of Security (WITS '02)*.To appear.
[12] R. Focardi and S. Rossi. Information Flow Security in Dynamic Contexts. Technical Report CS-2001-16, Dipartimento di Informatica, Università Ca' Foscari di Venezia, Italy, 2001.
[13] J. A. Goguen and J. Meseguer. Security Policy and Security Models. In *Proc. of the 1982 Symposium on Security and Privacy*, pages 11–20. IEEE Computer Society Press, 1982.
[14] A. Goralcikova and V. Koubek. A reduct and closure algorithm for graphs. In *Proc. of Mathematical Foundations of Computer Science (MFCS'79)*, volume 74 of *LNCS*, pages 301–307. Springer, 1979.
[15] P. C. Kannellakis and S. A. Smolka. CCS expressions, finite state processes, and three problems of equivalence. *Information and Computation*, 86(1):43–68, 1990.
[16] D. Kozen. Results on the Propositional μ-calculus. *Theoretical Computer Science*, 27:333–354, 1983.
[17] D. Lee and M. Yannakakis. Online minimization of transition systems. In *Proc. of 24th ACM Symposium on Theory of Computing (STOC'92)*, pages 264–274. ACM Press, 1992.
[18] D. Long, A. Browne, E. Clarke, S. Jha, and W. Marrero. An improved Algorithm for the Evaluation of Fixpoint expressions. In D. L. Dill, editor, *Proc. of Int. Conference on Computer Aided Verification (CAV'94)*, volume 818 of *LNCS*, pages 338–350. Springer, 1994.
[19] A. Mader. Modal μ-calculus, Model Checking, and Gauss elimination. In E. Brinksma, R. Cleaveland, K.G. T. Margaria Larsen, and B. Steffen, editors, *Proc. of Int. Conference on Tools and Algorithms for Construction and Analysis of Systems (TACAS'95)*, volume 1019 of *LNCS*, pages 72–88. Springer, 1995.
[20] R. Milner. *Communication and Concurrency*. Prentice-Hall, 1989.
[21] M. Müller-Olm. Derivation of Characteristic Formulae. *Electronic Notes in Theoretical Computer Science*, 18, 1998.
[22] R. Paige and R. E. Tarjan. Three partition refinement algorithms. *SIAM Journal on Computing*, 16(6):973–989, 1987.
[23] A. W. Roscoe. *The Theory and Practice of Concurrency*. Series in Computer Science. Prentice Hall, 1998.
[24] B. Steffen and A. Ingòlfsdòttir. Characteristic Formulae for Processes with Divergence. *Information and Computation*, 110(1):149–163, 1994.

A Formal Correspondence between Offensive and Defensive JavaCard Virtual Machines

Gilles Barthe[1], Guillaume Dufay[1], Line Jakubiec[2], and Simão Melo de Sousa[1,3]*

[1] INRIA Sophia-Antipolis, France
{Gilles.Barthe,Guillaume.Dufay,Simao.Desousa}@inria.fr
[2] Université de la Méditerranée, Marseille, France
Line.Jakubiec@lim.univ-mrs.fr
[3] Universidade da Beira Interior, Covilhã, Portugal

Abstract. Many formal specifications of the JavaCard Virtual Machine are defensive, in that they perform type-checking at run-time. In this paper, we show how to construct from such a defensive virtual machine an offensive one that does not perform type-checking at run-time. Further, we establish that the two machines coincide for the class of JavaCard programs that pass bytecode verification. Both the construction of the offensive virtual machine and its correctness proof are achieved using (non-standard) abstract interpretation techniques and have been fully formalized in the Coq proof assistant.

1 Introduction

JavaCard Open platform smartcards are small devices designed to integrate multiple applications on-board. Such applications, which include identity documents, electronic purses, loyalty applets and health records, are intended to coexist on the same card and communicate securely, and in principle, can be loaded on the card after its issuance to users.

JavaCard [16] is a popular programming language for open platform smartcards. According to the JavaCard Forum [15], JavaCard is the ideal choice for smart cards because (1) JavaCard programs are written in a subset of Java, hence JavaCard developers can benefit from the well-established Java technology; (2) the JavaCard security model enables multiple applications to communicate securely. Despite the discovery of several security breaches, see e.g. [13, 20], JavaCard has become *de facto* a standard for smartcard programming.

Reasoning about JavaCard The prospects of a widespread use of smartcards as identity documents and money devices put security issues at stake and has emphasized the necessity to develop formal models for verifying properties of the JavaCard platform. Over the last few years, intensive investigations have

* Simão Melo de Sousa is partially supported by the grant SFRH/BD/790/2000 from the Portuguese *Fundação para a Ciência e a Technologia*.

A. Cortesi (Ed.): VMCAI 2002, LNCS 2294, pp. 32–45, 2002.
© Springer-Verlag Berlin Heidelberg 2002

been carried in this direction, leading to several formal models of the JavaCard Virtual Machine and of the ByteCode Verifier. Despite impressive progress, see e.g. [14], much work remains to be done. Two crucial issues require particular attention:

- *Scalability.* Most formal specifications of the JavaCard platform only focus on a restricted subset of the language. This is clearly a problem because unexpected interactions between different features may lead to security breaches;
- *Accuracy.* Most formal specifications describe defensive virtual machines, i.e. virtual machines where values are tagged by their type and typing information is verified at run-time. In contrast, actual implementations of the virtual machine are so-called offensive and rely on successful bytecode verification to eliminate type verification at run-time.

Addressing both issues is crucial to gain confidence in the JavaCard platform. In [4], we address the first issue by providing an in-depth machine-checked account of the JavaCard platform, including a defensive virtual machine and a bytecode verifier. In this paper, we address the second issue by deriving an offensive virtual machine from a defensive one, and by showing that the two machines coincide on programs that have passed bytecode verification.

Apart from pursuing our earlier effort, our work brings evidence that:

- the formal verification of the relationship between the defensive virtual machine, the offensive virtual machine and bytecode verification scales up to the whole instruction set of the JavaCard Virtual Machine, including those instructions used for subroutines, exceptions, object handling and method calls that were left out from [8, 19, 25], where the relation between the three components was first considered;
- the construction of the offensive machine can be seen as a non-standard abstract interpretation of the defensive one (we say "non-standard" because the boolean-valued functions that relate to typing are abstracted as everywhere true), and that its correctness w.r.t. the defensive virtual machine can be seen as a non-standard statement of correctness of abstract interpretations. (See e.g. [10, 26] for some material and references on abstract interpretation.)

While the second insight has not been exploited directly in this paper, it suggests that the process can be automated. Such an automation falls beyond the scope of this paper but is currently being pursued in the context of Jakarta, see [3].

Contents The remaining of the paper is organized as follows: first in Section 2 we shortly introduce the Coq proof assistant. In Section 3, we give an overview of our earlier formalization of the defensive JavaCard Virtual Machine [4], that forms the starting point for the work reported here. In Section 4, we construct an offensive virtual machine from the defensive one. The correctness of the offensive virtual machine (as an abstract interpretation of the defensive one) is established in Section 5. The relationship with bytecode verification is discussed in Section 6. Finally, we conclude in Section 7 with related work and directions for future research.

Acknowledgments The importance of the offensive virtual machine was suggested to us by Lilian Burdy, Skander Kort and Jean-Louis Lanet, from Gemplus, during an evaluation [18] of the CertiCartes formalization.

2 A Primer on Coq

Coq [28] is a proof assistant based on the Calculus of Inductive Constructions. It combines a specification language (featuring inductive and record types) and a higher-order predicate logic (via the Curry-Howard isomorphism).

Our specifications of the JavaCard Virtual Machine only make a limited use of dependent types—a salient feature of Coq. This design choice was motivated by portability; by not using dependent types in an essential way (e.g. for partial function), our formalizations can be transposed easily to other proof assistants, including PVS and Isabelle. The development of the Jakarta toolset [3], that performs such kind of translations, has confirmed us in our choice.

We continue this primer with some notation. We use `*` to denote the cartesian product of two types, `(a,b)` to denote pairs, `[x:A] b` to denote a λ-abstraction, `(x:A) B` to denote a dependent function space and `A→B` to denote a non-dependent function space. An inductive type is declared with the keyword **`Inductive`**, its name, possibly some parameters, its type and a list of its constructors with their names. A record type `R` is declared with the keyword **`Record`** followed by its name, its type, and a description (name and type) of its fields. It is represented internally as an inductive type with a single constructor. Selectors are functions (defined by case-analysis) so we write `(l a)` instead of the more standard `a.l`. The latter notation is then used for qualified names where a construction `c` defined in a module `m` can be accessed with the notation `m.c`.

Finally, definitions are introduced by the **`Definition`** keyword and pattern matching over an inductive type is introduced by the **`Cases`** notation as shown in the following intuitive example:

```
Definition is_zero : bool := [n:nat]
  Cases n of O ⇒ true | (S p) ⇒ false end.
```

We point out that all functions in Coq are required to be terminating and total. To handle partial functions, we use the lift monad which is introduced in the Coq library through the parameterized inductive type:

```
Inductive Exc [A:Set] : Set :=
  value : A→(Exc A) | error : (Exc A).
```

For instance, the function that computes the head of a list is defined using `Exc` since the head of an empty list does not exist:

```
Definition head [A:Set,l:list A] : (Exc A) :=
  Cases l of
    nil        ⇒ (error A) |
    (cons x _) ⇒ (value A x)
  end.
```

3 CertiCartes: A Formal Executable Semantics of the JavaCard Platform

In a previous paper [4], we report on:

1. an executable specification of the defensive Java Card Virtual Machine JCVM;
2. an executable specification of the JavaCard ByteCode Verifier BCV;
3. a machine-checked proof of correctness of the ByteCode Verifier, stating that all programs that pass bytecode verification do not raise type errors at run-time.

Both specifications and proofs have been carried within the Coq proof assistant, and constitute one of the most in-depth machine-checked accounts of the JavaCard platform to date (more that 8.000 lines of codes for the specification and also 8.000 lines of proofs).

The formal semantics of the defensive JavaCard Virtual Machine, which forms the starting point for the work reported in this paper, is described by providing in Coq a representation of JavaCard programs, of JCVM memory model and of the semantics of the instructions. We briefly review these items below.

3.1 Representation of JavaCard Programs

JavaCard programs may be compiled to their Coq representation, that faithfully represents all JavaCard programs, using:

1. a Java compiler that produces a collection of class files;
2. a JavaCard converter that translates the class files into cap files;
3. the JCVM Tools (developed by B. Serpette, see [4]) that perform a number of verifications on cap files and translate a collection of cap files into their representation in Coq.

In our formalization, a JavaCard program only consists of a collection of classes, interfaces and methods (indexes to the constant pool have been solved by the JCVM Tools) defined as records. For instance, a method is declared as:

```
Record Method: Set := {
 signature    :((list type)*type); (* signature of the method     *)
 local        :nat;                (* number of local variables   *)
 bytecode     :(list Instruction); (* instructions to be executed *)
 is_static    :bool;               (* flag for static methods     *)
 handler_list:(list handler_type); (* exception handlers          *)
 method_id    :cap_method_idx;     (* index of the method         *)
 owner        :cap_class_idx;      (* index of the owner class    *)
}.
```

where in particular `Instruction` and `type` are inductive types enumerating respectively all the JavaCard bytecode names and the JavaCard type system.

3.2 Representation of JCVM Memory Model

The JCVM memory model is formalized by a type `state` that captures the possible states of the virtual machine during its execution. As suggested above, our memory model is typed, so as to allow for type-checking to be performed at run-time. More precisely, we start from the type of values of the virtual machine. A value is a pair made of the static type of the value and of an integer number:

```
Definition valu := type*Z.
```

and we propagate the type information through the memory model, e.g. through a frame, as described below:

```
Record frame : Set := {
  opstack     : (list valu);        (* operand stack          *)
  locvars     : (list valu);        (* local variables        *)
  method_loc  : cap_method_idx;     (* location of the method *)
  context_ref : Package;            (* context information    *)
  p_count     : bytecode_idx        (* program counter        *)
}.

Definition stack := (list frame).
```

Then, we represent objects, than can be either class instances or arrays, with an inductive (sum) type:

```
Inductive obj : Set :=
          Instance : type_instance → obj |
          Array    : type_array → obj.
```

Both `type_instance` and `type_array` are record types that contain all the relevant information for describing instances and arrays respectively. For example, a class instance is described by the index of the class from which the object is an instance, the instance variables (as a list of `valu`), the reference to the owning package and a flag to indicate whether the object is an entry point and whether it is a permanent or temporary entry point (entry points are used in the JavaCard security model for access control). Formally, we set:

```
Record type_instance : Set := {
  reference       : class_idx;
  contents_i      : (list valu);
  owner_i         : Package;
  entry_point     : bool;
  permanent_e_pt  : bool;
}.
```

Arrays are formalised in a similar fashion.

The heap, in which objects are stored, in naturally defined as a list of objects:

```
Definition heap := (list obj).
```

Finally, a state is defined as a triple:

```
Definition state := static_heap*heap*frame.
```

where `static_heap`, containing static fields of classes, is a list of `valu`.

3.3 Representation of JCVM Instructions

We formalize one-step execution by defining for each instruction a function of type `state` → `returned_state` (the result of one-step execution is tagged to witness normal or abrupt termination). For example, the function defining the `putstatic` bytecodes, that set a static field of a class and exist in four forms (for a reference, a byte or a boolean, a short and an int), is defined by:

```
Definition PUTSTATIC :=
[t:type][idx:static_heap_idx][st:state][cap:jcprogram]

(* Extracts topmost frame of the stack *)
Cases (get_topframe st) of
(value h) ⇒
  (*Extracts the head of the operand stack of the topmost frame*)
  Cases (head (opstack h)) of
  (value x) ⇒
    (* Extracts the idx-th element of the static heap *)
    Cases (Nth_elt (get_static_heap st) idx) of
    (value (tnod,vnod)) ⇒
      Cases t tnod of
        (Ref_)        (Ref_) ⇒ (res_putstatic_ref st x idx cap) |
        (Prim Byte)   (Prim Byte)    ⇒ (res_putstatic st x idx) |
        (Prim Byte)   (Prim Boolean) ⇒ (res_putstatic st x idx) |
        (Prim Short)  (Prim Short)   ⇒ (res_putstatic st x idx) |
        (Prim Int)    (Prim Int)     ⇒ (res_putstatic st x idx) |
        _             _              ⇒ (AbortCode type_error st)
      end |
    error ⇒ (AbortCode static_heap_error st)
    end |
  error ⇒ (AbortCode opstack_error st)
  end |
error ⇒ (AbortCode state_error st)
end.
```

Note that:

- the first argument `t` is there used to summarize in a single Coq function the four different `putstatic` bytecodes;
- if this first argument is `Byte`, the bytecode can be used to set a value of type `Byte` or `Boolean`;
- the `res_putstatic` and `res_putstatic_ref` functions construct a term of type `returned_state` corresponding to the resulting new state of the bytecode;
- the `AbortCode` function constructs a `returned_state` tagged to witness an abrupt termination and the reason of the error;
- the semantics embeds many of the checks that are usually performed at compile-time, including the type-checking verifications performed by the ByteCode Verifier.

Finally, we define a function exec_instruction that dispatches bytecode names from the inductive type Instruction to our formalization of the semantics of the bytecodes.

In the next section, we show how to construct from this defensive virtual machine an offensive virtual machine that does not perform type-checking at run-time.

4 The Offensive Virtual Machine

In this section, we flesh out the construction of an offensive virtual machine from the defensive machine described in the previous section. To start with, we remove typing information from values and set:

```
Definition valu := Z.
```

We notice that valu is defined in both defensive and offensive virtual machines, so we will use the notation for qualified names introduced in Section 2 wherever the two definitions are in the same scope. off_JCVM is the name of the module in which the offensive virtual machine is defined.

The definitions of frame and state remain unchanged but now use the redefined valu type. This leads to a simplified memory model in which type information is omitted wherever valu is used. Next, the semantics of each instruction is modified. More precisely, type-checking verifications are eliminated, as exemplified by the function:

```
Definition PUTSTATIC :=
[t:type][idx:static_heap_idx][st:state][cap:jcprogram]

Cases (get_topframe st) of
(value h) ⇒
  Cases (head (opstack h)) of
  (value x) ⇒
    Cases (Nth_elt (get_static_heap st) idx) of
    (value nod) ⇒
      Cases t of
        (Ref _)  ⇒ (res_putstatic_ref st x idx cap) |
        (Prim _) ⇒ (res_putstatic st x idx)
      end |
    error ⇒ (AbortCode static_heap_error st)
    end |
  error ⇒ (AbortCode opstack_error st)
  end |
error ⇒ (AbortCode state_error st)
end.
```

The type t is only used to discriminate the different PUTSTATIC bytecodes for which the semantics differs depending t is a primitive or reference type.

Note that the process of constructing the offensive virtual machine is inspired from abstract interpretation. Indeed, one can define a function alpha_off_valu of type valu → off_JCVM.valu that maps values of the defensive virtual machine to values of the offensive virtual machine, removing typing information:

```
Definition alpha_off_valu [v:valu] : off_JCVM.valu := (Snd v).
```

Then alpha_off_valu is extended to frame in the locations valu is used:

```
Definition alpha_off_frame [h:frame] : off_JCVM.frame :=
  (off_JCVM.Build_frame (map alpha_off_valu (opstack h))
                        (map alpha_off_valu (locvars h))
                        (method_loc h)
                        (context_ref h)
                        (p_count h)).
```

We define in a similar way alpha_off for states and alpha_off_rs for returned states. Hereafter, we will use off_state for off_JCVM.state and off_returned_state for off_JCVM.returned_state.

Finally, the offensive semantics of each instruction is defined in such a way that the diagram of Figure 1 commutes, provided the defensive virtual machine does not raise any type error (the AbortCode function will not be called with the type_error parameter). Note that we slightly depart from standard abstract interpretation because the construction of the offensive virtual machine assumes some checks made by the defensive virtual machine to be successful, and hence the diagram only commutes under the proviso that these checks are indeed successful.

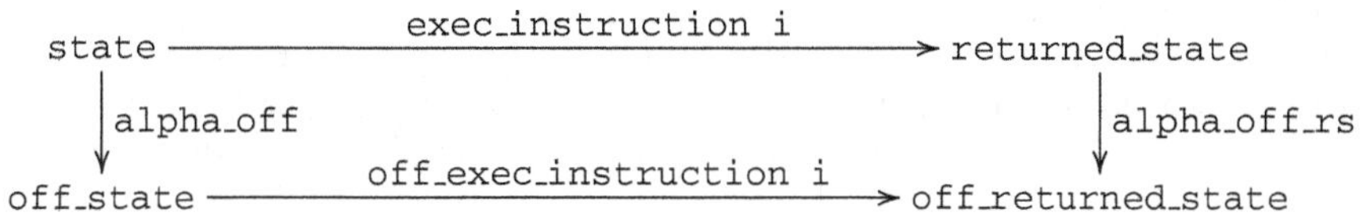

Fig. 1. Commutative diagram of defensive and offensive execution

In the next section, we present a formal proof of the diagram in Coq.

5 Equivalence of Offensive and Defensive Machines

The equivalence between offensive and defensive virtual machines is stated as a commutation property between both executions, under the assumption that defensive execution does not raise any typing error. Formally, we want to prove:

```
((execs n p) ≠ (AbortCode type_error state))) →
(alpha_off_rs (execs n p)) = (off_execs n (alpha_off p))
```

where `execs n p` (resp. `off_execs`) denotes the result of executing the defensive (resp. offensive) virtual machine n steps starting from the initial state associated to the JavaCard program p.

This is done in Coq by proving this property for each bytecode of the virtual machine. For the `putstatic` bytecode, it leads to the following statement:

```
Lemma PUTSTATIC_commut: (st:state)(t:type)(n:nat)(cap:jcprogram)
  let res = (exec_instruction (putstatic t n) st cap) in
  let off_res =
    (off_exec_instruction (putstatic t n) (alpha_off st) cap) in
  (~res = (AbortCode type_error st)) →
      (alpha_off_rs res cap) = off_res.
```

The proof is similar to the proof of commutation of the abstract virtual machine discussed in Section 6, and exploits a new package that performs inversion principles for functions [2]. In a nutshell, the tactic allows to split the proof of properties of the form $\forall \boldsymbol{x}.\ \phi(\boldsymbol{x}, f\boldsymbol{x})$, where f is a recursive function defined by a complex case analysis, into easier proofs of the form

$$\forall \boldsymbol{x}.\ s_1 = t_1 \rightarrow \ \ldots \ \rightarrow s_n = t_n \rightarrow \phi(\boldsymbol{x}, f\boldsymbol{x})$$

where the equalities correspond to one possible case of the function's definition, one subgoal per possible case. The tactic is very useful to prove commutation properties, as the equalities it generates often make the proof of $\phi(\boldsymbol{x}, f\boldsymbol{x})$ trivial.

The size of proof scripts for commutation properties of our virtual machines can be up to 8 times smaller than without the tactic. Indeed, we get directly a reduced goal whereas we had previously to decompose the state and rewrite the goal step by step. Furthermore, factorization of some part of the script is eased wherever same tactics are used for differents goals.

Using this tactic, under the context `st:state`, `t:type`, `n:nat`, `cap:jcprogram`, and if `G` is the term corresponding to the `PUTSTATIC_commut` lemma without the previous universal quantifiers, we will have to prove 40 subgoals such as:

- Subgoal 1:
  ```
  (sh:static_heap)(hp:heap) st=(sh,(hp,(nil frame))) →G
  ```
- Subgoal 2:
  ```
  (sh:static_heap)(hp:heap)(f:frame)(lf:(list frame))
  st=(sh,(hp,(cons h lf))) →(head (opstack h))=error →G
  ```
- Subgoal 8:
  ```
  (sh:static_heap)(hp:heap)(f:frame)(lf:(list frame))(x:valu)
  (z:Z)
  st=(sh,(hp,(cons h lf))) →(head (opstack h))=(value x) →
  (Nth_elt (get_static_heap st) idx)=(value((Prim Short),z)) →
  t=(Prim Int) →G
  ```
- Subgoal 9:
  ```
  (sh:static_heap)(hp:heap)(f:frame)(lf:(list frame))(x:valu)
  (z:Z)
  st=(sh,(hp,(cons h lf))) →(head (opstack h))=(value x) →
  (Nth_elt (get_static_heap st) idx)=(value ((Prim Int), z)) →
  t=(Prim Int) →G
  ```

The generated equalities are automatically rewritten into `G` leading to trivial proofs for all the generated subgoals. For the subgoal 9, where the execution behaves normally with `Int` types (`res_putstatic` has been called and unfolded), `G` is rewritten to:

```
 ~(Normal ((l_update_nth sh idx x),
          (hp,
          (cons (update_opstack (tail opstack h) h)
            (tail (cons h lf))))))
  =(off_JCVM.AbortCode type_error (sh,(hp,(cons h lf))))
→(alpha_off_rs (Normal
                ((l_update_nth sh idx x),
                (hp,
                (cons (update_opstack (tail opstack h) h)
                  (tail (cons h lf))))))
    cap)
 =(off_JCVM.Normal
      ((l_update_nth (alpha_off_sh sh) idx (alpha_off_valu x)),
       ((alpha_off_heap hp),
        (cons (off_JCVM.update_opstack
                     (lvalu2lovalu (tail (opstack h)))
                     (alpha_off_frame h))
          (tail (cons (alpha_off_frame h)
                  (alpha_off_lframe lf)))))))
```

The hypothesis is useless for this subgoal where the two results of the execution are equal.

6 Relation with Bytecode Verification

In [4], we construct an abstract virtual machine operating on types and derive from it an executable ByteCode Verifier by implementing a data-flow analysis as specified in Sun's specification. In this section, we briefly review this construction and show that both offensive and defensive virtual machines coincide on those programs that pass bytecode verification.

6.1 The Abstract Virtual Machine and Its Correctness Proof

As emphasized in the introduction, defensiveness results in having a type-checker hidden inside the JavaCard Virtual Machine. Subsequently, we can use abstraction techniques to flesh out type-checking. Concretely, the abstract JCVM is given by a notion of abstract state `abs_state`, derived from the notion of abstract value (with a slightly different type system due a special treatment of the type `ReturnAddress`):

```
Definition valu := abs_type.
```

an abstraction function `alpha_abs` of type:

```
state → abs_state
```

and an abstract semantics for each instruction as a function of type:

abs_state → list abs_state

Note that abstractions may lead to non-determinism (such as for the ifnull bytecode that branches to two different program counters), hence the abstract execution of an instruction may return several states, which we collect in a list.

Having defined the abstract virtual machine, one must establish the correctness of this virtual machine w.r.t. the defensive virtual machine. Again, correctness is expressed as a commuting diagram. Namely, the abstraction is shown correct by proving that, for every instruction, providing the defensive virtual machine does not raise exceptions, the diagram of Figure 2 relating defensive and abstract execution commutes—the function alpha_abs_rs of type returned_state → returned_abs_state extends alpha_off to returned states.

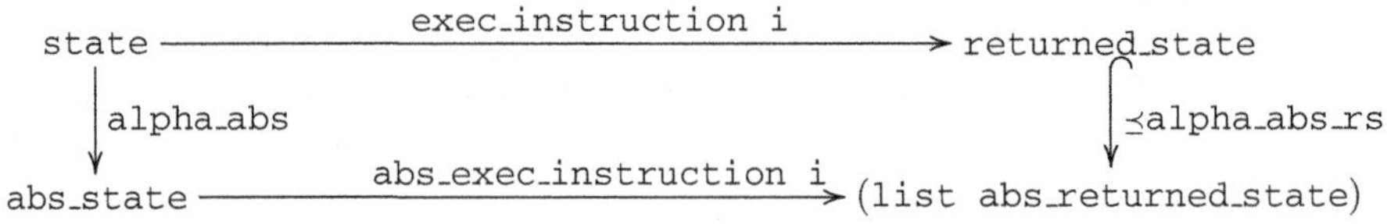

Fig. 2. Commutative diagram of defensive and abstract execution

The hooked vertical arrow on the right-hand side of the diagram means that the abstraction of the concrete returned state is, up to subtyping, a member of the list of abstract returned states.

6.2 Bytecode Verification and Its Correctness

The bytecode verifier is constructed from the abstract virtual machine using a data-flow analysis that iterates executing the abstract virtual machine by a process described in [4]. Formally, the function bcv:jcprogram → bool is defined by well-founded recursion and hence contains a proof of termination of the data-flow analysis. The correctness of the BCV states that, if bytecode verification is successful, then the function AbortCode will not be called, and hence that no typing error occurs at run-time.

The correctness proof of the ByteCode Verification, which uses the correctness of the abstraction, ensures that both defensive and offensive virtual machines coincide for those programs that pass bytecode verification. Formally, we do so by showing that for every program p:jcprogram such that bcv p = true, we have

(alpha_off (execs n p)) = (off_execs n (alpha_off p)).

7 Conclusion

We have shown how to construct an offensive JavaCard Virtual Machine from a defensive one. Further, we establish that the two machines coincide for the class of JavaCard programs that pass bytecode verification, thus providing a formal correspondence between the defensive virtual machine, the offensive virtual machine and bytecode verification. Both the construction of the offensive virtual machine and its correctness proof are cast in terms of (non-standard) abstract interpretations, which provide a rigorous justification of our methodology and opens the way for automated tool support.

Further, the constructions and verifications have been machine-checked in Coq, which together with the work reported in [4], provides us with one of the most in-depth machine-checked accounts of the JavaCard platform to date.

7.1 Related Work

The literature abounds with formal specifications of the Java and JavaCard Virtual Machine, see e.g. [6, 9, 19, 21, 22, 23, 24, 25, 27] to cite only a few. However it should be noted that, in general, these specifications only consider subsets of the the virtual machine and, often being tailored towards Java, do not consider specific aspects of JavaCard such as transactions and firewalls.

As emphasized in the introduction, only a few authors consider both an offensive and a defensive virtual machines. We briefly review their work and compare their approaches to ours.

- In their J-Book, Börger *et al.* [27] propose Abstract State Machines (ASMs) [29] based models of several Java virtual machines. In particular, they start from a trustful (offensive) machine that assumes programs to be successfully verified, and build from it a defensive machine which performs type checks before trustful execution. While their work also highlights the tight relationships between the two machines, their approach seems less practical for automated construction and validation of virtual machines. In particular, it does not seem as straightforward to build a tool that constructs automatically a defensive virtual machine from its offensive and abstract counterpart.
- In a series of papers [8, 19, 25], Casset, Lanet and Requet report on the use of the B method [1] for specifying the JavaCard platform. Like us, they start from a defensive virtual machine and use refinement to construct an offensive virtual machine and a bytecode verifier. The correctness proof of the offensive virtual machine is then expressed as the correctness proof of the refinement. Their methodology is similar to ours, but they only consider a subset of the virtual machine that does not include the JavaCard specificities and is "not representative of the tricky parts of the instruction set". Further, the B method is not suitable for establishing some important properties of the platform, such as the termination of the data-flow analysis used in bytecode verification.

7.2 Future Work

The methodology advocated in this paper is generic enough to be applied in a number of analyses related e.g. to initialization [11, 17], information flow [5, 7] and resource control [12]. We are currently applying this methodology to modified defensive virtual machines to extract stronger type systems for JavaCard. In order to facilitate these studies, we have undertaken the design and implementation of the Jakarta toolset, which aims at automating most of the construction and correctness proofs of the offensive and abstract virtual machines [3]. An offensive virtual machine has already been automatically built using the Jakarta toolset. We believe this line of work will provide valuable insight and tool support for designing the type systems of future versions of JavaCard.

References

[1] J.-R. Abrial. *The B-Book: Assigning Programs to Meanings.* Cambridge University Press, 1996.
[2] G. Barthe and P. Courtieu. Efficient Reasoning about Executable Specifications in Coq. Manuscript, 2002.
[3] G. Barthe, G. Dufay, M. Huisman, and S. Melo de Sousa. Jakarta: a toolset to reason about the JavaCard platform. In I. Attali and T. Jensen, editors, *Proceedings of e-SMART'01*, volume 2140 of *Lecture Notes in Computer Science*, pages 2–18. Springer-Verlag, 2001.
[4] G. Barthe, G. Dufay, L. Jakubiec, B. Serpette, and S. Melo de Sousa. A Formal Executable Semantics of the JavaCard Platform. In D. Sands, editor, *Proceedings of ESOP'01*, volume 2028 of *Lecture Notes in Computer Science*, pages 302–319. Springer-Verlag, 2001.
[5] C. Bernardeschi and N. De Francesco. Combining abstract interpretation and model checking for analysing security properties of java bytecode. In A. Cortesi, editor, *Proceedings of VMCAI'02*, volume 2xxx of *Lecture Notes in Computer Science*, 2002.
[6] Y. Bertot. Formalizing in Coq a type system for object initialization in the Java bytecode language. In G. Berry, H. Comon, and A. Finkel, editors, *Proceedings of CAV'01*, volume 2102 of *Lecture Notes in Computer Science*, pages 14–24. Springer-Verlag, 2001.
[7] P. Bieber, J. Cazin, V. Wiels, G. Zanon, P. Girard, and J.-L. Lanet. Electronic purse applet certification: extended abstract. In S. Schneider and P. Ryan, editors, *Proceedings of the workshop on secure architectures and information flow*, volume 32 of *Electronic Notes in Theoretical Computer Science.* Elsevier Publishing, 2000.
[8] L. Casset and J.-L. Lanet. A Formal Specification of the Java Byte Code Semantics using the B Method. In B. Jacobs, G. T. Leavens, P. Müller, and A. Poetzsch-Heffter, editors, *Proceedings of Formal Techniques for Java Programs.* Technical Report 251, 1999, Fernuniversität Hagen, Fernuniversität Hagen, 1999.
[9] R. M. Cohen. Defensive Java Virtual Machine Specification Version 0.5. Manuscript, 1997.
[10] P. Cousot. Abstract Interpretation Based Formal Methods and Future Challenges. In R. Wilhelm, editor, *Informatics — 10 Years Back, 10 Years Ahead*, volume 2000 of *Lecture Notes in Computer Science*, pages 138–156. Springer-Verlag, 2001.

[11] S. N. Freund and J. C. Mitchell. The type system for object initialization in the Java bytecode language. *ACM Transactions on Programming Languages and Systems*, 21(6):1196–1250, November 1999.

[12] A. Galland, D. Deville, G. Grimaud, and B. Folliot. Contrôle des ressources dans les cartes à microprocesseur. In *Proceedings of LTRE'02*, 2002.

[13] P. Girard. Which security policy for multiapplication smart cards? In *Proceedings of Usenix workshop on Smart Card Technology (Smartcard'99)*, 1999.

[14] P. Hartel and L. Moreau. Formalizing the Safety of Java, the Java Virtual Machine and Java Card. *ACM Computing Surveys*, 33:517–558, December 2001.

[15] JavaCard Forum. `http://www.javacardforum.org`

[16] JavaCard Technology. `http://java.sun.com/products/javacard`

[17] G. Klein and T. Nipkow. Verified bytecode verifiers. *Theoretical Computer Science*, 2002. Submitted.

[18] Gemplus Research Labs. Java Card Common Criteria Certification Using Coq. Technical Report, 2001.

[19] J.-L. Lanet and A. Requet. Formal Proof of Smart Card Applets Correctness. In J.-J. Quisquater and B. Schneier, editors, *Proceedings of CARDIS'98*, volume 1820 of *Lecture Notes in Computer Science*, pages 85–97. Springer-Verlag, 1998.

[20] M. Montgomery and K. Krishna. Secure Object Sharing in Java Card. In *Proceedings of Usenix workshop on Smart Card Technology, (Smartcard'99)*, 1999.

[21] J. Strother Moore, R. Krug, H. Liu, and G. Porter. Formal Models of Java at the JVM Level A Survey from the ACL2 Perspective. In S. Drossopoulou, editor, *Proceedings of Formal Techniques for Java Programs*, 2001.

[22] T. Nipkow. Verified Bytecode Verifiers. In F. Honsell and M. Miculan, editors, *Proceedings of FOSSACS'01*, volume 2030 of *Lecture Notes in Computer Science*, pages 347–363. Springer-Verlag, 2001.

[23] C. Pusch. Proving the soundness of a Java bytecode verifier specification in Isabelle/HOL. In W. R. Cleaveland, editor, *Proceedings of TACAS'99*, volume 1579 of *Lecture Notes in Computer Science*, pages 89–103. Springer-Verlag, 1999.

[24] Z. Qian. A Formal Specification of Java Virtual Machine Instructions for Objects, Methods and Subroutines. In J. Alves-Foss, editor, *Formal Syntax and Semantics of Java*, volume 1523 of *Lecture Notes in Computer Science*, pages 271–312. Springer-Verlag, 1999.

[25] A. Requet. A B Model for Ensuring Soundness of a Large Subset of the Java Card Virtual Machine. In S. Gnesi, I. Schieferdecker, and A. Rennoch, editors, *Proceedings of FMICS'00*, pages 29–46, 2000.

[26] D.A. Schmidt. Binary relations for abstraction and refinement. Technical Report 2000-3, Department of Computing and Information Sciences, Kansas State University, 2000.

[27] R. Stärk, J. Schmid, and E. Börger. *Java and the Java Virtual Machine - Definition, Verification, Validation.* Springer-Verlag, 2001.

[28] The Coq Development Team. *The Coq Proof Assistant User's Guide. Version 7.2*, January 2002.

[29] The ASM homepage. `http://www.eecs.umich.edu/gasm`

Analyzing Cryptographic Protocols in a Reactive Framework

R.K. Shyamasundar

School of Technology and Computer Science, Tata Institute of Fundamental Research, Mumbai 400005, India
shyam@tcs.tifr.res.in

Abstract. In this paper, we analyze the suitability of reactive frameworks for modelling and verification of cryptographic protocols. Our study shows that cryptographic protocols can be modelled easily and naturally including the communication feature of the Internet wherein a point-to-point communication could be interpreted as broadcast mechanism due to the underlying routing and LAN architectures. The reactive framework provides an effective modelling of attacks/intruders as well as the capturing of the security properties such as secrecy and authenticity as *observers*. The *observer-based* approach of synchronous reactive frameworks aids in the modelling of properties incrementally and the use of the simulate-compile-verify cycle of the synchronous programming environment. The anomalies that could arise due to possible concurrent runs of agents can be detected. For illustration purposes, we use the TMN protocol. We will also argue that the reactive frameworks also provide a basis for specifying cryptographic protocols.

1 Introduction

Public key encryptions are commonly used for secure communications over public computer networks. Development of e-commerce over the Internet has lead to a wide spectrum of secure protocols, called cryptographic protocols, that use cryptographic primitives for transactions. In these protocols, it is very important to ensure *security* as interactions take place over public networks that are basically insecure. In such protocols, it is very crucial to ensure:

- Messages meant of an agent cannot be read/accessed by others (*secrecy*).
- Guarantee genuineness of the sender of the message. (*authenticity*)

On any insecure network, there will be active attacks (attackers themselves are bona-fide users of the network!) to get information of other bona-fide agents by eavesdropping/impersonating other valid agents. Establishing secrecy and authenticity have two issues:

1. The possibility of breaking the encrypted message, and
2. Ensuring secrecy and authenticity of messages.

A. Cortesi (Ed.): VMCAI 2002, LNCS 2294, pp. 46–64, 2002.
© Springer-Verlag Berlin Heidelberg 2002

From the perspective of cryptographic protocol verification, it is the second aspect one is concerned with assuming that the encryption cannot be broken without the underlying secret key. The problem can be stated as follows:

Assuming the non-crackability of cryptographic primitives, establish that the protocol maintains secrecy and authenticity of transactions.

In the literature, techniques of establishing the correctness of classical distributed protocols have been adapted for establishing the secrecy/authenticity of the cryptographic protocols. Approaches can be broadly categorized as follows: (1) State Machine Models [11, 14], (2) π-Calculus Based Models [1], (3) Methods Based on Belief Logics [5], and (4) Theorem Prover based Methods [8, 3, 16, 4, 19, 9]. [17] provides an annotated bibliography.

In the area provably correct systems, there have been quite considerable efforts in the specification and verification of reactive systems [7]. The family of synchronous languages [2] has been well studied for the design and synthesis of provably correct reactive systems. Synchronous languages also support a powerful programming environment including verification. In this paper, we show that the techniques of modelling and verifying reactive systems in synchronous languages such as ESTEREL can be effectively used for verifying the correctness of cryptographic protocols. As ESTEREL has a precise formal semantics and powerful tool based techniques for verification, it is possible to model the protocol and the attacker cleanly and establish the security properties using its' simulate-compile-verify programming environment. The environment also permits us to find if flaw exists if concurrent runs of the protocol are allowed for the principals. Our reactive approach seems to satisfy some of the goals set by approaches of defining simples specification languages exclusively for cryptographic protocols [10]. Furthermore, the availability of *preemption* in ESTEREL allows the modelling of complex e-commerce protocols that use preemptive features at various points. Throughtout our presentation, we try to convey the underlying principles and intuition for the sake of simplicity and brevity.

2 Analysis of Cryptographic Protocols

Analysis of the cryptographic protocols is usually based on

1. *The model of the intruder*: The most widely used classical model of the intruder is that described in Dolev and Yao [6] where:
   (a) Intruder can obtain/decompose any message passing via the network.
   (b) Intruder can remember/insert messages using the data seen.
   (c) As the intruder is a legitimate user of the network, and can initiate a conversation with any user.
   (d) Given the key, the intruder can encrypt/decrypt a message.
   (e) Intruder *cannot* get partial information, guess the key or perform statistical tests, and
   (f) Encrypted message can neither be altered nor read without the key.

2. *Characteristics of Protocols*: The main characteristics are:
   (a) Roles of principals are finite.
   (b) Computational steps of each principal are finite.
   (c) All the messages are bounded in size.
   (d) Nonces (new messages) can be created.
   (e) Except for the Nonces all other entities are constants.

Informally speaking, the protocol is said to be correct under the above general model of the intruder and the characteristics of the protocol, if it is not possible for an intruder, say C, to get the key of some principal, say A, fraudulently while A is trying to transact with another principal, say B.

2.1 Issues in the Modelling of the Protocol and the Intruder

Protocols in general are operational descriptions of actions and reactions (responses). In general, they follow the principle that for every set (or sequence) of actions a finite set of reactions is expected. The general characteristics that needs to be catered/adhered to are:

1. Possible actions/roles that can be taken by the principals; while the roles of the intruder may be nondeterministic fashion, the reactions are deterministic.
2. Properties of communication medium and the Cryptographic primitives.
3. The operational structure of the protocol.
4. Protocol properties other than that are related to security.
5. Capabilities of the Attacker: eavesdropping over the network, sending fraudulent/forged messages, interception of messages etc. These capabilities are quite general and are not dependent on the protocol.
6. The general principles adhered to by the *Server* (like never re-issuing session keys or agents their Nonces).
7. Thus, the attacker is also a valid principal in the system and the intruder could be doing his genuine role as well as that of an attacker concurrently.
8. Security properties such as secrecy, authenticity as intended.

3 Modelling Cryptographic Protocols in Esterel

In this section, we discuss modelling cryptographic protocols using Esterel and use use the TMN protocol [18] studied in detail in [12] for illustrations. First, we shall consider the basic protocol to illustrate the modelling and subsequently, we shall discuss possible attacks on the protocol and the improvements needed to make the protocol *secure*.

Note 1. For illustrative purpose, we shall be using Esterel to model cryptographic protocols with a view to model and verify relative to various types of intruders. Note that the cryptographic protocols do require the manipulation of cryptographic primitives. However, in synchronous languages the general programming language features are usually borrowed from those existing in the host language such as C or java in which they are embedded. In our illustrations of modelling in ESTEREL, we abuse the usual notation of procedure calls and parameter transmissions for the sake of simplicity and succinctness. As the notation is fairly standard, no confusion should result. Such an interface for ESTEREL for cryptographic protocol analysis purposes is being built.

3.1 Basic TMN Protocol

TMN protocol [18] consists of three players: an *initiator* A, a *responder* B, and a *server* S who mediates between them for the generation of session keys. The protocol employs two methods of encryption:
a. Standard encryption: The function denoted E when applied to a message m produces an encrypted text that can be decrypted with a secret key. Further, the encrypted message can be decrypted only by the server. A typical example of such a method is the RSA encryption.
b. Vernam Encryption: This is written $V(k_1, k_2)$ and gives the bit-wise exclusive-or. It is be noted that $V(k_1, V(k_1, k_2)) = k_2$ and $V(k_2, V(k_1, k_2)) = k_1$.
Protocol: The protocol in the notation of [12] is given below:

`Message 1:` $A \rightarrow S$: $A.S.B.E(K_a)$
`Message 2:` $S \rightarrow B$: $S.B.A$
`Message 3:` $B \rightarrow S$: $B.S.A.E(K_b)$
`Message 4:` $S \rightarrow A$: $S.A.B.V(K_a,\ K_b)$

The simple model of the protocol corresponding to the above description is shown in Figure 1. We have used a bus rather than explicit channels as that resembles the model of the Internet structure (which is essentially a store forward network). The numbers over the messages shown in complete lines in Figure 1, correspond to the message numbers given above. The dotted lines with numbers with an apostrophe show the dual of picking up the message (corresponding to receipt).

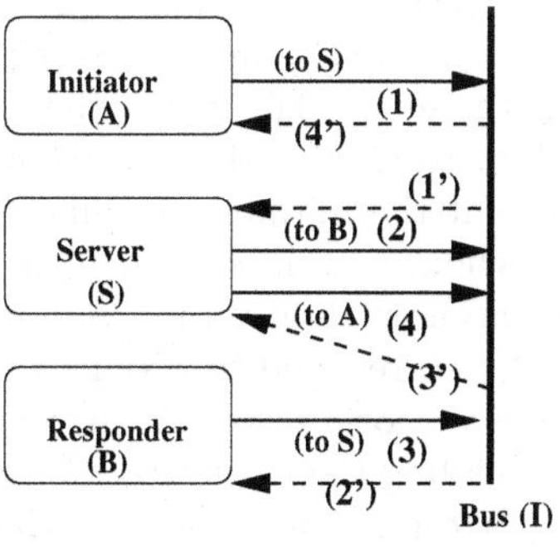

Fig. 1. Structure of the TMN Protocol

Note 2. We use $E(K_a)$ and $V(K_a, K_b)$ with the arguments explicitly even though only the respective values are seen rather than the components; explicit syntax helps us to keep track of different modules and parameter bindings.

3.2 Modelling the Basic TMN Protocol in Esterel

The model of communication used in ESTEREL is the broadcast mechanism; that is, whoever is ready to see /listen to a message can see/will get it at that point. Such a feature becomes handy in the modelling of the Internet which is a essentially a Store-Forward packet network (where message packets at any router can be seen by everyone who are on the same bus or access to it). This feature avoids the need of artificial channels for modelling communication as required in models based on CSP or CCS. Further, the orthogonality of concurrency and communication in ESTEREL makes it possible to model concurrent roles simultaneously. Specification of principals in ESTEREL taking the role of an initiator, responder and server respectively are shown in Figures 2, 3, and 4 respectively. The specification has been parameterized with respect to the behaviour of the principal. The labels on the statements are used for purposes of reference only. The overall TMN protocol with the above three agents is shown in Figure 5.

Note 3. The message structure is treated as a string from which the components can be extracted[1] by some function say, *Extract* (not shown).

Discussion: The three principals A,B and S are part of the TMN protocol. Each agent is doing some other computation other than that of participating in the protocol as required for transacting with other agents. Note that this a nonterminating behaviour. In the following, we shall informally discuss the actions performed by A as an initiator, B as a responder and S as a server.
Initiator: Labels $\ell_{i_0}, ...\ell_{i_3}$ correspond to actions with the interpretation: (i) await for some signal to initiate a session with a responder, (ii) make known to the server the intention to have a session with a responder with the underlying structure for the message packet, (iii) wait for some finite time for the server (which is indicated by the signal `tick`, and (iv) receive the response from the server as and when it sends the session key. Since, the underlying model assumes that the principals know how to extract the key given a priori known message structure, it follows easily that the initiator (in this case agent A) will get the key of the responder with whom it wanted to have a transaction (in this case agent B) using the simplification rules given for Vernam encryption earlier.
Responder: Labels $\ell_{r_0}, ...\ell_{r_3}$ correspond to actions with the interpretation: (i) await for request from the server for a response, (ii) waiting for some finite time before answering, and (iii) sending the requested information to the server.
Server: Labels $\ell_{s_0}, ...\ell_{s_3}$ correspond to actions having the interpretation: (i) awaiting for an initiator, (ii) waiting for sometime before sending the request to the responder, (iii) sending the request to the responder, (iv) awaiting a

[1] It must be noted, that in ESTEREL all such aspects are done as per the host language which can be C, Java etc.

```
module Initiator;
   input start; Is: some_string_type;
   output Ia : some_string_type;
   var Ka: key_bit_type;
       A: initiator_type; B: responder_type; S: server_type;
   loop
       ℓi0: await start;
       ℓi1: emit Ia(A,S,B,E(Ka));
                     %Structure:(sender.via,destination,encrypted_msg)%
       ℓi2: await tick;
       ℓi3: await Is(S,A,B,V(Ka,Kb))
success:
   endloop
end module
```

Fig. 2. Model of Initiator

```
module Responder;
   input Is: some_string_type;
   output Ib : some_string_type;
   var Kb: key_type;
       A: initiator_type; B: responder_type; S: server_type;
   loop   ℓr0: await immediate Is(S,B,A);
          ℓr1: await tick;
          ℓr2: emit Ib(B,S,A,E(Kb);
   endloop
end module
```

Fig. 3. Model of Responder

```
module Server:
   input Ia, Ib: some_string_type;
   output Is: some_string_type;
   var A: initiator_type; B: responder_type; S: server_type;
       key_initiator, key_receiver: key_type;
   loop ℓs0: await immediate Ia(A,S,B,E(Ka);
        A:= first(Ia(A,S,B,E(Ka)); B:= third(Ia(A,S,B,E(Ka));
        key_initiator:= getkey (Ia(A,S,B,E(Ka));
        ℓs1: await tick;
        ℓs2: emit Is(S,B,A);
        ℓs3: await Ib(B,S,A,E(KB));
        key_receiver:=getkey(Ir(B,S,A,E(Kb));
        ℓs4: await tick;
        ℓs5: emit Is(S,A,B, V(Ka,Kb))
   endloop
end module
```

Fig. 4. Model of Server

```
module TMN;
  input start;
  output Ia, Ib, Is: some_string_type;
  run initiator [Ia/Ia, Is/Is, Ka/Ka, A/A,B/B,S/S]
||
  run responder [Ib/Ib, Is/Is, Kb/Kb,A/A,B/B,S/S]
||
  run server;
end module
```

Fig. 5. Model of the TMN Protocol with Three Principals

response from the server - allowing it sometime for responding, (v) again awaiting before sending the information to the initiator and (vi) sending the required key information in the agreed structure to the initiator.

3.3 Characteristic Features of the Model

Capturing the roles and capabilities of the agents:

The model clearly articulates, the roles of agents, message packets, possible concurrent roles etc. To be more specific:

- The capabilities of the principals and the protocol followed by them are explicit.
- In the protocol, we have shown A to be performing the role of an initiator, B the role of a responder and S the role of a server. From the parameterized specifications, it is easy to see how the role of the principal can be changed and also several (finite) roles can be conceived concurrently.
- Further, I_a, I_b, I_s can be seen as packets that can be seen by the principals while being alert in the scope. This is one of the ways of abstracting the model of the public network with routers.

Verifying the proof obligations for message passing

- An initiator will get the key sent by the responder via the server given that responder and server react in finite time.
- Ignoring functional rewritings of the equation, the question corresponds to: $at(\ell_1) \leadsto after(\ell_{i_3})$ or in terms of messages I_a(A,S,B,E(K_a)) $\leadsto$ I_s(S,A,B,V(K_a, K_b)) where $at(p)$ $after(p)$ are the usual control predicates that indicate whether the control point is currently "at p" or has crossed "p" respectively.
- The inferences follow naturally from the automata constructed using the `Xeve` tool[2] for the above program and showing that the constructed automata is symbolically bisimilar to the automata corresponding to the trace $[I_a(A, S, B, E(K_a)) \quad I_s(S, A, B, V(K_a, K_b))]^*$ where "*" denotes the usual

[2] A proof tool based on symbolic bisimulation available for synchronous frameworks.

Kleene-star operation denoting finite a priori unbounded repetitions of the trace. Other implicit relations of the actions of the principals A,B and S can also be captured by similar trace structures.

3.4 Analyzing Security Properties

In this section, we shall discuss the analysis of security properties.

First, we generalize the model with several principals as shown in Figure 6 having m initiators and n responders. Note that the correspondence of initiators and responders need not be one-to-one physically.

```
module TMN-many;
  input start: boolean;
  output I_a1, ··· , I_am, I_b1, ··· , I_bn, I_s: some_string_type;
  run initiator [I_a1/I_a, I_s/I_s, K_a1/K_a, A_1/A, B_(1)/B,S/S]
            ...
|| run initiator [I_an/I_a, I_s/I_s, K_an/K_a, A_n/A, B_(m)/B,S/S]
|| run responder [I_b1/I_b, I_s/I_s, K_b1/K_b, A_(1)/A, B_1/B,S/S]
|| ...
|| run responder [I_bm/I_b, I_s/I_s, K_bm/K_b,A_(n)/A,B_m/B, S/S]
|| run server;
```

Fig. 6. Model of the TMN Protocol with Several Principals

Security Properties via Traces: Let A_i be the initiator and let B_j be the corresponding responder; we assume A_i is not the same as B_j. We say that *the protocol is secure under the assumption of non-crackability of the cryptographic primitive if the key, K_{b_j} sent by B_j to A_i via the server occurs only in the form $V(K_{a_i}, K_{b_j})$*. That is, for the latest request from A_i to B_j, there is no other message of the form $V(K_{a_r}, K_{b_j})$ for some $r \neq i$ message in the system. Now, let us see whether the protocol discussed above satisfies this property or a counterexample or an attack can be found. In the module structure shown in Figure 6, it can be seen that the module corresponding to the structure of the initiator or the responder for that instantiation can output only on that named output signal. That means, in the structure shown it is not possible to break security for the following reasons:

- ESTEREL is a lexically scoped typed language. Hence, unless the access to signals is explicitly given or derived under the scoping rules, the modules will not be able to access the signals. In the context shown, we have shown I_a being accessible only by A and the server, and I_b being accessible only by B and the server. In view of the strong typing, no intruder (which in this case has to be other than A or B) will be able send signals mimicking as other agents. In other words, the typing rules ensure that accessing messages not meant for it are out of bound for others.

– Considered in another way, the typing rules ensure the *authenticity* of the messages (i.e., the messages should have been sent by such and such a principal) that was perhaps implicit in the original protocol.

To model attacks wherein the intruders can see messages, create new messages etc., we need to derive a weaker structure than that shown in Figure 6. This is done by permitting each principal to access and broadcast on signals that are not necessarily meant for it. This is achieved by placing signals corresponding to the various initiators and responders in the lexical scope of all initiators and responders (or all valid principals). In this model, one cannot guarantee authenticity as will be seen later.

Note 4. It must be noted that ESTEREL permits concurrent incarnations of a module. For this reason, one could define explicit rules of *combination* when two signals are emitted concurrently.

4 Modelling Intruders, Attacks, and Analysis

The main capabilities of the intruder are:

1. Obtain any message, store them, and reinsert them at some point.
2. Decompose the plain text into different components, modify the components (no breaking is allowed) and insert the messages in the system.

Intruders following the above rules can be obtained by looking at the messages on the bus. Consider the modelling of an intruder corresponding to the messages emitted by the initiator shown in Figure 2. It may be noted that the initiator shown in Figure 2 emits only one message I_a(A,S,B,E(K_a)). As the server is unique, the messages constructed will have the server name unaltered as well as its position unchanged. The possible messages that can be generated or emitted with the capabilities as mentioned above on the message that is normally emitted by an initiator is given by (here, principal C is used to denote an intruder):

I_a(A,S,B,E(K_a))-- corresponds to emitting a message stored earlier;
I_a(A,S,B,E(K_c))-- Alter the key to that of agent C (intruder)
I_a(A,S,C,E(K_a))-- Responder is altered to C.
I_a(A,S,C,E(K_c))-- Responder as well as the key is changed to that of C
I_a(C,S,B,E(K_c))-- C becomes initiator

The other possible messages will not play any role; in fact, the third message shown above also does not play any useful role as the intruder will not be able to derive any useful information as it is its' (intruder) own key that is being passed. Interception (in a sense blocking!) is modelled by an "abort" statement and a signal "intercept" that is a local input signal to the intruder. Thus, when I_a and *intercept* are simultaneous, I_a would be intercepted. We have not shown the possibility of it being stored just for simplicity. An intruder, C, that alters the messages read from A as above, is given in Figure 7. In the figure, the signals, "zero, one, two, three, and four" are input signals that have been used to model

```
module Crude-init;
  input zero, one, two, three, four, intercept;
  loop
    abort
     await Ia(C,S,B,E(Kc));
     await immediate
      case zero do Ia(A,S,B,E(Ka));
      case one do emit Ia(A,S,B,E(Kc));
      case two do emit Ia(A,S,C,E(Ka)) ;
      case three do emit Ia(A,S,C,E(Kc));
      case four do emit Ia(C,S,B,E(Kc));
   when intercept;
  endloop
end module Crude-init
```

Fig. 7. Crude Intruder of Initiator

input nondeterminacy corresponding to the possibilities of emitting messages mentioned above.

On similar lines, one can construct intruders corresponding to the possible messages that can be seen *emitted* by the responder and server. *A parallel composition of all such intruders will be the actual intruder for the system*:

$||_i$ *crude* $-$ *init* $||_j$ *crude* $-$ *respond* $||_k$ *crude* $-$ *server*

will be the general intruder where i, j, and k denote the quantification over all messages that can be emitted by the initiator, responder and server respectively.

In the following, we shall consider some structured intruders that would illustrate the various attacks on the basic protocol described previously. It must be noted that the behaviours of these structured intruders will be contained in the behaviour of the general intruder constructed as above. These aspects will be discussed in the full paper. As concurrent incarnations of modules are possible, we can model finite concurrent roles.

Since the intruders are assumed to be valid principals of the system, without loss of any generality, we can assume that messages sent will have the well-defined syntactic structure. The attackers that mimic the roles of initiator, responder or the server of sessions can be obtained by decomposing the possible messages that could possibly be emitted and performing operations as detailed above. We shall illustrate the possibilities of attacks seen from the initiator module, the initiating agent being called A:

1. replacing the key of the initiator by its' own key which is realized by:

$$C_A \equiv initiator[I_a/I_a, I_s/I_s, K_c/K_a, A/A, B/B, S/S]$$

2. creating a new message as if A has initiated. This is given by,

$$C_A \equiv initiator[I_a/I_a, I_s/I_s, K_c/K_a, A/A, B/B, S/S]$$

The difference between (2) and (1) is that in (1) the message was in response to an initiation from the actual initiator A whereas in (2) a fraudulent message was created by the intruder C.

The module shown in Figure 8 combines the above two scenarios where input signals *one*, *two* represent signals that make the intruder decide the choice (this is where input indeterminacy comes into the picture). Actually the case corresponding to, *two*, is as good as C starting as an initiator. The other possibilities have been ignored as they don't seem to be structurally feasible. We have placed reactions pairwise (through the await-case statement) as the intruder once decides on a role will take the corresponding reaction.

```
module Intruder-init;
   input one, two;
         I_s: some_string_type;
   output I_a: some_string_type;
   var K_a: key_bit_type;
       A: initiator_type;
       B: responder_type;
       S: server_type;
   loop
       await
           case one  do emit I_a(A,S,B,E(K_c)); %change key%
           case two  do emit I_a(C,S,B,E(K_c)); % change A%
       end await
       await tick; % assume one is sustained till the nest reaction
                     of the await-case statement %
       await immediate
            case one do await immediate  I_s(S,A,B,V(K_c,K_b));
            case two do await immediate I_s(S,A,B,V(K_c,K_b))
       endawait;
   endloop
end module
```

Fig. 8. Model of General Intruder

On similar lines, the general intruder models can be obtained for playing the roles of responder and server. In short, breaking the message components and plain substitution makes it possible to perform attacks like (i) eavesdropping, (ii) mimicking an initiator, (iii) mimicking a responder, (iv) and mimicking as a server for the un-encrypted part (or plain text) etc. With concurrent roles being possible, attacks such as (a) concurrently mimicking as initiator and responder and (b) attack through concurrent sessions are possible. These are modelled using the parallel operator that permits concurrent instantiations of modules. The possibility of the initiator, A, starting two concurrent sessions will be discussed later. The work in [12] elucidates the various attacks on the TMN protocol using the CSP model checker elaborately. In the following section, we discuss these attacks and show how the attacks can be derived as instances of the general model discussed above.

Note 5. The interception of a message classically corresponds to somebody blocking (and picking) the message from reaching the actual destination. In the following, we have allowed the intruder from copying the packet and allowing it to reach the destination as pure interception does not lead to new possible attacks (note we have already modelled interception earlier). It must be noted that interception can be trivially modeled through a preemptive message. Interception will become relevant relative to questions like whether the initiator as well as the intruder are able to get the key etc.

4.1 Attacks in the Protocols

In this section, we shall illustrate the various attacks described in [12] as instances of the model discussed so far.

Intruder Mimicking Initiator: Operationally, the intruder mimicking the initiator can be described as follows:

- The intruder picks up the request of the initiator, say A, to some responder, say B.
- Sends the modified request (to denote as if it has come from initiator A). This is accomplished by replacing in the message digest its' own key in place of the key of the initiator.

As the intruder is also a valid principal in the system, the behaviour of an agent mimicking as A can be described by the following module:

$$C_A \equiv \mathit{initiator}[I_a/I_a, I_s/I_s, K_c/K_a, A/A, B/B, S/S]$$

The verification for this property is done by constructing an observer for repeated occurrences of the trace "I_a(A,S,B,E(K_a)) I_s(S,A,B,V(K_c, K_b))" as shown below:

```
module observer;
input Ia,    Is: some_string_type;
output alarm: alarm_type;
    loop
      await immediate Ia(A,S,B,E(Ka));
      await Is(S,A,B,V(Kc,Kb));
      present ?Is = (A,S,B,E(Ka))
                  then emit alarm
      else skip
      end present;
    end loop
end module observer
```

The observer when run along with the protocol emits the signal `alarm` depicting the underlying attack. Now, let us analyze further additional questions about security we can ask about the system having A, B, S and C_A as the principals (i.e. the system shown in Figure 5 along with C_A).

1. Does the intruder get k_b? That is, does C_A get the message "I_s(S,A,B, V(K_c, K_b))" in response to I_a(A,S,B,E(K_c))? The deduction of getting the key after this message is obtained, follows since the intruder is also a valid principal and hence, knows the underlying simplification rules.
   From the `Xeve` *(also by simulation through* `Xes`*), the answer is YES.*
2. Is it possible that the principal A also could have initiated the request and got the key concurrently?
   The answer is YES on the same lines as (1) above.
3. Is it possible that the principal A as well as the intruder C_A can get the keys concurrently?
   The answer is YES since it is possible to have multiple emissions of the same signal for which a proper *combination function*[2] can be defined in the program. In other words, both A and C_A will see two messages out of which only one can be decoded by each using the simplifications laws.
4. The affirmative answer to the above question leads to the question: Does the initiator detect that there could be an intruder? or Does the intruder smell that the actual principal could have been there and hence, it could have detected the possible existence of an intruder?
   The answer is YES again on the same lines of argument (3) given above.

Scenarios corresponding to above cases are: (i) A not actually initiating but initiated by C_A (ii) A and C_A initiating concurrently, (iii) only A initiating and (iv) neither A nor C_A initiating.

Intruder Mimicking Responder: Here, the intruder picks up the response of the server to the responder and sends it as if it was the responder itself except that it replaces its' key for the key of the responder. The corresponding module is: $C_B \equiv responder[I_b/I_b, I_s/I_s, K_c/K_b, A/A, B/B, S/S]$. Similar questions as in section 4.1 can be answered on the same way.

Concurrent Initiator- and Responder-Intruders: Here, the initiator initiates a run with itself mimicking as A and wanting to respond with B; when A indeed wants to have a session with B then the intruder responds as B. This could be treated as multiple roles for an intruder. The model corresponds to running the basic protocol shown in Fig. 5 in parallel with C_A and C_B as above. On the same lines as above, it can be shown that the principals could be deceived by the intruders. Assuming in the Internet, the packets are not destroyable except by those to whom it is meant for, the following question again can be answered affirmatively:

Is it possible that the initiator as well as the intruder would have got hold of the keys?

5 Modelling and Analysis of Modified TMN Protocol

The first modification of the TMN protocol to overcome the attacks discussed so far as discussed in [12] is as follows: the *initiator* and the *responder* share an explicit secret with the server and use them when sending messages to the server. Thus, the server matches the secret sent by the principal with its identity (again a secret known only to the Server and the agent itself). The modified protocol with the above mentioned changes [12] is shown below:

Message 1: $A \rightarrow S$: $A.S.B.E(s_a, K_a)$
Message 2: $S \rightarrow B$: $S.B.A$
Message 3: $B \rightarrow S$: $B.S.A.E(s_b, K_b)$
Message 4: $S \rightarrow A$: $S.A.B.V(K_a,\ K_b)$

The module structure shown in Figure 5 will remain the same except for the message structure and the additional secret the agents share with the server. The new model of the initiator, responder and the server are shown in Figures 9, 10, and 11 respectively with the modified TMN system shown in Figure 12.

Running the three modules shown in Figure 12 along with the model of the intruder shown in Figure 13, one arrives at the conclusion that that it is indeed the case the intruder can capture the secret key. On the same lines, one can show that it is also the case that it is quite possible that the initiator and the responder could get the clue that there is an intruder.

The attack as found in [12] (attacks 5.1 & 5.3) follows exactly as above; the difference from 5.1 and 5.3 as envisaged in [12] is that in 5.1 the message from the initiator has been intercepted and hence, it is not responding further whereas in 5.3 the initiator is continuing to respond. It is of interest to note that in the reactive framework, both of them are answered at one shot (in other words, one scenario comes for free).

The attack described in section 5.2 of [12] can be realized using the intruder $C_B \equiv$ initiator-I[$s_a, K_a/s_a, K_a,\ I_s/I_s$, A/A,C/B,S/S]
In this case, in the system consisting of A, B, S, and the intruder, C_B, the server, S, is responding to both the messages received from the initiator and the intruder. Thus, both A and C_B get the key K_a. This just corresponds to detecting the two messages (in fact, this is the question asked in section 4.1). It may be noted that the intruder is doing little more than than what it is supposed to do as it is assuming that the message is removed completely. (in fact, message 4' in attack 5.2 [12] will come by itself as the server is going to respond for the messages any way).

Attack of section 5.4 of [12] can be obtained using the same intruder as given above; the difference is that the initiator also gets the proper key.

```
module Initiator-I;
   input start; $I_s$: some_string_type;
   output $I_a$: some_string_type;
   var $K_a$: key_bit_type; $s_a$: sec_identity_type;
       A: initiator_type; B: responder_type; S: server_type;
   loop $\ell_{i_0}$: await start;
        $\ell_{i_1}$: emit $I_a$(A,S,B,E($s_a, K_a$));
           %(sender.via,destination,encrypted_msg and secret_share)%
        $\ell_{i_2}$: await tick;
        $\ell_{i_3}$: await $I_s$(S,A,B,V($K_a, K_b$))
   success: endloop
end module
```

Fig. 9. Modified Initiator

```
module Responder-I;
   input $I_s$: some_string_type;
   output $I_b$: some_string_type;
   var $K_b$: key_type; $s_b$: sec_identity_type;
       A: initiator_type; B: responder_type; S: server_type;
   loop $\ell_{r_0}$: await immediate $I_s$(S,B,A);
        $\ell_{r_1}$: await tick;
        $\ell_{r_2}$: emit $I_b$(B,S,A,E($s_b$, $K_b$);
   endloop
end module
```

Fig. 10. Modified Responder

```
module Server-I:
   input $I_a$, $I_b$: some_string_type;
   output $I_s$: some_string_type;
   var A: initiator_type; B: responder_type; S: server_type;
       key_initiator, key_receiver: key_type;
   loop $\ell_{s_0}$: await immediate $I_a$(A,S,B,E($s_a, K_a$);
      A:= first($I_a$(A,S,B,E($s_a, K_a$)); B:= third($I_a$(A,S,B,E($s_a, K_a$));
    key_initiator:= getkey ($I_a$(A,S,B,E($s_a, K_a$));
    $\ell_{s_1}$: await tick;
    $\ell_{s_2}$: emit $I_s$(S,B,A);
    $\ell_{s_3}$: await $I_b$(B,S,A,E($s_b, K_B$));key_receiver:=getkey($I_r$(B,S,A,E($s_b, K_b$));
    $\ell_{s_4}$: await tick;
    $\ell_{s_5}$: emit $I_s$(S,A,B, V($K_a, K_b$))
endloop
end module
```

Fig. 11. Modified Server

```
module TMN-imp;
  input strat;
  output Ia, Ib, Is: some_string_type;
  run initiator-I [sa,Ka/sa,Ka, Is/Is, A/A,B/B,S/S]
|| run responder-I [sb,Kb/sb,Kb,Is/Is, A/A,B/B,S/S]
|| run server-I
end module
```

Fig. 12. Modules of the Improved TMN Protocol

```
run initiator-I[sc,Kc/sa,Ka, Is/Is, C/A,B/B,S/S] % mimics initiator
|| run responder-I[sc,Kc/sb,Kb,Is/Is, A/A,C/B,S/S] % mimics responder
```

Fig. 13. Model of the Intruder

5.1 Further Strengthened TMN Protocol

The strengthened TMN for the attacks [12] wherein the identity of the agent with which communication is requested is encrypted is given below;

Message 1: $A \rightarrow S$: $A.S.E(B, s_a, K_a)$
Message 2: $S \rightarrow B$: $S.B.A$
Message 3: $B \rightarrow S$: $B.S.E(A, s_b, K_b)$
Message 4: $S \rightarrow A$: $S.A.B.V(K_a, K_b)$

ESTEREL model for the above protocol follows from the models shown earlier. The required proof obligation is: $I_a(A, S, E(B, s_a, K_a)) \leadsto I_s(S, A, B, V(K_a, K_b))$. This easily follows in the ESTEREL model.

Now, let us see whether some intruder can indeed try to get a key of a principal fraudulently. Our first task is to construct the intruder. By the rules of the intruder model, messages 1 and 3 cannot be changed meaningfully as encryption is tied down to identities as well as secrets with the servers which are by definition noncrackable. The only other message that can be be modified or inserted are message 2 (the possibilities being $S.B.C$ or $S.C.B$) and message 4 (the possibilities are $S.C.B.V(K_a, K_b)$, $S.A.C.V(K_a, K_b)$). Thus, the intruder will be simpler than that obtained earlier due to the strengthened message transmission. A simple analysis shows that the altered possibilities of message 4 are of no use to the intruder as the key cannot be decrypted by anyone else other than A as per the simplifications rules. Since the traces are finite, the observer constructed to find whether there will be a message of the form $I_a(S.A.B.V(K_c, K_b))$ in response to a message $I_a(A, S, E(B, s_a, K_a))$ will be false – establishing the security of the system.

5.2 Authenticity

Authenticity as defined in [12] is given below:

1. If a responder B completes a run of the protocol, say with A, then it must be the case that A must have been previously been trying to run the protocol with B. Note that it is never the case that B can conclude that A must have received the message sent by it. Further there should be a 1-1 relationship between the runs of A and B.
2. If an initiator A completes a run of the protocol, say with B, then B has previously been trying to run the protocol with B, then B has previously been trying to run the protocol with A; there should be a 1-1 relationship between the runs of A and B. Also, the two agents should agree on the value of the key established.

The trace for a proper correct run of the initiator and responder is:
$I_a(A, S, E(B, s_a, K_a))$, $I_s(S, B, A)$, $I_b(B, S, E(A, S_b, k_b)$, $I_s(S, A, B, V(K_a, K_b))$
Thus, if the system satisfies the property of authenticity, the above should be the only valid trace. However, the system will not only find the trace given above but also finds: $I_s(S, B, A)$, $I_b(B, S, E(A, S_b, k_b)$, $I_s(S, A, B, V(K_a, K_b))$
Hence, we can conclude that it is not the case that the strengthened protocol satisfies the property of authenticity. The reason for the failure of authenticity is that "message 2" can be emitted by the intruder in response to which the server can respond. Note that the intruder is also capable of emitting the first message which may be an old stored one. The server does not check whether the message has been responded to or not. Now, let us ask some question that relates to concurrent runs that can be modelled easily in the reactive framework.

Question: What happens if A wants to have concurrent runs with the restriction that the response from A to B should keep track of the explicit session?

As the protocol does not satisfy the property of authenticity, the above property cannot be obviously satisfied. The counter example can be found easily by modelling the observer and showing that the traces can be interleaved. We can also model nonces and iterative authentication protocols. We will not going into these aspects for want of space.

6 Synchronous Languages as Specification Languages for Cryptographic Protocols

One of the works [10] on cryptographic protocols is concerned with the specification of languages that would allow a simple derivation of the obligations and commitments of the principals involved in the protocol. A careful examination of ESTEREL shows that it satisfies the main objectives highlighted in [10] Considering the underlying typing rules, it is possible to distinctly arrive at the capabilities and visibilities of signals and variables. Using such information, we can arrive at the various obligations/commitments of the modules. For instance, the following scenarios can be arrived at from Figure 5:

1. A has the role of *initiator*, B of *responder* and S the role of *server*.
2. A sends its request on I_a and awaits response on I_s.
3. B awaits for requests on I_s and responds on I_s.
4. S awaits for requests/responses on I_a, I_b and forwards them on I_s.
5. Keys K_a and k_b should not be revealed to any intruder.

Through such an interpretation, one can formulate required properties as postulates and commitments – leading a good understanding of obligations.

7 Conclusions

The reactive framework seems to be quite suitable for the analysis of cryptographic protocols for the following reasons:

1. The languages are well defined and the semantics is captured nicely in terms of rewrite systems - thus,capturing the inductive definitions succinctly.
2. Language supports input indeterminacy with deterministic reactions. The underlying broadcast communication aids in capturing the router/broadcast features naturally that are needed for the modelling.
3. It has good simulate-compile-verify environment and permits checking some of the security and authenticity properties to be verified by simulation using *observer* criteria.
4. Modularity of the language permits to check properties with concurrent roles and runs; also, it can be used as a specification language.
5. Verification can be done via symbolic bisimulation or via model checking.
6. The availability of preemption allows us to model complex protocols that allow withdrawing of requests.

Most of the security properties can be captured as safety properties. These could be specified in various logics which can be directly translated as observers as envisaged above automatically; we shall not discuss further due to lack of space. Further, our experience shows that in analyzing cryptographic protocols, counter-example generating tools will have a useful role. We are also extending the study to real-life complex protocols such as SET [13] with preemption.

Acknowledgments

The work was done under the project " Design and Implementation of Secure Systems for E-Commerce", supported from MIT, New Delhi. Part of the work was done while the author was visiting Max-Planck Institut für Informatik, Saarbrücken. The author thanks Harald Ganzinger for the encouragement and several suggestions.

References

[1] M. Abadi, A. Gordon, *A Calculus for Cryptographic Protocols: The Spi Calculus*, 4th ACM Conf. on Computers and Communications Security, (1997) 36-47.
[2] G. Berry and G. Gonthier, *The* ESTEREL *Synchronous Programming Language: Design, semantics, Implementation*, SCP, 19 (2):87-152, November 1992.
[3] B. Blanchet, *An Efficient Cryptographic Protocol Verifier Based on Prolog Rules*, In 14th IEEE Computer Security Foundations Workshop (CSFW-14), Canada, 2001.
[4] D. Bolignano, *An approach to the formal verification of cryptographic protocols*, 3rd ACM Conf. on Computer and Communications Security, pp. 106-118, 1996.
[5] M. Burrows, M. Abadi, R. Needham, *A Logic of Authentication*, ACM Transactions on Computer Systems, 8(1), (1990) 18-36.
[6] D. Dolev, A. Yao, *On the Security of Public Key Protocols*, IEEE Trans. on Information Theory, 29(2), (1983) 198-208.
[7] D. Harel, A. Pnueli, *On the development of reactive systems: logics and models of concurrent systems*, Proc. NATO ASI Series, 477-498, Springer Verlag, 1985.
[8] R. Kemmerer, *Analyzing encryption protocols using formal verification techniques*, IEEE J. on Selected Areas in Communications, 7(4), (1989) 448-457.
[9] R. Kemmerer, C. Meadows and J. Millen, *Three Systems for Cryptographic Protocol Analysis*, J Cryptology (1994), 7:79-130.
[10] J.G. Larrecq, *Clap, a simple language for cryptographic protocols*, INRIA, 2001.
[11] G. Lowe, *Breaking and Fixing the Needham-Schroeder Public-Key Protocol Using FDR*, Proc. TACAS, LNCS 1055, 147-166, 1996, Springer Verlag.
[12] G. Lowe, and B. Roscoe, *Using CSP to detect errors in the TMN protocol*, In IEEE Tr. on Software Engg., v. 23, 10, 1997.
[13] Mastercard & VISA, *Secure Electronic Transaction Specification*, Books, 1-3, 1996.
[14] J.C. Mitchell, M. Mitchell, U. Stern, *Automated Analysis of Cryptographic Protocols Using Murϕ*, Proc. IEEE Symp. on Security and Privacy, 1997, 141-151.
[15] G. Pace, N. Halbwachs, and P. Raymond, *Counter-Example Generation in Symbolic Abstract Model Checking*, FMICS, 2001.
[16] L.C. Paulson, *The Inductive approach to verifying cryptographic protocols*, J. Computer Security, 6, 1998, 85-128.
[17] N. Raja and R.K. Shyamasundar, *A Cryptographic Protocol Analysis: an annotated bibliography*, Tutorial at Int. Conf. on Information Tech., Bhuvaneshwar, Dec. 2000.
[18] M. Tatebayashi, N. Matsuzaki, D. Neuman, *Key distribution protocol for digital mobile communication systems*, Proc. CRYPTO '89, (90) 324-333, Springer Verlag.
[19] C. Weidenbach, *Towards an automatic analysis of security protocols in first-order logic*, in H. Ganzinger, ed., 16th CADE-16, 1999, LNAI 1632, Springer, 378-382.

An Abstract Schema for Equivalence-Checking Games

Li Tan

Department of Computer Science
State University of New York at Stony Brook
Stony Brook, NY 11790 USA
tanli@cs.sunysb.edu

Abstract. Equivalence games have been shown as an efficient way to diagnose design systems. Nevertheless, like other diagnostic routines, equivalence games utilize the information already computed by equivalence checker during verification. Therefore, these diagnostic routines tightly gear to the data structure of checker being used, and their ability of migrating to a different checker is not always guaranteed. Moreover, different equivalence relations demand different game schemas, which makes it tedious to implement equivalence games. We solve the first problem by utilizing a generalized version of partition refinement tree (PRT) as an abstract of proof structures. With a little bookkeeping, a partition refinement-based checker is able to supply PRT as the evidence to support its result. The diagnostic routines built on PRTs are independent of equivalence checkers being used. PRTs may also be used to certify the equivalence-checking result.
To solve the second problem, we introduce a *semantics hierarchy*. Implementation following this hierarchy enjoys greater code sharing among different games. The prototype of this schema, including PRT-friendly algorithms and the architecture of semantics hierarchy, has been implemented on the Concurrency Workbench.

1 Introduction

The ability of generating diagnostic information is an important feature of a verification tool. In the case of equivalence checking, a tool usually returns a textual-based property satisfied by one process but not by the other. This could be a Hennessy-Milner logic formula in (weak-) bisimulation [HM85], a trace in language equivalence, or a failure in testing-based equivalence [Mai87]. Nevertheless, this information lacks of intuition, and is often inadequate for spotting errors in design systems.

Equivalence game [Sti87] has been shown to be an efficient way to help the user understand why or why not two processes are related. In equivalence game, user plays against computer to challenge the verification result. Computer convinces user about the correctness of result by showing that he has a strategy to win each and every play, no matter how user reacts. Nevertheless, there are certain difficulties in designing and implementing game semantics: first, like other

A. Cortesi (Ed.): VMCAI 2002, LNCS 2294, pp. 65–78, 2002.
© Springer-Verlag Berlin Heidelberg 2002

diagnostic routine, the construction of winning strategies utilize the information already computed during equivalence checking. Building games on a checker requires case-by-case study on the proof structure of individual checker, i.e., the data structure by which a checker reaches its result; second, each equivalence relation demands a unique definition of game. Implementing each game semantics separately turns out to be very tedious work.

We start to solve the first problem by abstracting in a "standard" form the proof structures of checkers, so diagnostic routines built on these abstract proof structures can migrant between checkers effortlessly. The abstract proof structure we are looking for turns out to be a generalized version of partition refinement tree (forest) (PRT). PRT serves as the evidence to support the result of equivalence checking. With some bookkeeping effort, a partition refinement-based algorithm can produce PRTs without compromising its complexity. PRT may also be used to certify the equivalence-checking result. Our study shows that PRT provides sufficient information for producing many diagnostics, including Hennessy-Miller logic formula in (weak-) bisimulation, trace in language equivalence, and failure suite in testing-based equivalence. Particularly in this paper we consider how to build equivalence-checking games on PRTs.

Different equivalence semantics demand different game schemas. Implementing them separately turns out to be a very tedious work. We introduce *semantic hierarchy* to promote code sharing between games, and make it easy to add a new game. The semantics hierarchy consists of three levels: at the top is an *abstract game*, which includes the common functionalities shared by all the (property-checking) games; in the middle is *equivalence game module*(*EQM*), which subsumes all the equivalence games; and on the bottom is semantics plug-ins (*plugins*), which include those functions unique for each individual game. The implementation following this hierarchy greatly improves the code sharing among games at appropriate levels. For example, one of *EQM*'s functions is to build *abstract* winning strategy by tracing PRTs. Semantics plug-ins will interpret this abstract winning strategy as the winning strategy for the targeting equivalence game. Therefore, each game don't have to implement its own function to handle PRTs. In most cases, to introduce a new equivalence game one only needs to supply relatively small *plugins*.

The introduction of PRTs and semantics hierarchy are two features making this schema distinct. Our experiments on CWB-NC has showed the combination of two dramatically reduced the implementation cost while adding flexibility and other nice features, including uniform interfaces and centralized bookkeeping.

This paper chooses bisimulation game and language equivalence game as examples to show how they can fit to this schema. The discussion on more complicate case of failure- and testing- equivalence games is left to the full version of this paper, available at `www.cs.sunysb.edu/~ tanli/bisgame.ps`. The rest of paper is organized as follows: section 2 prepares notations and definitions; section 3 introduces an abstract version of partition refinement tree as the standardized interface data structure between checkers and upper-level diagnostic routines. Section 4 introduces *semantics hierarchy*. Finally, section 5 discusses a prototype implemented on Concurrency Workbench of the New Century.

2 Preliminaries

2.1 Transition System and Equivalence Relations

We model the processes as labelled transition systems (*LTSs*). A labelled transition system is a triple $\langle S, A, \rightarrow \rangle$, where S is the set of states, A is the a set of actions containing visible actions $A - \{\tau\}$ and an internal action τ, and $\rightarrow \subseteq S \times A \times S$ is the transition relation. We shall write $s \xrightarrow{a} s'$ in lieu of $\langle s, a, s' \rangle \in \rightarrow$. We write $s \xrightarrow{a}$ if there exists a s' such that $s \xrightarrow{a} s'$, and $s \not\xrightarrow{a}$ if such s' doesn't exist. We denote $s \xrightarrow{a} \bullet$ for the set $\{s' \mid s \xrightarrow{a} s'\}$. We lift the notation of $\rightarrow$ to sets of states straightforwardly: $P \xrightarrow{a} P'$ iff $P' = \{s' \mid \exists s \in P.s \xrightarrow{a} s'\}$. A state s is stable if $s \not\xrightarrow{\tau}$. We refer to $s \xrightarrow{\bullet} = \{a \mid s \xrightarrow{a}\}$ as the set of initial actions of s. The notion of deterministic and non-deterministic transition systems is defined straightforwardly based on the behavior of their outgoing transitions.

Weak (Observational) transition relation $\Rightarrow$ is defined as below. Let $\beta \in (A - \{\tau\})^*$ be a sequence of visible actions, then,

1. $\overset{\epsilon}{\Rightarrow} = \xrightarrow{\tau^*}$, where $\xrightarrow{\tau^*}$ is the transitive and reflexive closure of $\xrightarrow{\tau}$.
2. $\overset{a\beta'}{\Rightarrow} = \overset{\epsilon}{\Rightarrow} \circ \xrightarrow{a} \circ \overset{\beta'}{\Rightarrow}$. where $\circ$ denotes relational composition.

We extend the notion of $\Rightarrow$ to sets of states: $P \overset{\beta}{\Rightarrow} P'$ iff $P' = \{s' \mid s \overset{\beta}{\Rightarrow} s'\}$. We refer to P^ϵ as P's ϵ-closure $\{s' \mid s \overset{\epsilon}{\Rightarrow} s'\}$. β is a trace of s_0 if there exists s' such that $s_0 \overset{\beta}{\Rightarrow} s'$. The language of $s_0 \in S$, written as $L(s_0)$, is defined as all the traces of s_0.

We now define semantics equivalences that relate processes (states in a transition system) on the basis of their behavior. In what follows, we fix the labelled transition transition $T = \langle S, A, \rightarrow \rangle$.

Definition 1. *Given a relation $\Pi \subseteq S \times S$, $\sim_\Pi$ is a Π-bisimulation iff $\sim_\Pi \subseteq \Pi$ and $s_0 \sim_\Pi s_1$ implies the following,*

1. $s_0 \xrightarrow{a} s_0' \Leftrightarrow \exists s_1'.s_1 \xrightarrow{a} s_1' \wedge s_0' \sim_\Pi s_1'$.
2. $s_1 \xrightarrow{a} s_1' \Leftrightarrow \exists s_0'.s_0 \xrightarrow{a} s_0' \wedge s_1' \sim_\Pi s_0'$.

Note that if $\Pi = S \times S$ then a Π-bisimulation is a bisimulation in the usual sense [Mil89].

Definition 2. *Let s_0 and s_1 be two states of T. $s_0 =_{may} s_1$ iff $L(s_0) = L(s_1)$.*

$=_{may}$ is also called *language equivalence relation.*

2.2 Computing Other Equivalence Relations as Bisimulation

[CH93] showed that many other equivalence relations, including language and testing equivalences, may be reduced to Π-bisimulation. Their idea is to first transform the original transition system to a new one which they call *reference transition system.* Computing an equivalence relation on original system is equivalent to compute a Π-bisimulation on *reference transition system.* [CH93] also suggests a family of reference transition systems, called *acceptance graph*, for language equivalence, failure equivalence, and testing equivalence. An *acceptance graph* is a deterministic transition system whose states are pairs of boolean value and set of states. In addition, each state q is labelled with a set of sets of actions $q.acc$. An *acceptance graph* for testing T on language equivalence, written $D(T) = \langle S_r, A_r, \rightarrow \rangle$, may be defined as below,

1. $S_r = \{\langle Q, false \rangle \mid Q = Q^\epsilon\}$
2. For each $t \in S_r$, $t.acc = \emptyset$
3. For $t_1 = \langle Q_1, b_1 \rangle$ and $t_2 = \langle Q_2, b_2 \rangle$, $t_1 \xrightarrow{a} t_2$ exactly when the following properties hold.
   (a) $a \neq \tau$
   (b) $(Q_1 \stackrel{a}{\Rightarrow} \bullet)^\epsilon = Q_2$

In other words, $D(T)$ is just the deterministic version of T. We denote $t.closed = b$ for the boolean value associated with the node $t = \langle Q, b \rangle$. $D(T)$ is a very simple acceptance graph in the sense that both $t.closed$ and $t.acc$ are trivial: they are always $false$ and $\emptyset$. We keep these two fields for the reason of compatibility. Testing and failure equivalence games need these two fields for maintaining divergence information.

The mapping function g associating each states in original system with a state in reference system can be defined as $g(p) = \langle \langle \{p\}^\epsilon \rangle, false \rangle$. Let $L(p)$ and $L(g(p))$ be the language accepted by p in T and that accepted by $g(p)$ in $D(T)$. Since $D(T)$ is merely the deterministic version of T on the relation $\Rightarrow$, we have $L(p) = L(g(p))$.

Theorem 1. *[CH93] $s_0 =_{may} s_1$ if and only if $g(s_0) \sim_\Pi g(s_1)$, where $g(s)$ is the state related to s in $D(T)$, and $\Pi = \{\langle t_1, t_2 \rangle \mid t_1.acc = t_2.acc\}$.*

Practically, if we only want to know whether $s_0 =_{may} s_1$, we only need to construct the part of $D(T)$ reachable from $g(s_0)$ or $g(s_1)$.

3 Partition Refinement Tree

A binary tree D is prefix-closed subset of $\{0,1\}^*$, where λ, the empty sequence, is the root of the tree. An edge is a tuple $\langle d, d.i \rangle \in E$ such that $d, d.i \in Q$. d is an internal node if d is the non-trivial prefix of some $d' \in D$, and it is a leaf otherwise. A binary tree D is complete if both $d.0$ and $d.1$ are in D for every internal node d. A forest of binary trees is the set of binary trees. We shall write $k\beta$ for the node β in k-th subtree.

In what follows, we fix the transition system $T = \langle S, A, \rightarrow \rangle$. We refer to $P \subseteq S$ as *stable* to $P' \subseteq S$ on action $a \in A$ iff either $Q = P$ or $Q = \emptyset$, where $Q = \{s \in P \mid \exists s' \in P'.s \xrightarrow{a} s'\}$. $P \subseteq S$ is *stable* to P' iff P is stable to P' on any action $a \in A$.

Definition 3. *A partition refinement tree (PRT) $\gamma = \langle D, \ell, \ell_s, \ell_a, T \rangle$ is a labelled complete binary tree D defined with respect to a LTS $T = \langle S, A, \rightarrow \rangle$. $\ell : D \rightarrow 2^S - \emptyset$ labels each node with a non-empty subset of S. $\ell_a : D \rightarrow A$ and $\ell_s : D \rightarrow D$ associates each* internal node *with an action and a node, respectively. In addition, ℓ_a and ℓ_s satisfies the following properties,*

1. *$\ell(\epsilon) = S$.*
2. *For each internal node d, $\ell(d.0) = \{s \in \ell(d) \mid \exists s' \in \ell_s(d).s \xrightarrow{\ell_a} s'\}$, and $\ell(d.1) = \ell(d) - \ell(d.0)$.*
3. *There is a well-founded order ω on D such that, for any $d \in D$, $d < d.i$ and $d \geq \ell_s(d)$ on ω.*

A node d is stable *to node d' and action a iff $\ell(d)$ is stable to $\ell(d')$ and a. A partition refinement tree is* stable *if, for any leaves q_1 and q_2, $\ell(q_1)$ is stable to $\ell(q_2)$ on any action.*

We refer to $\ell_s(q)$ and $\ell_a(q)$ as the *splitter* and *splitting action* of q. With the clear context we may avoid the formal discrimination of a node q and the set $\ell(q)$ it represents. Intuitively, when q splits with respect to a splitter $\ell_s(q)$ and a splitting action $\ell_a(q)$, its left child $\ell(q.0)$ contains those states of q which can make $\ell_a(q)$ transition to some states of $\ell_s(q)$, and the right child $q.1$ contains the rest of states in q which are not able to do so.

Most of properties of PRTs are clear to those reader who are familiar with the partition refinement-based algorithms (cf. [KS83]), except (3). The well-founded order ensures that the final partition represented by leaves is not "finer" than the partition induced by bisimulation. We need to introduce some definitions before we give the formal proof.

A stable partition on S is a partition Γ such that a block $P \in \Gamma$ is stable to any block $P' \in \Gamma$. A partition Γ is coarser than Γ', written $\Gamma' \sqsubseteq \Gamma$, iff for each $\mathbf{P} \in \Gamma$, there exists a $P' \in \Gamma'$ such that $P' \subseteq P$.

Lemma 1. *[PT87]*

1. *There is only one coarsest stable partition for any transition system, and*
2. *The coarsest stable partition is just the partition induced by bisimulation.*

Theorem 2. *Given a stable partition refinement tree $\gamma = \langle D, \ell, \ell_s, \ell_a, T \rangle$, $\Gamma_\gamma = \{\ell(q) \mid q \text{ is a leaf}\}$ is the partition induced by the bisimulation relation $\sim$.*

Proof. Let Γ is the coarsest stable partition. We need to show $\Gamma_\gamma = \Gamma$. Clearly from the definition of PRTs $\Gamma_\gamma \sqsubseteq \Gamma$. We only need to show that $\Gamma \sqsubseteq \Gamma_\gamma$.

We choose to prove a stronger condition: γ respects partition Γ, i.e., each node of γ is an union of some blocks in Γ. We use the contradiction to show this.

Let w be the well-founded order on D implied by the definition. Clearly the first node on w, the root, satisfies this. Assume that $d.k$ is the first node on w which violates the condition. We consider the case $k = 0$, while the case $k = 1$ can be proven similarly.

The assumption that $d.0$ is not the union of some classes in Γ implies the existence of s_i and s_j such that $s_i \in \ell(d.0)$, $s_j \notin \ell(d.0)$, and $\{s_i, s_j\} \subseteq P$ for some $P \in \Gamma$. Since d always appear before $d.i$ on w, s_i and s_j must be both in $\ell(q)$. Therefore, $s_j \in \ell(d.1)$. Moreover, By lemma 1, $\{s_i, s_j\} \subseteq P$ implies $s_i \sim s_j$.

By (2) in definition 3, there is a state $s'_i \in \ell(\ell_s(d))$ such that $s_i \stackrel{\ell_a(d)}{\rightarrow} s'_i$. Nevertheless, $s_i \sim s_j$ implies the existence of a s'_j such that $s_j \stackrel{\ell_a(d)}{\rightarrow} s'_j$ and $s'_i \sim s'_j$. Since d's splitter $\ell_s(d)$ cannot appear after d on w, $\ell_s(d)$ shall appear before $d.k$. Hence $\ell_s(d)$ should respect Γ by the assumption. It follows that s'_i and s'_j should be both in $\ell(\ell_s(d))$ because $s'_i \in \ell(\ell_s(d))$ and $s'_i \sim s'_j$. Therefore, $s_j \in \ell(d)$ can make an action $\ell_a(d)$ to a state in $\ell(\ell_s(d))$, hence $s_j \in \ell(d.0)$, which contradicts to the fact that $s_j \notin \ell(d.0)$. Thus, we proved that γ should respect Γ.

A partition refinement forest for a Π-bisimulation can be defined similarly. Each tree in the forest is a partition refinement tree, with one modification: the root of each tree now represents a unique block in the partition induced by Π instead of the set of all the states. One may prove in a similar manner that the leaves of a stable partition refinement forest implies the partition induced by $\sim_\Pi$.

Generating Partition Refinement Trees and Forests An execution of a partition refinement-based checker usually implies a partition refinement tree (forest). All we need to do is to construct a PRT from the information already existing in the internal data structures of checkers. To avoid too much details, we consider only a naive partition refinement-based algorithm. More sophistic refinement-based algorithms such as the three-way splitting algorithm [PT87], and Kernel-Auxiliary partition algorithm [TC01], may produce the refinement tree (forest) with similar modification.

Procedure $bisim(s_0, s_1, T = \langle S, A, \rightarrow\rangle)$
  $\Gamma = \{S\}$
  while Γ is not stable **do**
    Choose $P, P' \in \Gamma$ and an action a such that
    P is not stable w.r.t. to P and a.
    Replace P in Γ by $P_1 = \{s \in P \mid \exists s'.s \stackrel{a}{\rightarrow} s'\}$ and $P_2 = P - P_1$.
    if s_0 and s_1 in different blocks **then**
      return **false**
  return true.

We construct a PRT $\gamma = \langle D, \ell, \ell_s, \ell_a\rangle$ during the execution of $bisim(s_0, s_1)$. The main iteration maintains the following invariant for Γ,

For each block P in Γ, there is a leaf d in the current configuration of γ such that $\ell(d) = P$

Initially, γ has only one node ϵ with the label $\ell(\epsilon) = S$. Assume that P has been split by P' and a. Let d and d' be the current leaves related to P and P' by the above invariant. We create two children for d such that $\ell(d.0) = P_1$ and $\ell(d.1) = P_2$. Meanwhile, we also mark the splitter and splitting action for d as $\ell_s(d) = d'$ and $\ell_a(d) = a$.

Clearly the resulting PRTγ satisfies (1) and (2) of definition 3. To see (3), we may order the nodes by its splitting time. One may prove that this will yield a desired well-founded order.

In this example, the extra cost to construct a PRT won't exceed the time complexity of original algorithm. We found that the modification also won't increase the complexity of other more sophisticate algorithms. The space required to store ℓ_s and ℓ_a is linear to the size of tree. The space for storing ℓ is $O(|S|)$ because we only need to record $\ell(q)$ for each leaf q, and the states represented by an internal node can be constructed as the union of all the leaves in its subtree. Therefore, the extra space cost is linear to the size of transition system, which can be hidden by the complexity of checkers.

If two states s_0 and s_1 are not related, then PRT generated above may not necessarily be stable. However, if $s_0 \sim s_1$, then s_0 and s_1 should be in the same leaf , and the resulting PRT must be stable. Such refinement tree, for example, can be constructed by above procedure. This observation as well as lemma 2 gives the soundness and completeness of PRTs.

Theorem 3. *Given a labelled transition system $T = \langle S, A, \rightarrow \rangle$ and two states $s_0, s_1 \in S$, $s_1 \sim s_2$ if and only if there is a stable partition refinement tree γ for T such that s_0 and s_1 are in the same leaf.*

Verifying Partition Refinement Trees and Forests By theorem 3, we can verify the equivalence- checking result by verifying the validity of PRTs submitted by checkers. An independent verifier will check property (1), (2), and (3) on a candidate PRT γ. In addition, in the case that s_0 and s_1 are related, verifier also need to check the stability of γ. Most of mechanism of this verifier are clear, except checking (3). To check (3), we construct a graph $\beta = \langle Q, E \rangle$ from γ in which $\langle q, q' \rangle \in E$ if $\langle q, q' \rangle$ is an edge in γ, or, $q \neq q'$ and q is q''s splitter. Clearly (3) holds if and only if there is non-trivial loop [1] on β. Moreover, if such loop doesn't exist, then any topological order on β will yield a desired well-founded order. Therefore, checking (3) on γ can be done in $O(|\gamma|)$.

4 Equivalence Games

To define and implement an equivalence game, we introduce a three-level hierarchy by abstract levels of game semantics. At the top is an abstract game, which

[1] A loop is non-trivial iff it has more than one nodes

considers a generalized property-checking game. In the middle is a generalized equivalence game, which captures the common properties of all the equivalence games. On the bottom are individual games as instances of the generalized equivalence game. Also in this section, we will show how to efficient construct the winning strategy from PRTs.

4.1 Game Semantics Hierarchy

Abstract Game The purpose of a (property-checking) game is to determine whether or not property Φ is satisfied by a transition system. There are two players in a game: **I**, which believes that Φ holds, and **II**, which assumes the opposite. We use $A, B \cdots$ to range over $\{\mathbf{I}, \mathbf{II}\}$.

The definitions of a game shall specify the following aspects of game.

Configurations Q and initial configuration $c_0 \in Q$. A play $P = c_0 \cdots \in Q^*$ is a sequence of configurations.

Rules. The rules for valid next moves may be modelled as a function $\delta : Q^* \to 2^Q$. A play $P = c_0 c_1 \cdots$ is valid iff $c_{i+1} \in \delta(c_i)$. The rules should also declare the next player based on current configuration. This can be modelled as a function $p : Q \to \{\mathbf{I}, \mathbf{II}\}$. Player $p(c_i)$ shall choose the next move from $\delta(c_i)$.

Winning criteria. The winning criteria judges who wins the game. It can be written as a partial function $w : 2^{(Q^*)} \to \{\mathbf{I}, \mathbf{II}\}$. We require that the *winning criteria* is complete, that is, any play shall eventually have a winner. In what follows, we shall consider only non-trivial plays, that is, the play is valid and terminates whenever someone already wins the game.

Another important component of game is the *strategies* of players. Intuitively a strategy of player is a decision function by which a player chooses his next move. Formally a strategy for player A is a partial function σ_A such that $\sigma_A(c_i) \subseteq \delta(c_i)$ where $\sigma_A(c_i)$ is defined and $p(c_i) = A$. A strategy is *deterministic* if $\sigma_A(c_i)$ gives only one choice. A play $P = c_0 c_1 \cdots$ is under a strategy σ_A if $c_{i+1} \in \sigma_A(c_i)$ whenever $p(c_i) = A$. A strategy is complete if for any play P under the strategy σ_A, $\sigma_A(c_i)$ is defined whenever $p(c_i) = A$. A strategy σ_A is a winning strategy iff any play under σ_A will be won by A. It follows that at most one player has a winning strategy at any game.

When a game is used as a diagnostic routine, it have two physical players: computer and user. **I** and **II** will be referred as logical players, which can be seen as the roles the computer and user choose to play. Computer want to convince user about the correctness of property-checking result. Therefore, it always chooses to act as the player in favor of property-checking result. If the checker reports that Φ does hold for T, computer will choose to act as **II**, otherwise it acts as **I**. User takes the opposite role. We require that property-checking game is a fair game, i.e., if Φ is indeed true, then, **II** has a winning strategy, otherwise, **I** has a winning strategy. Therefore, computer always has a winning strategy in a fair game, if the property-checking result is correct.

There may exist more than one game schema for a property-checking semantics. Beyond the logic design, a good definition of game should also be understandable and helpful for diagnose design system.

A Generalized Equivalence Game The second level of semantics hierarchy is a generalized equivalence game, which can be seen as an instance of abstract game. In an equivalence game, The property in question is whether two processes (two states in a transition system) are related by some equivalence relation $=$. Configurations have the form either $F(q_0, q_1)$ or $S(q_0, q_1, i, b, q')$, where q_0, q_1, q' are the set of states, and $b \in B$ is a symbolic action. We refer to q_j as the side j, and B as the set of symbolic actions. A valid play P is an alternating sequence of F-configuration and S-configuration. Each round starts with a move from a F-configuration to a S-configuration, followed by a move from a S-configuration to F-configuration. The initial configuration is a F-configuration $F(q_0, q_1)$ such that $s_0 \in q_0$ and $s_1 \in q_1$.

The next player is determined by the form of current configuration. If it is a F-configuration, then **I** will be the next player, otherwise **II** will be the next player. The notion of valid moves relies on two transition relations different for each individual game: the nature transition $T_f : Q \to B \times Q$ and the matching transition $T_s : Q \times B \to 2^Q$, where $Q = 2^S$. Given T_f and T_s, the next move is determined as below. For a F-configuration $F(q_0^k, q_1^k)$, **I** will pick one side $i \in \{0, 1\}$, then choose a nature transition for q_i^k. The resulting S-configuration $S(q_0^k, q_1^k, i, b, q')$ satisfies that $\langle b, q' \rangle \in T_f(q_i^k)$. For $S(q_0^k, q_1^k, i, b, q')$, **II** matches **I**'s choice by choosing a matching transition for q_{1-i}^k. The resulting F-configuration $F(q_0^{k+1}, q_1^{k+1})$ satisfies $q_i^{k+1} = q'$ and $q_{1-i}^{k+1} \in T_s(q_{1-i}^k, b)$. The reason why we need two transition functions is that for some equivalence games the definition of transition in the first step is different from that in the second step. For example, in the weak bisimulation game the former refers to original transitions, while the latter refers to observational transitions.

The winning criteria includes those rules common to all the equivalence games, and the semantics-oriented rules different for each individual game. The latter is usually given in the term of an equivalence relation Π. The winning criteria checks only F-configuration. Let $P = F(q_0^0, q_1^0)S(\cdots)\cdots F(q_0^k, q_1^k)$ be a play, **I** wins the game if,

1. There exists an action b and a side i such that $\exists q'.(\langle b, q' \rangle \in tr_f(q_i^k))$ and $tr_s(q_{1-i}^k, b) = \emptyset$, i.e., Side i may fire an action b for which the other side cannot match; Or,
2. $\langle q_0^k, q_1^k \rangle \notin \Pi$.

II wins if **I** doesn't win and,

1. $tr_f(q_0^k) = tr_f(q_1^k) = \emptyset$, i.e., none of sides may fire an action; or,
2. The play is infinite. Since we are considering only the finite transition systems, this is equivalent to check whether a F-configuration $F(q_0^n, q_1^n)$ has been repeated.

Semantics Plug-Ins The lowest level of semantics hierarchy defines the part of semantics unique to each individual game. This includes the definition of initial configuration, the set of symbolic actions and two transition relations mentioned before: T_f and T_s. We will consider strong-bisimulation game and language (trace) equivalence game. The more complicate case of testing pre-ordering game are left for the full version of this paper.

Strong-bisimulation game. The property in question is the strong bisimulation relation $\sim$. In this game, each side contains only one single state. The initial configuration is $F(\{s_0\}, \{s_1\})$. The set of symbolic actions is just A, the set of actions of T. Both nature and matching transitions refer to the transition relations of T. Formally, we have $T_f(\{s\}) = \{\langle b, \{s'\}\rangle \mid s \xrightarrow{b} s'\}$ and $T_s(b, \{s\}) = \{\{s'\} \mid s \xrightarrow{b} s'\}$. There is no special semantics-oriented winning criteria for this game. Therefore, Π is just the universal transition. **I** wins a play $P = F(\{s_0\}, \{s_1\}) \cdots F(\{s_0^k\}, \{s_1^k\})$ if $\exists a.\ (s_i^k \xrightarrow{a}) \wedge (s_{1-i}^k \not\xrightarrow{a})$. **II** wins the game if $F(\{s_0^k\}, \{s_1^k\})$ has occurred before.

The complete definition of strong-bisimulation game can be assembled from its three-level definition. Nevertheless, it can be interpreted in the plain English easily as below. The game involves two players and two processes (i.e., sides). A play is a sequence of rounds. In each round **I** always goes first. He pick up a process and make an action on this process. **II** will choose the other process to show it too can fire the same action. If initial actions of two processes, then **I** wins. If a configuration has been repeated, then, **II** wins. To access the fairness of this game, one may refer to [Sti96].

Language (trace) equivalence game. The property in question is whether two processes have the same set of traces. The initial configuration $F(\{s_0\}^\epsilon, \{s_1\}^\epsilon)$ starts with the ϵ- closure of s_0 and s_1. The nature and matching transitions refer to an extended definition of weak transitions in term of sets of states. That is, $t_f(q) = \{\langle a, q'\rangle \mid q \stackrel{a}{\Rightarrow} q' \wedge q' \neq \emptyset\}$ and $t_s(b, q) = \{\langle b, q'\rangle \mid q \stackrel{a}{\Rightarrow} q' \wedge q' \neq \emptyset\}$. There is no need for semantics-oriented winning criteria in this game. i.e., Π is just the universal transition.

Apparently both t_f and t_s are deterministic. The proceeding of a play is controlled solely by **I**. **II** just passively matches the action chosen by **I** because the deterministic matching transition leaves no choice to **II**. Now we give the proof skeleton for the fairness: if **I** wins the play $P = F(\{s_0\}^\epsilon, \{s_1\}^\epsilon) S(\cdots) \cdots S(\cdots)$ $F(q_0^k, q_1^k)$ because q_i^k can make action a_{k+1} while q_{1-i}^k cannot, then, clearly there is a trace $\beta = a_0 a_1 \cdots a_{n+1}$ accepted by s_i but not by s_{1-i}. Therefore, **I** won't win the game if two sides have the same set of traces. The winning strategy for **II** is very simple: it just passively follows whatever action chosen by **I**. **II** will win the play because the winning criteria is complete. In the case that two states don't have the same set of traces, the computer as **I** just follows the trace not shared by both states. Clearly this will yield a winning strategy for the computer.

4.2 Constructing Winning Strategies Efficiently

To make the games defined above usable as a diagnostic routine, one needs to find an efficient way to construct a winning strategy for computer. Instead of building an algorithm exclusively for this purpose, we "recycle" the information already existing in proof structures of equivalence checkers. This information will be represented by partition refine trees (forests). We start with bisimulation game to show how to construct the winning strategy from PRTs.

Assume γ be the partition refinement tree for the problem $s_0 \sim s_1$. Recall that one side contains only one state in this game, we shall speak a side while actually refer to the state in this side. There are two cases, depending on whether two states are related.

1. $s_0 \not\sim s_1$. Therefore, s_0 and s_1 are in the different leaves of γ. We will form a winning strategy W_I for **I**. A play under W_I keeps the following invariant,

Two sides are always in different leaves of γ.

The initial configuration holds the invariant trivially. Now, let $F(q_0^k \equiv \{s_0^k\}, q_1^k \equiv \{s_1^k\})$ be the starting configuration of round k. By the invariant, s_0^k and s_1^k are in two different leaves, say d_0 and d_1. Let d be the closest common ancestor of d_0 and d_1. W.l.o.g., assume s_i^k be the state in the left child and s_{1-i}^k be the state in the right child. Computer will pick up the next configuration $S(q_0^k, q_1^k, i, b, q' \equiv \{s_i^{k+1}\})$ such that $b = \ell_a(d)$ is the splitting action of d and s_i^{k+1} is a b-derivative of s_i^k in d, i.e., $s_i^{k+1} \in (\ell_s(d) \cap s_i^k \xrightarrow{b} \bullet)$. By (2) of definition 3, such choice is always feasible. Moreover, no matter which s_{1-i}^k user will choose, it cannot be in the same leaf as s_i^{k+1}, as guaranteed by (2).

Now we show that **II** cannot win under W_I. First, the play cannot reach a configuration in which both side have no transitions, as **II** always can choose a side and make a transition. Second, the repetition of F-configuration under W_I implies that there is no well-founded order on the nodes of γ, therefore such repetition cannot exist. By the fairness of game, **I** has a winning strategy if **II** doesn't.

2. $s_0 \not\sim s_1$. Therefore, s_0 and s_1 are in the same leaf of γ, and γ is stable. The winning strategy W_{II} maintains the following invariant,

In any round, two sides are in the same leaf of γ

Assume that $F(s_0^k, s_1^k)$ is the starting configuration of round k, and **I** chooses b-derivates s_i^{k+1} as the successor of s_i^k. Let b_i be the leaf b_i which s_i^{k+1} is in. **II** chooses a b-derivative s_{1-i}^{k+1} as the successor of s_{1-i}^k such that s_{1-i}^{k+1} is in b_i. Following the argument similar to the above, one can show that this yields a winning strategy for **II**.

For other games, the winning strategies can be constructed by tracing those PRTs on the reference transition systems. We extend the notion of side to a tuple $p_i^k \equiv \langle q_i^k, s_{ri}^k \rangle$, where q_i^k is the side in original form, and s_{ri}^k is a state in the reference system related to q_i^k. We define h as the mapping function which associates the states (sides) in games with the states in its reference system. The technique of tracing PRTs in these games is similar to the one we used for bisimulation game: if two processes are not related, the winning strategy maintains the invariant that the pair of states related to current configuration are in different leaves. Otherwise, the pair of states shall be in the same leaf.

As we have identified that the function of tracing PRTs is common for all the equivalence games, it can be implemented as a part of equivalence game module.

It generates an abstract winning strategy, in which configuration is given in the term of states in the reference system. Semantics plugins will interpret these states as sides in the targeting game. The interpretation may be implemented in the form of a callback function $\langle q', b\rangle = T_c(p \equiv \langle q, s_r\rangle, s'_r, a)$, indicating, if s_r in the reference system makes action a to s'_r, side q shall make a symbolic action b to q'.

The definition of h and T_c is straightforward for the language equivalence game: for any side $\langle q, s\rangle$ in the extended form, q and s refer to the same set of states. That is, $h(q) = \langle q, closed\rangle$ for a side q in the game and $\langle q', closed\rangle$ in the reference system $D(T)$, and $T_c(p \equiv \langle q, s_r\rangle, s'_r \equiv \langle q', closed\rangle, a) = \langle a, q'\rangle$.

Let T_r and γ be the reference transition system and the PRTs for T_r. The detail of forming a winning strategy is below, depending on whether two processes are related.

1. s_0 and s_1 are related. Let $F(p_0^k \equiv \langle q_0^k, s_{r0}^k\rangle, p_1^k \equiv \langle q_1^k, s_{r1}^k\rangle)$ be the starting configuration of round k. s_{r0}^k and s_{r1}^k are in the different leafs of γ. *EQM* will choose side i, an action a and an a-derives s_{ri}^{k+1} of s_{ri}^k according to the splitting information of the closest common ancestor, as described before. The next configuration will be $S(p_0^k, p_1^k, i, a, p' \equiv \langle q', s_{ri}^{k+1}\rangle)$ such that $\langle b, q'\rangle = T_c(p_i^k, a, s_{ri}^{k+1})$.
2. s_0 and s_1 aren't related. Let $S(p_0^k \equiv \langle q_0^k, s_{r0}^k\rangle, p_1^k \equiv \langle q_1^k, s_{r1}^k\rangle, i, a, p' \equiv\equiv \langle q_i^{k+1}, s_{ri}^{k+1}\rangle)$ be the configuration after **I** moves in round k, then, *EQM* will choose the successor $s_{r(1-i)}^{k+1}$ of $s_{r(1-i)}^{k+1}$ such that s_{ri}^{k+1} and $s_{r(1-i)}^{k+1}$ are in the same leaf. The next configuration is $F(p_0^{k+1} \equiv \langle q_0^{k+1}, s_{r0}^{k+1}\rangle, p_1^{k+1} \equiv \langle q_1^{k+1}, s_{r1}^{k+1}\rangle)$, where q_{1-i}^{k+1} is the state related to $s_{r(1-i)}^{k+1}$ by T_c. That is, $\langle a, q_{1-i}^{k+1}\rangle = T_c(p_i^{k+1}, a, s_{r(1-i)}^{k+1})$.

The correctness of the winning strategy can be proven similarly as that for bisimulation game, although it may be slightly more complicate because of the use of reference systems. We leave it to readers.

5 Experimental Works

A prototype of this schema has been implemented on on Concurrency Workbench-the New Century (CWB-NC). CWB-NC is a verification toolkit for finite state systems which provides equivalence, preorder and model checking[CS96]. The part of architecture related to the equivalence games and other diagnostic routines are shown in Figure 1.

The input transition system is translated to a reference transition system, which is then checked by equivalence checkers. Currently CWB-NC has implemented Paige-Tarjan algorithm [PT87, Fer90] and Kernel-Auxiliary partition algorithm [TC01]. They both have been equipped with bookkeeping codes to produce PRTs.

The architecture of game routine follows the semantics hierarchy. Abstract game module is in charge of overall controlling: applying the rules, checking the

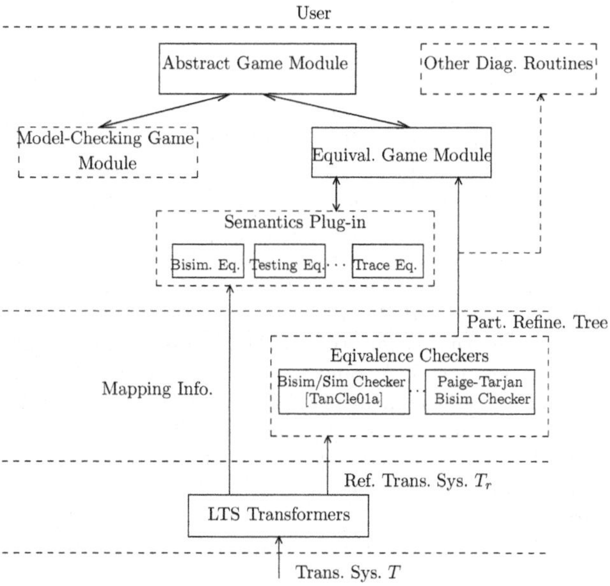

Fig. 1. Game Semantics Hierarchy on CWB-NC

winning condition, and providing common services, which include user interface and bookkeeping, etc. User's strategy is just to display a list of valid transitions and ask him to choose one as his next move. Hence, it is implemented as a part of user interface. The bookkeeping code maintains the history of a play, as required by the winning criteria. It also allow user to take back a few steps. One advantages of having the abstract game module have as many functions as possible is that they can be implemented consistently. For instance, the look and feel of bisimulation game is quite similar to those of language equivalence game because user interface has been implemented as part of abstract game module shared by all the games.

The equivalence game module (*EQM*) define the winning criteria, the rules, and computer strategy. The semantics plug-in supplies the semantics-oriented information, including Π as the special winning criteria, T_f, T_s, and T_c.

The abstract game module has 580 lines of Standard ML code. The equivalence game module (*EQM*) and preorder game module (*PRM*) are encoded as one single module with 547 lines of SML codes. The bisimulation game plug-in, observational equivalence game plug-in, language equivalence game plug-in, and testing equivalence game plug-in have 284, 417, 448, and 604 lines of code, respectively. We estimate that each game would need average 1,500 lines if it were implemented separately. According to our experience, it takes about one hour to write the language equivalence game plug-in. The prototype of this work is available at `ftp://ftp.cs.sunysb.edu/pub/CWB/working/playgame`.

References

[CH93] R. Cleaveland and M. C. B. Hennessy. Testing equivalence as a bisimulation equivalence. *Formal Aspects of Computing*, 5:1–20, 1993.

[CS96] R. Cleaveland and S. Sims. The NCSU concurrency workbench. In R. Alur and T. A. Henzinger, editors, *Computer Aided Verification (CAV '96)*, volume 1102 of *Lecture Notes in Computer Science*, pages 394–397, New Brunswick, New Jersey, July 1996. Springer-Verlag.

[Fer90] J.-C. Fernandez. An implementation of an efficient algorithm for bisimulation equivalence. *Sicence of Computer Programming*, 13:219–236, 1989/90.

[HM85] M. C. B. Hennessy and R. Milner. Algebraic laws for nondeterminism and concurrency. *Journal of the ACM*, 32(1):137–161, January 1985.

[KS83] P. C. Kanellakis and S. A. Smolka. CCS expressions, finite state processes, and three problems of equivalence. In *Proceedings of the 2nd ACM Symposium on the Principles of Distributed Computing*, Montreal, Canada, August 1983.

[Mai87] M. Main. Trace, failure and testing equivalences for communication, concurrency, and time. *International Journal of Parallel Programming*, 16(5):383–400, 1987.

[Mil89] R. Milner. *Communication and Concurrency.* International Series in Computer Science. Prentice Hall, 1989.

[PT87] R. Paige and R. E. Tarjan. Three partition refinement algorithms. *SIAM Journal of Computing*, 16(6):973–989, December 1987.

[Sti87] C. Stirling. Modal logics for communicating systems. *Theoretical Computer Science*, 49:311–347, 1987.

[Sti96] C. Stirling. Games and modal μ-calculus. In *Proceedings of the Third International Conference on Tools and Algorithms for the Construction and Analysis of Systems.* Springer-Verlag, 1996.

[TC01] L. Tan and R. Cleaveland. Simulation revisited. In *The 7-th International Conference on Tools and Algorithms for the Construction and Analysis of Systems*, volume 2031 of *Lecture Notes in Computer Science*, pages 480–495. Springer-Verlag, 2001.

Synchronous Closing of Timed SDL Systems for Model Checking

Natalia Sidorova[1] and Martin Steffen[2]

[1] Department of Mathematics and Computer Science
Eindhoven University of Technology
Den Dolech 2, P.O.Box 513,
5612 MB Eindhoven, The Netherlands
n.sidorova@tue.nl

[2] Institut für angewandte Mathematatik und Informatik
Christian-Albrechts-Universität
Preußerstraße 1–9,
24105 Kiel, Deutschland
ms@informatik.uni-kiel.de

Abstract. Standard model checkers cannot handle open reactive systems directly. Closing the system is commonly done by adding an environmental process. However, for model checking, the way of closing should be well-considered to alleviate the state-space explosion problem. This is especially true in the context of model checking SDL with its asynchronous message-passing communication because of a combinatorial explosion caused by all combinations of messages in the input queues.

In this paper we investigate a class of environmental processes for which the *asynchronous* communication scheme can safely be replaced by a *synchronous* one. Such a replacement is possible only if the environment is constructed under rather a severe restriction on the behavior, which can be partially softened via the use of a discrete-time semantics. We employ *data-flow analysis* to detect instances of variables and timers influenced by the data passing between the system and the environment.

1 Introduction

Model checking [7] is well-accepted for the verification of reactive systems. To alleviate the notorious state-space explosion problem, a host of techniques has been invented, including partial-order reduction [11, 25] and abstraction [19, 7, 9].

As standard model checkers, e.g., Spin [14], cannot handle open systems, one has to construct a closed model, and a problem of practical importance is how to *close* open systems. This is commonly done by adding an environment process that must exhibit at least all the behavior of the real environment. However, the way of closing should be well-considered to counter the state-space explosion problem. This is especially true in the context of model checking SDL-programs (*Specification and Description Language*) [22] with its *asynchronous*

A. Cortesi (Ed.): VMCAI 2002, LNCS 2294, pp. 79–93, 2002.
© Springer-Verlag Berlin Heidelberg 2002

message-passing communication model — sending arbitrary message streams to the unbounded input queues would immediately lead to an infinite state space, unless some assumptions restricting the environment behavior are incorporated in the closing process. Even so, adding an environment process may result in a combinatorial explosion caused by all combinations of messages in the input queues.

A desirable solution would be to construct an environment that communicates to the system *synchronously*. In [23] such an approach is considered for the simplest safe abstraction of the environment, the *chaotically* behaving environment: the outside chaos is *embedded* into the system's processes, which corresponds to the synchronous communication scheme. Though useful at a first verification phase, the chaotic environment may be too general. In the framework of the assume-guarantee paradigm, the environment should model the behavior corresponding to the verified properties of the components forming the environment. Here, we investigate for what kind of processes, apart from the chaotic one, the asynchronous communication can be safely replaced with the synchronous one. To make such a replacement possible, the system should be not reactive — it should either only send or only receive messages. However, since we are dealing with the discrete-time semantics [13, 3] of SDL, this requirement can be softened in that the restrictions are imposed on time slices instead of whole runs: in every time slice, the environmental process can either only receive messages, or it can both send and receive messages under condition that inputs do not change the state of the environment process.

Another problem the closing must address is that the *data* carried with the messages are usually drawn from some infinite data domains. For *data abstraction,* as in [23], we condense data exchanged with the environment into a single abstract value $\mathbb{T}$ to deal with the infinity of environmental data. We employ *data-flow analysis* to detect instances of chaotically influenced variables and timers and remove them. Based on the result of the data flow analysis, the system S is transformed into a *closed* system $S^\sharp$ which shows more behavior in terms of traces than the original one. For formulas of next-free LTL [21, 18], we thus get the desired property preservation: if $S^\sharp \models \varphi$ then $S \models \varphi$.

The rest of the paper is organized as follows. In Section 2 we fix syntax and semantics of the language. In Section 3 we describe under which condition the asynchronous communication with the environment can be replaced by synchronous one. In Section 4 we abstract from the data exchanged with the environment and give a data-flow algorithm to over-approximate the behavior. In Section 5 we discuss future work.

2 Semantics

In this section, we fix syntax and semantics of our analysis. As we take SDL [22] as source language, our operational model is based on asynchronously communicating state machines with top-level concurrency. The communication is done via *channels* and we assume a fixed set *Chan* of channel names for each program, with $c, c', \ldots$ as typical elements. The set of channel names is partitioned into $Chan_i$ and $Chan_o$, and we write $c_i, c'_o, \ldots$ to denote membership of a channel to one of these classes. A program *Prog* is given as the parallel composition $\Pi_{i=1}^{n} P_i$ of a finite number of processes. A process P is described by a tuple $(P, (in, out), Var, Loc, \sigma_{init}, Edg)$, where (in, out) are the finite sets of *input* resp. *output* channel names of the process, *Var* denotes a finite set of variables, and *Loc* denotes a finite set of *locations* or control states. We assume the sets of variables Var_i of processes P_i in a program $Prog = \Pi_{i=1}^{n} P_i$ to be disjoint. For a process P_i in a parallel composition, we write $\bar{P}$ for its environment, i.e., all processes except P. A mapping from variables to values is called a valuation; we denote the set of valuations by $Val = Var \rightarrow D$. We assume standard data domains such as $\mathbb{N}$, *Bool*, etc., where we write D when leaving the data domain unspecified, and we silently assume all expressions to be well-typed. $\Sigma = Loc \times Val$ is the set of states, where each process has one designated initial state $\sigma_{init} = (l_{init}, \eta_{init}) \in \Sigma$. An *edge* of the state machine describes a change of state by performing an *action* from a set *Act*; the set $Edg \subseteq Loc \times Act \times Loc$ denotes the set of edges.

As untimed actions, we distinguish (1) *input* over a channel c of a signal s containing a value to be assigned to a local variable, (2) *sending* over a channel c a signal s together with a value described by an expression, and (3) *assignments.* In SDL, each transition starts with an input action, hence we assume the inputs to be unguarded, while output and assignment are *guarded* by a boolean expression g, its guard. The three classes of actions are written as $c?s(x)$, $g \triangleright c!s(e)$, and $g \triangleright x := e$, respectively, and we use α, $\alpha' \ldots$ when leaving the class of actions unspecified. For an edge $(l, \alpha, \hat{l}) \in Edg$, we write more suggestively $l \longrightarrow_{\alpha} \hat{l}$. We assume for the non-timer guards, that at least one of them evaluates to true in each state. This assumption corresponds at the SDL source language level to the natural requirement that each conditional construct must cover all cases, for instance by having at least a default branch: The system should not block because of a non-covered alternative in a case-construct.

Time aspects of a system behavior are specified by actions dealing with *timers.* Each process has a finite set of timer variables (with typical elements $t, t'_1, \ldots$), where each timer variable consists of a boolean flag indicating whether the timer is active or not, together with a natural number value denoting its expiration time. A timer can be either *set* to a value, i.e., activated to run for the designated period, or *reset,* i.e., deactivated. Setting and resetting are expressed by guarded actions of the form $g \triangleright set\ t := e$ and $g \triangleright reset\ t$. If a timer expires, i.e., the value of a timer becomes zero, it can cause a *timeout,* upon which the timer is reset. The timeout action is denoted by $g_t \triangleright reset\ t$, where the timer guard g_t expresses the fact that the action can only be taken upon expiration.

The behavior of a single process is described by sequences of states $\sigma_{init} = \sigma_0 \rightarrow_{\lambda} \sigma_1 \rightarrow_{\lambda} \ldots$ starting from the initial one. The step semantics $\rightarrow_{\lambda} \subseteq \Sigma \times Lab \times \Sigma$ is given as a labeled transition relation between states. The labels differentiate between internal τ-steps, "*tick*"-steps, which globally decrease all active timers, and communication steps, either input or output, which are la-

$$\frac{l \longrightarrow_{c?s(x)} \hat{l} \in Edg}{(l,\eta) \rightarrow_{c_i?(s,v)} (\hat{l}, \eta_{[x\mapsto v]})}\ \textsc{Input} \qquad \frac{l \longrightarrow_{c?s'(x)} \hat{l} \in Edg \Rightarrow s' \neq s}{(l,\eta) \rightarrow_{c_i?(s,v)} (l,\eta)}\ \textsc{Discard}$$

$$\frac{l \longrightarrow_{g \,\triangleright\, c!(s,e)} \hat{l} \in Edg \qquad [\![g]\!]_\eta = true \qquad [\![e]\!]_\eta = v}{(l,\eta) \rightarrow_{c_o!(s,v)} (\hat{l},\eta)}\ \textsc{Output}$$

$$\frac{l \longrightarrow_{g \,\triangleright\, x:=e} \hat{l} \in Edg \qquad [\![g]\!]_\eta = true \qquad [\![e]\!]_\eta = v}{(l,\eta) \rightarrow_{\tau} (\hat{l}, \eta_{[x\mapsto v]})}\ \textsc{Assign}$$

$$\frac{l \longrightarrow_{g \,\triangleright\, set\ t:=e} \hat{l} \in Edg \qquad [\![g]\!]_\eta = true \qquad [\![e]\!]_\eta = v}{(l,\eta) \rightarrow_{\tau} (\hat{l}, \eta_{[t\mapsto on(v)]})}\ \textsc{Set}$$

$$\frac{l \longrightarrow_{g \,\triangleright\, reset\ t} \hat{l} \in Edg \qquad [\![g]\!]_\eta = true}{(l,\eta) \rightarrow_{\tau} (\hat{l}, \eta_{[t\mapsto off]})}\ \textsc{Reset}$$

$$\frac{l \longrightarrow_{g_t \,\triangleright\, reset\ t} \hat{l} \in Edg \qquad [\![t]\!]_\eta = on(0)}{(l,\eta) \rightarrow_{\tau} (\hat{l}, \eta_{[t\mapsto off]})}\ \textsc{Timeout}$$

$$\frac{(l \longrightarrow_{\alpha} \hat{l} \in Edg \Rightarrow \alpha \neq g_t \triangleright reset\ t) \qquad [\![t]\!]_\eta = on(0)}{(l,\eta) \rightarrow_{\tau} (l, \eta_{[t\mapsto off]})}\ \textsc{TDiscard}$$

$$\frac{blocked(\sigma)}{\sigma \rightarrow_{tick} \sigma_{[t\mapsto(t-1)]}}\ \textsc{Tick}_P$$

Table 1. Step semantics for process P

beled by a triple of channel name, signal, and transmitted value. Depending on location, valuation, and the potential next actions, the possible successor states are given by the rules of Table 1.

Inputting a value means reading a value belonging to a matching signal from the channel and updating the local valuation accordingly (rule Input), where $\eta \in Val$, and $\eta_{[x\mapsto v]}$ stands for the valuation equaling η for all $y \in Var$ except for $x \in Var$, where $\eta_{[x\mapsto v]}(x) = v$ holds instead. A specific feature of SDL-92 is captured by rule Discard: If the input value cannot be reacted upon at the current control state, i.e., if there is no input action originating from the location treating this signal, then the message is just discarded, leaving control state and valuation unchanged. Unlike input, output is guarded, so sending a message involves evaluating the guard and the expression according to the current valuation (rule Output). Assignment in Assign works analogously, except that the step is internal.

Concerning the temporal behavior, timers are treated in valuations as variables, distinguishing active and deactivated timer. The *set*-command activates a timer, setting its value to the specified time, *reset* deactivates it; both actions are guarded (cf. rules Set and Reset). A timeout may occur, if an active timer has expired, i.e., reached zero (rule Timeout).

$$\frac{}{(c,(s,v)::q) \rightarrow_{c_i!(s,v)} (c,q)}\ \textsc{Out} \qquad \frac{}{(c,q) \rightarrow_{c_o?(s,v)} (c,q::(s,v))}\ \textsc{In}$$

$$\frac{blocked(c,q)}{(c,q) \rightarrow_{tick} (c,q)}\ \textsc{Tick}_Q$$

Table 2. Step semantics for a queue

Time elapses by counting down active timers till zero, which happens in case no untimed actions are possible. In rule Tick, this is expressed by the predicate *blocked* on states: $blocked(\sigma)$ holds if no move is possible except either a clock-tick or a reception of a message, i.e., if $\sigma \rightarrow_\lambda$ for some label λ, then $\lambda = tick$ or $\lambda = c?(s,v)$. In other words, the time-elapsing steps are those with *least priority.* The counting down of the timers is written $\eta_{[t \mapsto (t-1)]}$, by which we mean, all currently active timers are decreased by one, i.e., $on(n+1) - 1 = on(n)$, non-active timers are not affected. Note that the operation is undefined for $on(0)$, which is justified later by Lemma 1.

In SDL, timeouts are often considered as specific timeout *messages* kept in the input queue like any other message, and timer-expiration consequently is seen as adding a timeout-message to the queue. We use an equivalent presentation of this semantics, where timeouts are not put into the input queue, but are modeled more directly by guards. The equivalence of timeouts-by-guards and timeouts-as-messages in the presence of SDL's asynchronous communication model is argued for in [3]. The time semantics chosen here is not the only one conceivable (see e.g. [5] for a broader discussion of the use of timers in SDL). The semantics we use is the one described in [13, 3], and is also implemented in DTSpin [2, 10], a discrete time extension of the Spin model checker.

In SDL's asynchronous communication model, a process receives messages via a single associated input queue. We write ϵ for the empty queue; $(s,v) :: q$ denotes a queue with message (s,v) (consisting of a signal s and a value v) at the head of the queue, i.e., (s,v) is the message to be input next; likewise the queue $q :: (s,v)$ contains (s,v) most recently entered. To facilitate the comparison of the asynchronous with the synchronous behavior of the environment, we model the queues implementing asynchronous channels explicitly as separate entities of the form (c,q), consisting of the channel name together with its queue content. In abuse of notation and to allow a uniform presentation of parallel composition below, we use the symbol σ not only for typical element of process states, but also for states (c,q) of queues. We require for the input and the output channel names of a queue that $in(c) = \{c_o\}$ and $out(c) = \{c_i\}$. The operational rules for queues are shown in Table 2.

In analogy to the tick-steps for processes, a queue can perform a tick-step iff the only steps possible are input or tick-steps, as captured again by the *blocked*-predicate (cf. rule Tick). Note that a queue is blocked and can therefore tick

$$\frac{\gamma_1 \rightarrow_{c!(s,v)} \hat{\gamma}_1 \qquad \gamma_2 \rightarrow_{c?(s,v)} \hat{\gamma}_2}{(\gamma_1, \gamma_2) \rightarrow_\tau (\hat{\gamma}_1, \hat{\gamma}_2)} \ \text{COMM}$$

$$\frac{\gamma_1 \rightarrow_\tau \hat{\gamma}_1}{(\gamma_1, \gamma_2) \rightarrow_\tau (\hat{\gamma}_1, \gamma_2)} \ \text{INTERLEAVE}_\tau$$

$$\frac{\gamma_1 \rightarrow_{c?(s,v)} \hat{\gamma}_1 \qquad c \notin out(\gamma_2)}{(\gamma_1, \gamma_2) \rightarrow_{c?(s,v)} (\hat{\gamma}_1, \gamma_2)} \ \text{INTERLEAVE}_{in}$$

$$\frac{\gamma_1 \rightarrow_{c!(s,v)} \hat{\gamma}_1 \qquad c \notin in(\gamma_2)}{(\gamma_1, \gamma_2) \rightarrow_{c!(s,v)} (\hat{\gamma}_1, \gamma_2)} \ \text{INTERLEAVE}_{out}$$

$$\frac{\gamma_1 \rightarrow_{tick} \hat{\gamma}_1 \qquad \gamma_2 \rightarrow_{tick} \hat{\gamma}_2}{(\gamma_1, \gamma_2) \rightarrow_{tick} (\hat{\gamma}_1, \hat{\gamma}_2)} \ \text{TICK}$$

Table 3. Parallel composition of R_1 and R_2

exactly if it is empty. Note further that a queue does not contain any timers. Hence, the counting down operation $[t \mapsto (t-1)]$ has no effect and is therefore omitted in the rule TICK$_Q$ of Table 2.

The semantics for parallel composition of processes or queues is given by the rules of Table 3. We call the parallel composition of one or more local states (either of processes or queues) a *configuration* and write $\gamma, \gamma'_1 \ldots \in \Gamma$ for typical elements. This means, γ is a vector of states of the participating processes or queues. Since we assumed that the variable sets of the components are all disjoint, we write $\gamma(x)$ for the value $\eta(x)$, for one state $\sigma = (l, \eta)$ being part of γ; analogously, we use the notation $[\![e]\!]_\gamma$ for the value of e in γ. The *initial* configuration of a parallel composition of components is given by the array of initial process states together with empty queues. We call a sequence of configurations $\gamma_{init} = \gamma_0 \rightarrow_\lambda \gamma_1 \rightarrow_\lambda \ldots$ starting from the initial configuration γ_{init} a *run*.

Communication between two partners is done by exchanging a common signal s and value v over a channel name c, as given by rule COMM. Note that by our conventions, $c \in out(\sigma_1)$ as well as $c \in in(\sigma_2)$. Note further that by the syntactic restrictions on the use of input and output channel names, only synchronization between one process and a queue can happen. As far as τ-steps and non-matching communication messages are concerned, each process can proceed on its own by rule INTERLEAVE. Each rule has a symmetric counterpart, which we elide. Finally, two components can perform a tick-step if both are able to do so.

By connecting processes with queues, the above semantics describes *asynchronous* communication. Synchronous communication for a channel name c is characterized similarly by identifying the names c_o and c_i such that the two processes *directly* communicate with each other. Furthermore, synchronous channels are not represented as queues in the system configuration.

Lemma 1. *Let S be a system and $\gamma \in \Gamma$ a configuration.*

1. *If $\gamma \rightarrow_{tick} \gamma'$, then $[\![t]\!]_\gamma \neq on(0)$, for all timers t.*
2. *If $\gamma \rightarrow_{tick}$, then for all queue states (c, q) in Γ, $q = \epsilon$.*

Proof. If, for part (1), $[\![t]\!]_\eta = on(0)$ for a timer t in a process P, then either TIMEOUT or TDISCARD of Table 1 allow a τ-step for P. Hence, P is not *blocked* and therefore cannot do a *tick*-step. Consequently, the system cannot perform a *tick*-step. Part (2) follows from the fact that a queue can only perform a *tick*-step exactly when it is empty. □

The following lemma expresses, that the blocked predicate is compositional in the sense that the parallel composition of processes is blocked iff each process is blocked.

Lemma 2. *For a configuration γ, blocked(γ) iff blocked(σ) for all states σ part of γ.*

3 Replacing Asynchronous with Synchronous Communication

In this section we specify under which conditions we can safely replace the asynchronous communication with an outside environment process, say E, by *synchronous* communication.

A general condition an asynchronously communicating process satisfies is that the process is always willing to accept messages, since the queues are unbounded. Hence, the environment process must be at least *input enabled:* it must always be able to react to messages, lest the synchronous composition will lead to more blockings. Thanks to the DISCARD-rule of Table 1, SDL-processes are input enabled, i.e., at least *input-discard* steps are possible, which throw away the message and do not changed the state of the process. Another effect of an input queue is that the queue introduces an arbitrary delay between reception of a message and the future reaction of the receiving process to this message. For an output, the effect is converse. This implies that the asynchronous process can be replaced by the analogous synchronous process as long as there are either only input actions or else only output actions, so the process is not reactive.[1] This is related to the so-called *Brock-Ackerman anomaly*, characterizing the difference between buffered and unbuffered communication [6].

Disallowing reactive behavior is clearly a severe restriction and only moderately generalizes completely chaotic behavior. One feature of the timed semantics, though, allows to loosen this restriction. Time progresses by *tick*-steps

[1] A more general definition would require that the process actions satisfy a *confluence* condition as far as the input and output actions are concerned, i.e., doing an input action does not invalidate the possibility of an output action, and vice versa. Also in this case, the process is not reactive, since there is no feed-back from input to output actions.

when the system is blocked. This especially means that when a *tick* happens, all queues of a system are empty (cf. Lemma 1). This implies that the restrictions need to apply only *per time slice*, i.e., at the steps between two ticks,[2] and not for the overall process behavior. Additionally we require that there are no infinite sequences of steps without a tick, i.e., there are no runs with *zero-time cycles*. This leads to the following definition.

Definition 3. *A reduction sequence is* tick-separated *iff it contains no zero-time cycle, and for every time slice of the sequence one of the following two conditions holds:*

1. *the time slice contains no output action;*
2. *the time slice contains no output over two different channels, and all locations in the time slice are input-discarding wrt. all inputs of that time slice.*

We call a process tick-separated, *if all its runs are tick-separated.*

Given a synchronous and an asynchronous versions of a process and two corresponding configurations $\gamma_s = \sigma_s$ and $\gamma_a = (\sigma_a, (c_i, q_i), (c_o^1, q_1), \ldots, (c_o^k, q_k))$. Then define $\trianglerighteq$ as $\gamma_a \trianglerighteq \gamma_s$, if $\sigma_a = \sigma_s$. Comparing the observable behavior of an asynchronous and a synchronous process, we must take into account that the asynchronous one performs more internal steps when exchanging messages with its queues, hence the comparison is based on a *weak* notion of transitions, ignoring the τ-steps: so define $\Rightarrow_\lambda$ as $\rightarrow_\tau^*\rightarrow_\lambda\rightarrow_\tau^*$ when $\lambda \neq \tau$, and as $\rightarrow_\tau^*$ else. Correspondingly, $\vec{\lambda}$ denotes a sequence of weak steps with labels from the sequence $\vec{\lambda}$.

Lemma 4. *Assume a synchronous and an asynchronous version P_s and P_a of a process and corresponding configurations γ_s and γ_a with $\gamma_a \trianglerighteq \gamma_s$, where the queues of γ_a are all empty. If $\gamma_a \Rightarrow_{\vec{\lambda}} \gamma_a'$ by a tick-separated reduction sequence, where $\vec{\lambda}$ does not contain a tick-step, and where the queues of γ_a' are empty, then there exists a sequence $\gamma_s \Rightarrow_{\vec{\lambda}} \gamma_s'$ with $\gamma_a' \trianglerighteq \gamma_s'$.*

Proof. We are given a sequence $\gamma_a = \gamma_0^a \rightarrow_{\lambda_0} \gamma_1^a \ldots \rightarrow_{\lambda_{n-1}} \gamma_n^a = \gamma_a'$, with the queues of γ_0^a and γ_n^a empty. According to the definition of tick-separation, we distinguish the following two cases:

Case 1: $\lambda_i \notin \{tick, c!(s,v)\}$, for all i

To get a matching reduction sequence of the synchronous system starting at γ_0^s, we apply the following renaming scheme. Input actions $\gamma_a \rightarrow_{c?(s,v)} \gamma_a'$ into the queue are just omitted (which means, they are postponed for the synchronous process). τ-steps $\gamma_a \rightarrow_\tau \gamma_a'$, inputting a value from the queue into the process, i.e., τ-steps justified by rule Input where the process does a step $\sigma \rightarrow_{c?(s,v)} \sigma'$ and the queue the corresponding output step by rule Out, are replaced by a direct input step $\gamma_s \rightarrow_{c?(s,v)} \gamma_s'$. Process internal τ-steps of the asynchronous system are identically taken by the synchronous system, as well. τ-steps caused by output actions from the process into a queue need not be dealt with, since

[2] A time slice of a run is a maximal subsequence of the run without *tick*-steps.

the sequence from γ_0^a to γ_n^a does not contain external output from the queues, and the queues are empty at the beginning and the end of the sequence.

It is straightforward to see that the sequence of steps obtained by this transformation is indeed a legal sequence of the synchronous system. Moreover, the last configurations have the same state component and, due to the non-lossiness and the Fifo-behavior of the input queue, both sequences coincide modulo τ-steps.

Case 2: no output over two different channels, input discarding locations
Similar to the previous case, the synchronous system can mimic the behavior of the asynchronous one adhering to the following scheme: τ-steps $\gamma_a \rightarrow_\tau \gamma_a'$, feeding a value from the process into the queue, i.e., τ-steps justified by rule OUTPUT where the process does a step $\sigma \rightarrow_{c!(s,v)} \sigma'$ and the queue the corresponding input step by rule IN, are replaced by a direct output step $\gamma_s \rightarrow_{c!(s,v)} \gamma_s'$. Input actions $\gamma_a \rightarrow_{c?(s,v)} \gamma_a$ into the queue are mimicked by a discard-step. Output steps from the queue of the asynchronous system are omitted, and so are τ-steps caused by internal communication from the input-queue to the process. All other internal steps are identically taken in both systems. The rest of the argument is analogous to the previous case. □

Note that $\gamma_a' \trianglerighteq \gamma_s'$ means that γ_s' is blocked whenever γ_a' is blocked.

Theorem 5. *If a process P is tick-separated, then $[\![P_s]\!]_{wtrace} = [\![P_a]\!]_{wtrace}$.*

Proof. There are two directions to show. $[\![P_s]\!]_{wtrace} \subseteq [\![P_a]\!]_{wtrace}$ is immediate: each communication step of the synchronous process P_s can be mimicked by the buffered P_a adding an internal τ-step for the communication with the buffer.

For the reverse direction $[\![P_a]\!]_{wtrace} \subseteq [\![P_s]\!]_{wtrace}$ we show that P_a is simulated by P_s according to the following definition of simulation, which considers as basic steps only tick-steps or else the sequence of steps within one time slice. A binary relation $R \subseteq \Gamma_1 \times \Gamma_2$ on two sets of configurations is called a *tick*-simulation, when the following conditions hold:

1. If $\gamma_1 \; R \; \gamma_2$ and $\gamma_1 \rightarrow_{tick} \gamma_1'$, then $\gamma_2 \rightarrow_{tick} \gamma_2'$ and $\gamma_1' \; R \; \gamma_2'$.
2. If $\gamma_1 \; R \; \gamma_2$ and $\gamma_1 \Rightarrow_{\vec{\lambda}} \gamma_1'$ for some γ_1' with $blocked(\gamma_1')$ where $\vec{\lambda}$ does not contain *tick*, then $\gamma_2 \Rightarrow_{\vec{\lambda}} \gamma_2'$ for some γ_2' with $blocked(\gamma_2')$.

We write $\gamma_1 \preceq_{tick} \gamma_2$ if there exists a tick simulation R with $\gamma_1 \; R \; \gamma_2$, and similarly for processes, $P_1 \preceq_{tick} P_2$ if their initial configurations are in that relation.

We define the relation $R \subseteq \Gamma_a \times \Gamma_s$ as $(l_s, \eta_s, ((c_i, q_0), (c_o^1, q_1), \ldots, (c_o^k, q_k))) \; R \; (l_s, \eta_s)$ iff $(l_s, \eta_s) = (l_a, \eta_a)$ and $q_i = \epsilon$ for all queues. To show that R is indeed a tick-simulation, assume $\gamma_a = (l, \eta, ((c_i, \epsilon), (c_o^1, \epsilon), \ldots, (c_o^k, \epsilon)))$ and $\gamma_s = (l, \eta)$ with $\gamma_a \; R \; \gamma_s$. There are two cases to consider.

Case: $\gamma_a \rightarrow_{tick} \gamma_a'$
where $\gamma_a' = \gamma_{a[t \mapsto (t-1)]}$. By the definition of the *tick*-step, $blocked(\gamma_a)$ must hold, i.e., there are no steps enabled except input from the outside or *tick*-steps. Since immediately $blocked(\gamma_s)$, also $\gamma_s \rightarrow_{tick} \gamma_{s[t \mapsto (t-1)]}$, which concludes the case.

Case: $\gamma_a \Rightarrow_{\vec{\lambda}} \gamma'_a$
where *blocked*(γ'_a) and $\vec{\lambda}$ does not contain a *tick*-label. The case follows directly from Lemma 4 and the fact that $\gamma'_a \trianglerighteq \gamma'_s$ where γ'_a is blocked implies that also γ'_s is blocked.

Since clearly the initial configurations are in relation R as defined above, this gives $P_a \preceq_{tick} P_s$. It can be shown by a standard argument, that this implies $[\![P_a]\!]_{wtrace} \subseteq [\![P_s]\!]_{wtrace}$, as required. □

4 Abstracting Data

In this section, we present a straightforward dataflow analysis marking variable and timer instances that may be influenced by the environment. It is a minor adaptation of the one from [23], taking care of channel communication.

4.1 Dataflow Analysis

The analysis works on a simple *flow graph* representation of the system, where each process is represented by a single flow graph, whose nodes n are associated with the process' actions and the flow relation captures the intra-process data dependencies. Since the structure of the language we consider is rather simple, the flow-graph can be easily obtained by standard techniques.

The analysis works on an abstract representation of the data values, where $\top$ is interpreted as value chaotically influenced by the environment and $\bot$ stands for a non-chaotic value. We write $\eta^\alpha, \eta^\alpha_1, \ldots$ for abstract valuations, i.e., for typical elements from $Val^\alpha = Var \to \{\top, \bot\}$. The abstract values are ordered $\bot \leq \top$, and the order is lifted pointwise to valuations. With this ordering, the set of valuations forms a complete lattice, where we write $\eta_\bot$ for the least element, given as $\eta_\bot(x) = \bot$ for all $x \in Var$, and we denote the least upper bound of $\eta^\alpha_1, \ldots, \eta^\alpha_n$ by $\bigvee_{i=1}^n \eta^\alpha_i$ (or by $\eta^\alpha_1 \vee \eta^\alpha_2$ in the binary case).

Each node n of the flow graph has associated an abstract transfer function $f_n : Val^\alpha \to Val^\alpha$, as given in Table 4, where α_n denotes the action associated with the node n of process P. The equations are mostly straightforward, describing the change the abstract valuations depending on the sort of action at the node. The only case deserving mention is the one for $c_i?s(x)$, whose equation captures the inter-process data-flow from a sending to a receiving actions (using c_i and c_o, we assume asynchronous communication in the analysis). In the equation $\bar{P}$ stands for the environment of P, i.e., the rest of the system. It is easy to see that the functions f_n are monotone.

Upon start of the analysis, at each node the variables' values are assumed to be defined, i.e., the initial valuation is the least one: $\eta^\alpha_{init}(n) = \eta_\bot$. This choice rests on the assumption that all local variables of each process are properly initialized. We are interested in the least solution to the data-flow problem given by the following constraint set:

$$
\begin{aligned}
f(c_i?s(x))\eta^\alpha &= \begin{cases} \eta^\alpha{}_{[x \mapsto \top]} & c \notin out(\bar{P}) \\ \eta^\alpha{}_{[x \mapsto \bigvee\{[\![e]\!]_{\eta^\alpha} \mid \alpha_{n'} = g \rhd c_o!s(e) \text{ for some node } n'\}]} & \text{else} \end{cases} \\
f(g \rhd c_o!s(e))\eta^\alpha &= \eta^\alpha \\
f(g \rhd x := e)\eta^\alpha &= \eta^\alpha{}_{[x \mapsto [\![e]\!]_{\eta^\alpha}]} \\
f(g \rhd \mathit{set}\ t := e)\eta^\alpha &= \eta^\alpha{}_{[t \mapsto on([\![e]\!]_{\eta^\alpha})]} \\
f(g \rhd \mathit{reset}\ t)\eta^\alpha &= \eta^\alpha{}_{[t \mapsto \mathit{off}]} \\
f(g_t \rhd \mathit{reset}\ t)\eta^\alpha &= \eta^\alpha{}_{[t \mapsto \mathit{off}]}
\end{aligned}
$$

Table 4. Transfer functions/abstract effect for process P

$$
\begin{aligned}
\eta^\alpha_{post}(n) &\geq f_n(\eta^\alpha_{pre}(n)) \\
\eta^\alpha_{pre}(n) &\geq \bigvee\{\eta^\alpha_{post}(n') \mid (n', n) \text{ in flow relation}\}
\end{aligned}
\tag{1}
$$

For each node n of the flow graph, the data-flow problem is specified by two inequations or constraints. The first one relates the abstract valuation η^α_{pre} before entering the node with the valuation η^α_{post} afterwards via the abstract effects of Table 4. The least fixpoint of the constraint set can be solved iteratively in a fairly standard way by a *worklist algorithm* (see e.g., [15, 12, 20]), where the worklist steers the iterative loop until the least fixpoint is reached (cf. Fig. 1).

---

input : the flow-graph of the program
output: $\eta^\alpha_{pre}, \eta^\alpha_{post}$;

$\eta^\alpha(n) = \eta^\alpha_{init}(n)$;
$WL = \{n \mid \alpha_n = ?s(x), s \in Sig_{ext}\}$;

repeat
  pick $n \in WL$;
  let $S = \{n' \in succ(n) \mid f_n(\eta^\alpha(n) \not\leq \eta^\alpha(n')\}$
  in
    for all $n' \in S$: $\eta^\alpha(n') := f(\eta^\alpha(n))$;
    $WL := WL \backslash n \cup S$;
until $WL = \emptyset$;

$\eta^\alpha_{pre}(n) = \eta^\alpha(n)$;
$\eta^\alpha_{post}(n) = f_n(\eta^\alpha(n))$

Fig. 1. Worklist algorithm

The worklist data-structure WL used in the algorithm is a set of elements, more specifically a set of nodes from the flow-graph, and where we denote by

$succ(n)$ the set of successor nodes of n in the flow graph in forward direction. It supports as operation to randomly pick one element from the set (without removing it), and we write $WL\backslash n$ for the worklist without the node n and $\cup$ for set-union on the elements of the worklist. The algorithm starts with the least valuation on all nodes and an initial worklist containing nodes with input from the environment. It enlarges the valuation within the given lattice step by step until it stabilizes, i.e., until the worklist is empty. If adding the abstract effect of one node to the current state enlarges the valuation, i.e., the set S is non-empty, those successor nodes from S are (re-)entered into the list of unfinished one. Since the set of variables in the system is finite, and thus the lattice of abstract valuations, the termination of the algorithm is immediate.

With the worklist as a set-like data structure, the algorithm is free to work off the list in any order. In praxis, more deterministic data-structures and traversal strategies are appropriate, for instance traversing the graph in a breadth-first manner (see [20] for a broader discussion or various traversal strategies). After termination the algorithm yields two mappings $\eta^{\alpha}_{pre}, \eta^{\alpha}_{post} : Node \rightarrow Val^{\alpha}$. On a location l, the result of the analysis is given by $\eta^{\alpha}(l) = \bigvee\{\eta^{\alpha}_{post}(\tilde{n}) \mid \tilde{n} = \tilde{l} \longrightarrow_{\alpha} l\}$, also written as η^{α}_{l}.

Lemma 6 (Correctness). *Upon termination, the the algorithm gives back the least solution to the constraint set as given by the equations (1), resp. Table 4.*

4.2 Program Transformation

Based on the result of the analysis, we transform the given system $S = P \parallel \bar{P}$ into an optimized one, denoted by $S^{\sharp}$, where the communication of P with its environment $\bar{P}$ is done synchronously, all the data exchanged is abstracted, and which is in a simulation relation with the original system.

The transformation given as a set of transformation rules for each process P, similar to the ones from [23]. As the transformation here is simpler (since it does not embed the environment process $\bar{P}$ by incorporating its effect directly into P) we omit the full set of rules. The transformation is straightforward: guards potentially influenced by the environment are taken non-deterministically, i.e., a guard g at a location l is replaced by *true*, if $[\![g]\!]_{\eta^{\alpha}_{l}} = \top$. Assignments of expressions whose value may depend on data from the environment are omitted. For timer guards whose value is indeterminate because of outside influence, we work with a 3-valued abstraction: *off* when the timer is deactivated, a value $on(\top)$ when the timer is active with arbitrary expiration time, and a value $on(\top^{+})$ for active timers, whose expiration time is arbitrary except immediate timeout; the latter two abstract values are represented by $on(0)$ and $on(1)$, respectively, and the non-deterministic behavior of the timer expiration is captured by arbitrarily postponing a timeout by setting back the value of the timer to $on(1)$. This is captured by adding edges according to:

$$\frac{[\![t]\!]_{\eta^{\alpha}_{l}} = \top}{l \longrightarrow_{gt \,\triangleright\, reset\ t} \longrightarrow_{set\ t:=1} l \in Edg^{\sharp}}\ \text{T-NoTimeout}$$

As the transformation only adds non-determinism, the transformed system $S^\sharp$ simulates S (cf. [23]). Together with Theorem 5, this guarantees preservation of LTL-properties as long as variables influenced by $\bar{P}$ are not mentioned. Since we abstracted external data into a single value, not being able to specify properties depending on externally influence data is not much of an additional loss of precision.

Lemma 7. *Let P_a and P_s be the asynchronous resp. synchronous variant of a process, and S be given as the parallel composition of a $P_a \parallel \bar{P}$, where $\bar{P}$ is the environment of P. Furthermore, let $S^\sharp = P_s^\sharp \parallel \bar{P}$ be defined as before, and φ a next-free LTL-formula mentioning only variables from $\{x \mid \neg\exists l \in Loc.\ [\![x]\!]_{\eta_l^\alpha} = \top\}$. Then $S^\sharp \models \varphi$ implies $S \models \varphi$.*

5 Conclusion

In this paper, we extended earlier work from [23] describing how to close an open, asynchronous SDL-process by a timed chaotic environment while avoiding the combinatorial state-explosion in the external buffers. The generalization presented here goes a step beyond complete arbitrary environmental behavior, using the timed semantics of the language and separating, more or less, input and output.

In the context of software-testing, [8] describes an a dataflow algorithm to close program fragments given in the C-language with the most general environment. The algorithm is incorporated into the *VeriSoft* tool. As in our paper, the assume an asynchronous communicating model and abstract away external data, but do not consider *timed* systems and their abstraction. As for model-checking and analyzing SDL-programs, much work has been done, for instance in the context of the Vires-project, leading to the IF-toolset [4]

A fundamental approach to model checking open systems is known as *module* checking [17][16]. Instead of transforming the system into a closed one, the underlying computational model is generalized to distinguish between transitions under control of the module and those driven by the environment. MOCHA [1] is a model checker for reactive modules, which uses alternating-time temporal logic as specification language.

For practical applications, we are currently extending the larger case study [24] using the chaotic closure to this more general setting. In the experiments, we are using a JAVA-implementation of the automatic closing and the data-flow algorithm for concrete SDL-92 resp. a discrete-time extension of the Spin model checker which we use in the verification. We proceed in the following way: after splitting an SDL system into subsystems following the system structure, properties of the subsystems are verified being closed with an embedded chaotic environment. Afterwards, the verified properties are encoded into an SDL process, for which a tick-separated closure is constructed. This closure is used as environment for other parts of the system. As the closure gives a safe abstraction of the desired environment behavior, the verification results can be transferred to the original system.

References

[1] R. Alur, T. A. Henzinger, F. Mang, S. Qadeer, S. K. Rajamani, and S. Tasiran. Mocha: Modularity in model checking. In A. J. Hu and M. Y. Vardi, editors, *Proceedings of CAV '98*, volume 1427 of *Lecture Notes in Computer Science*, pages 521–525. Springer-Verlag, 1998.

[2] D. Bošnački and D. Dams. Integrating real time into Spin: A prototype implementation. In S. Budkowski, A. Cavalli, and E. Najm, editors, *Proceedings of Formal Description Techniques and Protocol Specification, Testing, and Verification (FORTE/PSTV'98)*. Kluwer Academic Publishers, 1998.

[3] D. Bošnački, D. Dams, L. Holenderski, and N. Sidorova. Verifying SDL in Spin. In S. Graf and M. Schwartzbach, editors, *TACAS 2000*, volume 1785 of *Lecture Notes in Computer Science*. Springer-Verlag, 2000.

[4] M. Bozga, J.-C. Fernandez, L. Ghirvu, S. Graf, J.-P. Krimm, and L. Mounier. IF: An intermediate representation and validation environment for timed asynchronous systems. In J. Wing, J. Woodcock, and J. Davies, editors, *Proceedings of Symposium on Formal Methods (FM 99)*, volume 1708 of *Lecture Notes in Computer Science*. Springer-Verlag, Sept. 1999.

[5] M. Bozga, S. Graf, A. Kerbrat, L. Mounier, I. Ober, and D. Vincent. SDL for real-time: What is missing? In Y. Lahav, S. Graf, and C. Jard, editors, *Electronic Proceedings of SAM'00*, 2000.

[6] J. Brock and W. Ackerman. An anomaly in the specifications of nondeterministic packet systems. Technical Report Computation Structures Group Note CSG-33, MIT Lab. for Computer Science, Nov. 1977.

[7] E. Clarke, O. Grumberg, and D. Long. Model checking and abstraction. *ACM Transactions on Programming Languages and Systems*, 16(5):1512–1542, 1994. A preliminary version appeared in the Proceedings of POPL 92.

[8] C. Colby, P. Godefroid, and L. J. Jagadeesan. Automatically closing of open reactive systems. In *Proceedings of 1998 ACM SIGPLAN Conference on Programming Language Design and Implementation*. ACM Press, 1998.

[9] D. Dams, R. Gerth, and O. Grumberg. Abstract interpretation of reactive systems: Abstraction preserving $\forall$CTL*,$\exists$CTL*, and CTL*. In E.-R. Olderog, editor, *Proceedings of PROCOMET '94*. IFIP, North-Holland, June 1994.

[10] Discrete-time Spin. `http://win.tue.nl/~dragan/DTSpin.html`, 2000.

[11] P. Godefroid. Using partial orders to improve automatic verification methods. In E. M. Clarke and R. P. Kurshan, editors, *Computer Aided Verification 1990*, volume 531 of *Lecture Notes in Computer Science*, pages 176–449. Springer-Verlag, 1991. an extended Version appeared in ACM/AMS DIMACS Series, volume 3, pages 321–340, 1991.

[12] M. S. Hecht. *Flow Analysis of Programs*. North-Holland, 1977.

[13] G. Holzmann and J. Patti. Validating SDL specifications: an experiment. In E. Brinksma, editor, *International Workshop on Protocol Specification, Testing and Verification IX (Twente, The Netherlands)*, pages 317–326. North-Holland, 1989. IFIP TC-6 International Workshop.

[14] G. J. Holzmann. *Design and Validation of Computer Protocols*. Prentice Hall, 1991.

[15] G. Kildall. A unified approach to global program optimization. In *Proceedings of POPL '73*, pages 194–206. ACM, January 1973.

[16] O. Kupferman and M. Y. Vardi. Module checking revisited. In O. Grumberg, editor, *CAV '97, Proceedings of the 9th International Conference on Computer-Aided*

Verification, Haifa. Israel, volume 1254 of *Lecture Notes in Computer Science*. Springer, June 1997.

[17] O. Kupferman, M. Y. Vardi, and P. Wolper. Module checking. In R. Alur, editor, *Proceedings of CAV '96*, volume 1102 of *Lecture Notes in Computer Science*, pages 75–86, 1996.

[18] O. Lichtenstein and A. Pnueli. Checking that finite state concurrent programs satisfy their linear specification. In *Twelfth Annual Symposium on Principles of Programming Languages (POPL) (New Orleans, LA)*, pages 97–107. ACM, January 1985.

[19] D. Long. *Model Checking, Abstraction and Compositional Verification*. PhD thesis, Carnegie Mellon University, 1993.

[20] F. Nielson, H.-R. Nielson, and C. Hankin. *Principles of Program Analysis*. Springer-Verlag, 1999.

[21] A. Pnueli. The temporal logic of programs. In *Proceeding of the 18th Annual Symposium on Foundations of Computer Science*, pages 45–57, 1977.

[22] Specification and Description Language SDL, blue book. CCITT Recommendation Z.100, 1992.

[23] N. Sidorova and M. Steffen. Embedding chaos. In P. Cousot, editor, *Proceedings of the 8th Static Analysis Symposium (SAS'01)*, volume 2126 of *Lecture Notes in Computer Science*, pages 319–334. Springer-Verlag, 2001.

[24] N. Sidorova and M. Steffen. Verifying large SDL-specifications using model checking. In R. Reed and J. Reed, editors, *Proceedings of the 10th International SDL Forum SDL 2001: Meeting UML*, volume 2078 of *Lecture Notes in Computer Science*, pages 403–416. Springer-Verlag, Feb. 2001.

[25] A. Valmari. A stubborn attack on state explosion. *Formal Methods in System Design*, 1992. Earlier version in the proceeding of CAV '90 Lecture Notes in Computer Science 531, Springer-Verlag 1991, pp. 156–165 and in Computer-Aided Verification '90, DIMACS Series in Discrete Mathematics and Theoretical Computer Science Vol. 3, AMS & ACM 1991, pp. 25–41.

Automata-Theoretic Decision of Timed Games*

Marco Faella[1], Salvatore La Torre[1,2], and Aniello Murano[1,3]

[1] Università degli Studi di Salerno
mfaella,sallat,murano@dia.unisa.it
[2] University of Pennsylvania
[3] Rice University

Abstract. The solution of games is a key decision problem in the context of verification of open systems and program synthesis. We present an automata-theoretic approach to solve timed games. Our solution gives a general framework to solve many classes of timed games via a translation to tree automata, extending to timed games a successful approach to solve discrete games. Our approach relies on translating a timed automaton into a tree automaton that accepts all the trees corresponding to a given strategy of the protagonist. This construction exploits the region automaton introduced by Alur and Dill. We use our framework to solve timed Büchi games in exponential time, timed Rabin games in exponential time, CTL games in exponential time and LTL games in doubly exponential time. All these results are tight in the sense that they match the known lower bounds on these decision problems.

1 Introduction

The theory of games was originally introduced as a theoretical model for economic studies (see for example [20]). In the years, this theory has received an increasing interest by many researchers in both computer science and control theory. Games have been studied in the context of discrete [11,22,27,6], timed [9,8], and hybrid systems [14]. They provide a suitable framework for the program synthesis and the verification of *open systems*, that is, systems whose behavior depends on the current state as well as the behavior of the environment in which they are embedded.

The notion of open system naturally arises in the compositional modeling and design of *reactive systems*, that is systems that maintain an on-going interaction with their environment [7,22]. A reactive system can be seen as divided into many components interacting with each other, and each component can be modeled as an open system. In automated verification, systems are often modeled as *closed systems*, where a system behavior is completely determined by the current state. The verification problem can thus be phrased as: given an abstract model (transition system) M and a specification φ, we wish to determine if φ holds for

* This research was partially supported by the NSF awards CCR99-70925 and CCR99-88322, SRC award 99-TJ-688, DARPA ITO Mobies award F33615-00-C-1707, NSF ITR award, and by the MURST project "MEFISTO".

A. Cortesi (Ed.): VMCAI 2002, LNCS 2294, pp. 94–108, 2002.
© Springer-Verlag Berlin Heidelberg 2002

the computations of M (*model-checking*). Model-checking is a very successful technology which has been implemented in many tools.

The decision problem we consider in this paper is analogous to model-checking. We are given a specification and a game graph (alternating transition system), where the transitions are determined by the moves of two players. We wish to determine if a player has a strategy to ensure that, independently from the choices of the other player, the resulting computation satisfies the specification. We recall that for simple specifications such as "always p" and relatively to discrete-time systems, such model-checking games have already been implemented in the software MOCHA [5], and shown to be useful in construction of the most-general environments for automating assume-guarantee reasoning [1].

To refer to delays, time needs to be explicitly included in the model for a reactive system. In this paper we focus on timed games and model them as nondeterministic *timed automata* [3]: a finite automaton augmented with a finite set of real-valued *clocks*. The transitions of a timed automaton are enabled according to the current state, that is, the current *location* and the current clock values. In a transition, clocks can be instantaneously reset. The value of a clock is exactly the time elapsed since the last time it was reset. A clock constraint (*guard*) is associated to each transition with the meaning that a transition can be taken only if the associated guard is enabled. Moreover, a clock constraint (*invariant*) is also associated to each location with the meaning that the automaton can stay in a location as long as the corresponding invariant remains true.

When interpreting a nondeterministic timed automaton as a game graph, we capture the choices of the *protagonist* by the symbols associated with the transitions and nondeterminism is used to model the possible choices of the *antagonist*[1]. To model the case that the protagonist stays *idle* and the antagonist is moving, we use a special symbol denoted by ε. The case that both players stay idle is captured by letting time elapse in a location. A *play* of a timed game is thus constructed in the following way. At each time, a player declares how long it will wait idling and its next choice. At the time one of the players or both move, both players are allowed to redeclare their next move and the time they will issue it. That is, if a player moves before the other, this latter is allowed to change its last declared decision. Technically, a play is a run of the automaton modeling the game. The winning condition for the protagonist is expressed by a predicate over system behaviors (runs). Thus, the decision problem we wish to solve is to establish if the protagonist has a strategy to ensure that the resulting computations satisfy the winning condition.

A way to solve games is to reduce them to the emptiness problem for tree automata. This approach has been successfully exploited to solving discrete games [24,28]. In this paper we extend the automata-theoretic approach to solving timed games. We propose a general framework that can be used with any class of winning predicates over the untimed runs of a given timed automaton, which

[1] We recall that this formulation of games, which is asymmetric with respect to the two players, is substantially equivalent to the symmetric one, and thus our results can be stated also for the general case.

admit direct translation to a class of tree automata with decidable emptiness problem and closure under intersection. Given a timed automaton A and a winning predicate W we construct the tree automata A^T and A_W such that A^T accepts all the trees corresponding to a strategy of the protagonist in the game (A, W), and A_W accepts all the trees whose paths satisfy the predicate W and having arity (branching degree) upper bounded by the maximum arity among all the trees accepted by A^T. Thus, there exists a winning strategy of the protagonist in the game (A, W) if and only if the intersection between the languages accepted by A^T and A_W is not empty. To construct A^T we exploit the region automaton due to Alur and Dill [3].

We analyze in more detail the case of winning predicates expressed by temporal logic formulas. Temporal logic is a widely accepted formalism to specify and verify reactive systems introduced by Pnueli in 1977 [21]. Here we consider formulas of the logics CTL [12] and LTL [21]. Using our approach, we solve timed Büchi games in exponential time, timed Rabin games in exponential time, CTL games in exponential time and LTL games in doubly exponential time. Since timed reachability games are known to be EXPTIME-hard even if the antagonist is allowed to move only when the protagonist does [18], and LTL games are 2EXPTIME-hard [22], our results are complete. Combining our construction with the results on LTL generators from [6], we can prove an upper bound smaller than 2EXPTIME for meaningful subclasses of LTL timed games. Rectangular hybrid games with winning conditions expressed by LTL formulas were solved in [14], where the authors also prove EXPTIME-hardness of timed reachability games. The results from [14] subsumes our results on LTL timed games, but the approach we follow here is different, and mainly, we are giving a systematic way of solving timed games for different classes of winning predicates. Different formulations of games with winning conditions expressed by temporal logic formulas have been also considered in [4,15,16].

The rest of the paper is organized as follows. In Section 2, we introduce the definition and the notation relatively to timed games. We also briefly discuss the automata-theoretic approach to solve discrete games. In Section 3, we discuss the construction of a tree automaton accepting all the strategies of the protagonist in a timed game and give the complexity results on timed Büchi and Rabin games. The general algorithm to solve timed games and its application to timed games with winning conditions expressed by CTL and LTL formulas are discussed in Section 4. In Section 5 we give a few conclusions.

2 Timed Games

In this section we introduce the concept of timed game. We start defining discrete games and discuss an automata-theoretic approach to decide them. Then, we introduce timed games.

We model a game as a nondeterministic automaton along with a winning condition. The alphabet symbols (actions) of the automaton represent the choices of the *protagonist* and the nondeterminism is used to model the possible choices of the *antagonist*. To model the case that the protagonist stays *idle* and the antagonist is moving, we use a special symbol denoted by ε. Therefore, all transitions are to be considered joint moves of the two players, except transitions labeled with ε. In the following, we will denote by Σ^ε the set of symbols including the idle action ε, and, if not differently specified, by σ a member of Σ.

An automaton A is a tuple $(Q, \Sigma^\varepsilon, q_0, \Delta)$ where Q is a finite set of locations (or *vertices*), $q_0 \in Q$ is the initial location, and $\Delta \subseteq Q \times \Sigma^\varepsilon \times Q$ is the transition relation. A *run* of A is a sequence of locations $q_0 q_1 \dots q_k$ such that $(q_i, \sigma, q_{i+1}) \in \Delta$ for $i = 0, \dots, k-1$. We will also be interested in infinite runs, that is runs on ω-words over Σ^ε. An *ω-word* over a given alphabet Γ is a mapping from $\mathbb{N}$ into Γ, that is, an infinite sequence of symbols over Γ. Let $w = w_0 w_1 w_2 \dots$ be an ω-word, with w^i we denote the subsequence of w starting at position i, that is, the mapping defined by $w^i_n = w_{i+n}$. A game is a pair (A, W) where A is an automaton (*game graph*) and W is the winning condition, that is a predicate over ω-words of vertices. According to the kind of winning condition, we obtain different kinds of games. A *play* of a given game corresponds to a run of the automaton. A *strategy* is a function that with any run associates an action among those that are enabled. A strategy f has associated a tree t_f (*strategy tree*) in the following way:

- the root of t_f is $\langle q_0 \rangle$, and
- if $\langle q_0 \dots q_k \rangle$ is a node of t and $f(q_0 \dots q_k) = \sigma \in \Sigma^\varepsilon$, then $\langle q_0 \dots q_k q_{k+1} \rangle$ is a child of $\langle q_0 \dots q_k \rangle$ for all q_{k+1} such that $(q_k, \sigma, q_{k+1}) \in \Delta$.

A node $\langle q_0 \dots q_k \rangle$ of t_f is labeled by q_k. Thus, t_f has nodes corresponding to plays of the game constructed according to a strategy f. We observe that paths of t_f are in general not finite (i.e., t_f is an ω-tree), and thus are ω-words over Q. Given a game (A, W), a strategy f is *winning* if W holds on all the ω-words corresponding to paths of t_f. We consider the decision problem: "Is there a strategy satisfying the winning condition W?"

A way to solve games is to reduce them to the emptiness problem for a suitable class of ω-tree automata [24,28]. An ω-tree automaton is defined by a tuple (Q, Σ, q_0, Δ) where Q is a finite set of locations, $q_0 \in Q$ is the initial location, and Σ is an alphabet as in the definition of an automaton on ω-words. The only difference concerns the transition relation Δ, which here is a subset of $\cup_{i=1}^{K} (Q \times \Sigma \times Q^i)$, where K is a positive integer (called the *arity* of the automaton). A run of a tree automaton can thus be seen as a rewriting of a tree by locations, and generalizes the definition of run we have given for automata on ω-words in the obvious way. With a tree automaton we associate an acceptance condition which is usually a predicate over ω-words of locations (we will return on acceptance conditions for automata on ω-objects in Section 3.1). A tree is accepted by an automaton A if and only if there exists a run r of A such that all the paths of r satisfy the acceptance condition. See [26] for a survey on automata on ω-words and ω-trees.

Given a game (A, W) we construct a corresponding tree automaton A' accepting t_f for all the winning strategies f of (A, W) in the following way. The set of locations, the initial location, and the alphabet of A' are respectively the set of locations, the initial location, and the alphabet of A. The acceptance condition of A' is W, and the transition relation of A' is the set of the tuples $(q, \sigma, q_1, \dots, q_k)$ such that $(q, \sigma, q_1), \dots, (q, \sigma, q_k)$ are all the transitions on σ of A. It is easy to verify that A' accepts a tree t if and only if there exists a winning strategy f of (A, W) such that $t = t_f$.

We end this section by introducing timed games. We define timed games analogously to games via a nondeterministic *timed automaton* [3]. A timed automaton is a model of a real-time system. We assume that there is a central (real-valued) clock scanning time, and the model can use a finite set of *clock variables* (also simply named *clocks*) along with timing constraints to check the satisfaction of timing requirements. Each clock can be seen as a chronograph synchronized with the central clock. It can be read or set to zero (reset); after a reset, it restarts automatically. In each automaton, timing constraints are expressed by clock constraints. Let C be a set of clocks, the set of clock constraints $\Xi(C)$ contains:

- $x \leq y + c$, $x \geq y + c$, $x \leq c$ and $x \geq c$, where $x, y \in C$ and c is a natural number; we call such constraints *atomic* clock constraints;
- $\neg\delta$ and $\delta_1 \wedge \delta_2$ where $\delta, \delta_1, \delta_2 \in \Xi(C)$.

Furthermore, let $\mathbb{R}_+$ be the set of nonnegative real numbers, a *clock interpretation* is a mapping $\nu : C \longrightarrow \mathbb{R}_+$. If ν is a clock interpretation, λ is a set of clocks and d is a real number, we denote with $[\lambda \leftarrow 0](\nu + d)$ the clock interpretation that for each clock $x \in \lambda$ gives 0 and for each clock $x \notin \lambda$ gives the value $\nu(x) + d$.

A *timed automaton* A is a tuple $(Q, \Sigma^\varepsilon, q_0, C, \Delta, inv)$ where:

- Q is a finite set of locations;
- $q_0 \in Q$ is the initial location;
- C is a finite set of n clock variables;
- Δ is a finite subset of $Q \times \Sigma \times \Xi(C) \times 2^C \times Q$ (edges);
- $inv : Q \longrightarrow \Xi(C)$ maps each location q to its invariant $inv(q)$.

A *state* of a timed automaton A is a pair (q, ν) where $q \in Q$ and $\nu \in \mathbb{R}^n_+$. The *initial state* is the pair (q_0, ν_0) where $\nu_0(x) = 0$ for all $x \in C$. The semantics of a timed automaton is given by a transition system over the set of states. The transitions of this system are divided into *discrete steps* and *time steps*. A discrete step is $(q, \nu) \xrightarrow{\sigma} (q', \nu')$ where $(q, \sigma, \delta, \lambda, q') \in \Delta$, ν satisfies δ, $\nu' = [\lambda \leftarrow 0]\nu$, and ν' satisfies $inv(q')$. A time step is $(q, \nu) \xrightarrow{d} (q, \nu')$ where $d \in \mathbb{R}_+$, $\nu' = \nu + d$ and $\nu + d'$ satisfies $inv(q)$ for all $0 \leq d' \leq d$. A *step* is $(q, \nu) \xrightarrow{d,\sigma} (q', \nu')$ where $(q, \nu) \xrightarrow{d} (q, \nu'')$ and $(q, \nu'') \xrightarrow{\sigma} (q', \nu')$, for some $\nu'' \in \mathbb{R}^n$. A *timed word* $(\bar{\sigma}, \bar{\tau})$ over the alphabet Σ is such that $\bar{\sigma} \in \Sigma^*$, $\bar{\tau} \in \mathbb{R}^*_+$, and $|\bar{\sigma}| = |\bar{\tau}|$. In a timed word, each symbol σ_i at input is associated with a positive real number τ_i, which expresses (except for the first symbol σ_1) the time which has elapsed since the symbol σ_{i-1} was at input. Time τ_1 represents instead the time at which the symbol σ_1 appears at input assuming that the computation starts at time 0. A run r of a timed automaton A on a timed word $(\bar{\sigma}, \bar{\tau})$, where $\bar{\sigma} = \sigma_1 \dots \sigma_k$

and $\bar{\tau} = \tau_1 \dots \tau_k$, is a finite sequence $(q_0, \nu_0) \xrightarrow{\tau_1,\sigma_1} (q_1, \nu_1) \xrightarrow{\tau_2,\sigma_2} \dots \xrightarrow{\tau_k,\sigma_k} (q_k, \nu_k)$. We say that r starts at q_0 and ends at q_k. Also, for all $i \leqslant k$, we denote by r_i the run $(q_0, \nu_0) \xrightarrow{\tau_1,\sigma_1} (q_1, \nu_1) \xrightarrow{\tau_2,\sigma_2} \dots \xrightarrow{\tau_i,\sigma_i} (q_i, \nu_i)$, that is the prefix of r up to the i-th step. Finally, Run(A) is the set of all runs of A.

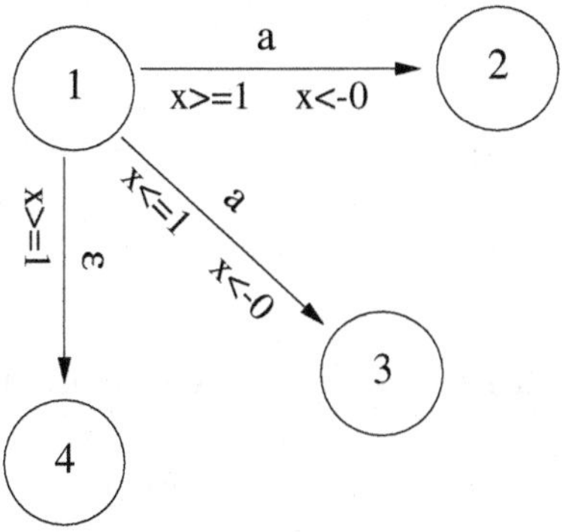

Fig. 1. A fragment of a timed game A.

In a timed game, both players can decide to stay idle for a while. We capture this case by time steps. A *play* of a timed game is constructed in the following way. At each time, a player declares how long it will wait idling until its next choice. At the time one of the players or both move, both players are allowed to redeclare their next move and the time they will issue it. That is, if a player moves before the other, this latter is allowed to change its former decision. A play is represented by a run of the automaton.

As instance, take the fragment of a one clock timed game depicted in figure 1, where the symbol above each edge is the action taken, while under the edge there is a timing constraint and possibly a clock reset. For sake of simplicity, the invariants on the locations are not shown and they are supposed to be *True*. Suppose that the game is in location 1, with clock x equal to zero and the current strategy of the protagonist is to take an a-move, after a delay of 1. Since at time $x = 1$ there are two a-moves enabled, the antagonist can choose which one is to be taken, and the game will proceed either to location 2 or to location 3. Notice that, since there is no ε-move enabled before time 1, this strategy does not allow the antagonist to move on his own.

Formally, a *timed game* is a tuple (A, W) where A is a timed automaton and W is a winning condition. A *strategy* is a function $\mathcal{F} : \mathit{Plays}(\mathcal{F}) \longrightarrow \mathbb{R}_+ \times \Sigma$, where $\mathit{Plays}(\mathcal{F}) \subseteq \mathrm{Run}(A)$, $(q_0, \nu_0) = (q_0, \bar{0}) \in \mathit{Plays}(\mathcal{F})$ and for all $r = (q_0, \nu_0) \xrightarrow{\tau_1,\sigma_1} (q_1, \nu_1) \xrightarrow{\tau_2,\sigma_2} \dots \xrightarrow{\tau_k,\sigma_k} (q_k, \nu_k)$ belonging to $\mathit{Plays}(\mathcal{F})$, it holds that for $i = 0, \dots, k-1$, either $\mathcal{F}(r_i) = (\tau_{i+1}, \sigma_{i+1})$ or $\mathcal{F}(r_i) = (d, \sigma)$, $\tau_{i+1} < d$ and $\sigma_{i+1} = \varepsilon$. In other words, a strategy gives the moves of the protagonist on each play which is "consistent" with the strategy itself and the case $\sigma_{i+1} = \varepsilon$ corresponds to a move of the antagonist taken before the next declared move of the protagonist. The set of ω-runs r such that any prefix of r is a play consistent with $\mathcal{F}$, is called the set of maximal plays of $\mathcal{F}$. Each strategy $\mathcal{F}$ has a *dense tree*[2] $T_{\mathcal{F}} = (S, \mu, b)$ associated with it, where:

- $S = Q \times \mathbb{R}^{|C|}$ the state space of A;
- $\mu(q, \nu) = q$;
- $b(q, \nu)$ is the set of suffixes starting from (q, ν) of maximal plays of $\mathcal{F}$.

A path in $T_{\mathcal{F}}$ is thus a maximal play of $\mathcal{F}$. Given a timed ω-word $w = (\bar{\sigma}, \bar{\tau})$, we define $\mathit{Untime}(w) = \bar{\sigma}$, that is the ω-word obtained by discarding the time occurrence of each symbol. A strategy $\mathcal{F}$ is *winning* if $\mathit{Untime}(r)$ satisfies the winning condition W for any maximal play r of $\mathcal{F}$.

3 From Timed Games to Tree Automata

In this section, we discuss how to extend to timed games the automata-theoretic approach to solve discrete games. This approach relies on the construction of a tree automaton accepting a non-empty language if and only if there exists a winning strategy of the protagonist in the given game. Our approach is based on the region automaton construction introduced by Alur and Dill in [3].

Consider a timed automaton $A = (Q, \Sigma^{\varepsilon}, q_0, C, \Delta, inv)$. By definition, its set of states is infinite. However, it can be partitioned in a finite number of equivalence classes, called *regions*, which are defined by a location and a *clock region*. Denoted by c_x the largest constant in clock constraints involving the clock variable x, a clock region is described by:

- a constraint of the type $c - 1 < x < c$, $x > c_x$, or $x = c$ for each clock variable x and a natural number $c \leq c_x$;
- the ordering of the fractional parts of the clock variables x such that $x < c_x$.

Thus, a clock region denotes a set of clock valuations. Given a clock valuation ν, $[\nu]$ denotes the clock region containing ν. A state (q, ν) belongs to a region $\langle q', \alpha \rangle$ if $q = q'$ and $\nu \in \alpha$. A clock region α is said to be *open* if for any clock variable x and $c \leq c_x$, $x = c$ does not hold in α. Otherwise α is said to be a *boundary* clock region. These definitions apply to regions in an obvious way. The key property of this equivalence relation is that all the valuations belonging to a region satisfy the same set of clock constraints from the given timed automaton. Consistently we say that a clock region α satisfies a constraint δ if ν satisfies δ for any $\nu \in \alpha$. A clock region α' is said to be a *time-successor* of a clock region α if and only if for all $\nu \in \alpha$ there is a $d \in \mathbb{R}_+$ such that $\nu + d \in \alpha'$. A *next time-successor* α' of α is a time-successor of α such that $\alpha' \neq \alpha$ and for all time-successors α'' of α such that $\alpha'' \notin \{\alpha, \alpha'\}$, α'' is also a time-successor of α'.

Denoted by ξ a symbol not in Σ^{ε}, the *region automaton* of A is a transition system defined by:

[2] For a general definition of dense tree see [2].

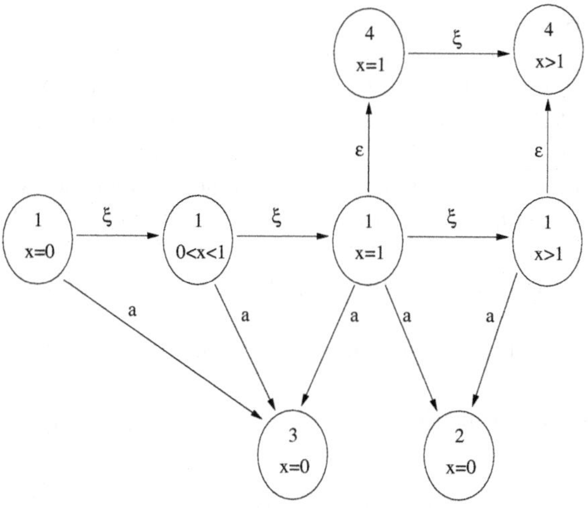

Fig. 2. The region automaton $R(A)$.

- the set of states $R(Q) = \{\langle q, \alpha\rangle \mid q \in Q$ and α is a clock region satisfying $inv(\mathrm{q})\}$;
- the transition rules $R(\Delta)$ such that:
  - $(\langle q, \alpha\rangle, \sigma, \langle q', \alpha'\rangle) \in R(\Delta)$ if and only if $(q, \sigma, \lambda, \delta, q') \in \Delta$, α satisfies δ, and $\alpha' = [\lambda \leftarrow 0]\alpha$ (σ-transition);
  - $(\langle q, \alpha\rangle, \xi, \langle q, \alpha'\rangle) \in R(\Delta)$ if and only if α' is the next time-successor of α (ξ-transition).

We denote by $R(A)$ the region automaton corresponding to A.

We observe that the action ξ captures the case that both players stay idle and let the time pass, while the other symbols in Σ^ε have the same meaning as in A. Given an A step $r = (q, \nu) \xrightarrow{d,\sigma} (q', \nu')$, define $[r]$ as $\langle q, [\nu]\rangle \xrightarrow{\xi} \langle q_0, \alpha_1\rangle \ldots \langle q_0, \alpha_{k-1}\rangle \xrightarrow{\xi} \langle q_0, \alpha_k\rangle \xrightarrow{\sigma} \langle q', [\nu']\rangle$ where $\alpha_0 = [\nu]$, α_{i+1} is the next successor of α_i, and $\nu + d \in \alpha_k$. ¿From the definition of $R(A)$, we have that $[r]$ is a run of $R(A)$ from $\langle q, [\nu]\rangle$ to $\langle q', [\nu']\rangle$. We can extend to any arbitrary run of A the previous definition. Clearly, it holds that if r is a run of A from (q, ν) to (q', ν') then $[r]$ is a run of A from $\langle q, [\nu]\rangle$ to $\langle q', [\nu']\rangle$. Given a strategy $\mathcal{F}$ in the game graph A we can analogously define a strategy $[\mathcal{F}]$ in $R(A)$.

The above observations would suggest to use $R(A)$ as a game graph in a discrete game corresponding to a game on A, however it is not obvious how to translate the winning conditions. To see this, suppose that the winning condition of the considered game defines a language which is not closed under stuttering, that is a language where repetitions of an assignment of atomic propositions matter. Since the ξ-transitions do not change the atomic propositions (the location remains the same), the winning condition may hold false on a run of $R(A)$ while it holds true on the corresponding run of A.

We solve this problem by constructing a tree automaton that hides the ξ-transitions and keeps the information relative to the ε-moves that can be taken by the antagonist while the protagonist chooses to stay idle. Namely, consider a state $\langle q, \alpha_1 \rangle$ of $R(A)$. Suppose that there exist a sequence of ξ-transitions from $\langle q, \alpha_i \rangle$ to $\langle q, \alpha_{i+1} \rangle$, for $i = 1, \ldots, k-1$ and $k \geq 1$, such that there is at least a σ-transition from $\langle q, \alpha_k \rangle$ for $\sigma \in \Sigma$. In the new transition system, we define a σ-transition from $\langle q, \alpha_1 \rangle$ to all the states $\langle q', \alpha' \rangle$ such that there exists a σ-transition from $\langle q, \alpha_k \rangle$ to $\langle q', \alpha' \rangle$.
Also, we add an ε-transition from $\langle q, \alpha_1 \rangle$ to all the states $\langle q', \alpha' \rangle$ such that:

- there exists an ε-transition from $\langle q, \alpha_i \rangle$ to $\langle q', \alpha' \rangle$ for some $i = 1, \ldots, k-1$, or
- there exists an ε-transition from $\langle q, \alpha_k \rangle$ to $\langle q', \alpha' \rangle$, if α_k is an open region and $k \neq 1$.

Given a state $\langle q, \alpha_1 \rangle$ of $R(A)$, if for all the time-successors α of α_1 there exist no σ-transition from $\langle q, \alpha \rangle$, then we define an ε-transition from $\langle q, \alpha_1 \rangle$ to all the states $\langle q', \alpha' \rangle$ such that there is an ε-transition from $\langle q, \alpha \rangle$ to $\langle q', \alpha' \rangle$ and α is a time-successor of α_1.

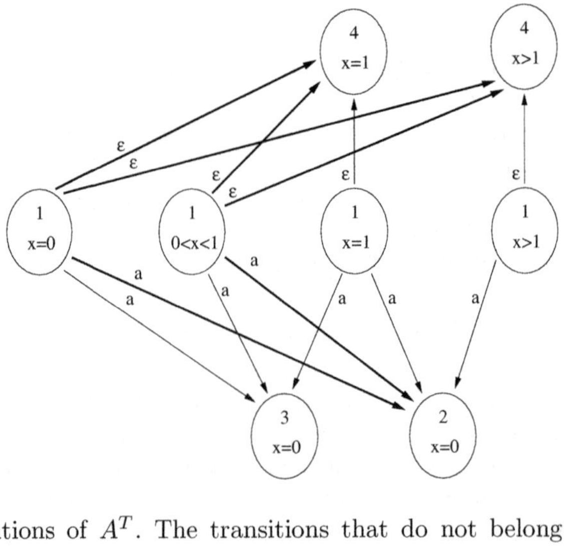

Fig. 3. Transitions of A^T. The transitions that do not belong to the region automaton are in boldface.

Let us take into consideration the A^T automaton depicted in figure 3. By comparing this automaton with the corresponding region automaton in figure 2, it can be seen that the transitions corresponding to the mere passage of time (ξ-transitions) have been removed, while others have been added. As instance, starting from region $\langle 1, x = 0 \rangle$, there is a new a-move, leading to $\langle 2, x = 0 \rangle$, which corresponds to the path $\langle 1, x=0\rangle$, $\langle 1, 0<x<1\rangle$, $\langle 1, x=1\rangle$,$\langle 2, x=0\rangle$ in the region automaton.

Since the winning conditions are predicates over the runs of the starting timed game, to complete the construction we need to define the transitions of the above tree automaton on locations of A. To do this, we simply replace each transition $(\langle q, \alpha\rangle, \sigma, \langle q_1, \alpha_1\rangle, \ldots, \langle q_k, \alpha_k\rangle)$ by $(\langle q, \alpha\rangle, q, \langle q_1, \alpha_1\rangle, \ldots, \langle q_k, \alpha_k\rangle)$.

We denote by A^T the tree automaton which is obtained by the above construction. (Notice that the action corresponding to a given transition can be easily determined by translating back a run of A^T into a run of $R(A)$.) From [3], we have that the number of regions of A is $O(|C|!\, 2^{|C|}\, \Pi_{x\in C}(2c_x+2))$. Thus, the following result holds.

Lemma 1. *The size of A^T is exponential in the size of the clock constraints and linear in the number of locations.*

By the construction of A^T, we have that the following theorem holds.

Theorem 1. *Given a timed game (A, W), each strategy $\mathcal{F}$ of the protagonist can be mapped into a tree t accepted by A^T, and vice-versa. Moreover, if $\mathcal{F}$ is winning then W holds on all the paths of t.*

3.1 Timed Büchi and Rabin Games

Here we briefly discuss some results that can be obtained directly from the construction presented in the first part of this section. In the next section we extend this approach to solving timed games to temporal logic games.

We recall that a *Büchi condition* asserts that at least a final location repeats infinitely often in an infinite run. That is, denoted by $Inf(r)$ the locations that repeat infinitely often in an infinite run r and by $W \subseteq Q$ a set of acceptance locations, the Büchi condition is expressed as $Inf(r) \cap W \neq \emptyset$. A *Rabin condition* is given by a set of pairs $\{(U_i, L_i) \mid i = 1, \ldots, k\}$ such that $U_i, L_i \subseteq Q$, and for some $i = 1, \ldots, k$, a vertex in U_i must repeat infinitely often and none of the vertices in L_i repeats infinitely often. Formally, the Rabin condition is: "there exists a pair (U_i, L_i) such that $Inf(r) \cap U_i \neq \emptyset$ and $Inf(r) \cap L_i = \emptyset$". Combining these two conditions with the definition of timed games, we define respectively *timed Büchi games* and *timed Rabin games.*

Given a timed Büchi game (A, W), define W' as the set $\{\langle q, \alpha\rangle \mid q \in W$ and α is a clock region of $A\}$. We have that A^T coupled with W' is a Büchi tree automaton which, by Theorem 1, accepts a tree t if and only if there exists a winning strategy of the protagonist in (A, W). We recall that the non-emptiness problem for Büchi tree automata is decidable in polynomial time [10]. Moreover, timed reachability games are EXPTIME-hard [14]. Thus by Lemma 1, the following result holds.

Theorem 2. *Timed Büchi games are* EXPTIME*-complete.*

We prove the same result on timed Rabin games. Given a timed Rabin game (A, W), for $(U_i, L_i) \in W$ define $U'_i = \{\langle q, \alpha\rangle \mid q \in U_i$ and α is a clock region of $A\}$

and $L'_i = \{\langle q, \alpha \rangle \mid q \in L_i$ and α is a clock region of $A\}$. Denote by W' the set $\{(U'_i, L'_i \mid (U_i, L_i) \in W\}$, we have that A^T coupled with W' is a Rabin tree automaton which, by Theorem 1, accepts a tree t if and only if there exists a winning strategy of the protagonist in (A, W). By Lemma 1 and the fact that the emptiness problem for Rabin tree automata can be solved in deterministic time $O((nm)^{cm})$ [22], where n is the number of locations, m is the number of pairs in the accepting set and c is a constant, we have the following result.

Theorem 3. *Timed Rabin games are* EXPTIME-*complete.*

4 A Solution to Timed Games

In this section we give a general algorithm to solve timed games with winning conditions that can be translated into a tree language accepted by a Rabin tree automaton, and using known results in the field of temporal logic, we apply it to solving CTL and LTL timed games.

Consider a timed game (A, W). By Theorem 1, it is possible to construct a tree automaton A^T such that for any strategy of the protagonist in (A, W) there exists a corresponding tree accepted by A^T and vice-versa. Let $K > 0$ be the maximum arity of a tree accepted by A^T. Suppose that it is possible to construct a tree automaton A_W accepting all the trees t with arity at most K such that W holds on all paths of t. Thus, by Theorem 1 we have that the language accepted by $A^T \cap A_W$ is non-empty is and only if there exists a winning strategy of the protagonist in the game (A, W). Since the automaton A^T is a Büchi tree automaton, it is sufficient that A_W is an automaton from a class of tree automata that are closed under intersection with respect Büchi automata and have a decidable emptiness problem. For example, A_W could be a Rabin, Büchi, Streett, or Muller tree automaton (see [26] for a survey on these classes of automata).

In the rest of the section we apply the above approach to solve CTL and LTL timed games.

4.1 Computation Tree Logic

Computation Tree logic (CTL) was introduced by Emerson and Clarke [12] as a powerful tool for specifying and verifying concurrent programs. Given a set of atomic propositions AP, a CTL formula is composed of atomic propositions, the boolean connectives *conjunction* ($\wedge$) and *negation* ($\neg$), and the linear-temporal operators *Next* ($\bigcirc$) and *Until* ($\mathcal{U}$) coupled with path quantifiers *for all paths* ($\forall$) and *for some path* ($\exists$). Formulas are built up in the usual way from the above operators and connectives, according to the following grammar

$$\varphi := p \mid \neg\varphi \mid \varphi \wedge \varphi \mid \forall\bigcirc\varphi \mid \exists\bigcirc\varphi \mid \forall(\varphi\,\mathcal{U}\,\varphi) \mid \exists(\varphi\,\mathcal{U}\,\varphi)$$

where p is an atomic proposition. The semantics of CTL is defined with respect to a *Kripke structure* $M = (S, \mu, R)$, where S is a countable set of states, $\mu : S \rightarrow$

2^{AP} maps each state to a set of atomic proposition true in that state, and R is a binary relation over S. A *path* in M is an infinite sequence of states $s_0, s_1, \ldots$ such that $(s_i, s_{i+1}) \in R$. Given a Kripke structure M, a CTL formula φ and a state $s \in S$, the satisfaction relation $(M, s) \models \varphi$, meaning that φ is true in M at s, is defined inductively as follows:

- if φ is an atomic proposition, then $(M, s) \models \varphi$ iff the truth assignment $\mu(s)$ satisfies φ;
- $(M, s) \models \neg\varphi$ iff $(M, s) \models \varphi$ does not hold;
- $(M, s) \models \varphi_1 \wedge \varphi_2$ iff $(M, s) \models \varphi_1$ and $(M, s) \models \varphi_2$;
- $(M, s) \models \forall \bigcirc \varphi$ iff $(M, s') \models \varphi$ for all $s' \in S$ such that $(s, s') \in R$;
- $(M, s) \models \exists \bigcirc \varphi$ iff $(M, s') \models \varphi$ for some $s' \in S$ such that $(s, s') \in R$;
- $(M, s) \models \forall(\varphi_1 \; \mathcal{U} \; \varphi_2)$ iff for every path $s_0, s_1, \ldots s_n$ with $s = s_0$, there exists $i \geq 0$ such that $(M, s_i) \models \varphi_2$, and $(M, s_j) \models \varphi_1$, for all j such that $0 \leq j < i$;
- $(M, s) \models \exists(\varphi_1 \; \mathcal{U} \; \varphi_2)$ iff there exist a path $s_0, s_1, \ldots s_n$ with $s = s_0$, and $i \geq 0$ such that $(M, s_i) \models \varphi_2$, and $(M, s_j) \models \varphi_1$, for all j such that $0 \leq j < i$.

Given a CTL formula φ and a positive integer K, it is possible to construct a Büchi tree automaton, of size exponential in the size of φ, which accepts all the ω-trees t with arity at most K such that: t is the unwinding of a Kripke structure M from a state s and $(M, s) \models \varphi$ [29]. Thus by Theorem 1, Lemma 1, and the fact that the emptiness problem for Büchi tree automata is decidable in polynomial time [10], the following theorem holds.

Theorem 4. *Given a timed game (A, φ) where φ is a* CTL *formula, the problem of deciding the existence of a winning strategy of the protagonist in (A, φ) is* EXPTIME-*complete.*

4.2 Linear Temporal Logic

Linear Temporal Logic (LTL) was introduced by Pnueli to specifying and verifying reactive systems [21]. Given a set of atomic propositions AP, an LTL formula is composed of atomic propositions, the boolean connectives *conjunction* ($\wedge$) and *negation* ($\neg$), the temporal operators *Next* ($\bigcirc$) and *Until* ($\mathcal{U}$). Formulas are built up in the usual way from the above operators and connectives, according to the following grammar

$$\varphi := p \mid \neg\varphi \mid \varphi \wedge \varphi \mid \bigcirc\varphi \mid \varphi \, \mathcal{U} \, \varphi$$

where p is an atomic proposition. Thus, the syntax of LTL formulas can be obtained by the syntax of CTL formulas by deleting the universal and existential quantifiers. The semantics of LTL formulas is given with respect to on an ω-word $w = w_0 w_1 \ldots w_n \ldots$ over the alphabet $\Sigma = 2^{AP}$. The satisfaction relation $w \models \varphi$ is defined in the standard way:

- if φ is an atomic proposition, then $w \models \varphi$ if and only if the assignment of atomic propositions specified by w_0 assigns φ true;

- $w \models \neg\varphi$ if and only if $w \models \varphi$ does not hold;
- $w \models \varphi_1 \wedge \varphi_2$ if and only if $w \models \varphi_1$ and $w \models \varphi_2$;
- $w \models \bigcirc\varphi$ if and only if $w^1 \models \varphi$;
- $w \models \varphi_1 \,\mathcal{U}\, \varphi_2$ if and only if there exists $i \geq 0$ such that $M, w^i \models \varphi_1$ and $w^j \models \varphi_2$ for all j such that $0 \leq j < i$.

For every LTL formula φ, it is possible to construct a nondeterministic Büchi automaton on ω-words accepting all models of φ. We will refer to such an automaton as a *generator* of models of φ. Since we need to construct a tree automaton, it is necessary to have a deterministic generator. In fact, given a positive integer K and a deterministic automaton on words A, a tree automaton accepting all the trees t with arity bounded above by K and such that any path of t is a word accepted by A, can be easily obtained by adding for any transition rule (q, σ, q') of A all the transition rules $(q, \sigma, q_1, \ldots, q_k)$ such that: $q_i = q'$ for $k = 1, \ldots, k$ and $k \leq K$. Clearly, such a construction does not work for nondeterministic automata.

A deterministic Rabin generator A_φ for an LTL formula φ of doubly exponential size can be obtained in the following way: from the formula φ, by the tableau construction, it is possible to construct a nondeterministic Büchi generator of size $2^{O(|\varphi|)}$ [19,30]; we recall that a Büchi automaton of size n can be determinized and the resulting deterministic Rabin automaton has $2^{O(n \log n)}$ states and n pairs [25]; thus, we determinize the Büchi generator for φ so obtaining a deterministic Rabin generator of doubly exponential size with exponentially many pairs. Notice that, in general, for a given formula φ, a deterministic Büchi generator may not exist but, when it exists, it has a doubly exponential size in the length of the formula (see [17]), and thus, the above construction is asymptotically optimal.

Consider now a game (A, φ) and denote by K the maximum arity of the trees accepted by A^T. Denote by A' the Rabin tree automaton corresponding to A_φ and constructed to accept trees of arity at most K. It is easy to construct a Rabin tree automaton $A^\cap$ accepting the intersection of the languages accepted by A^T and A'. From the above arguments, the size of $A^\cap$ is doubly exponential in the size of φ and, by Lemma 1, it is singly exponential in the size of A. Moreover, the number of pairs in the accepting condition of $A^\cap$ is exponential in the size of φ. We recall that, checking for the emptiness of a language accepted by a Rabin tree automaton with n locations and m pairs can be done in deterministic time $O((nm)^{cm})$ [22]. Thus, by Theorem 1 and the fact that LTL games are 2EXPTIME-hard [22], the following theorem holds.

Theorem 5. *Given a timed game (A, φ) where φ is an* LTL *formula, the problem of deciding the existence of a winning strategy of the protagonist in (A, φ) is 2*EXPTIME*-complete.*

We recall that the result stated in the above theorem is subsumed by the result proved in [14] for LTL rectangular hybrid games.

5 Conclusions

We presented an automata-theoretic approach to solve timed games. Our solution relies on the construction of a tree automaton accepting all the ω-trees corresponding to a strategy of the protagonist in the timed game. This approach can be used with any class of winning conditions admitting a direct translation to a class of tree automata with decidable emptiness problem and closure under intersection. We have analyzed in more detail the cases of winning conditions expressed by temporal logic formulas. We can solve timed Büchi games, timed Rabin games and CTL games in exponential time. Since timed reachability games are known to be EXPTIME-hard even if the antagonist is allowed to move only when the protagonist does [18], this results are also complete. We have also applied our approach to solving LTL games. The obtained procedure takes doubly exponential time, and since LTL games are 2EXPTIME-hard [22], our result is tight.

References

1. R. Alur, L. de Alfaro, T. Henzinger, and F. Mang. Automating modular verification. In *CONCUR'99: Concurrency Theory, Tenth Int. Conference*, LNCS 1664, pages 82–97, 1999.
2. R. Alur, C. Courcoubetis, and D.L. Dill. Model-checking in dense real-time. *Information and Computation*, 104(1):2 – 34, 1993.
3. R. Alur and D.L. Dill. A theory of timed automata. *Theoretical Computer Science*, 126:183 – 235, 1994.
4. R. Alur, T.A. Henzinger, and O. Kupferman. Alternating-time temporal logic. In *Proc. of the 38th IEEE Symposium on Foundations of Computer Science*, pages 100 – 109, 1997.
5. R. Alur, T. Henzinger, F. Mang, S. Qadeer, S. Rajamani, and S. Tasiran. MOCHA: Modularity in model checking. In *Proc. of the Tenth Int. Conference on Computer Aided Verification*, LNCS 1427, pages 521 – 525. Springer-Verlag, 1998.
6. R. Alur and S. La Torre. Deterministic generators and games for ltl fragments. In *Proc. of the 16th IEEE Symposium on Logic in Computer Science, LICS'01*, pages 291–300, 2001.
7. M. Abadi, L. Lamport, and P. Wolper. Realizable and unrealizable specifications of reactive systems. In *Proc. of the 16th Intern. Colloquium on Automata, Languages and Programming, ICALP'89*, LNCS 372, pages 1–17, 1989.
8. E. Asarin and O. Maler. As soon as possible: Time optimal control for timed automata. In *Proc. of the 2nd International Workshop on Hybrid Systems: Computation and Control*, LNCS 1569, pages 19 – 30. Springer-Verlag, 1999.
9. E. Asarin, O. Maler, A. Pnueli, and J. Sifakis. Controller synthesis for timed automata. In *Proc. IFAC Symposium on System Structure and Control*, pages 469 – 474. Elsevier, 1998.
10. J.R. Büchi and L.H. Landweber. Solving sequential conditions by finite-state stategies. *Trans. Amer. Math. Soc.*, 138:295 – 311, 1969.
11. A. Church. Logic, arithmetic, and automata. In *Proc. of the International Congress of Mathematics*, pages 23–35, 1962.

12. E.A. Emerson and E.M. Clarke. Using branching-time temporal logic to synthesize synchronization skeletons. *Science of Computer Programming*, 2:241 – 266, 1982.
13. E.A. Emerson and C.S. Jutla. The complexity of tree automata and logics of programs. In *Proc. of the 29th IEEE-CS Symposium on Foundations of Computer Science*, pages 328 – 337, 1988.
14. T.A. Henzinger, B. Horowitz, and R. Majumdar. Rectangular hybrid games. In *Proc. of the 10th International Conference on Concurrency Theory, CONCUR'99*, LNCS 1664, pages 320 – 335, 1999.
15. O. Kupferman and M.Y. Vardi. Module checking. In *Computer Aided Verification, Proc. Eighth Int. Workshop*, LNCS 1102, pages 75 – 86. Springer-Verlag, 1996.
16. O. Kupferman and M.Y. Vardi. Module checking revisited. In *Proc. of the 9th Intern. Conference on Computer Aided Verification, CAV'97*, LNCS 1254, pages 36 –47, June 1997.
17. O. Kupferman and M.Y. Vardi. Freedom, weakness, and determinism: From linear-time to branching-time. In *Proc. of the 13th IEEE Symposium on Logic in Computer Science*, pages 81 – 92, June 1998.
18. S. La Torre and M. Napoli. *Finite Automata on Timed ω-Trees.* To appear in *Theoretical Computer Science.*
19. O. Lichtenstein and A. Pnueli. Checking that finite-state concurrent programs satisfy their linear specification. In *Proc. of the 12th ACM Symposium on Principles of Programming Languages*, pages 97 – 107, 1985.
20. J. Von Neumann and O. Morgenstern. *Theory of Games and Economic Behavior.* Princeton University Press, 1944.
21. A. Pnueli. The temporal logic of programs. In *Proc. of the 18th IEEE Symposium on Foundations of Computer Science*, pages 46 – 77, 1977.
22. A. Pnueli and R. Rosner. On the synthesis of a reactive module. In *Proc. of the 16th ACM Symposium on Principles of Programming Languages*, pages 179 – 190, 1989.
23. M.O. Rabin. Decidability of second-order theories and automata on infinite trees. *Trans. Amer. Math. Soc.*, 141:1 – 35, 1969.
24. M.O. Rabin. Automata on infinite objects and Church's problem. *Trans. Amer. Math. Soc.*, 1972.
25. S. Safra. On the complexity of ω-automata. In *Proc. of the 29th IEEE Symposium on Foundations of Computer Science*, pages 319 – 327, 1988.
26. W. Thomas. Automata on infinite objects. In J. van Leeuwen, editor, *Handbook of Theoretical Computer Science*, volume B, pages 133 – 191. Elsevier Science Publishers, 1990.
27. W. Thomas. On the synthesis of strategies in infinite games. In Ernst W. Mayr and Claude Puech, editors, *12th Annual Symposium on Theoretical Aspects of Computer Science, STACS'95*, LNCS 900, pages 1 – 13. Springer-Verlag, 1995.
28. M.Y. Vardi. Verification of concurrent programs: the automata-theoretic framework. In *Proc. of the Second IEEE Symposium on Logic in Computer Science*, pages 167 – 176, 1987.
29. M.Y. Vardi and P. Wolper. Automata-theoretic techniques for modal logics of programs. *Journal of Computer and System Sciences*, 32:182 – 211, 1986.
30. M.Y. Vardi and P. Wolper. Reasoning about infinite computations. *Information and Computation*, 115:1 – 37, 1994.

Compositional Termination Analysis of Symbolic Forward Analysis

Witold Charatonik, Supratik Mukhopadhyay*, and Andreas Podelski

Max-Planck-Institut für Informatik
Im Stadtwald, 66123 Saarbrücken, Germany
{witold|supratik|podelski}@mpi-sb.mpg.de

Abstract. Existing model checking tools for infinite state systems, such as UPPAAL, HYTECH and KRONOS, use symbolic forward analysis, a possibly nonterminating procedure. We give termination criteria that allow us to reason compositionally about systems defined with asynchronous parallel composition; we can prove the termination of symbolic forward analysis for a composed system from the syntactic conditions satisfied by the component systems.
Our results apply to nonlinear hybrid systems; in particular to rectangular hybrid systems, timed automata and o-minimal systems. In the case of integer-valued systems we give negative results: forward analysis is not well-suited for this class of infinite-state systems.

1 Introduction

Recently, there has been a lot of research effort directed to automatic verification of infinite state systems. Research on decidability issues (e.g., [ACJT96, ACHH93, Boi98, LPY99, LPY00, HKPV95, CJ98]) has resulted in many nontrivial algorithms for the verification of different subclasses of infinite state systems. These results do not, however, imply the termination of the semi-algorithms on which practical tools are based (for example, the decidability of the model checking problem for timed automata does not entail termination for the symbolic forward analysis used in UPPAAL or HYTECH or KRONOS).

This paper addresses the termination for such a procedure in a compositional setting; we give sufficient *compositional* conditions for the termination of the symbolic forward analysis for nonlinear hybrid systems. We can prove the termination of this analysis for a composed system from the syntactic conditions satisfied by the components, without computing the explicit representation of the composition (which is usually exponentially bigger than the components). The conditions roughly express that, in each loop, the variables are initialized before they are used. Our sufficient conditions apply to several interesting examples such as the railroad crossing example. As a corollary we obtain termination for the subclass of *o-minimal* hybrid systems (for which backward analysis is known to be terminating [LPY99, LPY00]).

* Support from the grants NSF award CCR99-70925, SRC award 99-TJ-688, and DARPA ITO Mobies award F33615-00-C-1707 is gratefully acknowledged

A. Cortesi (Ed.): VMCAI 2002, LNCS 2294, pp. 109–125, 2002.
© Springer-Verlag Berlin Heidelberg 2002

Sufficient termination conditions for symbolic forward analysis seem interesting for three reasons. First, since they apply to concrete examples such as practical mutual exclusion protocols, they may shed a new light on the practical success of symbolic model checking for infinite-state systems (see e.g., [LPY95]). Second, for a concrete verification problem in a practical setting, the model to be checked can possibly be adapted to meet the sufficient termination conditions (e.g., by adding semantically redundant initializations of variables or hiding not used variables); we give such examples in the paper. This can be interesting to obtain a theoretical guarantee for a problem where practical termination has not yet been obtained. Such a guarentee is pragmatically useful in a limited sense, as follows. If one has waited for two hours for an experiment that is known to terminate theoretically, it may be worth to wait two hours more.

Third, our results suggest a potential optimization of the symbolic forward analysis procedure. Namely, the termination guarantees given in this paper continue to hold even when the fixpoint test is made more efficient by weakening it to *local entailment* (explained below; e.g., for linear arithmetic constraints over reals, the complexity of fixpoint test reduces from co-NP hard to polynomial; such a fixpoint test is used in the model checker UPPAAL [BLL+96] and in the model checker described in [DP99]).

2 Preliminaries

2.1 Infinite State Systems

We use guarded-command programs to specify (possibly infinite-state) transition systems. A guarded-command program consists of a set $\mathcal{E}$ of guarded commands e (called edges) of the form

$$e \equiv \ell : \gamma_e(\boldsymbol{x}) \; [\!] \alpha_e(\boldsymbol{x}, \boldsymbol{x'}); \; \texttt{goto} \; \ell'$$

where ℓ and ℓ' are labels ranging over a finite set of program locations, $\boldsymbol{x} = \langle x_1, \ldots, x_n \rangle$ is the tuple of program variables (ranging over a possibly infinite data domain); $\gamma_e(\boldsymbol{x})$ is a formula (the guard) whose free variables are among $\boldsymbol{x}$; $\alpha_e(\boldsymbol{x}, \boldsymbol{x'})$ is a formula (the action of e) whose free variables are among $\boldsymbol{x}, \boldsymbol{x'}$. Intuitively, the primed version of a variable stands for its value in the successor state after taking a transition through a guarded command. We allow more than one command labeled with the same location ℓ, which corresponds to a nondeterministic choice in the language.

We translate a guarded command e to the logical formula ψ_e simply by by replacing the guard $[\!]$ with conjunction and introducing a new variable L for locations.

$$\psi_e \equiv L = \ell \wedge \gamma_e(\boldsymbol{x}) \wedge L' = \ell' \wedge \alpha_e(\boldsymbol{x}, \boldsymbol{x'})$$

A state of the system is a pair $\langle \ell, \boldsymbol{v} \rangle$ consisting of the values for the location variable and for each program variable. The state $\langle \ell, \boldsymbol{v} \rangle$ can make a transition to the state $\langle \ell', \boldsymbol{v'} \rangle$ through the edge e provided that the values of ℓ for L, ℓ' for L', $\boldsymbol{v}$ for $\boldsymbol{x}$ and $\boldsymbol{v'}$ for $\boldsymbol{x'}$ define a solution for ψ_e. A run of the system is a sequence $\langle \ell^1, \boldsymbol{v^1} \rangle \longrightarrow \langle \ell^2, \boldsymbol{v^2} \rangle \longrightarrow \ldots$ such that for each $i = 1, 2, \ldots$ there exists an edge e such that the state $\langle \ell^i, \boldsymbol{v^i} \rangle$ can make a transition to the state $\langle \ell^{i+1}, \boldsymbol{v^{i+1}} \rangle$ through the edge e.

In this paper, we consider two basic classes of infinite state systems. In the first, we deal with the so-called hybrid systems in which the program variables range over the set of reals $\mathbb{R}$. Examples of such systems include the railroad crossing example and the Fischer's mutual exclusion protocol. In the second, the program variables range over the set of integers $\mathbb{Z}$, and the guard and the action formulas are arithmetic constraints. Examples of such systems include the bakery or ticket algorithms, the bounded buffer producer-consumer problem etc.

Systems with Integer-valued Variables. A system with integer-valued variables can be defined as a set of guarded commands as above where the variables $\boldsymbol{x}, \boldsymbol{x'}$ are interpreted over the set of integers $\mathbb{Z}$. We consider these systems in Section 5.

Hybrid Systems We write $OF(\mathbb{R})$ for the theory of the ordered field of reals; it is interpreted over the structure $\langle \mathbb{R}, <, +, \cdot, 0, 1 \rangle$.

A (possibly non-linear) hybrid system can be defined as a set of guarded commands as above where the guard $\gamma_e(\boldsymbol{x})$ is an $OF(\mathbb{R})$ formula, and the action $\alpha_e(\boldsymbol{x}, \boldsymbol{x'})$ is an $OF(\mathbb{R})$ formula given by

$$\alpha_e(\boldsymbol{x}, \boldsymbol{x'}) \;\equiv\; \exists z \geq 0 \; \exists \boldsymbol{x''} \; \delta_e(\boldsymbol{x}, \boldsymbol{x''}) \wedge \beta_{\ell'}(\boldsymbol{x''}, \boldsymbol{x'}, z).$$

Here, δ_e is an $OF(\mathbb{R})$ formula defining the "update" in e, and $\beta_{\ell'}$ is the $OF(\mathbb{R})$ formula defining the continuous evolution at the target location ℓ'. For example, in a timed system with two clocks x_1, x_2 where x_2 runs twice as fast as x_1, the action part of a command resetting the first clock would be $\exists z \geq 0 \; \exists x_1'' \exists x_2'' \; x_1'' = 0 \wedge x_2'' = x_2 \wedge x_1' = x_1'' + z \wedge x_2' = x_2'' + 2z$.

A transition according to a guarded command e represents an instantaneous 'jump' followed by a continuous evolution over time at the target location ℓ'. Namely, a state $\langle \ell, \boldsymbol{v} \rangle$ can make a transition through e to the state $\langle \ell', \boldsymbol{v'} \rangle$ if the values ℓ for the location variable L and $\boldsymbol{v}$ for the tuple of data variables $\boldsymbol{x}$ satisfy the guard $L = \ell \wedge \gamma_e(\boldsymbol{x})$ of e and there exists a $\boldsymbol{v''}$ such that $\boldsymbol{v}, \boldsymbol{v''}$ satisfies the update δ_e of e and there exists a real value d of the delay variable z such that $\boldsymbol{v'}$ is obtained from $\boldsymbol{v''}$ through continuous evolution over the delay d at the location ℓ'. A particular case of a transition in a hybrid system is the *time transition* (continuous evolution over time at a location) from the state $\langle \ell, \boldsymbol{v} \rangle$ to the state $\langle \ell, \boldsymbol{v'} \rangle$ where the update part $\delta(\boldsymbol{x}, \boldsymbol{x''})$ is simply the equality $\boldsymbol{x} = \boldsymbol{x''}$.

Rectangular hybrid systems A rectangular hybrid system is a hybrid system where the guards $\gamma_e(\boldsymbol{x})$ are conjunctions of constraints of the form $x_i \sim c_i$ where $\sim \in \{<, \leq, >, \geq\}$ and $c_i \in \mathbb{Z}$; the update part of the action formulas consists of the jump to a location with an initialization of some variables (the only allowed constraints are $L' = \ell'$, $x'' = x$ and $x'' \sim c$ where $c \in \mathbb{Z}$) and the continuous evolution $\beta_{\ell'}(\boldsymbol{x''}, \boldsymbol{x'}, z)$ is of the form $\bigwedge_{i=1}^{n} x_i'' + a_i z \sim x_i' \sim x_i'' + b_i z$ possibly in conjunction with location invariants of the form $c_i \sim x_i' \sim d_i$ where $a_i, b_i, c_i, d_i \in \mathbb{Z} \cup \{-\infty, +\infty\}$.

We will often use a notation like $\dot{x} \in [a, b)$ as a shortcut for $x'' + az \leq x' < x'' + bz$ and the notation $\dot{(x)} \in [a, b]$ as a shortcut for $x'' + az \leq x' \leq x'' + bz$. The continuous evolution of the timed system from the example above can be then described by $\dot{x_1} = 1, \dot{x_2} = 2$.

Timed automata Timed automata are particular case of rectangular hybrid systems where the update part consists of the jump to a location with reset of some clocks (the only allowed constraints are of the form $L' = \ell'$, $x'' = x$ and $x'' = 0$) and the continuous evolution is the increment of the clocks according to the time passing ($\beta_{\ell'}(\boldsymbol{x''}, \boldsymbol{x'}, z) \equiv \boldsymbol{x'} = \boldsymbol{x''} + z$), possibly in conjunction with location invariants of the form $x' \sim c$ where c is an integer.

O-minimal hybrid systems The o-minimal hybrid systems were introduced in [LPY99, LPY00], where it is shown that the *backward* analysis for these systems terminates. Our results generalize this one in two ways: we prove the termination of not only backward, but also forward analysis; second, our systems are less restrictive by allowing parallel composition and continuous change of variables between different locations.

Below we rephrase the definition from [LPY99, LPY00]. In o-minimal hybrid systems, the action formula $\alpha_e(\boldsymbol{x}, \boldsymbol{x'})$ of e is of the form $\alpha_e(\boldsymbol{x}, \boldsymbol{x'}) \equiv \exists z \geq 0 \exists \boldsymbol{x''}(\delta_e(\boldsymbol{x''}) \wedge \boldsymbol{x'} = exp^{zA_{\ell'}} \boldsymbol{x''})$ with free variables among $\{\boldsymbol{x}, \boldsymbol{x'}\}$, where the free variables in the "update" formula δ_e are among $\boldsymbol{x''}$, exp is the base of the natural logarithms, $A_{\ell'}$ is an $n \times n$ rational matrix that is either nilpotent or is diagonalizable with rational eigenvalues ($\boldsymbol{x'} = exp^{zA_{\ell'}} \boldsymbol{x''}$ represents the continuous evolution at the target location ℓ'). It can be shown [LPY99, LPY00] that in these cases, $\alpha_e(\boldsymbol{x}, \boldsymbol{x'})$ is definable in $OF(\mathbb{R})$. In the context of this paper, the most important property of o-minimal systems is that the action in the guarded command does not depend on the current values of variables (these values are relevant only for the guard of the command).

2.2 Parallel Composition

In this section we consider asynchronous parallel composition of hybrid systems [LPY95]. Parallel composition of integer-valued systems is considered in Section 5. We assume that the component programs do not share variables (except for the synchronizing labels). For the purpose of parallel composition, we assign to each guarded command a synchronizing label. Thus with each guarded-command program $\mathcal{S}$ we associate a (finite) set Σ of synchronizing labels and a mapping $lab : \mathcal{E} \longrightarrow \Sigma$ that assigns to each guarded command (or edge) a synchronizing label from Σ.

Given two guarded command programs $\mathcal{S}_1$ and $\mathcal{S}_2$ with label sets Σ_1 and Σ_2 and labeling functions lab_1 and lab_2 respectively, their parallel composition $\mathcal{S} = \mathcal{S}_1 || \mathcal{S}_2$ with set of synchronizing labels $\Sigma_1 \cup \Sigma_2$ and labeling function lab is defined as the set of all guarded commands of the form

$$e \equiv \langle \ell_1, \ell_2 \rangle : \gamma_e(\boldsymbol{x}, \boldsymbol{y}) \; [\!] \alpha_e(\boldsymbol{x}, \boldsymbol{y}, \boldsymbol{x'}, \boldsymbol{y'}); \; \mathsf{goto} \; \langle \ell_1', \ell_2' \rangle$$

with $lab(e) = \sigma$ such that either only $\mathcal{S}_1$ "moves" (i.e., takes a transition through an edge) while $\mathcal{S}_2$ undergoes continuous evolution at the same location (if the synchronizing label σ is in Σ_1 but not in Σ_2) or $\mathcal{S}_2$ "moves" while $\mathcal{S}_1$ undergoes continuous evolution at the same location (provided the synchronizing label σ is in Σ_2 but not in Σ_1) or both "move" (if the synchronizing label $\sigma \in \Sigma_1 \cap \Sigma_2$) with the same label $lab(e_1) = lab(e_2) = \sigma$.

Formally, the composed program $\mathcal{S}$ consists of all guarded commands of the form

$$e \equiv \langle \ell_1, \ell_2 \rangle : \gamma_e(\boldsymbol{x}, \boldsymbol{y}) \, [\!]\alpha_e(\boldsymbol{x}, \boldsymbol{y}, \boldsymbol{x}', \boldsymbol{y}'); \text{ goto } \langle \ell_1', \ell_2' \rangle$$

with $lab(e) = \sigma$ such that either

- • there is an edge $e_1 \equiv \ell_1 : \gamma_{e_1}(\boldsymbol{x}) \, [\!]\alpha_{e_1}(\boldsymbol{x}, \boldsymbol{x}')$; goto ℓ_1' in $\mathcal{S}_1$
  • $lab_1(e_1) = \sigma \in \Sigma_1 - \Sigma_2$
  • $\ell_2 = \ell_2'$ is a location in $\mathcal{S}_2$
  • $\gamma_e(\boldsymbol{x}, \boldsymbol{y}) \equiv \gamma_{e_1}(\boldsymbol{x})$
  • $\alpha_e(\boldsymbol{x}, \boldsymbol{y}, \boldsymbol{x}', \boldsymbol{y}') \equiv \exists z \geq 0 \; \varphi_{e_1}(\boldsymbol{x}, \boldsymbol{x}', z) \wedge \beta_{\ell_2}(\boldsymbol{y}, \boldsymbol{y}', z)$ where $\alpha_{e_1}(\boldsymbol{x}, \boldsymbol{x}') \equiv \exists z \geq 0 \; \varphi_{e_1}(\boldsymbol{x}, \boldsymbol{x}', z)$.
- Or same as the previous point but with the roles of $\mathcal{S}_1$ and $\mathcal{S}_2$ reversed.
- Or
  • there is an edge $e_1 \equiv \ell_1 : \gamma_{e_1}(\boldsymbol{x}) \, [\!]\alpha_{e_1}(\boldsymbol{x}, \boldsymbol{x}')$; goto ℓ_1' in $\mathcal{S}_1$ and an edge $e_2 \equiv \ell_2 : \gamma_{e_2}(\boldsymbol{y}) \, [\!]\alpha_{e_2}(\boldsymbol{y}, \boldsymbol{y}')$; goto ℓ_2' in $\mathcal{S}_2$
  • $lab_1(e_1) = lab_2(e_2) = \sigma \in \Sigma_1 \cap \Sigma_2$
  • $\gamma_e(\boldsymbol{x}, \boldsymbol{y}) \equiv \gamma_{e_1}(\boldsymbol{x}) \wedge \gamma_{e_2}(\boldsymbol{y})$
  • $\alpha_e(\boldsymbol{x}, \boldsymbol{y}, \boldsymbol{x}', \boldsymbol{y}') \equiv \exists z \geq 0 \; \varphi_{e_1}(\boldsymbol{x}, \boldsymbol{x}', z) \wedge \varphi_{e_2}(\boldsymbol{y}, \boldsymbol{y}', z)$ where $\alpha_{e_1}(\boldsymbol{x}, \boldsymbol{x}') \equiv \exists z \geq 0 \; \varphi_{e_1}(\boldsymbol{x}, \boldsymbol{x}', z)$ and $\alpha_{e_2}(\boldsymbol{y}, \boldsymbol{y}') \equiv \exists z \geq 0 \; \varphi_{e_2}(\boldsymbol{y}, \boldsymbol{y}', z)$.

A state of the composed program is a tuple $\langle \ell, \ell', \boldsymbol{v}, \boldsymbol{w} \rangle$ consisting of values of the locations and all variables. The semantics of the composed program is defined in the usual way. The parallel composition operation defined above is commutative and associative. For guarded command programs $\mathcal{S}_1, \ldots, \mathcal{S}_k$, we write $\mathcal{S}_1 || \ldots || \mathcal{S}_k$ to denote $(\ldots(\mathcal{S}_1 || \mathcal{S}_2) || \mathcal{S}_3) || \ldots) || \mathcal{S}_k)$. Tools like UPPAAL [BLL+96], HYTECH [HHWT95] use the kind of parallel composition described above (they also use urgent transitions; the framework described below can be easily made to take into account such urgent transitions).

2.3 Constraints Representing Sets of States

In this paper, by constraints we will mean $OF(\mathcal{R})$ formulas. We use constraints φ to represent certain sets of positions. We will consider only conjunctive constraints. A constraint φ is a conjunction of atomic constraints of the form $t \sim c$ where t is a term, $c \in \mathbb{Z}$ and $\sim \in \{>, <, \geq, \leq\}$. We identify solutions of the constraints with states of the system. We write $\mathcal{D}, \langle \ell, \boldsymbol{v} \rangle \models \varphi$ to denote that the state $\langle \ell, \boldsymbol{v} \rangle$ is a solution of the constraint φ where $\mathcal{D}$ is the structure under consideration, i.e., $\langle \mathbb{R}, <, +, \cdot, 0, 1 \rangle$. For a constraint φ, we define the denotation of φ, by $[\varphi]$ as $[\varphi] = \{\langle \ell, \boldsymbol{v} \rangle \mid \mathcal{D}, \langle \ell, \boldsymbol{v} \rangle \models \varphi\}$.

By a set of constraints we mean their disjunction; i.e., if Φ is a set of constraints then $[\Phi] = \bigcup_{\varphi \in \Phi} [\varphi]$. For two constraints φ and φ', we say that φ entails φ', denoted by $\varphi \models \varphi'$, if $[\varphi] \subseteq [\varphi']$. *We identify two constraints φ and φ' if they have the same denotations; i.e.,* $[\varphi] = [\varphi']$. It is known that given two constraints φ and φ' over reals, it is decidable whether $\varphi \models \varphi'$. For a constraint φ with free variables $\boldsymbol{x}$, by $\varphi(\boldsymbol{x}')$ we denote the constraint obtained by renaming the free variables $\boldsymbol{x}$ to $\boldsymbol{x}'$.

2.4 Constraint Transformer $\varphi \mapsto [\![w]\!](\varphi)$

The notion of constraint transformers is inspired by the notion of syntactic transformation monoids in classical automata theory [Eil76]. We write $e_1 \dots e_m$ for the word w obtained by concatenating the 'letters' $e_1, \dots, e_m$ (where each e_i is an edge of a guarded command program); thus, w is a word over the set of edges (or guarded commands) $\mathcal{E}$, i.e., $w \in \mathcal{E}^*$ (assuming that the target location of e_i is the source location of e_{i+1}). The *constraint transformer* with respect to an edge e is the successor constraint function $[\![e]\!]$ that assigns to a constraint φ with free variables $\boldsymbol{x}$ the constraint

$$[\![e]\!](\varphi) \equiv ((\exists \boldsymbol{x}(\varphi \wedge \psi_e))(\boldsymbol{x})).$$

Recall that ψ_e is a formula with free variables among $\boldsymbol{x}, \boldsymbol{x}'$; the variables $\boldsymbol{x}$ are here existentially quantified, and then the variables $\boldsymbol{x}'$ are renamed to $\boldsymbol{x}$. For example, if $\psi_e \equiv L = l_1 \wedge x_1 > 3 \wedge L' = l_2 \wedge \exists z. x_1' = z \wedge x_2' = x_2 + z$ then $[\![e]\!](L = l_1 \wedge x_1 > 1 \wedge x_2 = x_1 + 2) \equiv L = l_2 \wedge x_1 > 0 \wedge x_2 > 5$.

The successor constraint function $[\![w]\!]$ with respect to a string $w = e_1 \dots e_m$ of length $m \geq 0$ is the functional composition of the functions with respect to the edges $e_1, \dots, e_m$, i.e., $[\![w]\!] = [\![e_1]\!] \circ \dots \circ [\![e_m]\!]$. Thus $[\![\varepsilon]\!](\varphi) = \varphi$ and $[\![w.e]\!](\varphi) = [\![e]\!]([\![w]\!](\varphi))$. The solutions of $[\![w]\!](\varphi)$ are exactly the successors of the solutions of φ obtained by taking the sequence of transitions through the guarded commands $e_1, \dots, e_m$ (in that order).

We will next recall the definition of special classes of strings called cycles that correspond to cycles in the control graph of the system. We say that an edge of the form $\ell : \dots \texttt{goto}\ \ell'$ leads from the location ℓ to the location ℓ'. We canonically extend the terminology 'leads to' from edges e to strings w of edges.

Definition 1 (Cycle). *The string $w = e_1 \dots e_m$ of length $m \geq 1$ is a cycle if the sequence of edges $e_1, \dots, e_m$ lead from a location ℓ to itself. A cycle is* trivial *if it consists of one edge whose update part is the constraint $\boldsymbol{x}'' = \boldsymbol{x}$. A cycle $e_1 \dots e_m$ is called* simple *if it is not trivial and does not contain a proper subcycle.*

The notion of simple cycles will be used in providing sufficient termination conditions. We call an edge e an *entry* to a cycle w if it leads from a location outside the cycle to a location on the cycle; similarly, e is an *exit* from w if it leads from a location on the cycle to a location outside w.

Initializing strings A transformer $[\![w]\!]$ corresponding to the composition of transformers $[\![e_1]\!], \dots, [\![e_m]\!]$ can be presented by two constraints $\gamma_w(\boldsymbol{x})$ and $\alpha_w(\boldsymbol{x}, \boldsymbol{x}')$ such that for all φ we have $[\![w]\!](\varphi)(\boldsymbol{x}') \equiv \exists \boldsymbol{x}. \varphi(\boldsymbol{x}) \wedge \gamma_w(\boldsymbol{x}) \wedge \alpha_w(\boldsymbol{x}, \boldsymbol{x}')$ (for better readability we omit here the final renaming of the variables $\boldsymbol{x}'$ to $\boldsymbol{x}$). A string w is called *initializing* if the constraint α_w does not contain any occurrences of the variables $\boldsymbol{x}$; so whenever $\varphi(\boldsymbol{x}) \wedge \gamma_w(\boldsymbol{x})$ is satisfiable, the value of $[\![w]\!](\varphi)(\boldsymbol{x}')$ is simply $\alpha(\boldsymbol{x}')$. An initializing edge is an initializing string consisting of one edge.

We say that w is *weakly initializing* if the set of variables $\boldsymbol{x}$ can be split into two sets $\boldsymbol{x_1}$ and $\boldsymbol{x_2}$ such that $\alpha_w(\boldsymbol{x}, \boldsymbol{x}') \equiv \bigwedge_{x \in \boldsymbol{x_1}} x = x' \wedge \alpha'(\boldsymbol{x_2'})$. We call the variables in $\boldsymbol{x_1}$ the fixed variables of w. We say that a weakly initializing cycle w is *guarded* if either all its entries or all its exits are edges that initialize all fixed variables. Note that every initializing cycle is always guarded (the quantification is over the empty set of variables).

For the cases of non-linear hybrid systems (with the underlying theory being the theory of real closed fields), it can be effectively decided using the methods presented in [Lib00] whether a string is (weakly) initializing. Due to the lack of space we do not detail it out here.

3 Constraint Trees and Symbolic Forward Analysis

Given an infinite state system $\mathcal{S}$ with set of edges $\mathcal{E}$, we define the constraint tree for $\mathcal{S}$ as follows.

Definition 2 (Constraint Tree). *The constraint tree for $\mathcal{S}$ is an infinite tree whose domain is a subset of $\mathcal{E}^*$ (i.e., the nodes are strings over $\mathcal{E}$) that labels the node w by the constraint $[\![w]\!](\varphi^0)$ where φ^0 is the initial constraint.*

Clearly, the (infinite) disjunction of all constraints labeling a node of the constraint tree represents all reachable states of $\mathcal{S}$. We are now in a position to define symbolic forward analysis formally. A symbolic forward analysis is a traversal of (a finite prefix of) a constraint tree in a particular order. The following definition of a non-deterministic procedure abstracts away from that specific order.

Definition 3 (Symbolic Forward Analysis). *A symbolic forward analysis of an infinite state system $\mathcal{S}$ is a procedure that enumerates constraints φ_i labeling the nodes w_i of the constraint tree of $\mathcal{S}$ in a tree order such that the disjunction of the enumerated constraints represents all reachable states of $\mathcal{S}$. Formally,*

- *$\varphi_i = [\![w_i]\!](\varphi^0)$ for $0 \leq i < B$ where the bound B is either a natural number or ω,*
- *if w_i is a prefix of w_j then $i \leq j$,*
- *the disjunction $\bigvee_{0 \leq i < B} \varphi_i$ is equivalent to the disjunction $\bigvee_{0 \leq i < \omega} \varphi_i$.*

The number i is a leaf of a symbolic forward analysis if the node w_i is a leaf of the tree formed by all the nodes w_i where $0 \leq i \leq B$. We say that a symbolic forward analysis terminates if its bound B is finite. We define that a symbolic forward analysis terminates with local entailment if for all its leaves i there exists a $j < i$ such that the constraint φ_i entails the constraint φ_j (as a passing remark, we note that by changing the notion of local entailment, we can get a model checking procedure for liveness properties; we can change the notion of local entailment by requiring that for all leaves i, there exists a $j < i$ such that such that the constraint φ_j entails the constraint φ_i). In contrast, a symbolic forward analysis terminates with global entailment if for all its leaves i, the constraint φ_i entails the disjunction of the constraints φ_j where $j < i$. As discussed in the Introduction, model checking is more efficient with local entailment than with global entailment, both theoretically and practically. Many model checking tools for infinite state systems use local entailment (e.g., UPPAAL [BLL+96], which uses identity; the model checker for infinite state systems with integer-valued variables described in [DP99] also uses local entailment).

Proposition 1. *If every simple cycle of an infinite state system $\mathcal{S}$ is initializing wrt. all variables then symbolic forward analysis for the system terminates with local entailment.*

Proof. We show that the constraint transformer function associated with each initializing string w is either a constant function or unsatisfiable. Suppose that symbolic forward analysis for $\mathcal{S}$ does not terminate with local entailment. Hence, there must be an infinite path p along the constraint tree. Since we have only finitely many locations in $\mathcal{S}$, some of them must occur infinitely often along p, and thus p contains infinitely many occurrences of some simple cycle w; i.e., p is an element of the language $(\mathcal{E}^*.w)^\omega$. Now consider any two nodes $s_1 = w_1.w$ and $s_2 = w_2.w$ of p such that $s_1 < s_2$. Since the constraint transformer function labeling w is a constant function, the constraints labeling s_1 and s_2 are the same and the local entailment check between constraints at these two nodes terminates the analysis along path p, which contradicts the assumption that p is infinite. Hence symbolic forward analysis for $\mathcal{S}$ terminates with local entailment. □

As an immediate application of this proposition we get the following result.

Theorem 1. *Symbolic forward analysis of an o-minimal hybrid system terminates with local entailment.*

Proof. In an o-minimal system every edge and thus every cycle is initializing. □

It is worth noting that the same reasoning gives that backward analysis for o-minimal systems terminates, which was first proved in [LPY99, LPY00].

Proposition 2. *If every simple cycle of a rectangular hybrid system $\mathcal{S}$ is weakly initializing wrt. all variables and is guarded, then symbolic forward analysis for the system $\mathcal{S}$ terminates with local entailment.*

Proof. The reasoning here is similar to that of Proposition 1. In an infinite path p either we have two consecutive occurrences of the same simple cycle which is a constant function wrt. some variables and identity wrt. the others and thus the two constraints corresponding to the two occurrences are the same, or the cycle together with its entry or exit is a constant function. In the letter case, there are only finitely many different constant functions, and thus there must be two occurrences giving the same constraint. □

The propositions above give a termination criteria for forward analysis for infinite-state systems, but in order to apply them one needs an explicit representation of the system. However, usually systems are not represented explicitly but in form of parallel composition of several components. The computation of the explicit representation of a composed system gives an exponential blowup, which we want to avoid. In the following, we look for criteria on the components that allow the use of this proposition.

4 Compositional Reasoning about Termination

In this section, we show how to reason compositionally about sufficient termination conditions in our framework. We provide sufficient conditions on the individual components under which symbolic forward analysis of the parallel composition of n infinite state systems $\mathcal{S}_1, \dots, \mathcal{S}_n$ terminates.

First notice that just proving termination for individual components is not enough. Consider Figure 1. The figure shows two hybrid systems; each of them is o-minimal and hence symbolic forward analysis for each terminates. The first system consists of two locations ℓ_0 and ℓ_1 and one program variable x which increases with derivative 1 (i.e., $\dot{(x)} = 1$) in each location. There is an edge from ℓ_0 to ℓ_1 labeled a. The second system consists of a single location m_0 and an edge from m_0 to itself labeled b. The variable y is the only program variable; it increases with derivative 1 at the location m^0. The initial states (constraints) for both systems are respectively $L = \ell_0 \wedge x = 0$ and $L = m_0 \wedge y = 0$. The asynchronous parallel composition of the two systems is not o-minimal. To see this, consider the transition, where the first system stays (only the variable x increases as the time passes) and the second system moves. Since the value of the variable x after the transition depends on its value before the transition, the composed system is not o-minimal. In fact, symbolic forward analysis does not terminate here: in every iteration of the transition described above the variable x increases by at most two time units which is a non-terminating process.

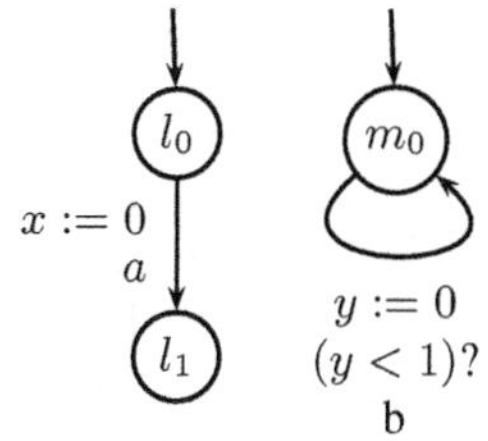

Fig. 1. Parallel composition of two o-minimal hybrid systems is not o-minimal

Theorem 2. *Let $\mathcal{S}_1, \ldots, \mathcal{S}_k$ be k infinite state systems with synchronizing alphabet sets $\Sigma_1, \ldots, \Sigma_k$. If*

- *each simple cycle $w = e_1 \ldots e_m$ ($m \geq 1$) of each $\mathcal{S}_i$ contains an e_j ($1 \leq j \leq m$) such that $lab(e_j) \in \Sigma_1 \cap \ldots \cap \Sigma_k$*
- *and for each $e \in w$ such that $lab(e) \in \Sigma_1 \cap \ldots \cap \Sigma_k$, e is an initializing edge*

then symbolic forward analysis for $\mathcal{S} = \mathcal{S}_1 || \ldots || \mathcal{S}_k$ terminates with local entailment.

Proof. We show that the constraint transformer function associated with each simple cycle in the composed is either a constant function or unsatisfiable.

Let $w = e_1 . \ldots . e_m$ be any simple cycle of $\mathcal{S}$. Then, there exists an edge e such that every component $\mathcal{S}_i$ "moves" on that edge: $lab(e) \in \bigcap_{i=1}^{k} \Sigma_i$. Let $e = e_j$. Consider the projection of e_j on any component $\mathcal{S}_i$. The projection will be an edge e' in this component and also $lab(e') \in \bigcap_{i=1}^{k} \Sigma_i$. Hence, by the assumption of the theorem, e is an initializing edge and the constraint transformer function associated with e is either a constant function or unsatisfiable. Let $w' = e_1 \ldots e_{j-1}$ and $w'' = e_{j+1} \ldots e_j$. Then the constraint transformer function associated with w is given by $[\![w]\!] = [\![w']\!] \circ [\![e_j]\!] \circ [\![w'']\!]$. Hence $[\![w]\!]$ is either a constant function or unsatisfiable. Therefore by Proposition 1, symbolic forward analysis with local entailment terminates. □

To see the applicability of our results, consider the two-process real time Fischer's mutual exclusion protocol given in Figure 2. The critical section is denoted by cs. The processes do not share real variables — the communication is through the synchronization labels. The set of synchronization labels Σ_1 of process P_1 is the set $\{a, b, g, p, t_1\}$ and that for process P_2 the set $\Sigma_2 = \{a, b, g, q, t_2\}$. Each process P_i has only one clock x_i. It can be seen that the protocol satisfies the conditions of Theorem 2: every cycle in each of the systems has an edge with a label in $\{a, b, g\}$. Hence, symbolic forward analysis for the composed system terminates. Note that to find it out we do not have to compute the composition of the two systems (which might be quite big) explicitly. Note also that the composed system is not o-minimal (for example in the transition labeled t_1 the clock x_2 is not reset) and hence the termination results from [LPY99, LPY00] do not apply here.

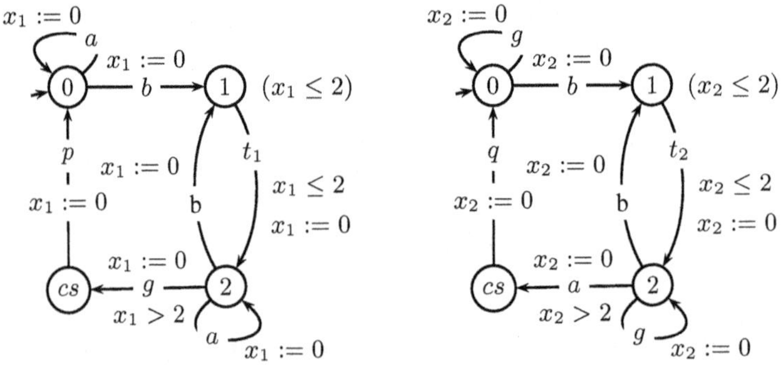

Fig. 2. Fischer's protocol for mutual exclusion of two timed processes

Note that Fischer's protocol is a parallel composition of timed automata. Theorem 2 does not use this fact. It is formulated for arbitrary hybrid systems (where the continuous evolution of particular components over the time might be completely different and thus time could be used as a source of additional communication between components), and can be used in particular to reason about parallel composition of o-minimal systems. The assumptions of the theorem are quite restrictive and are not enough to prove termination for the railroad-crossing example from [AD94, LS85]. It consists of the parallel composition of three components—the train, the gate and the controller. The transition systems (timed automata) for the three components are given in Figure 3. Although every simple cycle in every component is initializing, the assumptions of Theorem 2 are not satisfied since the intersection of $\{lower, down, raise, up\}$ with $\{approach, in, out, exit\}$ is empty.

In the case of timed automata, and more generally of rectangular hybrid systems, due to the uniform evolution of each automaton over the time, we can relax these restrictions. The termination of the forward analysis for the railroad-crossing example follows from Theorem 3 and Observation 1 below: it is enough to choose the controller as the system $\mathcal{A}_1$.

We say that a location ℓ in a rectangular hybrid system is *fixing* if the continuous change of all variables in ℓ satisfies $\dot{x} = 0$. A fixing location ℓ is *guarded* if all edges entering ℓ (or all edges leaving ℓ) initialize all variables of the system. We say that a location ℓ is time-bounded if either ℓ has an invariant $x \leq c$ (or $x < c$) and $\dot{x}$ is positive or it has an invariant $x \geq c$ (or $x > c$) and $\dot{x}$ is negative.

Theorem 3. *Let S be a parallel composition of rectangular non-zeno*[1] *hybrid systems, such that every simple cycle of every component is initializing and every fixing location is guarded. If in every simple cycle of the composed system every component either moves along some cycle or remains in a fixing or time-bounded location, then symbolic forward analysis terminates with local entailment.*

Proof. Suppose that there exists an infinite path p in the constraint tree. Some simple cycle C of the composed system must occur infinitely often along this path. Consider the projection of C on any of the components of the system: it is either a cycle of the component (and then it is initializing wrt. the variables of this component) or a single location that is time-bounded or fixing. If it is a time-bounded location, the system cannot stay at this location forever, therefore C must be a part of a bigger cycle C' in which every component moves or stays in a fixing location. The reasoning then follows the one of Proposition 2. □

The condition that every component moves in every simple cycle of the composed system is still not compositional, but in many cases it is not difficult to find sufficient compositional conditions implying this one—see the two observations below. The first of them applies e.g., to both Fischer's protocol and to timed-automaton version of the railroad crossing; the second to a hybrid version of railroad crossing present in the HYTECH distribution. Together with Theorem 3 above, these observation give sufficient compositional conditions for termination of the forward analysis.

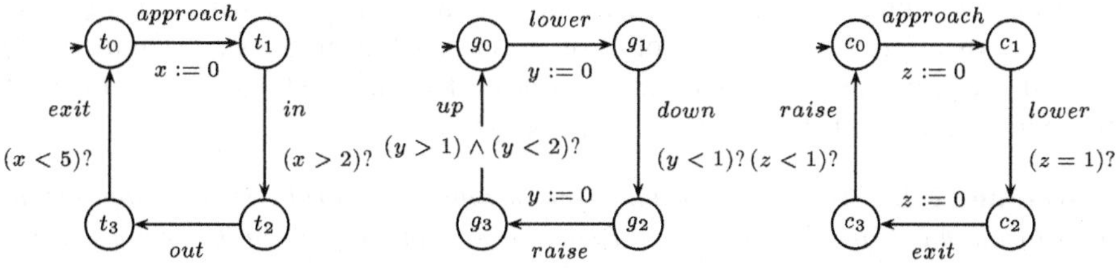

Fig. 3. Railroad crossing: Train, Gate and Controller as timed automata

Observation 1 *Let $\mathcal{A}_1, \ldots, \mathcal{A}_k$ be rectangular hybrid systems. If for all $i = 2, \ldots, k$ each simple cycle in $\mathcal{A}_1$ contains a synchronizing label from Σ_i, and each simple*

[1] Intuitively, a system is non-zeno [AH97] if it "allows" time to grow forever.

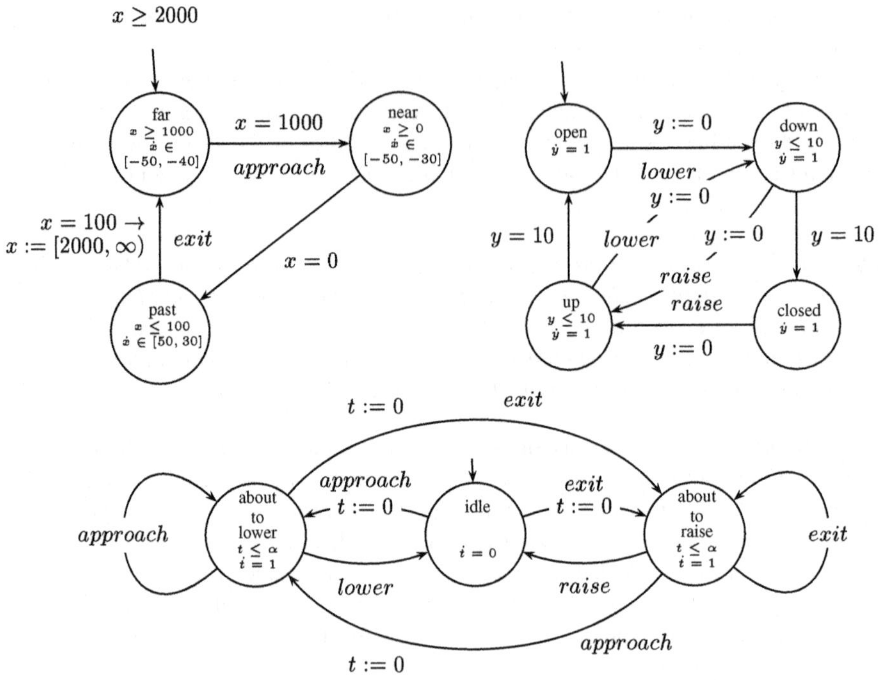

Fig. 4. Railroad crossing: Train, Gate and Controller as rectangular systems

cycle in $\mathcal{A}_i$ contains a synchronizing label from Σ_1 then in every simple cycle of $\mathcal{S} = \mathcal{A}_1 || \ldots || \mathcal{A}_k$ every component $\mathcal{A}_i$ moves.

Proof. The projection of any simple cycle C in the composed system on some of the components is a cycle. This cycle contains a synchronizing label from Σ_1, hence the projection of C on $\mathcal{A}_1$ is a cycle in $\mathcal{A}_1$, which for all i contains a synchronizing label from Σ_i. Therefore the projection of C on every component $\mathcal{A}_i$ is a cycle in $\mathcal{A}_i$ (in contrast, the projection of the only simple cycle of the composed system from Figure 1 on the first component is empty and thus not a cycle). □

Observation 2 *Let $A_1, \ldots, A_k$ be non-zeno rectangular hybrid systems. Suppose that every location is fixing time-bounded. Then in every simple cycle of the composed system every component either moves along some cycle or remains in a fixing or time-bounded location.*

The observation above applies e.g., to the hybrid version of the railroad crossing that can be found in the HYTECH distribution. Of course for this example the symbolic forward analysis terminates, but a very subtle change in the system may lead to non-termination. On Figure 4 we have modified this example by simply modeling the gate as a timed automaton; the other components are not changed at all, and the gate itself behaves essentially in the same way as the original one in HYTECH distribution.

Forward analysis for this example does not terminate, because for big enough values of the parameter α the gate may stay forever in the location open or closed, while the controller switches between about-to-lower and about-to-raise; every iteration of this cycle increases the values for the variable y by at most 2α, which is a nonterminating process. The observation above of course does not apply to this system (time is not bounded in locations open and closed), but it gives a hint how to improve the system such that the analysis terminates: changing $\dot{y}$ from 1 to 0 in both these locations forces the analysis to terminate without any essential changes in the behavior of the system (the variable y after leaving these locations is reset and thus its value is not needed; in particular both safety and liveness properties remain unchanged). Note that both these lacations are guarded (in fact they are doubly guarded: the entering edges initialize y to 10 and exit edges initialize y to 0).

We are implementing the static tests based on the observations above on the top of the model checker described in [DP99].

5 Integer-Valued Systems

The composed program $\mathcal{S} = \mathcal{S}_1 \parallel \mathcal{S}_2$ consists of all guarded commands of the form

$$e \equiv \langle \ell_1, \ell_2 \rangle : \gamma_e(\boldsymbol{x}, \boldsymbol{y}) \, [\!] \alpha_e(\boldsymbol{x}, \boldsymbol{y}, \boldsymbol{x}', \boldsymbol{y}'); \text{ goto } \langle \ell_1', \ell_2' \rangle$$

such that either there exists an edge $e_1 \equiv \ell_1 : \gamma_{e_1}(\boldsymbol{x}) \, [\!] \alpha_{e_1}(\boldsymbol{x}, \boldsymbol{x}'); \text{ goto } \ell_1'$ in $\mathcal{S}_1$ where $\gamma_e = \gamma_{e_1}, \ell_2' = \ell_2$ and $\alpha_e = \alpha_{e_1} \wedge \bigwedge_{y \in \boldsymbol{y} - \boldsymbol{x}} y' = y$, or the symmetrical condition with the roles of $\mathcal{S}_1$ and $\mathcal{S}_2$ reversed holds.

Integer-valued systems in general are not well-suited for symbolic forward analysis (without acceleration techniques such as widening) as the following observations show. We say that an edge e increments a variable x if the action α_e contains a conjunct $x' = x + 1$.

Proposition 3. *Suppose that a variable x has initially value 0 in a system $\mathcal{S} = \mathcal{S}_1 \parallel \ldots \parallel \mathcal{S}_n$, the component S_1 contains a simple cycle C with an edge e incrementing the variable x, and e is the only edge changing the value of x in $\mathcal{S}$. Then either C is executed only finitely many times in every infinite execution of $\mathcal{S}$ or forward analysis does not terminate.*

Sketch of proof. Suppose that C is executed infinitely many times. Then the constraint tree T for $\mathcal{S}$ contains an infinite path corresponding to this infinite execution. The nodes corresponding to the i-th execution of the cycle C in T are constraints containing a conjunct $x = i$, thus T contains infinitely many inequivalent constraints. □

The proposition above applies to many integer-valued protocols including the ticket protocol and bounded-buffer producer/consumer protocol. It does not, however apply to bakery protocol.

Observation 3 *Suppose that a variable x has initially value 0 in a system $\mathcal{S} = \mathcal{S}_1 \parallel \ldots \parallel \mathcal{S}_n$, the component S_i contains a simple cycle C_i with an edge with the action $x_{i+1 \bmod n} := x_i + 1$ and C_i does not modify $x_{i+2 \bmod n}$. Then forward analysis is not likely to terminate.*

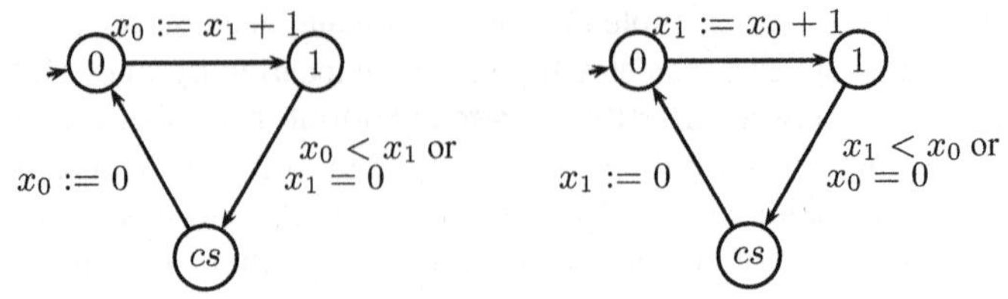

Fig. 5. Bakery protocol for mutual exclusion

The reason for possible non-termination of the forward analysis is an infinite execution of the system that consecutively increases the values of variables, thus creating infinitely many nonequivalent constraints in the constraint tree.

The observation above gives an idea of changing the protocol a little bit to make the analysis terminate: one can replace the action of the form $x := y+1$ by $x := [y+1, \infty)$, where the new value of x is any number greater than the value of y instead of concrete value $y+1$. The modified version of bakery protocol preserves its main property of mutual exclusion and starvation-freeness, but the forward analysis terminates. The above transformation can be applied on-the-fly as a widening operation.

6 Related Work

Reachability analysis for infinite state systems with integer valued variables has been considered by Berard and Fribourg [BF99] as well as by Fribourg and Olsen [FO97], but the authors do not provide any sufficient conditions for termination of their model checking procedure on any interesting class of systems.

Abdulla, Cerans, Jonsson and Tsay [ACJT96] as well as Finkel and Schnoebelen [FS98] gave a unifying framework for deriving decidability results for model checking for infinite state systems. However, their framework requires finding a well quasi-ordering on the states, which in many practical situations is not feasible. Besides, their method of deriving sufficient termination conditions for reachability analysis is monolithic; one has to consider the state-space of the composed system to show the termination of reachability analysis.

Comon and Jurski [CJ98] obtained decidability results for reachability analysis for a fragment of the class of multiple counter automata. They showed that the fixpoint of iterating transitions for this subclass of multiple counter automata is expressible in Presburger arithmetic. Again, their framework does not provide any means of reasoning about sufficient termination conditions compositionally.

Boigelot [Boi98] obtained sufficient conditions for termination of reachability analysis for infinite state systems with integer-valued variables based on graph-theoretic properties of the underlying control graphs. However, like the works mentioned above, his work does not provide a compositional way of reasoning about sufficient termination conditions.

Bultan, Gerber and Pugh [BGP97] presented a model checker for infinite state systems with integer-valued variables based on the Presburger solver from the Omega library [Pug92]. While [BGP97] provided model checking procedures for both safety and liveness properties, no sufficient conditions for termination of the procedures were provided.

Wong-Toi [WT95] has identified a subclass of linear hybrid systems called skewed clock automata that can be translated to timed safety automata. The subclass of skewed clock automata is closed under parallel composition. While symbolic backward analysis is guaranteed to terminate for skewed clock automata, symbolic forward analysis is possibly non-terminating for this subclass.

Non-linear hybrid systems have been considered by Lafferriere, Pappas and Yovine [LPY99, LPY00]. For the class of o-minimal hybrid systems, they proved the termination of symbolic backward analysis by showing that this class admits finite bisimulations. The reasoning about termination of symbolic backward analysis in [LPY99, LPY00] is not compositional.

Henzinger, Kopke, Puri and Varaiya [HKPV95] considered initialized rectangular automata, a subclass of linear hybrid systems, for which symbolic backward analysis is guaranteed to terminate. Henzinger [Hen95] considered hybrid automata with finite bisimulations for which symbolic backward analysis is guaranteed to terminate. But none of these works addressed the issue of compositional reasoning about sufficient termination conditions.

Lam and Brayton [LB93] considered alternating RQ timed automata closed under I/O composition. The class of alternating RQ automata is restrictive in the sense that it allows exactly one reset and exactly one query for each clock in an entire automaton. Moreover the notion of I/O composition that they used is much more restrictive than the notion of parallel composition used in this paper. It is also not known whether symbolic forward analysis for alternating RQ timed automata is guaranteed to terminate.

Namjoshi [Nam98] considered model checking for parameterized systems in which each process is finite state. In contrast, in this paper, we considered finite families of possibly infinite state systems.

In [MP99], we gave a framework for reasoning about syntactic sufficient termination conditions for timed automata. The present work is an extension of that framework to the more general context of hybrid systems as well as augmenting the framework with compositional reasoning.

References

[ACHH93] R. Alur, C. Courcoubetis, T.A. Henzinger, and P.-H. Ho. Hybrid automata: an algorithmic approach to the specification and verification of hybrid systems. In R.L. Grossman, A. Nerode, A.P. Ravn, and H. Rischel, editors, *Hybrid Systems I*, LNCS 736, pages 209–229. Springer-Verlag, 1993.

[ACJT96] P. Abdulla, K. Cerans, B. Jonsson, and T. K. Tsay. General decidability theorems for infinite state systems. In *LICS*, pages 313–321, 1996.

[AD94] R. Alur and D. Dill. A theory of timed automata. *Theoretical Computer Science*, 126(2):183–236, 1994.

[AH97] R. Alur and T. A. Henzinger. Modularity for timed and hybrid systems. In A. Mazurkiewicz and J. Winkowski, editors, *CONCUR'97: Concurrency Theory*, volume 1243 of *LNCS*, pages 74–88. Springer-Verlag, 1997.

[BF99] B. Berard' and L. Fribourg. Reachability analysis of (timed) petri nets using real arithmetic. In J. C. M. Baeten and S. Mauw, editors, *CONCUR: Concurrency Theory*, volume 1664 of *LNCS*, pages 178–193. Springer-Verlag, 1999.

[BGP97] T. Bultan, R. Gerber, and W. Pugh. Symbolic model checking of infinite state systems using presburger arithmetics. In Orna Grumberg, editor, *the 9th International Conference on Computer Aided Verification (CAV'97)*, LNCS 1254, pages 400–411. Springer, Haifa, Israel, July 1997.

[BLL+96] Johan Bengtsson, Kim. G. Larsen, Fredrik Larsson, Paul Petersson, and Wang Yi. Uppaal in 1995. In T. Margaria and B. Steffen, editors, *TACAS*, LNCS 1055, pages 431–434. Springer-Verlag, 1996.

[Boi98] Bernard Boigelot. *Symbolic Methods for Exploring Infinite State Spaces*. PhD thesis, Universite De Liege, Montefiore, Belgium, 1998.

[CJ98] H. Comon and Y. Jurski. Multiple Counters Automata, Safety Analysis, and Presburger Arithmetics. In Alan J. Hu and M. Y. Vardi, editors, *CAV'98: Computer Aided Verification*, volume 1427 of *LNCS*, pages 268–279. Springer-Verlag, 1998.

[DP99] G. Delzanno and A. Podelski. Model Checking in CLP. In R. Cleaveland, editor, *Proceedings of the 5th International Conference on Tools and Algorithms for Construction and Analysis of Systems (TACAS'99)*, volume 1579 of *LNCS*, pages 223–239. Springer-Verlag, March 1999.

[DT98] C. Daws and S. Tripakis. Model checking of real-time reachability properties using abstractions. In Bernhard Steffen, editor, *TACAS98: Tools and Algorithms for the Construction of Systems*, LNCS 1384, pages 313–329. Springer-Verlag, March/April 1998.

[Eil76] S. Eilenberg. *Automata, Languages and Machines*, volume B. Academic Press, 1976.

[FO97] L. Fribourg and H. Olsen. A Decompositional Approach for Computing Least Fixed Point of Datalog Programs with Z-counters. *Journal of Constraints*, 2(3-4):305–336, 1997.

[FS98] A. Finkel and P. Schnoebelen. Well-structured Transition Systems Everywhere! Technical Report LSV-98-4, Laboratoire Spécification et Vérification, Ecole Normale Supérieure de Cachan, 1998.

[Hen95] T.A. Henzinger. Hybrid automata with finite bisimulations. In Z. Fülöp and F. Gécseg, editors, *ICALP 95: Automata, Languages, and Programming*, LNCS 944, pages 324–335. Springer-Verlag, 1995.

[HHWT95] T.A. Henzinger, P.-H. Ho, and H. Wong-Toi. A user guide to HYTECH. In E. Brinksma, W.R. Cleaveland, K.G. Larsen, T. Margaria, and B. Steffen, editors, *TACAS 95: Tools and Algorithms for the Construction and Analysis of Systems*, LNCS 1019, pages 41–71. Springer-Verlag, 1995.

[HKPV95] T. A. Henzinger, P. W. Kopke, A. Puri, and P. Varaiya. What's decidable about hybrid automata? In *the 27th Annual Symposium on Theory of Computing*, pages 373–382. ACM Press, 1995.

[LB93] W. K. C. Lam and R. K. Brayton. Alternating RQ timed automata. In Costas Courcoubetis, editor, *the 5th International Conference on Computer-Aided Verification*, LNCS 697, pages 236–252. Springer-Verlag, June/July 1993.

[Lib00] L. Libkin. Variable independence, quantifier elimination, and constraint representations. In *ICALP: International Colloqium on Automata Languages and Programming*, 2000.

[LPY95] K.G. Larsen, P. Pettersson, and W. Yi. Compositional and symbolic model checking of real-time systems. In *Proceedings of the 16th Annual Real-time Systems Symposium*, pages 76–87. IEEE Computer Society Press, 1995.

[LPY99] G. Lafferriere, G. J. Pappas, and S. Yovine. A new class of decidable hybrid systems. In F. W. Vaandrager and J. H. van Schuppen, editors, *Hybrid Systems, Computation and Control*, volume 1569 of *LNCS*, pages 137–151, 1999.

[LPY00] G. Lafferriere, G. J. Pappas, and S. Yovine. O-minimal hybrid systems. *Mathematics of Control, Signals and Systems*, 13(1):1–21, March 2000.

[LS85] N. G. Leveson and J. L. Stolzy. Analyzing safety and fault tolerance using time petri nets. In H. Uhrig, C. Floyd, M. Nivat, and J. W. Thatcher, editors, *TAPSOFT: Theory and Practice of Software*, volume 186 of *LNCS*, pages 339–355. Springer, 1985.

[MP99] S. Mukhopadhyay and A. Podelski. Beyond region graphs: Symbolic forward analysis of timed automata. In C. Pandurangan, V. Raman, and R. Ramanujam, editors, *19th International Conference on the Foundations of Software Technology and Theoretical Computer Science*, volume 1738 of *LNCS*, pages 233–245, December 1999.

[Nam98] K. S. Namjoshi. *Ameliorating the State Explosion Problem.* PhD thesis, The Graduate School of the University of Texas at Austin, 1998.

[Pug92] W. Pugh. The omega test: a fast and practical integer programming algorithm for dependence analysis. *Communications of the ACM*, 8:102–104, 1992.

[WT95] H. Wong-Toi. *Symbolic Approximations for Verifying Real-Time Systems.* PhD thesis, Stanford University, 1995.

Combining Norms to Prove Termination

Samir Genaim[1], Michael Codish[1], John Gallagher[2], and Vitaly Lagoon[3]

[1] Dept. of Computer Science, Ben-Gurion University of the Negev, Israel
[2] Dept. of Computer Science, University of Bristol, United Kingdom
[3] Dept. of Computer Science and Software Eng., University of Melbourne, Australia

Abstract. Automatic termination analysers typically measure the size of terms applying norms which are mappings from terms to the natural numbers. This paper illustrates how to enable the use of size functions defined as tuples of these simpler norm functions. This approach enables us to simplify the problem of deriving automatically a candidate norm with which to prove termination. Instead of deriving a single, complex norm function, it is sufficient to determine a collection of simpler norms, some combination of which, leads to a proof of termination. We propose that a collection of simple norms, one for each of the recursive data-types in the program, is often a suitable choice. We first demonstrate the power of combining norm functions and then the adequacy of combining norms based on regular types.

1 Introduction

Termination analysis aims to determine that a given program definitely terminates on a given input. An analyser must guarantee a (correct) verdict within a finite amount of time. Such a tool typically reports either "yes" - it succeeded to prove termination, and in this case the program is guaranteed to terminate; or "no" - it did not succeed to prove termination. The quality of the tool is a function of its usability. A strong tool will succeed to prove termination for a wide range of terminating programs, preferably with less intervention from the user.

Proofs of termination are often based on size functions which map program states to the elements of a well founded domain. A proof follows by showing that the states encountered through computation decrease in size and in particular as the program goes through its loops. As the domain is well-founded and the size of the input is bounded, the size of the initial state can decrease only a finite number of times and hence the computation must terminate.

For logic programs, loops occur through recursion and it is the size of the predicate calls that is required to decrease between recursive calls. Termination analysers such as those described in [6, 19, 22] choose the natural numbers as the well-founded domain. Size is measured using so-called semi-linear norms [2] which map to the natural numbers and define the size of a term as the sum of the sizes of some of its arguments.

In this setting, a term is said to be *rigid* with respect to a given norm if its size does not change under instantiation. For example, assuming a list-length

A. Cortesi (Ed.): VMCAI 2002, LNCS 2294, pp. 126–138, 2002.
© Springer-Verlag Berlin Heidelberg 2002

norm (which indicates the number of elements in a list), both $[X, Y, Z]$ and $[X, Y, Z|Xs]$ contain 3 elements but only the first term is rigid as the length of the second term can change under instantiation. To illustrate the importance of this notion for termination analysis, consider the recursive clause of the *append*/3 relation: $append([X|Xs], Ys, [X|Zs]) \leftarrow append(Xs, Ys, Zs)$. To prove termination it does not suffice to observe that the length of the list in the first (and third) argument decreases in the recursive call (by one). One must also ensure that the argument is rigid when this clause is used. Otherwise the decrease in size could occur infinitely many times. Analysers hence maintain two types of information: about size — to detect a decrease; and about instantiation — to detect rigidity.

Instantiation information with respect to the given norm is obtained through abstract interpretation over the domain Pos of positive Boolean functions. The domain elements are interpreted as instantiation dependencies with respect to the given norm. For example, a formula of the form $x \wedge (y \rightarrow z)$ describes a program state in which x is definitely bound to a rigid term and there exists an instantiation dependency such that whenever y becomes bound to a rigid term then so does z. For details on Pos see [20].

Size relations express linear information about the sizes of terms with respect to a given norm function [1, 4, 7, 16]. For example, the relation $x \leq z \ \wedge \ y \leq z$ describes a program state in which the sizes of the terms associated with x and y are less or equal to the size of the term associated with z. Similarly, a relation of the form $z = x + y$ describes a state in which the sum of the sizes of the terms associated with x and y is equal to the size of the term associated with z. Several methods for inferring size relations are described in the literature [1, 4, 7, 8]. They differ primarily in their approach to obtaining a finite analysis as the abstract domain of size relations contains infinite chains.

This paper makes two contributions. First we address the situation where termination analysis should consider a combination of several norms. Namely, the size function used to prove termination combines several different measures on terms, perhaps because at least one of these measures decreases, or because a linear combination of the measures decreases. In many cases termination proofs follow due to the extra precision gained from dependencies between the size (and instantiation) information with respect to the different norms. In [17] the idea of using tuple of norm was used to increase the precision of *lower-bound time-complexity analysis*.

Second, we consider an alternative approach to guessing a suitable norm for termination analysis. Instead of trying to derive a single complex norm function (perhaps defined as a set of interdependent norms), we derive a collection of simpler norms, some combination of which, hopefully leads to a proof of termination. We do not specify how these norms should be combined. Instead, the system tries to find an appropriate combination. Of course, a general solution is impossible because if the program is terminating then there always exists a well founded domain and a size function which satisfy the requirements for the proof of termination [13].

Guessing a suitable norm reduces the level of intervention by the user and is often considered the main missing link in automatic termination analysis [10]. It has been recognised that type information provides a useful insight to this problem [3, 10, 21, 11, 12, 24] as recursive types represent recursive data-structures and thus identify potential sources of infinite recursion. We infer one norm per recursive data type in the program. Intuitively, for each type σ a corresponding norm $\|\cdot\|_\sigma$ counts the number of subterms of type σ in (typed) terms. This idea has been applied recently also in [24]. We take the extra step and propose that combining this collection of norms results in a very powerful technique not only for the inter-arguments size relations analysis but also for the instantiation dependency analysis.

Our presentation is based on regular types, expressed as deterministic "regular unary logic" (RUL) programs [25]. The types could either be declared or inferred, and we do not even require that the types are correct, although we are more likely to derive useful norms for proving termination if the types are correct and accurate.

Our aim is to generate norms from the types inferred by a recent type inference system [14]. This system does not use a "widening" to introduce recursive types. This means that recursion in the inferred types always reflects some recursive dependency in the program itself. For this reason it seems a promising starting point for deriving norms for termination analysis.

2 Preliminaries

Termination analysis for logic programs can be implemented (as for example in [6, 22]) using a technique termed abstract compilation. The program to be analysed is first abstracted, using the chosen norm, to corresponding constraint logic programs over CLP(R) and CLP(B) programs. These describe size and instantiation dependencies specified by the original program. The analyser characterises also size and instantiation for data occurring in loops. We do not detail the techniques in which this information is derived. Details can be found in the literature on termination analysis. See for example [9] for a survey and [6, 22] for specific analysers. Instead we limit our presentation on termination to the abstraction process to CLP(R) and explain intuitively the results obtained.

At the heart of the process is the choice of a norm. A semi-linear norm $|\cdot|$ is a mapping from terms to the natural numbers defined recursively such that $|X| = 0$ for a variable X and for each function symbol f/n in the underlying signature there is a statement of the form

$$|f(t_1, \ldots, t_n)| = c_f + \Sigma_{i \in I_f} |t_i|$$

where constant c_f and indecies $I_f \subseteq \{1, \ldots, n\}$ are determined by f/n.

In the examples we mention two norms: list-length (ll) which measures the number of elements of a list, and term-size (ts) which measures the number of nodes in the tree representation of a term. These are defined as:

$$\left|T\right|_{ll} = \begin{cases} 1 + \left|Xs\right|_{ll} & \text{if } T = [X|Xs] \\ 0 & \text{otherwise} \end{cases} \qquad \left|T\right|_{ts} = \begin{cases} 1 + \sum_{i=1}^{n} \left|t_i\right|_{ts} & \text{if } f/n \in \Sigma \text{ and } T = f(t_1,\ldots,t_n) \\ 0 & \text{otherwise} \end{cases}$$

The abstraction of a program with respect to a given norm is obtained by systematically replacing the predicate arguments in the program by corresponding abstract arguments. These are obtained by applying the norm to the argument, except that, whenever the norm is applied to a variable it is mapped to a fresh variable representing its size, instead of being mapped to 0. A given variable is mapped to the same size variable, wherever it occurs in a clause. For example, consider the *append*/3 relation depicted below (on the left), and its abstraction using the list-length norm (on the right). The concrete term [ ] is abstracted to 0 because $\left|[\,]\right|_{ll} = 0$ and the concrete term $[A|B]$ is abstracted to $1 + B1$ because $\left|[A|B]\right|_{ll} = 1 + \left|B\right|_{ll}$ which we denote as $1 + B1$. The CLP(R) program on the right is an abstraction of the concrete logic program on the left, in the sense that whenever $append(t_1, t_2, t_3)$ is a consequence of the concrete program, then $append(\left|t_1\right|_{ll}, \left|t_2\right|_{ll}, \left|t_3\right|_{ll})$ is a consequence of the abstract program.

```
append([],A,A).                      append(0,A1,A1).
append([A|B],C,[A|D]) :-             append(1+B1,C,1+D1) :-
    append(B,C,D).                       append(B1,C1,D1).
```

The *append* program specifies the relation $\{\ (x,y,z)\ |\ z = x.y\ \}$ (z equals the concatenation of x and y). The abstract program specifies the relation $\{\ (x,y,z)\ |\ z = x + y\ \}$ (the length of z is equal to the sum of the lengths of x and y). The instantiation analysis which can be obtained by applying a Pos analysis to the program on the right specifies the relation $\{\ (x,y,z)\ |\ x \wedge (y \leftrightarrow z)\ \}$ (x is rigid with respect to the norm and that y is rigid if and only if z is). A termination analysis based on the *list-length* norm infers also that all the loops in the program are of the form $append(x,y,z) \leftarrow append(u,v,w)$ with size information: $(u<x) \wedge (y=v) \wedge (w<z)$. From all of this information together it infers that the program terminates for queries in which the first or third arguments are instantiated to rigid terms. For details concerning the specific termination analyser we have extended in this work, see [6, 15].

3 Combining Norms

When basing termination analysis on program abstraction it is important to remember that variables occurring in the abstract program range over information about size and rigidity *with respect to* a given norm. This makes it difficult to apply one norm on one part of the program and another on a different part. First, one must know how to interpret values for each abstracted variable (with respect to which norm); and second, one must take care that variables abstracted by different norms do not interact (if different occurrences of variable X are abstracted by different norms then this can lead to problems). Both of these problems are solved if care is taken so that the two abstractions introduce distinct sets of abstracted variables. Namely, the abstraction of a variable X by the ith norm is X_i (interpreted as "the size of X by $norm_i$").

The key idea in this paper is to combine two or more norms by applying them simultaneously. This means that each argument in a predicate of the original program is replaced by two or more (renamed apart) abstract arguments each one specifying size and rigidity information with respect to the corresponding norm. The advantage of this approach is that inter-arguments relations can provide information about the dependencies with respect to each norm and between different norms. A similar phenomenon is observed in [12] where the authors abstract each argument by a single but different norm (depending on its type). However, we do not encounter the technical difficulties described in [12] by considering a semantic approach based on binary clauses as described in [6].

Example 1. Consider the program below (on the left) where some of the program points have been annotated (e.g., ⓐ). Termination analysis (of ground queries) using a list-length norm or a term-size norm does not succeed. The program contains three types of loops: (1) those where list-length is invariant but term-size decreases — recursive calls to point ⓐ, (2) those where list-length decreases but term-size increases — recursive calls to point ⓑ, and (3) those where both measures decrease — recursive calls to point ⓒ (keep in mind that $\left|0\right|_{ts} = 1$).

To perform a termination analysis combining the two norms each argument in the original program is abstracted first with respect to term-size and then with respect to list-length. The resulting abstract program is given below (on the right). Note that the two abstractions introduce disjoint sets of variables. Analysing this program indicates that all loops decrease in one of the two arguments which correspond respectively to the term-size and list-length of the original program. For ground queries both arguments are rigid (each with respect to the corresponding norm).

```
p([_]).
p([s(s(X)),Y|Xs]) :-
    ⓐ p([X,Y|Xs]),
    ⓑ p([s(s(s(s(Y))))|Xs]).
p([0|Xs]) :-
    ⓒ p(Xs).
```

```
p(2+X1,1).
p(4+X1+Y1+Xs1, 2+Xs2) :-
        p(2+X1+Y1+Xs1,2+Xs2),
        p(5+Y1+Xs1,1+Xs2).
p(2+Xs1,1+Xs2) :-
        p(Xs1,Xs2).
```

□

The previous example illustrates an argument for a program which is directly recursive. Our approach is not restricted to direct recursion as the termination analyzer we use makes all (indirect) loops explicit in terms of a direct recursion.

Example 2. Consider the program below (left) which multiplies the elements (natural numbers) in a (non-empty) list by iteratively replacing the first two elements by their multiplication. The program terminates if the list is ground. Attempting to prove this automatically using the term-size norm will indicate that the calls to *times* and *plus* are rigid (in their first and second arguments) and decrease in size (in their first arguments). So, corresponding calls to these predicates surely terminate. However the loop on *factor* does not decrease in term-size (we replace the first two elements by their multiplication). Termination for these loops can be shown using the list-length norm. This, on the other hand gives no useful information for *times* and *plus*. So, neither of the two single analyses provide a proof or termination.

The abstract program for the combined analysis is given below (right). Each argument in the original program is abstracted first with respect to term-size and then with respect to list-length. Analysing this program does give a proof of termination because in all loops one of the two abstract arguments corresponding to the first argument in the original program decreases in size and is rigid (with respect to the appropriate norm).

```
factor([X],X).                   factor(2+X1,1, X1,X2).
factor([X,Y|Xs],T) :-            factor(2+X1+Y1+Xs1,2+Xs2, T1,T2) :-
  times(X,Y,Z),                        times(X1,X2, Y1,Y2, Z1,Z2),
  factor([Z|Xs],T).                    factor(1+Z1+Xs1,1+Xs2, T1,T2).
times(0,X,0).                    times(1,0, X1,X2, 1,0).
times(s(X),Y,Z) :-               times(1+X1,0, Y1,Y2, Z1,Z2) :-
  times(X,Y,XY),                       times(X1,X2, Y1,Y2, XY1,XY2),
  plus(XY,Y,Z).                        plus(XY1,XY2, Y1,Y2, Z1,Z2).
plus(0,X,X).                     plus(1,0,X1,X2,X1,X2).
plus(s(X),Y,s(Z)):-              plus(1+X1,0, Y1,Y2, 1+Z1,0) :-
  plus(X,Y,Z).                         plus(X1,X2, Y1,Y2, Z1,Z2).
```
□

In the previous two examples we observe that when performing two separate analyses, each loop in the program decreases in size for at least one of two measures considered. The question is: Does this constitute a proof of termination? The answer depends on rigidity information. The point is that when observing a decreasing size with respect to one of the norms, we must observe also rigidity with respect to the same norm. For the above two examples, assuming that the initial query is ground (in the respective first arguments of p or *factor*), we can guarantee that each loop is both decreasing and rigid with respect to the appropriate norm (because rigidity with respect to term-size implies rigidity with respect to list-length). This is not always the case as demonstrated by the following example.

Example 3. For the following program neither of the two separate termination analyses, using list-length or term-size, detect a decrease in size for the loop on `t`. The combined analysis does give a proof of termination for queries in which the first argument of t is bound to a ground term. With the combined analysis we maintain a dependency between the term-size of N and the list-length of Xs in $ll(N, Xs)$ (they are equal).

```
t(N) :-                          ll(s(N),[X|Xs]) :- ll(N,Xs).
  ll(N,Xs),                      ll(0,[]).
  select(_,Xs,Xs1),              select(X,[Y|Xs],[Y|Ys]) :-
  ll(M,Xs1), t(M).                  select(X,Xs,Ys).
t(0).                            select(X,[X|Xs],Xs).
```
□

Correctness: The correctness of our approach is straightforward. All we have done is to implicitly duplicate the original arguments of each concrete predicate. E.g. the *plus* definition becomes:

```
plus(0,0, X,X, X,X).
plus(s(X),s(X), Y,Y, s(Z),s(Z)):- plus(X,X, Y,Y, Z,Z).
```

and clearly the success set of this program is isomorphic to the original. Then, each copy of an argument is abstracted with respect to a corresponding norm. Correctness follows because the different norms rename the copies apart and because the analyses (for size and instantiation dependencies) applied to each copy are known to be correct. At first it might seem that we could as well have done the analyses separately. But (1) this would complicate the specification of the termination check; and (2) by doing the analyses together we often derive (size and rigidity) dependencies between the different abstractions of various arguments. This sometimes helps provide termination proofs. These are the main differences between our approach and the one described in [24].

4 Norms from Types

In this section we reconsider how norms can be defined based on type information which may be inferred or provided. We refer (as do others) to such norms as *typed-norms*. This has been considered previously in [3, 10, 21, 11, 12, 24]. Inferring norms from type information makes sense as recursive types represent recursive data-structures and thus identify some potential sources of infinite recursion. Moreover, typed-norms are more refined than semi-linear norms because whereas semi-linear norms measure the size of a term T according to its prime functor (recursively, as a function of the size of its arguments), typed-norms define the size of T based on its type. This means that the same term can be measured differently depending on its type. This is particularly useful when the same function symbol may occur in different type contexts. Our construction is based on the notion of *regular types* [25]. The main intuition is that for each type σ defined in the program, a typed-norm $\|\cdot\|_\sigma$ counts the number of sub-terms of type σ in the (typed) term it is applied to. The novelty in our approach is to then compose the norms corresponding to the (recursive) types defined in the program. This leads to a powerful technique which avoids many of the problems encountered in previous works.

Regular Types: A *regular type* is a set of terms defined by a regular tree grammar. For our purposes, the formulation of regular tree grammars using regular unary logic (RUL) programs is convenient. An RUL program is a logic program consisting of clauses of the form: $\tau(f(X_1,\ldots,X_n)) \leftarrow \tau_1(X_1),\ldots,\tau_n(X_n)$, where $X_1,\ldots,X_n$ are distinct variables. If f has arity zero, then the body of the clause is *true*. An RUL program is deterministic if no two clause heads have a common instance. In this paper we assume deterministic RUL programs whenever we mention RUL programs. Let R be an RUL program, and τ be a predicate in

R. Then the *regular type* τ is the success set of τ in R. There is a distinguished regular type *any*, which represents the set of all terms over the signature.

Example 4. The following RUL program defines *list_of_nat*, the regular type consisting of the set of lists of natural numbers in successor notation.

```
list_of_nat([]).                      nat(0).
list_of_nat([X|Xs]) :-                nat(s(X)) :- nat(X).
    nat(X), list_of_nat(Xs).
```
□

We assume that each predicate p/n in a given program comes with a type declaration of the form ":–type($\tau_1, \ldots, \tau_n$)" where $\tau_1, \ldots, \tau_n$ are types defined in an accompanying RUL. In our examples we use declared types, but inferred types, or a combination of declared and inferred types can be used as well. The more accurate the types are, the more likely there are to derive useful norms for proving termination.

Example 5. The programs given in Examples 1 and 2 can be typed by adding the following declarations which assume the type definitions given in Example 4.

```
:- type p(list_of_nat).          :- type factor(list_of_nat,nat).
                                 :- type times(nat,nat,nat).
                                 :- type plus(nat,nat,nat).
```

These declarations be can inferred automatically using the goal directed analysis described in [14].

□

Defining Norms from Regular Types: The idea of type-based norms consists in associating each type σ used in the program with a corresponding norm function $\|\cdot\|_\sigma$. When applied to a term t of type τ (denoted $t{:}\tau$) $\|\cdot\|_\sigma$ counts the number of subterms of type σ within t. Typed norms can be computed directly from an RUL program simply by running the RUL on the term to be measured. For example, let σ and τ be RUL predicates and let t be a term of type τ. Then $\|t{:}\tau\|_\sigma$ is the number of calls to σ encountered when executing the query $\tau(t)$ (excluding calls in which the argument is a variable). In fact it is implemented as a meta-interpreter for RUL's which counts calls.

Typed-norm definitions are derived from an RUL program as follows: for each type σ defined in the program (excluding **any**) and clause $\tau(f(X_1, \ldots, X_n)) \leftarrow \tau_1(X_1), \ldots, \tau_n(X_n)$ we introduce an equation of the form

$$\|f(X_1, ..., X_n) : \tau\|_\sigma = c(\tau, \sigma) + \|X_1{:}\tau_1\|_\sigma + \ldots + \|X_n{:}\tau_n\|_\sigma$$

where $c(\tau, \sigma) = 1$ if $\tau = \sigma$, and 0 otherwise. In addition we assume that $\|t{:}\tau\|_{any} = 0$, for all $t{:}\tau$ and that $\|X{:}\tau\|_\sigma = 0$ where X is a variable, for all τ and σ.

Example 6. Consider the type definition from Example 4. There are two types and so we define two norm functions, one to count the number of subterms of type `list_of_nat` (denoted by l) and one to count the number of subterms of type `nat` (denoted by n) within a term (of type `list_of_nat` or of type `nat`). For instance, to evaluate $\| [s(0), s(s(0))] \|_l$ and $\| [s(0), s(s(0))] \|_n$ we count respectively the number of calls to `list_of_nat` and to `nat` in the derivation of the query "`?- list_of_nat([s(0),s(s(0))])`" (and this works out to 3 and 5). The typed-norms are defined as:

$$\|T\|_l = \begin{cases} 1 + \|Xs\|_l & \text{if } T = [X|Xs] \\ 1 & \text{if } T = [\,] \\ 0 & \text{if } T = s(X) \\ 0 & \text{if } T = 0 \\ 0 & \text{otherwise} \end{cases} \qquad \|T\|_n = \begin{cases} 1 + \|X\|_n & \text{if } T = s(X) \\ 1 & \text{if } T = 0 \\ \|X\|_n + \|Xs\|_n & \text{if } T = [X|Xs] \\ 0 & \text{if } T = [\,] \\ 0 & \text{otherwise} \end{cases}$$

□

Program abstraction with respect to typed norms is similar to the usual abstraction with respect to semi-linear norms. The abstraction for type σ replaces an argument of type τ by $\|t{:}\tau\|_\sigma$ except that typed variable $X{:}\tau$ is mapped to a corresponding size variable X_σ if the predicate defining σ is reachable from the predicate definition τ and otherwise to 0. Abstracting the programs shown in Examples 1 and 2 according to the *typed-norms* of Example 6 give similar results (except for constants) to the abstraction made in the Examples.

Example 7. The following program (14.4 in [23]) colors a map so that no two adjacent regions have the same color. The predicates *member*/2 and *select*/3 (omitted) are the standard predicates (see [23]). A map is represented as a list of regions where each region has a color (represented by a variable) and a list of colors (represented by variables) for the adjoining regions. An example initial query is given in the box (note the use of shared variables).

```
color_map([Region|Regions],Colors) :-
   color_region(Region,Colors),
   color_map(Regions,Colors).
color_map([],Colors).

color_region(region(Color,NBRs),Cs) :-
   select(Color,Cs,Cs1),
   members(NBRss,Cs1).

members([X|Xs],Ys) :-
   member(X,Ys),
   members(Xs,Ys).
members([],Ys).
```

```
?- color_map(
    [region(P,[E]),                 % portugal
     region(E,[F,P]),               % spain
     region(F,[E,I,S,B,G,L]),       % france
     region(B,[F,H,L,G]),           % belgium
     region(H,[B,G]),               % holland
     region(G,[F,A,S,H,B,L]),       % germany
     region(L,[F,B,G]),             % luxembourg
     region(I,[F,A,S]),             % italy
     region(S,[F,I,A,G]),           % switzerland
     region(A,[I,S,G])],            % austria
    [red,yellow,blue,white]).
```

Proving termination for this program is not straightforward and cannot be performed using the available termination analysers. The term-size norm is not suitable because the list of regions in the initial query contains variables (and hence is not rigid with respect to term-size). The list-length norm is not suitable because the first clause invokes a call to `color_region` which traverses the list of neighbours in that region (so even if the first argument in `color_map` is rigid, still the lists of neighbours inside the elements of that list are not rigid). A specialised semi-linear norm cannot be defined because the list functor occurs in two different type contexts (for regions and for neighbours) and should be treated differently in each. Using norms derived from types we obtain a suitable norm and a proof of termination. The types for this program are given as:

```
:- type color_map(list_of_region,list_of_color).
:- type color_region(region,list_of_color).
:- type select(color,list_of_color,list_of_color).
:- type members(list_of_color,list_of_color).
:- type member(color,list_of_color).
```

```
list_of_region([]).                      list_of_color([]).
list_of_region([X|Xs]) :-                list_of_color([X|Xs]) :-
    region(X), list_of_region(Xs).           color(X), list_of_color(Xs).
region(region(A,B)) :-                   color(red).     color(blue).
    color(A), list_of_color(B).          color(white).   color(yellow).
```

□

5 Implementation

The implementation of an analyser which supports the combination of norms and typed-norms is derived from the termination analyser described in [6] simply by changing the abstraction module. No other changes are necessary. The user provides a program and selects a set of norms and then the program is abstracted with respect to this selection. Norms can be selected from a predefined collection (like *listlength, termsize, etc,*) or defined by the user. Alternatively the user can supply types (inferred or declared) and specify that the analyser should use a combination of the corresponding typed-norms. For regular types we use the analyser described in [14]. The termination analyser can be accessed at `http://wwww.cs.bgu.ac.il/~mcodish/TeminWeb`.

6 Related Work

The idea of using type information to define norms has previously been studied by Bossi *et al.* [3], Martin *et al.* [21], Decorte *et al.* [10, 11, 12] and more recently by Vanhoof and Bruynooghe [24]. Our approach builds primarily on the techniques of Decorte *et al.* and of Vanhoof and Bruynooghe.

Decorte *et al.* observe in [10] and [11] that different predicate arguments can be measured by different (typed-) norms. The authors also observe that inter-arguments relations between different norms can provide useful information. Their work suffers from two restrictions. First, at most one typed-norm can be applied to a term of a given type. Second, as reported in [12], the use of different norms for different types renders the computation of inter-arguments relations far from trivial (they propose a solution based on a notion re-execution).

Vanhoof and Bruynooghe make the observation in [24] that interesting typed-norms can be defined by counting the number of subterms of a given type occurring in (typed-) terms. They address the "single norm per type" restriction of the Decorte *et al.*, observing that sometimes an argument should be measured by several different norms and they propose to consider a collection of norms, one per type defined in the program. However, to avoid the problems with inter-arguments relations described in [12] they perform a collection of separate analyses one for each norm. As a consequence there are no inter-arguments relations between arguments measured by different norms. However, the nature of their basic norms (counting in a term the number of subterms of a given type) is quite powerful and for many examples this leads to a proof of termination.

Our approach to combining norms simply by duplicating predicate arguments and applying the analyses simultaneously solves the problems encountered in both of the lines of work described above: we take the same collection of norms as proposed in [24]; we allow mixed norms (determined by different types); we allow several norms for arguments of the same type; we maintain inter-arguments size dependencies between different measures; and finally, if there are several candidate norms and it is not clear which (linear combination of different norms) is suitable then our system can find it automatically. This approach was also applied in [17] in the context of *lower-bound time-complexity analysis* to increase the precision of the inter-arguments size relations analysis.

The use of types to refine other program analyses has recently been considered in [5] and [18]. In those papers the authors observe that if a program is well-typed then only subterms of the same type can be unified. Hence, type information is used to refine the analysis of unifications in a program by considering for each type which of subterms can be matched. The idea of multiplying the arguments of predicates — one copy per type containing size information with respect to that type — closely resembles the approach used in [18] where for each type the corresponding copy of an argument contains its subterms of that type.

7 Conclusion

This paper describes a technique which enables a termination analyser to consider a combination of several (typed-) norms. The simple idea to replicate the arguments of a predicate for each norm goes a long way and solves many of the problems encountered in previous works. First because the analysis benefits from dependencies amongst different measures of the terms. Second because the analyser can discover which combination of the measures derived from the program's types is suitable to prove termination; and finally, because the implementation becomes straightforward.

References

[1] F. Benoy and A. King. Inferring argument size relationships with CLP(R). In *Sixth International Workshop on Logic Program Synthesis and Transformation (LOPSTR'96)*, pages 204–223, 1996.

[2] A. Bossi, N. Cocco, and M. Fabris. Proving termination of logic programs by exploiting term properties. In S. Abramsky and T.S.E. Maibaum, editors, *Proceedings of Tapsoft 1991*, volume 494 of *Lecture Notes in Computer Science*, pages 153–180. Springer-Verlag, Berlin, 1991.

[3] Annalisa Bossi, Nicoletta Cocco, and Massimo Fabris. Typed norms. In B. Krieg-Brückner, editor, *Proceeedings ESOP '92*, volume 582 of *Lecture Notes in Computer Science*, pages 73–92. Springer-Verlag, Berlin, 1992.

[4] A. Brodsky and Y. Sagiv. Inference of monotonicity constraints in Datalog programs. In *Proceedings of the Eighth ACM SIGACT-SIGART-SIGMOD Symposium on Principles of Database Systems*, pages 190–199, 1989.

[5] Maurice Bruynooghe, Wim Vanhoof, and Michael Codish. Pos(t): Analyzing dependencies in typed logic programs. Technical report, Presented at the Andrei Ershov Fourth International Conference on Perspectives of System Informatics, July 2001.

[6] M. Codish and C. Taboch. A semantic basis for the termination analysis of logic programs. *The Journal of Logic Programming*, 41(1):103–123, 1999.

[7] Patrick Cousot and Nicholas Halbwachs. Automatic discovery of linear restraints among variables of a program. In *Proceedings of the Fifth Annual ACM Symposium on Principles of Programming Languages*, pages 84–96, January 1978.

[8] D. De Schreye and K. Verschaetse. Deriving linear size relations for logic programs by abstract interpretation. *New Generation Computing*, 13(02):117–154, 1995.

[9] Danny De Schreye and Stefaan Decorte. Termination of logic programs: the never-ending story. *The Journal of Logic Programming*, 19 & 20:199–260, May 1994.

[10] Stefaan Decorte, Danny de Schreye, and Massimo Fabris. Automatic inference of norms: A missing link in automatic termination analysis. In Dale Miller, editor, *Logic Programming - Proceedings of the 1993 International Symposium*, pages 420–436, Massachusetts Institute of Technology, Cambridge, Massachusetts 021-42, 1993. The MIT Press.

[11] Stefaan Decorte, Danny De Schreye, and Massimo Fabris. Integrating types in termination analysis. Technical Report CW 222, K.U.Leuven, Department of Computer Science, January 1996.

[12] Stefaan Decorte, Danny De Schreye, and Massimo Fabris. Exploiting the power of typed norms in automatic inference of interargument relations. Technical Report CW 246, K.U.Leuven, Department of Computer Science, January 1997.

[13] R. W. Floyd. Assigning meanings to programs. In J.T Schwartz, editor, *Proceedings of Symposium in Applied Mathematics*, volume 19, Mathematical Aspects of Computer Science, pages 19–32, New York, 1967. American Mathematical Society, Providence, RI.

[14] J. Gallagher and G. Puebla. Abstract Interpretation over Non-Deterministic Finite Tree Automata for Set-Based Analysis of Logic Programs. In Shriram Krishnamurthi and C. R. Ramakrishnan, editors, *Practical Aspects of Declarative Languages, 4th International Symposium, PADL 2002, Portland, OR, USA, January 19-20, 2002*, volume 2257 of *Lecture Notes in Computer Science*, pages 243–261. Springer, 2002.

[15] Samir Genaim and Michael Codish. Inferring termination conditions for logic programs using backwards analysis. In R. Nieuwenhuis and A. Voronkov, editors, *Proceedings of the Eighth International Conference on Logic for Programming, Artificial Intelligence and Reasoning*, volume 2250 of *Lecture Notes in Artificial Intelligence*, pages 681–690. Springer-Verlag, December 2001.

[16] M. Karr. Affine relationships among variables of a program. *Acta Informatica*, 6:133–151, 1976.

[17] Andy King, Kish Shen, and Florence Benoy. Lower-bound time-complexity analysis of logic programs. In Jan Maluszynski, editor, *International Symposium on Logic Programming*, pages 261 – 276. MIT Press, November 1997.

[18] V. Lagoon and P. Stuckey. A framework for analysis of typed logic programs. In *FLOPS*, volume 2024 of *Lecture Notes in Computer Science*, pages 296–310. Springer-Verlag, Berlin, 2001.

[19] N. Lindenstrauss and Y. Sagiv. Automatic termination analysis of logic programs. In Lee Naish, editor, *Proceedings of the Fourteenth International Conference on Logic Programming*, pages 63–77, Leuven, Belgium, 1997. The MIT Press.

[20] K. Marriott and H. Søndergaard. Precise and efficient groundness analysis for logic programs. *ACM Letters on Programming Languages and Systems*, 2(1–4):181–196, 1993.

[21] Jon Martin and Andy King. Typed norms for typed logic programs. In *Logic Program Synthesis and Transformation*. Springer-Verlag, August 1996. Available at http://www.cs.ukc.ac.uk/pubs/1996/511.

[22] F. Mesnard and U. Neumerkel. Applying static analysis techniques for inferring termination conditions of logi programs. In *Static Analysis Symposium*, 2001.

[23] L. Sterling and E. Shapiro. *The Art of Prolog*. MIT Press, second edition, 1994.

[24] W. Vanhoof and M. Bruynooghe. When size does matter. Preproceedings of the Eleventh International Workshop on Logic-based Program Synthesis and Transformation (LOPSTR), November 2001.

[25] E. Yardeni and E.Y. Shapiro. A type system for logic programs. *Journal of Logic Programming*, 10(2):125–154, 1990.

Static Monotonicity Analysis for λ-definable Functions over Lattices*

Andrzej S. Murawski[1**] and Kwangkeun Yi[2***]

[1] Oxford University Computing Laboratory
Wolfson Building, Parks Roadd, Oxford OX1 3QD, UK
andrzej@comlab.ox.ac.uk
[2] ROPAS
Department of Computer Science
Korea Advanced Institute of Science & Technology
373-1 Kusong-dong Yusong-gu, Daejeon 307-701, Korea
kwang@cs.kaist.ac.kr

Abstract. We employ static analysis to examine monotonicity of functions defined over lattices in a λ-calculus augmented with constants, branching, meets, joins and recursive definitions. The need for such a verification procedure has recently arisen in our work on a static analyzer generator called Zoo, in which the specification of static analysis (input to Zoo) consists of finite-height lattice definitions and function definitions over the lattices. Once monotonicity of the functions is ascertained, the generated analyzer is guaranteed to terminate.

1 Motivation

We are currently involved in a project to build a program-analyzer generator (called "Zoo" [Yi01a, Yi01b]). One of the program analysis frameworks that Zoo supports is abstract interpretation [CC77, CC92]. Its user (analysis designer) defines an abstract interpreter in a specification language named "Rabbit". Zoo then compiles the input Rabbit program into an executable analyzer which, given an input program to analyze, derives a set of data-flow equations and solves them by fixpoint iterations.

Zoo, as of now, is less discerning than desirable; it does not check whether the user-specified abstract interpreter defines a correct and terminating analysis. It blindly generates an executable program without verifying that the input specification qualifies for static analysis. Assuring correctness and termination of the specified abstract interpreter has been the responsibility of the designer (Zoo's user) so far.

* This work is supported by Creative Research Initiatives of the Korean Ministry of Science and Technology.

** On leave from Nicholas Copernicus University, Toruń, Poland.

*** ROPAS - Research On Program Analysis System (http://ropas.kaist.ac.kr), National Creative Research Initiative Center, KAIST, Korea.

A. Cortesi (Ed.): VMCAI 2002, LNCS 2294, pp. 139–153, 2002.
© Springer-Verlag Berlin Heidelberg 2002

To overcome these shortcomings, we have designed a static analysis method by which Zoo can check monotonicity of the input abstract interpreters. An abstract interpreter consists of lattice definitions and definitions of functions over the lattices. Once it is known that the functions are monotonic, the generated analyzers are guaranteed to terminate (because Zoo allows only finite-height lattices). By using the analysis, Zoo can statically estimate monotonicity of the input functions and consequently reject analyzers whose specification is possibly not monotonic.

Existing results [Vor00, DGL$^+$99, GGLR98, Sch96] on monotonicity verification in learning theory have turned out hardly adoptable in our case. They are restricted to boolean lattices and concern functions $\{0,1\}^n \rightarrow \{0,1\}$. Though finite distributive lattices can be embedded in a product of the boolean lattices [Rut65], Zoo also supports non-distributive lattices which are prevalent in static analysis. The above-mentioned algorithms are probabilistic, and as such are allowed to err with some small probability. In our generalized case, finding a tight bound on this probability of mistakes seems a formidable job. Besides, only functions in extenso seem to have been studied thus far, whereas we also have access to the definitions. This makes the problem amenable to static analysis. Furthermore, what if conventional static analysis can reliably ensure monotonicity with a reasonable accuracy? This is the approach we took and we present the outcome in this paper.

2 Setting

Let L_1 and L_2 be lattices. A function $f : L_1 \longrightarrow L_2$ is monotonic (respectively anti-monotonic) if and only if for all $x \leq y$, we have $f(x) \leq f(y)$ (respectively $f(y) \leq f(x)$). If a function is both monotonic and anti-monotonic, it is constant. Analogously, for functions of many arguments, we can define monotonicity and anti-monotonicity with respect to the ith argument.

Our goal is to design a static procedure that can certify whether a function between two lattices is monotonic or not. The source language is Rabbit [Yi01a], the input specification language of the Zoo system. For brevity of presentation, we only consider its core here:

$$
\begin{array}{rll}
e ::= & c & \text{constant (lattice point)} \\
| & x & \text{variable} \\
| & \lambda x.e & \text{function} \\
| & \mathit{fix}\ f\ e & \text{recursive definition} \\
| & e\ e & \text{application} \\
| & e \sqcup e & \text{join operation} \\
| & e \sqcap e & \text{meet operation} \\
| & \mathit{if}\ e \sqsubseteq e\ \mathit{then}\ e\ \mathit{else}\ e & \text{branching}
\end{array}
$$

Values in this language are either lattice elements or functions over lattices. c is a constant expression denoting a lattice element. The *if* expression branches, as usual, depending on whether the conditional partial-order relation holds or not.

In the actual Rabbit language [Yi01a] one can also compute elements in lattices of various kinds: product lattices, powerset lattices, function lattices, and lattices with user-defined orders.

Throughout the paper we write $e(x_1, \cdots, x_n)$ if $\{x_1, \cdots, x_n\}$ are the free variables of e. We also write $e(c_1, \cdots, c_n)$ when a constant c_i is substituted for each x_i in e.

3 Monotonicity Checking by an Effect Type System

Given an expression e of the core language, our monotonicity check will determine conservatively for each $1 \leq i \leq n$ whether the operation

$$(x_1, \cdots, x_n) \mapsto e(x_1, \cdots, x_n)$$

is monotonic, anti-monotonic, or constant with respect to the ith argument. This monotonicity behavior will be summarized in a table. For example, the expression $x \sqcup c$ defines $\{x \mapsto \text{monotonic}, \textit{else} \mapsto \text{constant}\}$: monotonic for the free variable x, constant for other variables. As another example take *if* $x \sqsubseteq c$ *then* $\top$ *else* $\bot$. Here the monotonicity is captured by $\{x \mapsto \text{anti-monotonic}, \textit{else} \mapsto \text{constant}\}$, because the values change from $\top$ to $\bot$ (decreasing) as x increases.

We present the verification procedure as an effect-type inference system with typing judgments of the form

$$\Gamma \vdash e : \tau, me.$$

The judgments should be read as "under type environment Γ, expression e has type τ and monotonicity behavior me". The monotonicity behavior is a finite function

$$me \;\in\; ME = Var \stackrel{\text{fin}}{\rightarrow} M$$

from the set of variables to the set M of *monotonicity tokens*:

$$M = \{0, +, -, \top\}.$$

We normally write me in table form $\{\cdots\}$. Monotonicity tokens have the following meaning:

$$\begin{aligned}
[\![0]\!] &= \{f \mid x \sqsubseteq y \text{ implies } f(x) = f(y) \text{ if } f(x), f(y) \text{ terminate}\}\\
[\![+]\!] &= \{f \mid x \sqsubseteq y \text{ implies } f(x) \sqsubseteq f(y) \text{ if } f(x), f(y) \text{ terminate}\}\\
[\![-]\!] &= \{f \mid x \sqsubseteq y \text{ implies } f(y) \sqsubseteq f(x) \text{ if } f(x), f(y) \text{ terminate}\}\\
[\![\top]\!] &= \text{all functions}
\end{aligned}$$

and hence they form a diamond-shaped lattice:

$$0 \sqsubseteq + \sqsubseteq \top, \quad 0 \sqsubseteq - \sqsubseteq \top.$$

The order on M can be extended to ME in a point-wise fashion:

$$me_1 \sqsubseteq me_2 \;\; \textit{iff} \;\; \forall x \in Var. me_1(x) \sqsubseteq me_2(x).$$

The type environment Γ is a finite function from variables to effect types:

$$\Gamma \in Var \overset{\text{fin}}{\to} EffectType.$$

Effect types t are types paired with monotonicity effects:

$$EffectType \;\; t ::= (\tau, me)$$

Types τ are either ground types ι denoting lattices[1] or function types $(\tau, me) \to (\tau, me)$ with effects for both the argument and the result:

$$Type \;\; \tau ::= \iota \mid (\tau, me) \to (\tau, me)$$

The monotonicity behavior me of a function will be described with the aid of *monotonicity expressions*, which are generated as follows:

$$\begin{aligned} me ::= &\ \bar{0} \mid \bar{+} \mid \bar{-} \mid \{x \mapsto m\} \\ \mid &\ me[m/x] \mid @\ me\ me\ me \\ \mid &\ \textbf{if}\ me\ me\ me\ me\ \phi \mid \textbf{ifc}\ me\ me\ \phi \end{aligned}$$

$\bar{0}$, $\bar{+}$ and $\bar{-}$ denote respectively all-constant, all-monotonic, and all-antimonotonic behavior. m stands for any monotonicity token and $\{x \mapsto +\}$ means monotonic in x and constant for others, i.e. the induced function is independent of variables other than x. Similarly, for $\{x \mapsto -\}$ and $\{x \mapsto \top\}$. $me[m/x]$ denotes a table which is the same as me except that the entry for x is m. In what follows we will define the operators @, **if**, and **ifc** as we introduce the typing rules. ϕ denotes a parameter whose meaning will be explained later.

A constant expression remains constant for any variable, hence $\bar{0}$:

$$\frac{}{\Gamma \vdash c : \iota, \bar{0}} \qquad \text{(CON)}$$

The identity function is monotonic, so a variable should be declared as monotonic with respect to itself:

$$\frac{\Gamma(x) = (\tau, me)}{\Gamma \vdash x : \tau, me[+/x]} \qquad \text{(VAR)}$$

The monotonicity of the join operation is compositional:

$$\frac{\Gamma \vdash e_1 : \tau, me_1 \quad \Gamma \vdash e_2 : \tau, me_2}{\Gamma \vdash e_1 \sqcup e_2 : \tau, me_1 \sqcup me_2} \qquad \text{(LUB)}$$

Note that this means that the monotonicity of the two subexpressions is reflected by the monotonicity of the whole term. For example, if e_1 is monotonic and e_2 is anti-monotonic, the result is unknown ($\top$). The same applies to the meet

[1] Our results are independent of the choice of lattices denoted by ground types.

operation. The monotonicity of the expression $e_1 \sqcap e_2$ also corresponds to $me_1 \sqcup me_2$.

The rule for lambda expressions is similar to that of any standard effect-type system. The monotonicity behaviors of the argument and the body (result) are used to annotate the function type. Note that the potential effect of the result can be weaker than that of the body ($me' \sqsubseteq me$). This relaxation makes the rule safely less restrictive; without it we would have to reject programs in which two functions of varying monotonicity are called in the same application. Lastly, the behavior of a lambda expression is identical to that of its body, except that the new function is independent of the freshly bound parameter:

$$\frac{\Gamma + x : (\tau_1, me_1) \vdash e : \tau_2, me_2' \quad me_2' \sqsubseteq me_2}{\Gamma \vdash \lambda x.e : (\tau_1, me_1) \to (\tau_2, me_2), me_2[0/x]} \quad \text{(LAM)}$$

The rule for recursion requires that the body and the name have the same effect types:

$$\frac{\Gamma + f : (\tau, me) \vdash e : \tau, me}{\Gamma \vdash \mathit{fix}\ f\ e : \tau, me[0/f]} \quad \text{(FIX)}$$

For application we introduce a special operator @:

$$\frac{\Gamma \vdash e_1 : (\tau_1, me_1) \to (\tau_2, me_2), me_3 \quad \Gamma \vdash e_2 : \tau_1, me_1}{\Gamma \vdash e_1\ e_2 : \tau_2, @\ me_1\ me_2\ me_3} \quad \text{(APP)}$$

Although @ could just be defined as taking joins, we can do better for an increased accuracy. First, suppose the function to be called is fixed. When both its body and the argument exhibit the same monotonicity (both increasing or both decreasing), the result of the application will be monotonic (increasing). When one is monotonic (increasing) and the other is anti-monotonic (decreasing), then the application is anti-monotonic (decreasing). When one of the two (body or argument) remains constant, the result is constant. Now, consider the situation in which the function itself is changing, for example, monotonically. Then the application is monotonic only when the argument and the body combined are monotonic. The behavior is unpredictable if the argument and the body combined are anti-monotonic. All these cases (and the remaining ones) are accounted for by:

$$@\ me_{\text{arg}}\ me_{\text{body}}\ me_{\text{ftn}} = (me_{\text{arg}} \otimes me_{\text{body}}) \sqcup me_{\text{ftn}}$$

where $me_1 \otimes me_2$ is the pointwise (commutative and monotonic) "multiplication of signs": $+ \otimes + = +$, $- \otimes - = +$, $+ \otimes - = -$ and $0 \otimes \text{any} = 0$.

The case of the conditional expression is quite involved because of the **if** operator:

$$\frac{\Gamma \vdash e_1 : \tau', me_1 \quad \Gamma \vdash e_2 : \tau', me_2 \quad \Gamma \vdash e_3 : \tau, me_3 \quad \Gamma \vdash e_4 : \tau, me_4}{\Gamma \vdash \mathit{if}\ e_1 \sqsubseteq e_2\ \mathit{then}\ e_3\ \mathit{else}\ e_4 : \tau, \mathbf{if}\ me_1\ me_2\ me_3\ me_4\ \Phi} \quad \text{(IF)}$$

Before we present a definition of **if**, let us note that it is wrong to join the monotonicity behaviors of the two branches. For example, *if* $x \sqsubseteq c$ *then* $\top$ *else* $\bot$ has constant branches but it decreases (switches from $\top$ to $\bot$) as x increases. Thus, we have to examine whether the monotonicity behavior is preserved at the point of the switch and thereafter. We need to know two details: (1) in which direction (from true to false or the reverse) the *if*-condition changes, and (2) whether the consequent change of branches preserves the monotonicity. Our point-wise definition of $\dot{\mathbf{if}}$:

$$\dot{\mathbf{if}}\ me_1\ me_2\ me_3\ me_4\ \Phi = \{x \mapsto \dot{\mathbf{if}}\ me_1(x)\ me_2(x)\ me_3(x)\ me_4(x)\ \Phi \mid x \in \mathit{Var}\}$$

is based on a conservative approximation of the two pieces of information. Assuming, for simplicity, that there exists only one free variable that can occur in each e_i, the four representative cases in the definition of $\dot{\mathbf{if}}$ are as follows:

$me_1(x)$	$me_2(x)$	$me_3(x)$	$me_4(x)$	Φ	$\dot{\mathbf{if}}\ me_1(x) \cdots me_4(x)\ \Phi$
$-$	$+$	$+$	$+$	$e_3(\bot) \sqsupseteq e_4(\top)$	$+$
$-$	$+$	$-$	$-$	$e_3(\bot) \sqsubseteq e_4(\top)$	$-$
$+$	$-$	$+$	$+$	$e_3(\top) \sqsubseteq e_4(\bot)$	$+$
$+$	$-$	$-$	$-$	$e_3(\top) \sqsupseteq e_4(\bot)$	$-$

For example, the first row captures the case when the boolean value of $e_1 \sqsubseteq e_2$ switches from false to true (because e_1 is decreasing and e_2 is increasing). Thus, if the maximal value in the 'false' branch (i.e. $e_4(\top)$, because e_4 is monotonic) does not exceed the minimal value in the 'true' branch ($e_3(\bot)$), we can conclude that the whole *if*-expression is monotonic. In general, for expressions with several variables, the extrema are calculated on the basis of the monotonicity table, e.g. if $e_3(x_1, x_2, x_3)$ defines $\{x_1 \mapsto +, x_2 \mapsto -, x_3 \mapsto +\}$, the smallest value will be $e_3(\bot, \top, \bot)$.

The Φ parameter ensures that monotonicity will be preserved at the switching point. The monotonicity tokens for e_1 and e_2 give a conservative estimate of the direction of the switch. The four cases we have distinguished handle all the posibilities in which monotonicity of the aggregate expression is predictable, provided the participating functions are monotonic or anti-monotonic. There are a few more cases taking constant functions into account. The required results for those are easily derivable from the above table, e.g.

$me_1(x)$	$me_2(x)$	$me_3(x)$	$me_4(x)$	Φ	$\dot{\mathbf{if}}\ me_1(x) \cdots me_4(x)\ \Phi$
$-$	$+$	0	0	$e_3(\bot) \sqsupseteq e_4(\top)$	$+$
$+$	$-$	0	0	$e_3(\top) \sqsupseteq e_4(\bot)$	$-$
$+$	0	0	0	$e_3(\top) \sqsupseteq e_4(\bot)$	$-$
0	0	0	0	irrelevant	0

The complete definition can be found in Appendix A.

Note, for example, that the (IF) rule can be instantiated to:

$$\frac{x : t \vdash e_1 : \tau, \{x \mapsto -\} \quad x : t \vdash e_2 : \tau, \{x \mapsto +\}}{x : t \vdash \mathit{if}\ e_1 \sqsubseteq e_2\ \mathit{then}\ \top\ \mathit{else}\ \bot : \iota, \{x \mapsto +\}}$$

$$\frac{x:t \vdash e_1 : \tau, \{x \mapsto +\} \quad x:t \vdash e_2 : \tau, \{x \mapsto -\}}{x:t \vdash \mathit{if}\ e_1 \sqsubseteq e_2\ \mathit{then}\ \top\ \mathit{else}\ \bot : \iota, \{x \mapsto -\}}$$

and further to:

$$\frac{x:t \vdash x : \tau, \{x \mapsto +\} \quad x:t \vdash \bot : \tau, \bar{0}}{x:t \vdash \mathit{if}\ x \sqsubseteq \bot\ \mathit{then}\ \top\ \mathit{else}\ \bot : \iota, \{x \mapsto -\}}$$

We can sharpen the (IF) rule for the case in which the condition is of the special shape $x \sqsubseteq c$, which actually occurs quite frequently in program analysis specifications. Here the true-false boundary is clearly known and we exploit that in order to define **ifc**:

$$\frac{\Gamma \vdash e_3 : \tau, me_3 \quad \Gamma \vdash e_4 : \tau, me_4}{\Gamma \vdash \mathit{if}\ x \sqsubseteq c\ \mathit{then}\ e_3\ \mathit{else}\ e_4 : \tau, \mathbf{ifc}\ x\ me_3\ me_4\ \Phi} \quad \text{(IFC)}$$

When we increase x, the value switches from e_3 to e_4 at points directly above c in the associated lattice. Let $\widehat{c}$ be the set of such elements:

$$\widehat{c} = \{\, x \mid x \sqsupset c,\ \forall y.(x \sqsupseteq y \sqsupset c \Rightarrow x = y)\} \,.$$

We can gain more precision if we use $\widehat{c}$ to determine whether switches preserve monotonicity. For instance, suppose e_3 and e_4 have one free variable and both are monotonic with respect to it. Then if $e_3(c)$ does not exceed $e_4(d)$ for every $d \in \widehat{c}$, then the whole *if*-expression is also monotonic. Hence, we can define **ifc** to be

$$\mathbf{ifc}\ x\ me_3\ me_4\ \Phi = \{y \mapsto \begin{cases} \dot{\mathbf{ifc}}\ me_3(y)\ me_4(y)\ \Phi, & \text{if } y = x \\ me_3(y) \sqcup me_4(y), & \text{otherwise} \end{cases} \mid y \in \mathit{Var}\}$$

where $\dot{\mathbf{ifc}}$ (assuming that e_3 and e_4 have one free variable) is defined by:

$me_3(x)$	$me_4(x)$	Φ	$\dot{\mathbf{ifc}}\ me_3(x)\ me_4(x)\ \Phi$
$+$	$+$	$\forall d \in \widehat{c}.\ e_3(c) \sqsubseteq e_4(d)$	$+$
$+$	0	$\forall d \in \widehat{c}.\ e_3(c) \sqsubseteq e_4(d)$	$+$
0	$+$	$\forall d \in \widehat{c}.\ e_3(c) \sqsubseteq e_4(d)$	$+$
$-$	$-$	$\forall d \in \widehat{c}.\ e_3(c) \sqsupseteq e_4(d)$	$-$
$-$	0	$\forall d \in \widehat{c}.\ e_3(c) \sqsupseteq e_4(d)$	$-$
0	$-$	$\forall d \in \widehat{c}.\ e_3(c) \sqsupseteq e_4(d)$	$-$
0	0	irrelevant	0

If e_3,e_4 have occurrences of more variables, one should use c and d with a combination of $\bot$ and $\top$ depending on the monotonicity of e_3 and e_4 with respect to the other variables. The Φ condition is statically computable when the set $\widehat{c}$ of the associated lattice is finite and no recursive calls have to be made to evaluate the relevant expressions.

4 Soundness

First we introduce some notation. For $s, s' \in ME$ we write $s \sqsubseteq s'|_x$ iff $s(x) \sqsubseteq s'(x)$ and $s(y) = s'(y)$ for $y \neq x$. Given lattice elements v, v', a monotonicity behavior $me \in ME$, and a variable x we define $v\ me(x)\ v'$ by:

$$v\ me(x)\ v' = \begin{cases} v = v', & me(x) = 0 \\ v \sqsubseteq v', & me(x) = + \\ v \sqsupseteq v', & me(x) = - \end{cases}$$

Next let $v : (\tau, me)$ be a logical relation between lattice elements and types satisfying:

$$\begin{array}{ll} c : (\iota, \bar{0}) & \text{iff true} \\ (\lambda x.e, s) : (t_1 \to t_2, me) & \text{iff} \\ & (1)\ v_1 : t_1 \text{ and } s + x : v_1 \vdash e \Rightarrow v_2 \text{ implies } v_2 : t_2 \\ & (2)\ s \sqsubseteq s'|_y,\ v_1 : t_1, \\ & \quad s + x : v_1 \vdash e \Rightarrow v_2,\ s' + x : v_1 \vdash e \Rightarrow v_2' \\ & \quad \text{implies } v_2\ me(y)\ v_2' \end{array}$$

where $s \vdash e \Rightarrow v$ means that v is the result of evaluating e in the value environment s. We write $s \models \Gamma$ when the value environment s respects the type environment Γ:

$$\frac{}{\emptyset \models \emptyset} \qquad \frac{s \models \Gamma \quad v : t}{s + x : v \models \Gamma + x : t}$$

Now we are ready to state the correctness result:

Theorem 1. *If $\Gamma \vdash e : \tau, me$ then $s \models \Gamma$, $s' \models \Gamma$, $s \sqsubseteq s'|_x$, $s \vdash e \Rightarrow v$, and $s' \vdash e \Rightarrow v'$ imply $v\ me(x)\ v'$.*

Proof. By structural induction on e.

Case $\Gamma \vdash \lambda x.e : (\tau_1, me_1) \to (\tau_2, me_2), me_2[0/x]$.

Let $s \models \Gamma$, $s' \models \Gamma$, $s \sqsubseteq s'|_y$, $s \vdash \lambda x.e \Rightarrow (\lambda x.e, s)$, and $s' \vdash \lambda x.e \Rightarrow (\lambda x.e, s')$. We have to show: $(\lambda x.e, s)\ me[0/x](y)\ (\lambda x.e, s')$,
i.e. to show that for $v_1 : (\tau_1, me_1)$, $s + x : v_1 \vdash e \Rightarrow v_2$ and $s' + x : v_1 \vdash e \Rightarrow v_2'$ implies $v_2\ me[0/x](y)\ v_2'$

- When $y = x$.
  Then $s + x : v_1 = s' + x : v_1$.
  Thus $s + x : v_1 \vdash e \Rightarrow v_2$ and $s' + x : v_1 \vdash e \Rightarrow v_2'$
  imply $v_2 = v_2'$, thus $v_2\ (me[0/x](y))\ v_2'$.
- When $y \neq x$.
  By definition, $\Gamma + x : (\tau_1, me_1) \vdash e : \tau_2, me_2'$ and $me_2' \sqsubseteq me_2$.
  Observe that $s + x : v_1 \sqsubseteq s' + x : v_1|_y$,
  $s + x : v_1 \models \Gamma + x : (\tau_1, me_1)$, and $s' + x : v_1 \models \Gamma + x : (\tau_1, me_1)$.
  Let $s + x : v_1 \vdash e \Rightarrow v_2$ and $s' + x : v_1 \vdash e \Rightarrow v_2'$.
  Then by IH, $v_2\ me'(y)\ v_2'$, i.e. $v_2\ me(y)\ v_2'$ because $me' \sqsubseteq me$,
  so $v_2\ (me[0/x](y))\ v_2'$.

The reasoning in other cases is pretty much similar and uses the arguments we have outlined informally when introducing the system. □

5 Algorithm

Our effect-type system is a little different from conventional effect systems. In [TT94, TT93, TJ92, TJ91] effects are constant symbols and the only operation involved is set-union. In this paper effects (monotonicity tables) are subject to other operations: $\otimes$, **if** and **ifc**. Hence, we cannot solely rely on the unification procedure [Rob65] for type inference.

Our algorithm consists of two phases: we derive constraints for types and monotonicity effects first, then we solve the constraints. There are two kinds of constraints: for types (τ) and for monotonicity behaviors (me). The type constraints will be solved by unification [Rob65] and the monotonicity constraints – by fixpoint iteration. Unification is applicable to the type constraints because they are simply equality constraints with variables for the latent-effects. Its result will provide us with some additional monotonicity constraints about the latent effects of function types. Then conventional fixpoint iteration can be applied to the monotonicity constraints since every operator (@, **if**, and **ifc**) on the constraints is monotonic. Because the least model for the constraints is equivalent to the least fixed point of the corresponding equations [CC95], the algorithm will give the best approximation of monotonicity that can be inferred in our type system.

5.1 Extraction of Constraints

Each constraint ρ will be a monotonicity formula constructed according to the following rules:

$$\begin{aligned}\rho ::= &\ \tau_1 \dot{=} \tau_2 \mid me_1 \supseteq me_2\\ &\mid \exists\alpha.\rho \mid \exists\beta.\rho\\ &\mid \rho_1, \rho_2\end{aligned}$$

where variables are allowed to occur in types τ and monotonicity behaviors me:

$$\begin{aligned}\tau\ &::= \text{as before} \mid \alpha \text{ (type variable)}\\ me &::= \text{as before} \mid \beta \text{ (monotonicity variable)}\end{aligned}$$

We write α_i for type variables, and β_i for monotonicity variables. The validity $\vdash \rho$ of the formula ρ is defined as follows. $\{x/y\}\rho$ denotes ρ in which x has been substituted for y.

$$\frac{}{\vdash \tau \dot{=} \tau} \qquad \frac{me_1 \sqsupseteq me_2}{\vdash me_1 \supseteq me_2} \qquad \frac{\vdash \{\tau/\alpha\}\rho}{\vdash \exists\alpha.\rho} \qquad \frac{\vdash \{me/\beta\}\rho}{\vdash \exists\beta.\rho} \qquad \frac{\vdash \rho_1 \quad \vdash \rho_2}{\vdash \rho_1, \rho_2}$$

We extract the associated monotonicity formula from an expression e using a recursive procedure $C(\Gamma, e, \tau, me)$. It has linear time complexity (with respect to the size of e). The size of the generated formula is also linear in e's size:

$$
\begin{aligned}
C(\Gamma, c, \tau, me) &= \tau \doteq \iota, \quad me \supseteq \bar{0} \\
C(\Gamma, x, \tau, me) &= \text{let } (\tau', me') = \Gamma(x) \text{ in} \\
&\quad \tau \doteq \tau, \quad me \supseteq me'[+/x] \\
C(\Gamma, \lambda x.e, \tau, me) &= \exists \alpha_1 \alpha_2 \beta_1 \beta_2. \\
&\quad \tau \doteq (\alpha_1, \beta_1) \to (\alpha_2, \beta_2), \\
&\quad C(\Gamma + x : (\alpha_1, \beta_1), e, \alpha_2, \beta_2), \\
&\quad me \supseteq \beta_2[0/x] \\
C(\Gamma, \text{fix } f\ e, \tau, me) &= \exists \beta. \\
&\quad C(\Gamma + f : (\tau, \beta), e, \tau, \beta) \\
&\quad me \supseteq \beta[0/f] \\
C(\Gamma, e_1\ e_2, \tau, me) &= \exists \alpha \beta_1 \beta_2 \beta_3. \\
&\quad C(\Gamma, e_1, (\alpha, \beta_1) \to (\tau, \beta_2), \beta_3), \\
&\quad C(\Gamma, e_2, \alpha, \beta_1), \\
&\quad me \supseteq @\ \beta_1\ \beta_2\ \beta_3 \\
C(\Gamma, e_1 \sqcup e_2 \text{ or } e_1 \sqcap e_2, \tau, me) &= \exists \beta_1 \beta_2. \\
&\quad C(\Gamma, e_1, \tau, \beta_1), \quad C(\Gamma, e_2, \tau, \beta_2), \\
&\quad me \supseteq \beta_1 \sqcup \beta_2 \\
C(\Gamma, \textit{if } e_1 \sqsubseteq e_2 \textit{ then } e_3 \textit{ else } e_4, \tau, me) &= \exists \alpha \beta_1 \beta_2 \beta_3 \beta_4. \\
&\quad C(\Gamma, e_1, \alpha, \beta_1), \quad C(\Gamma, e_2, \alpha, \beta_2), \\
&\quad C(\Gamma, e_3, \tau, \beta_3), \quad C(\Gamma, e_4, \tau, \beta_4), \\
&\quad me \supseteq \mathbf{if}\ \beta_1\ \beta_2\ \beta_3\ \beta_4\ \Phi \\
C(\Gamma, \textit{if } x \le c \textit{ then } e_3 \textit{ else } e_4, \tau, me) &= \exists \beta_3 \beta_4. \\
&\quad C(\Gamma, e_3, \tau, \beta_3), \quad C(\Gamma, e_4, \tau, \beta_4), \\
&\quad me \supseteq \mathbf{ifc}\ \beta_3\ \beta_4\ \Phi
\end{aligned}
$$

It is easy to see that the validity of the generated formula $C(\Gamma, e, \tau, me)$ is equivalent to the typing judgment $\Gamma \vdash e : \tau, me$. Below we give part of the proof in the case of lambda expressions.

Theorem 2. $\vdash C(\Gamma, e, \tau, me)$ *iff* $\Gamma \vdash e : \tau, me'$ *and* $me' \sqsubseteq me$.

Proof. By structural induction on e.
Case $\lambda x.e$.

$\Rightarrow$ Suppose $C(\Gamma, \lambda x : e, \tau, me)$ holds.
Then there exist τ_1, τ_2, b_1, b_2 such that
$\tau = (\tau_1, b_1) \to (\tau_2, b_2)$, $C(\Gamma + x : (\tau_1, b_1), e, \tau_2, b_2)$ and $b_2[0/x] \sqsubseteq me$.
By IH $\Gamma + x : (\tau_1, b_1) \vdash e : \tau_2, b_2'$ and $b_2' \sqsubseteq b_2$.
By (LAM) $\Gamma \vdash \lambda x.e : (\tau_1, b_1) \to (\tau_2, b_2), b_2[0/x]$,
i.e. $\Gamma \vdash \lambda x.e : \tau, me'$ and $me' \sqsubseteq me$.

$\Leftarrow$ Assume $\Gamma \vdash \lambda x.e : \tau, me'$ and $me' \sqsubseteq me$.
By (LAM), $\tau = (\tau_1, b_1) \to (\tau_2, b_2)$, $\Gamma + x : (\tau_1, b_1) \vdash e : \tau_2, b_2'$ where $b_2' \sqsubseteq b_2$ and $me' = b_2[0/x]$.
By IH we get $\vdash C(\Gamma + x : (\tau_1, b_1), e, \tau_2, b_2)$.
Since $b_2[0/x] \sqsubseteq me$, $C(\Gamma, \lambda x : e, \tau, me)$ is true.

□

5.2 Solving the Constraints

We observe two properties of the generated monotonicity formula $C(\Gamma, e, \alpha, \beta)$. Firstly, in every occurrence of (τ, me), me is a variable β_i. This is quite obvious, because the property holds at the only two places where such a latent type is formed (lambda abstraction and application). Secondly, every me_1 in $me_1 \sqsupseteq me_2$ is a variable β_i. This is because for every generated monotonicity constraint $me_1 \sqsupseteq me_2$ the left-hand-side me_1 is the last parameter to C, which is a monotonicity variable β_i for every recursive call to C.

Thanks to the first property, the unification procedure can be applied to the type constraints $\{\tau \doteq \tau' \in C(\Gamma, e, \alpha, \beta)\}$, and the resultant substitution involves only monotonicity variables β_i.

Each item β'/β in the substitution is equivalent to the monotonicity contraints $\beta' \sqsupseteq \beta$ and $\beta \sqsupseteq \beta'$. This set of unification-driven contraints, together with the monotonicity contraints from $C(\Gamma, e, \alpha, \beta)$, constitute the equations (e.g. "$\beta \sqsupseteq me_1, \cdots, \beta \sqsupseteq me_k$" as "$\beta = me_1 \sqcup \cdots \sqcup me_k$") whose least solution corresponds to the the least model of the original contraints [CC95]. The least solution is computed by iteration: starting from $\bar{0}$ for every me_i we repeatedly apply the right-hand-sides of the equations to the intermediate result. This procedure terminates with the least fixed point, because the operators involved $(@, \mathbf{if}, \mathbf{ifc}, \sqcup)$ are all monotonic.

Complexity. The constraint extraction procedure C takes linear time in the size of the input program. The number of generated constraints (type equations and monotonicity constraints) is also linear. Then unification takes linear time with respect to the number of type equations. Because there are $O(n)$ indeterminates (me_i) where n is the program size, the iteration will take $O(n^2)$ steps in the worst case, since no chain in the lattice $Var \to \{0, +, -, \top\}$ can be longer than $2 \times |Var|$ (Var is here the finite set of free variables occurring in the input program). The overall time complexity is therefore $O(n^3)$, because each equation computes a new monotonicity behavior me_i whose size is $O(|Var|)$ and constant time is needed for table look-up for each operator.

6 Conclusion

We have introduced a method of monotonicity verification for λ-definable functions over arbitrary finite-height lattices. Static monotonicity analysis seems an interesting problem on its own and apparently not much work has been done in that area. Our interest in this topic was motivated by Zoo [Yi01a, Yi01b], which is a program-analyzer generator. Now that it can automatically check whether the input specification is monotonic or not, termination of the specified analysis is guaranteed if the outcome of the test is positive. Thus we can prevent Zoo from generating divergent analyzers, or from generating extra "joining" operations [LCVH92, LCVH94] necessary to enforce the monotonicity of fixpoint iterations. Our work may also suggest a similar solution for other existing program-analyzer generators like PAG [Mar98].

Our verification procedure is an effect-type system, which can be classified as mono-variant flow-insensitive analysis. Its effectiveness remains to be investigated and experiments are underway for existing program analyses (e.g. conventional data flow analyses [ASU86, YH93] and exception analyses [YR01, YR97]). We would also like to make the rules more liberal by employing other static analysis tools to estimate the boundary region in the conditional expression. It seems that there is not too much scope for improvement in the rest of cases.

Acknowledgments We thank ROPAS members at KAIST and the anonymous referees for their helpful comments. We are grateful to Youil Kim, Oukseh Lee, and Naoki Kobayashi for corrections and suggestions of improvements. Andrzej Murawski would like to express gratitude to ROPAS for the warm and cordial hospitality extended to him during his visit.

References

[ASU86] Alfred V. Aho, Ravi Sethi, and Jeffrey D. Ullman. *Compilers: Principles, Techniques, and Tools.* Addison-Wesley, 1986.

[CC77] Patrick Cousot and Radhia Cousot. Abstract interpretation: A unified lattice model for static analysis of programs by construction or approximation of fixpoints. In *Proceedings of The ACM SIGPLAN-SIGACT Symposium on Principles of Programming Languages*, pages 238–252, 1977.

[CC92] Patrick Cousot and Radhia Cousot. Abstract interpretation frameworks. *Journal of Logic Computation*, 2(4):511–547, 1992. Also as a tech report: Ecole Polytechnique, no. LIX/RR/92/10.

[CC95] Patrick Cousot and Radhia Cousot. Compositional and inductive semantic definitions in fixpoint, equational, constraint, closure-condition, rule-based and game-theoretic form. In *Lecture Notes in Computer Science*, volume 939, pages 293–308. Springer-Verlag, proceedings of the 7th international conference on computer-aided verification edition, 1995.

[DGL+99] Yevgeniy Dodis, Oded Goldreich, Eric Lehman, Sofya Raskhodnikova, Dana Ron, and Alex Samorodnitsky. Improved testing algorithms for monotonicity. Number Report TR99-107 in Electronic Colloquium on Computational Compleity, June 1999.

[GGLR98] Oded Goldreich, Shafi Goldwasser, Eric Lehman, and Dand Ron. Testing monotonicity. In *Proceedings of the 39th Annual Symposium on Foundations of Computer Science*, 1998.

[LCVH92] B. Le Charlier and P. Van Hentenryck. A universal top-down fixpoint algorithm. Technical Report TR-CS-92-25, Brown University, Dept. of Computer Science, May 1992. (also as a technical report of Institute of Computer Science, University of Namur).

[LCVH94] B. Le Charlier and P. Van Hentenryck. Experimental Evaluation of a Generic Abstract Interpretation Algorithm for Prolog. *ACM Transactions on Programming Languages and Systems*, 16(1):35–101, January 1994.

[Mar98] Florian Martin. PAG – an efficient program analyzer generator. *International Journal on Software Tools for Technology Transfer*, 2(1):46–67, 1998.

[Rob65] J. A. Robinson. A machine-oriented logic based on the resolution principle. *Journal of the ACM*, 12(1):23–41, 1965.

[Rut65] D.E. Rutherford. *Introduction to Lattice Theory.* Hafner Publishing Company, New York, 1965.

[Sch96] Winfrid G. Schneeweiss. A necessary and sufficient criterion for the monotonicity of boolean functions with deterministic and stochastic. *IEEE Transactions on Computers*, 45(11):1300–1302, November 1996.

[TJ91] Jean-Pierre Talpin and Pierre Jouvelot. Type, effect and region reconstruction in polymorphic functional languages. In *Proceedings of Functional Programming Languages and Computer Architecture*, 1991.

[TJ92] Jean-Piere Talpin and Pierre Jouvelot. Polymorphic type, region and effect inference. *Journal of Functional Programming*, 2(3):245–271, July 1992.

[TT93] Mads Tofte and Jean-Pierre Talpin. A theory of stack allocation in polymorphically typed languages. Technical Report Technical Report 93/15, Department of Computer Science, Copenhagen University, July 1993.

[TT94] Mads Tofte and Jean-Pierre Talpin. Implementation of the typed call-by-value λ-calculus using a stack of regions. In *Proceedings of The ACM SIGPLAN-SIGACT Symposium on Principles of Programming Languages*, pages 188–201, January 1994.

[Vor00] Andrei Voronenko. On the complexity of the monotonicity verification. In *Proceedings of the 15th Annual IEEE Conference on Computational Complexity*, pages 4–7, July 2000.

[YH93] Kwangkeun Yi and Williams Ludwell Harrison III. Automatic generation and management of interprocedural program analyses. In *Proceedings of The ACM SIGPLAN-SIGACT Symposium on Principles of Programming Languages*, pages 246–259, January 1993.

[Yi01a] Kwangkeun Yi. *Program Analysis System Zoo.* Research On Program Analysis: National Creative Research Center, KAIST, July 2001. `http://ropas.kaist.ac.kr/zoo/doc/rabbit-e.ps`.

[Yi01b] Kwangkeun Yi. System Zoo: towards a realistic program analyzer generator, July 2001. Seminar talk at ENS, Paris. `http://ropas.kaist.ac.kr/~kwang/talk/ens01/ens01.ps`.

[YR97] Kwangkeun Yi and Sukyoung Ryu. Towards a cost-effective estimation of uncaught exceptions in SML programs. In *Proceedings of the 4th International Static Analysis Symposium*, volume 1302 of *Lecture Notes in Computer Science*, pages 98–113. Springer-Verlag, 1997.

[YR01] Kwangkeun Yi and Sukyoung Ryu. A cost-effective estimation of uncaught exceptions in Standard ML programs. *Theoretical Computer Science*, 273(1), 2001. (to appear).

A Operator Definition

Full definition of $\dot{\textbf{if}}$, assuming only a single variable can occur freely in e_3 and e_4. Note that the operation is monotonic. For missing cases, the results are equal to $\top$.

$me_1(x)$	$me_2(x)$	$me_3(x)$	$me_4(x)$	Φ	**if** $me_1(x) \cdots me_4(x)$ Φ
−	+	+	+	$e_3(\bot) \sqsupseteq e_4(\top)$	+
0	+	+	+	$e_3(\bot) \sqsupseteq e_4(\top)$	+
−	0	+	+	$e_3(\bot) \sqsupseteq e_4(\top)$	+
−	+	0	+	$e_3(\bot) \sqsupseteq e_4(\top)$	+
−	+	+	0	$e_3(\bot) \sqsupseteq e_4(\top)$	+
0	0	+	+	irrelevant	+
0	+	0	+	$e_3(\bot) \sqsupseteq e_4(\top)$	+
0	+	+	0	$e_3(\bot) \sqsupseteq e_4(\top)$	+
−	0	0	+	$e_3(\bot) \sqsupseteq e_4(\top)$	+
−	0	+	0	$e_3(\bot) \sqsupseteq e_4(\top)$	+
−	+	0	0	$e_3(\bot) \sqsupseteq e_4(\top)$	+
−	0	0	0	$e_3(\bot) \sqsupseteq e_4(\top)$	+
0	+	0	0	$e_3(\bot) \sqsupseteq e_4(\top)$	+
0	0	+	0	irrelevant	+
0	0	0	+	irrelevant	+
+	−	+	+	$e_3(\top) \sqsubseteq e_4(\bot)$	+
0	−	+	+	$e_3(\top) \sqsubseteq e_4(\bot)$	+
+	0	+	+	$e_3(\top) \sqsubseteq e_4(\bot)$	+
+	−	0	+	$e_3(\top) \sqsubseteq e_4(\bot)$	+
+	−	+	0	$e_3(\top) \sqsubseteq e_4(\bot)$	+
0	−	0	+	$e_3(\top) \sqsubseteq e_4(\bot)$	+
0	−	+	0	$e_3(\top) \sqsubseteq e_4(\bot)$	+
+	0	0	+	$e_3(\top) \sqsubseteq e_4(\bot)$	+
+	0	+	0	$e_3(\top) \sqsubseteq e_4(\bot)$	+
+	−	0	0	$e_3(\top) \sqsubseteq e_4(\bot)$	+
+	0	0	0	$e_3(\top) \sqsubseteq e_4(\bot)$	+
0	−	0	0	$e_3(\top) \sqsubseteq e_4(\bot)$	+
−	+	−	−	$e_3(\bot) \sqsubseteq e_4(\top)$	−
0	+	−	−	$e_3(\bot) \sqsubseteq e_4(\top)$	−
−	0	−	−	$e_3(\bot) \sqsubseteq e_4(\top)$	−
−	+	0	−	$e_3(\bot) \sqsubseteq e_4(\top)$	−
−	+	−	0	$e_3(\bot) \sqsubseteq e_4(\top)$	−
0	0	−	−	irrelevant	−
0	+	0	−	$e_3(\bot) \sqsubseteq e_4(\top)$	−
0	+	−	0	$e_3(\bot) \sqsubseteq e_4(\top)$	−
−	0	0	-	$e_3(\bot) \sqsubseteq e_4(\top)$	−
−	0	-	0	$e_3(\bot) \sqsubseteq e_4(\top)$	−
-	+	0	0	$e_3(\bot) \sqsubseteq e_4(\top)$	−
−	0	0	0	$e_3(\bot) \sqsubseteq e_4(\top)$	−
0	+	0	0	$e_3(\bot) \sqsubseteq e_4(\top)$	−
0	0	−	0	irrelevant	−
0	0	0	−	irrelevant	−

(continued)

$me_1(x)$	$me_2(x)$	$me_3(x)$	$me_4(x)$	Φ	**if** $me_1(x) \cdots me_4(x)$ Φ
+	−	−	−	$e_3(\top) \sqsupseteq e_4(\bot)$	−
0	−	−	−	$e_3(\top) \sqsupseteq e_4(\bot)$	−
+	0	−	−	$e_3(\top) \sqsupseteq e_4(\bot)$	−
+	−	0	−	$e_3(\top) \sqsupseteq e_4(\bot)$	−
+	−	−	0	$e_3(\top) \sqsupseteq e_4(\bot)$	−
0	−	0	−	$e_3(\top) \sqsupseteq e_4(\bot)$	−
0	−	−	0	$e_3(\top) \sqsupseteq e_4(\bot)$	−
+	0	0	−	$e_3(\top) \sqsupseteq e_4(\bot)$	−
+	0	−	0	$e_3(\top) \sqsupseteq e_4(\bot)$	−
+	-	0	0	$e_3(\top) \sqsupseteq e_4(\bot)$	−
−	0	0	0	$e_3(\top) \sqsupseteq e_4(\bot)$	−
0	−	0	0	$e_3(\top) \sqsupseteq e_4(\bot)$	−
0	0	0	0	irrelevant	0

A Refinement of the Escape Property*

Patricia M. Hill[1] and Fausto Spoto[2]

[1] School of Computing, University of Leeds, UK
hill@comp.leeds.ac.uk
[2] Dipartimento di Informatica, Verona, Italy
Ph.: +44 01132336807, Fax: +44 01132335468
spoto@sci.univr.it

Abstract Escape analysis of object-oriented languages determines, for every program point, the *escape property* $\mathcal{E}$ *i.e.,* the set of the creation points of the objects reachable from some variables. An approximation of $\mathcal{E}$ is useful to stack allocate dynamically created objects and to reduce the overhead of synchronisation in Java-like languages. $\mathcal{E}$ can itself be used for escape analysis, but it is very imprecise. We define here a refinement $\mathcal{ER}$ of $\mathcal{E}$, in the sense that $\mathcal{ER}$ is more concrete than $\mathcal{E}$ and, hence, leads to a more precise escape analysis than $\mathcal{E}$.

1 Introduction

Escape analysis should determine which dynamically created data structures will not *escape* from their creating method. This information allows us to allocate these structures to the stack instead of the heap. Compared to heap allocation, stack allocation reduces the garbage collection overhead at run-time. Moreover, in the case of object-oriented languages such as Java, a knowledge of those objects that cannot *escape* the methods of their creating threads can be used to remove unnecessary synchronisations when the objects are accessed.

In [8], an escape analysis for object-oriented languages is defined on an *escape property* $\mathcal{E}$ which is an abstract interpretation of concrete states. This property collects, for each program point, the set of creation points of objects reachable at that point from the variables and fields in scope. That analysis, although very imprecise, was shown in [8] to be sometimes more precise than other escape analyses proposed in literature [3, 4, 7, 12, 15]. Hence, in [8] we concluded that these other analyses are not a concretisation of $\mathcal{E}$ itself and that, for improved precision, a *refinement* of $\mathcal{E}$ *i.e.,* a more concrete domain than $\mathcal{E}$, should be constructed. This paper defines the refinement $\mathcal{ER}$ by splitting the sets of creation points in $\mathcal{E}$ into subsets, one for each variable or field. Our implementation of $\mathcal{ER}$ confirms that it is indeed more precise than $\mathcal{E}$.

2 Overview

We illustrate our domain $\mathcal{ER}$ through its implementation inside a static analyser for simple object-oriented languages, called LOOP [13]. Escape analysis is typi-

* This work has been funded by EPSRC grant GR/R53401.

A. Cortesi (Ed.): VMCAI 2002, LNCS 2294, pp. 154–166, 2002.
© Springer-Verlag Berlin Heidelberg 2002

```
class figure :
field next : figure
method def() : void is empty
method rot(a : angle) : void is empty
method draw() : void is empty

class square extends figure :
fields side, x, y : int
field rotation : angle
method def() : void is
  this.side := 1;
  this.x, this.y := 0;
  this.rotation := new angle;   {π1}
  this.rotation.degree = 0;
method rot(a : angle) : void is
  this.rotation := a;
method draw() : void is
  % something using this.rotation here...

class circle extends figure :
fields radius, x, y : int
method def() : void is
  this.radius := 1;
  this.x, this.y := 0;
method draw() : void is
  % put something here...
```

```
class angle :
field degree : int
method acute() : int is
  out := this.degree < 90;

class main :
method main(n : figure) : void is
  f : figure;
  f := new square;     {π2}
  f.def();
  rotate(f);           {w1}
  f := new circle;     {π3}
  f.def();
  f.next = n;
  while(f)
    rotate(f);         {w2}
    f := f.next
method rotate(f : figure) : void is
  a : angle;
  a := new angle;      {π4}
  f.rot(a);
  a.degree := 0;
  while (a.degree < 360)
    a.degree := a.degree + 1;
    f.draw();
```

Fig. 1. An example of program.

cally used to stack allocate objects which do not *escape* their creating method. Thus we direct the analysis of LOOP over the program points immediately after a call to a method which creates the data structure we want to stack allocate.

To see how the domain $\mathcal{ER}$ can be used for escape analyses, consider the program in Figure 1. We assume that main is called with n bound to a list of circles and we direct the analysis on the program points w_1 and w_2 which follow a rotate(f) call. If the creation point π_4 is not reachable from f in w_1 or w_2, then the angles created by that call can be stack allocated. With the domain $\mathcal{E}$ (Section 5), we analyse the program starting from an abstract state $\{\overline{\pi}, \pi_3\}$, the collection of all the creation points for circles (π_3) and for main ($\overline{\pi}$). With the new domain $\mathcal{ER}$ (Section 6), we analyse it instead starting from an abstract state which binds n and the field next to $\{\pi_3\}$, hence distributing the creation points over variables and fields. Using $\mathcal{E}$, LOOP computes at w_1 and w_2 the abstract information $\{\overline{\pi}, \pi_1, \pi_2, \pi_3, \pi_4\}$. All we can conclude is that the creation point π_4 might be reachable in both w_1 and w_2. Using $\mathcal{ER}$, it computes:

$$w_1 : \left\langle \begin{bmatrix} \mathtt{f} \mapsto \{\pi_2\}, \mathtt{n} \mapsto \{\pi_3\}, \\ \mathtt{out} \mapsto *, \mathtt{this} \mapsto \{\overline{\pi}\} \end{bmatrix}, \begin{bmatrix} \mathtt{rotation} \mapsto \{\pi_1, \pi_4\}, \\ \mathtt{next} \mapsto \{\pi_3\}, \mathtt{degree} \mapsto *, \ldots \end{bmatrix} \right\rangle \quad \text{and}$$

$$w_2 : \left\langle \begin{bmatrix} \texttt{f} \mapsto \{\pi_3\}, \texttt{n} \mapsto \{\pi_3\}, \\ \texttt{out} \mapsto *, \texttt{this} \mapsto \{\overline{\pi}\} \end{bmatrix}, \begin{bmatrix} \texttt{rotation} \mapsto \varnothing, \\ \texttt{next} \mapsto \{\pi_3\}, \texttt{degree} \mapsto *, \ldots \end{bmatrix} \right\rangle .$$

The value $*$ means that the corresponding variable is of type *int*, hence no object is bound to it. As before, we can conclude that in w_1 an object created in π_4 might be reachable from `f`. Namely, `f` is allowed to be bound to an object created in π_2 which has class `square`. This class has a field `rotation` which may contain an object created in π_4. On the other hand, in w_2 we can conclude that no object created in π_4 can be reachable from `f`. Namely, `f` can only be bound to an object created in π_3, which is hence a `circle`, and thus has no field which can be created in π_4. Note that $\mathcal{ER}$ provides even more information. Namely, it says that in w_2 *no* object created in π_4 is reachable. This does not mean that they have not been created. For instance, in w_2 an object has been created in π_4 by the call `rotate(f)` just before w_1. But that object is not reachable anymore in w_2. This information is useful for the static prediction for garbage collection.

3 Preliminaries

The *(co-)domain* of a function f is $\mathsf{dom}(f)$ ($\mathsf{rng}(f)$). A total (partial) function is denoted by $\mapsto$ ($\rightarrow$). We denote by $[v_1 \mapsto t_1, \ldots, v_n \mapsto t_n]$ a function f whose domain is $\{v_1, \ldots, v_n\}$ and such that $f(v_i) = t_i$ for $i = 1, \ldots, n$. An *update* of f is denoted by $f[w_1 \mapsto d_1, \ldots, w_m \mapsto d_m]$, where the domain of f may be enlarged. By $f|_s$ ($f|_{-s}$) we denote the *restriction* of f to $s \subseteq \mathsf{dom}(f)$ (to $\mathsf{dom}(f) \setminus s$). If $\mathsf{dom}(f) \subseteq \mathsf{rng}(f)$ and $f(x) = x$ then x is a *fixpoint* of f. The set of fixpoints of f is $\mathsf{fp}(f)$. A definition like $S = \langle a, b \rangle$, with a and b meta-variables, silently defines the selectors $s.a$ and $s.b$ for $s \in S$. An element x will often stand for the singleton set $\{x\}$.

A pair $\langle C, \leq \rangle$ is a *poset* if $\leq$ is reflexive, transitive and antisymmetric on C. A poset is a *complete lattice* when *least upper bounds* (lub) and *greatest lower bounds* (glb) always exist. If $\langle C, \leq \rangle$ and $\langle A, \preceq \rangle$ are posets, then $f : C \mapsto A$ is *(co-)additive* if it preserves lub's (glb's). It is a *lower closure operator* (*lco*) if it is *monotonic*, *reductive* ($f(c) \leq c$ for every $c \in C$) and *idempotent* ($ff(c) = f(c)$ for every $c \in C$).

In abstract interpretation (AI) [5], a *Galois connection* between two posets $\langle C, \leq \rangle$ and $\langle A, \preceq \rangle$ (the *concrete* and the *abstract* domain) is a pair of monotonic maps $\alpha : C \mapsto A$ and $\gamma : A \mapsto C$ such that $\gamma\alpha$ is extensive and $\alpha\gamma$ is reductive. It is a *Galois insertion* if $\alpha\gamma$ is the identity map *i.e.*, if A does not contain *useless* elements. This is equivalent to α being onto, or γ one-to-one. The *abstraction* α and the *concretisation* γ determine each other. If C and A are complete lattices and α is additive, it is the abstraction map of a Galois connection.

4 The Framework of Analysis

In this paper we build on the *watchpoint semantics* for the static analysis of object-oriented programs [14]. That framework allows us to derive a compositional and *focused* analyser from the specification of a domain of abstract states

$$\mathcal{K} = \{\texttt{angle}, \texttt{figure}, \texttt{square}, \texttt{circle}, \texttt{main}\}$$

$$\texttt{square} \leq \texttt{figure}, \quad \texttt{circle} \leq \texttt{figure} \quad \text{and reflexive cases}$$

$$F(\texttt{angle}) = [\texttt{degree} \mapsto int] \quad F(\texttt{figure}) = [\texttt{next} \mapsto \texttt{figure}] \quad F(\texttt{main}) = []$$

$$F(\texttt{square}) = \begin{bmatrix} \texttt{next} \mapsto \texttt{figure}, \texttt{side} \mapsto int, \texttt{squarex} \mapsto int \\ \texttt{squarey} \mapsto int, \texttt{rotation} \mapsto \texttt{angle} \end{bmatrix}$$

$$F(\texttt{circle}) = [\texttt{circlex} \mapsto int, \texttt{circley} \mapsto int, \texttt{next} \mapsto \texttt{figure}, \texttt{radius} \mapsto int]$$

Fig. 2. The static information of the program in Figure 1.

and of some operations which work over them. Then we do not have to consider any problem like scoping, recursion and name clash, since they are already solved by the watchpoint semantics. Moreover, using that framework we can measure the precision of the analysis by measuring that of the domain.

We introduce the states [9] which are the concrete domain of a version of the watchpoint semantics [14] for object-oriented programs. We refer to [9] for the concrete operations over those states and to [14] for the construction of the semantics from those states and operations. Hence some definitions contained in [9, 14] will be omitted here.

We assume that we analyse programs of a simple object-oriented language, whose only basic type is *int*. All other types are called *classes*. A *typing* assigns types to a finite set of variables. The variable `this` must be bound to a class.

Definition 1. *Let Id be a set of* identifiers, $\mathcal{K}$ *a finite set of* classes *ordered by a* subclass relation $\leq$ *such that* $\langle \mathcal{K}, \leq \rangle$ *is a poset and* $\texttt{main} \in \mathcal{K}$. *Let Type be the set* $\{int\} + \mathcal{K}$. *We extend* $\leq$ *to Type by defining* $int \leq int$. *Let* $Vars \subseteq Id$ *be a set of* variables *such that* $\texttt{this} \in Vars$. *We define*

$$Typing = \{\tau : Vars \to Type \mid \mathsf{dom}(\tau) \text{ is finite, if } \texttt{this} \in \mathsf{dom}(\tau) \text{ then } \tau(\texttt{this}) \in \mathcal{K}\}.$$

Types and typings are initialised as $\mathsf{init}(int) = 0$, $\mathsf{init}(\kappa) = nil$ *for* $\kappa \in \mathcal{K}$ *and* $\mathsf{init}(\tau)(v) = \mathsf{init}(\tau(v))$ *for* $\tau \in Typing$ *and* $v \in \mathsf{dom}(\tau)$.

A class contains local variables (*fields*). Then *Fields* is a set of maps which bind each class to the typing of its fields. We require that different fields have different names, and that the variable `this` cannot be a field.

Definition 2. $Fields = \{F : \mathcal{K} \mapsto Typing \mid \texttt{this} \notin \mathsf{dom}(F(\kappa)) \text{ for all } \kappa \in \mathcal{K}\}$. *We require that if* $F \in Fields$, $\kappa_1, \kappa_2 \in \mathcal{K}$ *and* $f \in \mathsf{dom}(F(\kappa_1)) \cap \mathsf{dom}(F(\kappa_2))$ *then* $F(\kappa_1)(f) = F(\kappa_2)(f)$.

We use the *static information* of the program to be analysed.

Definition 3. *The* static information *of a program consists of a poset* $\langle \mathcal{K}, \leq \rangle$ *and a map* $F \in Fields$.

Figures 1 and 2 show a program and its static information. The fields `x` and `y` of the classes `square` and `circle` have been disambiguated.

Definition 4. *We assume that we have a finite set Π of* creation points. *A map $k : \Pi \mapsto \mathcal{K}$ relates every creation point with the class of the objects it creates. A hidden creation point $\overline{\pi} \in \Pi$,* internal *to the operating system, creates objects of class* `main`. *Then we define $k(\overline{\pi}) = \mathtt{main}$. Every other $\pi \in \Pi$ decorates a* `new` *κ statement in the program. Then we define $k(\pi) = \kappa$. Let $\pi \in \Pi$ and $F \in Fields$. We define $F(\pi) = F(k(\pi))$.*

Look at Figure 3. *Locations* are references to memory cells. *Values* are integers, locations or *nil*. *Frame* is a set of maps from variables to values. The values must be consistent with the type of the variables. For instance, class variables must be bound to a location or to *nil*. An *object* contains its creation point and the frame of its fields. *Memory* is a set of maps from locations to objects. As in [8], we use here a more concrete notion of object than in [9], since they have a creation point, essential for the subsequent abstraction into a domain for escape analysis.

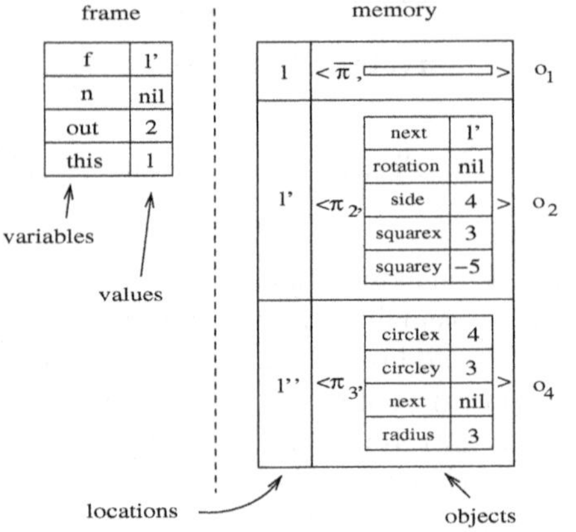

Fig. 3. Frame ϕ_1 and memory μ_1 for $\tau = [\mathtt{f} \mapsto \mathtt{figure}, \mathtt{n} \mapsto \mathtt{figure}, \mathtt{out} \mapsto int, \mathtt{this} \mapsto \mathtt{main}]$.

Definition 5. *Let Loc be an infinite set of* locations, *Value* $= \mathbb{Z} + Loc + \{nil\}$ *and $\tau \in Typing$. We define* frames, objects *and* memories *as*

$$Frame_\tau = \left\{ \phi \in \mathsf{dom}(\tau) \mapsto Value \;\middle|\; \begin{array}{l} \textit{for every } v \in \mathsf{dom}(\tau) \\ \;\textit{if } \tau(v) = int \textit{ then } \phi(v) \in \mathbb{Z} \\ \;\textit{if } \tau(v) \in \mathcal{K} \textit{ then } \phi(v) \in \{nil\} \cup Loc \end{array} \right\}$$

$$Obj = \{\langle \pi, \phi \rangle \mid \pi \in \Pi,\ \phi \in Frame_{F(\pi)}\}$$

$$Memory = \{\mu \in Loc \to Obj \mid \mathsf{dom}(\mu) \textit{ is finite}\} .$$

Example 1. Let τ be as in Figure 3 *i.e.*, the typing at program point w_1 in Figure 1. Let $l, l' \in Loc$. The set $Frame_\tau$ contains $\phi_1 = [\mathtt{f} \mapsto l', \mathtt{n} \mapsto nil, \mathtt{out} \mapsto 2, \mathtt{this} \mapsto l]$ (Figure 3), but it does not contain $\phi_2 = [\mathtt{f} \mapsto 2, \mathtt{n} \mapsto l', \mathtt{out} \mapsto -2, \mathtt{this} \mapsto l]$, because `f` is bound to 2 in ϕ_2 (while it has class `figure` in τ).

Example 2. An object o_1 created at the hidden creation point $\overline{\pi}$ has class $k(\overline{\pi}) =$ `main` (Definition 4). Since $F(\mathtt{main}) = []$ (Figure 2), we have $o_1 = \langle \overline{\pi}, [] \rangle$ (Figure 3). Objects created at π_2 have class $k(\pi_2) = \mathtt{square}$ (Figure 1). Examples of such objects (where $l, l' \in Loc$), consistent with $F(\mathtt{square})$, are (Figure 3)

$$o_2 = \langle \pi_2, [\mathtt{next} \mapsto l', \mathtt{rotation} \mapsto nil, \mathtt{side} \mapsto 4, \mathtt{squarex} \mapsto 3, \mathtt{squarey} \mapsto -5] \rangle,$$
$$o_3 = \langle \pi_2, [\mathtt{next} \mapsto nil, \mathtt{rotation} \mapsto l, \mathtt{side} \mapsto 4, \mathtt{squarex} \mapsto 3, \mathtt{squarey} \mapsto -5] \rangle.$$

Objects created at π_3 have class $k(\pi_3) = \texttt{circle}$ (Figure 1). An example of such objects, consistent with $F(\texttt{circle})$, is (Figure 3)

$$o_4 = \langle \pi_3, [\texttt{circlex} \mapsto 4, \texttt{circley} \mapsto 3, \texttt{next} \mapsto nil, \texttt{radius} \mapsto 3] \rangle \ .$$

Example 3. Let $l, l', l'' \in Loc$ be distinct and o_1, o_2, o_3, o_4 from Example 2. Then *Memory* contains (for μ_1, see Figure 3)

$$\mu_1 = [l \mapsto o_1, l' \mapsto o_2, l'' \mapsto o_4] \quad \mu_2 = [l \mapsto o_2, l' \mapsto o_1] \quad \mu_3 = [l \mapsto o_2, l' \mapsto o_3] \ .$$

We define a notion of type correctness which guarantees that variables are bound to locations which contain objects allowed by the type of the variables.

Definition 6. *Let* $\tau \in Typing$, $\phi \in Frame_\tau$ *and* $\mu \in Memory$. *We say that* ϕ *is* weakly τ-correct *w.r.t.* μ *if for every* $v \in \mathsf{dom}(\phi)$ *such that* $\phi(v) \in Loc$ *we have* $\phi(v) \in \mathsf{dom}(\mu)$ *and* $k((\mu\phi(v)).\pi) \leq \tau(v)$.

We strengthen the correctness notion of Definition 6 by requiring that it holds for the fields of the objects in memory also.

Definition 7. *Let* $\tau \in Typing$, $\phi \in Frame_\tau$ *and* $\mu \in Memory$. *We say that* ϕ *is* τ-correct *w.r.t.* μ, *and we write* $(\phi, \mu) : \tau$, *if*

1. ϕ *is weakly* τ*-correct w.r.t.* μ *(Definition 6),*
2. *for every* $o \in \mathsf{rng}(\mu)$ *we have that* $o.\phi$ *is weakly* $F(o.\pi)$*-correct w.r.t.* μ.

Example 4. Let τ, ϕ_1 and μ_1 be as in Figure 3 and μ_2 and μ_3 as in Example 3.

- $(\phi_1, \mu_1) : \tau$ (Figure 3). Condition 1 of Definition 7 holds because $\{v \in \mathsf{dom}(\phi_1) \mid \phi_1(v) \in Loc\} = \{\texttt{this}, \texttt{f}\}$, $\{l, l'\} \subseteq \mathsf{dom}(\mu_1)$, $k(\mu_1(l).\pi) = k(o_1.\pi) = k(\overline{\pi}) = \texttt{main} = \tau(\texttt{this})$ and $k(\mu_1(l').\pi) = k(o_2.\pi) = k(\pi_2) = \texttt{square} \leq \texttt{figure} = \tau(\texttt{f})$. Condition 2 holds because $\mathsf{rng}(\mu_1) = \{o_1, o_2, o_4\}$, $o_1.\phi = []$, $\mathsf{rng}(o_4.\phi) \cap Loc = \varnothing$, $\mathsf{rng}(o_2.\phi) \cap Loc = \{l'\}$, $l' \in \mathsf{dom}(\mu_1)$ and $k(\mu_1(l').\pi) = \texttt{square} \leq \texttt{figure} = F(o_2.\pi)(\texttt{next})$.
- $(\phi_1, \mu_2) : \tau$ does not hold, since condition 1 of Definition 7 does not hold. Namely, $\tau(\texttt{this}) = \texttt{main}$, $k((\mu_2\phi_1(\texttt{this})).\pi) = k(o_2.\pi) = k(\pi_2) = \texttt{square}$ and $\texttt{square} \not\leq \texttt{main}$.
- $(\phi_1, \mu_3) : \tau$ does not hold, since condition 2 of Definition 7 does not hold. Namely, $o_3 \in \mathsf{rng}(\mu_3)$ and $o_3.\phi$ is not $F(o_3.\pi)$-correct *w.r.t.* μ_3, since we have that $o_3.\phi(\texttt{rotation}) = l$, $\texttt{square} \not\leq \texttt{angle}$ but $k(\mu_3(l).\pi) = k(o_2.\pi) = k(\pi_2) = \texttt{square}$ and $F(o_3.\pi)(\texttt{rotation}) = F(\texttt{square})(\texttt{rotation}) = \texttt{angle}$.

The state of the computation is a pair consisting of a frame and a memory. The variable `this` in the domain of the frame must be bound to an object.

Definition 8. *Let* $\tau \in Typing$. *We define the* states

$$\Sigma_\tau = \left\{ \langle \phi, \mu \rangle \,\middle|\, \begin{array}{l} \phi \in Frame_\tau,\ \mu \in Memory,\ (\phi, \mu) : \tau, \\ if\ \texttt{this} \in \mathsf{dom}(\tau)\ then\ \phi(\texttt{this}) \neq nil \end{array} \right\} \ .$$

Example 5. In Example 4, we have $\langle \phi_1, \mu_1 \rangle \in \Sigma_\tau$ (Figure 3) but $\langle \phi_1, \mu_2 \rangle \notin \Sigma_\tau$.

Every AI of $\wp(\Sigma_\tau)$ induces an AI of the semantics [14]. This has been used to define in [8] the escape property $\mathcal{E}$, which we briefly introduce in Section 5.

5 The Escape Property $\mathcal{E}$

Since escape analysis *over*approximates, for every program point p, the set of creation points of the objects reachable in p from some variable or field in scope, we first define a notion of *reachable* objects.

Definition 9. *Let $\tau \in$ Typing, $\sigma = \langle \phi, \mu \rangle \in \Sigma_\tau$ and $S \subseteq \Sigma_\tau$. The set of the objects* reachable *in σ is $O_\tau(\sigma) = \{O^i_\tau(\sigma) \mid i \geq 0\}$ where*

$$\begin{aligned} O^0_\tau(\sigma) &= \varnothing \\ O^{i+1}_\tau(\sigma) &= \{\mu\phi(v) \mid v \in \mathsf{dom}(\tau),\ \phi(v) \in Loc\} \ \cup \\ &\qquad \cup \{\mu(o.\phi(f)) \mid o \in O^i_\tau(\sigma),\ f \in \mathsf{dom}(F(o.\pi)),\ o.\phi(f) \in Loc\} \ . \end{aligned}$$

We define $\alpha^{\mathcal{E}}_\tau(S) = \{o.\pi \mid \sigma \in S$ and $o \in O_\tau(\sigma)\} \subseteq \Pi$.

Note that variables and fields of type *int* do not contribute to $\alpha^{\mathcal{E}}_\tau$.

Example 6. In Figure 3, we have $O_\tau(\langle \phi_1, \mu_1 \rangle) = \{o_1, o_2\}$, $\alpha^{\mathcal{E}}_\tau(\langle \phi_1, \mu_1 \rangle) = \{\overline{\pi}, \pi_2\}$ and $o_4 \notin O_\tau(\langle \phi_1, \mu_1 \rangle)$, since o_4 is not reachable from the variables of ϕ_1.

In general, it is $\mathsf{rng}(\alpha^{\mathcal{E}}_\tau) \neq \wp(\Pi)$, since $\alpha^{\mathcal{E}}_\tau$ is not necessarily onto. This means that if we chose $\wp(\Pi)$ as abstract domain, it would contain useless elements (Section 3). We look hence only for those elements of $\wp(\Pi)$ which belongs to $\mathsf{rng}(\alpha^{\mathcal{E}}_\tau)$. Namely, for every $S \in \wp(\Pi)$ we define $\delta_\tau(S)$ as the largest subset of S which contains only those creation points deemed useful by the typing τ. Note that if there are no possible creation points for `this`, all creation points are useless.

Definition 10. *Let $\tau \in$ Typing and $S \subseteq \Pi$. We define $\delta_\tau(S) = \cup\{\delta^i_\tau(S) \mid i \geq 0\}$ with*

$$\begin{aligned} \delta^0_\tau(S) &= \varnothing \\ \delta^{i+1}_\tau(S) &= \begin{cases} \varnothing & \textit{if } \mathtt{this} \in \mathsf{dom}(\tau) \textit{ and there is no } \pi \in S \textit{ s.t. } k(\pi) \leq \tau(\mathtt{this}) \\ \cup\{\{\pi\} \cup \delta^i_{F(\pi)}(S) \mid \kappa \in \mathsf{rng}(\tau) \cap \mathcal{K},\ \pi \in S,\ k(\pi) \leq \kappa\} & \textit{otherwise.} \end{cases} \end{aligned}$$

Lemma 1. *Let $\tau \in$ Typing and $i \in \mathbb{N}$. The maps δ^i_τ and δ_τ are lco's.*

The following result proves that δ_τ can be used to define $\mathsf{rng}(\alpha^{\mathcal{E}}_\tau)$.

Lemma 2. *Let $\tau \in$ Typing. Then $\mathsf{fp}(\delta_\tau) = \mathsf{rng}(\alpha^{\mathcal{E}}_\tau)$.*

Lemma 2 allows us to assume that $\alpha^{\mathcal{E}}_\tau : \wp(\Sigma_\tau) \mapsto \mathsf{fp}(\delta_\tau)$. Moreover, it justifies the following definition of the simplest domain $\mathcal{E}$ for escape analysis. It coincides with the *escape property* itself.

Definition 11. *Let $\tau \in$ Typing. The* escape property *is $\mathcal{E}_\tau = \mathsf{fp}(\delta_\tau)$, ordered by set inclusion.*

Example 7. Let τ be as in Figure 3. We have

$$\mathcal{E}_\tau = \varnothing \cup \{S \in \wp(\Pi) \mid \overline{\pi} \in S \text{ and if } \pi_1 \in S \text{ or } \pi_4 \in S \text{ then } \pi_2 \in S\}\ .$$

The constraint on $\mathcal{E}_\tau$ says that to reach an `angle` (created in π_1 or in π_4) from the variables in $\mathsf{dom}(\tau)$, we must be able to reach a `square` (created in π_2).

Proposition 1. *Let $\tau \in$ Typing. The map $\alpha^{\mathcal{E}}_\tau$ is strict, additive and onto i.e., it is the abstraction map of a Galois insertion from $\wp(\Sigma_\tau)$ to $\mathcal{E}_\tau$.*

For the best approximations over $\mathcal{E}$ of the operations in [9], see [8].

6 The Refined Domain $\mathcal{ER}$

We define here a *refinement* $\mathcal{ER}$ of the domain $\mathcal{E}$ of Section 5, in the sense that $\mathcal{ER}$ is a concretisation of $\mathcal{E}$ (Proposition 3).

An abstract value (compare with Definition 5) is $*$, which approximates the integers, or $S \subseteq \Pi$, which approximates *nil* and all locations containing an object created in some creation point in S. An abstract frame maps variables to abstract values consistent with their type.

Definition 12. *Let $\mathit{Value}^{\mathcal{ER}} = \{*\} \cup \wp(\Pi)$ and $\tau \in$ Typing. Then*

$$\mathit{Frame}^{\mathcal{ER}}_\tau = \left\{ \phi \in \mathsf{dom}(\tau) \mapsto \mathit{Value}^{\mathcal{ER}} \;\middle|\; \begin{array}{l} \text{for every } v \in \mathsf{dom}(\tau) \\ \quad \text{if } \tau(v) = \mathit{int} \text{ then } \phi(v) = * \\ \quad \text{if } \tau(v) \in \mathcal{K} \text{ and } \pi \in \phi(v) \\ \qquad \text{then } k(\pi) \le \tau(v) \end{array} \right\}.$$

Example 8. Let τ be as in Figure 3. We have

$$[\mathtt{f} \mapsto \{\pi_2\}, \mathtt{n} \mapsto \{\pi_2, \pi_3\}, \mathtt{out} \mapsto \varnothing, \mathtt{this} \mapsto \{\overline{\pi}\}] \in \mathit{Frame}^{\mathcal{ER}}_\tau$$
$$[\mathtt{f} \mapsto \{\overline{\pi}, \pi_2\}, \mathtt{n} \mapsto \{\pi_2, \pi_3\}, \mathtt{out} \mapsto \varnothing, \mathtt{this} \mapsto \{\overline{\pi}\}] \notin \mathit{Frame}^{\mathcal{ER}}_\tau\ ,$$

since $k(\overline{\pi}) = \mathtt{main}$, $\tau(\mathtt{f}) = \mathtt{figure}$ and $\mathtt{main} \not\le \mathtt{figure}$.

The map ε *extracts* the creation points of the objects bound to the variables.

Definition 13. *Let $\tau \in$ Typing. The map $\varepsilon_\tau : \wp(\Sigma_\tau) \mapsto \mathit{Frame}^{\mathcal{ER}}_\tau$ is such that, for every $S \subseteq \Sigma_\tau$ and $v \in \mathsf{dom}(\tau)$,*

$$\varepsilon_\tau(S)(v) = \begin{cases} * & \text{if } \tau(v) = \mathit{int} \\ \{(\mu\phi(v)).\pi \mid \langle \phi, \mu \rangle \in S \text{ and } \phi(v) \in \mathit{Loc}\} & \text{if } \tau(v) \in \mathcal{K}. \end{cases}$$

Example 9. In Figure 3, we have $\varepsilon_\tau(\langle \phi_1, \mu_1 \rangle) = [\mathtt{f} \mapsto \{\pi_2\}, \mathtt{n} \mapsto \varnothing, \mathtt{out} \mapsto *, \mathtt{this} \mapsto \{\overline{\pi}\}]$.

Because of Definition 2, the typing $\overline{\tau}$ *of all the fields* is well-defined.

Definition 14. *We define* $\overline{\tau} = \cup\{F(\kappa) \mid \kappa \in \mathcal{K}\}$. *Let* $\tau \in$ *Typing such that* $\mathsf{dom}(\tau) \subseteq \mathsf{dom}(\overline{\tau})$ *and* $\phi \in Frame_\tau$. *Its* extension $\overline{\phi} \in Frame_{\overline{\tau}}$ *is such that, for every* $v \in \mathsf{dom}(\overline{\tau})$,

$$\overline{\phi}(v) = \begin{cases} \phi(v) & \text{if } v \in \mathsf{dom}(\tau) \\ \mathsf{init}(\overline{\tau}(v)) & \text{otherwise (Definition 1).} \end{cases}$$

Example 10. Consider Figure 2. We have

$$\overline{\tau} = \begin{bmatrix} \mathtt{circlex} \mapsto int, \mathtt{circley} \mapsto int, \mathtt{degree} \mapsto int \\ \mathtt{next} \mapsto \mathtt{figure}, \mathtt{radius} \mapsto int, \mathtt{rotation} \mapsto \mathtt{angle} \\ \mathtt{side} \mapsto int, \mathtt{squarex} \mapsto int, \mathtt{squarey} \mapsto int \end{bmatrix} .$$

Let $\phi = [\mathtt{circlex} \mapsto 12, \mathtt{circley} \mapsto 5, \mathtt{next} \mapsto l, \mathtt{radius} \mapsto 5] \in F(\mathtt{circle})$, with $l \in Loc$. We have

$$\overline{\phi} = \begin{bmatrix} \mathtt{circlex} \mapsto 12, \mathtt{circley} \mapsto 5, \mathtt{degree} \mapsto 0, \mathtt{next} \mapsto l, \mathtt{radius} \mapsto 5 \\ \mathtt{rotation} \mapsto nil, \mathtt{side} \mapsto 0, \mathtt{squarex} \mapsto 0, \mathtt{squarey} \mapsto 0 \end{bmatrix} .$$

An abstract memory is an abstract frame for the collection of the fields of all classes. The abstraction map computes the abstract memory by extracting the creation points of the fields of the reachable objects of the concrete memory.

Definition 15. *Let* $\tau \in$ *Typing and* $Memory^{\mathcal{ER}} = Frame^{\mathcal{ER}}_{\overline{\tau}}$. *We define the map* $\alpha^{\mathcal{ER}}_\tau : \wp(\Sigma_\tau) \mapsto \{\bot\} \cup (Frame^{\mathcal{ER}}_\tau \times Memory^{\mathcal{ER}})$ *such that, for* $S \subseteq \Sigma_\tau$,

$$\alpha^{\mathcal{ER}}_\tau(S) = \begin{cases} \bot & \text{if } S = \varnothing \\ \langle \varepsilon_\tau(S), \varepsilon_{\overline{\tau}}(\{\langle \overline{o.\phi}, \sigma.\mu\rangle \mid \sigma \in S \text{ and } o \in O_\tau(\sigma)\})\rangle & \text{otherwise.} \end{cases}$$

Example 11. In Figure 3, we have (compare with Example 6. The fields not represented are implicitly bound to $*$)

$$\alpha^{\mathcal{ER}}_\tau(\langle \phi_1, \mu_1\rangle) = \left\langle \begin{bmatrix} \mathtt{f} \mapsto \{\pi_2\}, \mathtt{n} \mapsto \varnothing \\ \mathtt{out} \mapsto *, \mathtt{this} \mapsto \{\overline{\pi}\} \end{bmatrix}, \begin{bmatrix} \mathtt{next} \mapsto \{\pi_2\} \\ \mathtt{rotation} \mapsto \varnothing, \ldots \end{bmatrix} \right\rangle .$$

Like $\alpha^{\mathcal{E}}_\tau$ (Section 5), also the map $\alpha^{\mathcal{ER}}_\tau$ is not necessarily onto.

Example 12. Let $\tau = [\mathtt{c} \mapsto \mathtt{circle}]$. From a $\mathtt{circle}$ is not possible to reach an object of type $\mathtt{angle}$. Then there is no $\sigma \in \Sigma_\tau$ such that $\alpha^{\mathcal{ER}}_\tau(\sigma)$ is equal to the abstract state $s = \langle [\mathtt{c} \mapsto \{\pi_3\}], [\mathtt{next} \mapsto \varnothing, \mathtt{rotation} \mapsto \{\pi_1\}, \ldots]\rangle$.

Hence, we define a map ρ which collects the *reachable* creation points from an abstract frame and memory, and a map ξ which forces to $\varnothing$ the fields of type class of the objects which have no reachable creation point.

Definition 16. *Let $\tau \in Typing$. We define $\rho_\tau : Frame^{\mathcal{ER}}_\tau \times Memory^{\mathcal{ER}} \mapsto \wp(\Pi)$ and $\xi_\tau : \{\bot\} \cup (Frame^{\mathcal{ER}}_\tau \times Memory^{\mathcal{ER}}) \mapsto \{\bot\} \cup (Frame^{\mathcal{ER}}_\tau \times Memory^{\mathcal{ER}})$ as $\rho_\tau(s) = \cup\{\rho^i_\tau(s) \mid i \geq 0\}$, where*

$$\rho^0_\tau(\langle\phi,\mu\rangle) = \varnothing$$
$$\rho^{i+1}_\tau(\langle\phi,\mu\rangle) = \{\pi \in \phi(v) \mid v \in \mathsf{dom}(\tau),\ \tau(v) \in \mathcal{K}\} \ \cup$$
$$\cup\, \{\pi \in \mu(f) \mid \pi' \in \rho^i_\tau(\langle\phi,\mu\rangle),\ f \in \mathsf{dom}(F(\pi')),\ F(\pi')(f) \in \mathcal{K}\}$$

and

$$\xi_\tau(\bot) = \bot$$
$$\xi_\tau(\langle\phi,\mu\rangle) = \begin{cases} \bot & \textit{if } \mathtt{this} \in \mathsf{dom}(\tau) \textit{ and } \phi(\mathtt{this}) = \varnothing \\ \langle\phi, \cup\{\mu|_{\mathsf{dom}(F(\pi))} \mid \pi \in \rho_\tau(\langle\phi,\mu\rangle)\} \cup \mathsf{init}(\overline{\tau})\rangle & \textit{otherwise.} \end{cases}$$

Example 13. In Example 12, we have $\rho_\tau(s) = \{\pi_3\}$ and hence

$$\xi_\tau(s) = \langle[\mathsf{c} \mapsto \{\pi_3\}], [\mathtt{next} \mapsto \varnothing, \mathtt{rotation} \mapsto \varnothing, \ldots]\rangle\ .$$

Lemma 3. *Let $\tau \in Typing$. The map ξ_τ is an lco.*

The map ξ_τ can be used to define $\mathsf{rng}(\alpha^{\mathcal{ER}}_\tau)$.

Lemma 4. *Let $\tau \in Typing$. Then $\mathsf{fp}(\xi_\tau) = \mathsf{rng}(\alpha^{\mathcal{ER}}_\tau)$.*

Lemma 4 allows us to assume that $\alpha^{\mathcal{ER}}_\tau : \wp(\Sigma_\tau) \mapsto \mathsf{fp}(\xi_\tau)$, and justifies the following definition.

Definition 17. *Let $\tau \in Typing$. We define $\mathcal{ER}_\tau = \mathsf{fp}(\xi_\tau)$, ordered by pointwise set-inclusion (with the assumption that $* \subseteq *$ and $\bot \subseteq x$ for every $x \in \mathcal{ER}_\tau$).*

Proposition 2. *Let $\tau \in Typing$. The map $\alpha^{\mathcal{ER}}_\tau$ is strict, additive and onto i.e., it is the abstraction map of a Galois insertion from $\wp(\Sigma_\tau)$ to $\mathcal{ER}_\tau$.*

We have explicitly calculated the optimal approximations induced by $\mathcal{ER}$ of all the concrete operations over states defined in [9]. We do not have space to fully describe them here. They are similar to those of the Palsberg and Schwartzbach's domain for *class analysis* [10] as formulated in [9]. However, $\mathcal{ER}$ observes the fields of just the reachable objects (Definition 15), while Palsberg and Schwartzbach observe the fields of all objects in memory. As an example, consider the operations $\mathsf{get\_var}^v$, which loads the value of the variable v in an accumulator called *res*, and $\mathsf{restrict}^{vs}$, which removes the variables in the set vs from the frame of the state. Their optimal approximations over $\mathcal{ER}$ are

$$\mathsf{get\_var}^v_\tau(\langle\phi,\mu\rangle) = \langle\phi[res \mapsto \phi(v)],\mu\rangle \qquad \mathsf{restrict}^{vs}_\tau(\langle\phi,\mu\rangle) = \xi_\tau(\langle\phi|_{-vs},\mu\rangle)\ .$$

In the case of $\mathsf{restrict}$, we remove the variables in vs from the abstract frame and, through ξ_τ, we force to $\varnothing$ the fields of type class of the objects which hence have no reachable creation point. Thus the result of restrict belongs to $\mathcal{ER}_{\tau|_{-vs}}$ (Definition 17).

We show now how an element $s \in \mathcal{E}$ can be *implemented* by an element of $\mathcal{ER}$. The idea is that every variable or field must be bound in $\mathcal{ER}$ to all those creation points in s compatible with its type.

Definition 18. *Let $\tau \in Typing$ and $s \subseteq \Pi$. We define $\vartheta_\tau(s) \in Frame_\tau^{\mathcal{ER}}$ such that, for every $v \in \mathsf{dom}(\tau)$,*

$$\vartheta_\tau(s)(v) = \begin{cases} * & \text{if } \tau(v) = int \\ \{\pi \in s \mid k(\pi) \le \tau(v)\} & \text{if } \tau(v) \in \mathcal{K}. \end{cases}$$

The implementation *$\theta_\tau(s) \in \mathcal{ER}_\tau$ of $s \in \mathcal{E}_\tau$ is $\theta_\tau(s) = \xi_\tau(\langle \vartheta_\tau(s), \vartheta_{\overline{\tau}}(s)\rangle)$.*

Example 14. Let τ be as in Figure 3 and $s = \{\overline{\pi}, \pi_1, \pi_2, \pi_3\} \in \mathcal{E}_\tau$ (Example 7). Then

$$\theta_\tau(s) = \left\langle \begin{bmatrix} \mathtt{f} \mapsto \{\pi_2, \pi_3\}, \mathtt{n} \mapsto \{\pi_2, \pi_3\} \\ \mathtt{out} \mapsto *, \mathtt{this} \mapsto \{\overline{\pi}\} \end{bmatrix}, \begin{bmatrix} \mathtt{next} \mapsto \{\pi_2, \pi_3\} \\ \mathtt{rotation} \mapsto \{\pi_1\}, \ldots \end{bmatrix} \right\rangle.$$

Proposition 3 proves the correctness of the implementation of Definition 18. It is based on the following result.

Lemma 5. *Let $\tau \in Typing$, $\sigma \in \Sigma_\tau$ and $s \in \mathcal{E}_\tau$. We have $\theta_\tau(s) \in \mathcal{ER}_\tau$. Moreover, we have $\alpha_\tau^{\mathcal{E}}(\sigma) \subseteq s$ if and only if $\alpha_\tau^{\mathcal{ER}}(\sigma) \subseteq \theta_\tau(s)$.*

Proposition 3. *Let $\tau \in Typing$, $s \in \mathcal{E}_\tau$ and $\gamma_\tau^{\mathcal{E}}$ and $\gamma_\tau^{\mathcal{ER}}$ be the concretisation maps induced by the abstraction maps of Definitions 9 and 15, respectively. We have $\gamma_\tau^{\mathcal{E}}(s) = \gamma_\tau^{\mathcal{ER}}(\theta_\tau(s))$ and hence $\gamma_\tau^{\mathcal{E}}(\mathcal{E}_\tau) \subseteq \gamma_\tau^{\mathcal{ER}}(\mathcal{ER}_\tau)$.*

Proof. By Lemma 5, for every $s \in \mathcal{E}_\tau$ we have [5]

$$\gamma_\tau^{\mathcal{E}}(s) = \{\sigma \in \Sigma_\tau \mid \alpha_\tau^{\mathcal{E}}(\sigma) \subseteq s\} = \{\sigma \in \Sigma_\tau \mid \alpha_\tau^{\mathcal{ER}}(\sigma) \subseteq \theta_\tau(s)\} = \gamma_\tau^{\mathcal{ER}}(\theta_\tau(s)).$$

The inclusion proved in Proposition 3 is strict, in general.

Example 15. Let τ be as in Figure 3. By Example 7 we have $\#\mathcal{E}_\tau \le 2^4$ and $\#\mathcal{ER}_\tau > \#Frame_\tau^{\mathcal{ER}} \ge 2^4$.

7 Discussion

Abstract domains for escape analysis have been developed for both functional and object-oriented languages. For functional languages, the escape analysis first defined in [11] was later made more efficient [6] and then extended to some imperative constructs and applied to very large programs [2]. For object-oriented languages, there have been a number of approaches to escape analysis [3, 4, 7, 8, 12, 15]. In [12], a *lifetime analysis* propagates the *sources* of data structures.

In [3] integer *contexts* are used to specify the part of a data structure which can escape. Both [4] and [15] use *connection graphs* to represent the concrete memory although, in [15] these graphs are slightly more concrete than those used in [4]. In [7], a program is translated to a constraint, whose solution is the set of *escaping* variables. In [8], an escape analysis for object-oriented languages was defined on the *escape property* $\mathcal{E}$ and shown to be sometimes more precise than these other escape analyses.

In this paper, we have refined the escape property $\mathcal{E}$ defined in [8] to give the domain $\mathcal{ER}$ and derive the abstract analyser directly from the abstract domain. Observe that the relation between the refined domain $\mathcal{ER}$ and $\mathcal{E}$ is similar to that between the Palsberg and Schwartzbach's class analysis [9, 10] and the *rapid type analysis* [1] although, while all objects stored in memory are considered in [1, 9, 10], only those actually reachable from some variable or field are considered by the domains $\mathcal{E}$ and $\mathcal{ER}$ (Definitions 9 and 15).

The escape analysis using the domain $\mathcal{ER}$ has been defined and implemented for the simple object-oriented language given in [14]. We are currently generalising the semantics to the Java bytecode. We will then be able to apply $\mathcal{ER}$ to the Java bytecode and to provide an experimental evaluation.

References

[1] D. F. Bacon and P. F. Sweeney. Fast Static Analysis of C++ Virtual Function Calls. In *Proc. of OOPSLA'96*, volume 31(10) of *ACM SIGPLAN Notices*, pages 324–341, New York, 1996. ACM Press.

[2] B. Blanchet. Escape Analysis: Correctness Proof, Implementation and Experimental Results. In *25th ACM SIGPLAN-SIGACT Symposium of Principles of Programming Languages (POPL'98)*, pages 25–37, San Diego, CA, USA, January 1998. ACM Press.

[3] B. Blanchet. Escape Analysis for Object-Oriented Languages: Application to Java. In *1999 ACM SIGPLAN Conference on Object-Oriented Programming Systems, Languages and Applications (OOPSLA'99)*, volume 34(1) of *SIGPLAN Notices*, pages 20–34, Denver, Colorado, USA, November 1999.

[4] J.-D. Choi, M. Gupta, M. J. Serrano, V. C. Sreedhar, and S. P. Midkiff. Escape Analysis for Java. In *1999 ACM SIGPLAN Conference on Object-Oriented Programming Systems, Languages and Applications (OOPSLA'99)*, volume 34(10) of *SIGPLAN Notices*, pages 1–19, Denver, Colorado, USA, November 1999.

[5] P. Cousot and R. Cousot. Abstract Interpretation: A Unified Lattice Model for Static Analysis of Programs by Construction or Approximation of Fixpoints. In *Proc. of POPL'77*, pages 238–252, 1977.

[6] A. Deutsch. On the Complexity of Escape Analysis. In *24th ACM SIGPLAN-SIGACT Symposium on Principles of Programming Languages (POPL'97)*, pages 358–371, Paris, France, January 1997. ACM Press.

[7] D. Gay and B. Steensgaard. Fast Escape Analysis and Stack Allocation for Object-Based Programs. In D. A. Watt, editor, *Compiler Construction, 9th International Conference, (CC'00)*, volume 1781 of *Lecture Notes in Computer Science*, pages 82–93, Berlin, Germany, March 2000. Springer-Verlag.

[8] P. M. Hill and F. Spoto. A Foundation of Escape Analysis. Submitted for publication. Available from `http://www.sci.univr.it/~spoto/papers.html`, 2002.

[9] T. Jensen and F. Spoto. Class Analysis of Object-Oriented Programs through Abstract Interpretation. In F. Honsell and M. Miculan, editors, *Proc. of FOSSACS 2001*, volume 2030 of *Lecture Notes in Computer Science*, pages 261–275, Genova, Italy, April 2001. Springer-Verlag.

[10] J. Palsberg and M. I. Schwartzbach. Object-Oriented Type Inference. In *Proc. of OOPSLA'91*, volume 26(11) of *ACM SIGPLAN Notices*, pages 146–161. ACM Press, November 1991.

[11] Y. G. Park and B. Goldberg. Escape Analysis on Lists. In *ACM SIGPLAN'92 Conference on Programming Language Design and Implementation*, volume 27(7) of *SIGPLAN Notices*, pages 116–127, San Francisco, California, USA, June 1992.

[12] C. Ruggieri and T. P. Murtagh. Lifetime Analysis of Dynamically Allocated Objects. In *15th ACM Symposium on Principles of Programming Languages (POPL'88)*, pages 285–293, San Diego, California, USA, January 1988.

[13] F. Spoto. The LOOP Analyser. `http://www.sci.univr.it/~spoto/loop/`.

[14] F. Spoto. Watchpoint Semantics: A Tool for Compositional and Focussed Static Analyses. In P. Cousot, editor, *Proc. of the Static Analysis Symposium, SAS'01*, volume 2126 of *Lecture Notes in Computer Science*, pages 127–145, Paris, July 2001. Springer-Verlag.

[15] J. Whaley and M. C. Rinard. Compositional Pointer and Escape Analysis for Java Programs. In *1999 ACM SIGPLAN Conference on Object-Oriented Programming Systems, Languages and Applications (OOPSLA'99)*, volume 34(1) of *SIGPLAN Notices*, pages 187–206, Denver, Colorado, USA, November 1999.

Storage Size Reduction by In-place Mapping of Arrays

Remko Tronçon[1], Maurice Bruynooghe[1], Gerda Janssens[1], and Francky Catthoor[2]

[1] Katholieke Universiteit Leuven, Department of Computer Science
Celestijnenlaan 200A, B-3001 Heverlee, Belgium
{remko,maurice,gerda}@cs.kuleuven.ac.be
[2] IMEC/DESICS, Kapeldreef 75, B-3001 Heverlee, Belgium
catthoor@imec.be

Abstract. Programs for embedded multimedia applications typically manipulate several large multi-dimensional arrays. The energy consumption per access increases with their size; the access to these large arrays is responsible for a substantial part of the power consumption. In this paper, an analysis is developed to compute a bounding box for the elements in the array that are simultaneously in use. The size of the original array can be reduced to the size of the bounding box and accesses to it can be redirected using modulo operations on the original indices. This substantially reduces the size of the memories and the power consumption of accessing them.

1 Introduction

The design of embedded systems starts with code in a high level programming language (typical C) implementing the algorithms required by the processing of the input signals received by these systems (e.g., video images, ...). Typical for the involved algorithms is that they manipulate large multi-dimensional arrays. A direct translation of this code in an embedded system results in a design with large memory banks. A large share of the total cost and power consumption of such designs is due to data transfer and storage.

The DESICS group at IMEC has developed a Data Transfer and Storage Exploration (DTSE) methodology[4] that aims to reduce the memory requirements and data transfer costs of such designs. In a first step, the program is brought into a single assignment form[9] where each memory cell is written at most once. Typically, this further increases the memory usage of the program (as extra dimensions are introduced for arrays with elements that are written several times). However, this form simplifies the dependencies between read and write statements, and hence facilitates transformations of loop nests that bring consumers of data closer to the producers and shortens the time span between the creation (write event) of a data element and its last consumption (read event). These transformations reduce the number of data elements that are in-use (live) at any time in the program. Moreover, all introduced overhead is afterwards

A. Cortesi (Ed.): VMCAI 2002, LNCS 2294, pp. 167–181, 2002.
© Springer-Verlag Berlin Heidelberg 2002

```
for (i=0; i =< 4; i++)
  for (j=0; j =< 9; j++)
      if (j >= 2)
          /* P_1 */
          A[i][j] = ... ;
      /* P_2 */
      if (i>=2 && j >= 2 && j =< 8)
          ... = A[i][j] + A[i-2][j+1];
```

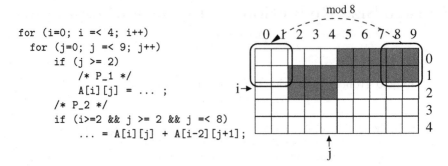

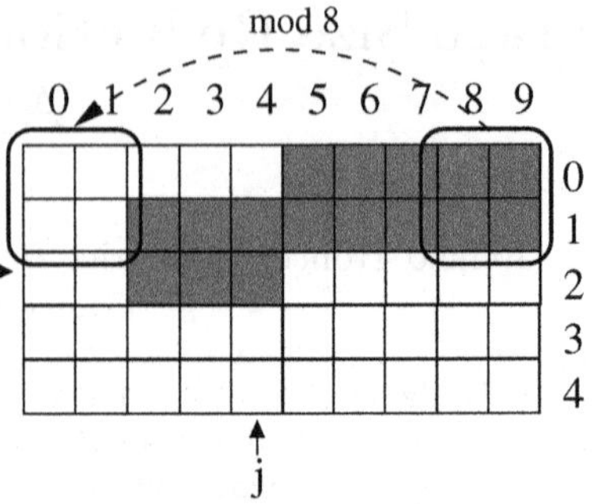

Fig. 1. Live elements of an array. The picture on the right indicates for program point P_2 what elements of the array contain a value that will be used in the future, given the current values of i and j.

removed again, so even in the worst case no penalty is introduced. In practical cases, the more explicit search space allows better solutions than what can be achieved using the multiple assignment code.

To reduce the size of the arrays, De Greef[7, 5, 6] considers all possible linearizations of an array (for an n-dimensional array there are $n!$ orderings; moreover, elements in a given dimension can be placed in increasing or in decreasing order, hence there are $2^n n!$ possible linearizations) and computes what is at any time the largest distance in the linearized array between two live elements. This distance for the chosen linearization (+1) is then the size required for the array.

In this paper we develop a different approach to approximate the optimal size of a n-dimensional array. In a first phase we compute in each program point a description of the data elements of the array that are live (they contain a value that will be read in the future) as a set of areas, where each area is described by a conjunction of equality ($=$) and inequality ($\leq$) constraints. The purpose of the second phase is to compute values $(w_1, \ldots, w_n)$ that can be used as operands in modulo operations that redirect all accesses to the array; i.e., an access $A[exp_1] \ldots [exp_n]$ is replaced by an access $A[exp_1 \ mod \ w_1] \ldots [exp_n \ mod \ w_n]$. This mapping has to preserve the correctness of the program, i.e., two distinct elements live in the same program point should not be mapped by the modulo operations to the same element. The values $(w_1, \ldots, w_n)$ (the window or bounding box) determine the size required for storing the array.

A small example illustrating our approach is depicted in Fig. 1. If we look at the program point P_2, we can see that only a part of the array is in-use. The part is determined by the current values of surrounding iterators i and j. As can be seen in the illustration, if we apply 'mod 8' in the second dimension of all the accesses, the last 2 elements are mapped back to the first 2 (empty) locations. The same can be applied for the first dimension, this time with 'mod 2'. So, we can replace each access `A[exp₁][exp₂]` by `A[exp₁ mod 2][exp₂ mod 8]`, resulting in a 2×8 (=16) element array, instead of the original 50 element array. Note that, if we linearize our array first, we can only apply 'mod 20', because the distance between first and last live element is at least 19.

Assumptions. We apply our transformation on programs written in a subset of the C language. This subset only allows assignments, `if-then-else` statements, and `for`-loops. Additionally, we assume that the code is in accordance with the following requirements:

- The program is in *single assignment* form, i.e., each array element is written at most once (it can be read several times).
- The index expressions used in the array accesses, the conditions of the `if-then-else` statements and the lower and upper bounds of the iterators in the `for`-loops are linear in the iterators of the surrounding `for`-loops[1].
- Array elements that are assigned a value, will also be read in the future.

While these assumptions are quite strong, programs produced by applying the DTSE methodology[4] meet them. In section 6, we will reconsider them.

Organisation of paper. Section 3 describes how to compute the live elements in each program point and discusses the complexity. In section 4 it is described how to compute the size of the window. Section 5 reports on the results obtained with a prototype in the CLP(Q) extension of SICStus Prolog. Finally, section 6 discusses possible extensions and related work.

2 Preprocessing

In a very first step of our approach, we perform some transformations on the source program in order to simplify the code.

- As only one array at a time is analysed, only the `for`-loop statements and the statements that access the array of interest are kept.
- Some transformations are applied to simplify the structure of the `if`-statements. This includes hoisting of accesses common to the `then` and `else` branches out of the `if`-statement and replacement of nested `if`-statements by simple ones.

These steps decrease the number of program points and hence the cost of the further analysis. Note that the final program can be transformed into a program consisting only of `for`-loops, and assignments annotated with the conditions under which the assignment is executed, e.g.,

```
for (...)
    ⟨Cond1⟩ : A[expi][expj] = ;
    for (...)
        ⟨Cond2⟩ : A[expk][expl] = A[expm][expn];
...
```

[1] Of the form $c_0 + c_1 i_1 + \ldots + c_k i_k$ with $c_0, \ldots, c_k$ constants and $i_1, \ldots, i_k$ the iterators of the surrounding `for`-loops.

$P_0^b \rightarrow W_0^b = \emptyset, R_0^b = R_0^{'b}$
for $(i_1 = l_1;\ i_1 \leq u_1;\ i_1{+}{+}\ )$
$\quad P_1^b \rightarrow W_1^b(ic_1) = W_0^b \cup W_1^{'b}(ic_1), R_1^b(ic_1) = R_0^a \cup R_1^{'b}(ic_1)$
$\quad$ **for** $(i_2 = l_2;\ i_2 \leq u_2;\ i_2{+}{+})$
$\quad\quad P_2^b \rightarrow W_2^b(ic_1, ic_2) = W_1^b(ic_1) \cup W_2^{'b}(ic_1, ic_2),$
$\quad\quad\quad R_2^b(ic_1, ic_2) = R_1^a(ic_1) \cup R_2^{'b}(ic_1, ic_2)$
$\quad\quad \ldots$
$\quad\quad$ **for** $(i_m = l_m;\ i_m \leq u_m;\ i_m{+}{+})$
$\quad\quad\quad P_m^b \rightarrow W_m^b(ic_1, \ldots, ic_m) = W_{m-1}^b(ic_1, \ldots, ic_{m-1}) \cup W_m^{'b}(ic_1, \ldots, ic_m),$
$\quad\quad\quad\quad R_m^b(ic_1, \ldots, ic_m) = R_{m-1}^a(ic_1, \ldots, ic_{m-1}) \cup R_m^{'b}(ic_1, \ldots, ic_m)$
$\quad\quad\quad \langle Cond \rangle$ **A:** $\mathrm{A}[exp_1^w][exp_2^w]\ldots[exp_n^w] = \mathrm{A}[exp_1^r][exp_2^r]\ldots[exp_n^r]$
$\quad\quad\quad P_m^a \rightarrow W_m^a(ic_1, \ldots, ic_m) = W_m^b(ic_1, \ldots, ic_{m-1}) \cup W_m^{'a}(ic_1, \ldots, ic_m),$
$\quad\quad\quad\quad R_m^a(ic_1, \ldots, ic_m) = R_{m-1}^a(ic_1, \ldots, ic_{m-1}) \cup R_m^{'a}(ic_1, \ldots, ic_m)$
$\quad\quad$ **end for**
$\quad\quad \ldots$
$\quad\quad P_2^a \rightarrow W_2^a(ic_1, ic_2) = W_1^b(ic_1) \cup W_2^{'a}(ic_1, ic_2),$
$\quad\quad\quad R_2^a(ic_1, ic_2) = R_1^a(ic_1) \cup R_2^{'a}(ic_1, ic_2)$
$\quad$ **end for**
$\quad P_1^a \rightarrow W_1^a(ic_1) = W_0^b \cup W_1^{'a}(ic_1), R_1^a(ic_1) = R_0^a \cup R_1^{'a}(ic_1)$
end for
$P_0^a \rightarrow W_0^a = W_0^{'a}, R_0^a = \emptyset$

Fig. 2. Schematical representation of a program with one read and one write operation **A**, under condition $\langle Cond \rangle$.

The assignments may contain an empty left-hand side or right-hand side.

3 Liveness Analysis

In this section we describe how to compute for each program point the sets containing the elements that are live for a given array. As explained in the introduction, elements are *live* or *in-use* in a program point if they have been written when control reaches the program point and will be read later on. Clearly, for a program point inside a nest of `for`-loops, which elements are live depends on the current values of the iterators of the surrounding `for`-loops.

3.1 Written Elements

Past Iteration Spaces. To compute the written elements due to an assignment labelled A, we first determine for each program point P_i the *past iteration space* of the assignment A. The past iteration space defines the set of iterations for which the statement A has been executed given that control is in P_i and given the values of the surrounding iterators. In the example of Figure 1, the past iteration space in P_1 will be a 2-dimensional set of points (depending on i_c and j_c) of the form

$$PI_1(i_c, j_c) = \{(x, y) \mid \ldots\}$$

where $(x, y) \in PI_1(i_c, j_c)$, means: if the current value of iterator i is i_c, and the current value of j is j_c, then A has been executed in the iteration where i was x and j was y. We will represent these past iteration spaces by (parameterized) *integral polyhedra.*

Definition 1 (Integral Polyhedron). *An integral polyhedron is the set of solutions to a finite system of linear inequalities on integer valued variables. Equivalently, the intersection of a finite number of linear half-spaces in* $\mathbb{Z}^n$.

Note that an n-dimensional parametrized polyhedron with 2 parameters $PI(i_c, j_c)$ can always be represented by a normal $n+2$ dimensional polyhedron, by taking the parameters i_c and j_c extra dimensions. In the example, PI_1 then is defined as

$$PI_1 = \{(x, y, i_c, j_c) \mid \ldots\}$$

We now define the past iteration spaces for the basic case of 1 assignment (and its condition) surrounded by m `for`-loops. With m surrounding `for`-loops, we can distinguish $2m+2$ different past iteration spaces that can be associated with the program points $P^b_0, \ldots, P^b_m, P^a_m, P^a_0$ as shown in Figure 2, i.e., P^b_0 is the first program point, the program point $P^b_k (k > 0)$ is the first program point of the kth `for`-loop, P^a_m is the first program point after the assignment, and $P^a_k (k < m)$ is the first program point after exiting the $(k+1)^{\text{th}}$ `for`-loop (in other program points, the past iteration space is identical to that of the preceding program point in the schema of Figure 2). We use $ic_1, \ldots, ic_m$ as variables denoting the current values of respectively the iterators $i_1, \ldots, i_m$. Note that l_k and u_k are respectively the lower and upper bound of the `for`-loop with iterator i_k[2]

First we define the iterator spaces PI^b_k associated with the points P^b_k. With *Cond* the condition under which the assignment is executed, we define:

$$
\begin{aligned}
PI^b_0 &\equiv \emptyset \\
PI^b_1(ic_1) &\equiv PI^b_0 \cup \{(j_1, \ldots, j_m) \mid \underline{l_1 \le j_1 < ic_1} \wedge l_2 \le j_2 \le u_2 \wedge \\
&\qquad \ldots \wedge l_m \le j_m \le u_m \wedge Cond\,\} \\
PI^b_2(ic_1, ic_2) &\equiv PI^b_1(ic_1) \cup \{(j_1, \ldots, j_m) \mid j_1 = ic_1 \wedge \underline{l_2 \le j_2 < ic_2} \wedge \\
&\qquad l_3 \le j_3 \le ic_3 \wedge \ldots \wedge l_m \le j_m \le u_m \wedge Cond\,\} \\
&\ \vdots \\
PI^b_k(ic_1, \ldots, ic_k) &\equiv PI^b_{k-1}(ic_1, \ldots, ic_{k-1}) \cup \{(j_1, \ldots, j_m) \mid
\end{aligned}
$$

[2] Recall that the lower and upper bound are a linear combination of the surrounding current iterator values $ic_1, \ldots, ic_{k-1}$.

$$\begin{aligned}
&j_1 = ic_1 \wedge \ldots \wedge j_{k-1} = ic_{k-1} \wedge \\
&\underline{l_k \le j_k < ic_k} \wedge l_{k+1} \le j_{k+1} \le u_{k+1} \wedge \ldots \wedge \\
&l_m \le j_m \le u_m \wedge Cond \;\} \;(\forall 2 \le k \le m)
\end{aligned}$$

$$\vdots$$

$$\begin{aligned}
PI^b_m(ic_1, \ldots, ic_m) \equiv PI_{m-1}(ic_1, \ldots, ic_{m-1}) \cup \{(j_1, \ldots, j_m) \mid \\
j_1 = ic_1 \wedge \ldots \wedge j_{m-1} = ic_{m-1} \wedge \\
l_m \le j_m < u_m \wedge Cond\}
\end{aligned}$$

This is equivalent to

$$PI^b_k(ic_1, \ldots, ic_k) \equiv \{(j_1, \ldots, j_k) \mid (j_1, \ldots, j_k) <_l (ic_1, \ldots, ic_k) \wedge Cond\}$$

where $<_l$ represents the *lexicographic order* on tuples. If *Cond* is a disjunction, then these sets fall apart in multiple polyhedra. Note that the current iterator values ic_j by which these polyhedra are parametrized are constrained by the bounds l_j and u_j; these constraints are omitted.

These definitions can be explained as follows: in P^b_0, statement A has not been executed at all (i.e., $PI^b_0 \equiv \emptyset$). In P^b_1, A has been considered for execution for iterator values $(j_1, \ldots, j_n)$ such that j_1 precedes the current iterator ic_1 (as the statement has not yet been considered for $j_1 = ic_1$ when control is in P^b_1). As for the other iterator values $j_2, \ldots, j_m$, the statement is considered (and executed if *Cond* is true) for all possible iterations within the bounds (i.e., $\forall k : 2 \le k \le m\ ,\ l_k \le j_k \le u_k$). This gives the above formula for $PI^b_1(ic_1)$. More generally, for program point P^b_k $(1 \le k \le m)$, the statement has been executed for the same values as in program point P^b_{k-1}, and in addition for a number of iterations where $j_1 = ic_1, \ldots, j_{k-1} = ic_{k-1}$, namely the iterations of the kth `for`-loop preceding its current iteration ic_k (hence $l_k \le j_k < ic_k$); for those iterations, all values for $j_{k+1}, \ldots, j_m$ within their respective bounds $[l_{k+1}, u_{k+1}], \ldots, [l_m, u_m]$ are considered, giving the formula for $PI^b_k(ic_1, \ldots, ic_n)$.

For the program points $P^a_k (k > 0)$, the difference with P^b_k is that the statement has also been considered (and executed if *Cond* is true) for the iterations with $j_1 = ic_1, \ldots, j_k = ic_k$ (and all possible values for the iterators $j_{k+1}, \ldots, j_m$). This change in the second component of the definition results in:

$$\begin{aligned}
PI^a_m(ic_1, \ldots, ic_m) \equiv PI^b_{m-1}(ic_1, \ldots, ic_{m-1}) \cup \{(j_1, \ldots, j_m) \mid \\
j_1 = ic_1 \wedge j_2 = ic_2 \;\wedge \ldots \wedge l_m \le j_m \le ic_m \wedge Cond \;\}
\end{aligned}$$

$$\vdots$$

$$\begin{aligned}
PI^a_k(ic_1, \ldots, ic_k) \equiv PI^b_{k-1}(ic_0, \ldots, ic_{k-1}) \cup \{(j_1, \ldots, j_k) \mid \\
j_1 = ic_1 \wedge \ldots \wedge j_{k-1} = ic_{k-1} \wedge l_k \le j_k \le ic_k \wedge \\
l_{k+1} \le j_{k+1} \le u_{k+1} \wedge \ldots \wedge\; l_m \le j_m \le u_k \wedge Cond \;\}
\end{aligned}$$

$$\vdots$$

$$\begin{aligned}
PI^a_0 \equiv \{(j_1, \ldots, j_m) \mid l_1 \le j_1 \le u_1 \wedge l_2 \le j_2 \le u_2 \wedge \\
\ldots \wedge\; l_m \le j_m \le u_m \wedge Cond \;\}
\end{aligned}$$

For $k = 0$, the statement is considered for all iterations of all loops.

For example, for the first assignment of Figure 1, we obtain:

$$\begin{aligned}
PI_0^b &\equiv \emptyset \\
PI_1^b(i_c) &\equiv \{(i,j) \mid 0 \le i < i_c \wedge 0 \le j \le 9\} \\
PI_2^b(i_c, j_c) &\equiv \{(i,j) \mid 0 \le i < i_c \wedge 0 \le j \le 9\} \cup \\
&\quad\; \{(i,j) \mid i = i_c \wedge 0 \le j < j_c\} \\
PI_2^a(i_c, j_c) &\equiv \{(i,j) \mid 0 \le i < i_c \wedge 0 \le j \le 9\} \cup \\
&\quad\; \{(i,j) \mid i = i_c \wedge 0 \le j \le j_c\} \\
PI_1^a(i_c) &\equiv \{(i,j) \mid 0 \le i \le i_c \wedge 0 \le j \le 9\} \\
PI_0^a(i_c) &\equiv \{(i,j) \mid 0 \le i \le 4 \wedge 0 \le j \le 9\}
\end{aligned}$$

We now sketch how past iteration spaces can be computed in two passes. In the first pass, we add an iteration space for the current iterator values in the program point following assignment. I.e., in P_m^a, we add the iterator space

$$\{(j_1, \ldots, j_m) \mid j_1 = ic_1 \wedge \ldots \wedge j_m = ic_m \wedge Cond\}$$

Moreover, we propagate iteration spaces from program point to program point. This is trivial but for a program point P_k^a following the exit of `for`-loop $k+1$. We must eliminate the parameter ic_{k+1} in $j_{k+1} = ic_{k+1}$. Given the bounds l_{k+1} and u_{k+1} on ic_{k+1}, projecting out ic_{k+1} results in the constraint $l_{k+1} \le j_{k+1} \le u_{k+1}$. Doing this projection at the exits of all `for`-loops, at the end of the first iteration we have $(\forall k)$

$$\begin{aligned}
PI_k^{*b} &\equiv \emptyset \\
PI_k^{*a} &\equiv \{(j_1, \ldots, j_n) \mid j_1 = ic_1 \wedge \ldots \wedge j_k = ic_k \wedge \\
&\qquad l_{k+1} \le j_{k+1} \le u_{k+1} \wedge \ldots \wedge l_m \le j_m \le u_m\}
\end{aligned}$$

Note that this polyhedron covers the difference between PI_k^b and PI_k^a.

In the second iteration, upon entry of a for loop relevant for the statement of interest, the standard propagation from the previous program point takes care of the component PI_{k-1}^b in PI_k^b. In addition, we use the value of P_k^a computed during the first iteration for constructing the second component of P_k^b. This is simply achieved by replacing $j_k = ic_k$ by $l_k \le j_k < ic_k$. In the points P_k^a following the assignment, the projected polyhedron with the constraint $l_k \le j_k < ic_k$ can be merged with the polyhedron from the first iteration (having the constraint $j_k = ic_k$) to obtain $l_k \le j_k \le ic_k$. After this second iteration, all program points are annotated with the iteration spaces of all assignments.

Written Elements. Using the past iteration spaces, it is easy to describe which elements of the array have been written due to assignment A. Since indexing an array is simply a transformation from iterator space into 'array space', applying the same transformation on the past iteration spaces results in the elements that have been written in past iterations. Hence, we apply the following transformation t on all past iteration spaces (can be performed during the second iteration of the iteration space computation)

$$t : \mathrm{Z}^m \rightarrow \mathrm{Z}^n : (x_1, \ldots, x_m) \rightarrow (exp_1, \ldots, exp_n)$$

where m is the number of surrounding iterators, n is the number of dimensions of A, and $exp_1, \ldots, exp_n$ are the linear index expressions (in function of $x_1, \ldots, x_n$) used in the assignment. In terms of PI, this means (as illustrated in Figure 2) that

$$\begin{aligned}
&W_0^b \equiv \emptyset \\
&W_k^b \equiv t(PI_k^b) \equiv t(PI_{k-1}^b \cup PI_k^{'b}) \equiv W_{k-1}^b \cup W_k^{'b} \\
&W_k^a \equiv t(PI_k^a) \equiv t(PI_{k-1}^b \cup PI_k^{'a}) \equiv W_{k-1}^b \cup W_k^{'a}
\end{aligned}$$

For example, an expression `A[2*i+j]` would map a 2-dimensional iteration space

$$\begin{aligned}
I(i_c, j_c) \equiv \{(i,j) \mid 0 \leq i < i_c \wedge 0 \leq j \leq 9\} \\
\cup \{(i,j) \mid i = i_c \wedge 0 \leq j \leq j_c\}
\end{aligned}$$

to a 1-dimensional array space

$$\begin{aligned}
W(i_c, j_c) \equiv \{(x) \mid x = 2 * i + j \wedge 0 \leq i < i_c \wedge 0 \leq j \leq 9\} \\
\cup \{(x) \mid x = 2 * i + j \wedge i = i_c \wedge 0 \leq j \leq j_c\}
\end{aligned}$$

3.2 To Be Read Elements

The analysis to determine which elements will be read in the future is very similar to the previous one. Instead of computing the past iteration spaces, we use the *future iteration spaces*, describing for which iterations A still has to be executed (hence now P_k^b has a union of polyhedra that is larger than the corresponding one in P_k^a, namely the one involving the current iterator ic_k.

Computing the future iteration spaces can be done by 'reversing' the program, and doing the past iteration space analysis. Reversing the program not only means reversing the program points, but also reversing the bounds in the expressions. For example, the first (relevant) program point in this analysis would be P_1^a, in which FI_1^a would become

$$\begin{aligned}
FI_1^a(ic_1) \equiv \{(j_1, \ldots, j_m) \mid \underline{ic_1 < j_1 \leq u_1} \wedge l_2 \leq j_2 \leq u_2 \wedge \\
\ldots \wedge\ l_m \leq j_m \leq u_m \wedge Cond\ \}
\end{aligned}$$

Again, by applying t on the future iteration spaces, we obtain all elements of the array that will be read later on.

After these steps, we obtain for every program point a set of polyhedra describing all the elements of the array that have been written, and a set of polyhedra describing all elements that will be read. Note that the polyhedra of written elements are disjoint when *Cond* does not contain overlapping disjunctions (because of the single assignment property of our code), but that the 'to be read' polyhedra may overlap due to multiple reads of the same element.

3.3 Live Elements

Finally, the elements that are live in a program point have to be computed. Doing so requires to intersect the set of all written elements with the set of all elements to be read. This means intersecting the union of 'written' polyhedra with the union of the 'to be read' polyhedra we computed in the previous section, which in turn means taking the pairwise intersection of all polyhedra of 'written' elements with all polyhedra of 'to be read' elements.
Typically, many sets are empty for all values of the current iterators within their bounds (e.g., $l_k \leq j_k < ic_k \wedge ic_k < j_k \leq u_k$). It is important for the complexity of the window computation to remove them as soon as possible.

3.4 Properties

With the conventions of Figure 2, one can infer from the descriptions of the iteration spaces that $W_j^{'b} \subseteq W_j^{'a}$, $W_{j+k}^b \subseteq W_j^b$, and $W_{j+k}^a \subseteq W_j^a$. Similarly, $R_j^{'a} \subseteq R_j^{'b}$, $R_{j+k}^b \subseteq R_j^b$, and $R_{j+k}^a \subseteq R_j^a$. These inequalities could be used to reduce the number of emptiness tests. For example, if the set R_0^b of some written element has an empty intersection with the set W_0^a, then $R_j^* \cap W_k^? = \emptyset$ in all program points (with $*$ and $?$ either a or b).

3.5 Complexity

For a write statement at depth m there are (at most) $2m$ different sets $W_i^{'*}$ and similar, for a read statement at depth n, there are (at most) $2n$ different sets $R_j^{'*}$. Hence the number of different constraints $W_i^{'*} \cap R_j^{'*}$ is bounded by $4nm$ and the total number of emptiness tests by $4d^2rw$ with d the maximal nesting of `for`-loops, w the number of writes and r the number of reads.

4 Computing the Window

As explained in the introduction, we want to find values for a window $\boldsymbol{W} = (w_1, \ldots, w_n)$ such that $w_1 * \ldots * w_n$ is minimal and that replacing all array accesses $A[exp_1] \ldots [exp_n]$ by $A[exp_1 \ mod \ w_1] \ldots [exp_n \ mod \ w_n]$ preserves the correctness of the program. Correctness is preserved if there is no program point with distinct live elements $(x_1, \ldots, x_n)$ and $(y_1, \ldots, y_n)$ such that $x_1 \ mod \ w_1 = y_1 \ mod \ w_1 \wedge \ldots \wedge x_n \ mod \ w_n = y_n \ mod \ w_n$. To solve this problem, we proceed in two steps: first we compute an underestimation for $\boldsymbol{W}$, and then we search for an optimal solution.

As a result of the preceding liveness analysis, we can assume that every program point P_j is annotated with a set of polyhedra $\{L_{j,1}(ic_1, \ldots, ic_j), \ldots, L_{j,n_j}(ic_1, \ldots, ic_j)\}$ where the integer solutions of $L_{j,k}(ic_1, \ldots, ic_j)$, a conjunction of constraints, specify a set of live array elements. Note that $ic_1, \ldots, ic_j$ are the current values of the iterators surrounding the program point P_j. For simplicity of notation we include here all surrounding iterators in the parameter list, though not all live areas depend on all parameters. When solving the constraint problems below, it is important to take into account the bounds on the current iterators $(l_1 \leq ic_1 \leq u_1, \ldots)$.

Underestimation for w_i. To compute the underestimation w'_i for w_i, we start with $w'_i = 1$ and iterate over all areas $L_{j,k}(ic_1, \ldots, ic_j)$ until w'_i is a plausible solution for all of them. By the latter, we mean that by applying mod w'_i in the ith dimension of $L_{j,k}$, no 2 elements are mapped onto the same element. This is equivalent to the following set having no solution:

$$\begin{cases} (x_{1,1}, \ldots, x_{1,i-1}, x_{1,i}, x_{1,i+1}, \ldots, x_{1,n}) \in L_{j,k}(ic_1, \ldots, ic_j) \\ (x_{1,1}, \ldots, x_{1,i-1}, x_{2,i}, x_{1,i+1}, \ldots, x_{1,n}) \in L_{j,k}(ic_1, \ldots, ic_j) \\ x_{1,i} \bmod w'_i = x_{2,i} \bmod w'_i \\ x_{1,i} \neq x_{2,i} \end{cases}$$

When some $L_{j,k}(ic_1, \ldots, ic_j)$ violates the condition, then w'_i is incremented in steps of 1 until the test succeeds. After iterating over all polyhedra $L_{j,k}(ic_1, \ldots, ic_j)$, our final underestimate may still create conflicts in some areas. Indeed, one can construct areas with holes such that the test succeeds for some value w'_i but not for $w'_i + 1$. As it is an inexpensive test, one can better continue until the test succeeds for all areas $L_{j,k}(ic_1, \ldots, ic_j)$. For our benchmarks however, the value obtained at the end of the first iteration is always the final lower bound.

The search for a solution. In the last step we check whether the underestimate $(w'_1, \ldots, w'_n)$ is a correct window in all program points. If not, we adjust our underestimate until it is. To check a program point P_j and to adjust the lower bound if needed, we consider a sequence of n tests for each pair of areas in the live set of the program point (including pairs of the same area). If all succeed, the underestimate is correct for the pair at hand; if the ith test fails, failure is due to a conflict involving index i and w'_i is increased by 1. The ith test on $L_{j,k}(ic_1, \ldots, ic_j)$ and $L_{j,l}(ic_1, \ldots, ic_j)$ verifies that the constraint S_i has no solution[3]:

$$S_i \equiv \begin{cases} (x_{1,1}, \ldots, x_{1,n}) \in L_{j,k}(ic_1, \ldots, ic_j) \\ (x_{2,1}, \ldots, x_{2,n}) \in L_{j,l}(ic_1, \ldots, ic_j) \\ \forall m \leq i : x_{1,m} \bmod w'_m = x_{2,m} \bmod w'_m \\ \exists m \leq i : x_{1,m} \neq x_{2,m} \end{cases}$$

The above approach does not guarantee an optimal solution. Using a different order for the dimensions of the array, one may find a conflict for a different dimension. However, one can expect that it results in a tight upper bound. Eventually, one could search for better solutions in the space between the original lower bound and the current best solution. For the benchmarks we have, the lower bound is often a solution. If not, only one dimension is adjusted to obtain the optimal solution.

[3] The test must also be performed for $k = l$.

Benchmark	*#A*	*Mem. Bef.*	*Mem. Aft.*	*Mem. DG1*	*Mem. DG2*	*Time Liveness*	*Time Window*
`updating_svd`	6	6038	613	314	224	1m12s	15s
`wavelet_2D`	11	14742	1008	3038	1008	2m15s	49s
`edge_detection`	19	20389	567	576	576	57s	13s
`gsm_autocorr`	17	21668	529	529	529	1m31s	15s
`vocoder`	201	335715	2366	2403	2403	21m30s	4m19s

Table 1. Benchmark Results

The number of tests in a program point is quadratic in the number of live areas of the program point. In principle one could exploit the relationships between the live areas of different program points to reduce the total number of tests. In our current implementation we do not exploit this as the total execution time is dominated by the liveness analysis.

5 Implementation

To be able to solve the problems from section 3 and 4, we need a solver that can solve inequalities over the domain of the integral numbers. The *CLP(Q)* library[11] included in *SICStus Prolog*[2], which we used to build a prototype of our approach, allows this.

As test programs, we used several kernels of multimedia applications: an updating singular value decomposition algorithm (used in radar applications), the kernel of a 2-dimensional wavelet compression algorithm, an edge-detection algorithm, a voice coder algorithm, and a GSM autocorrelation algorithm. The timings and memory gain of these benchmarks after applying our prototype tool on a *Pentium II-300Mhz* are shown in Table 1. The second column shows the number of arrays present in the benchmarks. The third column gives the sum of the initial sizes of all arrays (in memory cells) in the benchmark, while the following column shows the sum of the sizes of the windows we computed. The last two columns indicate the time needed to perform the liveness analysis as described in section 3 (which is dominated by the test on the emptiness of the polyhedra), and to compute the window as described section 4 (the sum of both times is the total time needed for our approach). The current prototype is very straightforward and performs all tests in all program points, sometimes doing the same test in different program points, and not exploiting the relationships described in section 3.4. The columns *DG1* and *DG2* give sizes obtained with another technique. A description of that technique and a discussion of differences is in section 6.

As can be seen, the time for the liveness analysis is dominating. In section 3.5, we derived that the number of emptiness checks during the liveness analysis is bounded by $4d^2rw$, with d the depth of the deepest `for`-loop, and with r and w respectively the number of reads and writes present in the program. We have

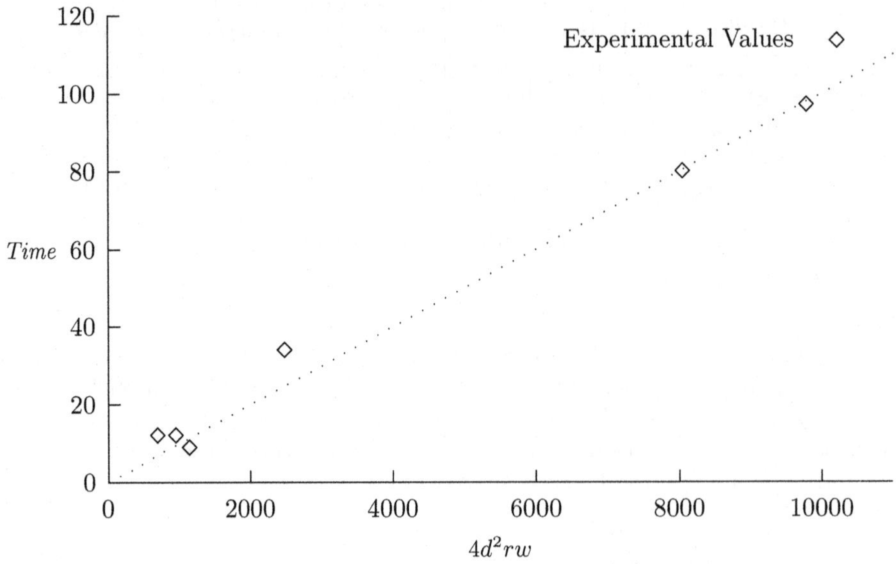

Fig. 3. Complexity of liveness analysis. The value $4d^2rw$ is plotted against the actual liveness analysis time for some arrays. The experimental values are plotted as ◇.

measured these values for the most time-consuming arrays in our benchmarks, and plotted the results in Figure 3. As can be seen, there is a strong correlation between the estimated number of emptiness checks and the time for the liveness analysis.

It has to be noted that there are libraries around which are better suited for the problems described in this paper, such as *Polylib* [20] with its $\mathcal{Z}$-polyhedra extensions [14], the *Parma Polyhedra Library*[1]. We expect much better run-times when using these libraries.

6 Discussion

About the assumptions. Our analysis can be applied to programs that are designed within the DTSE methodology [4]. However, other programs will not meet the strong assumptions stated in section 1. The analysis remains correct for programs that are not single-assignment. However, spurious live areas will be introduced and one can expect a serious deteriorisation of the precision of the results. Another technique, also useful within the overall DTSE methodology, would be to develop tools to transform programs into single assignment form [9]. The other requirement is that bounds of `for`-loops and conditions in

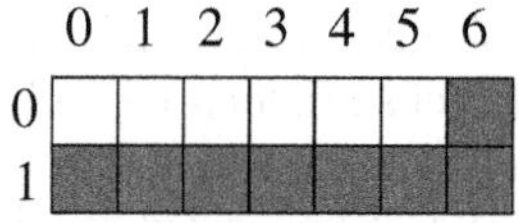

Fig. 4. Overlapping elements on boundary

`if-then-else` are linear in the iterators of the surrounding `for`-loops. In absence of this, one could consider the use of known approaches within abstract interpretation to infer intervals that safely approximate the possible values for bounds and conditions. Again, this could introduce precision loss.

Comparison with De Greef. Another approach of in-place mapping is the technique of De Greef[7, 5, 6]. This technique first linearizes a multi-dimensional array, and then computes the window for this array. Given a linearization, array indices are mapped to addresses in a one dimensional array. For each read write pair, a constraint is built that formalises at which time points the memory cells are live (points in a two dimensional space: the array index and the time). Finally, for each pair of such constraints, an optimisation problem is solved that computes the largest distance in memory between two points that are live at the same time, one point in the solution space of the first constraint, the other in the solution space of the second constraint. The results obtained with this approach are shown in the column *DG1* of Table 1. A refinement that projects away invariant dimensions (dimensions that do not carry dependencies over loops) improves the results as shown in column *DG2*. The number of optimisation problems to be solved for one linearization is of the order $(wr)^2$ with w and r respectively the number of writes and reads. This is worse than the complexity of our liveness analysis (d^2wr). Moreover, the number of linearizations quickly increases with the dimension n of the array ($2^n n!$). The tool of De Greef is implemented in C and uses the `LP_SOLVE` [3] solver. The analysis times for the benchmarks are in the range of 20 seconds to 15 minutes.

Our approach improves upon the tool of De Greef in situations where the size of the array can be reduced in any dimension as in the example shown in Figure 1 because any linearization contains a number of unused elements. Also situations where the array contains holes (e.g., an array where only the even numbered rows are used) lead to better results (however, such examples did not occur in our benchmarks; perhaps designers avoid them because they know it leads to non-optimal results). On the other hand, there are also cases where linearization is better. An example is shown in Figure 4. The set of live elements does not fit in a 1×7 box because of the one element on the boundary. This forces us to enlarge the first dimension by 1, resulting in an array of 2×7 elements. If the array is first linearized, only 8 elements are needed. Such situations do occur a few times in the benchmarks. They are responsible for the cases where our approach gives worse results than De Greef. For example, in the benchmark `updating_svd` there is a 20×100 array where linearization gives a size 101. We find a window of 2×100 with size 200. One can remark here that the window size allows to determine how many cells are located on boundary planes and hence to estimate what is the maximal gain one can expect if a particular linearization is tried (in the example of Figure 4, if linearized row by row, the maximal possible gain is 6 cells out of 14; if ordered column by column, the maximal possible gain is 1 cell out of 14). This suggests to apply a combined approach where our analysis is followed by a linearization for arrays where linearization could potentially give large additional savings.

Other related work. Within logic programming, there are several works aiming at compile-time analysis with the purpose of reusing memory cells once the last reference to them has passed (e.g., [8, 10, 13]).

For what concerns the reuse of the storage of multidimensional arrays, the problem was formally identified by Verbauwhede et al.[18]. A first systematic approach, for a fixed linearization of the array was developed by Vanhoof et al.[17].

Quilleré and Rajopadhye[15, 16] study the problem for the single assignment language ALPHA, which imposes similar assumptions on the input code (except that they also handle parametrized code). First, as many dimensions as possible are projected out, after which a windowing technique is applied on the resulting array. However, they use a different optimization criterion.

Other works[19, 12] take a broader view. They develop transformations that change the control flow so that the amount of live memory cells is reduced.

Acknowledgements

We are indebted to Saumya Debray for providing us with an initial parser that could turn the benchmarks into logic programs readable by SICStus Prolog.

References

[1] *PPL: The Parma Polyhedra Library.* `http://www.cs.unipr.it/ppl/`.
[2] *SICStus Prolog 3.8.6.* Swedish Institute of Computer Science, `http://www.SICStus.se`.
[3] M. Berkelaar. *Lp_solve Mixed Integer Linear Programming solver 2.0.* Available at `ftp://ftp.es.ele.tue.nl/pub/lp_solve`, 1995.
[4] Francky Catthoor, Sven Wuytack, Eddy De Greef, Florin Balasa, Lode Nachtergale, and Arnout Vandecapelle. *Custom Memory Management Methodology: Exploration of Memory Organisation for Embedded Multimedia Design.* Kluwer Academic Publishers, 1998.
[5] E. De Greef, F. Catthoor, and H. De Man. Reducing storage size for static control programs mapped onto parallel architectures. In *Proceedings of Dagstuhl Seminar on Loop Parallelization*, 1996.
[6] E. De Greef, F. Catthoor, and H. De Man. Memory size reduction through storage order optimization for embedded parallel multimedia applications. In *Proceedings of the Workshop on Parallel Processing and Multimedia of the International Parallel Processing Symposium*, pages 84–98, 1997.

[7] Eddy De Greef. *Storage Size Reduction for Multimedia Applications.* PhD thesis, Katholieke Universiteit Leuven, Faculteit Toegepaste Wetenschappen, Jan 1998.

[8] Saumya K. Debray. On copy avoidance in single assignment languages. In David S. Warren, editor, *Proceedings of the Tenth International Conference on Logic Programming*, pages 393–407. The MIT Press, 1993.

[9] P. Feautrier. Dataflow analysis of array and scalar references. *International Journal of Parallel Programming*, 20(1):23–53, 1991.

[10] Gudjón Gudjónsson and William H. Winsborough. Compile-time memory reuse in logic programming languages through update in place. *ACM Transactions on Programming Languages and Systems*, 21(3):430–501, May 1999.

[11] Christian Holzbaur. *OFAI clp(q,r) Manual, Edition 1.3.3.* Austrian Research Institute for Artificial Intelligence, Vienna, TR-95-09, 1995.

[12] V. Lefebvre and P. Feautrier. Optimizing storage size for static control programs in automatic parallelizers. In *Proc. EuroPar Conference, Passau, Germany*, volume 1300 of *LNCS*, pages 356–363. Springer Verlag, Aug. 1997.

[13] Nancy Mazur, Gerda Janssens, and Maurice Bruynooghe. A module based analysis for memory reuse in Mercury. In John Lloyd, Veronica Dahl, Ulrich Furbach, Manfred Kerber, Kung-Kiu Lau, Catuscia Palamidessi, Luis Moniz Pereira, Yehoshua Sagiv, and Peter J. Stuckey, editors, *Computational Logic - CL 2000, UK, Proceedings*, volume 1861 of *LNAI*, pages 1255–1269. Springer-Verlag, 2000.

[14] Sunder Phani Kumar Nookala Nookala and Tanguy Risset. A library for doing $\mathcal{Z}$-polyhedral computations. Technical Report 1330, Institut de Recherche en Informatique et Systèmes Aléatoires, May 2000.

[15] Fabien Quilleré and Sanjay Rajopadhye. Optimizing memory usage in the polyhedral model. In *Massively Parallel Computer Systems Conf.*, 1998.

[16] Fabien Quilleré and Sanjay Rajopadhye. Optimizing memory usage in the polyhedral model. In *ACM Transactions on Programming Languages and Systems (TOPLAS), Volume 22, Issue 5*, pages 773–815, Sept. 2000.

[17] J. Vanhoof, I. Bolsens, and H. De Man. Compiling multi-dimensional data streams into distributed DSP ASIC memory. In *Proc. IEEE Int. Conf. Comp. Aided Design, Santa Clara CA*, pages 272–275, 1989.

[18] I. Verbauwhede, F. Catthoor, J. Vandewalle, and H. De Man. Background memory management for the synthesis of algebraic algorithms on multi-processor DSP chips. In *Proc. VLSI'89, Int. Conf. on VLSI, Munich, Germany*, pages 209–218, 1989.

[19] D. Wilde and S. Rajopadhye. Memory reuse analysis in the polyhedral model. In *Proc. EuroPar Conference, Lyon, France*, volume 1123 of *LNCS*, pages 389–397. Springer Verlag, 1996.

[20] Doran K. Wilde. A library for doing polyhedral computations. Technical Report 785, Institut de Recherche en Informatique et Systèmes Aléatoires, December 1993.

Verifying BDD Algorithms through Monadic Interpretation*

Sava Krstić[1] and John Matthews[2]

[1] Oregon Graduate Institute
krstic@cse.ogi.edu
[2] Compaq Cambridge Research Lab
John.Matthews@compaq.com

Abstract. Many symbolic model checkers use *Binary Decision Diagrams* (BDDs) to efficiently determine whether two Boolean formulas are semantically equivalent. For realistic problems, the size of the generated BDDs can be enormous, and constructing them can easily become a performance bottleneck. As a result, most state-of-the-art BDD programs are written as highly optimized imperative C programs, increasing the risk of soundness defects in their implementation. This paper describes the use of *monadic interpreters* to formally verify BDD algorithms at a higher level of abstraction than the original C program, but still at a concrete enough level to retain their essential imperative features. Our hope is then that verification of the original C program can be achieved by strictly localized refinement reasoning.
During this work we encountered the surprising fact that modeling imperative recursive algorithms monadically often results in logical functions that are both partial and nestedly-recursive in their (hidden) state parameters, making termination proofs difficult.

1 Introduction

Confidence in results produced by verification tools varies. Counterexamples we can directly check. A theorem prover's claim of the validity of a formula can be checked by an independent tool that tests the validity of derivations recorded in proof scripts. But when a model checker says that a formula is true, such independent checking is untenable for large examples. Since large examples are what model checkers are made for, trusting their results seems tantamount to trusting correctness of their design.

Model checkers are usually built on top of a BDD (binary decision diagrams) package, or some other set of efficiently implemented algorithms for representing and manipulating boolean formulas. Verifying the correctness of a model checker thus naturally splits into two parts: verification of the model checking algorithms assuming correctness of the BDD package, and verification of the BDD package.

* The research reported in this paper was supported by the National Science Foundation Grants EIA-0072761 and CDA-9703218, Compaq Computer Corporation, and Intel Corporation.

A. Cortesi (Ed.): VMCAI 2002, LNCS 2294, pp. 182–195, 2002.
© Springer-Verlag Berlin Heidelberg 2002

Recent work of Reif et al. [RRSV00] successfully carried out the first verification task for the model checker RAVEN. The focus of this work is on the second task and our goal is to provide a technique for proving correctness of high performance BDD packages.

The efficiency of modern BDD programs is achieved at the expense of often highly complex code structure, for example by implementing custom hash tables and garbage collection routines, employing tricks with unused bits in pointers, and so on. To avoid runtime overhead, the code is written in a low level language, usually C. Our goal of formally verifying such algorithms *as originally written* distinguishes our work from other proofs of BDD algorithms [HPPR98, VGPA00, Sum00].

BDD libraries are hierarchical: More complex programs are built on top of a set of atomic primitives using standard programming constructs. In this paper we decompose the verification problem accordingly into two steps: verifying an abstraction of the program with the primitives specified axiomatically, and then a refinement proof that the C implementation of the primitives and programming constructs is faithful to the abstraction. This paper concentrates on the first step, although we hope the reader will be convinced that the axioms governing the primitives can be justified by purely local reasoning over their C implementations, and that our logical characterization of the standard programming constructs (e.g., sequencing of statements and use of local variables) is faithful to the corresponding C semantics.

We adopted an abstraction method called *monadic interpretation* for the first step; it is particularly suitable for higher order logic theorem provers such as *Isabelle/HOL* (in the sequel, *Isabelle*). In particular, local C variables that are statically assigned to only once (the common case) are abstracted to *logical* function parameters, allowing the theorem prover to automatically carry out routine inferences about variable creation, renaming, and substitution.

We begin in Section 2 by giving an informal description of a basic BDD package. Monadic interpreters are briefly described in Section 3. The BDD routines are then monadically interpreted as *Isabelle* functions in Section 4. The most complicated of the library programs (`Apply`) is a recursively defined partial function, which presents a difficulty for *Isabelle*, where all functions are total. How we deal with recursion and model the program `Apply` is explained in Section 5. Then in Section 6 we state the correctness properties of non-atomic programs and comment on their proofs. We comment on what is needed to refine our abstraction to C in Section 7.

We hope the relevance of this paper goes beyond its immediate objective. It presents, by means of an extensive example, a method, based on monadic interpretation and refinement, for proving correctness of imperative programs that use complicated recursion, manipulate complex state, and raise exceptions.

2 Basic BDD Package

A binary decision diagram is a rooted directed acyclic graph in which every node represents a boolean function. Two special nodes represent the two constant functions. Every other node u has an associated variable x and two child nodes l and h. The boolean function represented by the node u is defined recursively by $f_u = \text{ if } x \text{ then } f_l \text{ else } f_h$. Bryant [Bry86] originally proved that every function is represented by a unique reduced ordered BDD, where *reduced* means that no two nodes represent the same function, and *ordered* means that variable names are totally ordered and that every node's variable name precedes the variable names of its children.

Following the exposition in [And96], we give now a fairly abstract description of a typical implementation of (reduced, ordered) BDDs and a small package of programs, sufficient to define a tautology checker. It contains some underspecified basic types and atomic functions, and a few more complex but fully specified C programs. In the next two sections we will show how all this naturally translates into *Isabelle*.

We abstract the global state used by the BDD package as two tables: `BDD` and `HASH`. The first table represents the storage pool of BDD nodes, and the second is a hash table that memoizes a reverse mappingu from the contents of a node to its address. Node addresses are represented by the abstract type *node*.

Specifically, each entry of `BDD` associates to a node `u` a unique triple `(i,l,h)`, where `i` is a natural number (the *level* of `u`) and `l` an `h` are nodes (the *low* and *high children* of `u`). The level of a node is the position of the node's variable name in the given variable ordering. Each entry in `HASH` maps a triple `(i,l,h)` to a unique node.

There are two special nodes `TrueNode` and `FalseNode`; the atomic procedure `initializeState` replaces the current state with the initial state whose tables associate the special nodes with the triples `(0,TrueNode,TrueNode)` and `(0,FalseNode,FalseNode)` respectively, and contain no other entries.

The accessor functions `lookupLev`, `lookupLow` and `lookupHigh` take a node `u` as an argument, and return the components `i`, `l` and `h` of the triple the table `BDD` associates with `u`. What, if anything, these functions return in the case when `u` is not in the table `BDD` is left unspecified. Similarly, the function `lookupH` takes a triple `(i,l,h)` as input, and returns the node associated by `HASH` to this triple. Again, we do not know what `lookupH` returns if the input triple is not in the table `HASH`. However, there is another function, `member`, which also takes triples `(i,l,h)` as inputs and returns a boolean value that is `True` if and only if the triple is in the table `HASH`.

The simple function `bool2node` maps `True` and `False` to `TrueNode` and `FalseNode` respectively, while `node2bool` does the opposite, being unspecified for "non-boolean" inputs.

The function `getFreshNode` takes no input and returns a node that is not already in the table `BDD`, raising an exception if there are no free nodes left.

The list of atomic programs is completed with `insertNode` and `insertH`. Both take as input a quadruple `(i,l,h,u)` consisting of a level and three nodes, have no output, but change the state. The effect of **insertNode** is the update of BDD by an entry that associates u with (i,l,h). The **insertH** similarly updates HASH.

The remaining programs are defined by combining the atomic ones by means of standard constructs: sequencing, conditionals, and recursion. Shown below is the program Mk, the only one in the package that directly calls the updating functions insertNode and insertH, thus guaranteeing that all higher-level BDD programs preserve some critical properties of the state, for example that the two tables are inverses. (See Section 5 for the complete state invariant.)

```
node Mk(int i, node l, node h) {
  if (l == h)
    return l;
  else if (member(i,l,h))
    return lookupH(i,l,h);
  else {
    node u = getFreshNode();
    insertNode(i,l,h,u);
    insertH(i,l,h,u);
    return u;
  }
}
```

The program Apply takes a binary boolean operation *op* and two nodes, and returns a node representing the boolean function one could otherwise obtain by applying *op* to boolean functions represented by the two input nodes. It is the most complicated program in the package and is defined recursively as follows.

```
node Apply(opFn op, node u, node v) {
  int i = lookupLev(u);
  int j = lookupLev(v);
  if (i == j)
    if (i == 0) return bool2node((*op)(node2bool(u),node2bool(v)));
    else {
      node l1 = lookupLow(u);
      node l2 = lookupLow(v);
      node h1 = lookupHigh(u);
      node h2 = lookupHigh(v);
      return Mk(i,Apply(op,l1,l2),Apply(op,h1,h2));
    }
  else if (i < j) {
    node l = lookupLow(v);
    node h = lookupHigh(v);
    return Mk(j,Apply(op,u,l),Apply(op,u,h));
  }
  else {
    node l = lookupLow(u);
    node h = lookupHigh(u);
    return Mk(i,Apply(op,l,v),Apply(op,h,v));
  }
}
```

The program Apply is used by another program Build to produce a node representing the boolean function defined by a given boolean expression. Build is defined by primitive recursion over the structure of the expression. Finally, we have the program TautChecker which just initializes the state, invokes Build with its input expression, and returns a boolean value: True if and only if the node returned by Build is TrueNode.

In the next section we will see how all the above code can be more or less directly translated into *Isabelle*, so instead of giving the C code for Build and TautChecker here, we refer to their *Isabelle* definitions in Section 4.

3 Monadic Interpretation

Variants and extensions of Floyd-Hoare logic [AO97] are the most commonly used frameworks for verifying imperative programs. The complexity of our programs forces to adopt an alternative, more flexible, even if less investigated and automated approach. We proceed by modeling BDD programs as functions in higher order logic, in the style of monadic interpreters [Mog91, LHJ95]. Generally, a *monadic interpreter* translates source programs of input type A and output type B into functions of type $A \Rightarrow M\, B$ in the target functional language, where the type constructor M is a suitable *monad* that encapsulates the *notion of computation* used by the source language. Different source languages get interpreted by means of different monads. The target language for us will be *Isabelle*, and the source language would be a fragment of C large enough to describe BDD programs. For our purposes, a so-called "state with exceptions" monad is the appropriate choice. With it, a program of input type A and output type B gets interpreted as a function that given an element of A and a state returns a new state together with either an element of B or the memory overflow exception.

Postponing the definition of the state type St, the definition of the monad is as follows.

```
datatype 'a except = OutOfMem | Rslt 'a

types 'a M = "St ⇒ St × 'a except"

constdefs return :: "'a ⇒ 'a M"                          ("η")
          "return ≡ λa s. (s, Rslt a)"
           bind :: "['a M, 'a ⇒ 'b M] ⇒ 'b M"         (infixr "▷" 60)
          "bind ≡ λm f s. let s' = fst (m s) in  case snd (m s)
                           of OutOfMem  ⇒ (s', OutOfMem)
                            | Rslt a    ⇒ f a s'"
```

Every instance of a monad has two distinguished operations: *return* (η) and *bind* ($\triangleright$). The η operator is used to represent effect-free computations, such as the evaluation of pure expressions and functions. The notion of "effect" varies by monad; in our case an effect is either a change in the global state or the raising of an out-of-memory exception. The $\triangleright$ operator simultaneously captures the notions of program sequencing and local variable declaration. The expression $m \triangleright f$ has the effect of first performing the computation m; assuming m returns normally, then f is applied to m's return value, which results in a new computation that is then performed. The $\triangleright$ operator also ensures that state changes and exceptions are propagated correctly between m and f.

Proper monads are required to obey three algebraic identities: *unit laws*

$$(\eta\ x) \triangleright f = f\ x \qquad\qquad m \triangleright (\lambda x.\ \eta\ x) = m$$

and *associativity of* $\triangleright$

$$m \triangleright (\lambda x.\ p[x] \triangleright f) = (m \triangleright (\lambda x.\ p[x])) \triangleright f$$

Here $p[x]$ indicates that the bound variable x is allowed to occur free in p but not in f, since x's scope is being restricted on the right-hand side. It is straightforward to prove the above laws hold for our *Isabelle* definitions of `return` and `bind`. Once proved, the laws can then be used to simplify complex monadic expressions.

The rules of higher order logic guarantee that the logical bound variables, which represent local program variables, are re-scoped and renamed as necessary to maintain program equivalence. The monadic representation of programs also allows program recursion to be naturally modeled as logical recursion, as we will see in Section 5. In the next section, we show how the BDD package primitives are axiomatized as monadic computations in our state-with-exceptions monad.

4 Modeling the Basic Package

The following *Isabelle* code models the global state of our BDD package.

```
types  Level = nat

typedecl Node

record NodeRecord =  lev :: Level  low :: Node  high :: Node

types  BDD = "Node ⇒ NodeRecord"
      HASH = "NodeRecord ⇒ Node"

typedecl St

consts  bdd        :: "St ⇒ BDD"
        hash       :: "St ⇒ HASH"
        activeNode :: "St ⇒ Node ⇒ bool"
        activeRcrd :: "St ⇒ NodeRecord ⇒ bool"
```

Thus, the type `Node` is left undefined and so is `St`, but we know that we can extract the two tables from the state. The intuition that the table `BDD` is mathematically a partial function of type `Node ⇒ NodeRecord` is represented in *Isabelle* (where all functions are total) by declaring the table to be a total function of that type, and specifying its domain of definition separately by the function `activeNode`. Similar remarks apply to the table *HASH*. The important thing to notice, however, is that whatever concrete implementation of the BDD package we later come up with, it should be possible to define the functions `bdd`, `hash`, `activeNode` and `activeRcrd`.

`TrueNode` and `FalseNode` are declared as constants of type `Node`, and since this type is unspecified, we add an axiom saying that these two nodes are distinct. The initial values `initBDD`, `initHASH`, `initActiveNode` and `initActiveRcrd` are straighforward to define, and then `initializeSt` is introduced by an axiom.

```
consts initializeSt :: "unit M"
axioms initializeSt_ax :
  "initializeSt s = (s',x) ⟹ bdd s' = initBDD ∧ hash s' = initHASH
   ∧ activeNode s' = initActiveNode ∧ activeRcrd s' = initActiveRcrd"
```

Other atomic functions are also introduced by axioms[1]. We show three; the remaining ones are similar or simpler. (The notation `f (u := a)` used in `insertNode_ax` is for function update.)

```
consts lookupLev :: "Node ⇒ Level M"
axioms lookupLev_ax : "⟦lookupLev u s = (s',p); activeNode s u⟧
     ⟹ s' = s ∧ p = Rslt (lev (bdd s u))"

consts getFreshNode :: "Node M"
axioms getFreshNode_ax :
  "getFreshNode s = (s', Rslt u) ⟹ ¬(activeNode s u)"

consts insertNode :: "Level × Node × Node × Node ⇒ unit M"
axioms insertNode_ax : "insertNode (i,l,h,u) s = (s',p) ⟹
              p               = Rslt ()
            ∧ bdd s'          = (bdd s) (u := ⦇lev = i, low = l, high = h⦈)
            ∧ activeNode s'   = (activeNode s) (u := True)
            ∧ hash s'         = hash s
            ∧ activeRcrd s'   = activeRcrd s"
```

Non-atomic programs `Mk`, `Build` and `TautChecker` are fully specified as follows and the recursively defined `Apply` is discussed in the next section.

```
constdefs Mk ::  "Level × Node × Node ⇒ Node M"
          "Mk ≡  λ(i,l,h).
                 if l=h then η l
                 else member (i,l,h) ▷ (λx.
                   if x then lookupH (i,l,h)
                   else getFreshNode ▷ (λu.
                        insertNode (i,l,h,u) ▷ (λp.
                        insertH (i,l,h,u))))"
```

[1] There is no danger of inconsistency with these axioms; after the refinement step (Section 7) they will be theorems. We could have also introduced our underspecified functions in a purely definitional manner by means of the ε-operator.

```
consts  Build :: "Exp ⇒ Node M"
primrec  "Build (Var i) = Mk (i+1,TrueNode,FalseNode)"
    "Build (Const b) = bool2node b"
    "Build (Exp' oper e1 e2) =
                Build e1 ▷ (λu.
                Build e2 ▷ (λv.
                Apply (oper,u,v)))"

constdefs TautChecker :: "Exp ⇒ bool M"
          "TautChecker ≡ λe.
             initializeSt ▷ (λx.
             Build e ▷ (λu.
             η (u = TrueNode)))"
```

The input tupe of *Build* is that of boolean expressions:

```
datatype Exp = Var nat | Const bool | Exp' Op  Exp  Exp
```

Note that the variable *Var i* is represented by the level *i+1*; the level zero of the BDD table is reserved for *TrueNode* and *FalseNode*.

5 Modeling Recursive Programs (*Apply*)

The definition of *Apply* and the proof of the corresponding recursion theorem is the most difficult part of this work. Even though *Isabelle* has a sophisticated *recdef* mechanism [NP] for recursive definitions with user-supplied well-founded relation or a measure function to justify termination, this method is difficult to apply in our case, mostly because of nested recursion we have to deal with.

Pondering the definition in Section 2, one realizes that even a hand proof of termination of `Apply` requires effort. The ultimate reason for termination is clear: in an ordered BDD (and only those we would like to consider), the level goes down when passing children nodes, so in all recursive calls of `Apply` the level decreases either for both node arguments, or decreases for the "higher", while the other stays the same. Thus, in order to prove that the arguments decrease in recursive calls, it is necessary to work with a restricted set of states, described by a predicate *goodSt* that needs to be preserved by `Apply`. A workable invariant *goodSt* is the conjunction of three properties: (1) being ordered; (2) having inverse *bdd* and *hash* tables; (3) the two tables associate *TrueNode* and *FalseNode* with *TrueRcrd* and *FalseRcrd* respectively, and among active records only these two have level zero.

In *Isabelle* notation, the type of *Apply* is *Op × Node × Node ⇒ Node M*, which is the same as *Op × Node × Node ⇒ St ⇒ St × Node except*; later we will use the shorthand *Z* for it. The *Op* argument is of little significance here, so *Apply* is practically a function of two arguments of type *Node* and one of type *St*. We can expect *Apply* to terminate only if its *St* argument is good. But there must be restrictions on the node arguments as well: they must be present in the state. We capture these restrictions using the node-state relation *u in s* defined as the conjunction of *goodSt s* and *activeNode u s*. Thus, *Apply* must be modeled as a partial function, with restrictions on its state and node arguments. The expected recursion theorem takes these restrictions as assumption.

theorem *Apply_Recursion:*
  "⟦u in s; v in s⟧ ⟹ Apply (oper,u,v) s = F Apply (oper,u,v) s"

Here *F* is the *Isabelle* function of type *Z ⇒ Z*, obtained by a direct monadic translation of the C code for `Apply` in Section 2. In principle, the *recdef* package can handle recursive definitions of partial functions by defining the partial function as a total function whose value is arbitrary outside its "real" domain of definition, and by proving the recursion theorem with the proviso that the argument belongs to that domain, just as in our example. However, there is an additional difficulty that *recdef* cannot easily deal with, viz. the presence of *nested recursion*—a recursive call whose argument contains another recursive call.

Back to the informal definition of `Apply`, consider for example the second of the three lines in which recursion occurs; in expanded form this piece of code could read like this:

```
node ll = Apply(op,u,l);
node hh = Apply(op,u,h);
node w  = Mk(j,ll,hh)
```

After the first call to `Apply`, the state changes, so perhaps `u` and `h` are not even active indices in the new state's BDD table. How do we know then that the second call terminates? We may say that the new state, being the result of an application of `Apply`, must contain the old state intact. But this is circular reasoning, assuming a property of `Apply` before this function has been defined. Our inductive proof of termination of `Apply` must thus be organized as a simultaneous proof of termination and the desired property that `Apply` increases the state. A careful analysis shows that a stronger invariant *goodFn* (predicate on *Z*) is necessary; it is the conjuction of three properties: (1) increasing state; (2) output node is active in the new state; (3) the level of the output node is not larger than the levels of the input nodes.

Note that nesting is not immediately seen in the definition given in Section 2 because the state is not implicitly mentioned in the program text, being an extra hidden argument. If we made it explicit, the three lines above would look like this:

```
(ll,s1) = Apply'(op,u,l,s)
(hh,s2) = Apply'(op,u,h,s1)
(w,s3)  = Mk'(j,ll,hh,s2)
```

exposing the nesting first in

```
hh = fst(Apply'(op,u,h, snd(Apply'(op,u,l,s))))
```

Generalizing this observation, note that nested recursion occurs in every recursively defined imperative program in which there is a sequence of commands containing two recursive calls.

Nested recursion is difficult to treat by automatic tools. In [Sli00], Slind demonstrates that *recdef* can be used even in such cases, but some additional more or less ad hoc arguing is inevitable to make it work. We devised and formulated in *Isabelle* a systematic approach that reduces the problem of justifying a nested recursive definition and proving the appropriate recursion theorem to two specific proof obligations. To make it work, in addition to the measure function (or well-founded ordering) as in *recdef*, the user has to supply a *specification*—property of the function being defined that is needed to prove termination. A brief explanation of the basic form of the method follows; full development will appear elsewhere [KM].

Given a functional $F : (A \Rightarrow B) \Rightarrow (A \Rightarrow B)$ and a well-founded relation $\prec$ on A, one can prove that F has a unique fixed point (that is, a function $f : A \Rightarrow B$ satisfying $f\ x = F\ f\ x$) if it satisfies the *contraction condition*

$$\forall f\ g\ x.\ (\forall y.\ y \prec x \longrightarrow f\ y = g\ y) \longrightarrow F\ f\ x = F\ g\ x$$

This is a fixed point theorem à la Banach, and we can immediately generalize it by considering a non-empty predicate $S : (A \Rightarrow B) \Rightarrow \mathsf{bool}$ and asserting that if S is invariant under F (that is, $S\ f \longrightarrow S\ (F\ f)$), then a weakened contraction condition

$$\forall f\ g\ x.\ (\forall y.\ y \prec x \longrightarrow f\ y = g\ y) \wedge S\ f \wedge S\ g \longrightarrow F\ f\ x = F\ g\ x$$

guarantees the existence of a fixpoint of F and its uniqueness among functions satisfying S.

The weakened form of the last uniqueness result is a drawback, especially in the application to program semantics. When a recursive program is interpreted as a fixpoint of a functional in HOL, the situation is clean when that fixpoint is unique, and not quite so when we have uniqueness only among the set of functions satisfying a certain predicate. We obtained a satisfying solution by strengthening both the invariance and contraction conditions. It works for invariants specified as input-output relations. Precisely, given F and $\prec$ as before, and given a relation $R : A \Rightarrow B \Rightarrow \mathsf{bool}$, the two conditions

$$\forall f.\ (\forall y.\ y \prec x \longrightarrow R\ y\ (f\ y)) \longrightarrow R\ x\ (f\ x)$$
$$\forall f\ g\ x.\ (\forall y.\ y \prec x \longrightarrow f\ y = g\ y \wedge R\ y\ (f\ y)) \longrightarrow F\ f\ x = F\ g\ x$$

are sufficient to guarantee the existence and (unrestricted) uniqueness of a fixpoint of F.

Finally, we need to generalize the last result to cover the possibility of non-termination of the limit function outside a specified set of inputs. That set being described by a predicate $D : A \Rightarrow \mathsf{bool}$, the final form of the invariance and contraction conditions reads as follows.

$$\forall f.\ (\forall y.\ D\ y \wedge y \prec x \longrightarrow R\ y\ (f\ y)) \longrightarrow R\ x\ (f\ x)$$
$$\forall f\ g\ x.\ D\ x \wedge (\forall y.\ D\ y \wedge y \prec x \longrightarrow f\ y = g\ y \wedge R\ y\ (f\ y)) \longrightarrow F\ f\ x = F\ g\ x$$

Now we can formulate a fixpoint theorem that can be used to justify nested recursive definitions.

Theorem 1. *Suppose the last two conditions are satisfied. Then there exists a function* $f : A \Rightarrow B$ *such that*

$$\forall x.\, D\, x \longrightarrow f\, x = F\, f\, x$$

Moreover, f *is unique in the sense that every other function* g *satisfying this same conditional fixpoint equation satisfies also* $\forall x.\, D\, x \longrightarrow g\, x = f\, x$.

The theorem can be proved in *Isabelle* and then instantiated by taking: (1) F to be the functional defining `Apply`; (2) the well-ordering $\prec$ induced by the measure function given by the maximum of the levels of input nodes in the input state; (3) R to be the input-output relation defining the invariant `goodFn`; (4) the predicate D saying that both input nodes are present in the input state. As a result, we obtain the definition of `Apply` together with the quoted theorem `Apply_Recursion`.

6 Correctness

Once the definition and recursion theorem for `Apply` become available, the proof of its correctness and then the correctness of `Build` and `TautChecker` are straightforward. The only interesting auxiliary function is the interpretation function `IntNode` that specifies how a node and a state containing the node determine a boolean function.

```
consts IntNode :: "Node × St ⇒ BoolFn"
recdef IntNode "measure (λ(u,s). lev' u s)"
  "IntNode us = (let u = fst us; s = snd us in
     if u in s then
       (if u = TrueNode then TrueFn
        else if u = FalseNode then FalseFn
        else λ env. if env ((lev' u s) - 1)
                    then IntNode (low' u s, s) env
                    else IntNode (high' u s, s) env)
    else arbitrary)"
```

As for the new notation, `lev' u s` , `low' u s` and `high' u s` are abbreviations for the components of the record `bdd s u`, the type `BoolFn` is just `"Env ⇒ bool"`, and the environment type `Env` is `"Var ⇒ bool"`.

Correctness of `Apply` asserts the relationship between the interpretations of the two input nodes and the output node. To state it we need the obvious version of `Apply` for boolean functions: `BoolFnApply oper f g env = oper (f env) (g env)`.

```
theorem Apply_Correct: "⟦u in s; v in s; Apply (oper,u,v) s=(s',Rslt w)⟧
  ⟹ IntNode (w,s') = BoolFnApply oper (IntNode (u,s)) (IntNode (v,s))"
```

Correctness of `Build` is the statement saying that the interpretation of the node constructed by `Build` is the boolean function represented (via the obvious function `IntExp`) by the expression given as input to `Build`.

theorem *Build_Correct:* "⟦goodSt s; Build e s = (s',Rslt u)⟧ ⟹
    IntNode (u,s') = IntExp e"

Correctness of the tautology checker is its soundness property:

theorem *TautChecker_Correct:*
    "out (TautChecker e) s = Rslt True ⟹ IntExp e = TrueFn"

One can also prove the completeness of the tautology checker, saying that if it terminates with the result `False`, then the input expression is not a tautology.

7 Completing the Refinement

Formalization of the complete ANSI C language is a formidable challenge but within reach, as demonstrated by current work of Norish [Nor98] and Papaspyrou [Pap01]. Ideally, verification of C programs would use such a formalization, but for proving properties of a small set of programs partial formalizations could also be acceptable. BDD programs, for example, can be written in a small fragment of C that we can with little pain interpret monadically in *Isabelle*.

We have already produced translations of non-atomic BDD programs and made them a part of an *Isabelle* theory presented in Section 4. It remains to add translations of atomic programs and derive the correctness of the whole translated package. Since *Isabelle* does not directly support refinement of its theories, we would have to manually modify the theory file described in Section 4 as follows.

First, the unspecified types `St` and `Node` are declared to be equal to the state and node type used by the C functions. The functions `bdd`, `hash`, `activeNode`, `activeRcrd` that extract the abstract tables from the concrete representation of the state should at this point have straightforward definitions. Finally, atomic functions are given their concrete definitions and the axiom we previously had for each of them is now a theorem that needs to be proved.

Clearly, the abstract BDD package of Section 4 can be refined this way to more than one C implementation. The complexity of the implementation will not affect the proof of the top-level correctness; it will only show up in the level of difficulty for the refinement proofs of atomic functions.

Leaving further development to future work, a couple of remarks are in order about features that are critical for good performance, but left out in this work. First is the memoization of `Apply` results. Adding it would indeed complicate some of our proofs, but the main reason for this omission is ongoing work where we expect to formalize a general result about equivalence of recursive programs with their versions optimized by memoization. Then we have garbage collection, omitted in the initial phase of this research for reasons of simplicity and irrelevance for the proof of correctness of the tautology checker. Adding it is possible at almost no cost in changing existing proofs. Concretely, reference counts would be added to node records, together with the pertinent atomic functions. The garbage collector would be called by a refined `getFreshNode`, so we would need to reprove correctness of that routine assuming the correctness of the garbage collector.

8 Related Work

Filliâtre seems to be the first to explore monadic interpretation for verifying imperative programs. In [Fil01], he presents a far-reaching generalization of the Floyd-Hoare method, applicable to programs written in an *ML*-like functional language, with recursion and references. In the framework of the *Coq* theorem prover, he uses a generalized monadic translation and suitable program annotations to automatically generate simpler proof obligations from a given correctness statement. The elegance and power of this system notwithstanding, it is not clear how well it handles programs with nested recursion. It would be interesting to see whether the specification predicates (mentioned in Section 5) we found necessary to prove termination of such functions could be added as annotations in this framework.

Verification of BDD algorithms has been a subject of active research and the papers [HPPR98], [VGPA00] and [Sum00] offer proofs done with proof assitants *PVS*, *Coq* and *ACL2* respectively. Some go beyond our work so far in that they cover memoization and/or garbage collection. A common goal of these papers is to extend the prover with a certified BDD package by means of reflection available in their respective systems. The resulting packages have high-confidence and encouraging performance, though still substantially below those of the corresponding C-coded implementations.

BDD algorithms are modeled in [VGPA00, Sum00] as functional programs in "state-threading" style, while the "perfect hashing" trick used in [HPPR98] makes the state constant. Complexity of the proof effort and the proof assistants' idiosyncrasies imposed limitations on the form of some of these programs could be expressed. For example, extra counter parameters are used in [VGPA00] for recursive BDD programs, even though they are not needed for the algorithm being defined. In contrast, our work is an attempt to verify BDD algorithms "in the wild", that is, expressed as closely as possible to the form they appear in existing C implementations. Thus, we have emphasized monadic style and worked hard to allow natural program definitions even if they involve nested recursion.

9 Conclusions

We have made progress towards our ultimate goal of verifying current C language-based model checkers. Adopting the monadic interpretation technique, we have defined an abstract version in *Isabelle* of the imperative code implementing standard BDD algorithms. At this level, we proved correctness of the BDD programs, including the BDD tautology checker. A shallow embedding of a small fragment of C will allow interpretation of the actual C code. By refinement, verifying correctness of the C code will be, in virtue of theorems presented in this paper, reduced to proving precisely identified properties of (only) the atomic BDD functions in the C package.

Acknowledgments

We thank John Launchbury and anonymous referees for useful comments on the paper.

References

[And96] H. R. Andersen. An Introduction to Binary Decision Diagrams. Internet, September 1996.

[AO97] K. R. Apt and E.-R. Olderog. *Verification of sequential and concurrent programs.* Springer-Verlag, 1997.

[Bry86] R. E. Bryant. Graph-based algorithms for Boolean function manipulation. *IEEE Transactions on Computers*, C-35(8):677–691, August 1986.

[Fil01] J.-C. Filliâtre. Verification of Non-Functional Programs using Interpretations in Type Theory. *Journal of Functional Programming*, 2001.

[HPPR98] F. W. von Henke, S. Pfab, H. Pfeifer, and H. Rueß. Case Studies in Meta-Level Theorem Proving. In J. Grundy and M. Newey, editors, *Proc. Intl. Conf. on Theorem Proving in Higher Order Logics (TPHOLS)*, Lecture Notes in Computer Science, pages 461–478. Springer LNCS 1479, September 1998.

[KM] S. Krstić and J. Matthews. Nested recursive definitions in *Isabelle/HOL*. In preparation.

[LHJ95] S. Liang, P. Hudak, and M. P. Jones. Monad transformers and modular interpreters. In *Conference record of POPL '95, 22nd ACM SIGPLAN-SIGACT Symposium on Principles of Programming Languages*, pages 333–343, New York, NY, USA, January 1995. ACM Press.

[Mog91] E. Moggi. Notions of computation and monads. *Information and Computation*, 93:55–92, 1991.

[Nor98] M. Norrish. *C formalised in HOL.* PhD thesis, University of Cambridge Computer Laboratory, 1998.

[NP] T. Nipkow and L. Paulson. *Isabelle/HOL* tutorial.

[Pap01] N. S. Papaspyrou. Denotational semantics of ANSI C. *Computer Standards and Interfaces*, 23:169–185, 2001.

[RRSV00] W. Reif, J. Ruf, G. Schellhorn, and T. Vollmer. Do you trust your model checker? In W. A. Hunt Jr. and S. D. Johnson, editors, *Formal Methods in Computer Aided Design (FMCAD).* Springer LNCS 1954, November 2000.

[Sli00] K. Slind. Another look at nested recursion. In M. Aagaard and J. Harrison, editors, *Proc. Intl. Conf. on Theorem Proving in Higher Order Logics (TPHOLS)*, Lecture Notes in Computer Science, pages 498–518. Springer LNCS 1869, August 2000.

[Sum00] R. Sumners. Correctness proof of a BDd manager in the context of satisfiability checking. Technical Report TR-00-29, The University of Texas at Austin, Department of Computer Sciences, November 2000.

[VGPA00] K. N. Verma, J. Goubalt-Larrecq, S. Prasad, and S. Arun-Kumar. Reflecting BDDs in Coq. In J. He and M. Sato, editors, *Proc. 6th Asian Computing Science Conference (ASIAN)*, Lecture Notes in Computer Science, pages 162–181. Springer LNCS 1961, November 2000.

Improving the Encoding of LTL Model Checking into SAT*

Alessandro Cimatti[1], Marco Pistore[1], Marco Roveri[1], and Roberto Sebastiani[1,2]

[1] ITC-IRST, Trento, Italy
{cimatti,pistore,roveri}@irst.itc.it
[2] Dept. of Information and Communication Technology – University of Trento, Italy
rseba@science.unitn.it

Abstract. Bounded Model Checking (BMC) is a technique for encoding an LTL model checking problem into a problem of propositional satisfiability. Since the seminal paper by Biere et al. [2], the research on BMC has been primarily directed at achieving higher efficiency for solving reachability properties. In this paper, we tackle the problem of improving BMC encodings for the full class of LTL properties. We start noticing some properties of the encoding of [2], and we exploit them to define improvements that make the resulting boolean formulas smaller or simpler to solve.

1 Motivations and Goals

Model Checking [8,7] is a powerful technique for verifying systems and detecting errors at early stages of the design process, which is obtaining wide acceptance in industrial settings. In Model Checking, the specification is expressed in temporal logic —either Computation Tree Logic (CTL) or Linear temporal Logic (LTL)— and the system is modeled as a finite state machine (FSM). A traversal algorithm verifies exhaustively whether the FSM satisfies the property or not. Symbolic Model Checking uses Ordered Boolean Decision Diagrams (BDDs) [4] to encode the FSM [5,11].

Recently a new approach for Symbolic Model Checking has been proposed, called Bounded Model Checking (BMC), which is based on SAT techniques [2]. Given a FSM M and an LTL specification f, the idea is to look for counter-examples of maximum length k, and to generate a boolean formula which is satisfiable if and only if such counter-example exists. The boolean formula is

* The fourth author is sponsored under the MURST COFIN99 project "Model checking and satisfiability: development of novel decision procedures and comparative evaluation and experimental analysis in significant application areas – Moses", protocol number 9909261583. The first, second and fourth authors are sponsored by the CALCULEMUS! IHP-RTN EC project, contract code HPRN-CT-2000-00102, and have thus benefited of the financial contribution of the Commission through the IHP program.

A. Cortesi (Ed.): VMCAI 2002, LNCS 2294, pp. 196–207, 2002.
© Springer-Verlag Berlin Heidelberg 2002

then given as input to a SAT solver. If the formula is satisfiable, the satisfying assignment returned is converted into a counter-example execution path.

Since then, the research on bounded model checking has mainly focused on using effective data structures to encode boolean expression [1,16] or on customizing SAT procedures for BMC problems [14]. Moreover, most work have restricted to the very particular subproblem of reachability [3,1,14,9]. For the general case, no alternative encoding than that in [2] has been proposed so far.

In this paper, we analyze the encoding of [2], we reveal and prove some basic properties of the encoding, and we use these properties to define some improvements which make the resulting boolean formula smaller or simpler to solve. Some of these improvements are currently implemented in the NuSMV symbolic model checker [6] (NuSMV is available at `http://nusmv.irst.itc.it`).

2 The Basic Encoding

We briefly recall some basic notions and a description of the BMC encoding, as proposed in [2]. We omit any formal description of the semantics of LTL and of LTL model checking, which can be found there.

We consider LTL formulas in negative normal form, which are defined as follows: a propositional literal is a LTL formula; if h and g are LTL formulas, then $h \wedge g$, $h \vee g$, $\mathbf{X}g$, $\mathbf{G}g$, $\mathbf{F}g$, $h\mathbf{U}g$ and $h\mathbf{R}g$ are LTL formulas, $\mathbf{X}$, $\mathbf{G}$, $\mathbf{F}$, $\mathbf{U}$ and $\mathbf{R}$ being the standard "next", "globally", "eventually", "until" and "releases" temporal operators respectively. We denote by $depth(f)$ the maximum level of nesting of temporal operators in f. A Kripke Structure M is a tuple $\langle S, I, T, \mathcal{L} \rangle$ with a finite set of states S, a set of initial states $I \subset S$, a transition relation $T \subseteq S \times S$ and a labeling function $\mathcal{L} : S \rightarrow \mathcal{P}(\mathcal{A})$, $\mathcal{A}$ being the set of atomic propositions.

Given M, an LTL formula f and an integer $k \geq 0$, the existential bounded model checking problem $M \models_k \mathbf{E}f$, meaning "there exist an execution path of M of length k satisfying the temporal property f", is equivalent to the satisfiability problem of a boolean formula $[[M, f]]_k$ defined as follows:

$$[[M, f]]_k := \; [[M]]_k \wedge \; [[f]]_k \tag{1}$$

where

$$[[M]]_k := I(s_0) \wedge \bigwedge_{i=0}^{k-1} T(s_i, s_{i+1}), \tag{2}$$

$$[[f]]_k := (\neg L_k \wedge \; [[f]]_k^0) \vee \bigvee_{l=0}^{k} (\;_lL_k \wedge \; _l[[f]]_k^0), \tag{3}$$

$_lL_k := T(s_k, s_l)$, $L_k := \bigvee_{l=0}^{k} \;_lL_k$, $[[f]]_k^i$ and $_l[[f]]_k^i$ are described in Table 1. (If f is boolean, we denote by f_i the value of f at step i.) Intuitively,

- $[[M, f]]_k$ represents the paths of length k which are compatible with the initial conditions and the transition relation, and satisfy f;

f	$[[f]]_k^i$	$_l[[f]]_k^i$
p	p_i	p_i
$\neg p$	$\neg p_i$	$\neg p_i$
$h \wedge g$	$[[h]]_k^i \wedge [[g]]_k^i$	$_l[[h]]_k^i \wedge {}_l[[g]]_k^i$
$h \vee g$	$[[h]]_k^i \vee [[g]]_k^i$	$_l[[h]]_k^i \vee {}_l[[g]]_k^i$
$\mathbf{X}g$	$[[g]]_k^{i+1}$ *if* $i < k$ $\bot$ *otherwise.*	$_l[[g]]_k^{i+1}$ *if* $i < k$ $_l[[g]]_k^l$ *otherwise.*
$\mathbf{G}g$	$\bot$	$\bigwedge_{j=min(i,l)}^{k} {}_l[[g]]_k^j$
$\mathbf{F}g$	$\bigvee_{j=i}^{k} [[g]]_k^j$	$\bigvee_{j=min(i,l)}^{k} {}_l[[g]]_k^j$
$h\mathbf{U}g$	$\bigvee_{j=i}^{k} \left([[g]]_k^j \wedge \bigwedge_{n=i}^{j-1} [[h]]_k^n \right)$	$\bigvee_{j=i}^{k} \left({}_l[[g]]_k^j \wedge \bigwedge_{n=i}^{j-1} {}_l[[h]]_k^n \right) \vee$ $\bigvee_{j=l}^{i-1} \left({}_l[[g]]_k^j \wedge \bigwedge_{n=i}^{k} {}_l[[h]]_k^n \wedge \bigwedge_{n=l}^{j-1} {}_l[[h]]_k^n \right)$
$h\mathbf{R}g$	$\bigvee_{j=i}^{k} \left([[h]]_k^j \wedge \bigwedge_{n=i}^{j} [[g]]_k^n \right)$	$\bigwedge_{j=min(i,l)}^{k} {}_l[[g]]_k^j \vee$ $\bigvee_{j=i}^{k} \left({}_l[[h]]_k^j \wedge \bigwedge_{n=i}^{j} {}_l[[g]]_k^n \right) \vee$ $\bigvee_{j=l}^{i-1} \left({}_l[[h]]_k^j \wedge \bigwedge_{n=i}^{k} {}_l[[g]]_k^n \wedge \bigwedge_{n=l}^{j} {}_l[[g]]_k^n \right)$

Table 1. Recursive definition of $[[f]]_k^i$ and $_l[[f]]_k^i$.

- $[[M]]_k$ represents the paths which are compatible with the initial conditions and the transition relation;
- $[[f]]_k$ represents the paths which satisfy f;
- $_lL_k$ represents the transition from step k to step l, which induces a loop;
- L_k represents the disjunction of every transitions from step k to a step l;
- $[[f]]_k^0$ represents the paths which satisfy f, if there is no loop from step k to any step $l \leq k$;
- $_l[[f]]_k^0$ represents the paths which satisfy f, if there is a loop from step k to step l.

Of course, the method is not complete, in the sense that, if $[[M, f]]_k$ is unsatisfiable (that is, $M \not\models_k \mathbf{E}f$) then nothing can be said about the existence of paths of length $\geq k$. [1] Of course, there is a maximum value of k, called the *diameter* of the problem, after which we can conclude there is no solution. Unfortunately, such value is typically very big and very hard to compute [3]. Thus, the typical technique is to generate and solve $[[M, f]]_k$ for increasing values of $k = 0, 1, 2, 3, \ldots$, until either a satisfying path is found, or a given timeout is reached.

Notice that, a path of length k satisfying an LTL formula f (i.e. such that $M \models_k \mathbf{E}f$) corresponds to a counter-example for the universal model checking problem $M \models \mathbf{A}\neg f$, meaning "for all computation path the LTL property $\neg f$ is satisfied".

[1] This should not be a surprise, as LTL model checking is PSPACE-complete, while SAT is NP-complete.

3 Problems with the Basic Encoding

In this paper we assume that all the boolean formulas are represented by binary directed acyclic graphs (DAGs) so that all common subformulas are shared. [2] These formulas keep reasonably small, but are not canonical, in the sense that the DAG representation of logically equivalent formulas is not unique. The DAG representing $[[M, f]]_k$ is CNF-ized by means of a labeling CNF conversion (see. e.g., [12,10]). Remarkably, this conversion avoids the exponential explosion in size, but forces the introduction of new boolean variables. Moreover, the resulting formula is not logically equivalent to the previous one, but it is only equally satisfiable.

A key problem with the encoding described in Section 2 is that in many cases it produces redundant formulas. For instance, if we consider the standard reachability problem s.t. $f = \mathbf{F}g$ with g boolean and we apply straightforwardly (3) and the encodings of Table 1, we have:

$$[[\mathbf{F}g]]_k = \left((\neg \bigvee_{l=0}^{k} {}_lL_k \wedge \bigvee_{j=0}^{k} g_j) \vee \bigvee_{l=0}^{k} ({}_lL_k \wedge \bigvee_{j=0}^{k} g_j) \right) . \tag{4}$$

The DAG structure allows for sharing the $\bigvee_{j=0}^{k} g_j$ and ${}_lL_k$ terms, but it cannot simplify (4) any further. On the other hand, we will see later that in this case $[[\mathbf{F}g]]_k = \bigvee_{j=0}^{k} g_j$, that is, all the ${}_lL_k$ terms can be dropped.

In general, there are often simplifications which can be done, e.g., by simply applying DeMorgan's rules and/or the associativity of conjuncts and disjuncts, or by recognizing properties due to the semantics of subformulas. In this paper we identified some of these simplifications, thus allowing for their application in the encoding algorithm. The identified simplifications aim to speed up the SAT solver in answering the submitted problem.

4 Optimizations to the Encoding

Analyzing (1), (2), (3) and the inductive definitions of $[[f]]_k^i$ and ${}_l[[f]]_k^i$ in Table 1, we notice some properties which allow for introducing significant improvements in the size of the encodings. In the following we denote by $f \models g$ propositional model entailment.

4.1 Removing the "$\neg L_k$" Component

Property 1. For all LTL formulas f and for all i, l, k s.t. $0 \leq i \leq k$ and $0 \leq l \leq k$,

$$[[f]]_k^i \models {}_l[[f]]_k^i \tag{5}$$

[2] Noteworthy cases of efficient implementation of DAGs are Reduced Boolean Circuits (RBCs) [1] and Boolean Expression Diagrams (BEDs) [16].

Proof. The result comes from the inductive definitions of $[[f]]_k^i$ and ${}_l[[f]]_k^i$ in Table 1, by induction on the structure of f. We recall that, in propositional logic, if $f_1 \models g_1$ and $f_2 \models g_2$, then $f_1 \wedge f_2 \models g_1 \wedge g_2$ and $f_1 \vee f_2 \models g_1 \vee g_2$, and $h \models h[g_1/f_1]^+$, where $h[g_1/f_1]^+$ is obtained by substituting positive occurrences of f_1 with g_1 in h.

– If $f \in \{p, \neg p\}$, then $[[f]]_k^i = {}_l[[f]]_k^i$.

We assume by inductive hypothesis that $[[h]]_k^i \models {}_l[[h]]_k^i$ and $[[g]]_k^i \models {}_l[[g]]_k^i$. Thus:

– $[[h]]_k^i \wedge [[g]]_k^i \models {}_l[[h]]_k^i \wedge {}_l[[g]]_k^i$ and $[[h]]_k^i \vee [[g]]_k^i \models {}_l[[h]]_k^i \vee {}_l[[g]]_k^i$.
– $[[\mathbf{X}g]]_k^i \models {}_l[[\mathbf{X}g]]_k^i$ and $[[\mathbf{G}g]]_k^i \models {}_l[[\mathbf{G}g]]_k^i$, as $\bot \models f$ for every f.
– $[[\mathbf{F}g]]_k^i \models {}_l[[\mathbf{F}g]]_k^i$, $[[h\mathbf{U}g]]_k^i \models {}_l[[h\mathbf{U}g]]_k^i$, $[[h\mathbf{R}g]]_k^i \models {}_l[[h\mathbf{R}g]]_k^i$, as they are all in the form " $[[f]]_k^i \models [[f]]_k^i[\mathbf{h}/\ {}_l\mathbf{h}, \mathbf{g}/\ {}_l\mathbf{g}]^+ \vee F^*$", where $[[f]]_k^i[\mathbf{h}/\ {}_l\mathbf{h}, \mathbf{g}/\ {}_l\mathbf{g}]^+$ is the formula obtained by substituting the positive occurrences of $[[h]]_k^j$'s and $[[g]]_k^j$'s with the respective ${}_l[[h]]_k^j$'s and ${}_l[[g]]_k^j$'s in $[[f]]_k^i$.

□

Property 2. The boolean expression $[[f]]_k$ defined in (3) is logically equivalent to

$$[[f]]_k^0 \vee \bigvee_{l=0}^{k} (\ {}_lL_k \wedge\ {}_l[[f]]_k^0). \qquad (6)$$

Proof. If μ is a model for $(\neg L_k \wedge [[f]]_k^0) \vee \bigvee_{l=0}^k (\ {}_lL_k \wedge\ {}_l[[f]]_k^0)$, then it is trivially a model also for $(\ [[f]]_k^0 \vee \bigvee_{l=0}^k (\ {}_lL_k \wedge\ {}_l[[f]]_k^0))$. Vice-versa, if μ is a model for $(\ [[f]]_k^0 \vee \bigvee_{l=0}^k (\ {}_lL_k \wedge\ {}_l[[f]]_k^0))$, then either it is a model for $\bigvee_{l=0}^k (\ {}_lL_k \wedge\ {}_l[[f]]_k^0)$ or it is not. In the first case, μ is also a model for (3). In the second case, $\mu \models [[f]]_k^0$ and, for every l, $\mu \not\models (\ {}_lL_k \wedge\ {}_l[[f]]_k^0)$. From Property 1 for every l $\mu \models {}_l[[f]]_k^0$, thus $\mu \not\models {}_lL_k$. Therefore, $\mu \models \neg L_k$, and thus it is a model for (3).

□

Thus, in (3) the "$\neg L_k$" component is redundant and can be dropped.

4.2 Encodings Ad Hoc when $depth(f) \leq 1$

In this section we borrow from [13] some ideas from their encodings of CTL specifications of the form $\{\mathbf{AX}g, \mathbf{AG}g, \mathbf{AF}g, \mathbf{A}[h\mathbf{U}g], \mathbf{A}[h\mathbf{R}g]\}$, with h and g boolean, which we generalize to every LTL formula f s.t. $depth(f) \leq 1$. [3]

Property 3. If ${}_l[[f]]_k^0$ does not vary with l (we denote it by ${}_*[[f]]_k^0$), then we have:

$$[[f]]_k = [[f]]_k^0 \vee (L_k \wedge\ {}_*[[f]]_k^0). \qquad (7)$$

[3] Notice that our encodings are dual w.r.t. those defined in [13] as here f is the negation of the specification.

Proof. From (6), we have:

$$\begin{aligned}[[f]]_k &= [[f]]^0_k \vee \bigvee_{l=0}^{k}(\,_lL_k \wedge \,_*[[f]]^0_k) \\ &= [[f]]^0_k \vee (\bigvee_{l=0}^{k} \,_lL_k \wedge \,_*[[f]]^0_k) \\ &= [[f]]^0_k \vee (L_k \wedge \,_*[[f]]^0_k).\end{aligned}$$

□

Property 4. If $_l[[f]]^0_k$ does not vary with l, and if there exists a formula F^*_k such that $_l[[f]]^0_k$ can be rewritten as $_l[[f]]^0_k = (\,[[f]]^0_k \vee F^*_k)$, then we have:

$$[[f]]_k \;=\; [[f]]^0_k \vee (L_k \wedge F^*_k). \tag{8}$$

Proof. Starting from (7), we can factorize the common term $[[f]]^0_k$:

$$\begin{aligned}[[f]]_k &= [[f]]^0_k \vee (L_k \wedge (\,[[f]]^0_k \vee F^*_k)) \\ &= [[f]]^0_k \vee (L_k \wedge \,[[f]]^0_k) \vee (L_k \wedge F^*_k) \\ &= [[f]]^0_k \vee (L_k \wedge F^*_k).\end{aligned}$$

□

As a particular case, if $_l[[f]]^0_k = [[f]]^0_k$, then $F^*_k = \bot$ and thus $[[f]]_k = [[f]]^0_k$.

Property 5. If $depth(f) \leq 1$, then $_l[[f]]^0_k = \,_*[[f]]^0_k$ does not vary with l. Thus, by Property 3 we have:

$$[[f]]_k \;=\; [[f]]^0_k \vee (L_k \wedge \,_*[[f]]^0_k). \tag{9}$$

Proof. The result comes from Table 1 by induction on the structure of f.

- If $f \in \{p, \neg p\}$, then $_l[[f]]^i_k$ does not vary with l, for every i.
- If $_l[[h]]^i_k$ and $_l[[g]]^i_k$ do not vary with l, then neither do $_l[[h]]^i_k \wedge \,_l[[g]]^i_k$ and $_l[[h]]^i_k \vee \,_l[[g]]^i_k$, for every i.

If h and g are boolean, then $_l[[g]]^i_k$ and $_l[[h]]^i_k$ do not vary with l, for every i. Thus:

- If $i = 0$, then $i < k$ except when $k = 0$, in which case $l = i = k = 0$. Thus, $_l[[\mathbf{X}g]]^0_k$ does not vary with l.
- $min(0, l) = 0$, thus $_l[[\mathbf{G}g]]^0_k$ $_l[[\mathbf{F}g]]^0_k$ do not vary with l.
- as $i = 0$, the terms $\bigvee_{j=l}^{i-1} \cdots$ are null. Thus, $_l[[h\mathbf{U}g]]^0_k$ and $_l[[h\mathbf{R}g]]^0_k$ do not vary with l.

□

Thus, when $depth(f) \leq 1$, $[[f]]_k$ can be rewritten into the much simpler expression (9) or even into (8) if $_l[[f]]^0_k = [[f]]^0_k \vee F^*_k$ for some F^*_k.

f	$[[f]]_k^0$	${}_*[[f]]_k^0$	$[[f]]_k$
g	g_0	g_0	g_0
$\mathbf{X}g$	g_1 *if* $k > 0$ $\bot$ *otherwise.*	g_1 *if* $k > 0$ g_0 *otherwise.*	g_1 *if* $k > 0$ ${}_0L_0 \wedge g_0$ *otherwise.*
$\mathbf{G}g$	$\bot$	$\bigwedge_{j=0}^{k} g_j$	$L_k \wedge \bigwedge_{j=0}^{k} g_j$
$\mathbf{F}g$	$\bigvee_{j=0}^{k} g_j$	$\bigvee_{j=0}^{k} g_j$	$\bigvee_{j=0}^{k} g_j$
$h\mathbf{U}g$	$\bigvee_{j=0}^{k} \left(g_j \wedge \bigwedge_{n=0}^{j-1} h_n\right)$	$\bigvee_{j=0}^{k} \left(g_j \wedge \bigwedge_{n=0}^{j-1} h_n\right)$	$\bigvee_{j=0}^{k} \left(g_j \wedge \bigwedge_{n=0}^{j-1} h_n\right)$
$h\mathbf{R}g$	$\bigvee_{j=0}^{k} \left(h_j \wedge \bigwedge_{n=0}^{j} g_n\right)$	$\bigwedge_{j=0}^{k} g_j \ \vee$ $\bigvee_{j=0}^{k} \left(h_j \wedge \bigwedge_{n=0}^{j} g_n\right)$	$\bigvee_{j=0}^{k} \left(h_j \wedge \bigwedge_{n=0}^{j} g_n\right) \vee$ $(L_k \wedge \bigwedge_{j=0}^{k} g_j)$

Table 2. $[[f]]_k^i$, ${}_*[[f]]_k^i$ and $[[f]]_k$, $f \in \{g, \mathbf{X}g, \mathbf{G}g, \mathbf{F}g, h\mathbf{U}g, h\mathbf{R}g\}$, h, g boolean.

Example 1. Consider the LTL model checking problem $M \models \mathbf{A}((h\mathbf{U}g) \rightarrow \mathbf{G}p)$, and its corresponding BMC problem $M \models_k \mathbf{E}f$, f being $((h\mathbf{U}g) \wedge \mathbf{F}\neg p)$, h, g and p being boolean. We have $[[f]]_k^0 = {}_l[[f]]_k^0 = \bigvee_{j=0}^{k} \left(g_j \wedge \bigwedge_{n=0}^{j-1} h_n\right) \wedge \bigvee_{j=0}^{k} \neg p_j$, $F^* = \bot$, thus from (8), $[[f]]_k = [[f]]_k^0$.

◇

This is not a formula of the kind addressed by [13]. However, if we restrict to $f \in \{g, \mathbf{X}g, \mathbf{G}g, \mathbf{F}g, h\mathbf{U}g, h\mathbf{R}g\}$ with h, g boolean, then we can apply (9) and obtain the same results as in [13], as shown in Table 2.

As final remark we can notice that, when $depth(f) > 1$ it is in general the case that $[[f]]_k^i$ is not a subformula of ${}_l[[f]]_k^i$. This property can be exploited to simplify the work of the SAT solver as it will be shown in Section 5.

4.3 Handling Fairness Constraints: f = GFg, g boolean

We consider here the encoding of fairness constraints, that is, LTL formulas in the form "$\mathbf{GF}g$", g being a boolean formula. From Table 1 we have that $[[\mathbf{GF}g]]_k^i = \bot$ and that

$$ {}_l[[\mathbf{GF}g]]_k^0 = \bigwedge_{i=0}^{k} \bigvee_{j=min(i,l)}^{k} g_j. \tag{10} $$

We subdivide the external conjunction in two parts: for $i < l$, —outside the loop— and for $i \geq l$ —inside the loop. Inside the first conjunct, we further subdivide the disjunction in two parts: for $i < l$, —outside the loop— and for $i \geq l$ —inside the loop (11). The underlined term $\bigvee_{j=l}^{k} g_j$ in both conjuncts of (11) does not vary with i, thus we can take it out from their respective conjunctions:

$$
\begin{aligned}
{}_l[[\mathbf{GF}g]]_k^0 &= \bigwedge_{i=0}^{l-1}\left(\bigvee_{j=i}^{l-1} g_j \vee \underline{\bigvee_{j=l}^{k} g_j}\right) \wedge \bigwedge_{i=l}^{k}\underline{\bigvee_{j=l}^{k} g_j} &(11)\\
&= \left(\bigwedge_{i=0}^{l-1}\bigvee_{j=i}^{l-1} g_j \vee \underline{\bigvee_{j=l}^{k} g_j}\right) \wedge \underline{\bigvee_{j=l}^{k} g_j}\\
&= \bigvee_{j=l}^{k} g_j . &(12)
\end{aligned}
$$

Intuitively, ${}_l[[\mathbf{GF}g]]_k^0$ holds if and only if g_j holds in at least one of the internal states of the loop. From (3) and (12) we have thus:

$$
[[\bigwedge_r \mathbf{GF}g^{(r)} \wedge f]]_k = \bigvee_{l=0}^{k}\left({}_lL_k \wedge \bigwedge_r \bigvee_{j=l}^{k} g_j{}^{(r)} \wedge {}_l[[f]]_k^0 \right) \tag{13}
$$

which represents the case of bounded model checking $M \models_k \mathbf{E}f$ under the set of fairness constraints $\{\mathbf{GF}g^{(r)}\}_r$. Intuitively, (13) means "there is a loop in which f holds s.t., for each $g^{(r)}$, there is a state s_j in the loop in which $g^{(r)}$ holds". Again, if ${}_l[[f]]_k^0$ does not depend on l, it can be extracted from the disjunction:

$$
[[\bigwedge_r \mathbf{GF}g^{(r)} \wedge f]]_k = {}_*[[f]]_k^0 \wedge \bigvee_{l=0}^{k}\left({}_lL_k \wedge \bigwedge_r \bigvee_{j=l}^{k} g_j{}^{(r)} \right) . \tag{14}
$$

Notice that, if we have only one fairness constraint $\mathbf{GF}g$, we can rewrite (13) as:

$$
\begin{aligned}
[[\mathbf{GF}g \wedge f]]_k &= \bigvee_{l=0}^{k}\left(\bigvee_{j=l}^{k} g_j \wedge {}_lL_k \wedge {}_l[[f]]_k^0\right)\\
&= \bigvee_{l=0}^{k}\bigvee_{j=l}^{k} (g_j \wedge ({}_lL_k \wedge {}_l[[f]]_k^0))\\
&= \bigvee_{j=0}^{k}\bigvee_{l=0}^{j} (g_j \wedge {}_lL_k \wedge {}_l[[f]]_k^0)\\
&= \bigvee_{j=0}^{k}\left(g_j \wedge \bigvee_{l=0}^{j}({}_lL_k \wedge {}_l[[f]]_k^0)\right) . &(15)
\end{aligned}
$$

Intuitively, (15) means "there is a state s_j in which g holds, s.t. there is a loop containing s_j in which f holds". This means lifting to the top of the formula the boolean constraint g_j –which typically come straightforwardly from primary inputs.

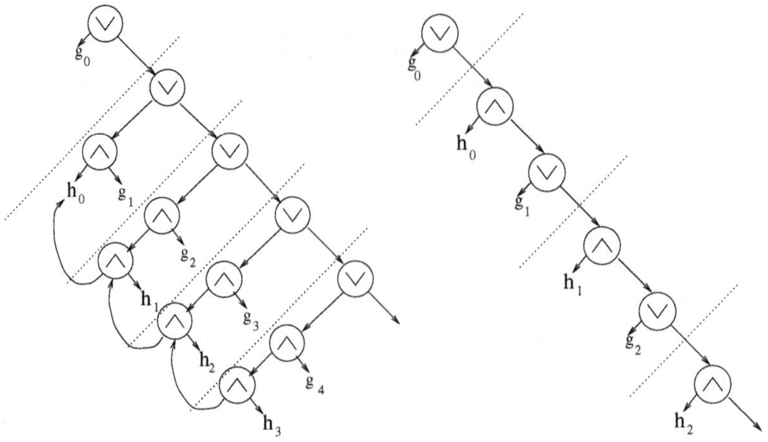

Fig. 1. $[[h\mathbf{U}g]]_k^0 = \; _l[[h\mathbf{U}g]]_k^0$, g, h boolean. Left: as in (16). Right: as in (17).

4.4 "Tableau-Style" Encodings for f = hUg and f = hRg

Consider $f = h\mathbf{U}g$, h and g being generic LTL formulas. From Table 1, for $i = 0$ we have that

$$[[h\mathbf{U}g]]_k^0 = \begin{array}{l} (\ [[g]]_k^0 \qquad\qquad\qquad\qquad\qquad\qquad \vee \\ ((\ [[g]]_k^1 \wedge \ [[h]]_k^0 \qquad\qquad\qquad\qquad)\vee \\ ((\ [[g]]_k^2 \wedge (\ [[h]]_k^0 \wedge [[h]]_k^1\ ) \qquad\qquad)\vee \\ ((\ [[g]]_k^3 \wedge ((\ [[h]]_k^0 \wedge [[h]]_k^1\ ) \wedge [[h]]_k^2\ )\ )\vee \\ \quad \ldots \qquad\qquad\qquad\qquad\qquad\qquad \ldots \\ ))))\ldots)) \end{array} \tag{16}$$

we notice that each $[[h]]_k^i$ is a common conjunct from the $i+2$-th conjunction onward. Thus, factorizing iteratively the $[[h]]_k^i$'s, we obtain:

$$[[h\mathbf{U}g]]_k^0 = \begin{array}{l} (\ [[g]]_k^0 \vee \\ \quad (\ [[h]]_k^0 \wedge (\ [[g]]_k^1 \vee \\ \qquad\qquad (\ [[h]]_k^1 \wedge (\ [[g]]_k^2 \vee \\ \qquad\qquad\qquad (\ [[h]]_k^2 \wedge (\ [[g]]_k^3 \vee \\ \ldots \qquad\quad \ldots \qquad\quad \ldots \\ )\,)) \qquad\quad)) \qquad\quad)) \qquad\quad \ldots \end{array} \tag{17}$$

Analogous transformations can be done for $[[h\mathbf{U}g]]_k^i$, $_l[[h\mathbf{U}g]]_k^0$ and $_l[[h\mathbf{U}g]]_k^i$.

A comparison of the (DAG of the) encodings in (16) and (17), with h and g boolean, is represented in Figure 1. The second encoding requires about $2 \cdot k$ new nodes, while the first, even with the best factorization, requires about $3 \cdot k$ nodes.

Intuitively, the encoding (17) can be seen as a straightforward application of the recursive expansion:

$$h\mathbf{U}g = g \vee (h \wedge \mathbf{X}(h\mathbf{U}g)), \tag{18}$$

which is the basis of the tableau encoding of LTL formulas into automata [15]. For this reason, we call this kind of encodings "tableau-style". Analogous encodings can be produced for $[[h\mathbf{R}g]]_k^i$ and $_l[[h\mathbf{R}g]]_k^i$.

The tableau-style encodings are logically equivalent to those of Table 1, thus properties 1 and 2 still hold and, if $depth(f) \leq 1$, then we still have that $_*[[h\mathbf{U}g]]_k^0 = [[h\mathbf{U}g]]_k^0$ and $_*[[h\mathbf{R}g]]_k^0 = \bigwedge_{j=0}^k g_j \vee [[h\mathbf{R}g]]_k^0$. As a consequence, the optimizations described in Sections 4.1 and 4.2 apply to tableau-style encodings as well.

5 Adding Implicit Constraints

Property 1 suggests a further optimization to apply to (3) to speed up the work of the SAT solver. In Section 4.2 we noticed that if $depth(f) > 1$, then $[[f]]_k^i$ is not necessarily a subformula of $_l[[f]]_k^i$. Thus, when the SAT solver has assigned (the labeling variable of) $[[f]]_k^i$ to true, in general it may need extra search to infer that the $_l[[f]]_k^i$'s are true; vice-versa, when it has assigned one $_l[[f]]_k^i$ to false, it may need extra search to infer that $[[f]]_k^i$ is false.

Thus, the idea is to add a series of constraints to the resulting DAG of $[[M,f]]_k$, to speed up the search. If g is a subformula of f s.t. $depth(f) > depth(g) > 1$, then for every i and l such that $[[g]]_k^i$ and $_l[[g]]_k^i$ occur in the DAG of $[[M,f]]_k$, the subformula:

$$\neg [[g]]_k^i \vee {}_l[[g]]_k^i \tag{19}$$

is added to the DAG of $[[M,f]]_k$.

As both $[[g]]_k^i$ and $_l[[g]]_k^i$ already occur in the DAG, the subformula (19) is simply a binary clause in the labeling variables of $[[g]]_k^i$ and $_l[[g]]_k^i$. Thus, when the SAT solver has assigned (the labeling variable of) $[[g]]_k^i$ to true, then it assigns to true also all the $_l[[g]]_k^i$'s by simple unit propagation, and vice-versa. If $depth(f) = depth(g) > 1$, then only the $_l[[g]]_k^0$'s occur in the DAG of $[[M,f]]_k$, thus only the constraints in $\neg [[g]]_k^0 \vee {}_l[[g]]_k^0$ are added, for all l. On the whole, this corresponds to add to the DAG of $[[M,f]]_k$ the formula

$$\bigwedge_{\substack{g \subseteq f:\\ depth(g) =\\ depth(f) > 1}} \bigwedge_{l=0}^{k} (\neg [[g]]_k^0 \vee {}_l[[g]]_k^0) \wedge \bigwedge_{\substack{g \subset f:\\ depth(f) >\\ depth(g) > 1}} \bigwedge_{i=0}^{k} \bigwedge_{l=0}^{k} (\neg [[g]]_k^i \vee {}_l[[g]]_k^i), \tag{20}$$

which corresponds to add $O(k^2 \cdot |f|)$ binary constraints.

6 Exploiting the Associativity Order

The main reason why we use DAGs to represent propositional formulas is that they allow for sharing a lot of subformulas, reducing thus the size and number of extra variables of the resulting CNF-ized formula submitted to the SAT solver [12,10]. Unfortunately, using DAG representation does not help to recognize as identical two formulas which differ only modulo associativity of $\wedge, \vee$, like, e.g., $(p \wedge (q \wedge r))$ and $(p \wedge q) \wedge r))$. When encoding complex LTL formulas the problem becomes very relevant, and it requires some care.

Consider for example the case of $f = h\mathbf{U}g$, with h and g boolean, and consider the j-th disjunct $\bigwedge_{n=0}^{j-1} h_n$ in Table 2. If the conjuncts are associated left-to-right:

$$j: \quad (h_1 \wedge (h_2 \wedge (\ldots \wedge (h_{j-2} \wedge h_{j-1}))) \ldots))) \tag{21}$$

$$j+1: \quad (h_1 \wedge (h_2 \wedge (\ldots \wedge (h_{j-2} \wedge (h_{j-1} \wedge h_j)))) \ldots))), \tag{22}$$

then the DAGs cannot share any sub-formula of the conjunction. If, instead, the conjuncts are associated right-to-left:

$$j: \quad ((((\ldots (h_1 \wedge h_2) \ldots \wedge h_{j-2}) \wedge h_{j-1}) \tag{23}$$

$$j+1: \quad ((((\ldots (h_1 \wedge h_2) \ldots \wedge h_{j-2}) \wedge h_{j-1}) \wedge h_j) \tag{24}$$

then the DAGs share the components $((((\ldots (h_1 \wedge h_2) \ldots \wedge h_i)$, as in Figure 1 (left). If we consider instead the example of $f = \mathbf{GF}g$ with g boolean (13), in order to let the DAG share the common disjuncts, the terms $G_l^k = \bigvee_{j=l}^k g_j$ must be associated in the opposite way:

$$G_l^k: \quad (g_l \vee (g_{l+1} \vee \ldots (g_{k-2} \vee (g_{k-1} \vee g_k)) \ldots)))) \tag{25}$$

$$G_{l+1}^k: \quad (g_{l+1} \vee \ldots (g_{k-2} \vee (g_{k-1} \vee g_k)) \ldots))). \tag{26}$$

Thus, using DAGs with more complex LTL formulas, it is very important to decide each time the best associativity order of the conjuncts to maximize the sharing of common nodes by DAGs.

7 Conclusions and Future Works

In this paper we identified some simplifications of the encoding of bounded model checking problems into propositional satisfiability problems. These simplifications aim to reduce the effort of the SAT solvers in this problem. We are currently integrating the defined optimizations within NuSMV. Preliminary experiments on the problems proposed in [2] (not reported here for lack of space) confirm that these optimizations lead to a reduction on the size of the CNF formulas submitted to the SAT solver, and to a significant reduction in the time required by the SAT solver to return an answer.

Future work goes in two main directions. The first one consists in completing the integration of all the simplifications defined in this paper within NuSMV. The second direction consists in performing an exhaustive experimental analysis aimed, from one hand, to show the effectiveness of the devised simplifications, and from the other hand, to possibly discover new ones. A crucial point to perform a detailed experimental analysis is the lack of a standard benchmark suite for evaluating the performances of the encoding algorithms. As part of this task, we are working on the definition of a benchmark suite for bounded model checking problems.

References

1. P. A. Abdullah, P. Bjesse, and N. Een. Symbolic Reachability Analysis based on SAT-Solvers. In *Sixth Int.nl Conf. on Tools and Algorithms for the Construction and Analysis of Systems (TACAS'00)*, 2000.
2. A. Biere, A. Cimatti, E. M. Clarke, and Yunshan Zhu. Symbolic Model Checking without BDDs. In *Proc. TACAS'99*, pages 193–207, 1999.
3. A. Biere, E. Clarke, R. Raimi, and Y. Zhu. Verifying safety proeprties of a power pc microprocessor using symbolic model checking without BDDs. In *Proc CAV99*, volume 1633 of *LNCS*, pages 60–71, Berlin, 1999. Springer.
4. R. E. Bryant. Symbolic Boolean manipulation with ordered binary-decision diagrams. *ACM Computing Surveys*, 24(3):293–318, September 1992.
5. J. R. Burch, E. M. Clarke, K. L. McMillan, D. L. Dill, and L. J. Hwang. Symbolic Model Checking: 10^{20} States and Beyond. *Information and Computation*, 98(2):142–170, June 1992.
6. A. Cimatti, E. M. Clarke, F. Giunchiglia, and M. Roveri. NuSMV : a new symbolic model checker. *International Journal on Software Tools for Technology Transfer (STTT)*, 2(4), March 2000.
7. E. Clarke, O. Grumberg, and D. Long. Model Checking. In *Proceedings of the International Summer School on Deductive Program Design*, Marktoberdorf, Germany, 1994.
8. E.M. Clarke, E.A. Emerson, and A.P. Sistla. Automatic verification of finite-state concurrent systems using temporal logic specifications. *ACM Transactions on Programming Languages and Systems*, 8(2):244–263, 1986.
9. F. Copty, L. Fix, E. Giunchiglia, G. Kamhi, A. Tacchella, and M. Vardi. Benefits of Bounded Model Checking at an Industrial Setting. In *Proc. CAV'2001*, LNCS, Berlin, 2001. Springer.
10. E. Giunchiglia and R. Sebastiani. Applying the Davis-Putnam procedure to non-clausal formulas. In *Proc. AI*IA'99*, number 1792 in Lecture Notes in Artificial Intelligence. Springer Verlag, 1999.
11. K.L. McMillan. *Symbolic Model Checking.* Kluwer Academic Publ., 1993.
12. D.A. Plaisted and S. Greenbaum. A Structure-preserving Clause Form Translation. *Journal of Symbolic Computation*, 2:293–304, 1986.
13. D. Sheridan and T. Walsh. Clause Forms Generated by Bounded Model Checking. In *Proc. Eighth Workshop on Automated Reasoning: Bridging the Gap between Theory and Practice*, University of York, March 2001.
14. O. Shtrichmann. Tuning SAT checkers for bounded model checking. In *Conference of Computer Aided Verification*, volume 1855 of *LNCS*, pages 480–494, Berlin, 2000. Springer.
15. M. Y. Vardi and P. Wolper. Automata-Theoretic Techniques for Modal Logics of Programs. *Journal of Computer and System Sciences*, 32:183–221, 1986.
16. P. F. Williams, A. Biere, E. M. Clarke, and A. Gupta. Combining Decision Diagrams and SAT Procedures for Efficient Symbolic Model Checking. In *Proc. CAV'2000*, volume 1855 of *LNCS*, pages 124–138, Berlin, 2000. Springer.

Automatic Verification of Probabilistic Free Choice*

Lenore Zuck[1], Amir Pnueli[1,2], and Yonit Kesten[3]

[1] New York University, New York
zuck@cs.nyu.edu
[2] Weizmann Institute of Science, Rehovot, Israel
amir@wisdom.weizmann.ac.il
[3] Ben-Gurion University, Beer-Sheva, Israel
yKesten@bgumail.bgu.ac.il

Abstract. We study *automatic* methods for establishing P-validity (validity with probability 1) of *simple* temporal properties over finite-state probabilistic systems. The proposed approach replaces P-validity with validity over a non-probabilistic version of the system, in which probabilistic choices are replaced by non-deterministic choices constrained by *compassion* (strong fairness) requirements. "Simple" properties are temporal properties whose only temporal operators are $\Diamond$ (eventually) and its dual $\Box$ (always). In general, the appropriate compassion requirements are "global," since they involve global states of the system. Yet, in many cases they can be transformed into "local" requirements, which enables their verification by model checkers. We demonstrate our methodology of translating the problem of P-validity into that of verification of a system with local compassion requirement on the "courteous philosophers" algorithm of [LR81], a parameterized probabilistic system that is notoriously difficult to verify, and outline a verification of the algorithm that was obtained by the TLV model checker.

1 Introduction

Probabilistic elements have been introduced into concurrent systems in the early 1980s to provide solutions (with high probability) to problems that do not have deterministic solutions. Among the pioneers of probabilistic protocols were ([LR81, Rab82]). One of the most challenging problems in the study of probabilistic protocols has been their formal verification. While methodologies for proving safety (invariance) properties still hold for probabilistic protocols, formal verification of their liveness properties has been, and still is, a challenge. The main difficulty stems from the two types of nondeterminism that occur in such programs: Their asynchronous execution, that assumes a hostile (though somewhat fair) scheduler, and the nondeterminism associated with the probabilistic actions, that assumes an even-handed scheduler.

* This research was supported in part by the John von Neumann Minerva Center for Verification of Reactive Systems, The European Community IST project "Advance", and ONR grant N00014-99-1-0131.

A. Cortesi (Ed.): VMCAI 2002, LNCS 2294, pp. 208–224, 2002.
© Springer-Verlag Berlin Heidelberg 2002

It had been realized that if one only wants to prove that a certain property is *P-valid*, i.e., holds with probability 1 over all executions of a system, this can be accomplished, for finite-state systems, in a manner that is completely independent of the precise probabilities. Decidability of P-validity had been first established in [HSP82] for termination properties over finite-state systems, using a methodology that is graph-theoretic in nature. The work in [PZ86b] extends the [HSP82] method and presents deductive proof rules for proving P-validity for termination properties of finite-state program. The work in [PZ86a, PZ93] presents sound and complete methodology for establishing P-validity of general temporal properties over probabilistic systems, and [VW86, PZ86a, PZ93] describe model checking procedure for the finite-state case.

The emerging interest in embedded systems brought forth a surge of research in automatic verification of parameterized systems, that, having unbounded number of states, are not easily amendable to model checking techniques. In fact, verification of such systems is known to be undecidable [AK86]. Much of the recent research has been devoted to identifying conditions that enable automatic verification of such systems, and abstraction tools to facilitate the task (e.g., [KP00, APR$^+$01, EN95, EN96, EK00, PRZ01].)

Many of the probabilistic protocols that have been proposed and studied (e.g., [LR81, Rab82, PZ86b, CLP84]) are parameterized. An obvious question is therefore whether we can combine verification tools of parameterized systems with those of probabilistic ones. The work in [PZ86b] provides several examples of deductive verification of *parameterized* probabilistic systems, including the *free philosophers* algorithm of [LR81] that guarantees livelock freedom of the system. A verification of the more complex *courteous philosophers* algorithm of [LR81] is in [L85], using a methodology that cannot be automated.

The main additional difficulty encountered when verifying probabilistic programs is "probabilistic fairness" – the fairness requirement over computations that suffices to replace measure-theoretic considerations. In this paper we study the problem of *automatic* verification of P-validity of probabilistic systems using a method that is also applicable to the verification of parameterized probabilistic systems. We show how, for the case of *simple* temporal properties, probabilistic systems can be translated into non-probabilistic systems by replacing the probabilistic fairness with *compassion* (strong fairness.) "Simple" properties are temporal properties whose only temporal operator are $\diamondsuit$ (eventually) and its dual $\square$ (always). While this, of course, impairs the expressive power of the properties proven, it encompasses almost all properties of probabilistic protocols that have been studied. The compassion requirements obtained, however, are many and global (i.e., are with respect to global states.) Consequently, the systems obtained are not easily accommodated by most model checkers, that expect compassion requirements to be local. In many cases, and almost all of those we have studied, it is possible to transform the new compassion requirements into few local ones.

We demonstrate our methodology of translating the problem of P-validity into that of verification of a system with local compassion requirement on the "courteous philosopher" algorithm of [LR81], a parameterized probabilistic system that is notoriously difficult to verify. We describe the automatic verification of the algorithm obtained using TLV [PS96], the Weizmann Institute's programmable model checker.

2 Fair Discrete Systems

As a computational model for reactive systems we take the model of *fair discrete systems* (FDS) [KP00], which is a slight variation on the model of *fair transition system* [MP95]. Under this model, a system $\mathcal{S} : \langle V, \mathcal{O}, W, \Theta, \rho, \mathcal{J}, \mathcal{C} \rangle$ consists of the following components:

- V: A finite set of typed *system variables*, containing data and control variables. A state s is an assignment of type-compatible values to the system variables V. For a set of variables $U \subseteq V$, we denote by $s[U]$ the set of values assigned by state s to the variables U. The set of states over V is denoted by Σ. In this paper, we assume that Σ is finite.
- $\mathcal{O} \subseteq V$: A subset of *observable variables.* These are the variables which can be externally observed.
- $W \subseteq V$: A subset of *owned* variables. These are variables which only the system itself can modify. All other variables can also be modified by steps of the environment.
- Θ: The *initial condition* – an *assertion* (first-order state formula) characterizing the initial states.
- ρ: A *transition relation* – an assertion $\rho(V, V')$, relating the values V of the variables in state $s \in \Sigma$ to the values V' in an ρ-successor state $s' \in \Sigma$.
- $\mathcal{J}$: A set of *justice* (*weak fairness*) *requirements*. The justice requirement $J \in \mathcal{J}$ is an assertion, intended to guarantee that every computation contains infinitely many J-states (states satisfying J).
- $\mathcal{C}$: A set of *compassion* (*strong fairness*) *requirements*. Each compassion requirement is a pair $\langle p, q \rangle \in \mathcal{C}$ of assertions, intended to guarantee that every computation containing infinitely many p-states also contains infinitely many q-states.

We require that every state $s \in \Sigma$ has at least one ρ-successor. This is often ensured by including in ρ the *idling* disjunct $V = V'$ (also called the *stuttering* step). In such cases, every state s is its own ρ-successor. A system is said to be *closed* if $W = V$, i.e., all variables are owned by the system.

Let $\sigma : s_0, s_1, s_2, ...,$ be an infinite sequence of states, φ be an assertion, and let $j \geq 0$ be a natural number. We say that j is a φ-position of σ if s_j is a φ-state.

Let $\mathcal{S}$ be an FDS for which the above components have been identified. We define an (*open*) *computation* of $\mathcal{S}$ to be an infinite sequence of states $\sigma : s_0, s_1, s_2, ...,$ satisfying the following requirements:

- *Initiality:* s_0 is initial, i.e., $s_0 \models \Theta$.
- *Consecution:* For each $j = 0, 1, ...,$
  - $s_{2j+1}[W] = s_{2j}[W]$. That is, s_{2j+1} and s_{2j} agree on the interpretation of the owned variables W.
  - s_{2j+2} is a ρ-successor of s_{2j+1}.
- *Justice:* For each $J \in \mathcal{J}$, σ contains infinitely many J-positions
- *Compassion:* For each $\langle p, q \rangle \in \mathcal{C}$, if σ contains infinitely many p-positions, it must also contain infinitely many q-positions.

According to this definition, system and environment steps strictly interleave. Since both the system and environment allow stuttering steps, this is not a serious restriction.

For an FDS $\mathcal{S}$, we denote by $\mathit{Comp}(\mathcal{S})$ the set of all computations of $\mathcal{S}$. A *property* is a (next- and previous-free) propositional linear time temporal logic, possibly including past operators, over the states of $\mathcal{S}$. A property φ is *valid* over $\mathcal{S}$ is $\sigma \models \varphi$ for every $\sigma \in \mathit{Comp}(\mathcal{S})$.

Systems $\mathcal{S}_1$ and $\mathcal{S}_2$ are *compatible* if their sets of owned variables are disjoint, and the intersection of their variables is observable in both systems. For compatible systems $\mathcal{S}_1$ and $\mathcal{S}_2$, the *parallel composition* of $\mathcal{S}_1$ and $\mathcal{S}_2$, denoted by $\mathcal{S}_1 \parallel \mathcal{S}_2$, is the FDS whose sets of variables, observable variables, owned variables, justice, and compassion sets are the unions of the corresponding sets in the two systems, whose initial condition is the conjunction of the initial conditions, and whose transition relation is the disjunction of the two transition relations. Thus, a step in an execution of the new system is a step of system $\mathcal{S}_1$, or a step of system $\mathcal{S}_2$, or an environment step.

An *observation* of $\mathcal{S}$ is a projection of $\mathcal{S}$-computation onto $\mathcal{O}$. We denote by $\mathit{Obs}(\mathcal{S})$ the set of all observations of $\mathcal{S}$. Systems $\mathcal{S}_C$ and $\mathcal{S}_A$ are said to be *comparable* if they have the same sets of observable variables, i.e., $\mathcal{O}_C = \mathcal{O}_A$. System $\mathcal{S}_A$, is said to be an *abstraction* of the comparable system $\mathcal{S}_C$, denoted $\mathcal{S}_C \sqsubseteq \mathcal{S}_A$ if $\mathit{Obs}(\mathcal{S}_A) \subseteq \mathit{Obs}(\mathcal{S}_C)$. The abstraction relation is reflexive, transitive, and compositional, that is, whenever $\mathcal{S}_C \sqsubseteq \mathcal{S}_A$ then $(\mathcal{S}_C \parallel Q) \sqsubseteq (\mathcal{S}_A \parallel Q)$. It is also *property restricting*. That is, if $\mathcal{S}_C \sqsubseteq \mathcal{S}_A$ then $\mathcal{S}_A \models p$ implies that $\mathcal{S}_C \models p$.

All our concrete examples are given in SPL (Simple Programming Language), which is used to represent concurrent programs (e.g., [MP95, MAB+94]). Every SPL program can be compiled into an FDS in a straightforward manner. In particular, every statement in an SPL program contributes a disjunct to the transition relation. For example, the assignment statement

$$\ell_0\colon\ y := x + 1;\ \ \ell_1\colon$$

can be executed when control is at location ℓ_0. When executed, it assigns $x+1$ to y while control moves from ℓ_0 to ℓ_1. This statement contributes to ρ the disjunct

$$\rho_{\ell_0}\colon \quad at\_\ell_0 \ \wedge\ at\_\ell_1' \ \wedge\ y' = x + 1 \ \wedge\ x' = x.$$

The predicates at_ℓ_0 and at_ℓ_1' stand, respectively, for the assertions $\pi_i = 0$ and $\pi_i' = 1$, where π_i is the control variable denoting the current location within the process to which the statement belongs.

3 Parameterized Systems and Their Verification

A *parameterized FDS* is a system $\mathcal{S}(N) = P[1] \parallel \ldots \parallel P[N]$, where the $P[i]$'s are symmetric SPL programs. For each value of $N > 0$, $\mathcal{S}(N)$ is an instantiation of an FDS. We are interested in properties that hold for every process in the system. Because of symmetry, we can express them in terms of one process, say $P[1]$. Thus, we are interested in properties of the type $\varphi(1)$, where $\varphi(1)$ is a temporal formula referring only to variables that are known to $P[1]$. The problem of parameterized verification is to show that $\varphi(1)$ is valid (P-valid) over $\mathcal{S}(N)$ *for every* N. A similar situation exists if we are interested in properties, such as mutual exclusion, which involve two contiguous processes. In this case, we can test these properties by checking whether a property $\psi(1,2)$ holds for the specific processes $P[1]$ and $P[2]$, for every value of $N > 2$.

Parametric verification is known to be undecidable (see, e.g., [AK86]). Recent research has focused on methodologies to identify systems and properties for which the problem of parametric verification is decidable, and, for these systems, to provide for semi- or fully- automatic verification.

One of the main ideas that have been proposed is to identify some number, say N_0, such that validity of $\varphi(1)$ over $\mathcal{S}[N']$ for every $N' \leq N_0$ suffices to establish its validity for all $N' \geq N$ [APR+01, EN95, EN96, EK00, PRZ01].

To prove the liveness property of a parameterized system, we propose a variant of the network invariant strategy of [KP00] (see also [WL89, BCG86, CGJ95], [KM95]). The approach is described by:

1. Divine a *network invariant* $\mathcal{I}$ which is an FDS intended to provide an abstraction for the parallel composition of $P_2 \parallel \cdots \parallel P_n$ for any $n \geq c$ for some small constant c.
2. Confirm that $\mathcal{I}$ is indeed a network invariant, by verifying that $P_2 \sqsubseteq \mathcal{I}$ and that $(\mathcal{I} \parallel P_2) \sqsubseteq \mathcal{I}$.
3. Model check $P_1 \parallel \mathcal{I} \models p$.
4. Conclude that $S(N) \models p$ for every $N > 1$.

The crucial step in establishing that a candidate $\mathcal{I}$ is a good network invariant is in proving the refinement ($\sqsubseteq$) relation between systems. Usually, the abstract system has significantly more non-determinism than the concrete system. Thus, showing the every concrete step has a unique abstract step that maps to it (and preserves the value of the observable variables) may be quite complicated. Indeed, it has been our experience that a significant part of the effort of proving refinement is devoted to "guiding" TLV to find the abstract step that maps to a concrete step.

4 Example: Deterministic Dining Philosophers

The purpose of this example is twofold: To show a parameterized system and outline its verification, and to present the problem of the dining philosophers that we look at more carefully in Section 6.

Assume there are $N > 2$ processes (philosophers) arranged in a ring (sitting around a table) numbered counter-clockwise $P_1, \ldots, P_N$. Let $i \oplus 1 = (i \bmod N) + 1$ and $i \ominus 1 = (i - 2 \bmod N) + 1$. These definitions lead to the facts that $N \oplus 1 = 1$ and $1 \ominus 1 = N$. Every two adjacent philosophers, P_i and $P_{i\oplus 1}$, share a common fork, $y[i \oplus 1]$. A description of a typical portion of the table is in Fig. 1. Philosophers spend most of their lives thinking (non-critical), however, occasionally a philosopher may become hungry. In order to eat, a philosopher needs to obtain both its adjacent forks. A solution to the dining philosophers problem is a program for the philosophers, that guarantees that no two adjacent philosophers eat simultaneously, and that every hungry philosopher eventually eats. It is well known that if the system is fully symmetric, there are no deterministic solutions to the problem. An almost symmetric solution, using semaphores for the forks, is presented in the SPL program described in Fig. 2. The system is "almost symmetric" since all processes, but one, follow the same protocol, while the singled out process ($P[1]$) follows a different protocol: A "regular' philosopher $P[i]$, $i > 1$, reaches first for its left fork and then for its right fork. The "contrary" philosopher $P[1]$ reaches first for its right fork and then for its left fork.

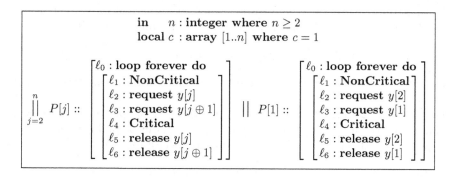

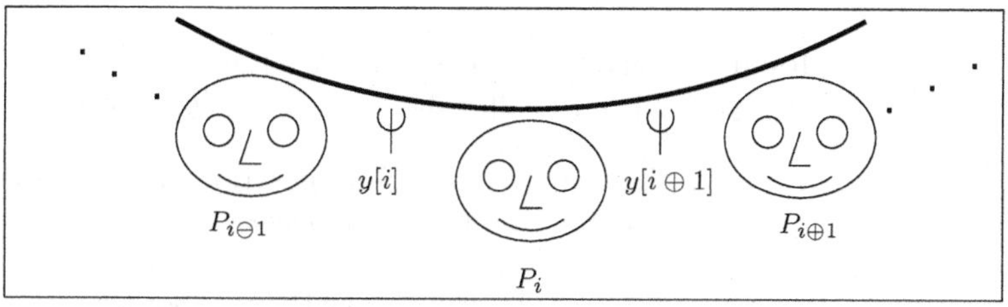

Fig. 1. Part of The Table

$$
\begin{array}{l}
\textbf{in} \quad n : \textbf{integer where } n \geq 2 \\
\textbf{local } c : \textbf{array } [1..n] \textbf{ where } c = 1
\end{array}
$$

$$
\mathop{\Big\|}_{j=2}^{n} P[j] :: \left[\begin{array}{l}
\ell_0 : \textbf{loop forever do} \\
\quad \left[\begin{array}{l}
\ell_1 : \textbf{NonCritical} \\
\ell_2 : \textbf{request } y[j] \\
\ell_3 : \textbf{request } y[j \oplus 1] \\
\ell_4 : \textbf{Critical} \\
\ell_5 : \textbf{release } y[j] \\
\ell_6 : \textbf{release } y[j \oplus 1]
\end{array}\right]
\end{array}\right]
\quad \Big\| \quad P[1] :: \left[\begin{array}{l}
\ell_0 : \textbf{loop forever do} \\
\quad \left[\begin{array}{l}
\ell_1 : \textbf{NonCritical} \\
\ell_2 : \textbf{request } y[2] \\
\ell_3 : \textbf{request } y[1] \\
\ell_4 : \textbf{Critical} \\
\ell_5 : \textbf{release } y[2] \\
\ell_6 : \textbf{release } y[1]
\end{array}\right]
\end{array}\right]
$$

Fig. 2. A deterministic solution with one contrary philosopher.

The liveness property of the system is:

$$\square(at\_\ell_2[1] \;\rightarrow\; \diamondsuit(at\_\ell_4[1])),$$

We now outline two different (and successful) network invariant strategies used for obtaining the liveness property of the protocol. In both, we view each regular philosopher as a system $P(\mathit{left}, \mathit{right})$, where the semaphores *left* and *right* are the only observables. We seek an invariant $\mathcal{I}(\mathit{left}, \mathit{right})$ which is an abstraction of the philosophers chain

$$S[k] :: \left[\begin{array}{l}\textbf{local } f : \textbf{array}[2..k] \textbf{ of boolean where } f = 1 \\ P(\mathit{left}, f[2]) \parallel P(f[2], f[3]) \parallel \cdots \parallel P(f[k], \mathit{right})\end{array}\right]$$

for every $k \geq 2$. This means that any $(\mathit{left}, \mathit{right})$-observation of $S[k]$ is matched by a corresponding $(\mathit{left}, \mathit{right})$-observation of $\mathcal{I}(\mathit{left}, \mathit{right})$.

Abstraction 1: The "*two-halves*". Observing how the two border members of $S[k]$ manipulate the obesrvables *left* and *right*, led, after experimentation to an abstraction consisting of the composition of a *left half* philosopher and a *right half* philosopher, as presented in Fig. 3.

$$L(\mathit{left}) :: \left[\begin{array}{l}\ell_0 : \textbf{loop forever do} \\ \left[\begin{array}{l}\ell_1 : \textbf{NonCritical} \\ \ell_2 : \textbf{request } \mathit{left} \\ \ell_3 : \textbf{idle} \\ \ell_4 : \textbf{Critical} \\ \ell_5 : \textbf{release } \mathit{left} \\ \ell_6 : \textbf{skip}\end{array}\right]\end{array}\right] \parallel R(\mathit{right}) :: \left[\begin{array}{l}m_0 : \textbf{loop forever do} \\ \left[\begin{array}{l}m_1 : \textbf{NonCritical} \\ m_2 : \textbf{idle} \\ m_3 : \textbf{request } \mathit{right} \\ m_4 : \textbf{Critical} \\ m_5 : \textbf{skip} \\ m_6 : \textbf{release } \mathit{right}\end{array}\right]\end{array}\right]$$

Extra Compassion: $(at\_\ell_3 \wedge \mathit{right} > 0,\; at\_\ell_4)$

Fig. 3. The two-halves Network Invariant

The additional compassion requirement reflects the possibility that the leftmost process in $S[2]$ may only deadlock while requesting its right fork (at ℓ_3) if the rightmost process can eventually always holds on to its right fork. To show that an arbitrary regular philosopher never starves, it is suffices to verify

$$(\mathcal{I} \parallel P \parallel \mathcal{I} \parallel R) \quad \models \quad (at\_\ell_2 \;\rightarrow\; \diamondsuit\; at\_\ell_4)$$

where R is a contrary philosopher and the locations in the property refer to P.

Abstraction 2: The "*four-by-three*". An alternate simpler invariant can be obtained by taking $\mathcal{I} = S[3]$, i.e. a chain of 3 (unmodified) philosophers.
To prove that this is an invariant, it is sufficient to establish

$$(p[1] \parallel p[2] \parallel p[3] \parallel p[4]) \sqsubseteq (P[5] \parallel P[6] \parallel P[7])$$

i.e., that 3 philosophers can faithfully emulate 4 philosophers.

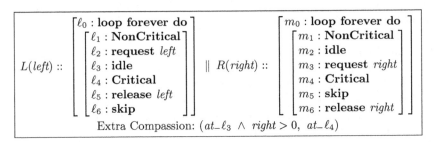

This is established by letting $P[5]$ mimic $p[1]$ and $P[7]$ mimic $p[4]$. As to $P[6]$, it can remain idle until it finds out that $S[4]$ is 2 (internal) steps away from a *guaranteed deadlock* (all of $p[1], \ldots, p[4]$ remain stuck at location ℓ_2), at which point $P[6]$ joins $P[5]$ and $P[7]$ in order to form a similar deadlock at the abstract level. This requires the capability of clairvoyance, which has been implemented within TLV.

5 Adding to and Removing Probabilities from FDSs

We describe the formal model for probabilistic discrete systems (PDS) and P-validity. We then show how, when establishing P-validity of simple properties, PDS's can be translated into FDSs.

5.1 PDS: Adding Probabilities to FDSs

A *probabilistic discrete system* (PDS) $\mathcal{S}$: $\langle V, \mathcal{O}, W, \Theta, \rho, \mathcal{J}, \mathcal{C}, \mathcal{P}\rangle$ consists of an FDS $\langle V, \mathcal{O}, W, \Theta, \rho, \mathcal{J}, \mathcal{C}\rangle$ and a *probabilistic fairness condition* $\mathcal{P}$ containing tuples of the form $\langle p;\ \alpha_1 : q_1, \ldots, \alpha_n : q_n\rangle$, where $q_1, \ldots, q_n$ are mutually disjoint state assertions, and $\sum_{i=1}^{n} \alpha_i = 1$. It is also required that p is disjoint of any of the q_i's. Intuitively, the meaning of a probabilistic fairness condition $\langle p;\ \alpha_1 : q_1, \ldots, \alpha_n : q_n\rangle$ is that whenever the system moves from a p-state into a state satisfying $\bigvee_{i=1}^{n} q_i$, it moves into a q_i-state with probability α_i. Let s be a p-state. It is required that s has precisely $n+1$ successors, s (itself) and $s_1, \ldots, s_n$, where s_i satisfies q_i, for every $i = 1, \ldots, n$.

The following definition applies to a PDS with a single probabilistic tuple $\langle p;\ \alpha_1 : q_1, \ldots, \alpha_n : q_n\rangle$. Its generalization to systems with more than one such tuple is straightforward.

An (open) *computation tree* of a PDS is formed as follows:

- The root of the tree is any state which is initial, i.e. satisfies Θ.
- Every node s at level $2j$ has a single descendant which is an environment successor of s,i.e. a state $\widetilde{s}$ such that $\widetilde{s}[W] = s[W]$.
- Every node s at level $2j+1$ which is not a p-state, has a single descendant which is a ρ-successor of s.
- Every node s at level $2j+1$ which is a p-state has either itself s as a single descendant, or the n descendants $s_1, \ldots, s_n$.

Such a tree induces a probability measure over all the infinite paths that can be traced in the tree, where each edge from s to s_i is assigned the probability a_i. A computation tree is called *admissible* if the measure of paths which are just and compassionate is 1.

Following [PZ93], we say that a temporal property φ is *P-valid* over a computation tree T_σ if the measure of paths in that satisfy φ is 1. (See [PZ93] for a detailed description and definition of the measure space.) Similarly, φ is *P-valid over the PDS $\mathcal{S}$* if it is P-valid over every admissible computation tree of $\mathcal{S}$.

Much work has been devoted to replacing the measure space required in the definition of P-validity by "simpler" notion of fairness. In particular, we have been searching for a definition of "x-fairness" of computation, such that φ would be P-valid iff it is satisfied by every x-fair computation of $\mathcal{S}$. Such is the α-fairness of [PZ93]: For a past temporal logic formula χ, a computation $\sigma = s_0, \ldots$ is *α-fair with respect to* χ if, for every probabilistic fairness condition $\langle p; \alpha_1 : q_1, \ldots, \alpha_n : q_n \rangle$,

$$s_0, \ldots, s_j \models \chi \wedge p \quad \text{and} \quad s_{j+1} \models q_1 \vee \ldots \vee q_n \qquad \text{for infinitely many } j\text{'s}$$

implies

$$s_0, \ldots, s_j \models \chi \wedge p \quad \text{and} \quad s_{j+1} \models q_\ell \qquad \text{for infinitely many } j\text{'s}$$

for every $\ell = 1, \ldots, n$.

In other words, if the computation reaches a "p to $\bigvee q_i$" transition infinitely many times from χ-prefices, then each mode of the transition should be taken infinitely many times from χ-prefices. A computation if *α-fair* iff it is α-fair with respect to *every* past temporal formula χ. A result of [PZ93] is:

Theorem 1. *A temporal property φ is P-valid over $\mathcal{S}$ iff every α-fair computation of $\mathcal{S}$ satisfies φ.*

While α-fairness is sound and complete, it is hardly satisfactory, since it calls for establishing α-fairness with respect to "every past formula." The work in [PZ93] also presents a model checking procedure of finite state PDSs against temporal specification that do not have the temporal operators $\bigcirc$ and $\mathcal{U}$. That is, the temporal properties whose P-validity is established in the model checking can include all the past operators, but the only future operator they can have is $\diamondsuit$ (and its dual, $\square$). The model checking procedure there involves constructing the closure of the (negation of the) property, building an atom graph where each atom node is a maximal logically-consistent subset of formulae in the closure that correspond to program states, and nodes are connected if they do so in both the tableau of the property and the program itself.

A careful examination of this model checking procedure reveals that in order to establish P-validity over finite state PDSs and $\{\bigcirc, \mathcal{U}\}$-less properties, it suffices to consider computations that are α-fair only with respect to every past formula that appears in the closure of the property. Consequently, we have:

Corollary 1. *Given a finite-state PDS $\mathcal{S}$ and a $\{\bigcirc, \mathcal{U}\}$-less property φ. Then φ is P-valid over $\mathcal{S}$ iff for every past formula χ appearing the in the closure of φ, every $\mathcal{S}$-computation that is α-fair with respect to χ satisfies φ.*

5.2 Removing Probabilities from PDSs

Consider *simple temporal properties* that do no include any of the past, or the future $\bigcirc$ and $\mathcal{U}$ operators. Thus, simple temporal properties include, as their only temporal operators, $\diamondsuit$ and it dual, $\square$. The work in [SZ93] includes an extensive study of this class.

While at first glance it may seem that this class of simple temporal properties is extremely restrictive, it is actually a rather inclusive class, since it accommodates all the safety, and most of the progress properties one usually wants to prove about PDSs. E.g., mutual exclusion usually has the form $\square(\text{trying}_i \rightarrow \diamondsuit\, \text{critical}_i)$ which is a simple temporal property.

The closure of a simple temporal property includes no past formulae. Consequently, we can replace α-fairness by fairness with respect to every state assertion. We call this notion of fairness γ-fairness. Formally, a $\mathcal{S}$-computation σ is γ-fair if it is α-fair with respect to every state assertion. Note that for a finite-state system, the relevant state assertions are the states themselves (in fact, the γ comes from "global", since this is fairness with respect to the global states.)

We can therefore conclude from Corollary 1:

Corollary 2. *Given a finite PDS $\mathcal{S}$ and a simple temporal property φ. Then φ is P-valid over $\mathcal{S}$ iff every $\mathcal{S}$-computation that is γ-fair satisfies φ.*

Corollary 2 implies that, in order to prove that a simple temporal property is P-valid over a finite PDS, it suffices to prove that it is satisfied over all (just and compassionate) computations of the system where if the probabilistic choice is made infinitely many times from a given state, then each outcome of that probabilistic choice should be taken from that state. Hence, each probabilistic fairness condition $\langle p; \alpha_1 : q_1, \ldots, \alpha_n : q_n \rangle$ can be translated into a *set of compassion* requirements that includes every pair of states $\langle s, s' \rangle$ such that s is a p-state and s' is a q_i-state for some i. For a set $\mathcal{P}$ of probabilistic fairness requirements, denote by $\mathcal{C}(\mathcal{P})$ the set of compassion properties obtained by replacing each condition in $\mathcal{P}$ by the corresponding set of compassion requirements. We then have:

Theorem 2. *Given a finite PDS $\mathcal{S} : \langle V, \Theta, \rho, \mathcal{J}, \mathcal{C}, \mathcal{P} \rangle$. Let $\mathcal{S}' : \langle V, \Theta, \rho, \mathcal{J}, \mathcal{C} \cup \mathcal{C}(\mathcal{P}) \rangle$ be the FDS obtained from $\mathcal{S}$ by translating the probabilistic fairness conditions of $\mathcal{S}$ into compassion requirements. Then for every simple temporal property φ,*

$$\varphi \text{ is P-valid over } \mathcal{S} \quad \text{iff} \quad \varphi \text{ is valid over } \mathcal{S}'$$

While Theorem 2 implies that PDSs can be translated into FDSs, a straightforward application of the idea may lead to systems that are not manageable by current model checkers. The reason for this is that the state assertions appearing in the probabilistic fairness conditions are usually local, while the assertions appearing in the new compassion requirements are usually global. For example, in the probabilistic fairness condition, p is usually of the form $at\_\ell_x[i]$ and the q_j's are of the form $at\_\ell_{y_j}[i]$, stating that "from any global state where $P[i]$ is about to take a probabilistic choice whose outcomes are to move it from location x to locations $y_1, \ldots, y_n$, each with a positive probability, it should reach each of these locations from that global state infinitely many times." Each compassion requirement $\langle s, s'_j \rangle$ we obtain has on the left one of the global states where $P[i]$ is in location x, and on the right a set of states where it is in location y_j. We cannot combine the left-hand-side s-s into a single compassion requirement, since this has the undesirable effect of allowing a computation where, e.g., $P[i]$ always gets to y_1 from certain states, and always to y_2 from others. Thus, unless somehow manipulated, we will end up with too many compassion requirements that are global, both are undesirable properties for the purpose of model checking. Note that the situation gets completely out of hand when dealing with parameterized systems. There, the number of compassion requirements one may end up with if not careful is exponential in the size of the code of a single process.

Consequently, a crucial step in establishing P-validity of simple properties using existing model checking technique is then to "localize" the compassion requirements and to minimize their number. While we have no general methodology of doing that, we succeeded to do it for many interesting cases. The most complex case is described in the next section.

6 The [LR81] Dining Philosophers Protocol

In Lehmann and Rabin's *Courteous Philosophers Algorithm* the forks are shared variables that are set when held and reset when on the table. In addition to the forks, adjacent philosophers share a $lastL[i \oplus 1]$ variable, initially -1, and after one of the them eats, denoting whether it's the left (P_i) philosopher that last ate or the right. Each philosopher P_i has additional boolean variables (written by it and read by its immediate neighbours), $signR[i]$ which denotes its wish to eat to its left neighbor ($P_{i\ominus 1}$) and $signL[i]$ which denotes its wish to eat to its right neighbor ($P_{i\oplus 1}$).

The algorithm is a refinement of the "Free Philosophers" algorithm, in the same paper, were each hungry philosopher chooses randomly whether to wait to its left or right fork first, and, after (and if) it obtains it, waits until the other fork is available. The Free Philosophers are guaranteed, however, only that eventually *some* philosopher eats. The Courteous Philosophers are similar to the free ones, the difference being that a courteous philosopher can pick up its first fork only if its partner (on that side) is either not hungry or is the last to have eaten between the two of them. An SPL code of the protocol is described in Fig. 4.[1]

The justice requirements and probabilistic fairness conditions of the system are the obvious ones, and there are no compassion requirements. Since the property we want to establish is the liveness property

$$\Box(at\_\ell_1[1] \;\rightarrow\; \Diamond\, at\_\ell_8[1]),$$

which is a simple property, we proceed to translate the probabilistic fairness into compassion requirements.

[1] In the protocol, as presented in [LR81], the instructions appearing in lines 9–11 are not atomic. Making them atomic, as we did in our presentation doesn't impair the proof since none of these non-atomic assignments are observable to a single process. It does, however, reduce state space for model-checking.

in N : **integer where** $N \geq 2$
local $signL, signR, y,$: **array** $[1..N]$ **of boolean init** 0
local $lastL$: **array** $[1..N]$ **of** $\{-1, 0, 1\}$ **init** -1

$\overset{N}{\underset{i=1}{\|}} P[i] ::$
loop forever do
- ℓ_0 : **non-critical**
- ℓ_1 : $signL[i] := 1; signR[i] := 1;$ **goto** $\{0.5 : \ell_2; 0.5 : \ell_5\}$
- ℓ_2 : **await** $\neg y[i] \;\wedge\; (\neg signR[i \ominus 1] \;\vee\; lastL[i] = 1)$
  and then $y[i] := 1$
- ℓ_3 : **If** $y[i \oplus 1] = 0$
  then $y[i \oplus 1] := 1$; **goto** ℓ_8
- ℓ_4 : $y[i] := 0$; **goto** ℓ_1
- ℓ_5 : **await** $\neg y[i \oplus 1] \;\wedge\; (\neg signL[i \oplus 1] \;\vee\; lastL[i \oplus 1] = 0)$
  and then $y[i \oplus 1] := 1$
- ℓ_6 : **If** $y[i] = 0$
  then $y[i] := 1$; **goto** ℓ_8
- ℓ_7 : $y[i \oplus 1] := 0$; **goto** ℓ_1
- ℓ_8 : **Critical**
- ℓ_9 : $signL[i] := 0; signR[i] := 0$
- ℓ_{10} : $lastL[i] := 0, lastL[i \oplus 1] := 1$
- ℓ_{11} : $y[i] := 0; y[i \oplus 1] := 0$

Fig. 4. The Courteous Philosophers

A naive replacement of the probabilistic fairness properties by compassion will lead to roughly 12^N global compassion requirements which is unacceptable. To minimize and localize the requirements, we employed a combination of studying the system (and its deductive proof in [L85]) and experimentation with proving the liveness property for $N = 3, 4$ using TLV. The chain of reductions we went through is as follows.

The deductive proof focuses, at each step, only on two adjacent processes. It seemed therefore reasonable to localize the compassion, and to require it from each processes only with respect to its immediate neighbours. This led to including in the compassion set of each process i the requirements:

$$\langle at\_\ell_1[i] \;\wedge\; cond,\; at\_\ell_2[i] \;\wedge\; cond \rangle, \quad \langle at\_\ell_1[i] \;\wedge\; cond,\; at\_\ell_5[i] \;\wedge\; cond \rangle$$

for every

$$cond \in \left\{ \begin{array}{l} at\_\ell_{8..11,0..1}[i \ominus 1], at\_\ell_{2,3}[i \ominus 1], at\_\ell_4[i \ominus 1], at\_\ell_{5,6}[i \ominus 1], at\_\ell_7[i \ominus 1] \\ at\_\ell_{8..11,0..1}[i \oplus 1], at\_\ell_{2,3}[i \oplus 1], at\_\ell_4[i \oplus 1], at\_\ell_{5,6}[i \oplus 1], at\_\ell_7[i \oplus 1] \end{array} \right\}$$

The process of deriving small and local compassion sets is non-algorithmic in nature, however, the result can always be automatically verified.

To provide an automatic proof of the liveness property of the protocol, we first reduced the state space, by eliminating the variables $y[i], signL[i], signR[i]$, whose values can be uniquely determined by the locations of the relevant processes. We also compressed all the actions performed in locations $\ell_8 - \ell_{11}$ into a single statement labeled ℓ_8. All of these reductions do not alter significantly the behavior of the processes but simplify its verification. This leads to the protocol described in Fig. 5.

$$\mathop{\Big\|}_{i=1}^{N} P[i] :: \left[\begin{array}{l} \textbf{in} \quad N: \quad \textbf{integer where } N \geq 2 \\ \textbf{local } \mathit{lastL} : \textbf{array } [1..N] \textbf{ of } \{-1,0,1\} \textbf{ init } -1 \\ \textbf{loop forever do} \\ \quad \left[\begin{array}{l} \ell_0 : \textbf{non-critical} \\ \ell_1 : \textbf{goto } \{0.5 : \ell_2; 0.5 : \ell_5\} \\ \ell_2 : \textbf{await } \mathit{at\_}\ell_0[i \ominus 1] \ \vee \ \mathit{at\_}\ell_{0..5}[i \ominus 1] \wedge (\mathit{lastL}[i] \neq 0) \\ \ell_3 : \textbf{if } \mathit{at\_}\ell_{1,2,5..7}[i \oplus 1] \textbf{ then go to } \ell_8 \\ \ell_4 : \ \textbf{go to } \ell_1 \\ \ell_5 : \textbf{await } \mathit{at\_}\ell_0[i \oplus 1] \ \vee \ \mathit{at\_}\ell_{1,2,5..7}[i \oplus 1] \wedge (\mathit{lastL}[i] \neq 1) \\ \ell_6 : \textbf{if } \mathit{at\_}\ell_{0..5}[i \ominus 1] \textbf{ then go to } \ell_8 \\ \ell_7 : \ \textbf{go to } \ell_1 \\ \ell_8 : \textbf{Critical; } \mathit{lastL}[i] := 0; \ \mathit{lastL}[i \oplus 1] := 1 \end{array}\right] \end{array}\right]$$

Fig. 5. Location-based Courteous Philosophers

Using TLV we established the property

$$\square\, \mathit{at\_}\ell_5[i] \quad \Longrightarrow \quad \diamondsuit \square (\mathit{at\_}\ell_5[i \oplus 1] \ \wedge \ \mathit{lastL}[i \oplus 1] = 1) \tag{1}$$

for every i. From this, by induction around the philosophers ring, we can show that if one process gets stuck at ℓ_5 then all processes eventually get stuck at ℓ_5, with $\mathit{lastL}[1] = \cdots = \mathit{lastL}[N] = 1$. Since the only statement which modifies any of the $\mathit{lastL}[i]$ variables is ℓ_8, which sets $\mathit{lastL}[i]$ to 0, and $\mathit{lastL}[i \oplus 1]$ to 1, we conclude that the situation $\mathit{lastL}[1] = \cdots = \mathit{lastL}[N] = 1$ is unreachable. Therefore, no process can get stuck at location ℓ_5. In a symmetric way, we can show that no process ever gets stuck at location ℓ_2.

This allows us to add the justice properties $\neg \mathit{at\_}\ell_2[i], \neg \mathit{at\_}\ell_5[i]$ to the justice set of each process. Thus, from now on, we restrict our attention to *progressive philosophers* which are guaranteed not to get stuck at either ℓ_2 or ℓ_5.

Next, we follow the ideas developed in Section 4 and view each philosopher $P[i]$ as a system $P(\mathit{lloc}, \mathit{cloc}, \mathit{rloc}, \mathit{clst}, \mathit{rlst})$, whose observables are, respectively, $\mathit{lloc} = P[i \ominus 1].\mathit{loc}$, $\mathit{cloc} = P[i].\mathit{loc}$, $\mathit{rloc} = P[i \oplus 1].\mathit{loc}$, $\mathit{clst} = \mathit{lastL}[i]$, and $\mathit{rlst} = \mathit{lastL}[i \oplus 1]$. We seek an invariant $\mathcal{I}(\mathit{elloc}, \mathit{lloc}, \mathit{rloc}, \mathit{erloc}, \mathit{llst}, \mathit{erlst})$ which is an abstraction of the following philosophers chain $S[k]$:

$$\left[\begin{array}{llll} \textbf{in} & \mathit{elloc}, \mathit{erloc} : & [0..8] \\ \textbf{in-out} & \mathit{llst}, \mathit{erlst} : & [-1..1] \textbf{ where } \mathit{llst}, \mathit{erlst} = -1 \\ \textbf{out} & \mathit{lloc}, \mathit{rloc} : & [0..8] \textbf{ where } \mathit{lloc}, \mathit{rloc} = 0 \\ \textbf{local} & \mathit{loc} : & \textbf{array}[2..k{-}1] \textbf{ of } [0..8] \textbf{ where } \mathit{loc} = 0 \\ & \mathit{lastL} : & \textbf{array}[2..k] \textbf{ of } [-1..1] \textbf{ where } \mathit{lastL} = -1 \\ \multicolumn{4}{l}{P(\mathit{elloc}, \mathit{lloc}, \mathit{loc}[2], \mathit{llst}, \mathit{lastL}[2]) \parallel \cdots \parallel P(\mathit{loc}[k{-}1], \mathit{rloc}, \mathit{erloc}, \mathit{lastL}[k], \mathit{erlst})} \end{array}\right]$$

for every $k \geq 2$.

Abstraction 1: The "*two-halves*". As in the same abstraction of the deterministic case, we obtain an abstraction consisting of the composition of a *left-half* philosopher and a *right-half* philosopher. This abstraction is presented in Fig. 6.

in $elloc, erloc : [0..8]$
in-out $llst, erlst : [-1..1]$ **where** $llst, erlst = -1$
out $lloc, rloc : [0..8]$ **where** $lloc, rloc = 0$

loop forever do
- ℓ_0 : **non-critical**
- ℓ_1 : **goto** $\{\ell_2, \ell_5\}$
- ℓ_2 : **await** $elloc = 0 \vee elloc \in \{0..5\} \wedge llst \neq 0$
- ℓ_3 : **go to** $\{\ell_4, \ell_8\}$
- ℓ_4 : **go to** ℓ_1
- ℓ_5 : **skip**
- ℓ_6 : **if** $elloc \in \{0..5\}$ **then go to** ℓ_8
- ℓ_7 : **go to** ℓ_1
- ℓ_8 : **Critical**; $llst := 0$

$\|$

loop forever do
- m_0 : **non-critical**
- m_1 : **goto** $\{m_2, m_5\}$
- m_2 : **skip**
- m_3 : **if** $erloc \in \{1, 2, 5..7\}$ **then go to** m_8
- m_4 : **go to** m_1
- m_5 : **await** $erloc = 0 \vee erloc \in \{1, 2, 5..7\} \wedge erlst \neq 1$
- m_6 : **go to** $\{m_7, m_8\}$
- m_7 : **go to** m_1
- m_8 : **Critical**; $erlst := 1$

Extra Compassion: $(at\_\ell_{2..4} \wedge at\_m_{5..7},\quad at\_\ell_8 \vee at\_m_8)$

Fig. 6. A two-halves abstraction for the Courteous Philosophers

The additional compassion property $\langle at\_\ell_{2..4} \wedge at\_m_{5..7}, at\_\ell_8 \vee at\_m_8 \rangle$ reflects a remote interaction between the two end processes.

Using TLV, we model checked that the network invariant, so derived, is inductive, and, that properly connected to a full philosopher, the system satisfies the liveness property.

Abstraction 2: The "*five-by-four*". As in the deterministic case, the "$k+1$-by-k" abstraction has the potential of being much simpler. Unlike the deterministic case, this cannot be done for $k = 3$ because of the additional ($lastL$) variables. There is a reason to believe that it can be accomplished for $k = 4$. We describe here the ideas that lead us to this belief. However, since model-checking this abstraction requires running nine processes, we have so far failed in checking it in TLV, hence we just sketch the main ideas.

Thus, we take $\mathcal{I} = S[4]$, that is, a chain of 4 (unmodified) philosophers, and prove that

$$(p[1] \parallel p[2] \parallel p[3] \parallel p[4] \parallel p[5]) \sqsubseteq (P[6] \parallel P[7] \parallel P[8] \parallel P[9])$$

i.e., that 4 philosophers can faithfully emulate 5 philosophers (and the observable variables.)

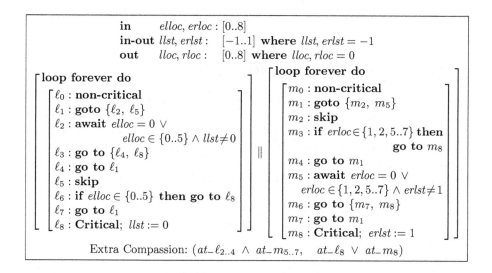

This is established by letting $P[6]$ mimic $p[1]$ and $P[9]$ mimic $p[5]$. The middle processes, $P[7]$ and $P[8]$, remain mostly idle. The only scenario in which $P[7]$ has to move is when $p[1]$ gives up its left fork, i.e., the system moves from a $at\_\ell_3[1]$-state into a $at\_\ell_4[1]$-state. Similarly, $P[8]$ has to move only in the symmetric situation with respect to $p[5]$ (moving from ℓ_6 into to ℓ_7). In each of these cases, it is possible to let the relevant middle process get hold of the fork it shares with its external neighbour, so that to justify the neighbour's failure to obtain the fork. It is also possible to do it in a way the will guarantee compassion of the abstract system.

7 Conclusion and Future Research

In this paper we studied the problem of proving P-validity (validity with probability 1) of "simple" LTL specifications over finite state program. We showed how probabilistic fairness can be replaced by compassion (strong fairness), thus reducing the problem of proving P-validity of probabilistic program to that of verifying (strongly) fair programs. The compassion requirements so obtained are generally global, i.e., are expressed relative to global state of the system. In order to model-check such properties, the compassion requirements must be local, i.e., expressed relative to states of single processes. Once one obtains local compassion properties, establishing P-validity of simple properties can be fully automatic.

We demonstrated our ideas by providing a formal proof for the Courteous Philosophers algorithm of Lehman and Rabin, a notoriously difficult to formally verify. (Indeed, this is the first published verification of it.) The protocol is a somewhat involved protocol that is both parameterized and probabilistic. We are happy to report that we succeeded in obtaining the proofs using the Weizmann programmable model checker TLV.

The main drawback of our method is the ad-hoc manner in which we "localized" the compassion properties. We are attempting to develop better methodologies and tools to assist us in this step. We are also studying more examples, e.g., parameterized probabilistic mutual exclusion protocols.

Another issue, closely related to the work here, is the notion of abstraction and tools for its verification. The research reported here helped us identify some extensions of the notion of abstraction (notably, clairvoyance and stuttering) that can considerably improve our tools. We are currently attempting to find more such extensions. Thus, we hope to soon be able to automatically establish the "five-to-four" abstraction reported at the end of the previous section.

References

[AK86] K. R. Apt and D. Kozen. Limits for automatic program verification of finite-state concurrent systems. *Information Processing Letters*, 22(6), 1986.

[APR+01] T. Arons, A. Pnueli, S. Ruah, J. Xu, and L. Zuck. Parameterized verification with automatically computed inductive assertions. In *Proc.* 13rd *Intl. Conference on Computer Aided Verification (CAV'01), volume 2102 of* Lect. Notes in Comp. Sci., *Springer-Verlag*, pages 221–234, 2001.

[BCG86] M.C. Browne, E.M. Clarke, and O. Grumberg. Reasoning about networks with many finite state processes. In *Proc. 5th ACM Symp. Princ. of Dist. Comp.*, pages 240–248, 1986.

[CGJ95] E.M. Clarke, O. Grumberg, and S. Jha. Verifying parametrized networks using abstraction and regular languages. In *6th International Conference on Concurrency Theory (CONCUR'95)*, pages 395–407, 1995.

[CLP84] S. Cohen, D. Lehmann, and A. Pnueli. Symmetric and economical solutions to the mutual exclusion problem in a distributed system. *Theor. Comp. Sci.*, 34:215–225, 1984.

[EK00] E.A. Emerson and V. Kahlon. Reducing model checking of the many to the few. In *17th International Conference on Automated Deduction (CADE-17)*, pages 236–255, 2000.

[EN95] E. A. Emerson and K. S. Namjoshi. Reasoning about rings. In *Proc. 22th ACM Conf. on Principles of Programming Languages, POPL'95*, San Francisco, 1995.

[EN96] E.A. Emerson and K.S. Namjoshi. Automatic verification of parameterized synchronous systems. In *R. Alur and T. Henzinger, editors,* Proc. 8th Intl. Conference on Computer Aided Verification (CAV'96)*, volume 1102 of* Lect. Notes in Comp. Sci.*, Springer-Verlag,* 1996.

[HSP82] S. Hart, M. Sharir, and A. Pnueli. Termination of probabilistic concurrent programs. In *Proc. 9th ACM Symp. Princ. of Prog. Lang.*, pages 1–6, 1982.

[KM95] R.P. Kurshan and K.L. McMillan. A structural induction theorem for processes. *Information and Computation*, 117:1–11, 1995.

[KP00] Y. Kesten and A. Pnueli. Control and data abstractions: The cornerstones of practical formal verification. *Software Tools for Technology Transfer*, 4(2):328–342, 2000.

[L85] Zuck L. Interim report to PhD Committee. Technical report, Weizmann Institute of Sciences, 1985.

[LR81] D. Lehmann and M.O. Rabin. On the advantages of free choice: A symmetric and fully distibuted solution to the dining philosophers problem. In *Proc. 8th ACM Symp. Princ. of Prog. Lang.*, pages 133–138, 1981.

[MAB+94] Z. Manna, A. Anuchitanukul, N. Bjørner, A. Browne, E. Chang, M. Colón, L. De Alfaro, H. Devarajan, H. Sipma, and T.E. Uribe. STeP: The Stanford Temporal Prover. Technical Report STAN-CS-TR-94-1518, Dept. of Comp. Sci., Stanford University, Stanford, California, 1994.

[MP95] Z. Manna and A. Pnueli. *Temporal Verification of Reactive Systems: Safety.* Springer-Verlag, New York, 1995.

[PRZ01] A. Pnueli, S. Ruah, and L. Zuck. Automatic deductive verification with invisible invariants. In *Proc. 7th Intl. Conference on Tools and Algorithms for the Construction and Analysis of Systems (TACAS'01)*, volume 2031, pages 82–97, 2001.

[PS96] A. Pnueli and E. Shahar. A platform for combining deductive with algorithmic verification. In *R. Alur and T. Henzinger, editors,* Proc. 8th Intl. Conference on Computer Aided Verification (CAV'96)*, volume 1102 of* Lect. Notes in Comp. Sci.*, Springer-Verlag,* pages 184–195, 1996.

[PZ86a] A. Pnueli and L. Zuck. Probablistic verification by tableaux. In *Proc. First IEEE Symp. Logic in Comp. Sci.*, pages 322–331, 1986.

[PZ86b] A. Pnueli and L. Zuck. Verification of multiprocess probabilistic protocols. *Distributed Computing*, 1:53–72, 1986.

[PZ93] A. Pnueli and L.D. Zuck. Probabilistic verification. *Inf. and Cont.*, 103(1):1–29, 1993.

[Rab82] M.O. Rabin. The choice coordination problem. *Acta Informatica*, 17:121–134, 1982.

[SZ93] A.P. Sistla and L.D. Zuck. Reasoning in a restricted temporal logic. *Inf. and Cont.*, 102(2):167–195, 1993.

[VW86] M.Y. Vardi and P. Wolper. An automata-theoretic approach to automatic program verification. In *Proc. First IEEE Symp. Logic in Comp. Sci.*, pages 332–344, 1986.

[WL89] P. Wolper and V. Lovinfosse. Verifying properties of large sets of processes with network invariants. In J. Sifakis, editor, *Automatic Verification Methods for Finite State Systems*, volume 407 of *Lect. Notes in Comp. Sci.*, pages 68–80. Springer-Verlag, 1989.

An Experiment in Type Inference and Verification by Abstract Interpretation

Roberta Gori and Giorgio Levi

Dipartimento di Informatica, Università di Pisa, Pisa, Italy
{gori, levi}@di.unipi.it

Abstract This paper describes an experiment in the definition of tools for type inference and type verification of ML-like functional languages, using abstract interpretation techniques. We first show that by extending the Damas-Milner type inference algorithm, with a (bounded) fixpoint computation (as suggested by the abstract interpretation view, i.e. by a slight variation of one of the type abstract semantics in [7]), we succeed in getting a better precision and solving some problems of the ML type inference algorithm without resorting to more complex type systems (e.g. polymorphic recursion). We then show how to transform the analyzer into a tool for type verification, using an existing verification method based on abstract interpretation. The resulting type verification method can be exploited to improve the ML type inference algorithm, when the intended type of functions is specified by the programmer.

1 Introduction

The experiment, described in this paper, has two main aims:

- getting a better insight in the relation between type rules, type inference algorithms and abstract interpretation;
- testing the applicability to functional programs of an approach to program verification [16,4], originally developed for logic programs.

We have therefore chosen a well-understood property, i.e., types in functional languages à la ML. This property was extensively studied from the *type systems* viewpoint. There exist notions of type, where types are represented by (possibly quantified) terms. These include, for example, principal monotypes [15], polytypes with monomorphic recursion [17,13] and polytypes with polymorphic recursion [20]. Each of these notions has a corresponding correct (often non-complete) type inference algorithm. Some of these algorithms have been reconstructed [18,19] as *computations of an abstract semantics*, according to abstract interpretation theory. Cousot [7] has shown how to derive by abstract interpretation a hierarchy of type systems and type inference algorithms, including all the above mentioned ones.

In this paper, we consider the case of the ML's type system (where polymorphism is allowed inside the let construct only). The corresponding type inference

A. Cortesi (Ed.): VMCAI 2002, LNCS 2294, pp. 225–239, 2002.
© Springer-Verlag Berlin Heidelberg 2002

algorithm is the Damas-Milner algorithm [17,13], which is equivalent to one of the abstract semantics in the Cousot's hierarchy [7]. The interested reader can find in that paper

- the detailed derivation of such an abstract semantics from a concrete semantics, which is the collecting version of the denotational semantics of eager untyped λ-calculus;
- the formal definition of the abstract domain.

Let us just note that the abstract semantics corresponding to the Damas-Milner type inference algorithm is obtained in [7] by abstracting a polymorphic recursion semantics (à la Mycroft [20]). The last abstraction step removes the (abstract) fixpoint computation, which would be needed in the case of recursive functions. This is due to the fact that the goal is to reconstruct the Damas-Milner algorithm, which does not provide any fixpoint computation. The issue of fixpoint computations for typing recursive functions is not even mentioned in the early papers on the ML type inference algorithm [17,13]. Mycroft's paper [20], which provides a type system and a type inference algorithm intended to capture polymorphic recursion, describes a fixpoint computation and mentions the termination problem. The abstract interpretation view provides a better insight into this problem. [18,19] show that the solution chosen by the Damas-Milner algorithm to handle recursion (essentially a unification after the first iteration) can be understood as the application of a widening operator. In abstract interpretation, widening operators, which provide an upper approximation of the abstract least fixpoint, are used to speed up the analysis (at the expense of precision) and are known to be essential to guarantee the termination of the analysis, when the abstract domain is non-Noetherian, i.e., contains infinite increasing chains. Some kind of widening is needed in our type abstract semantics, since the abstract domain is non-Noetherian. However, there might exist widenings which are more precise than the one used in the Damas-Milner algorithm. Monsuez [18,19] discusses some of these widenings in the context of an abstract semantics with polymorphic recursion equivalent to the Mycroft's one [20].

We have decided to apply a family of widening operators in the Damas-Milner's algorithm, by using exactly the ML's type system without polymorphic recursion. Each widening operator is indexed by an integer k and is roughly described as follows. We try to find the least fixpoint using at most k iterations. If we fail, we apply the unification-based operation used in the Damas-Milner's algorithm (which uses therefore exactly our widening indexed by 1). In principle, this should allow us to compute more precise types, essentially because we can get the least fixpoint. Of course, we cannot guarantee to always compute the most general (principal) type, because of the approximation inherently associated to the widening operators.

The resulting family of abstract semantics lie between the Damas-Milner and the Mycroft semantics in the Cousot's hierarchy. They are more precise than the first one, because of better fixpoint approximations. They are less precise than the last one, since they do not allow polymorphic recursion.

The aim of the experiment is to check whether the improvement in precision holds in practice, i.e., whether there exist sensible ML programs, for which we are able to infer a type which is more general (more precise) than the one inferred by the ML's type inference algorithm. We have then implemented (in the language OCAML [22]) a parametric abstract interpreter, corresponding to our family of abstract semantics. The implementation, apart from the case of recursion, is very close to the implementation of the Damas-Milner algorithm shown in [6].

The result of the experiment is positive. As we will show in Section 3.1, we succeed in inferring more precise types, simply by computing better approximations of the fixpoints in the abstract semantics of recursive functions, without resorting to more complex type systems (e.g. polymorphic recursion).

The second part of the experiment, described in Section 4, is related to type verification. The aim is to apply a verification method [16,5,4], originally developed for logic programs, to functional programs. The verification method is based on abstract interpretation. As we will see in Section 2, the core of the method consists in the application of the "abstract functional" associated to recursive definitions. Such a functional is an explicit component of our type interpreter, used inside the (bounded) fixpoint computation. Hence transforming our type analyzer into a type verifier is an almost straightforward task, requiring just a few lines of additional code, as was the case for other programming paradigms [3].

Finally, in Section 5 we discuss a simple extension of the ML type inference algorithm, which uses our approach to type verification and which is applicable when the intended type of functions is specified by the programmer.

2 Abstract Interpretation and Verification

Abstract interpretation [8,9] is a general theory for approximating the semantics of discrete dynamic systems, originally developed by Patrick and Radhia Cousot, in the late 70's. The *abstract semantics* is an approximation of the concrete one, where exact (concrete) values are replaced by (abstract) properties, modeled by an abstract domain.

In abstract interpretation based static program analysis we compute an abstract fixpoint semantics. Assume we have a semantic evaluation function $\mathcal{T}_P$ on a concrete domain $(\mathbb{C}, \sqsubseteq)$, whose least fixpoint $\mathrm{lfp}_{\mathbb{C}}(\mathcal{T}_P)$ is the (concrete) semantics of the program P. The class of properties we want to consider is formalized as an abstract domain $(\mathbb{A}, \leq)$, related to $(\mathbb{C}, \sqsubseteq)$ by a Galois connection $\alpha : \mathbb{C} \rightarrow \mathbb{A}$ and $\gamma : \mathbb{A} \rightarrow \mathbb{C}$ (abstraction and concretization functions). The corresponding *abstract semantic evaluation function* $\mathcal{T}_P^{\alpha}$ is systematically derived from $\mathcal{T}_P$, α and γ. The resulting abstract semantics $\mathrm{lfp}_{\mathbb{A}}(\mathcal{T}_P^{\alpha})$ is a correct approximation of the concrete semantics by construction, i.e., $\alpha(\mathrm{lfp}_{\mathbb{C}}(\mathcal{T}_P)) \leq \mathrm{lfp}_{\mathbb{A}}(\mathcal{T}_P^{\alpha})$, and no additional "correctness" theorems need to be proved. The abstract semantics $\mathrm{lfp}_{\mathbb{A}}(\mathcal{T}_P^{\alpha})$ models a safe approximation of the property of interest: if the property is verified in $\mathrm{lfp}_{\mathbb{A}}(\mathcal{T}_P^{\alpha})$ it will also be verified in $\mathrm{lfp}_{\mathbb{C}}(\mathcal{T}_P)$. An analysis method based on the computation of the abstract semantics $\mathrm{lfp}_{\mathbb{A}}(\mathcal{T}_P^{\alpha})$ is effective only if the least fixpoint is reached in finitely many iterations, i.e., if the abstract domain is Noetherian. If this is not the case, *widening operators* can be used to ensure termination. Widening operators [11] give an upper approximation of the least fixpoint and guarantee termination by introducing further approximation.

Abstract interpretation was shown [10,12] to be very useful to understand, organize and synthesize proof methods for *program verification*. We consider here one specific approach to the generation of abstract interpretation-based partial correctness conditions [16], which is used also in abstract debugging [1,5,2]. The aim of verification is to define conditions which allow us to formally prove that a program behaves as expected, i.e., that the program is correct w.r.t. a given specification, a description of the program's expected behavior.

The ideas behind this approach are the following.

- An element $\mathcal{S}_\alpha$ of the domain $(\mathbb{A}, \leq)$ is the specification, i.e., the abstraction of the intended concrete semantics.
- The *partial correctness* of a program P w.r.t. a specification $\mathcal{S}_\alpha$ can be expressed as

$$\alpha(\mathrm{lfp}_{\mathbb{C}}(\mathcal{T}_P)) \leq \mathcal{S}_\alpha. \tag{1}$$

- Since condition (1) requires the computation of the concrete fixpoint semantics, it is not effectively computable. Then, we can prove instead the condition

$$\mathrm{lfp}_{\mathbb{A}}(\mathcal{T}_P^\alpha) \leq \mathcal{S}_\alpha \tag{2}$$

  which implies partial correctness (by soundness of the abstract semantics). Note that an abstract fixpoint computation is still needed. Hence, condition (2) is effective only if the abstract domain is Noetherian or if we use widening operators.
- A simpler condition, which is the abstract version of Park's *fixpoint induction* [21], is a *sufficient* condition for (2) (by fixpoint theorems), and, therefore, for partial correctness,

$$\mathcal{T}_P^\alpha(\mathcal{S}_\alpha) \leq \mathcal{S}_\alpha. \tag{3}$$

  This condition does not require the computation of fixpoints and can, therefore, be used for proving properties described by non-Noetherian domains.

Both sufficient conditions require an abstract domain $(\mathbb{A}, \leq)$, such that

- the intended abstract behavior (specification) $\mathcal{S}_\alpha \in \mathbb{A}$ has a finite representation;
- $\leq$ is a decidable relation.

3 Type Inference via Abstract Interpretation: The Case of Recursive Functions

Our language is a small variation of untyped λ-calculus as considered in [7], with let and mutual recursion. Monotypes (with variables) are Herbrand terms, built with the basic type *int*, (type) variables and the (functional) type constructor $\rightarrow$. A value of the abstract domain is a pair consisting of a *monotype* and an *idempotent substitution*. An abstract environment H maps identifiers to (possibly) universally quantified abstract values, to cope with let-polymorphism. An abstract value is transformed into a quantified abstract value by a function gen_H, which universally quantifies all the type variables not occurring in the environment H. Substitutions are always restricted to the set of type variables occurring in the environment. The abstract partial order relation is defined in terms of the relations on terms and substitutions. Namely, $(t_1, \theta_1) \leq (t_2, \theta_2)$ if there exists a substitution σ such that $t_2 = t_1\sigma$ and $\theta_2 = \theta_1 \cdot \sigma$. As usual, elements of the abstract domain are equivalence classes w.r.t. the corresponding equivalence relation. The *lub* operation can easily be defined by means of the unification algorithm. The bottom element $\perp$ is a pair consisting of a type variable and the empty substitution. The equivalence class corresponding to the top element contains all the pairs, whose first component is the distinguished term *Notype*. Note that the abstract domain is non-Noetherian since there exist infinite ascending chains.

We will just show the abstract semantics of recursive functions. The case of mutual recursion (used in some examples) is handled in a similar way. For all the other constructs, the abstract semantics is the one computed by the Damas-Milner algorithm. In particular, we will show the rules corresponding to the *let rec* construct, viewed as a declaration, whose abstract semantics returns an abstract environment. The following rules define (or use) several transition relations. The first two relations define type inference for declarations and expressions. In both relations, the integer k identifies the specific widening to be used.

- $\leadsto_k^d$: *environment* $*$ *declaration* $->$ *environment*
- $\leadsto_k^e$: *environment* $*$ *expression* $->$ *abstractvalue*

The other two relations define the application of the functional associated to the recursive definition and the widening.

- $\Rrightarrow_{T_P}$: *environment* $*$ *declaration* $->$ *environment*
- $\Rightarrow_{wid}$: *environment* $*$ (*declaration* $*$ *integer*) $->$ *environment*

$$\frac{H[f \leftarrow \perp] \vdash (\text{let rec } f = e,\ k) \Rightarrow_{wid} H_1}{H \vdash \text{let rec } f = e \leadsto_k^d H_1}(Rec)$$

$$\frac{k > 0, H \vdash \text{let rec } f = e \Rrightarrow_{T_P} H_1, H(f) = H_1(f)}{H \vdash (\text{let rec } f = e,\ k) \Rightarrow_{wid} H[f \leftarrow gen_H(H(f))]}(Wid\ 1)$$

$$\frac{\begin{array}{c} k > 1, H \vdash \text{let rec } f = e \Rrightarrow_{T_P} H_1, H(f) \neq H_1(f), \\ H_1 \vdash (\text{let rec } f = e,\ \text{k-1}) \Rightarrow_{wid} H_2 \end{array}}{H \vdash (\text{let rec } f = e,\ k) \Rightarrow_{wid} H_2}(Wid\ 2)$$

$$\frac{\begin{array}{c}H \vdash \text{let rec } f = e \Rrightarrow_{T_P} H_1, H(f) \neq H_1(f), \\ H(f) = (\tau, \gamma), H_1(f) = (\tau_1, \gamma_1)\end{array}}{H \vdash (\text{let rec } f = e,\ 1) \Rightarrow_{wid} H[f \leftarrow gen_H(lub((\tau\gamma_1, \epsilon), (\tau_1, \gamma_1)))]}(Wid\ 3)$$

$$\frac{H \vdash e \rightsquigarrow_k^e \sigma}{H \vdash \text{let rec } f = e\ \ \Rrightarrow_{T_P} H[f \leftarrow \sigma]}(T_P)$$

H, H_1, H_2 are type environments, τ, τ_1 are monotypes, γ, γ_1 are idempotent substitutions and σ is an abstract value. The rule (Rec) starts the widening by binding the recursive function name f to the bottom element in the abstract domain (a fresh variable and the empty substitution ϵ). The rule (T_P) applies the functional to an environment containing an approximation for f. The other 3 rules define the widening algorithm. Rule $(Wid\ 1)$ finds the least fixpoint. Rule $(Wid\ 2)$ performs another iteration. Rule $(Wid\ 3)$ computes the approximation, by using the *lub* operation, after k iterations. Note that gen_H is only used when the final abstract value is inserted in the environment (and not for the approximations). This does not allow polymorphic recursion.

3.1 Examples of Type Inference

The transition relation $\rightsquigarrow_k^d$ is implemented by a function *typeinfer* : *declaration* $\rightarrow$ *env* $\rightarrow$ *int* $\rightarrow$ *env*, where the integer parameter is used to choose the specific widening operator. When the control parameter is set to -1, no widening is used and the system tries to compute the least fixpoint without using any widening (with possible non-termination). For the current presentation we will represent programs using the syntax of ML [1]. We will also use the ML's notation for the abstract values. In particular, the result will not contain quantifiers and substitutions. The environments are represented as lists of elements of the form *identifier* $\leftarrow$ *monotype*.

The declaration (taken from [7])

```
# let rec f f1 g n x = if n=0 then g(x)
     else f(f1)(function x -> (function h -> g(h(x)))) (n-1) x f1;;
This expression has type ('a -> 'a) -> 'b but is here used with type 'b.
```

cannot be typed by the Damas-Milner's algorithm (the underlined expression is the one to which the type error message applies). The expression defines the function $f\ f_1\ g\ n\ x = g(f_1^n(x))$ which has the type $(`a \rightarrow `a) \rightarrow (`a \rightarrow `b) \rightarrow int \rightarrow `a \rightarrow `b$. This type is correctly computed (by a fixpoint computation) in [7], by using a more complex type system (a polytype system à la Church-Curry). We show that we infer the same type, simply by using a suitable widening. If we use the widening corresponding to $k = 1$, we obtain the same result of the Damas-Milner's algorithm, i.e., f cannot be typed.

[1] The abstract syntax of the language, together with the type abstract interpreter and verifier can be found at ⟨`http://www.di.unipi.it/~levi/typesav/pagina2.html`⟩.

```
# typeinfer ``let rec f f1 g n x = if n=0 then g(x)
      else f(f1)(function x -> (function h -> g(h(x)))) (n-1) x f1''
      emptyenv 1;;
- : env = [f <- Notype]
```

However, the widening with $k = 3$ succeeds in inferring a type for f.

```
# typeinfer ``let rec f f1 g n x = if n=0 then g(x)
      else f(f1)(function x -> (function h -> g(h(x)))) (n-1) x f1''
      emptyenv 3;;
- : env = [f <- ('a -> 'a) -> ('a -> 'b) -> int -> 'a -> 'b]
```

The inferred type is indeed the least fixpoint.

```
# typeinfer ``let rec f f1 g n x = if n=0 then g(x)
      else f(f1)(function x -> (function h -> g(h(x)))) (n-1) x f1''
      emptyenv (-1);;
- : env = [f <- ('a -> 'a) -> ('a -> 'b) -> int -> 'a -> 'b]
```

We show the sequence of abstract values (approximations for f) computed in the example.

1. step 0:
   $\tau_0 =$ `'a1`
   $\gamma_0 = \epsilon$
2. step 1:
   $\tau_1 =$ `'a5->('a4->'a2)->int->'a4->'a2`,
   $\gamma_1 =$`'a1` $\leftarrow$`'a5->('a3->(('a3->'a4)->'a2))->int->'a4->('a5->'a2)`$\}$
3. step 2:
   $\tau_2 =$ `('a7->'a7)->('a7->'a6)->int->'a7->'a6`,
   $\gamma_2 =\{$`'a2`$\leftarrow$ `('a7->'a7)->'a6`, `'a4`$\leftarrow$`'a7`$\}$
4. step 3:
   $\tau_3 =$ `('a->'a) ->('a->'b)->int->'a->'b`,
   $\gamma_3 =\{$`'a6`$\leftarrow$ `('a->'a)->'b`, `'a7`$\leftarrow$`'a`$\}$

Note that at step 3 we reach the fixpoint since $(\tau_2, \gamma_2) = (\tau_3, \gamma_3)$ (both γ_2 and γ_3 are empty when restricted to the global environment). The sequence is obviously increasing. Looking at the sequence, we can also check the result we would obtain using a less precise widening, in particular, the ML widening ($k = 1$). In this case, we would use the rule (Wid 3) after step 1. The computation of the $lub((\tau_0\gamma_1, \epsilon), (\tau_1, \gamma_1)$ would lead to the computation of the solved form of the equation

```
'a5->('a4->'a2)->int->'a4->'a2 =
'a5->('a3->(('a3->'a4)->'a2))->int->'a4->('a5->'a2).
```

The unification algorithm would generate the unsolvable equation

```
'a2=('a3->'a3)->'a2,
```

which explains the ML type error message. The result of the *lub* operation is therefore the top abstract value, i.e., the declaration cannot be typed. When the widening terminates by using rule (*Wid* 3) we always compute an upper approximation of the least fixpoint, i.e., a less precise type.

The next example shows that widening is really needed to avoid non-termination.

```
# let rec f x = f;;
This expression has type 'a -> 'b but is here used with type 'b
# typeinfer ''let rec f x = f'' emptyenv 10;;
- : env = [f <- Notype]
# typeinfer ''let rec f x = f'' emptyenv (-1);;
does not terminate.
```

Our last example is similar to the one (defined on lists) shown in [20], as a motivation for polymorphic recursion. The Damas-Milner's algorithm does not compute the expected type for the function *apply*, which should be $('a \rightarrow' b \rightarrow' b) \rightarrow' a \rightarrow' b \rightarrow int \rightarrow' b$.

```
# let rec apply f x y n = if n = 0 then y else apply f x (f x y) (n - 1)
  and times x n = apply (function z -> function w -> z + w) x 0 n;;
val apply : (int -> int -> int) -> int -> int -> int -> int = <fun>
val times : int -> int -> int = <fun>
```

We obtain the same approximation with the ML widening ($k = 1$).

```
# typeinfer
 ''let rec apply f x y n = if n = 0 then y else apply f x (f x y) (n - 1)
  and times x n = apply (function z -> function w -> z + w) x 0 n''
  emptyenv 1;;
  - : env = [apply <- (int -> int -> int) -> int -> int -> int -> int;
             times <- int -> int -> int]
```

However, if we perform two more iterations, we succeed in getting the expected type (which turns out to be also the least fixpoint).

```
# typeinfer
 ''let rec apply f x y n = if n = 0 then y else apply f x (f x y) (n - 1)
  and times x n = apply (function z -> function w -> z + w) x 0 n''
  emptyenv 3;;
  - : env = [apply <- ('a -> 'b -> 'b) -> 'a -> 'b -> int -> 'b;
             times <- int -> int -> int]
```

Note again that, using the ML widening, we compute an abstract value by means of rule (*Wid* 3). Such a value is less precise than the one which is computed by a better widening, using rule (*Wid* 1). The above declaration would correctly be typed by Mycroft [20], by using a more powerful type system with polymorphic recursion (and an explicit fixpoint computation).

Our first conclusion is that a very simple extension of the ML's type inference algorithm (more precise widenings) would make it more precise and solve some of the problems, which were believed to require more powerful notions of types. As a side remark, the idea of approximating (by means of widenings) abstract fixpoints comes naturally from the concrete semantics, if the type inference algorithm is viewed as the computation of an abstract semantics. It is not that straightforward if one starts from the classical typing rules.

4 Type Verification by Abstract Fixpoint Induction

The abstract interpreter for type inference is the function
typeinfer : *declaration* $\rightarrow$ *env* $\rightarrow$ *int* $\rightarrow$ *env*. If we want to verify a single declaration, the specification $\mathcal{S}_\alpha$ (abstraction of the intended semantics), to be used in conditions (2) and (3) of Section 2, should be a type environment specifying the intended types of

- global names
- names defined in the declaration

A specification is always finite and we can easily define a decidable partial order relation $\leq_{env}$ on type environments by lifting the partial order relation $\leq$. Both sufficient conditions are therefore effective. Note that the resulting verification methods are compositional, since we verify a single declaration, by using the specification (environment) $\mathcal{S}_\alpha$ to determine the types of the global names.

The implementation of the verification condition (2) ($\mathrm{lfp}_{\mathbb{A}}(\mathcal{T}_P^\alpha) \leq \mathcal{S}_\alpha$, inference and comparison) is straightforward:
infercheck : *declaration* $\rightarrow$ *specification* $\rightarrow$ *int* $\rightarrow$ *bool*, is defined by one line of ML code

```
infercheck (d:declaration) (S:environment) (k:int) =
(typeinfer d S k) ≤env  S.
```

Note that the integer parameter is again used to choose the widening to be used in type inference.

As already mentioned, our types abstract domain is non-Noetherian. This is therefore a typical case for application of the approach based on the effective sufficient condition (3) ($\mathcal{T}_P^\alpha(\mathcal{S}_\alpha) \leq \mathcal{S}_\alpha$), which does not require fixpoint computations (and widenings). Note that the specification $\mathcal{S}_\alpha$ is related to the functions defined by the top-level declaration only. The specification does not assign types to lower level recursive functions. Therefore we can only infer their types, using a suitable widening. This is the reason why the function
check : *declaration* $\rightarrow$ *specification* $\rightarrow$ *int* $\rightarrow$ *bool*,
which implements condition (3), has the usual integer parameter. *check* is the same as *infercheck*, for non-recursive declarations. In the case of a recursive declaration, *infercheck* simply applies the rule (T_P), where the initial environment is the specification. The case of mutual recursion is similar and is not discussed here, since we did not provide the rules for mutual recursion.

It is worth noting that *check* is in general more efficient than *infercheck*. Moreover, even if condition (2) is stronger than condition (3), *infercheck* is not always stronger than *check*. As we will show later, because of the widening, *infercheck* can sometimes be weaker than *check*.

In the following section we show and discuss some examples.

4.1 Examples of Verification

In the following examples, specifications have exactly the same format of environments in Section 3.1, i.e., they are lists of elements of the form *identifier* $\leftarrow$ *monotype*.

The first example shows the compositional nature of our verifier. Here the function *fact* is defined in terms of two (global) functions. In the verification of *fact*, we just consider the types for the global functions as defined in the specification.

```
# let rec pi f a b = if a > b then 1 else (f a) * (pi f (a +1) b)
  let id x = x let fact = pi id 1;;
val pi : (int -> int) -> int -> int -> int = <fun>
val id : 'a -> 'a = <fun>
val fact : int -> int = <fun>

# check ''let fact = pi id 1''
   [pi <- (int -> int) -> int -> int -> int; id <- 'a -> 'a;
   fact <- int -> int] 1;;
- : bool = true
```

The next example involves let-polymorphism. The two occurrences of the polymorphic function *id* are allowed to take different instances of the type given in the specification.

```
# let id x = x
 let g = id id;;
val id : 'a -> 'a = <fun>
val g : 'b -> 'b = <fun>
# check ''let g = id id''  [ id <- 'a -> 'a; g <- 'b -> 'b ] 1;;
- : bool = true
```

The next example considers the function *f* of Section 3, which cannot be typed by ML. The inductive verifier *check* succeeds in showing that the function satisfies a specification with the correct type. On the contrary, *infercheck* (with the ML widening) fails, because of the approximation of the analyzer. As already mentioned, *infercheck* can sometimes be worse than *check*, exactly because of the widening.

```
# check ''let rec f f1 g n x = if n=0 then g(x)
           else f(f1)(function x -> (function h -> g(h(x)))) (n-1) x f1''
    [f <- ('a -> 'a) -> ('a -> 'b) -> int -> 'a -> 'b] 1;;
- : bool = true
```

```
# infercheck ''let rec f f1 g n x = if n=0 then g(x)
            else f(f1)(function x -> (function h -> g(h(x)))) (n-1) x f1''
    [f <- ('a -> 'a) -> ('a -> 'b) -> int -> 'a -> 'b] 1;;
- : bool = false
```

check correctly fails, if the specification gives "too general" a type.

```
# check ''let rec f f1 g n x = if n=0 then g(x)
            else f(f1)(function x -> (function h -> g(h(x)))) (n-1) x f1''
    [f <- ('a -> 'c) -> ('a -> 'b) -> int -> 'a -> 'b] 1;;
- : bool = false
```

check sometimes fails (it is just a sufficient condition!), even if the function satisfies the specification. In these cases, with a suitable number of iterations, *infercheck* can perform better. This is shown by the following example, where the specification gives to f a (correct) "ground" type.

```
# check ''let rec f f1 g n x = if n=0 then g(x)
            else f(f1)(function x -> (function h -> g(h(x)))) (n-1) x f1''
    [f <- (int -> int) -> (int -> int) -> int -> int -> int] 1;;
- : bool = false
# infercheck ''let rec f f1 g n x = if n=0 then g(x)
           else f(f1)(function x -> (function h -> g(h(x)))) (n-1) x f1''
    [f <- (int -> int) -> (int -> int) -> int -> int -> int] 3;;
- : bool = true
```

Our last example reconsiders the mutual recursion example of Section 3. We show that (as expected) *infercheck* (with the ML widening) fails with the first specification (while *check* succeeds). They both succeed with the second specification.

```
# check
  ''let rec apply f x y n = if n = 0 then y else apply f x (f x y) (n - 1)
  and times x n = apply (function z -> function w -> z + w) x 0 n''
[apply <- ('a -> 'b -> 'b) -> 'a -> 'b -> int -> 'b;
 times <- int -> int -> int] 1;;
- : bool = true
# infercheck
  ''let rec apply f x y n = if n = 0 then y else apply f x (f x y) (n - 1)
  and times x n = apply (function z -> function w -> z + w) x 0 n''
[apply <- ('a -> 'b -> 'b) -> 'a -> 'b -> int -> 'b;
 times <- int -> int -> int] 1;;
- : bool = false
# check
  ''let rec apply f x y n = if n = 0 then y else apply f x (f x y) (n - 1)
  and times x n = apply (function z -> function w -> z + w) x 0 n''
[apply <- (int -> int -> int) -> int -> int -> int -> int;
 times <- int -> int -> int] 1;;
- : bool = true
# infercheck
  ''let rec apply f x y n = if n = 0 then y else apply f x (f x y) (n - 1)
  and times x n = apply (function z -> function w -> z + w) x 0 n''
```

```
[apply <- (int -> int -> int) -> int -> int -> int -> int;
 times <- int -> int -> int] 1;;
- : bool = true
```

5 Verification and Inference with Type Specifications

We consider now the problem of how type verification might be used to extend a type inference algorithm to cope with user-defined type specifications. For the sake of simplicity, we will just consider the construct defining recursive functions, which is the only construct for which inductive verification is not simply the composition of inference and comparison.

The classical typing rule for recursion, with the Damas-Milner type system, is (we use the notation of [7]):

$$\frac{H[f \leftarrow \tau] \vdash \lambda x.e \Rightarrow \tau}{H \vdash \mu f.\lambda x.e \Rightarrow \tau}, \tag{4}$$

where H is a type environment and τ is a monotype with variables. The rule clearly shows that τ is a fixpoint of the functional associated to the recursive definition. When using the rule for type inference, we have to devise an algorithm to compute τ. The rule can instead directly be used for type checking, if τ is provided by the user as a type declaration (*specification*). The modified rule taking into account type specifications is

$$\frac{H[f \leftarrow \tau] \vdash \lambda x.e \Rightarrow \tau}{H \vdash (\mu f.\lambda x.e : \tau) \Rightarrow \tau}. \tag{5}$$

Is this rule actually used by the ML's type checking algorithm? The answer is that this is not the case, at least in the OCAML implementation, as shown by the following examples

```
# let rec (f: ('a -> 'a) -> ('a -> 'b) -> int -> 'a -> 'b) =
    function f1 -> function g -> function n -> function x ->
    if n=0 then g(x)
    else f(f1)(function x -> (function h -> g(h(x)))) (n-1) x f1;;
This expression has type ('a -> 'a) -> 'b but is here used with type 'b
# let rec (apply: ('a -> 'b -> 'b) -> 'a -> 'b -> int -> 'b) =
    function f -> function x -> function y -> function n ->
    if n = 0 then y else apply f x (f x y) (n - 1)
  and (times: int -> int -> int) = function x -> function  n ->
    apply (function z -> function w -> z + w) x 0 n;;
val apply : (int -> int -> int) -> int -> int -> int -> int = <fun>
val times : int -> int -> int = <fun>
```

which suggest that type inference is performed first, with the approximation induced by the ML widening, without actually using the specified types, which are both fixpoints, as already shown in Section 3.1. This reminds our verification condition (2) ($\mathrm{lfp}_{\mathbb{A}}(\mathcal{T}_P^{\alpha}) \leq \mathcal{S}_{\alpha}$, inference and comparison), which, as already noted, can be weaker, because of the widening.

In general, we could accept a specification even if it is not a fixpoint, yet it is satisfied by the recursive definition, i.e., if it is an instance of the type that would be inferred. If the function satisfies σ, then σ is the inferred type, i.e., specifications are prescriptive, provided they are satisfied. The extended typing rule is then:

$$\frac{H[f \leftarrow \sigma] \vdash \lambda x.e \Rightarrow \tau \quad \tau \leq \sigma}{H \vdash (\mu f.\lambda x.e : \sigma) \Rightarrow \sigma}. \tag{6}$$

Note that now σ is a pre-fixpoint of the functional associated to the recursive definition. Note also that the premise of the rule is exactly our condition (3).

The ML type inference algorithm might extend its precision in type inference by using rule 6, even without using more precise widenings, because no widening is required when the user specifies the expected type.

6 Open Problems and Conclusions

We have shown that the choice of a better widening in our family can improve the precision of the inferred type, because, by increasing the number of iterations, we might reach the least fixpoint. However, if we consider two widenings, different in the number of iterations, both terminating by using the rule (Wid 3), we might wonder which is the relation among the computed abstract values. In principle, the most precise widening (the one with more iterations) might lead to a less precise result, unless we get to the fixpoint. In all the examples we have considered in our experiment, when termination is achieved by rule (Wid 3), the result does not depend on the number of iterations. We are currently investigating whether this property holds in general.

The main conclusion of our experiment is that abstract interpretation techniques can help in the development of inference and verification tools in the type systems approach. Type systems are very important to handle a large class of properties, not only in functional and object-oriented programming, but also in calculi related to concurrency and mobility. The type system directly reflects the property we are interested in and the typing rules are usually easy to understand. The main problem is that it is often hard to move from the typing rules to the type inference algorithm. Systematic techniques are needed to systematically help in the transformation of typing rules into type inference algorithms. We believe that abstract interpretation provides some of these techniques.

Examples of problems which might be tackled using abstract interpretation techniques are

- The identification of the information which needs to be added to the types in order to perform an accurate inference. For example, the Damas-Milner algorithm uses idempotent substitutions. This is essentially the same problem in abstract interpretation, when one needs to move from the property of

interest to a (more concrete) abstract domain, in order to achieve a better precision in the abstract computation. The relation among the two problems was explicitly shown by [18]: in the case of Mycroft's algorithm [20], the additional information is a kind of relational information, very often used in abstract domains. It is worth noting that the theory of abstract interpretation provides techniques for the refinement of domains [14], which can be very useful to systematically transform the property of interest into a good abstract domain.
- How to solve computational problems which are not explicitly shown in the typing rules, such as fixpoint approximation. We have shown that abstract interpretation can help, by providing a theory which tells us when we can safely compute abstract fixpoints and when and how we should use widening operators.
- How to handle user-provided type specifications. As we have shown, when the user is allowed to specify types (whatever property is represented by the type), verification techniques based on abstract interpretation can usefully be embedded in the inference algorithm.

As a last remark, we have shown that when the user is allowed to specify types (whatever property is represented by the type), verification techniques based on abstract interpretation can usefully be embedded in the inference algorithm.

Acknowledgments. The authors thank the reviewers of the first version of this paper for their comments and suggestions.

References

1. F. Bourdoncle. Abstract Debugging of Higher-Order Imperative Languages. In *Programming Languages Design and Implementation '93*, pages 46–55, 1993.
2. F. Bueno, P. Deransart, W. Drabent, G. Ferrand, M. Hermenegildo, J. Maluszynski, and G. Puebla. On the Role of Semantic Approximations in Validation and Diagnosis of Constraint Logic Programs. In M. Kamkar, editor, *Proceedings of the AADEBUG'97*, pages 155–169, 1997.
3. M. Comini, R. Gori, and G. Levi. How to Transform an Analyzer into a Verifier. In R. Nieuwenhuis and A. Voronkov, editors, *Proceedings of the 8th International Conference on Logic for Programming, Artificial Intelligence and Reasoning*, volume 2250 of *Lecture Notes in Artificial Intelligence*. Springer-Verlag, Berlin, 2001.
4. M. Comini, R. Gori, G. Levi, and P. Volpe. Abstract Interpretation based Verification of Logic Programs. In S. Etalle and J.-G. Smaus, editors, *Proceedings of the Workshop on Verification of Logic Programs*, volume 30 of *Electronic Notes in Theoretical Computer Science*. Elsevier Science Publishers, 2000.
5. M. Comini, G. Levi, M. C. Meo, and G. Vitiello. Abstract Diagnosis. *Journal of Logic Programming*, 39(1-3):43–93, 1999.
6. G. Cousineau and M. Mauny. *The Functional Approach to Programming*. Cambridge University Press, 1998.
7. P. Cousot. Types as abstract interpretations . In *Conference Record of the 24th ACM Symp. on Principles of Programming Languages* , pages 316–331. ACM Press, 1997.

8. P. Cousot and R. Cousot. Abstract Interpretation: A Unified Lattice Model for Static Analysis of Programs by Construction or Approximation of Fixpoints. In *Proceedings of Fourth ACM Symp. Principles of Programming Languages*, pages 238–252, 1977.
9. P. Cousot and R. Cousot. Systematic Design of Program Analysis Frameworks. In *Proceedings of Sixth ACM Symp. Principles of Programming Languages*, pages 269–282, 1979.
10. P. Cousot and R. Cousot. Abstract Interpretation Frameworks. *Journal of Logic and Computation*, 2(4):511–549, 1992.
11. P. Cousot and R. Cousot. Comparing the Galois Connection and Widening/Narrowing Approaches to Abstract Interpretation. In M. Bruynooghe and M. Wirsing, editors, *Proceedings of PLILP'92*, volume 631 of *Lecture Notes in Computer Science*, pages 269–295. Springer-Verlag, 1992.
12. P. Cousot and R. Cousot. Inductive Definitions, Semantics and Abstract Interpretation. In *Proceedings of Nineteenth Annual ACM Symp. on Principles of Programming Languages*, pages 83–94. ACM Press, 1992.
13. L. Damas and R. Milner. Principal type-schemes for functional programs. In *Proceedings of the Ninth Annual ACM Symposium on Principles of Programming Languages*, pages 207–212. ACM Press, 1982.
14. G. Filè, R. Giacobazzi, and F. Ranzato. A Unifying View on Abstract Domain Design. *ACM Computing Surveys*, 28(2):333–336, 1996.
15. J.R. Hindley. The principal type-scheme of an object in combinatory logic. *Transaction American mathematical Society*, 146:29–60, 1969.
16. G. Levi and P. Volpe. Derivation of Proof Methods by Abstract Interpretation. In C. Palamidessi, H. Glaser, and K. Meinke, editors, *Principles of Declarative Programming. 10th International Symposium, PLILP'98*, volume 1490 of *Lecture Notes in Computer Science*, pages 102–117. Springer-Verlag, 1998.
17. R. Milner. A theory of type polymorphism in programming. *Journal of Computer and Systems Sciences*, 17-3:348–375, 1978.
18. B. Monsuez. Polymorphic typing by abstract interpretation. In R. Shyamasundar, editor, *Proceedings of Foundation of Software Technology and Theoretical Computer Science*, volume 652 of *Lecture Notes in Computer Science*, pages 217–228. Springer-Verlag, 1992.
19. B. Monsuez. Polymorphic types and widening operators. In P.Cousot, M.Falaschi, G. File', and A.Rauzy, editors, *Proceedings of Static Analysis*, volume 724 of *Lecture Notes in Computer Science*, pages 224–281. Springer-Verlag, 1993.
20. A. Mycroft. Polymorphic type schemes and recursive definitions. In G. Goos and J. Hartmanis, editors, *Proceedings of the International Symposium on Programming*, volume 167 of *Lecture Notes in Computer Science*, pages 217–228. Springer-Verlag, 1984.
21. D. Park. Fixpoint Induction and Proofs of Program Properties. *Machine Intelligence*, 5:59–78, 1969.
22. D. Rémy and J. Vouillon. Objective ML:An effective object-oriented extension to ML. *Theory and Practice of Object-Systems*, 4(1):27–50, 1998.

Weak Muller Acceptance Conditions for Tree Automata*

Salvatore La Torre[1,2], Aniello Murano[2,3], and Margherita Napoli[2]

[1] University of Pennsylvania
[2] Università degli Studi di Salerno
{sallat,murano,napoli}@unisa.it
[3] Rice University

Abstract. Over the last decades the theory of finite automata on infinite objects has been an important source of tools for the specification and the verification of computer programs. Trees are more suitable than words to model nondeterminism and thus concurrency. In the literature, there are several examples of acceptance conditions that have been proposed for automata on infinite words and then have been fruitfully extended to infinite trees (*Büchi*, *Rabin*, and *Muller* conditions). The type of acceptance condition can influence both the succinctness of the corresponding class of automata and the complexity of the related decision problems. Here we consider, for automata on infinite trees, two acceptance conditions that are obtained by a relaxation of the Muller acceptance condition: the *Landweber* and the *Muller-Superset* conditions. We prove that Muller-Superset tree automata accept the same class of languages as Büchi tree automata, but using more succinct automata. Landweber tree automata, instead, define a class of languages which is not comparable with the one defined by Büchi tree automata. We prove that, for this class of automata, the emptiness problem is decidable in polynomial time, and thus we expand the class of automata with a tractable emptiness problem.

1 Introduction

Since its early days the theory of finite automata had an astonishing impact in computer science. Several models of automata have been extensively studied and applied to many fields. In the sixties, with their pioneering work, Büchi [1, 2], McNaughton [11], and Rabin [12] enriched this theory by introducing finite automata on infinite objects. The connections between such automata and the logic theories have been fruitfully investigated and have originated automata-theoretic approaches to reduce decision problems in the field of mathematical logics to automata decision problems.

* This research was partially supported by the NSF award CCR99-70925, NSF grant CCR-9988322, SRC award 99-TJ-688, DARPA ITO Mobies award F33615-00-C-1707, NSF ITR award, and the MURST in the framework of project "Metodi Formali per la Sicurezza" (MEFISTO)

A. Cortesi (Ed.): VMCAI 2002, LNCS 2294, pp. 240–254, 2002.
© Springer-Verlag Berlin Heidelberg 2002

Automata on infinite words and trees turned out to be very useful for those areas of computer science where nonterminating computations are studied. They give a unifying paradigm to specify, verify, and synthesize nonterminating systems [7, 15, 16]. A system specification can be translated to an automaton, and thus, questions about systems and their specifications are reduced to decision problems in the automata theory. For example, the satisfiability of a specification and the correctness of a system with respect to its specification can be often reduced to the nonemptiness problem and the containment of languages accepted by automata. It is thus important to study classes of automata for which checking for the emptiness of a language is not computationally expensive and the closure under complementation and intersection hold.

As abstract models of systems, trees are more suitable than words to model the nondeterminism, which is also useful to model concurrent programs (nondeterministic interleaving of atomic processes). It is worth noticing that some concurrent programs, such as operating systems, communication protocols, and air-traffic control systems, are intrinsically nondeterministic and nonterminating. Moreover, by using trees we can express the existential path quantifier, and thus we are able to express lower bounds on nondeterminism and concurrency. This feature turns out to be greatly helpful in applications such as program synthesis [3, 4].

In the literature, several acceptance conditions on infinite words have been fruitfully extended to infinite trees, such as Büchi, Muller, and Rabin conditions. The kind of acceptance condition we choose usually influences both the succinctness of the model and the complexity of the decision algorithms. While for Büchi tree automata the emptiness problem is decidable in polynomial time, for Rabin tree automata it is NP-complete. On the other hand, Büchi tree automata are not closed under language complementation, while Rabin tree automata are. Since Rabin tree automata are strictly more expressive than Büchi tree automata, in terms of the class of accepted languages, it is worth searching for new models of automata with interesting closure properties and tractable decision problems, that capture languages besides those characterized by the Büchi paradigm.

For automata on infinite objects, the acceptance is defined with respect to the set of states which are visited infinitely often while reading the input. For example, for a Büchi tree automaton some of the states are declared accepting, and a tree t is accepted if and only if on all the paths of t at least an accepting state is visited infinitely often. For Muller tree automata, a family of set of states $F = \{F_1, F_2, \ldots, F_n\}$ is declared accepting, and a tree t is accepted if and only if on each path of t the set of states which are visited infinitely often belongs to F, that is, it is one of the accepting sets. In this paper, we study two new acceptance conditions for tree automata: *Landweber* and *Muller-Superset* acceptance conditions. These conditions are obtained by relaxing the Muller condition in the following way. The Landweber condition requires that, on each path of the input tree, the set of states which are visited infinitely often is contained in one of the accepting sets, while the Muller-Superset condition requires the opposite, that is, on each path of the input tree, one of the accepting sets is contained in the set of states which are visited infinitely often. With Landweber tree automata, we extend to infinite trees the acceptance condition introduced by Landweber in 1969, relatively to deterministic finite automata on infinite words [8]. Hossley studied the nondeterministic version of such automata [6]. Here, we study both the deterministic and the nondeterministic version of the corresponding tree automata.

For Landweber tree automata, we prove that the class of languages which are accepted by the deterministic model is strictly contained in the class defined by the nondeterministic one. We also prove that both classes are closed under union and intersection but not under complementation. We compare these classes to those accepted by Büchi and Muller tree automata in both deterministic and nondeterministic paradigms. It is also worth noticing that the class of languages accepted by Büchi tree automata is not comparable with that accepted by Landweber tree automata. We prove that the emptiness problem for Landweber tree automata is decidable in polynomial time. From the result on the comparison with Büchi tree automata, we thus obtain an alternative class of tree languages for which there exists a polynomial time decision algorithm.

The class of languages accepted by Muller-Superset tree automata turns out to coincide with the class of languages accepted by Büchi tree automata, in both the deterministic and the nondeterministic versions. An interesting feature of this paradigm is that automata from this class are usually more succinct than Büchi tree automata. We prove that for every language L accepted by a minimal Muller-Superset tree automata S, L is accepted by a minimal Büchi tree automata B such that $size(S) \leq size(B) \leq 2^{O(size(S))}$.

The rest of the paper is organized as follows. In Section 2, we give the definitions and recall some results on the theory of finite automata on infinite trees. In Section 3, we study the Muller-Superset tree automata and compare them with the Büchi tree automata. In Section 4, we extend the Landweber acceptance condition to tree automata, and study the corresponding model with a major emphasis on the main closure properties and the comparison between deterministic and nondeterministic paradigms. Relationships among Büchi, Landweber and Muller classes of languages are studied in Section 5. In Section 6, we prove that the emptiness problem for Landweber tree automata is decidable in polynomial time. Finally, we give a few conclusions in Section 7.

2 Automata on ω-trees

In this section, we introduce some notations that will be used in the rest of this paper. We also recall the definitions and the main results concerning Büchi, Muller, and Rabin tree automata.

Let Σ be a finite alphabet and $\text{DOM} = \{0, 1, \ldots, k-1\}^*$. We define an infinite k-ary Σ-tree t as a map $t : \text{DOM} \to \Sigma$. In the following, unless differently stated, an infinite k-ary Σ tree will be referred simply as a tree. For each tree t, the element in DOM are the nodes of the tree and the empty word ϵ corresponds to the root. If u is a node of a tree then ui is the i-th child of the node u. We say that a symbol $a \in \Sigma$ occurs in a tree t if there exists $u \in$ DOM such that $t(u) = a$. Let u, $v \in$ DOM, we say that u *precedes* v, denoted as $u < v$, if there exists an $x \in$ DOM such that $v = ux$. Let $\pi \subseteq$ DOM, π is a path of t if it is a maximal subset of DOM linearly ordered by $<$. If $\pi \subseteq$ DOM is a path of t, then t/π denotes the restriction of the function t to the set π. We say that a symbol $a \in \Sigma$ occurs in a tree t if there exists $u \in$ DOM such that $t(u) = a$. Moreover, we say that a occurs infinitely often in t/π if there exists an infinite number of nodes $u \in \pi$ such that $t(u) = a$. Let t be a tree and π a path of t, with $Inf(t/\pi)$ we denote the set $\{a \in \Sigma \mid a \text{ occurs infinitely often in } t/\pi\}$. Given a tree t and a node $u \in$ DOM, we define the *subtree* of t rooted in u as the tree t_u such that $t_u(v) = t(uv)$ for $v \in$ DOM. Let Σ be a finite alphabet, we denote by T^ω_Σ the set of Σ-valued trees. A language is a subset of T^ω_Σ. In the following we will deal exclusively with infinite binary trees (DOM $= \{0,1\}^*$). All the results we obtain also hold for k-ary trees. According to the definition of a subtree, we use t_0 and t_1 to denote, respectively, the left and right subtree of t. Moreover, we denote by π_0 the leftmost path in a tree, that is $\pi_0 = \{0\}^*$, and by π_1 the rightmost one, i.e. $\pi_1 = \{1\}^*$.

Now we give some basic definitions from the theory of automata on infinite trees. We start by recalling some well-known acceptance conditions. In the literature several acceptance conditions on infinite trees have been considered. Here we recall those defining Büchi, Muller, and Rabin automata. Other paradigms such as Streett automata, turned out to be equivalent to Muller automata.

Definition 1. *A finite automaton on infinite trees (TA) is a tuple $A = \langle Q, \Sigma, \delta, Q_0, F\rangle$ where $Q \neq \emptyset$ is a finite set of states, Σ is an alphabet, $\delta \subseteq Q \times \Sigma \times Q \times Q$ is the transition relation, $Q_0 \subseteq Q$ is the set of initial states, and F is an acceptance condition.*

A deterministic automaton on infinite trees (DTA) is a TA with $|Q_0| = 1$ and δ is a total function $\delta : Q \times \Sigma \to Q \times Q$. To describe the behaviour of a TA, we recall the notion of run.

Definition 2. *Let $A = \langle Q, \Sigma, \delta, Q_0, F\rangle$ be a TA and $t :$ DOM $\to \Sigma$ be an infinite tree. A run r of A on t is a tree $r :$ DOM $\to Q$ such that $r(\epsilon) \in Q_0$, and $(r(u), t(u), r(u0), r(u1)) \in \delta$, for all $u \in$ DOM.*

With $Run_A(t)$ we denote the set of runs of A on t. Clearly, if A is deterministic, then $|Run_A(t)| = 1$. An infinite tree is accepted by A if there exists a *successful* run r of A on t, that is r satisfies the acceptance conditions on all its paths. Moreover, with $T(A)$ we denote the language recognized by A.

The Büchi tree automaton (BTA) was defined by Rabin [13] who gave to these automata the name of *special automata.* A (D)BTA B is a (D)TA with a Büchi acceptance condition expressed by a set of states F. This condition requires that at least one accepting state occurs infinitely often. Thus, given a $t \in T^\omega_\Sigma$, a run $r \in Run_B(t)$ is successful if and only if for each path π of r, $Inf(r/\pi) \cap F \neq \emptyset$. With (D)BTA we denote also the class of languages accepted by (deterministic) Büchi tree automata.

The Muller condition is given as a family of sets of states $F = \{F_1, \ldots, F_m\}$ and requires that the states that repeat infinitely often are exactly the states from one of accepting sets. Thus, a (deterministic) Muller tree automaton ((D)MTA) M is a (D)TA with family $F = \{F_1, \ldots, F_m\}$. Given a $t \in T_\Sigma^\omega$, a run $r \in Run_M(t)$ is successful if and only if for each path π of r, there exists a set $F_i \in F$ such that $Inf(r/\pi) = F$. With (D)MTA we denote also the class of languages accepted by (deterministic) Muller tree automata.

Finally, a (deterministic) Rabin tree automaton ((D)RTA) R is a (D)TA along with a family of set of states $F = \{(F_1, G_1), \ldots, (F_m, G_m)\}$. Given a tree t, a run $r \in Run_R(t)$ is successful if and only if for each path π of r, there exists a pair $(F_i, G_i) \in F$ such that $Inf(r/\pi) \cap F_i \neq \emptyset$ and $Inf(r/\pi) \cap G_i = \emptyset$. With RTA we denote also the class of languages accepted by a Rabin tree automata.

We recall the main results for the introduced classes of tree automata. Since the class of languages accepted by Rabin tree automata coincides with that accepted by Muller tree automata, when we compare the classes of languages we will refer only to MTA. In Figure 1 we summarize the relationships among the considered classes of tree automata [9, 10, 13].

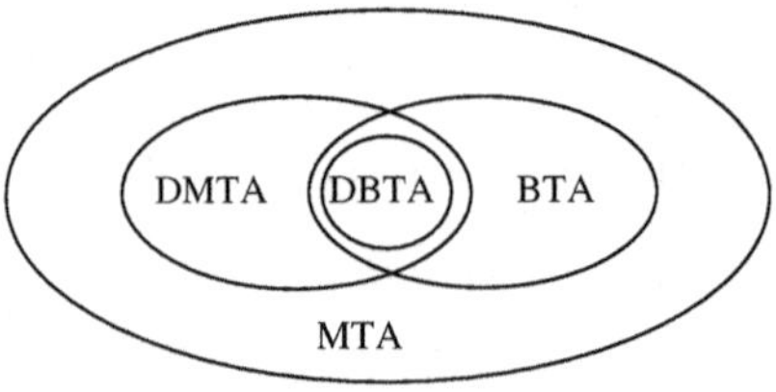

Fig. 1. Relationships among (D)BTA and (D)MTA.

In Figure 2 we list some languages along with their ranking relatively to the classification illustrated in Figure 1. For all of these languages, we assume that $\Sigma = \{a, b\}$. We will use them in the following.

Languages	Ranking
$T_1 = \{t \in T_\Sigma^\omega \mid \exists\ \pi$ such that $a \notin Inf(t/\pi)\}$	BTA - DMTA
$T_2 = \{t \in T_\Sigma^\omega \mid \forall\ \pi$, either $a \notin Inf(t/\pi)$ or $b \notin Inf(t/\pi)\}$	$DMTA - BTA$
$T_3 = \{t \in T_\Sigma^\omega \mid \forall\ x \in \pi_0,\ t/\pi_0(x) = a\}$	$DBTA$
$T_4 = \{t \in T_\Sigma^\omega \mid \forall\ \pi,\ a \in Inf(t/\pi)$ and $b \in Inf(t/\pi)\}$	$DBTA$
$T_5 = \{t \in T_\Sigma^\omega \mid a \notin Inf(t/\pi_0)\}$	$BTA - DBTA$
$T_6 = \{t \in T_\Sigma^\omega \mid \forall\ \pi,\ a \in Inf(t/\pi)\}$	$DBTA$

Fig. 2. Some tree languages and their classification.

In the following remark, we summarize the closure properties of the above classes of automata and languages.

Remark 1.

- DMTA, DBTA, and BTA are closed under intersection and union, but they are not closed under complementation.
- MTA is closed under intersection, union, and complementation.

In the following remark, we recall some known results on the decision problems of Büchi and Rabin tree automata.

Remark 2.

- The emptiness problem for BTA is decidable [13], and is LOGSPACE-complete for PTIME [15].
- The non-emptiness problem for RTA is NP-complete [12, 5].

Given a TA $A = \langle Q, \Sigma, \delta, Q_0, F\rangle$, we define the size of A, denoted by $Size(A)$, as the sum of the sizes of Q, δ, and F. Let T be a language, we define the size of T, denoted by $Size_{TA}(T)$, as the minimum over the sizes of the TA's recognizing T, that is, $Size_{TA}(T) = Size(A)$ where A is a TA such that $T(A) = T$ and for every TA A' such that $T(A') = T$, $Size(A) \leq Size(A')$. We refer to such a TA A as a minimal TA for T.

3 Muller-Superset Tree Automata

In this section, we study the Muller-Superset acceptance condition, a new acceptance condition for tree automata obtained by using the superset operation, instead of the equality, in the Muller acceptance paradigm. We prove that Muller-Superset tree automata define the same class of languages as Büchi tree automata, in both the deterministic and nondeterministic cases. We also show that Muller-Superset tree automata are at least as much succinct as Büchi tree automata and in some cases the gain can be exponential. We start by defining this class of automata.

A Muller-Superset tree automaton (*STA*) S is a TA with acceptance condition $F = \{F_1, \ldots, F_m\}$. A tree $t \in T_\Sigma^\omega$ is accepted by an STA S if and only if there exists a run $r \in Runs_S(t)$ satisfying the condition that for every path π of r, the inclusion $Inf(r/\pi) \supseteq F_i$ holds for some $F_i \in F$. Moreover, with (D)STA we also denote the class of languages accepted by (deterministic) Muller-Superset tree automata. In the next example we give a DSTA accepting the language T_4.

Example 1. Let $S = \langle\{q_0, q_a, q_b\}, \Sigma, \delta, \{q_0\}, \{\{q_a, q_b\}\}\rangle$ be a DSTA where $\delta = \{(q, x, q_x, q_x) \mid q \in Q \text{ and } x \in \Sigma\}$. A tree $t \in T(S)$ if and only if there exists a run $r \in Runs_S(t)$ such that for all paths π of r, the set $\{q_a, q_b\}$ is contained by $Inf(r/\pi)$, and thus if and only if for all paths π of t, it holds $\{a, b\} \subseteq Inf(t/\pi)$. Hence, we have that $T(S) = T_4$.

In the following theorem, we show that the classes DBTA and DSTA are equivalent. We prove it by showing that for every DBTA B that recognizes a language T, there exists a DSTA S that recognizes the same language T and vice-versa. Besides, using the corresponding reductions, we show that for every language T accepted by a DSTA, $Size_{DSTA}(T) \leq Size_{DBTA}(T) \leq 2^{\mathcal{O}(Size_{DSTA}(T))}$.

Theorem 1. *The classes DBTA and DSTA coincide. Moreover, for a given tree language* T, $Size_{DSTA}(T) \leq Size_{DBTA}(T) \leq 2^{\mathcal{O}(Size_{DSTA}(T))}$.

Proof. To prove that $DBTA \subseteq DSTA$, we use a simple automata construction involving only the accepting set. Given a DBTA $B = \langle Q, \Sigma, \delta, Q_0, F \rangle$, we construct a DSTA $S = \langle Q, \Sigma, \delta, Q_0, F' \rangle$ where $F' = \{\{q_i\} \mid q_i \in F\}$. A tree $t \in T(B)$ if and only if there exists an $r \in Run_B(t)$ such that for each path π of r, we get $Inf(r/\pi) \cap F \neq \emptyset$, and thus if and only if there exists a $F_i \in F'$ such that $F_i \subseteq Inf(r/\pi)$. Hence, $t \in T(B)$ if and only if $t \in T(S)$. If B is a minimal $DBTA$ such that $T(B) = T$, by the above construction and the fact that $Size_{DSTA}(T) \leq Size(S)$, we get $Size_{DSTA}(T) \leq Size_{DBTA}(T)$.

Now, let us prove that $DBTA \supseteq DSTA$. Let $S = \langle Q, \Sigma, \delta, Q_0, F \rangle$ be a DSTA and $H = \{W \in \mathcal{P}(Q) \mid \forall F_i \in F, F_i \not\subseteq W\}$, that is H contains only sets of states W such that for any F_i W is either strictly contained in F_i or not comparable with it. Let $B = \langle Q \times H, \Sigma, \delta', Q_0 \times \emptyset, Q \times \emptyset \rangle$ be a DBTA such that $((q, X), a, (q_1, X_1), (q_2, X_2)) \in \delta'$ if $(q, a, q_1, q_2) \in \delta$ and for $i = 1, 2$:

$$X_i = \begin{cases} \emptyset & \text{if } \exists F_j \in F \text{ such that } F_j \subseteq X \cup \{q_i\}, \\ X \cup \{q_i\} & \text{otherwise.} \end{cases}$$

The automaton B enters an accepting state if and only if all the states of an accepting set $F_j \in F$ have been visited. Thus, a tree $t \in T(S)$ if and only if $t \in T(B)$. Since the number of sets in H is at most exponential in the size of Q, we have that $Size(B)$ is bounded above by $2^{\mathcal{O}(Size_{DSTA}(T))}$. Thus, $Size_{DBTA}(T) \leq 2^{\mathcal{O}(Size_{DSTA}(T))}$. □

Given a DSTA S accepting a language T, using the above algorithm we can construct a DBTA B accepting T with an exponential blow-up in the size of the automaton S. In the next example, we show a matching lower-bound for this construction. In particular we define a class of languages and a corresponding Muller-Superset tree automata S such that a minimal DBTA B accepting $T(S)$ is such that $Size(B)$ is at least exponential in $Size(S)$.

Example 2. Let $\Sigma = \Sigma_a \cup \Sigma_b$ where $\Sigma_a = \{a_1, \ldots, a_n\}$ and $\Sigma_b = \{b_1, \ldots, b_n\}$, and $T = \{t \in T^{\omega}_{\Sigma} \mid \forall \pi \text{ of } t, \{a_i, b_i\} \in Inf(t/\pi) \text{ for some } i \text{ such that } 1 \leq i \leq n\}$. We show that T is accepted by a DSTA S with $Size(S) = 4n^2 + 4n$ and a minimal DBTA B accepting T is such that $Size(B) \geq 2^n$. Let $S = \langle Q, \Sigma, \delta, \{q_{a_1}\}, F \rangle$ be a DSTA with $Q = \{q_x \mid x \in \Sigma\}$, $F = \bigcup_{i=1}^{n} \{q_{a_i}, q_{b_i}\}$, and $\delta = \{(q, x, q_x, q_x) \mid q \in Q$ and $x \in \Sigma\}$. Trivially $T(S) = T$ and $Size(S) = 4n^2 + 4n$.

Now we prove by contradiction that $Size_{DBTA}(T) \geq 2^n$. Assume that B is a DBTA with less than 2^n states such that $T = T(B)$. Notice that any tree t such that for any path π, $t/\pi = (wb_i)^{\omega}$, where $w \in \Sigma_a^*$, $b_i \in \Sigma_b$ and w contains a_i, belongs to T. For a word $w \in \Sigma_a^*$, we define $symbols(w) = \{x_i \mid x_i \in \Sigma_a$ and $w = w' x_i w''\}$, that is the set of symbols from Σ_a which occur in w. Define the equivalence $\equiv$ over Σ_a^* as $w \equiv w'$ if and only if $symbols(w) = symbols(w')$. Clearly $\equiv$ has index 2^n. Given a word w, consider a tree t^w such that w is the prefix of the word labeling the leftmost path of t^w. Since B has less than 2^n

states, there exist two words w and w' such that: $w \not\equiv w'$ and, the runs of B on t^w and $t^{w'}$ reach, on the leftmost path, the same state after reading, respectively, w and w'. Let $a_i \in symbols(w)$ and $a_i \notin symbols(w')$. Consider now a tree t whose leftmost path is labeled by $(wb_i)^\omega$ and a tree t' whose leftmost path is labeled by $(w'b_j)^\omega$ for some b_j such that $a_j \in symbols(w')$. Clearly both t and t' belong to T, thus, the corresponding runs r and r' of B are accepting runs. Let t'' be a tree which differs from t' only in the leftmost path which is labeled by $(w'b_i)^\omega$. Such t'' does not belong to T but by the above assumptions we have that the only run of B on t'' is accepting, and thus we have a contradiction.

We end this section showing that Büchi and Muller-Superset tree automata capture the same class of languages also in the nondeterministic case.

Theorem 2. *The classes BTA and STA coincide. Moreover, for a given tree language T, $Size_{STA}(T) \leq Size_{BTA}(T) \leq (Size_{STA}(T))^3$.*

Proof. To prove that $BTA \subseteq STA$, we can use the same construction as we have used in the deterministic case. We recall that that construction also proves $Size_{STA}(T) \leq Size_{BTA}(T)$.

Now let us prove that $BTA \supseteq STA$. Let $S = \langle Q, \Sigma, \delta, Q_0, F\rangle$ be an STA, where $F = \{F_1, \ldots, F_n\}$. We assume that the states from F_h are numbered from 0 to $n_h - 1$, where $n_h = |F_h|$, according to any arbitrary order. Define $B = \langle Q', \Sigma, \delta', Q'_0, F'\rangle$ as the BTA with set of states $Q' = \{[q, h, i] \,|\, q \in Q, 1 \leq h \leq n$ and $0 \leq i \leq n_h\}$, set of initial states $Q'_0 = \{[q, h, 0] \,|\, q \in Q_0$ and $1 \leq h \leq n\}$, accepting set $F' = \{[q, h, n_h] \,|\, q \in Q$ and $1 \leq h \leq n\}$ and transition relation δ' defined as follows. For any transition $(q, a, q_1, q_2) \in \delta$, we add the tuples $([q, h, i], a, [q_1, h_1, i_1], [q_2, h_2, i_2])$ such that at least one between h_1 and h_2 is equal to h, and for $j = 1, 2$ we have that if $h_j \neq h$ then $i_j = 0$, otherwise if $h_j = h$ then

- $i_j = i + 1$, if $i < n_h$ and q is the i-th state of the set F_h,
- $i_j = 0$, if $i = n_h$, and
- $i_j = i$, in all the other cases.

For each path, the automaton B nondeterministically guesses a set of accepting states F_h and checks that all the states from this set are visited infinitely often. Thus, $T(B) = T(S)$. By the above construction we have that the size of Q' is $|F|\,|Q|$, $\delta' = O(n\,|\delta|\,|F|)$ and $|F'| = n\,|Q|$. Thus, we get that $Size(B) \leq (Size(S))^3$, and $Size_{BTA}(T) \leq (Size_{STA}(T))^3$ holds. □

4 Landweber Tree Automata

In this section, we introduce the *Landweber* acceptance condition, a new acceptance condition on infinite trees obtained by using the subset operation, instead of the equality, in the Muller acceptance condition. We study for the corresponding class of languages the main closure properties and we compare the classes of languages accepted by the deterministic and the nondeterministic Landweber tree automata. The considered model extends to trees, in the usual way, the acceptance condition introduced by Landweber for automata on ω-words [8].

A *Landweber* tree automaton (LTA) L is a TA with accepting condition $F = \{F_1, \ldots, F_m\}$. A tree $t \in T_\Sigma^\omega$ is accepted by L if and only if there exists a run $r \in Run_L(t)$ satisfying the condition that for every path π of r, the containment $Inf(r/\pi) \subseteq F_i$ holds for some $F_i \in F$. Moreover, with (D)LTA we denote the class of languages accepted by (deterministic) Landweber tree automata. Directly from the definition we have that LTA is contained in MTA.

In the following example, we give a DLTA accepting the language T_2.

Example 3. Let $L = \langle \{q_a, q_b\}, \{a, b\}, \delta, \{q_a\}, \{\{q_a\}, \{q_b\}\}\rangle$ be a DLTA where $\delta = \{(q, a, q_a, q_a), (q, b, q_b, q_b) \mid q \in Q\}$. The automaton L changes its state to q_a (respectively, q_b) whenever an occurrence of a (respectively, b) is read. Thus, $t \in T(L)$ if and only if on each path there are either finitely many occurrences of b or finitely many occurrences of a, that is if and only if $t \in T_2$. Hence, $T_2 \in$DLTA.

We show now that, also for this new acceptance condition, nondeterminism strictly increases the accepting power of the model.

Theorem 3. *$DLTA \subset LTA$.*

Proof. To prove this result we provide a language in LTA which is not in DLTA. Namely, we show that $T_1 \in$LTA-DLTA.

Let L be the LTA $\langle \{q_0, q_1, q_2\}, \{a, b\}, \delta, \{q_0\}, \{\{q_1, q_2\}\}\rangle$ such that δ is given by $\{(q_0, x, q_0, q_1), (q_0, x, q_1, q_0), (q_1, x, q_1, q_1), (p, b, q_1, q_2), (p, b, q_2, q_1) \mid x \in \{a, b\}$ and $p \in \{q_0, q_2\}\}$. L nondeterministically chooses a path in the input tree and checks if there is a finite number of a's. This check is carried out by guessing the last occurrence of a on the selected path. Thus, a tree is accepted if and only if it is possible to select a path with a finite number of a's. Hence, $T_1 = T(L)$.

To complete the proof, suppose that there is a DLTA L accepting T_1. Let $t \in T_1$ such that t_0 is entirely labeled by a, and t_1 is entirely labeled by b and let r be a successful run from $Run_L(t)$. Consider now the tree t' obtained from t by exchanging the two subtrees t_0 and t_1, that is $t'_0 = t_1$ and $t'_1 = t_0$. Obviously, $t' \in T_1$, and let r' be a successful run of L on t'. Replace t'_1 for t_1 in t, and call the obtained tree t''. Clearly, $t'' \notin T_1$. Since L is deterministic, and r and r' are successful runs, we have that replacing r'_1 for r_1 in r, we obtain a successful run of L on t''. Thus, $t'' \in T(L)$ and hence we get a contradiction. □

By standard automata constructions we can prove the following theorem:

Theorem 4. *(D)LTA is closed under union and intersection.*

Now we informally introduce a new notation that will be used to prove the non closure under complementation of (D)LTA. Let Σ be a finite alphabet and let $c \notin \Sigma$ be a new symbol, we denote by $T_\Sigma^{(c)}$ the set of trees with both infinite and finite paths valued on $\Sigma \cup \{c\}$ with the restriction that c cannot label internal nodes and all the symbols in Σ can only label internal nodes. Let $t, t' \in T_\Sigma^{(c)}$, we denote by $t \cdot_c t'$ the tree obtained from t by replacing each occurrence of c with t' (*c-concatenation*). For $T \in T_\Sigma^{(c)}$, the ωc-concatenation of t denoted by $t^{\omega c}$ is the tree in T_Σ^ω obtained by iterating the *c-concatenation* on t.

The following theorem states the nonclosure under complementation of both the introduced classes.

Theorem 5. *(D)LTA is not closed under complementation.*

Proof. To prove this result we show that there is a language in DLTA whose complement with respect to T_Σ^ω is not in LTA. In the Example 3, we have given a DLTA accepting T_2. Consider now $T = \{t \in T_\Sigma^\omega \mid \exists\ \pi$ *such that* $a \in Inf(t/\pi)$ and $b \in Inf(t/\pi)\}$. Clearly T is the complement of T_2 with respect to T_Σ^ω. Suppose that there exists an LTA L such that $T(L) = T$. Thus, there exists $t \in T$ such that $Inf(t/\pi_0) = \{a, b\}$, $Inf(t/\pi) \subset \{a, b\}$ for any path $\pi \neq \pi_0$, and for any natural number h, there exists a natural number $m \geq h$ such that $t(0^i) = b$ for $m \leq i \leq n + m$, where n is the number of states of L. Let r be a successful run of L on t such that $Inf(r/\pi_0) \subseteq F_i$ for a given i. Thus, there exist j and k such that $m \leq j < k \leq m + n$ and $r(0^j) = r(0^k) \in F_i$. We can decompose r (respectively, t) in three parts as follows:

- r' (resp. t') is obtained from r (resp. t) by replacing the subtree r_{0^j} (resp. t_{0^j}) with a sole node labeled by c.
- r'' (resp. t'') is obtained from r_{0^j} (resp. t_{0^j})by replacing r_{0^k} (resp. t_{0^k}) with a sole node labeled by c.
- r''' (resp. t''') is r_{0^k} (resp. t_{0^k}).

Thus, $r = r' \cdot_c r'' \cdot_c r'''$ and $t = t' \cdot_c t'' \cdot_c t'''$. Directly from the above properties of r and t, we get that the run $r' \cdot_c r''^{\omega c}$ is a successful run of L on $t' \cdot_c t''^{\omega c}$. But for the choice of j and k this tree contains only paths with a finite number of a. Hence, we contradict the hypothesis that $T(L) = T$. □

Notice that the above proof is sufficient to show also that T_4 is not LTA.

5 Language Comparisons

In this section we compare the classes of languages (D)BTA, (D)MTA, and (D)LTA. To prove our results we use the languages along their rank listed in Figure 2.

The following theorem states the results of the comparisons involving DLTA.

Theorem 6.

1. *DLTA and (D)BTA are not comparable.*
2. *DLTA $\cup$ DBTA $\subset$ DMTA.*

Proof. From example 3 we have that $T_2 \in$ DLTA. Since we know that $T_2 \notin$ BTA, and $T_4 \in$ DBTA-DLTA, we obtain that DLTA and (D)BTA are not comparable. From the relationships summarized in Figure 1 and a trivial automata construction we get DLTA $\cup$ DBTA $\subseteq$ DMTA. To prove the strict containment we use $T = \{t \in T_\Sigma^\omega \,|\, t_0 \in T_2 \text{ and } t_1 \in T_4\}$. Obviously, $T \notin$ DLTA $\cup$ DBTA. We know that T_2 and T_4 is in DMTA and thus part 2 holds. □

Comparisons between LTA and the remaining classes are established in the following lemma.

Theorem 7.

1. *LTA and (D)BTA are not comparable.*
2. *LTA and DMTA are not comparable.*
3. *For $X, Y, Z \in \{LTA, BTA, DMTA\}$ such that $X \neq Y$, $X \neq Z$ and $Y \neq Z$, we have that $X \not\subseteq Y \cup Z$.*
4. *LTA $\cup$ BTA $\cup$ DMTA $\subset$ MTA.*

Proof. Part 1 is a direct consequence of $T_4 \in DBTA - LTA$, and $T_2 \in LTA - BTA$. We know from the table in Figure 2 and the results in section 4 that $T_1 \in$ LTA-DMTA and $T_4 \in$ DMTA-LTA, thus, part 2 holds. To prove part 3 we only need to consider three cases: (a) LTA $\not\subseteq$ BTA $\cup$ DMTA, (b) BTA $\not\subseteq$ LTA $\cup$ DMTA, and (c) DMTA $\not\subseteq$ BTA $\cup$ LTA. Consider the case (a). Let $T = \{t \in T_\Sigma^\omega \,|\, t_0 \in T_1 \text{ and } t_1 \in T_2\}$. We have that $T \notin$ DMTA $\cup$ BTA since $T_1 \notin$ DMTA and $T_2 \notin$ BTA, but $T \in$ LTA since by the results in section 4 we know that T_1 and T_2 belong to LTA. The proofs of cases (b) and (c) are analogous. In particular, for (b) we may use $T = \{t \in T_\Sigma^\omega \,|\, t_0 \in T_1 \text{ and } t_1 \in T_4\}$ and for (c) we may use $T = \{t \in T_\Sigma^\omega \,|\, t_0 \in T_2 \text{ and } t_1 \in T_4\}$. For part 4, we observe that, by a simple automata construction involving only the accepting sets, it is possible to prove that LTA $\subseteq$ MTA. Thus, from Figure 1, we have that DMTA $\cup$ BTA $\cup$ LTA $\subseteq$ MTA. Let $T = \{t \in T_\Sigma^\omega \,|\, t_0 \in T_1 \text{ and } t_{10} \in T_2 \text{ and } t_{11} \in T_4\}$, we obtain $T \notin$ DMTA $\cup$ BTA $\cup$ LTA since $T_1 \notin$ DMTA, $T_2 \notin$ BTA, and $T_4 \notin$ LTA. It easy to verify that T is instead accepted by an MTA. □

In the following theorem we complete the study of the relationships among the introduced classes of languages by pointing out the existence of languages in particular subclasses.

Theorem 8.

1. *DLTA $\cap$ DBTA $\cap$ DMTA $\neq \emptyset$.*
2. $((LTA \cap DMTA) - BTA) \neq \emptyset$, $((BTA \cap LTA) - DMTA) \neq \emptyset$ *and* $((BTA \cap DMTA) - LTA) \neq \emptyset$.
3. $((DLTA \cap BTA) - DBTA) \neq \emptyset$.
4. $((BTA \cap DMTA) - (DBTA \cup LTA)) \neq \emptyset$.

Proof. It is easy to prove that $T_3 \in$ DLTA, thus, from the table in Figure 2, T_3 belongs to the intersection of DLTA, DBTA, and DMTA. Hence, part 1 holds. Part 2 directly follows from the classification of the languages T_1, T_2 and T_4.

Part 3 can be proved by using T_5. For part 4, consider $T = \{t \in T^{\omega}_{\Sigma} \,|\, t_0 \in T_4$ and $t_1 \in T_5\}$. Since $T_4 \notin$ LTA and $T_5 \notin$ DBTA we have that $T \notin$ LTA ∪ DBTA. Since $T_4, T_5 \in$ DMTA ∩ BTA, we have that $T \in$ DMTA ∩ BTA. □

It is an open problem to determine whether DLTA = DMTA ∩ LTA. Our conjecture is that this is the case. Our main motivation is that a language to be accepted nondeterministically by an LTA and deterministically by an MTA, cannot contain trees that require nondeterministic guesses on the paths on which the automaton must check for a given property. Thus, nondeterminism can be only used along the paths. Since every path is an infinite word and the nondeterministic and deterministic paradigms of finite automata on infinite sequences of characters with Landweber acceptance condition are equivalent, we expect our conjecture to hold.

Assuming that our conjecture is true the relationships among the introduced classes of languages is reported in Figure 3. Notice that according to the results presented in this section, any region denoted in the diagram is not empty.

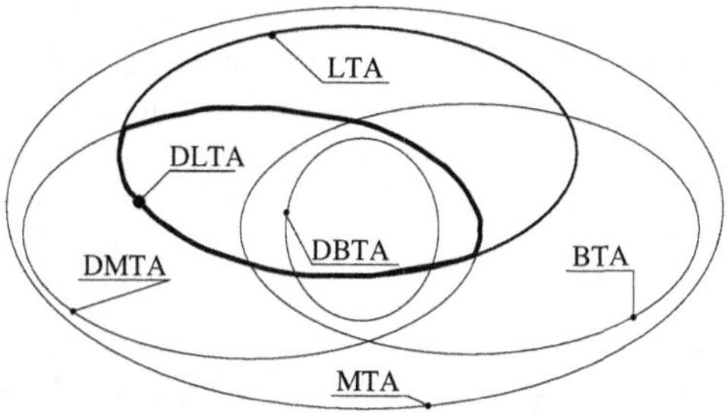

Fig. 3. Relationships between (D)BTA, (D)MTA and (D)LTA.

6 The Emptiness Problem for *LTA*

In this section we deal with the emptiness problem for Landweber tree automata. From Theorem 7 we have that the class *LTA* is not comparable with *BTA* and is strictly contained in *MTA*. We observe that a Landweber condition can be directly translated to a Rabin condition by a very simple construction. Given a Landweber tree automaton $L = \langle Q, \Sigma, \delta, Q_0, F \rangle$ where $F = \{F_1, \ldots, F_m\}$, a Rabin tree automaton accepting $T(L)$ is $R = \langle Q, \Sigma, \delta, Q_0, F' \rangle$, where $F' = \{(F_1, Q - F_1), \ldots, (F_m, Q - F_m)\}$. By this construction and the result that any non-empty language accepted by a Rabin tree automaton contains a regular tree [14], we have the following lemma.

Lemma 1. *Any non-empty language accepted by a Landweber tree automaton contains a regular tree.*

Algorithm 1.
$P \leftarrow Q'$
repeat
$P' \leftarrow P$
$P \leftarrow \emptyset$
for $(q, a, q_1, q_2) \in \delta$ such that $q \in P'$ **do**
if $(p, p' \in \{q_1, q_2\}, p \neq p', p \in Q''$ **and** $p' \in P')$ **or** $q_1, q_2 \in P'$ **then**
$P \leftarrow P \cup \{q\}$
enddo
until $P' = P$
return $Reach(Q'' \cup P)$

Fig. 4. Algorithm for computing $Accept(Q', Q'')$.

Since the constructed automaton R is linear in the size of the starting automaton L, and the non-emptiness problem for Rabin tree automata is NP-complete [5, 12], we get a nondeterministic polynomial time algorithm to solve the non-emptiness problem for Landweber tree automata. In the following, we indeed prove that checking for the emptiness of Landweber tree automata can be done in deterministic polynomial time and thus, under the theoretical assumption that "$P \neq NP$", it turns out to be simpler than for Rabin tree automata. Before proving the claimed result on the LTA emptiness problem we give some notation.

Consider a Landweber tree automaton $L = \langle Q, \Sigma, \delta, Q_0, F \rangle$ where $F = \{F_1, \ldots, F_m\}$. A *finite portion* of a run r is a subtree r' of r such that all paths in r' are finite. We refer to the last nodes of all paths in r' as *leaves*. For a set of states $Q' \subseteq Q$, we define $Reach(Q')$ as the set of all the states from which there exists a finite portion of a run whose leaves are labeled with states in Q'. This set can be computed in time linear in $|Q'| + |\delta|$, by using a simple algorithm of backward reachability.

For a transition $e = (q, a, q_1, q_2) \in \delta$, we define the *graph induced* by e as the directed graph whose vertices are q, q_1, and q_2, and whose edges are (q, q_1) and (q, q_2). This definition generalizes to sets of transitions in an obvious way. Moreover, we define a *graph embedded* in L as the graph induced by the transitions from a $\delta' \subseteq \delta$ such that for any $q \in Q$ there exists at most a transition from q in δ'. Given two sets $Q', Q'' \subseteq Q$, by $Accept(Q', Q'')$ we denote a set of states $q \in Q$ such that there exists a graph G embedded in L such that q is a vertex of G and along every maximal simple path of G starting from q either a state in Q'' or a cycle over only states from Q' are reached. Clearly, $Accept(\emptyset, P) = Reach(P)$ and $Accept(P, \emptyset)$ is $Reach(P')$ where $P' = \cup_{i=1}^{k} P_i$ such that for any $i = 1, \ldots, k$, $P_i \subseteq P$ and there exists a graph G_i which is embedded in L, has P_i as set of vertices, and is a strongly connected component (i.e., from any vertex of G all the other vertices of G can be reached). The set $Accept(Q', Q'')$ can be computed by the algorithm in Figure 4.

Lemma 2. *Algorithm 1 computes* $Accept(Q', Q'')$ *in* $O(|Q'|\,|\delta| + |Q''|)$ *time.*

The following theorem holds.

Theorem 9. *The emptiness problem for LTA is decidable in polynomial time.*

Proof. Consider a Landweber tree automaton $L = \langle Q, \Sigma, \delta, Q_0, F\rangle$ where $F = \{F_1, \ldots, F_m\}$. A procedure to decide "$T(L) = \emptyset$?" is given by the recurrence $\Gamma_0 = \cup_{i=1}^{m} Accept(F_i, \emptyset)$ and $\Gamma_{j+1} = \cup_{i=1}^{m} Accept(F_i, \Gamma_j)$. Let Γ be the least fixed-point of the above recurrence, our decision algorithm outputs YES, if $\Gamma \cap Q_0 = \emptyset$, and NO, otherwise. We observe that the least fixed-point of the above recurrence is reached in at most $|Q|$ iterations. Thus, by Lemma 2 and the fact that *Reach*(P) can be done in linear time, computing Γ requires $O(m\,|\delta|\,|Q|^2)$ time and hence can be computed in polynomial time. To complete the proof we need to show that $T(L)$ is not empty if and only if $\Gamma \cap Q_0$ is not empty. The converse direction is a direct consequence of the definition of the set Γ and the definition of the Landweber acceptance condition. Consider now the forward direction. From Lemma 1 we have that $T(L)$ is not empty if and only if there exists a regular tree belonging to $T(L)$. Consider now a finite graph G corresponding to an accepting regular run of L (i.e., a run on a regular tree). We claim that G must contain at least a strongly connected component over states from a given $F_i \in F$. To prove this we observe that if this is not the case then there is an infinite path π of G, and thus of the corresponding regular tree, that does not satisfy the acceptance condition, i.e., for any $F_i \in F$ it holds that on π the set of states that repeat infinitely often is not contained in F_i. This property ensures that some of the vertices of such G correspond to states belonging to Γ_0. By a similar argument we can prove that at the i-th iteration of the above algorithm at least one new state, among those corresponding to vertices of G, is added to Γ_i, and this is repeated until all such states are added. Since G corresponds to an accepting run of L, then also a state from Q_0 is eventually added to some Γ_i, and thus, is contained in Γ. Hence, we get that if $T(L)$ is not empty then $\Gamma \cap Q_0$ is not empty, and we are done. □

7 Conclusions

In this paper we have studied two new acceptance conditions for tree automata: the Landweber and the Muller-Superset acceptance conditions. These conditions are relaxations of the Muller acceptance condition. We have shown that Muller-Superset tree automata capture the same class of languages as Büchi tree automata, and that automata from this class can be more succinct than Büchi tree automata. For Landweber tree automata we have studied both the nondeterministic and the deterministic paradigms, and compared the corresponding classes of languages to those characterized by Büchi and Muller tree automata. The class of languages accepted by Landweber tree automata is orthogonal to that accepted by Büchi tree automata. For this class we have studied the main closure properties and the emptiness problem. Our main result is that the emptiness problem for Landweber tree automata is decidable in polynomial time, and thus we enlarge the class of ω-tree languages that can be characterized by automata with a tractable emptiness problem. Besides the intrinsic interest in such a theoretical result, the emptiness problem of automata is closely related to decision problems in mathematical logics and also to the specification and verification of systems. Future developments of this research will take in account these aspects. Finally, the Landweber acceptance condition naturally expresses the complement of the Büchi condition. Given a Büchi condition F its complementation is given by the Landweber condition $\{Q - F\}$, where Q is the set of states of the automaton. This suggests a very simple way of characterizing the complement of deterministic Büchi tree automata by nondeterministic Landweber tree automata with only one accepting set. The nondeterminism is needed to nondeterministically select a path to check for the violation of the Büchi condition.

References

[1] J.R. Büchi. Weak second-order arithmetic and finite automata. *Z. Math Logik Grundlag. Math.*, 6:66 – 92, 1960.

[2] J.R. Büchi. On a decision method in restricted second-order arithmetic. In *Proc. of the International Congress on Logic, Methodology, and Philosophy of Science 1960*, pages 1 – 12. Stanford University Press, 1962.

[3] E.M. Clarke and E.A. Emerson. Design and synthesis of synchronization skeletons using branching time temporal logic. In *Proc. of Workshop on Logic of Programs*, LNCS 131, pages 52 – 71. Springer-Verlag, 1981.

[4] E.A. Emerson and J.Y. Halpern. Sometimes and not never revisited: On branching versus linear time. *Journal of the ACM*, 33(1):151 – 178, 1986.

[5] E.A. Emerson and C.S. Jutla. The complexity of tree automata and logics of programs. In *Proc. of the 29th IEEE-CS Symposium on Foundations of Computer Science*, pages 328 – 337, 1988.

[6] R. Hossley. *Finite tree Automata and ω-Automata.* PhD thesis, MIT, Cambridge, Massachussets, 1970.

[7] R.P. Kurshan. *Computer-aided Verification of Coordinating Processes: the automata-theoretic approach.* Princeton University Press, 1994.

[8] L. H. Landweber. Decision problems for ω-automata. *Mathematical System Theory*, 3:376 – 384, 1969.

[9] S. La Torre and M. Napoli. Finite automata on timed ω-trees. *Theoretical Computer Science*, To appear.

[10] S. La Torre and M. Napoli. Timed tree automata with an application to temporal logic. *Acta Informatica*, 38(2):89–116, 2001.

[11] R. McNaughton. Testing and generating infinite sequences by a finite automaton. *Information and Control*, 9:521 – 530, 1966.

[12] M.O. Rabin. Decidability of second-order theories and automata on infinite trees. *Trans. Amer. Math. Soc.*, 141:1 – 35, 1969.

[13] M.O. Rabin. Weakly definable relations and special automata. *Mathematical Logic and Foundations of Set theory*, 1970.

[14] M.O. Rabin. Automata on Infinite Objects and Church's Problem. *Amer. Mathematical Soc.*, 1972.

[15] M.Y. Vardi and P. Wolper. Automata-theoretic techniques for modal logics of programs. *Journal of Computer and System Sciences*, 32:182 – 211, 1986.

[16] M.Y. Vardi and P. Wolper. Reasoning about infinite computations. *Information and Computation*, 115:1 – 37, 1994.

A Fully Abstract Model for Higher-Order Mobile Ambients*

Mario Coppo and Mariangiola Dezani-Ciancaglini

Dipartimento di Informatica – Università di Torino
{coppo,dezani}@di.unito.it

Abstract. Aim of this paper is to develop a filter model for a calculus with mobility and higher-order value passing. We will define it for an extension of the Ambient Calculus in which processes can be passed as values. This model turns out to be fully abstract with respect to the notion of contextual equivalence where the observables are ambients at top level.

1 Introduction

The *Ambient Calculus* [8] is a calculus of mobile computation that allows active processes to move between sites and interact with them. Owing to its interest a number of studies on various foundational aspects of this or derived systems have been recently developed. The subject of these investigations have been mainly type systems (finalized to the proof of various properties like safe communications [9] or security [7,17,6]), proof systems [10], abstract interpretations [19] and flow analysis [13]. In [11] a denotational model has been proposed for a very basic subset of the language, in which only mobility primitives where present. Aim of this paper is to extend this model to a language in which processes can be exchange as values inside ambients. Our approach is similar to that of [3], but in our language we do not have a separate set of expressions (including an explicit λ operator) which can be communicated. In the resulting language, however, the λ-calculus can be directly simulated.

One main difficulty in defining models of the Ambient Calculus is that of finding an abstract counterpart to the notion of mobility. A promising tool for overcoming this difficulty seems the notion of "logical" semantics in which domains are described by abstract filters of logical formulas expressing properties of the terms of the calculus. In filter models, moreover, terms are interpreted as the sets of their computational properties (types). This makes them an interesting basis for the study and development of analysis tools. Filter models have been successfully applied, for instance, to the study of normalization properties of lambda terms [16].

In this paper we define, in particular, a model for a variant of the Ambient Calculus with synchronous higher-order value passing and a new "selfopen" primitive so. The so action is strongly related to the *acid* operation of [8] and allows the simulation of objective moves [8]. Our model turns out to be fully abstract with respect to the notion

* Partially supported by MURST Cofin'00 AITCFA Project, MURST Cofin'01 COMETA Project, IST-2001-33477 DART Project and IST-2001-322222 MIKADO Project.

A. Cortesi (Ed.): VMCAI 2002, LNCS 2294, pp. 255–271, 2002.
© Springer-Verlag Berlin Heidelberg 2002

of contextual equivalence defined in [18]. The same model is also adequate with respect to the calculus obtained by eliminating the so action, but in this case it is not fully abstract.

The “logical” approach to denotational semantics goes back to [25], and has been advocated in [1] as a general paradigm unifying, among other things, type assignment, logic of programs and logical characterizations of behaviors of concurrent processes such as Hennessy-Milner logic. A main advantage of this approach is that it produces a denotational model in the sense that the denotation of a term is given in a compositional way. This has been used in [4] and [2] for λ-calculus. In the same line are the studies concerning extensions of λ-calculus by means of operators with concurrent features like [23,5,14,15]. In [5], in particular, the intersection type operator is seen as the basic tool to represent nondeterministic choice in the “may” perspective.

In [21] Hennessy presents the first denotational model of higher-order concurrent processes based on a compromise between type systems and modal logic. The resulting filter model turns out to be fully abstract with respect to an operational semantics based on a notion of testing and “may” convergency. A similar result has been proved in [20] for a kernel of the language FACILE. A filter model for higher-order processes which is adequate but not complete with respect to the “must” testing as been proposed in [22]. The same approach is used in [12] to build a filter model of the π-calculus which is fully abstract for “may” convergence.

The type system used for the definition of the model can also be seen as a proof system to express ambient and process properties. Proof systems with these aims have also proposed by Cardelli and Gordon (see e.g. [10]). Sangiorgi's paper [24] provides a careful study of the equivalence on mobile ambients induced by the *ambient logic* of [10]. The logic turns out to be strongly intensional, equating mainly structurally equivalent processes: for example it distinguishes between the processes $in\, a.in\, a.\mathbf{0}$ and $in\, a.\mathbf{0} \mid in\, a.\mathbf{0}$, which are observationally equivalent. Therefore the ambient logic seems not suitable to be taken as a basis for the construction of a model of contextual semantics, where properties need to have an extensional meaning.

2 The Language

The calculus of Selfopening Mobile Ambients, introduced in [11], is an extension of the calculus of Mobile Ambients [8] obtained by adding a new primitive action so. In the Ambient Calculus a process has no way of opening the ambient a in which he is running raising itself one level up. This kind of action is allowed by the so primitive. This primitive is quite similar to the *acid* primitive discussed by Cardelli and Gordon in [8]. The main difference is that *acid* does not mention the ambient dissolved while so does. This can be crucial in defining a type system for avoiding unwanted uses of so. Processes can be exchanged as values with the standard input and output primitives of the synchronous Ambient Calculus. We leave out here restriction: its introduction could be investigated following the lines of [12].

Ambients and Processes

Let $\mathcal{V}$ be a set of *process variables*, ranged over by $X,\ Y, \ldots$. Let $\mathcal{L}$ be a set of *ambient names* ranged over by $a, b, c \ldots$ and $\mathcal{M}$ be the set of *actions*, ranged over by $\mathsf{m}, \mathsf{n}, \ldots$, containing $in\, a$, $out\, a$, $open a$, $so\, a$ for all ambients $a \in \mathcal{L}$, and (X), $\langle P \rangle$ for all process variables X and processes P. The set $\mathcal{P}$ of *processes* (ranged over by $P,\ Q,\ R, \ldots$) is defined by

$$\mathcal{P} ::= \mathbf{0} \mid \mathcal{V} \mid \mathcal{M}.\mathcal{P} \mid \mathcal{L}[\mathcal{P}] \mid \mathcal{P} \,|\, \mathcal{P} \mid !\mathcal{P}.$$

$\mathcal{M}^{\updownarrow} \subseteq \mathcal{M}$ will denote the set of *mobility actions* containing only $in\, a$, $out\, a$, $open\, a$, $so\, a$ for all ambients $a \in \mathcal{L}$.
We assume that "." takes precedence over "|". So $\mathsf{m}.\alpha \,|\, \beta$ is read $(\mathsf{m}.\alpha)|\beta$.

As customary, the relation of structural congruence $\equiv$ is defined as the minimal reflexive, transitive and symmetric relation which is a congruence and moreover:

- satisfies $!P \equiv !P \,|\, P$;
- includes α-conversion;
- makes the operator $|$ commutative, associative, with $\mathbf{0}$ as neutral element.

The behavior of processes is then represented by the reduction relation defined in Figure 1. Note that the *so* action allows a process to open its enclosing ambient. This action is orthogonal to the other mobility actions (in , out , $open$) and cannot be internally simulated in the standard Ambient Calculus.

$(red\ in)$	$a[in\, b.P \,|\, Q] \,|\, b[R]]$	$\to b[a[P \,|\, Q] \,|\, R]$
$(red\ out)$	$a[b[out\, a.P \,|\, Q] \,|\, R]$	$\to a[R] \,|\, b[P \,|\, Q]$
$(red\ selfopen)$	$a[so\, a.P \,|\, Q]$	$\to P \,|\, Q$
$(red\ open)$	$open\, a.P \,|\, a[Q]$	$\to P \,|\, Q$
$(comm)$	$(X).P \,|\, \langle Q \rangle.R$	$\to P[X := Q] \,|\, R$
$(R-par)$	$P \to Q$	$\Rightarrow P \,|\, R \to Q \,|\, R$
$(R-amb)$	$P \to Q$	$\Rightarrow n[P] \to n[Q]$
$(R-\equiv)$	$P' \equiv P' \;\; P \to Q \;\; Q \equiv Q'$	$\Rightarrow P' \to Q'$

Fig. 1. Reduction

Observational Equivalence

In the ambient calculus the natural candidates to represent observables are the ambients. The following definition of observational preorder takes the notion of observable proposed in the original system [18].

Definition 1. *(i) We say that process* P exhibits *an ambient* a*, notation* $P \Downarrow a$ *if* $P \to^* a[Q] \mid R$ *for some processes* Q, R.
(ii) $P \sqsubseteq Q$ *if for all closing context* $\mathcal{C}[\,]$ *and ambients* a*:* $\mathcal{C}[P] \Downarrow a \Rightarrow \mathcal{C}[Q] \Downarrow a$.
(iii) $P \cong Q$ *if* $P \sqsubseteq Q$ *and* $Q \sqsubseteq P$.

Remark 1. Note that $P \to Q$ implies $Q \sqsubseteq P$, but in general $P \not\cong Q$. For instance let $P_1 = open\, a.\mathbf{0} \mid a[b[\mathbf{0}]]$ and $P_2 = b[\mathbf{0}]$. Then $P_1 \to P_2$ but $P_1 \not\cong P_2$ (take $\mathcal{C}[\,]$ as $[-]$).

3 Types

Like in type assignment systems for polymorphic λ-calculus, types are seen as properties of type-free objects rather than domains in which objects live. Types are intended to provide partial information about the processes they are associated with. Our language of types must be expressive enough to completely characterize process behaviors. We need, thus, to consider both the ambient, mobility actions and parallel composition as type constructors. The (binary) type constructor for input actions is $(-).-$, which correspond to the $\to$ function type constructor. We use here this notation for uniformity with the other type constructors. Similarly $\langle - \rangle.-$ is the type constructor for output actions. A type $\langle \sigma \rangle.\alpha$ represents processes which can produce an output of type σ and then leave a continuation of type α. For technical reasons (see Remark 2 of Section 5) we need to restrict the set of types allowed in the input-output fields of types.

The conjunction type constructor is added to represent nondeterminism. Type ω represents a property that is true of all processes. The set $\mathcal{T}$ of *types* (ranged over by α, β, $\gamma, \ldots$) is then defined by

$$\mathcal{T} ::= \omega \mid \mathcal{M}^{\updownarrow}.\mathcal{T} \mid \langle \mathcal{T}^{-} \rangle.\mathcal{T} \mid (\mathcal{T}^{-}).\mathcal{T} \mid \mathcal{L}[\mathcal{T}] \mid \mathcal{T} | \mathcal{T} \mid \mathcal{T} \wedge \mathcal{T},$$

where $\mathcal{T}^{-} \subseteq \mathcal{T}$ is the subset of *simple* types, ranged over by σ, $\tau, \ldots$, containing all types without occurrences of the $\wedge$ operator. Intersection represent "may" nondeterminism. A process has type $\alpha \wedge \beta$ if it can possibly exhibit, although in different reduction paths, both property α and property β. We make the convention that $\wedge$ has the lowest precedence.

In connecting types to processes we must consider two distinct formal systems. One is to represent the logical structure of types, determined by their entailment relation (denoted $\leq$), and one to assign types to processes.

The logical structure of types is formalized as a partial order relation representing entailment. We write $\alpha \leq \beta$ to mean that property α entails property β. We write $\alpha \simeq \beta$ if $\alpha \leq \beta \leq \alpha$. Let $\simeq$ be the equivalence relation induced by $\leq$.

The formal rules for type entailment are represented in Figure 2. We say that two actions m and n *match* if either $\mathsf{m} \equiv (\sigma)$, $\mathsf{n} \equiv \langle \tau \rangle$ or $\mathsf{n} \equiv (\sigma)$, $\mathsf{m} \equiv \langle \tau \rangle$, and in both cases $\tau \leq \sigma$.

As pointed out in Remark 1 of Section 2, the execution of an action corresponds to a loss of capabilities. This is formalized by the axioms of the group "Reduction". Rule $(out - in)$ takes into account the fact that, in rule $(red\ in)$, after the consumption of the $in\, a$ action, the process inside a is always able to perform a sequence $out\, a,\ in\, a$ of

- Commutativity and distributivity of $|$

$$(|1)\quad \alpha\,|\,\beta \simeq \beta\,|\,\alpha \qquad\qquad (|2)\quad (\alpha\,|\,\beta)\,|\,\gamma \simeq \alpha\,|\,(\beta\,|\,\gamma)$$

- Axioms for ω:

$$(\omega 1)\quad \alpha \leq \omega \qquad\qquad (\omega 2)\quad \alpha \simeq \alpha\,|\,\omega$$

- Distributivity of $\wedge$

$$\begin{array}{ll} ([\,]\wedge) & a[\alpha \wedge \beta] \simeq a[\alpha] \wedge a[\beta] \\ (|\wedge) & \alpha\,|\,(\beta \wedge \gamma) \simeq (\alpha\,|\,\gamma) \wedge (\beta\,|\,\gamma) \\ (.\wedge) & \mathsf{m}.(\alpha \wedge \beta) \simeq \mathsf{m}.\alpha \wedge \mathsf{m}.\beta \end{array}$$

- Sequentialization

$$\begin{array}{lll} (.|_1) & \mathsf{m}.\alpha\,|\,\beta \leq \mathsf{m}.(\alpha\,|\,\beta) & \\ (.|_2) & \mathsf{m}.\alpha\,|\,\mathsf{n}.\beta \simeq \mathsf{m}.(\alpha\,|\,\mathsf{n}.\beta) \wedge \mathsf{n}.(\mathsf{m}.\alpha\,|\,\beta) & \text{if } \mathsf{m} \text{ and } \mathsf{n} \text{ do not match} \\ (comm) & (\sigma).\beta\,|\,\langle\tau\rangle.\gamma \simeq \beta\,|\,\gamma \wedge (\sigma).(\beta\,|\,\langle\tau\rangle.\gamma) \wedge \langle\tau\rangle.((\alpha).\beta\,|\,\gamma) & \text{if } \tau \leq \sigma \end{array}$$

- Reduction

$$(in)\quad a[in\, b.\alpha\,|\,\beta]\,|\,b[\gamma] \leq b[a[\alpha\,|\,\beta]\,|\,\gamma] \qquad (out)\quad a[b[out\, a.\alpha\,|\,\beta]\,|\,\gamma] \leq a[\gamma]\,|\,b[\alpha\,|\,\beta]$$

$$(selfopen)\quad a[so\, a.\,\alpha\,|\,\beta] \leq \alpha\,|\,\beta \qquad (open)\quad open\, a.\alpha\,|\,a[\beta] \leq \alpha\,|\,\beta$$

$$(out{-}in)\quad in\, a.out\, a.in\, a.\alpha \leq in\, a.\alpha \qquad (in{-}out)\quad out\, a.in\, a.out\, a.\alpha \leq out\, a.\alpha$$

- Congruence

$$(cg-[\,])\ \frac{\alpha \leq \beta}{a[\alpha] \leq a[\beta]} \qquad (cg-action)\ \frac{\alpha \leq \beta}{\mathsf{m}.\alpha \leq \mathsf{m}.\beta}$$

$$(cg-())\ \frac{\sigma' \leq \sigma}{(\sigma).\alpha \leq (\sigma').\alpha} \qquad (cg-\langle\rangle)\ \frac{\sigma \leq \sigma'}{\langle\sigma\rangle.\alpha \leq \langle\sigma'\rangle.\alpha}$$

$$(cg-|)\ \frac{\alpha \leq \gamma \quad \beta \leq \delta}{\alpha\,|\,\beta \leq \gamma\,|\,\delta}$$

- Transitivity

$$(trans)\ \frac{\alpha \leq \beta \quad \beta \leq \gamma}{\alpha \leq \gamma}$$

- Logical

$$(\wedge - r)\quad \alpha \wedge \beta \leq \beta \qquad (\wedge - l)\quad \alpha \wedge \beta \leq \alpha$$

$$(\wedge - id)\quad \alpha \leq \alpha \wedge \alpha \qquad (\wedge - \leq)\ \frac{\alpha \leq \alpha' \quad \beta \leq \beta'}{\alpha \wedge \beta \leq \alpha' \wedge \beta'}$$

Fig. 2. Type Entailment Rules

actions. A similar motivation holds for rule $(in - out)$. Sangiorgi [24] calls *stuttering* this phenomenum.

Axiom $(.\mid_2)$ represents the fact that two parallel processes can perform two distinct actions in any order. Axiom $(.\mid_1)$ is a consequence of this. If the two processes can communicate (axiom $(comm)$) we must take into account also this possibility. Axioms $(\omega 1)$, $(\omega 2)$ and rule $(cg-\mid)$ imply that $\alpha \mid \beta \leq \alpha$, i.e. parallel composition corresponds to increase of capabilities. Note also that, using $(\wedge - id)$, $(\omega 1)$, $(\mid 1)$, $(cg-\mid)$, $(\wedge - \leq)$, $(\omega 2)$, we get $\alpha \mid \beta \leq \alpha \wedge \beta$. As usual output is covariant (rule $(cg - \langle\rangle)$), while input is contravariant (rule $(cg - ())$).

Types will be always considered modulo $\simeq$. Note that $\simeq$ is preserved by both intersection and parallel composition with ω. The operators $\mid$ and $\wedge$ are associative so, for instance, we can write unambiguously $\alpha \mid \beta \mid \gamma$. Parallel composition of types are also considered modulo permutations, and intersection of types are considered modulo permutations and repetitions (rules $(\wedge - id)$, $(\wedge - l)$, $(\wedge - r)$).

A parallel composition $\alpha_1 \mid \ldots \mid \alpha_n$ will sometimes be denoted by $\overrightarrow{\alpha}$ in *vector* notation. An intersection of types $\alpha_1 \wedge \ldots \wedge \alpha_n$ will be denoted by $\bigwedge_{i \in [1 \ldots n]} \alpha_i$. In this case $\beta \propto \bigwedge_{i \in [1 \ldots n]} \alpha_i$ denote that $\beta \equiv \alpha_i$ for some $(1 \leq i \leq n)$.

A crucial technical notion is that of normal type.

Definition 2. *(i) The set $\mathcal{N} \subset \mathcal{T}$ of* normal *types is defined inductively in the following way:*

1. $\omega \in \mathcal{N}$.
2. $\omega \mid \phi \in \mathcal{N}$ *where* $\phi \in \mathcal{N}$.
3. $\mathsf{m}.\phi \in \mathcal{N}$ *where* $\mathsf{m} \in \mathcal{M}$ *and* $\phi \in \mathcal{N}$.
4. $a[\phi] \in \mathcal{N}$ *where* $\phi \in \mathcal{N}$.
5. $\phi \mid a[\psi] \in \mathcal{N}$ *where* $\phi, \psi \in \mathcal{N}$.

(ii) A normal type is easy *if it is normal and is of the form 3.*

Let $\phi, \psi, \xi, \chi ...$ range over normal types. In general a normal type different from ω has the form $\phi \mid a_1[\psi_1] \mid \ldots \mid a_n[\psi_n]$ (or $\phi \mid \overrightarrow{a[\psi]}$ in vector notation) where ϕ can be missing or is easy or ω and $n \geq 0$.

Note that normal types do not contain intersections. A normal type represents a process in which, in each ambient, there is at most one possible action that can be performed. Nondeterminism is left, however, since in the same normal type different actions can be enabled in different ambients.

Definition 3. *Let $\simeq_0$ be the equivalence relation defined by the rules obtained by replacing $\leq$ by $\simeq_0$ in the rules* $(\mid 1)$, $(\mid 2)$, $(\omega 2)$, $([\,]\wedge)$, $(\mid \wedge)$, $(.\wedge)$, $(.\mid_2)$, $(comm)$ *and* $(trans)$ *of Figure 2.*

We can show by structural induction on types that each type has a unique normal form modulo permutations and parallel composition with ω.

Lemma 1. *For all $\alpha \in \mathcal{T}$ there is a unique type $\bigwedge_{i \in I} \phi_i$, where ϕ_i $(i \in I)$ are normal types such that $\alpha \simeq_0 \bigwedge_{i \in I} \phi_i$. We call it the* normal form *of α, denoted $nf(\alpha)$.*

Ambients are inactive with respect to normal forms in the following sense.

Lemma 2. *Let $\phi, \overrightarrow{a[\psi]}$ be normal types. Then $\phi \propto nf(\alpha)$ iff $\phi \mid \overrightarrow{a[\psi]} \propto nf(\alpha \mid \overrightarrow{a[\psi]})$.*

Lemma 3. *Let $nf(\alpha) = \bigwedge_{i \in I} \phi_i$. Then*

1. $nf(a[\alpha])) = \bigwedge_{i \in I} a[\phi_i]$;
2. $nf(\mathsf{m}.\alpha)) = \bigwedge_{i \in I} \mathsf{m}.\phi_i$;
3. *Let $nf(\beta)) = \bigwedge_{j \in J} \psi_j$. Then $nf(\alpha \mid \beta) = \bigwedge_{i \in I, j \in J} nf(\phi_i \mid \psi_j)$.*

The entailment relation can be specialized to normal types. Let $\leq_N \subset \mathcal{N} \times \mathcal{N}$ denote this relation, defined by the rules of Figure 3.

In the rules for $\leq_N$ the r.h.s. is naturally a normal type whenever the l.h.s. is normal, except for rules $(open^N)$ and $(selfopen^N)$, since the parallel composition of two normal types is not normal, in general.

The following lemma is crucial for representing the entailment properties of normal types.

Lemma 4. *Let ϕ, ψ, ξ, χ be normal types such that $\phi \leq_N \psi$ and $\xi \leq_N \chi$. Then for all $\nu \propto nf(\psi \mid \chi)$ there is $\mu \propto nf(\phi \mid \xi)$ such that $\mu \leq_N \nu$.*

Proof sketch. It is enough to prove the lemma assuming $\phi \leq_N \psi$ and $\xi \equiv \chi$. The general property can be easily obtained by transitivity. The proof is then by induction on the proof of $\phi \leq_N \psi$. The most difficult cases are when $\leq_N$ has been obtained by rules $(open^N)$ and $(selfopen^N)$. The proof of these cases requires a careful analysis of the shape of the normal forms and is not given here.

The main lemma of this section relates normal forms and $\leq_N$ to $\leq$.

Lemma 5. *Let $\alpha \leq \beta$. Then for all $\psi \propto nf(\beta)$ there exists $\phi \propto nf(\alpha)$ such that $\phi \leq_N \psi$.*

Proof. By induction on the proof of $\leq$. The most difficult case is that of rule $(cg - \mid)$ which is handled using Lemmas 4 and 3(3).

Corollary 1. *Let ϕ, ψ be normal types. Then $\phi \leq \psi$ iff $\phi \leq_N \psi$.*

4 Type Inference

It is rather natural to devise type assignment rules for ambients and processes. They are represented in Figure 4, where $\Gamma : \mathcal{V} \rightharpoonup \mathcal{T}^-$ is a mapping from process variables to simple types. Let $\Gamma[X := \sigma]$ denote the mapping equal to Γ except that its value at X is σ. As usual processes are considered modulo renaming of bound variables.

The system $\vdash$ has only introduction rules for the various constructors: elimination rules are replaced by rule $(\leq)$.

We can prove by a simple induction on deductions a generation lemma.

– Commutativity and distributivity of $|$

$$(\,|\,1^N) \quad \phi \,|\, \psi \simeq_N \psi \,|\, \phi \text{ provided } \phi \,|\, \psi \text{ is normal}$$
$$(\,|\,2^N) \quad (\phi \,|\, \psi) \,|\, \xi \simeq_N \phi \,|\, (\psi \,|\, \xi) \text{ provided } (\phi \,|\, \psi) \,|\, \xi \text{ is normal}$$

– Sequentialization

$$(.\,|\,_1^N) \quad \mathsf{m}.\phi \,|\, \overrightarrow{a[\psi]} \leq \mathsf{m}.(\phi \,|\, \overrightarrow{a[\psi]})$$

– Axioms for ω:

$$(\omega 1^N) \quad \phi \leq_N \omega \qquad\qquad (\omega 2^N) \quad \phi \,|\, \omega \simeq_N \phi$$

– Reduction

$$\begin{array}{ll}
(in^N) & a[in\, b.\phi \,|\, \overrightarrow{c[\psi]}] \,|\, b[\xi] \leq_N b[a[\phi \,|\, \overrightarrow{c[\psi]}] \,|\, \xi] \\
(out^N) & a[b[out\, a.\phi \,|\, \overrightarrow{c[\psi]}] \,|\, \xi] \leq_N a[\xi] \,|\, b[\phi \,|\, \overrightarrow{c[\psi]}] \\
(selfopen^N) & a[so\, a.\phi \,|\, \overrightarrow{c[\chi]}] \,|\, \psi \leq_N \xi \,|\, \overrightarrow{c[\chi]} \quad \text{for all } \xi \propto nf(\phi \,|\, \psi) \\
(open^N) & open\, a.\phi \,|\, a[\psi] \leq_N \xi \quad \text{for all } \xi \propto nf(\phi \,|\, \psi) \\
(out{-}in^N) & in\, a.out\, a.in\, a.\phi \leq in\, a.\phi \\
(in{-}out^N) & out\, a.in\, a.out\, a.\phi \leq out\, a.\phi
\end{array}$$

– Congruence

$$(cg{-}[\,]^N) \quad \frac{\phi \leq_N \psi}{a[\phi] \leq_N a[\psi]} \qquad\qquad (cg{-}action^N) \quad \frac{\phi \leq_N \psi}{\mathsf{m}.\phi \leq_N \mathsf{m}.\psi}$$

$$(cg-()^N) \quad \frac{\sigma' \leq \sigma}{(\sigma).\phi \leq_N (\sigma').\phi} \qquad\qquad (cg-\langle\rangle^N) \quad \frac{\sigma \leq \sigma'}{\langle\sigma\rangle.\phi \leq_N \langle\sigma'\rangle.\phi}$$

$$(cg{-}\,|\,^N) \quad \frac{\phi \leq_N \phi' \quad \psi \leq_N \psi'}{\phi \,|\, a[\psi] \leq_N \phi' \,|\, a[\psi']}$$

– Transitivity

$$(trans^N) \quad \frac{\phi \leq_N \psi \quad \psi \leq_N \xi}{\phi \leq_N \xi}$$

Fig. 3. Entailment Rules for Normal Types

Lemma 6 (Generation Lemma).

1. *$\Gamma \vdash \boldsymbol{0} : \alpha$ iff $\alpha \simeq \omega$;*
2. *$\Gamma \vdash \mathsf{m}.P : \alpha$ and $\mathsf{m} \in \mathcal{M}^{\updownarrow}$ iff $\Gamma \vdash P : \beta$ and $\mathsf{m}.\beta \leq \alpha$ for some β;*

$$(\omega)\quad \Gamma \vdash P : \omega \qquad\qquad (\mathsf{m}^{\updownarrow})\quad \frac{\Gamma \vdash P : \alpha \quad \mathsf{m} \in \mathcal{M}^{\updownarrow}}{\Gamma \vdash \mathsf{m}.P : \mathsf{m}.\alpha}$$

$$(input)\quad \frac{\Gamma[X := \sigma] \vdash P : \alpha}{\Gamma \vdash (X).P : (\sigma).\alpha} \qquad\qquad (output)\quad \frac{\Gamma \vdash P : \sigma \quad \Gamma \vdash Q : \alpha}{\Gamma \vdash \langle P \rangle.Q : \langle \sigma \rangle.\alpha}$$

$$(amb)\quad \frac{\Gamma \vdash P : \alpha}{\Gamma \vdash a[P] : a[\alpha]} \qquad\qquad (\,|\,)\quad \frac{\Gamma \vdash P : \alpha \quad \Gamma \vdash Q : \beta}{\Gamma \vdash P \,|\, Q : \alpha \,|\, \beta}$$

$$(!)\quad \frac{\Gamma \vdash P : \alpha \quad \Gamma \vdash !P : \beta}{\Gamma \vdash !P : \alpha \,|\, \beta} \qquad\qquad (\leq)\quad \frac{\Gamma \vdash P : \alpha \quad \alpha \leq \beta}{\Gamma \vdash P : \beta}$$

$$(\wedge I)\quad \frac{\Gamma \vdash P : \alpha \quad \Gamma \vdash P : \beta}{\Gamma \vdash P : \alpha \wedge \beta}$$

Fig. 4. Type Inference Rules

3. $\Gamma \vdash (X).P : \alpha$ *iff* $\Gamma[X := \sigma_i] \vdash P : \beta_i$ *for* $(1 \leq i \leq n)$, *and* $(\sigma_1).\beta_1 \wedge \ldots \wedge (\sigma_n).\beta_n \leq \alpha$ *for some* $\beta_1, \ldots, \beta_n, \sigma_1, \ldots, \sigma_n$;
4. $\Gamma \vdash \langle P \rangle.Q : \alpha$ *iff* $\Gamma \vdash P : \sigma$, $\Gamma \vdash Q : \beta$ *and* $\langle \sigma \rangle.\beta \leq \alpha$ *for some* σ, β;
5. $\Gamma \vdash a[P] : \alpha$ *iff* $\Gamma \vdash P : \beta$ *and* $a[\beta] \leq \alpha$ *for some* β;
6. $\Gamma \vdash P \,|\, Q : \alpha$ *iff* $\Gamma \vdash P : \beta$, $\Gamma \vdash Q : \gamma$ *and* $\beta \,|\, \gamma \leq \alpha$ *for some* β, γ;
7. $\Gamma \vdash !P : \alpha$ *iff* $\Gamma \vdash P : \beta_i$ *for* $(1 \leq i \leq n)$ *and* $\beta_1 \,|\, \ldots \,|\, \beta_n \leq \alpha$ *for some* $\beta_1, \ldots, \beta_n$.

Lemma 6 says that the types of a term can be obtained in an uniform way from the types of its subterms, and this will guarantee the compositionality of the filter model we will build in the next section.

Since we are in a "may" perspective, it is natural that a process P offers all the capabilities offered by one of its reducts Q (may be more). At the type assignment level this means that types are preserved under subject expansion. Of course subject reduction should not hold; for example, the reduction of a process P with the rule (*red open*) produces a process that in general offers less ambients (and so has less types). Instead congruent processes have the same types. Both properties can be proved by induction on the definitions of $\equiv$ and $\rightarrow^*$ using Lemma 6.

Lemma 7 (Subject Congruence). $P \equiv Q$ *and* $\Gamma \vdash Q : \alpha \;\Rightarrow\; \Gamma \vdash P : \alpha$.

Lemma 8 (Subject Expansion). $P \rightarrow^* Q$ *and* $\Gamma \vdash Q : \alpha \;\Rightarrow\; \Gamma \vdash P : \alpha$.

5 The Filter Model

We capitalize on the type assignment system of previous section for defining a filter model of the ambient calculus. We mainly follow the development line of [12].

Let $\langle D; \sqsubseteq \rangle$ be a preorder. A subset L of D is a *filter* if L is a non-empty upper set, i.e., $l \in L$ and $l \sqsubseteq l'$ imply $l' \in L$, and every finite subset of L has a greatest lower bound in L.

Consider the set $\mathcal{T}$ of types with the inclusion $\leq$ defined in Section 3. The greatest lower bound of a finite non-empty set of types is the intersection of the types in the set. It is standard to prove that the of filters over $\mathcal{T}$ is a domain in the usual sense.

Lemma 9. *The set $\mathcal{F}(\mathcal{T})$ of filters over $\mathcal{T}$ ordered by set inclusion is a consistently complete algebraic lattice.*

If $A \subseteq \mathcal{T}$ is a non-empty set of types then $\uparrow A$ denotes the filter generated by A, obtained by closing A under finite intersection and (by upper closing A under) $\leq$. Let $\widetilde{par} : \mathcal{F}(\mathcal{T}) \times \mathcal{F}(\mathcal{T}) \to \mathcal{F}(\mathcal{T})$ be the function defined by $\widetilde{par}(F, G) = \uparrow \{\alpha \mid \beta \mid \alpha \in F \text{ and } \beta \in G\}$.

We can now give an interpretation of processes in $\mathcal{F}(\mathcal{T})$. Let Env be the set of environments, i.e.mappings $\rho : \mathcal{V} \to \mathcal{F}(\mathcal{T})$.

Definition 4. *The function $[\![-]\!] : Env \to \mathcal{P} \to \mathcal{F}(\mathcal{T})$ is defined in the following way:*

- $[\![\mathit{0}]\!]_\rho = \uparrow \{\omega\}$
- $[\![act\ a.P]\!]_\rho = \uparrow \{act\ a.\alpha \mid \alpha \in [\![P]\!]_\rho\}$ *where* $act \in \{in\,, out\,, open\,, so\}$
- $[\![a[P]]\!]_\rho = \uparrow \{a[\alpha] \mid \alpha \in [\![P]\!]_\rho\}$
- $[\![(X).P]\!]_\rho = \uparrow \{(\sigma).\alpha \mid \alpha \in [\![P]\!]_{\rho[X:=\uparrow\{\sigma\}]}\}$
- $[\![\langle P\rangle.Q]\!]_\rho = \uparrow \{\langle\sigma\rangle.\alpha \mid \sigma \in [\![P]\!]_\rho \text{ and } \alpha \in [\![Q]\!]_\rho\}$
- $[\![P \mid Q]\!]_\rho = \widetilde{par}([\![P]\!]_\rho, [\![Q]\!]_\rho)$
- $[\![!P]\!]_\rho = fix(\lambda X \in \mathcal{F}(\mathcal{T}).\, \widetilde{par}([\![P]\!]_\rho, X))$,

where σ ranges over simple types.

The basic property of the filter model is that the interpretation of a term is defined by the set of its types. Define $\Gamma \models \rho$ if, for all X in the domain of Γ, $\Gamma(X) = \sigma$ implies $\sigma \in \rho(X)$.

Theorem 1. $[\![P]\!]_\rho = \{\alpha \in \mathcal{T} \mid \text{for some } \Gamma\text{: } \Gamma \models \rho \text{ and } \Gamma \vdash P : \alpha\}$.

From rules (ω), $(\leq)$, and $(\wedge)$ we have that $[\![P]\!]_\rho \in \mathcal{F}(\mathcal{T})$ for all P and ρ. Subject expansion can now be rephrased into the following statement:

$$\text{if } P \to^* Q \text{ then } [\![P]\!]_\rho \supseteq [\![Q]\!]_\rho \text{ for all } \rho.$$

The inclusion on filters induces an ordering on terms.

Definition 5. *Let $P, Q \in \mathcal{P}$. $P \sqsubseteq_F Q$ if and only if $[\![P]\!]_\rho \subseteq [\![Q]\!]_\rho$ for all ρ.*

The order relation $\sqsubseteq_F$ can be easily characterized by means of the deducibility of types as follows.

Proposition 1. *Let $P, Q \in \mathcal{P}$. $P \sqsubseteq_F Q$ if and only if $\Gamma \vdash P : \alpha$ implies $\Gamma \vdash Q : \alpha$ for all Γ, α.*

We will prove that the filter model exactly mirrors the operational semantics, i.e., that it is adequate and complete, i.e. it is fully abstract.

Adequacy

The adequacy proof requires a double induction on types and deductions. Following a standard methodology, we split this induction by introducing a realizability interpretation of types as sets of terms. The underlying idea is that a process P belongs to the interpretation of a type α if and only if α can be derived for P.

First we give an interpretation of simple types, and then we build the interpretation of all types, taking into account Lemmas 1 and 5. In defining the interpretation of types we will use a somewhat stronger notion of reduction over processes.

Definition 6. *The reduction relation $\rightsquigarrow$ over $\mathcal{P}$ is defined by adding to the rules of Fig. 1 the following rules:*

$$
\begin{array}{ll}
(seq) & \mathsf{m}.P \mid Q \rightsquigarrow \mathsf{m}.(P \mid Q) \\
(red-out-in) & in\, a.out\, a.in\, a.P \rightsquigarrow in\, a.P \\
(red-in-out) & out\, a.in\, a.out\, a.P \rightsquigarrow out\, a.P
\end{array}
$$

where in rule (seq) we do not allow capturing of free variables when m is an input action.

Note that, as in the case of $\rightarrow$, the relation $\rightsquigarrow$ corresponds to a loss of capabilities. It is easy to verify that $\rightsquigarrow$ does not modify the notion of convergence, i.e. that $P \Downarrow a$ iff $P \rightsquigarrow^* a[Q] \mid R$ for some processes Q, R. A standard induction on the definition of $\rightsquigarrow$ shows that the subject expansion property holds also with respect to $\rightsquigarrow$ reductions.

Lemma 10. $P \rightsquigarrow^* Q$ *and* $\Gamma \vdash Q : \alpha \quad \Rightarrow \quad \Gamma \vdash P : \alpha$.

The interpretation of normal types as sets of terms is given by induction on the *weight* of normal and simple types defined as follows:

$$
\begin{array}{ll}
|\omega| = 1 & |\mathsf{m}.\sigma| = 1 + |\sigma| \text{ if } \mathsf{m} \in \mathcal{M}^{\updownarrow} \\
|(\sigma).\tau| = 1 + |\sigma| + |\tau| & |\langle\sigma\rangle.\tau| = 1 + |\sigma| + |\tau| \\
|a[\sigma]| = 1 + |\sigma| & |\sigma \mid \tau| = 1 + |\sigma| + |\tau|
\end{array}
$$

It is easy to verify that, if $nf(\sigma) = \bigwedge_{i\in I} \phi_i$, then for all $i \in I$ we get $|\phi_i| \leq |\sigma|$. This is crucial for the soundness of the following definition.

Let $\mathcal{P}^0$ be the set of *closed processes*.

Definition 7. *The interpretation of normal types is defined by:*

1. $[\![\omega]\!] = \mathcal{P}^0$.
2. *If* $\mathsf{m} \in \mathcal{M}^{\updownarrow}$ *then* $[\![\mathsf{m}.\phi]\!] = \{P \in \mathcal{P}^0 \mid P \rightsquigarrow^* \mathsf{m}.Q \text{ such that } Q \in [\![\phi]\!]\}$.
3. *Let* $nf(\sigma) = \bigwedge_{i\in I} \phi_i$. *Then*
   $[\![(\sigma).\phi]\!] = \{P \in \mathcal{P}^0 \mid P \rightsquigarrow^* (X).Q \text{ such that } \forall S \in \bigcap_{i\in I} [\![\phi_i]\!].\ Q[X := S] \in [\![\phi]\!]\}$.
4. *Let* $nf(\sigma) = \bigwedge_{i\in I} \phi_i$. *Then*
   $[\![\langle\sigma\rangle.\phi]\!] = \{P \in \mathcal{P}^0 \mid P \rightsquigarrow^* \langle S\rangle.Q \text{ such that } Q \in [\![\phi]\!] \text{ and } S \in \bigcap_{i\in I} [\![\phi_i]\!]\}$.
5. $[\![a[\phi]]\!] = \{P \in \mathcal{P}^0 \mid P \rightsquigarrow^* a[Q] \mid R \text{ such that } Q \in [\![\phi]\!]\}$.
6. $[\![\phi \mid a[\psi]]\!] = \{P \in \mathcal{P}^0 \mid P \rightsquigarrow^* Q \mid a[R] \text{ such that } Q \in [\![\phi]\!] \text{ and } R \in [\![\psi]\!]\}$.

We need to prove the soundness of the normal type inclusion relation with respect to the interpretation of normal types. To this aim we need the following Lemma.

Lemma 11. *Let ϕ, ψ be normal types. Then $P \in [\![\phi]\!]$ and $Q \in [\![\psi]\!]$ imply $P \mid Q \in [\![\xi]\!]$ for all $\xi \propto nf(\phi \mid \psi)$.*

The soundness of the type inclusion relation can be shown by induction on $\leq_N$ definition. The most interesting case are axioms $(open^N)$ and $(selfopen^N)$, which can be handled using Lemma 11.

Lemma 12. *Let ϕ, ψ be normal types. Then $\phi \leq_N \psi$ implies $[\![\phi]\!] \subseteq [\![\psi]\!]$.*

We can now define the interpretation of all types.

Definition 8. *The interpretation of arbitrary types is defined by:*

$$[\![\alpha]\!] = \bigcap_{\phi \propto nf(\alpha)} [\![\phi]\!].$$

We need the soundness of the type inclusion relation with respect to the interpretation of types.

Lemma 13. *If $\alpha \leq \beta$ then $[\![\alpha]\!] \subseteq [\![\beta]\!]$.*

As expected the type interpretation perfectly matches the type assignment system. Let $FV(P) = \{X_1, \ldots, X_n\}$: define

$$\Gamma \models P : \alpha \iff \forall Q_1 \in [\![\Gamma(X_1)]\!], \ldots, Q_n \in [\![\Gamma(X_n)]\!].P[X_1 := Q_1] \ldots [X_n := Q_n] \in [\![\alpha]\!].$$

Theorem 2 (Soundness and completeness of $\vdash$). *$\Gamma \vdash P : \alpha$ iff $\Gamma \models P : \alpha$.*

Proof. Soundness is proved by induction on the derivation of $\Gamma \vdash P : \alpha$, using Lemma 13 for rule $(\leq)$.
As for completeness, by definition it suffices to show that if $\Gamma \models P : \phi$ then $\Gamma \vdash P : \phi$, when ϕ is normal. This proof can be done by induction on $|\phi|$ using Subject Expansion with respect to $\rightsquigarrow^*$ (Lemma 10).

Now we are able to characterize convergency by means of typing.

Lemma 14 (Resource property). *Let $P \in \mathcal{P}^0$. Then $\Gamma \vdash P : a[\omega]$ iff $P \Downarrow a$.*

Proof. $\Gamma \vdash P : a[\omega]$ iff (by Theorem 2) $P \in [\![a[\omega]]\!]$ iff (by Definition 7) $P \rightsquigarrow^* a[Q] \mid R$ for some processes Q, R.

We can now conclude the adequacy proof.

Theorem 3 (Adequacy). *If $P \sqsubseteq_F Q$ then $P \sqsubseteq Q$.*

Proof. If $\mathcal{C}[P] \Downarrow a$ then by Lemma 14 we get $\Gamma \vdash \mathcal{C}[P] : a[\omega]$. This together with $P \sqsubseteq_F Q$ imply $\Gamma \vdash \mathcal{C}[Q] : a[\omega]$, so we can conclude $\mathcal{C}[Q] \Downarrow a$ using again Lemma 14.

Completeness

Our completeness proof relies on building *test terms* $T_\phi^{x,y}$, where ϕ is a normal type and x, y are fresh ambient names with respect to ϕ. Their intended behavior is that, for all normal types ϕ, $x[P] \mid T_\phi^{x,y} \Downarrow y$ iff $\Gamma \vdash P : \phi$. The process P under testing is formerly enclosed in an ambient x for technical convenience.

In building these terms it is useful to have a process which exhibits ambient y iff it is in parallel with a process which exhibits all ambients $x_1, \dots, x_n$.

Lemma 15. *Let w be a fresh ambient name. Let's define*

$$H^{x_1,\dots,x_n \Rightarrow y} = w[in\, x_1.out\, x_1 \dots in\, x_n.out\, x_n.y[out\, w]] .$$

Then $H^{x_1,\dots,x_n \Rightarrow y} \mid P \Downarrow y$ iff $P \Downarrow x_i$ for all $i \in \{1, \dots, n\}$.

To define test terms we will use *characteristic terms*. If σ is a simple type, the characteristic term C_σ is the "typical" term of type σ, i.e. we require that $\vdash \mathsf{C}_\sigma : \sigma$ and that

$$\vdash \mathsf{C}_\sigma : \alpha \text{ implies } \vdash Q : \alpha \text{ for all } Q \in [\![\sigma]\!].$$

Test terms and characteristic terms are build by simultaneous induction on the weight of normal types (defined at page 265). We define a test term for each normal type and a characteristic term for each simple type. We assume to have an unlimited source of ambient names, and to be able to pick new ambients names without clashing with the ambient names occurring in the processes we are testing.

Definition 9 (Test and Characteristic Terms).

Let ϕ be a normal type and σ a simple type. The test terms $T_\phi^{x,y}$ *and* characteristic terms C_σ *are defined by induction the weight of normal and simple types in the following way.*

Test terms:

- $T_\omega^{x,y} = p[in\, x.out\, x.y[out\, p]]$
- $T_{\omega \mid \phi}^{x,y} = T_\phi^{x,y}$
- $T_{in\, a.\phi}^{x,y} = a[p[in\, x.so\, p.out\, a.in\, v.in\, z]] \mid v[z[open\, x.t[out\, z.out\, v.open\, v.open\, a]]] \mid open\, t \mid T_\phi^{z,y}$
- $T_{out\, a.\phi}^{x,y} = p[in\, x.so\, p.in\, v.in\, a.in\, z] \mid v[a[z[open\, x.t[out\, z.out\, v.open\, v.open\, a]]]] \mid open\, t \mid T_\phi^{z,y}$
- $T_{open\, a.\phi}^{x,y} = p[in\, x.so\, p.a[in\, v.in\, z]] \mid v[z[open\, x.t[out\, z.out\, v.open\, v]]] \mid open\, t \mid T_\phi^{z,y}$
- $T_{so\, a.\phi}^{x,y} = p[in\, x.so\, p.in\, v.in\, z.in\, a] \mid v[z[a[open\, x.t[out\, z.out\, v.open\, v]]]] \mid open\, t \mid T_\phi^{z,y}$
- $T_{(\sigma).\phi}^{x,y} = p[in\, x.so\, p.in\, v.in\, z] \mid v[z[open\, x \mid \langle \mathsf{C}_\sigma \rangle.t[out\, z.out\, v.open\, v]]] \mid open\, t \mid T_\phi^{z,y}$

- $T^{x,y}_{(\sigma).\phi} = p[in\, x.so\, p.in\, v.in\, z] \mid$
  $v[z[open\, x \mid (X).t[T^{q_1,w_1}_{\phi_1} \mid q_1[X] \mid \ldots \mid T^{q_n,w_n}_{\phi_n} \mid q_n[X]$
  $\mid H^{w_1,\ldots,w_n \Rightarrow w} \mid open\, w.out\, z.out\, v.open\, v]]] \mid open\, t \mid T^{z,y}_{\phi}$
  where $\bigwedge_{i\in[1\ldots n]} \phi_i = nf(\sigma)$.

- $T^{x,y}_{a[\psi]} = p[in\, x.in\, a.so\, p.out\, x.in\, v.in\, w]$
  $\mid v[w[open\, a.t[out\, w.out\, v.open\, v]]] \mid open\, t \mid T^{w,y}_{\psi}$

- $T^{x,y}_{\phi \mid a[\psi]} = p[in\, x.in\, a.so\, p.out\, x.in\, v.in\, w]$
  $\mid v[w[open\, a.t[out\, w.out\, v.open\, v]]] \mid open\, t \mid T^{x,q}_{\phi} \mid T^{w,z}_{\psi} \mid H^{q,z \Rightarrow y}$

Characteristic terms:

- $C_\omega = \mathbf{0}$
- $C_{\mathsf{m}.\sigma} = \mathsf{m}.C_\sigma$ *if* $\mathsf{m} \in \mathcal{M}^{\updownarrow}$
- $C_{\langle\sigma\rangle.\tau} = \langle C_\sigma\rangle.C_\tau$
- $C_{(\sigma).\tau} = (X).(T^{q_1,w_1}_{\phi_1} \mid q_1[X] \mid \ldots \mid T^{q_n,w_n}_{\phi_n} \mid q_n[X] \mid H^{w_1,\ldots,w_n \Rightarrow y} \mid open\, y.C_\tau)$
  where $\bigwedge_{i\in[1\ldots n]} \phi_i = nf(\sigma)$.
- $C_{a[\sigma]} = a[C_\sigma]$
- $C_{\sigma \mid \tau} = C_\sigma \mid C_\tau$

where we assume that all ambient names ($p, q, v, w, x, y, z, \ldots,$ *except* a*) introduced in the definition of each* $T^{x,y}_{\phi}$ *are fresh. We call them the* extra names *of* $T^{x,y}_{\phi}$*, denoted* $EN(T^{x,y}_{\phi})$*. Similarly for* C_σ*.*

We can roughly summarize the behaviors of the test terms in the following way:

- $T^{x,y}_{\mathsf{m}.\phi}$ for a mobility action m:
  - the process $p[\,]$ moves the process $x[\,]$ inside the ambient z (which is inside the ambient v);
  - the process inside the ambient z opens x in an environment which allows the process formerly enclosed in x to consume m;
  - if the test is successful the process $t[\,]$ goes at top level and opens the ambient v;
  - the remaining process inside the ambient z will be tested by $T^{z,y}_{\phi}$.
- $T^{x,y}_{(\sigma).\phi}$:
  - the process $p[\,]$ moves the process $x[\,]$ inside the ambient z (which is inside the ambient v);
  - the process inside the ambient z opens the ambient x and offers then as output the characteristic term C_σ;
  - if the output is consumed the process $t[\,]$ goes at top level and opens the ambient v;
  - the remaining process inside the ambient z will be tested by $T^{z,y}_{\phi}$.
- $T^{x,y}_{\langle\sigma\rangle.\phi}$:
  - the process $p[\,]$ moves the process $x[\,]$ inside the ambient z (which is inside the ambient v);
  - the process inside the ambient z opens the ambient x and takes an input;

  - if the input satisfies all tests ϕ_i for $i \in \{1, \ldots, n\}$ (where $\bigwedge_{i \in [1 \ldots n]} \phi_i = nf(\sigma)$) then the process $t[\,]$ goes at top level and opens the ambient v;
  - the remaining process inside the ambient z will be tested by $T^{z,y}_{\phi}$.

- $T^{x,y}_{\phi \,|\, a[\psi]}$:
  - first the process $p[\ ]$ moves the process $a[\ ]$ inside the ambient w (which is inside the ambient v);
  - then the process $t[\,]$ goes at top level and opens the ambient v;
  - the remaining processes inside the ambients x, w will be tested respectively by the terms $T^{x,q}_{\phi}$ and $T^{w,z}_{\psi}$. The process $H^{q,z \Rightarrow y}$ lastly checks that both tests are successful.

Note that all the terms $T^{x,y}_{\phi}$ are reducible only when they are put in parallel with the ambient x and can exhibit y at top level only when reduced. So all of them must interact with x in the proper way to do the job. The basic property of test terms is the following.

Lemma 16. *1.* $\vdash \mathsf{C}_\sigma : \alpha$ *iff* $\sigma \leq \alpha$.
2. Let $P \in \mathcal{P}^0$ *be a process containing no occurrences of any ambient name belonging to* $EN(T^{x,y}_{\phi})$*. Then* $x[P] \,|\, T^{x,y}_{\phi} \Downarrow y$ *iff* $\vdash P : \phi$.

Remark 2. Note that characteristic terms do not seem to exist for arbitrary types containing intersection. The natural choice would be to take $\mathsf{C}_{\sigma \wedge \tau} = \mathsf{C}_\sigma + \mathsf{C}_\tau$ where $+$ is the nondeterministic choice operator, but it does not seem possible to represent $+$ our system.

Completeness now follows easily.

Theorem 4 (Completeness). *If* $P \sqsubseteq Q$ *then* $P \sqsubseteq_F Q$.

Proof. If $P \not\sqsubseteq_F Q$ then there are Γ, α such that $\Gamma \vdash P : \alpha$ and $\Gamma \not\vdash Q : \alpha$. Then by Lemmas 1, 5, and rule $(\leq)$ there is a normal type ϕ such that $\Gamma \vdash P : \phi$ and $\Gamma \not\vdash Q : \phi$. Let $\tau = (\sigma_1).\ldots.(\sigma_n).\phi$, where $FV(P \,|\, Q) = \{X_1, \ldots, X_n\}$ and $\Gamma(X_i) = \sigma_i$ for $i \in \{1, \ldots, n\}$. By Lemma 16 we get that $T^{x,y}_{\phi} \,|\, x[(X_1).\ldots.(X_n).P] \Downarrow y$ and $T^{x,y}_{\phi} \,|\, x[(X_1).\ldots.(X_n).Q] \not\Downarrow y$. So we conclude $P \not\sqsubseteq Q$.

6 Final Remarks

If we drop from our language the *so* primitive, leaving then only the standard mobility actions of the Ambient Calculus, we have immediately that $\mathcal{F}(\mathcal{T})$ is also a model of the resulting language. This model is adequate ($P \sqsubseteq_F Q$ implies$P \sqsubseteq Q$) but not fully abstract. To show this take, for instance:

$$P_1 = a[b[out\ c]]$$
$$P_2 = a[b[open\ d]] \,|\, d[in\ b.out\ c]$$

The process P_1 and P_2 are incomparable in the model (we can find proper types separating them) but operationally, in the standard Ambient Calculus, we have $P_1 \sqsubseteq P_2$. In fact both exhibit the ambient a which contains only an ambient b. To show that $P_1 \not\sqsubseteq P_2$ we should find a context allowing to exercise the action *out* c in P_1. But to obtain this we need to enclose b in an ambient c and this is possible only if we eventually open a. In this case, in a may perspective, we cannot avoid that d jumps into b and is opened there, allowing P_2 to show the same behavior as P_1. Instead using the *so* action we are able to build a context that separatesP_1 and P_2.

We are aware that *so* can cause undesired behaviors, but we are confident that a suitable type discipline can avoid them. The design of such a discipline will be subject of further investigations.

Acknowledgements

We are grateful to Daniel Hirschkoff and to the anonymous referees for their useful comments and suggestions.

References

1. S. Abramsky. Domain theory in logical form. *Annals of Pure and Applied Logic*, 51(1-2):1–77, 1991.
2. S. Abramsky and C.-H. L. Ong. Full abstraction in the lazy lambda calculus. *Information and Computation*, 105(2):159–267, 1993.
3. T. Amtoft, A. J. Kfoury, and S. M. Pericas-Geertsen. What are polymorphically-typed ambients? In *ESOP'01*, volume 2028 of *LNCS*, pages 206–220, Berlin, 2001. Springer-Verlag.
4. H. Barendregt, M. Coppo, and M. Dezani-Ciancaglini. A filter lambda model and the completeness of type assignment. *The Journal of Symbolic Logic*, 48(4):931–940, 1983.
5. G. Boudol. Lambda-calculi for (strict) parallel functions. *Information and Computation*, 108(1):51–127, 1994.
6. M. Bugliesi and G. Castagna. Secure safe ambients. In *POPL'01*, pages 222–235, New York, 2001. ACM Press.
7. L. Cardelli, G. Ghelli, and A. D. Gordon. Mobility types for mobile ambients. In *ICALP'99*, volume 1644 of *LNCS*, pages 230–239, Berlin, 1999. Springer-Verlag.
8. L. Cardelli and A. D. Gordon. Mobile ambients. In *FoSSaCS'98*, volume 1378 of *LNCS*, pages 140–155, Berlin, 1998. Springer-Verlag.
9. L. Cardelli and A. D. Gordon. Types for mobile ambients. In *POPL'99*, pages 79–92, New York, 1999. ACM Press.
10. L. Cardelli and A. D. Gordon. Anytime, anywhere. modal logics for mobile ambients. In *POPL'00*, pages 365–377, New York, 2000. ACM Press.
11. M. Coppo and M. Dezani-Ciancaglini. A fully abstract model for mobile ambients. In *TOSCA'01*, volume 62 of *ENTCS*. Elsevier Science, 200X. to appear.
12. F. Damiani, M. Dezani-Ciancaglini, and P. Giannini. A filter model for mobile processes. *Mathematical Structures in Computer Science*, 9(1):63–101, 1999.
13. P. Degano, F. Levi, and C. Bodei. Safe ambients: Control flow analysis and security. In *ASIAN'00*, volume 1961 of *LNCS*, pages 199–214, Berlin, 2000. Springer-Verlag.
14. M. Dezani-Ciancaglini, U. de'Liguoro, and A. Piperno. Finite models for conjunctive-disjunctive λ-calculi. *Theoretical Computer Science*, 170(1–2):83–128, 1996.
15. M. Dezani-Ciancaglini, U. de'Liguoro, and A. Piperno. A filter model for concurrent λ-calculus. *SIAM Journal on Computing*, 27(5):1376–1419, 1998.

16. M. Dezani-Ciancaglini and S. Ghilezan. A lambda model characterizing computational behaviors of terms. In *RPC'01*, pages 100–118. Tohoku University, 2001.
17. M. Dezani-Ciancaglini and I. Salvo. Security types for safe mobile ambients. In *ASIAN'00*, volume 1961 of *LNCS*, pages 215–236, Berlin, 2000. Springer-Verlag.
18. A. D. Gordon and L. Cardelli. Equational properties of mobile ambients. In *FoSSaCS'99*, volume 1578 of *LNCS*, pages 212–226, Berlin, 1999. Springer-Verlag.
19. R. R. Hansen, J. G. Jensen, F. Nielson, and H. R. Nielson. Abstract interpretation of mobile ambients. In *SAS'99*, number 1694 in LNCS, pages 134–148, Berlin, 1999. Springer-Verlag.
20. C. Hartonas and M. Hennessy. Full abstractness for a functional/concurrent language with higher-order value-passing. *Information and Computation*, 145(1):64–106, 1998.
21. M. Hennessy. A fully abstract denotational model for higher-order processes. *Information and Computation*, 112(1):55–95, 1994.
22. M. Hennessy. Higher-order process and their models. In *ICALP'94*, volume 820 of *LNCS*, pages 286–303, Berlin, 1994. Springer-Verlag.
23. C.-H. L. Ong. Non-determinism in a functional setting. In *LICS'93*, pages 275–286, Montreal, Canada, 1993. IEEE Computer Society Press.
24. D. Sangiorgi. Extensionality and intensionality of the ambient logic. In *POPL'01*, pages 4–13, New York, 2001. ACM Press.
25. D. S. Scott. Domains for denotational semantics. In *ICALP'82*, volume 140 of *LNCS*, pages 577–613, Berlin, 1982. Springer-Verlag.

A Simulation Preorder for Abstraction of Reactive Systems

Ferucio Laurenţiu Ţiplea and Aurora Ţiplea

Faculty of Computer Science
"Al. I. Cuza" University
6600 Iaşi, Romania
fltiplea@mail.dntis.ro

Abstract. We present a *simulation preorder* for reactive systems modeled by *fair Kripke structures* whose transition relation is divided into two parts, *internal* and *external*. The first one models the internal behaviour of the system, while the second one is used to model the interaction with an environment. We show that our simulation preorder preserves a substantial subset of $\forall CTL^*$. Then, we present an *abstraction* technique for systems composed by multiple modules and we show that each such system is smaller in the simulation preorder than its "augmented" components. We illustrate our abstraction methodology by applying it to *Petri net reactive systems*.

1 Introduction and Preliminaries

In the last decade a lot of progress has been made in the development of methods for formal verification, such as model checking and deductive verification. In spite of this progress, many realistic systems are still too large to be handled. Thus, it is important to find techniques that can be used in conjunction with these methods to extend the size of the systems that can be verified. Two such techniques, generally recognized as the only methods can ever scale up to handle industrial-size design and verification, are the *abstraction* and *modularization* which break the task of verifying a large system into several smaller tasks of verifying simpler systems. Modularization exploits the modular structure of a complex system composed of multiple processes running in parallel. In such systems it is essential to study and analyse each process as a *reactive system* [11]. That is because, from the point of view of each process, the rest of the system can be viewed as an environment that continuously interacts with the process. Then, an obvious strategy is to derive properties (proofs) of the whole system from partial (local) properties involving (abstractions of) its modules (components). An elegant way to do that is to define a preorder relation capturing the idea of "more behaviors" and to use a logic whose semantics relate to the preorder. The preorder should preserve the satisfaction of formulas of the logic in the sense that, if a formula is true for a model, a clear specified variant of it should also be true for every model which is smaller in the preorder. Additionally, a system should be smaller in the preorder than its individual components.

A. Cortesi (Ed.): VMCAI 2002, LNCS 2294, pp. 272–288, 2002.
© Springer-Verlag Berlin Heidelberg 2002

Related work Much work has been done following a line like that described above. The approach in [6] introduces the logic $\forall CTL^*$ and gives a compositional simulation preorder on Kripke structure with Streett fairness conditions, but no difference between internal and external steps is made. In [9] it is shown that this simulation relation remains compositional too if the Streett fairness constraints are replaced by Rabin fairness conditions.

In [3], the authors start with an abstract $\forall CTL^*$ formula φ^a evaluated over the abstract system and show how to translate it into a concrete formula φ. The survey in [4] deals with the simpler case in which the abstraction does not concern the variables on which the property φ depends. Therefore, $\varphi^a = \varphi$.

In the Alur and Henzinger's approach of reactive modules [1], the set of variables of a module is partitioned into internal, interface and external variables. The preorder $\preceq$ they introduce captures the fact that the module P has possible more interface and external variables than the specification Q, whenever $P \preceq Q$. Thus, P has possible fewer traces than Q. The abstraction is done by identifying a subset Y of interface variables and collapsing consecutive rounds of the original module P until one of the variables in Y changes its value. It is shown that the abstraction is compositional w.r.t. the preorder on modules.

The methodological paper [8] reviews the two main tools of compositionality and abstraction in the framework of linear temporal logic. Here, the abstraction acts on observable variables .

These papers do not present a simulation relation appropriate for reactive systems with strict distinction between internal and external steps.

Contribution In this paper we model reactive systems by fair Kripke structures with Büchi fairness constraints. From the beginning, we make a clear distinction between internal and external steps by dividing the transition relation into two parts, *internal* and *external.* The first one models the internal behaviour of the system, while the second one is used to model the interaction with an environment.

We introduce a new simulation preorder which captures two basic aspects:

(1) a system K_1 may be embedded into a system K_2 having "more behaviour";
(2) the system K_2 may abstract from some parts of the behaviour of K_1 by collapsing several consecutive steps into a single one.

While (1) is a general property that should be achieved by any simulation preorder, (2) is that that makes our simulation preorder different from those known from the literature [1,6,4,9,8]. In the particular case of empty external relations, our simulation preorder is that from [6] except for the fact that we use fairness constraints given as Büchi but not as Streett conditions.

The logic we use is a substantial subset of $\forall CTL^*$ which we prove is preserved by the simulation relation. That is, we show that a *delayed version* $\hat{\varphi}$ of a $\forall CTL^*$ formula φ holds in a structure K_1 whenever φ holds in K_2 and there is a simulation preorder from K_1 to K_2.

Based on this simulation relation we propose a new abstraction technique that can be described as follows. Given a system $K_1 \circ K_2$, which is the asynchronous composition of K_1 and K_2, we abstract from the internal variables of K_2 obtaining a new structure $K_{1,2}$. The structure $K_{1,2}$ collapses consecutive external steps performed by K_2 in $K_1 \circ K_2$ by only one internal step in K_1. Therefore, its state space is smaller than the state space of $K_1 \circ K_2$. Moreover, we prove that there is a simulation preorder from $K_1 \circ K_2$ to $K_{1,2}$.

The simulation preorder and the abstraction technique we propose are different than the ones found in the literature. We think that they are very suitable to be used when abstracting of components of composed systems.

Finally, we illustrate our abstraction methodology by applying it to Petri net reactive modules.

Overview The paper is organized as follows. The rest of this section presents the logic we use and its semantics given by fair Kripke structures. The simulation preorder and some of its basic properties are given in section 2. The next section presents the asynchronous composition of fair Kripke structures and the abstraction methodology we propose. This methodology is illustrated in section 4 by applying it to Petri net reactive systems. We conclude with a summary and some directions for future work.

Temporal logic We use the *universal branching-time temporal logic* $\forall CTL^*$ to specify properties of reactive systems [6]. There are two types of formulas in $\forall CTL^*$, *path* and *state formulas*. Their syntax is given by the following rules ($\mathcal{A}$ is a set of atomic propositions, $p \in \mathcal{A}$, φ is a state formula, and ψ is a path formula):

(i) $\varphi := \mathbf{true}|\mathbf{false}|p|\neg p|\varphi \vee \varphi|\varphi \wedge \varphi|\forall(\varphi)$;

(ii) $\psi := \varphi|\psi \vee \psi|\psi \wedge \psi|X\psi|\psi U\psi|\psi V\psi$.

The semantics of this logic is given as usual [6] by using *fair Kripke structures* [4] (*structures*, for short) $K = (Q, Q_0, \mathcal{A}, \mathcal{L}, \rho, \mathcal{F})$, where Q is a finite set of *states*, $Q_0 \subseteq Q$ is a set of *initial states*, $\mathcal{A}$ is a finite set of *atomic propositions*, $\mathcal{L} : Q \to \mathcal{P}(\mathcal{A})$ is a function that labels each state with the set of atomic propositions true in that state, $\rho \subseteq Q \times Q$ is a *transition relation*, and $\mathcal{F} \subseteq \mathcal{P}(Q)$ is a set of *fairness constraints* given as Büchi acceptance conditions ($\mathcal{P}(A)$ is the powerset of A).

The fairness requirements intend to guarantee that every path (infinite computation in K) contains infinitely many states from each $A \in \mathcal{F}$. Formally, a *path* (*starting* or *beginning at* q_0) in a structure K is an infinite sequence of states $\sigma = q_0 q_1 q_2 \cdots$ satisfying $q_i \,\rho\, q_{i+1}$, for all $i \geq 0$. The path σ is called *fair* if $inf(\sigma) \cap A \neq \emptyset$ for all $A \in \mathcal{F}$, where $inf(\sigma)$ is the set of states having infinitely many occurrences in σ.

If φ is a state formula, the notation $K, q \models \varphi$ means that φ *holds at state* q in the structure K. Similarly, $K, \sigma \models \varphi$ means that φ *holds along path* σ in the structure K. When φ is true in all initial states of K we write $K \models \varphi$.

2 A Simulation Preorder

In this section we define a preorder relation capturing the idea of "more behaviors" and show that it preservs the satisfaction of $\forall CTL^*$ formulas via the delaying operation. First of all we will make a basic assumption valid for the rest of the paper (another two will be made in the next section):

- the transition relation ρ of each structure K is the union of two given binary relations on states, $\rho = \rho^i \cup \rho^e$, not necessarily disjoint. The relation ρ^i models the *internal state-changes* in K (that is, proper atomic steps performed by K), and ρ^e models *external state-changes* in K (that is, state-changes caused by the environment). Usually, ρ^e is not completely known, but we can approximate it starting from the remark that in many real cases we know the response of an environment to an output of the module.

Each structure K_j, $j = 0, 1, 2, \ldots$, we will consider is assumed to have the components $K_j = (Q_j, Q_0^j, \mathcal{A}_j, \mathcal{L}_j, \rho_j, \mathcal{F}_j)$, where $\rho_j = \rho_j^i \cup \rho_j^e$.

Definition 2.1 *Let K_1 and K_2 be two structures, and $\mathcal{A} \subseteq \mathcal{A}_1 \cap \mathcal{A}_2$. Let q and q' be states in K_1 and K_2, respectively. A* simulation from (K_1, q) to (K_2, q') w.r.t. $\mathcal{A}$ *is a binary relation $H \subseteq Q_1 \times Q_2$ such that $(q, q') \in H$ and, for all q_0 and q_0', if $(q_0, q_0') \in H$ then:*

(1) $\mathcal{L}_1(q_0) \cap \mathcal{A} = \mathcal{L}_2(q_0') \cap \mathcal{A}$;

(2) for every fair path $\sigma = q_0 q_1 \cdots$ in K_1 there is a fair path $\sigma' = q_0' q_1' \cdots$ in K_2 and a decomposition of σ, $\sigma = q_{i_0} \cdots q_{i_1} \cdots q_{i_2} \cdots$ where $i_0 = 0$, such that for all $j \geq 0$ the following hold:

- $(i_{j+1} = i_j + 1 \wedge (q_{i_j}, q_{i_{j+1}}) \in \rho_1^e \Rightarrow (q_j', q_{j+1}') \in \rho_2^e \wedge (q_{i_{j+1}}, q_{j+1}') \in H)$;
- $(i_{j+1} = i_j + 1 \wedge (q_{i_j}, q_{i_{j+1}}) \in \rho_1^i \Rightarrow (q_j', q_{j+1}') \in \rho_2 \wedge (q_{i_{j+1}}, q_{j+1}') \in H)$;
- $(i_{j+1} > i_j + 1 \Rightarrow (q_j', q_{j+1}') \in \rho_2^e \wedge (q_{i_{j+1}}, q_{j+1}') \in H)$.

To indicate that two fair paths σ and σ' correspond as in Definition 2.1(2) we write $H(\sigma, \sigma')$. When there is a simulation relation from (K_1, q) to (K_2, q') w.r.t. $\mathcal{A}$ we will write $(K_1, q) \prec_{\mathcal{A}} (K_2, q')$.

A binary relation H is a *simulation from K_1 to K_2 w.r.t. $\mathcal{A}$* if

$$(\forall q \in Q_0^1)(\exists q' \in Q_0^2)((K_1, q) \prec_{\mathcal{A}} (K_2, q')).$$

We will use the notation $K_1 \prec_{\mathcal{A}} K_2$ whenever there is a simulation from K_1 to K_2 w.r.t. $\mathcal{A}$. In the case $\rho_1^e = \rho_2^e = \emptyset$ and $\mathcal{A} = \mathcal{A}_2 \subseteq \mathcal{A}_1$ our definition of simulation is that from [6] (except for the fact that we use fairness constraints given as Büchi but not as Streett acceptance conditions).

Proposition 2.1 *The simulation relation $\prec_{\mathcal{A}}$ is a preorder (i.e., a reflexive and transitive order) on structures whose set of atomic propositions include $\mathcal{A}$.*

The preorder $\prec_{\mathcal{A}}$ captures the fact that consecutive steps in K_1 are collapsed into a single step in K_2 or, equivalently, a single step in K_2 is broken into multiple consecutive steps in K_1, whenever $K_1 \prec_{\mathcal{A}} K_2$. Therefore, the preorder $\prec_{\mathcal{A}}$ preserves, up to a delay, formulas of $\forall CTL^*$. Intuitively, by delaying o formula we mean that the "next" operator becomes "eventually" etc. Formally, consider the operators $\Diamond$ and $\overline{U}$ given by "$\Diamond\varphi$ iff $\mathbf{true}\,U\varphi$" and "$\varphi\,\overline{U}\psi$ iff $\varphi\,U(\varphi \wedge \psi)$", and call them *eventually* and *until with equality*.

Let φ be a formula. Denote by $\overline{\varphi}$ the formula obtained from φ by replacing all the occurrences of U by $\overline{U}$, and by $\hat{\varphi}$ the formula defined inductively as follows:

- if $\varphi = \mathbf{true}, \mathbf{false}, p$ or $\neg p$, then $\hat{\varphi} = \varphi$;
- if $\varphi = \varphi_1 \vee \varphi_2$ ($\varphi = \varphi_1 \wedge \varphi_2$, $\varphi = \forall(\varphi_1)$, resp.), then $\hat{\varphi} = \hat{\varphi}_1 \vee \hat{\varphi}_2$ ($\hat{\varphi} = \hat{\varphi}_1 \wedge \hat{\varphi}_2$, $\hat{\varphi} = \forall(\hat{\varphi}_1)$, resp.);
- if $\varphi = X\varphi_1$ ($\varphi = \varphi_1 U \varphi_2$, $\varphi = \varphi_1 V \varphi_2$, resp.), then $\hat{\varphi} = \Diamond\hat{\varphi}_1$ ($\hat{\varphi} = (\Diamond\hat{\varphi}_1)\,U\hat{\varphi}_2$, $\hat{\varphi} = \hat{\varphi}_1 V(\Diamond\hat{\varphi}_2)$, resp.).

The formula $\hat{\varphi}$ is called the *delayed version* of the formula φ. We can also apply this construction to formulas $\overline{\varphi}$ by replacing the operator U by $\overline{U}$.

Theorem 2.1 *Let K_1 and K_2 be two structures. Then, for every two states q and q' of K_1 and K_2, respectively, and every two fair paths σ and σ' in K_1 and K_2, respectively, if H is a simulation from (K_1, q) to (K_2, q') w.r.t. a set $\mathcal{A} \subseteq \mathcal{A}_1 \cap \mathcal{A}_2$ and $H(\sigma, \sigma')$ holds true, then for every $\forall CTL^*$ formula φ over $\mathcal{A}$ we have:*

(1) if φ is a state formula and $q' \models \overline{\varphi}$ then $q \models \hat{\overline{\varphi}}$;

(2) if φ is a path formula and $\sigma' \models \overline{\varphi}$ then $\sigma \models \hat{\overline{\varphi}}$.

An immediate consequence of the Theorem 2.1 is the following result.

Corollary 2.1 *Let K_1 and K_2 be two structures and $\mathcal{A} \subseteq \mathcal{A}_1 \cap \mathcal{A}_2$. If $K_1 \prec_{\mathcal{A}} K_2$ then, for every $\forall CTL^*$ formula φ over $\mathcal{A}$, $K_2 \models \overline{\varphi}$ implies $K_1 \models \hat{\overline{\varphi}}$.*

3 Asynchronous Composition of Structures

We consider in this section an asynchronous composition of structures which captures the idea that two structures execute concurrently by performing steps in an interleaved way. First, we will make two basic assumptions:

- the states of each structure K will be considered as *interpretations* over a finite set V of typed variables. That is, each state q is a function assigning to each variable $v \in V$ a value $q(v)$ in its domain. For the case of finite-state systems we have to assume that all variables range over finite domains. We also assume that with each set V, a subset $V^e \subseteq V$ is specified. V^e defines the set of *external* or *interface variables* that are used by the system to communicate with an environment. The set $V^i = V - V^e$ is the set of *internal variables* [1] of K; it is related to the relation ρ^e by[2]:

$$(\forall q, q')((q, q') \in \rho^e \Rightarrow q|_{V^i} = q'|_{V^i}).$$

That is, the environment may update only the external variables, whereas the system may update all the variables. From now on we will assume that for a system K_j, $j = 0, 1, 2, \ldots$, its sets of variables are denoted by V_j, V_j^e and V_j^i, whitout adding them to the tuple defining K.

- the fairness constraints we consider are of the form $\mathcal{F} = \mathcal{F}^i \cup \mathcal{F}^e$, where $\mathcal{F}^i \subseteq \mathcal{P}(Dom(\rho^i))$ and $\mathcal{F}^e \subseteq \mathcal{P}(Dom(\rho^e))$ ($Dom(\rho)$ denotes the domain of the relation ρ). The sets in $\mathcal{F}^i$ are called *internal fairness constraints*, whereas those in $\mathcal{F}^e$ are called *external fairness constraints*. These fairness requirements intend to capture the idea that the environment is given the chance to interfere with the system (by entering infinitely many times in states where the communication with the environment is possible), but also the system may have a proper behaviour (by entering infinitely many times in states where internal steps may be done).

Two structures K_1 and K_2 are called *compatible* if $V_1^i \cap V_2^i = \emptyset$ and $V_1^e = V_2^e$. The first condition requires that a variable can only be owned by one of the systems, whereas the second condition requires that the external variables are common for both systems.

Definition 3.1 *Let K_1 and K_2 be two compatible structures. The* asynchronous composition *of K_1 and K_2 is the structure $K_1 \circ K_2 = (Q, Q_0, \mathcal{A}, \mathcal{L}, \rho, \mathcal{F})$, where:*

(1) the set Q of states consists of all the interpretations q of $V = V_1^i \cup V^e \cup V_2^i$, where $V^e = V_1^e = V_2^e$, such that $q|_{V_1}$ and $q|_{V_2}$ are states in K_1 and K_2, respectively, and $\mathcal{L}_1(q|_{V_1}) \cap \mathcal{A}_2 = \mathcal{L}_2(q|_{V_2}) \cap \mathcal{A}_1$;

(2) $Q_0 = \{q \in Q | q|_{V_1} \in Q_0^1 \wedge q|_{V_2} Q_0^2\}$;

(3) $\mathcal{A} = \mathcal{A}_1 \cup \mathcal{A}_2$;

(4) $\mathcal{L}(q) = \mathcal{L}_1(q|_{V_1}) \cup \mathcal{L}_2(q|_{V_2})$ for all $q \in Q$ (the definition of Q avoids the existence of atomic propositions p both true and false at q);

(5) $(q, q') \in \rho$ iff
- *$(q|_{V_1}, q'|_{V_1}) \in \rho_1$ and $q'|_{V_2^i} = q|_{V_2^i}$, or*
- *$(q|_{V_2}, q'|_{V_2}) \in \rho_2$ and $q'|_{V_1^i} = q|_{V_1^i}$.*

If a step performed in one of the systems is external (internal), then the corresponding step in K is external (internal). A step may be both external and internal;

(6) $\mathcal{F} = \{\{q \in Q | q|_{V_1} \in A_1\} | A_1 \in \mathcal{F}_1\} \cup \{\{q \in Q | q|_{V_2} \in A_2\} | A_2 \in \mathcal{F}_2\}$.

---

[1] The distinction between internal and interface variables is similar to the distinction between controlled and external variables in the Alur and Henzinger's formalism of reactive modules ([1]), or to the distinction between unobservable owned variables and observable variables in the formalism of fair Kripke structures as given in ([8]).

[2] For a function $f : A \to B$ and a subset $C \subseteq A$, $f|_C$ denotes the restriction of f to C.

States of the composition are "pairs" of component states that agree on the common variables and on the common atomic propositions. Each transition of the composition involves a transition of one of the two components.

It is straightforward but tedious to prove that asynchronous parallel composition is commutative and associative (up to isomorphism).

For a structure K we denote by $Reach(K)$ the set of all *reachable states* in K, that is $Reach(K) = \{q \in Q | \exists q_0 \in Q_0 : (q_0, q) \in \rho^*\}$ (ρ^* stands for the reflexive and transitive closure of ρ). Given two compatible structures K_1 and K_2, consider a new structure $K_{1,2} = (Q_1, Q_0^1, \mathcal{A}_1, \mathcal{L}_1, \rho_{1,2}, \mathcal{F}_{1,2})$ defined as follows:

- $\rho_{1,2}^i = \rho_1^i$, $\rho_{1,2}^e = \rho_1^e \cup \bar{\rho}_2^e \cup \bar{\rho}_2^i$;
- $\bar{\rho}_2^e$ is the set of all pairs $(q_1|_{V_1}, q_2|_{V_1})$, where q_1 and q_2 are states in $K_1 \circ K_2$, $q_1 \in Reach(K_1 \circ K_2)$, $(q_1|_{V_2}, q_2|_{V_2}) \in \rho_2^e$ and $q_1|_{V_1^i} = q_2|_{V_1^i}$;
- $\bar{\rho}_2^i$ is the set of all pairs $(q_1|_{V_1}, q_2|_{V_1})$ such that there is a sequence of states $q_1 = q_1^1, \ldots, q_1^n = q_2$ in $K_1 \circ K_2$ with the properties: $q_1 \in Reach(K_1 \circ K_2)$, $(q_1^j|_{V_2}, q_1^{j+1}|_{V_2}) \in \rho_2^i$ and $q_1^j|_{V_1^i} = q_1^{j+1}|_{V_1^i}$ for all $1 \leq j < n$;
- $\mathcal{F}_{1,2} = \mathcal{F}_1 \cup \overline{\mathcal{F}}_2$, $\overline{\mathcal{F}}_2 = \{\{q|_{V_1} | q \in Reach(K_1 \circ K_2) \wedge q|_{V_2} \in A_2\} | A_2 \in \mathcal{F}_2\}$.

The structure $K_{1,2}$ is obtained from $K_1 \circ K_2$ by abstracting from (the internal behavior of) K_2 as follows: the internal steps in $K_{1,2}$ are exactly the internal steps in K_1; the external steps in K_1 and K_2 became external in $K_{1,2}$ and, moreover, sequences of consecutive internal steps in K_2 lead to external steps in $K_{1,2}$. The fairness constraints in K_2 lead to fairness constraints in $K_{1,2}$, which are external as we prove below.

Proposition 3.1 *The set $\overline{\mathcal{F}}_2$ defined as above is a set of external fairness constraints in $K_{1,2}$.*

The following theorem is the basis of our abstraction technique.

Theorem 3.1 *Let K_1 and K_2 be two compatible structures. Then,*
(1) $K_1 \circ K_2 \prec_{\mathcal{A}_1} K_{1,2}$;
(2) for every $\forall CTL^*$ formula φ over $\mathcal{A}_1$, $K_{1,2} \models \overline{\varphi}$ implies $K_1 \circ K_2 \models \hat{\overline{\varphi}}$.

What we have already done in this section acts as an abstraction methodology. Given a system $K_1 \circ K_2$, we abstract from the internal variables of K_2 obtaining $K_{1,2}$. The structure $K_{1,2}$ collapses consecutive steps in $K_1 \circ K_2$ by a single one, ensuring a simulation from $K_1 \circ K_2$ to $K_{1,2}$. The number of states in $K_{1,2}$ is reduced in comparison with $K_1 \circ K_2$ (the number of arcs could be increased but this is not as important as the reduction in the number of states is).

It is generally recognized that abstractions are not efficient if all the variables in a system are *visible* (if we cannot abstract from the internal variables of K_2, in our case – see [4] and [8] for more comments). On the other side, to have a good abstraction it is important to produce exactly $\rho_{1,2}^e$, or to produce approximations sufficiently closed to $\rho_{1,2}^e$ so that we can still verify interesting properties of the system. More comments about this will be provided in the end of the next section.

4 Application to Petri Net Reactive Modules

In this section we will show how the results from the previous sections can be translated to Petri net reactive modules.

4.1 Petri Net Reactive Modules

Recall first a few concepts regarding Petri nets (for details the reader is referred to [12]). A *marked Petri net* is a tuple $\gamma = (\Sigma, M_0)$, where:

(i) $\Sigma = (S, T, F, W)$ is a *Petri net* (S and T are two finite sets (of *places* and *transitions*, respectively), $S \cap T = \emptyset$, $F \subseteq (S \times T) \cup (T \times S)$ is the *flow relation*, and $W : (S \times T) \cup (T \times S) \to \mathbf{N}$ is the *weight function* of Σ verifying $W(x, y) = 0$ iff $(x, y) \notin F$);

(ii) $M_0 \in \mathbf{N}^S$ is a *marking* of Σ, i.e. a function from S into the set $\mathbf{N}$ of natural numbers, called the *initial marking*.

The *transition relation* of a net γ states that a transition t is *enabled* at a marking M, denoted by $M[t\rangle_\gamma$, if $M(s) \geq W(s, t)$ for all $s \in S$. If t is enabled at M, then it can occur yielding a new marking M' given by $M(s) = M(s) - W(s, t) + W(t, s)$ for all $s \in S$; we denote this by $M[t\rangle_\gamma M'$. The transition relation is usually extended to sequences of transitions. When there is a sequence $w \in T^*$ such that $M_0[w\rangle_\gamma M$ we say that M is *reachable*.

A *Petri net module* (*module*, for short) [14] is a couple $\mathcal{M} = (\gamma, S^c)$, where $\gamma = (\Sigma, M_0)$ is a marked Petri net called the *underlying net* of $\mathcal{M}$, and S^c is a subset of places of γ, called the *set of interface* or *shared places* of $\mathcal{M}$; $S^i = S - S^c$ is the *set of internal places* of $\mathcal{M}$.

The interface places are used by a module $\mathcal{M}$ to interact with an environment which updates, from time to time, the content of these places. Such an interaction can be mathematically modelled by a binary relation $R \subseteq \mathbf{N}^{S^c} \times \mathbf{N}^{S^c}$ on markings on S^c. A pair $(M^c, \overline{M}^c)$ means that the environment reads the content M^c of the interface places and then update it to $\overline{M}^c$. From the module $\mathcal{M}$ point of view this updating is done in exactly one step. A couple $\mathcal{J} = (\mathcal{M}, R)$, where $\mathcal{M}$ is a module and $R \subseteq \mathbf{N}^{S^c} \times \mathbf{N}^{S^c}$, is called an *environmental module* (*e-module*, for short); $\mathcal{M}$ is called the *underlying module*, and R the *environment*, of $\mathcal{J}$. E-modules are mainly used to describe in a compact way the behaviour of modules; they abstract from some parts of the behavior of modules by collapsing many consecutive steps into a single one. Let $\mathcal{J} = (\mathcal{M}, R)$ be an e-module. The *transition relation* of $\mathcal{J}$ is the binary relation $[\cdot\rangle_\mathcal{J}$ on $\mathbf{N}^S$ given by:

$$\begin{aligned} M[x\rangle_\mathcal{J} M' \Leftrightarrow {} & x \text{ is a transition and } M[x\rangle_\gamma M', \quad \text{or} \\ & x = (M^c, \overline{M}^c) \in R \text{ and } M|_{S^c} = M^c \text{ and } M' = M - M^c + \overline{M}^c, \end{aligned}$$

for all $M, M' \in \mathbf{N}^S$, where $M - M^c$ denotes the marking given by $(M - M^c)(s) = M(s) - M^c(s)$ for $s \in S^c$, and $(M - M^c)(s) = M(s)$ otherwise (in a similar way we define $M + M^c$).

It is important to note that the environment of an e-module may update the content of the interface places whenever it is possible. That is, for any reachable marking M, the environment may change the marking on S^c to $\overline{M}^c$, whenever $M|_{S^c} = M^c$ and $(M^c, \overline{M}^c) \in R$. Then, the module can execute further [3].

We define now the *asynchronous parallel composition* of modules. In order to avoid some annoying and totally unessential things for our purposes we assume given two disjoint countable sets $\mathcal{S}$ and $\mathcal{T}$, and all the nets we consider have the sets of places and transitions included in $\mathcal{S}$ and $\mathcal{T}$, respectively. For a finite set $S^c \subset \mathcal{S}$ and a marking M_0^c on S^c (that is, $M_0^c : S^c \to \mathbf{N}$) consider the set $PN(S^c, M_0^c)$ of all modules whose set of places includes S^c and whose initial marking agrees with M_0^c on S^c. Two modules $\mathcal{M}_0$ and $\mathcal{M}_1$ in this set are called *compatible* if $S_0 \cap S_1 = S^c$ and $T_0 \cap T_1 = \emptyset$.

Let $\mathcal{M}_1, \mathcal{M}_2 \in PN(S^c, M_0^c)$ be two compatible modules. The *asynchronous parallel composition* of $\mathcal{M}_1$ and $\mathcal{M}_2$, denoted by $\mathcal{M}_1 \circ \mathcal{M}_2$, is the component-wise union of $\mathcal{M}_1$ and $\mathcal{M}_2$, that is:

- $\mathcal{M}_1 \circ \mathcal{M}_2 = (\gamma, S^c)$, $\gamma = (\Sigma, M_0)$, and $\Sigma = (S, T, F, W)$;
- S, T, F, W, and M_0 are the union of the sets of places, transitions, flow relations, weight functions, and markings of $\mathcal{M}_1$ and $\mathcal{M}_2$, respectively.

Two e-modules $\mathcal{J}_1 = (\mathcal{M}_1, R_1)$ and $\mathcal{J}_2 = (\mathcal{M}_2, R_2)$ are called *compatible* when their underlying modules are compatible. The asynchronous parallel composition can be extended to compatible e-modules by $\mathcal{J}_1 \circ \mathcal{J}_2 = (\mathcal{M}_1 \circ \mathcal{M}_2, R_1 \cup R_2)$.

4.2 Abstraction of Petri Net Reactive Modules

Now, we show how the methodology we developed in the first sections can be applyied to safe Petri net modules. A net (module) is *n-safe*, where $n \in \mathbf{N}$, if $M(s) \leq n$ for all reachable markings M and places s; it is called *safe* when it is n-safe, for some $n \in \mathbf{N}$.

To each safe net γ we associate a *Kripke structure without fairness constraints* $K(\gamma) = (Q, Q_0, \mathcal{A}, \mathcal{L}, \rho)$ as follows:

- regard places as variables which range over finite sets of positive integers. Then, the set of states is the set of all interpretations of variables (markings of γ componentwise bounded by some integer n). The only initial state is the initial marking;
- we may define a set $\mathcal{A}$ of atomic propositions using the variables in S and the constants, functions and predicates over the corresponding domains (as in [11], p. 182). These propositions should be either true or false at a marking (state) M, and they will be used to define state and path formulas.

[3] The approach we considered for an environment, and for the corresponding transition rule, does not take into account the internal structure neither of the module nor of the environment. This one could appear unrealistic. But, we want to use e-modules for abstraction purposes, and if we should take into consideration the entire internal structure of the module and of the environment then such a purpose can be never reached. However, an intermediate variant of taking into account partial information about their internal structure (or to use something like semaphor variables) could be an worthy idea.

Let $\mathcal{L}$ be the function which associate to each marking M the set of all atomic propositions in $\mathcal{A}$ satisfied at M;

- the transition relation is specified by the set of transitions of γ in an obvious way; that is, $(M, M') \in \rho$ iff there is a transition t such that $M[t\rangle_\gamma M'$. The relation ρ is considered internal ($\rho = \rho^i$).

We may also add to $K(\gamma)$ a set $\mathcal{F}$ of fairness constraints getting in such a way a fair Kripke structure $K(\gamma, \mathcal{F})$ associated to γ.

We suppose from now on that for every net (module, e-module) there is given a set of atomic propositions (referring to its set of markings). Moreover, we will assume that whenever we merge (combine) two markings M_1 and M_2 which agree on some places (in order to obtain a marking of the composed net, module or e-module), the propositions that are satisfied at the new marking are exactly those that are satisfied at M_1 and M_2 [4].

We extend the notations above to modules and e-modules by:

- for a safe module $\mathcal{M} = (\gamma, S^c)$, $K(\mathcal{M})$ is obtained from $\mathcal{K}(\gamma)$ by considering S^c as the set of external (interface) variables;
- for a safe e-module $\mathcal{J} = (\mathcal{M}, R)$, $K(\mathcal{J})$ is obtained from $K(\mathcal{M})$ by adding the external transition relation
$$\rho^e = \{(M, M') \in \mathbf{N}^S \times \mathbf{N}^S | M'|_{S^i} = M|_{S^i} \ \wedge \ (M|_{S^c}, M'|_{S^c}) \in R\}$$
to the transition relation of $\mathcal{M}$;
- for a safe module $\mathcal{M}$ (e-module $\mathcal{J}$) and a set $\mathcal{F}$ of fairness constraints, $K(\mathcal{M}, \mathcal{F})$ ($K(\mathcal{J}, \mathcal{F})$) is the structure obtained by adding $\mathcal{F}$ to the 5-tuple $K(\mathcal{M})$ ($K(\mathcal{J})$). For e-modules, the fairness constraints we use are like in Section 3.

The pairs $(\gamma, \mathcal{F})$ ($(\mathcal{M}, \mathcal{F})$, $(\mathcal{J}, \mathcal{F})$) as above are called *fair nets* (*modules, e-modules*). The simulation and satisfaction relations are defined for them by means of the structures they induce. For example, for two fair safe e-modules $(\mathcal{J}_1, \mathcal{F}_1)$ and $(\mathcal{J}_2, \mathcal{F}_2)$ we write:

- $(\mathcal{J}_1, \mathcal{F}_1) \prec_{\mathcal{A}} (\mathcal{J}_2, \mathcal{F}_2)$ for $K(\mathcal{J}_1, \mathcal{F}_1) \prec_{\mathcal{A}} K(\mathcal{J}_2, \mathcal{F}_2)$, and
- $(\mathcal{J}_1, \mathcal{F}_1) \models \varphi$ for $K(\mathcal{J}_1, \mathcal{F}_1) \models \varphi$.

Let $(\mathcal{J}_1, \mathcal{F}_1)$ and $(\mathcal{J}_2, \mathcal{F}_2)$ be two compatible fair e-modules whose underlying modules are elements of $PN(S^c, M_0^c)$. Define their composition $(\mathcal{J}_1, \mathcal{F}_1) \circ (\mathcal{J}_2, \mathcal{F}_2)$ by $(\mathcal{J}_1 \circ \mathcal{J}_2, \mathcal{F})$, where $\mathcal{F}$ is defined as in Definition 3.1. Further, consider the fair e-module $(\mathcal{J}_{1,2}, \mathcal{F}_{1,2})$, where:

- $\mathcal{J}_{1,2} = (\gamma_1, R_{1,2})$, and $R_{1,2} = R_1 \cup R_2' \cup R_2''$;
- R_2' is the set of all pairs $(M|_{S^c}, M'|_{S^c}) \in R_2$, where M is reachable in $\mathcal{J}_1 \circ \mathcal{J}_2$;
- R_2'' is the set of all pairs $(M|_{S^c}, M'|_{S^c})$, where M is reachable in $\mathcal{J}_1 \circ \mathcal{J}_2$ and $M'|_{S_2}$ is reachable from $M|_{S_2}$ (in γ_2) by at least one transition occurrence;

[4] It was pointed out in [5] that in the case of 1-safe nets we may restrict the set of atomic propositions to propositions p_s, where s is a place, with the following meaning: a marking M satisfies p_s iff it marks the place s. Clearly, for such nets, our supposition trivially holds. Anyway, it is not a severe restriction for the case of safe nets.

- $\mathcal{F}_{1,2} = \mathcal{F}_1 \cup \overline{\mathcal{F}}_2$, where $\overline{\mathcal{F}}_2 = \{\{M|_{S_1} | M$ is reachable in $\mathcal{J}_1 \circ \mathcal{J}_2 \wedge M|_{S_2} \in A_2\} | A_2 \in \mathcal{F}_2\}$.

The following theorem makes the connection between modules and structures.

Theorem 4.1 *Let $(\mathcal{J}_1, \mathcal{F}_1)$ and $(\mathcal{J}_2, \mathcal{F}_2)$ be two compatible fair e-modules whose underlying modules are elements of $PN(S^c, M_0^c)$. If $\mathcal{J}_1 \circ \mathcal{J}_2$ is safe, then:*
(1) $K((\mathcal{J}_1, \mathcal{F}_1) \circ (\mathcal{J}_2, \mathcal{F}_2)) = K(\mathcal{J}_1, \mathcal{F}_1) \circ K(\mathcal{J}_2, \mathcal{F}_2)$;
(2) $(\mathcal{J}_1, \mathcal{F}_1) \circ (\mathcal{J}_2, \mathcal{F}_2) \prec_{A_1} (\mathcal{J}_{1,2}, \mathcal{F}_{1,2})$;
(3) $(\mathcal{J}_{1,2}, \mathcal{F}_{1,2}) \models \overline{\varphi}$ implies $(\mathcal{J}_1, \mathcal{F}_1) \circ (\mathcal{J}_2, \mathcal{F}_2) \models \hat{\overline{\varphi}}$, for every $\forall CTL^*$ formula φ over the set of atomic proposition of $\mathcal{J}_1$.

Let $\mathcal{M}_1, \mathcal{M}_2 \in PN(S^c, M_0^c)$ be two compatible modules, $\mathcal{M} = \mathcal{M}_1 \circ \mathcal{M}_2$, and let M be a reachable marking in $\mathcal{M}$. We say that the pair $(M^c, \overline{M}^c)$ of markings on S^c is *induced by $\mathcal{M}_2$ at M in $\mathcal{M}$* if there is a reachable marking $\overline{M}$ in $\mathcal{M}$ such that $M|_{S^c} = M^c$, $\overline{M}|_{S^c} = \overline{M}^c$, and $\overline{M}$ is reachable from M only by occurrences of transitions in $\mathcal{M}_2$, but at least by one occurrence. The set of all pairs induced by $\mathcal{M}_2$ at reachable markings of $\mathcal{M}$ is called the *relation induced* by $\mathcal{M}_2$ in $\mathcal{M}$.

When the set $\mathcal{F}$ of fairness constraints of a fair e-module $(\mathcal{J}, \mathcal{F})$ contains only the set of all reachable markings, then all paths of the e-module are fair. In such a case we may simplify the pair $(\mathcal{J}, \mathcal{F})$ to $\mathcal{J}$ (but understanding that all the paths of $\mathcal{J}$ are fair). Composition of such e-modules leads to such an e-module (all paths are fair). Then, directly from the theorem above we obtain:

Corollary 4.1 *Let $\mathcal{M}_1, \mathcal{M}_2 \in PN(S^c, M_0^c)$ be two compatible modules. If $\mathcal{M}_1 \circ \mathcal{M}_2$ is safe, then for every $\forall CTL^*$ formula φ over the set of atomic proposition of $\mathcal{M}_1$, $\mathcal{J} \models \overline{\varphi}$ implies $\mathcal{M}_1 \circ \mathcal{M}_2 \models \hat{\overline{\varphi}}$, where $\mathcal{J} = (\mathcal{M}_1, R)$ and R is the relation induced by $\mathcal{M}_2$ in $\mathcal{M}_1 \circ \mathcal{M}_2$.*

This corollary tells us how properties of components are transferred to the entire system. As we have already mentioned, the main goal is to find an approximation of the relation induced by a component, sufficiently closed to the real relation induced on the interface places. A very convenient case is when a module $\mathcal{M} = \mathcal{M}_1 \circ \mathcal{M}_2$ is context-free w.r.t. $\mathcal{M}_1$ or $\mathcal{M}_2$, that is, if for every pair $(M^c, \overline{M}^c)$ induced by $\mathcal{M}_1$ ($\mathcal{M}_2$) and for every reachable marking M in $\mathcal{M}$, if $M|_{S^c} = M^c$ then $\mathcal{M}_1$ ($\mathcal{M}_2$) can induce $(M^c, \overline{M}^c)$ at M.

This is the case of the module $\mathcal{M} = \mathcal{M}_1 \circ \mathcal{M}_2$ in Figure 1 which is context-free w.r.t. both $\mathcal{M}_1$ and $\mathcal{M}_2$ (places are represented by circles, transitions by boxes, the flow relation by arcs – all of them are weighted by 1 – and the initial marking is presented by putting $M_0(s)$ tokens into the circle representing the place s; the set of interface places is $\{s_1, s_2, s_3\}$). Then, $\mathcal{J}_1 = (\mathcal{M}_1, R_1)$, where

$$R_1 = \{((0,1,1),(0,1,1)), ((0,1,1),(0,1,0)), ((0,1,0),(0,1,0)), ((0,1,0),(0,1,1)), ((1,0,1),(1,0,1)), ((1,0,1),(1,0,0))\},$$

is an e-module which ensures a simulation from $\mathcal{M}$ to it. The state space of $\mathcal{M}$ is reduced to the state space of $\mathcal{M}_1$ (we have to add some more arcs, corresponding

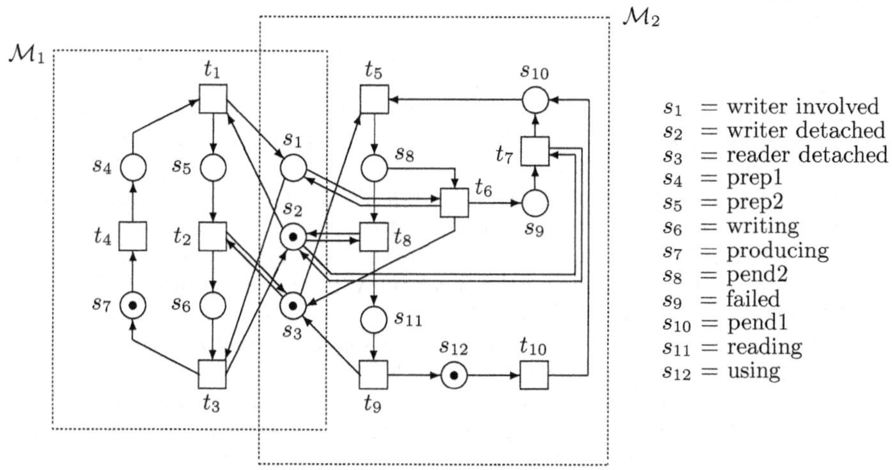

Fig. 1. A Petri Net model for the Owicki-Lamport Mutex algorithm [13]

to R_1, but this is not as important as the reduction of the state space is). Therefore, properties of $\mathcal{J}_1$ can be transferred to $\mathcal{M}$.

Conclusions

We partition the transition relation of a Kripke structure into two parts, internal and external. This allows an appropriate modeling of reactive systems. We propose a simulation preorder suitable for use with such Kripke structures. The preorder captures the relation between a component and a system containing that component, treating the transition relation of that component as internal in the system. We identify a substantial subset of $\forall CTL^*$, which is appropriate to be used with our preorder. We also propose an abstraction method, and illustrate its application to Petri net reactive modules. There are two parts of this method: first, we decompose the system into modules and compute the relation induced by some submodules, and second, we check the satisfaction of properties in the "augmented" modules.

Finding efficient methods to describe or approximate the relation induced by submodules is of great importance for practical applications. For Petri net reactive modules, we discuss briefly how to approximate the relation induced by a component into a system. Possible future work is to identify classes of systems with good properties for automated approximation.

Acknowledgement We thank Daniel Kröning for helpful suggestions and discussions.

References

1. R. Alur, Th.A. Henziger: *Reactive Modules*, in: Proc. of the 11th IEEE Symposium on Logic in Computer Science LICS, 1996, 207–218.
2. E.M. Clarke, E.A. Emerson: *Synthesis of Synchronizations Skeletons for Branching Time Temporal Logic*, in: Workshop on Logic of Programs, Yorktown Heights, May 1981, LNCS 131, Springer-Verlag, 1981.
3. E.M. Clarke, O. Grumberg, D.E. Long: *Model Checking and Abstraction*, ACM Trans. Prog. Lang. Sys., 16(5), 1994, 1512–1542.
4. E.M. Clarke, O. Grumberg, D.E. Long: *Model Checking*, in: Model Checking, Abstraction and Composition, vol 152 of NATO ASI Series F, Springer-Verlag, 1996, 477-498.
5. J. Esparza, S. Melzer: *Model Checking LTL Using Constraint Programming*, Technical Report, Technische Universität München, 1997.
6. O. Grumberg, D.E. Long: *Model Checking and Modular Verification*, ACM Transactions on Programming Languages and Systems 16, 1994, 843–871 (a short version in Proceedings of CONCUR'91, LNCS 527, 1991, 250-265).
7. Y. Kersten, A. Pnueli, L. Raviv: *Algorithmic Verification of Linear Temporal Logic Specifications*, in: Proc. of the 25th International Colloquium on Automata, Languages, and Programming ICALP'98, LNCS 1443, Springer-Verlag, 1998, 1–16.
8. Y. Kersten, A. Pnueli: *Modularization and Abstraction: The Keys to Practical Formal Verification*, in: Proc. of the 23rd International Symposium on Mathematical Foundations of Computer Science MFCS'98, LNCS 1450, Springer-Verlag, 1998, 54–71.
9. O. Kupferman, M.Y. Vardi: *Modular Model Checking*, in: Proc. of the International Symposium "Compositionality: The Significant Difference" COMPOS'97, Bad Malente (Germany), Sept 8–12, 1997, LNCS 1536, Springer-Verlag, 1998, 381–401.
10. B. Kurshan: *Analysis of Discrete Event Coordination*, in: Proc. of the REX Workshop on Stepwise Refinement of Distributed Systems, Models, Formalisms, Correctness (J.W. Bakker, W.-P. de Roever, G. Rozenberg, eds.), LNCS 430, Springer-Verlag, 1989, 414-453.
11. Z. Manna, A. Pnueli: *The Temporal Logic of Reactive and Concurrent Systems. Specification*, Springer-Verlag, 1992.
12. W. Reisig: *Petri Nets*, Springer-Verlag, 1985.
13. W. Reisig: *Elements of Distributed Algorithms. Modeling and Analysis with Petri Nets*, Springer-Verlag, 1998.
14. F.L. Ţiplea, A. Ţiplea: *Petri Net Reactive Modules*, Tech. Report 1999-7, Universität Augsburg, Institut für Informatik, 1999, 50pp.

5 Appendix: Proofs

Proposition 2.1 The simulation relation $\prec_{\mathcal{A}}$ is a preorder (i.e., a reflexive and transitive order) on structures whose set of atomic propositions include $\mathcal{A}$.

Proof. The relation $H = \{(q,q) | q \in Q\}$ is a simulation from K to K w.r.t. $\mathcal{A}$. Thus, $\prec_{\mathcal{A}}$ is reflexive.

Assume that H_1 is a simulation from K_1 to K_2 w.r.t. $\mathcal{A}$, and H_2 is a simulation from K_2 to K_3 w.r.t. $\mathcal{A}$. Let H_3 be the usual product of the binary relations H_1 and H_2. We show that H_3 is a simulation from K_1 to K_3 w.r.t. $\mathcal{A}$.

First of all we note that $\mathcal{L}_1(q) \cap \mathcal{A} = \mathcal{L}_3(q'') \cap \mathcal{A}$, for all $(q,q'') \in H_3$. Indeed, for each $(q,q'') \in H_3$ there is a state q' in H_2 such that $(q,q') \in H_1$ and $(q',q'') \in H_2$. Since H_1 and H_2 are simulations, it follows that

$$\mathcal{L}_1(q) \cap \mathcal{A} = \mathcal{L}_2(q') \cap \mathcal{A} = \mathcal{L}_3(q'') \cap \mathcal{A},$$

which proves our statement above.

For each initial state q_0 in K_1 there is an initial state q'_0 in K_2 such that H_1 is a simulation from (K_1, q_0) to (K_2, q'_0) w.r.t. $\mathcal{A}$. Similarly, there is an initial state q''_0 in K_3 such that H_2 is a simulation from (K_2, q'_0) to (K_3, q''_0) w.r.t. $\mathcal{A}$. Let

$$\sigma = q_0 q_1 \cdots = q_{i_0} \cdots q_{i_1} \cdots q_{i_2} \cdots$$

and $\sigma' = q'_0 q'_1 \cdots$ be fair paths in K_1 and K_2, respectively, as in Definition 2.1 ($i_0, i_1, \ldots$ specify the decomposition of σ). For the fair path σ' there is a fair path $\sigma'' = q''_0 q''_1 \cdots$ in K_3 and a decomposition of σ',

$$\sigma' = q'_0 q'_1 \cdots = q'_{j_0} \cdots q'_{j_1} \cdots q'_{j_2} \cdots$$

as in Definition 2.1. We will define recursively a partition of σ

$$\sigma = q_0 q_1 \cdots = q_{k_0} \cdots q_{k_1} \cdots q_{k_2} \cdots$$

such that $H_3(\sigma, \sigma'')$ holds. There are several cases to be considered.

Case 1: $i_1 = 1 = j_1$. Clearly, if $(q_0, q_1) \in \rho_1^e$ then $(q'_0, q'_1) \in \rho_2^e$ and, consequently, $(q''_0, q''_1) \in \rho_3^e$. Moreover, $(q_1, q'_1) \in H_1$ and $(q'_1, q''_1) \in H_2$, which shows that $(q_1, q''_1) \in H_3$. We consider in this case $k_1 = 1$, and the decomposition of σ continues with σ^1, $(\sigma')^1$ and $(\sigma'')^1$ ($H_1(\sigma^1, (\sigma')^1)$ and $H_2((\sigma')^1, (\sigma'')^1)$) hold).

Case 2: $i_1 = 1$ and $j_1 > 1$. Consider $k_1 = i_{j_1}$. It is easy to verify that $(q_{k_1}, q'_{j_1}) \in H_1$ and $(q'_{j_1}, q''_1) \in H_2$; therefore, $(q_{k_1}, q''_1) \in H_3$. The decomposition of σ continues with σ^{k_1}, $(\sigma')^{j_1}$ and $(\sigma'')^1$.

The other two cases, $i_1 > 1$ and $j_1 = 1$, and $i_1 > 1$ and $j_1 > 1$, can be discussed in a similar way. We conclude that $\prec_{\mathcal{A}}$ is transitive and, therefore, $\prec_{\mathcal{A}}$ is a preorder. □

Theorem 2.1 Let K_1 and K_2 be two structures. Then, for every two states q and q' of K_1 and K_2, respectively, and every two fair paths σ and σ' in K_1

and K_2, respectively, if H is a simulation from (K_1, q) to (K_2, q') w.r.t. a set $\mathcal{A} \subseteq \mathcal{A}_1 \cap \mathcal{A}_2$ and $H(\sigma, \sigma')$ holds true, then for every $\forall CTL^*$ formula φ over $\mathcal{A}$ we have:

(1) if φ is a state formula and $q' \models \overline{\varphi}$ then $q \models \hat{\overline{\varphi}}$;
(2) if φ is a path formula and $\sigma' \models \overline{\varphi}$ then $\sigma \models \hat{\overline{\varphi}}$.

Proof. We prove the theorem by induction on the structure of $\overline{\varphi}$.

Base: If $\overline{\varphi}$ is **true** or **false**, the result is trivial. If $\overline{\varphi} = p$ for $p \in \mathcal{A}$, then $q' \models p$ iff $p \in \mathcal{L}_2(q')$. By the definition of simulation, $\mathcal{L}_1(q) \cap \mathcal{A} = \mathcal{L}_2(q') \cap \mathcal{A}$, and so $p \in \mathcal{L}_1(q)$ iff $p \in \mathcal{L}_2(q')$. Thus, $q \models p$. The case $\varphi = \neg p$ for $p \in \mathcal{A}$ is similar to the previous one.

Induction: There are several cases.

1. $\overline{\varphi} = \overline{\varphi}_1 \wedge \overline{\varphi}_2$, a state formula. Then,
$$\begin{aligned} q' \models \overline{\varphi} &\Rightarrow q' \models \overline{\varphi}_1 \text{ and } q' \models \overline{\varphi}_2 \\ &\Rightarrow q \models \hat{\overline{\varphi}}_1 \text{ and } q \models \hat{\overline{\varphi}}_2 \text{ (induction hypothesis)} \\ &\Rightarrow q \models \hat{\overline{\varphi}} \end{aligned}$$
The same reasoning holds if $\overline{\varphi}$ is a path formula (replacing q' by σ' and q by σ).
2. $\overline{\varphi} = \overline{\varphi}_1 \vee \overline{\varphi}_2$, a state or path formula. This case is similar to the previous case.
3. $\overline{\varphi} = \forall(\overline{\varphi}_1)$, a state formula ($\varphi_1$ is a path formula). Suppose $q' \models \overline{\varphi}$. Let σ_1 be a fair path in K_1 starting at q. By the definition of simulation relation, there is a fair path σ_2 in K_2 starting at q' and such that $H(\sigma_1, \sigma_2)$ holds. Then,
$$\begin{aligned} q' \models \overline{\varphi} &\Rightarrow \sigma_2 \models \overline{\varphi}_1 \text{ (definition of } \models) \\ &\Rightarrow \sigma_1 \models \hat{\overline{\varphi}}_1 \text{ (induction hypothesis)} \end{aligned}$$
As σ_1 has been arbitrarily chosen, we obtain $q \models \hat{\overline{\varphi}}$.
4. If φ is a path formula consisting of only a state formula and $\sigma' \models \overline{\varphi}$, then the initial state of σ' satisfies $\overline{\varphi}$. By the induction hypothesis, the initial state of σ will satisfy $\hat{\overline{\varphi}}$. Thus, $\sigma \models \hat{\overline{\varphi}}$.
5. $\overline{\varphi} = X\overline{\varphi}_1$, a path formula. Suppose $\sigma' \models \overline{\varphi}$. Then, $(\sigma')^1 \models \overline{\varphi}_1$. Since $H(\sigma, \sigma')$ holds, there is $i_1 \geq 1$ such that $H(\sigma^{i_1}, (\sigma')^1)$ holds. Therefore, by the induction hypothesis, $\sigma^{i_1} \models \hat{\overline{\varphi}}_1$, and so $\sigma \models \Diamond\hat{\overline{\varphi}}_1 = \hat{\overline{\varphi}}$.
6. $\overline{\varphi} = \overline{\varphi}_1 \overline{U} \overline{\varphi}_2$, a path formula. Suppose $\sigma' \models \overline{\varphi}$. Then, there is $j \geq 0$ such that $(\sigma')^j \models \overline{\varphi}_1 \wedge \overline{\varphi}_2$ and, for all $0 \leq i < j$, $(\sigma')^i \models \overline{\varphi}_1$.
The definition of simulation leads to the existence of an $i_j \geq j$ such that $H(\sigma^{i_j}, (\sigma')^j)$ holds, and from the induction hypothesis we obtain $\sigma^{i_j} \models \hat{\overline{\varphi}}_1 \wedge \hat{\overline{\varphi}}_2$. Clearly, $\sigma^i \models \Diamond\hat{\overline{\varphi}}_1$, for all $0 \leq i \leq i_j$, and so $\sigma \models \hat{\overline{\varphi}}$.
7. $\overline{\varphi} = \overline{\varphi}_1 V \overline{\varphi}_2$, a path formula. The argument in this case is similar to that for the previous case.

The theorem is proved. □

Proposition 3.1 The set $\overline{\mathcal{F}}_2$ defined as above is a set of external fairness constraints in $K_{1,2}$.

Proof. The fairness constraints in $\overline{\mathcal{F}}_2$ are obtained from the (internal and external) fairnes constraints in $\mathcal{F}_2$. We consider the next two cases:

- if A_2 is an external fairness constraint in $\mathcal{F}_2$, then every state $q \in Reach(K_1 \circ K_2)$ with the property $q|_{V_2} \in A_2$ verifies also $q|_{V_2} \in Dom(\rho_2^e)$, and so $q|_{V_1} \in Dom(\bar{\rho}_2^e)$;
- if A_2 is an internal fairness constraint in $\mathcal{F}_2$, then every state $q \in Reach(K_1 \circ K_2)$ with the property $q|_{V_2} \in A_2$ verifies also $q|_{V_2} \in Dom(\rho_2^i)$, and so $q|_{V_1} \in Dom(\bar{\rho}_2^i)$.

Therefore, for every fairness constraint $A_2 \in \mathcal{F}_2$ we have

$$\{q|_{V_1} | q \in Reach(K_1 \circ K_2) \ \wedge \ q|_{V_2} \in A_2\} \subseteq Dom(\bar{\rho}_2^i \cup \bar{\rho}_2^e),$$

which shows that $\overline{\mathcal{F}}_2$ is a set of external fairness constraints in $K_{1,2}$. □

Theorem 3.1 Let K_1 and K_2 be two compatible structures. Then,
(1) $K_1 \circ K_2 \prec_{\mathcal{A}_1} K_{1,2}$;
(2) for every $\forall CTL^*$ formula φ over $\mathcal{A}_1$, $K_{1,2} \models \overline{\varphi}$ implies $K_1 \circ K_2 \models \hat{\overline{\varphi}}$.

Proof. (1) Let $K = K_1 \circ K_2$. Consider $H = \{(q, q|_{V_1}) | q \in Q\}$ and show that H is a simulation from $K = K_1 \circ K_2$ to $K_{1,2}$ w.r.t. $\mathcal{A}_1$.

For every state $q \in Q$ we have:

$$\begin{aligned} \mathcal{L}(q) \cap \mathcal{A}_1 &= (\mathcal{L}_1(q|_{V_1}) \cup \mathcal{L}_2(q|_{V_2})) \cap \mathcal{A}_1 \\ &= (\mathcal{L}_1(q|_{V_1}) \cap \mathcal{A}_1) \cup (\mathcal{L}_2(q|_{V_2}) \cap \mathcal{A}_1) \\ &= \mathcal{L}_1(q|_{V_1}) \cup (\mathcal{L}_1(q|_{V_1}) \cap \mathcal{A}_2) \qquad \text{(definition of } Q) \\ &= \mathcal{L}_1(q|_{V_1}). \end{aligned}$$

Then, we note that for every initial state q_0 in K, $q_0|_{V_1}$ is an initial state in $K_{1,2}$.

Let $\sigma = q_0 q_1 q_2 \cdots$ be a fair path in K. Decompose the path σ,

$$\sigma = q_{i_0} \cdots q_{i_1} \cdots q_{i_2} \cdots$$

such that, for all $j \geq 0$, the following requirements are satisfied:
(a) if $i_{j+1} = i_j + 1$, then $(q_{i_j}|_{V_1}, q_{i_{j+1}}|_{V_1}) \in \rho_1$ or $(q_{i_j}|_{V_2}, q_{i_{j+1}}|_{V_2}) \in \rho_2^e$;
(b) if $i_{j+1} \geq i_j + 1$, then $(q_{i_j}|_{V_2}, q_{i_{j+1}}|_{V_2}) \in (\rho_2^i)^+$, $q_{i_j}|_{V_1} = \cdots = q_{i_{j+1}-1}|_{V_1}$, $q_{i_j}|_{V_1^i} = q_{i_{j+1}}|_{V_1^i}$.

Define now a path σ' of $K_{1,2}$ by modifying the path σ as follows:

- keep all (a)-type steps (but restrict all states to V_1);
- replace each (b)-type sequence by $(q_{i_j}|_{V_1}, q_{i_{j+1}}|_{V_1})$.

Clearly, this is an infinite path of $K_{1,2}$. We will prove that this path is fair. Let $A \in \mathcal{F}_{1,2}$.

Case 1: $A \in \mathcal{F}_1$. Then, $A' = \{q \in Q | q|_{V_1} \in A\}$ is a fairness constraint in K. Since σ is a fair path it follows that $inf(\sigma) \cap A' \neq \emptyset$, and so there is $q \in Q \cap inf(\sigma)$. It is enough to show that $q|_{V_1}$ occurs infinitely many times in σ'. In fact, the only problem we encounter is the following one: "condensing" a (b)-type sequence by its left and right most states we may loose some occurrences of q and, therefore, of $q|_{V_1}$. However, at least one occurrence of $q|_{V_1}$ is kept in the left or right most state, and this is enough to ensure that $q|_{V_1}$ occurs infinitely many times in σ'.

Case 2: $A \in \overline{\mathcal{F}}_2$. Then, there is a fairness constraint $A_2 \in \mathcal{F}_2$ such that

$$A = \{q|_{V_1} | q \in Reach(K_1 \circ K_2) \ \wedge \ q|_{V_2} \in A_2\}.$$

But, the set $A' = \{q \in Q | q|_{V_2} \in A_2\}$ is a fairness constraint in K, and so there is $q \in A'$ occurring infinitely many times in σ. Moreover, q is reachable in K and $q|_{V_1} \in Dom(\bar{\rho}_2^{\mathrm{l}} \cup \bar{\rho}_2^{\mathrm{e}})$ (as we have shown above the theorem). By a similar argument as in Case 1 we can prove that $q|_{V_1} \in inf(\sigma')$. Hence, $inf(\sigma') \cap A \neq \emptyset$.

Therefore, the path σ' is fair and it is straightforward to prove that $H(\sigma, \sigma')$ holds. Thus, H is a simulation from $K_1 \circ K_2$ to $K_{1,2}$ w.r.t. $\mathcal{A}_1$.

(2) follows directly from (1) and Corolary 2.1. □

Theorem 4.1 Let $(\mathcal{J}_1, \mathcal{F}_1)$ and $(\mathcal{J}_2, \mathcal{F}_2)$ be two compatible fair e-modules whose underlying modules are elements of $PN(S^c, M_0^c)$. If $\mathcal{J}_1 \circ \mathcal{J}_2$ is safe, then:
(1) $K((\mathcal{J}_1, \mathcal{F}_1) \circ (\mathcal{J}_2, \mathcal{F}_2)) = K(\mathcal{J}_1, \mathcal{F}_1) \circ K(\mathcal{J}_2, \mathcal{F}_2)$;
(2) $(\mathcal{J}_1, \mathcal{F}_1) \circ (\mathcal{J}_2, \mathcal{F}_2) \prec_{\mathcal{A}_1} (\mathcal{J}_{1,2}, \mathcal{F}_{1,2})$;
(3) for every $\forall CTL^*$ formula φ over the set of atomic proposition of $\mathcal{J}_1$, $(\mathcal{J}_{1,2}, \mathcal{F}_{1,2}) \models \overline{\varphi}$ implies $(\mathcal{J}_1, \mathcal{F}_1) \circ (\mathcal{J}_2, \mathcal{F}_2) \models \hat{\overline{\varphi}}$.

Proof. If $\mathcal{J}_1 \circ \mathcal{J}_2$ is safe, then $\mathcal{J}_1$ and $\mathcal{J}_2$ are safe. Then, (1) follows immediately from definitions (see also the assumption on composing markings at the beginning of the section), and (3) from (2) and Theorem 3.1.

(2) Let $K_1 = K(\mathcal{J}_1, \mathcal{F}_1)$ and $K_2 = K(\mathcal{J}_2, \mathcal{F}_2)$. We have:

$$K((\mathcal{J}_1, \mathcal{F}_1) \circ (\mathcal{J}_2, \mathcal{F}_2)) = K(\mathcal{J}_1, \mathcal{F}_1) \circ K(\mathcal{J}_2, \mathcal{F}_2) = K_1 \circ K_2 \prec_{\mathcal{A}_1} K_{1,2}.$$

By the remark that $K_{1,2} = K(\mathcal{J}_{1,2}, \mathcal{F}_{1,2})$ we get (2). □

Corollary 4.1 Let $\mathcal{M}_1, \mathcal{M}_2 \in PN(S^c, M_0^c)$ be two compatible modules. If $\mathcal{M}_1 \circ \mathcal{M}_2$ is safe, then for every $\forall CTL^*$ formula φ over the set of atomic proposition of $\mathcal{M}_1$, $\mathcal{J} \models \overline{\varphi}$ implies $\mathcal{M}_1 \circ \mathcal{M}_2 \models \hat{\overline{\varphi}}$, where $\mathcal{J} = (\mathcal{M}_1, R)$ and R is the relation induced by $\mathcal{M}_2$ in $\mathcal{M}_1 \circ \mathcal{M}_2$.

Proof. Considering $\mathcal{J}_1 = (\mathcal{M}_1, \emptyset)$ and $\mathcal{J}_2 = (\mathcal{M}_2, \emptyset)$, the e-module $\mathcal{J}_{1,2}$ is just the e-module $\mathcal{J}$ in Theorem 4.1. Moreover, $\mathcal{F}_{1,2}$ contains the set of all reachable marking in $\mathcal{M}_1$ and also a subset, possible strict, of this one. However,

$$\gamma_1 \circ \gamma_2 \prec_{\mathcal{A}_1} (\mathcal{J}_{1,2}, \mathcal{F}_{1,2}) = (\mathcal{J}, \mathcal{F}_{1,2}) \prec_{\mathcal{A}_1} \mathcal{J}.$$

Then, $\mathcal{J} \models \overline{\varphi}$ implies $\mathcal{M}_1 \circ \mathcal{M}_2 \models \hat{\overline{\varphi}}$. □

Approximating ATL* in ATL

Aidan Harding[1], Mark Ryan[1], and Pierre-Yves Schobbens[2]

[1] School of Computer Science, University of Birmingham, Edgbaston, Birmingham B15 2TT, UK
[2] Institut d'Informatique, Facultés Universitaires de Namur, Rue Grandgagnage 21, 5000 Namur, Belgium

Abstract. Alternating Time Temporal Logic (ATL) [2] has proved useful in specifying systems that can be viewed as the parallel composition of a set of *agents*. It has tool-support for model checking and simulation in the form of MOCHA [1]. ATL* is a more expressive form of ATL which provides a more natural way to write specifications. Whilst ATL can be model checked in linear time (relative to the size of the model), ATL* is 2EXPTIME-complete [2]. Here we present a method of "translating" an ATL* formula, into ATL so that model checking can then be performed. This method cannot, in general, be entirely exact but instead produces a strong and a weak bound. From these we may be able to infer whether the original formula was satisfied. To minimise the number of undecided cases, the bounds must be as close as possible to the original. Exact translations help to ensure that this is so, and we have identified a subset of ATL* which can be translated without loss. Case studies support the method by showing that most ATL* formulae attempted did yield conclusive results, even after approximation.

1 Introduction

The aim of this work is to provide a method of model checking ATL* specifications using a model checker for ATL. Model checking ATL* directly is infeasible, so we have taken the option of rewriting a given ATL* property φ, into a pair of ATL properties, φ_s and φ_w where φ_s is stronger and φ_w is weaker than φ. By checking these two properties, we may be able to infer whether or not φ is satisfied. There is some uncertainty in the method, because φ_s and φ_w do not capture *all* of the information in φ. In some cases this abstraction of the formula may be too coarse, making it impossible for the method to discern whether φ is true or not. To add to the accuracy and sophistication of our method, exact (i.e. information preserving) transformations on ATL* formulae are used, wherever possible.

1.1 Why ATL*?

ATL* [2] is a temporal logic for reasoning about systems composed of *agents*. It is desirable to write specifications in ATL* rather than CTL* or LTL because

A. Cortesi (Ed.): VMCAI 2002, LNCS 2294, pp. 289–301, 2002.
© Springer-Verlag Berlin Heidelberg 2002

it allows us to distinguish between the possible choices of agents, which are the sources of non-determinism. By recognising the agents in a system, it is possible to separate out properties which would otherwise remain hidden.

A formal look at ATL and ATL* is deferred until Section 2, but first we look at a motivating example for their use. Consider a basic phone system. A natural question to ask about it is *"Can two users, i and j, cooperate such that in the future, they will be talking to one and other"*. The idea of their cooperation is that we wish to exclude paths such as those where i never dials j, or j goes off-hook every time the connection is being attempted. We allow for the rest of the system to be as awkward as possible e.g. another phone k may try to interfere by also dialling j and the exchange may solve the conflict by favouring k. In CTL, this cannot be expressed – it is only possible to write about all computation paths or the existence of at least one. However, in ATL we can write about the paths enforceable by the cooperation of i and j: $\langle\langle i, j\rangle\rangle \mathrm{F}(i.talking \wedge i.callee = j)$. Clearly there are many other systems where ATL* is beneficial, allowing us to reason about the capabilities of sets of agents in cooperation/opposition.

Just as CTL* generalises CTL by allowing temporal operators to be nested directly, ATL* generalises ATL. ATL* can be more useful than ATL due to this extra expressiveness. It provides all of the advantages of LTL whilst retaining the ability to reason about the capabilities of agents. LTL specifications are claimed to be easier to write in [8], and to be more useful for reasoning about concurrent systems in [6]. By using ATL*, we have the best of both worlds (in expressivity).

1.2 Approximating ATL* in ATL

Since ATL* is strictly more expressive than ATL, we cannot hope to translate all possible formulae exactly from ATL* into ATL. The complexity of model checking ATL is linear in the size of the model, whilst model checking ATL* directly is doubly exponential [2]. Our method is a partial solution to the problem of model checking ATL* – it returns within a feasible time, but may lose some of the original information. In essence, this is achieved by approximating a single property φ, into two properties φ_s and φ_w which surround the original property with a strong and a weak bound such that:

$$\varphi_s \Rightarrow \varphi \Rightarrow \varphi_w \tag{1.1}$$

We can then model check the ATL formulae with MOCHA [1, 10] to deduce the satisfaction of φ. If we find φ_s to be true, then φ is true; If we find φ_w to be false, then φ is false; If φ_s is false and φ_w is true, we cannot decide whether φ is true or false.

It is essential to minimise the number of times our method may come back undecided. This means ensuring that the strong and weak bound are as close as possible to φ. To do this, we use exact equivalences, where possible. These equivalences are designed to make φ in some sense, better with each application i.e. they should make the property closer to ATL than it was before. When no more equivalences are applicable, approximation is used to copy path quantifiers over temporal operators e.g.

$$\langle\langle A\rangle\rangle \mathrm{FG}\varphi \rightsquigarrow \begin{array}{ll} \langle\langle A\rangle\rangle \mathrm{F}\langle\langle A\rangle\rangle \mathrm{G}\varphi & \text{(strong)} \\ \langle\langle A\rangle\rangle \mathrm{F}\exists \mathrm{G}\varphi & \text{(weak)} \end{array}$$

After each approximation, equivalences are applied until either the formula is in ATL or more approximation is needed. With the complete set of approximations provided, any well-formed ATL* formula can be translated into into a pair of well-formed ATL formulae.

The rest of the paper is organised as follows: Section 2 summarises the syntax and semantics of ATL; Section 3 lists the exact equivalences used in the translation process; Section 4 covers the approximations used in the translation process; Section 5 considers the practicalities of the method as a term rewriting system; Section 6 has a model of a telephone system with ATL* specifications which have been translated and checked with MOCHA; Finally, Section 7 draws some conclusions.

2 Alternating-Time Temporal Logic

Alternating-Time Temporal Logic [2] (ATL) is a temporal logic for reasoning about *reactive systems* comprised of *agents*. It contains the usual temporal operators (next, always, until) plus cooperation modalities $\langle\langle A\rangle\rangle\varphi$, where A is a set of agents. This modality quantifies over the set of behaviours and means that A have a collective strategy to enforce φ, whatever the choices of the other players. ATL generalises CTL, and similarly ATL* generalises CTL*, μ-ATL generalises the μ-calculus. These logics can be model-checked by generalising the techniques of CTL, often with the same complexity.

This section contains a brief review of ATL, as we have used it in this paper. For a more detailed treatment, the interested reader is referred to [2].

2.1 Alternating Transition Systems

ATL is interpreted over Alternating Transition Systems (ATS) which are Kripke structures, extended to represent the choices of agents.

An ATS is a 5-tuple $\langle \Pi, \Sigma, Q, \pi, \delta\rangle$ where

- Π is a set of propositions
- Σ is a set of agents
- Q is a set of states
- $\pi : Q \rightarrow 2^{\Pi}$ maps each state to the propositions which are true in that state
- $\delta : Q \times \Sigma \rightarrow 2^{2^Q}$ is a transition function from a state, q, and an agent, a, to the set of a's choices. a's choices are sets of states, and one particular choice is taken, Q_a. The next state of the system is the intersection of the choices of all agents $\bigcap_{a\in\Sigma} Q_a$.
  The transition function is *non-blocking* and *unique* i.e. for every state, the intersection of all possible choices of all agents is singleton.

For two states q, q' and an agent a, q' is an *a-successor* of q if there exists some $Q' \in \delta(q,a)$ such that $q' \in Q'$. The set of a-successors of q is denoted $succ(q,a)$. For two states q and q', q' is a *successor* of q if $\forall a \in \Sigma\ q' \in succ(q,a)$. A computation, λ, is defined as an infinite sequence of states $q_0, q_1, q_2, \ldots$ such that for all $i \geq 0$, q_{i+1} is the successor of q_i.

Subsegments of a computation path $\lambda = q_1, q_2, \ldots$ are denoted by postfixing an interval in square brackets. For example, $\lambda[i,j] = q_i, \ldots, q_j$, $\lambda[i,\infty] = q_i, \ldots$ and $\lambda[i] = q_i$.

2.2 ATL Syntax

Let Π be a set of atomic propositions and Σ a set of agents. The syntax of ATL is given by

$$\varphi ::= p \mid \top \mid \neg\varphi \mid \varphi_1 \vee \varphi_2 \mid \langle\langle A \rangle\rangle(\varphi_1\, \mathcal{U}\, \varphi_2) \mid \langle\langle A \rangle\rangle(\varphi_1\, \mathcal{R}\, \varphi_2)$$

where $p \in \Pi$ and $A \subseteq \Sigma$[1]. We use the usual abbreviations for $\rightarrow$, $\wedge$ in terms of $\neg$, $\vee$. The operator $\langle\langle\ \rangle\rangle$ is a path quantifier, and $\mathcal{U}$ (*until*) and $\mathcal{R}$ (*release*) are temporal operators. As in CTL, we write $\mathrm{F}\varphi$ for $\top\, \mathcal{U}\, \varphi$ and $\mathrm{G}\varphi$ for $\bot\, \mathcal{R}\, \varphi$.

While the formula $\langle\langle A \rangle\rangle\psi$ means that the agents in A can cooperate to make ψ true (they can "enforce" ψ), the dual formula $[[A]]\psi$ means that the agents in A cannot cooperate to make ψ false (they cannot "avoid" ψ) i.e. $[[A]]\psi \equiv \neg\langle\langle A \rangle\rangle\neg\varphi$

Since ATL is a generalisation of CTL, we can use CTL as shorthand for some cases of ATL i.e. write $\forall\psi$ for $\langle\langle\emptyset\rangle\rangle\psi$ and $\exists\psi$ for $\langle\langle\Sigma\rangle\rangle\psi$. The logic ATL* generalises ATL in the same way that CTL* generalises CTL, namely by allowing path quantifiers and temporal operators to be nested arbitrarily.

2.3 ATL* Semantics

In ATL*, there are two types of formulae: *state formulae* are evaluated over states, and denoted here as φ; *path formulae* are evaluated over computation paths, and denoted ψ. To define the semantics of ATL*, the notion of *strategies* is used. A strategy for an agent a is a mapping $f_a : Q^+ \rightarrow 2^Q$ such that for all $\lambda \in Q^*$ and all $q \in Q$, we have $f_a(\lambda \cdot q) \in \delta(q,a)$. The strategies map finite prefixes of λ-computations to a choice in $\delta(q,a)$ as suggested by the strategy.

The *outcome* of a strategy must also be defined. For a state q, a set of agents A, and a family of strategies $F_A = \{f_a | a \in A\}$ the outcomes of F_A from q are denoted $out(q, F_A)$. They are the q-computations that the agents in A can enforce by following their strategies. $\lambda = q_0, q_1, q_2 \ldots$ is in $out(q, F_A)$ if $q = q_0$ and for all positions $i \geq 0$ q_{i+1} is a successor of q_i satisfying $q_{i+1} \in \bigcap_{a \in A} f_a(\lambda[0,i])$.

The semantics of ATL* are defined inductively:

- $\lambda \models p$ iff $p \in \pi(\lambda[0])$
- $\lambda \models \neg\varphi$ iff $\lambda \not\models \varphi$

[1] Following Lamport's warning that the X operator leads to over-specification [7] and for simplicity, we differ from [2] by omitting X.

- $\lambda \models \varphi_1 \vee \varphi_2$ iff $\lambda \models \varphi_1$ or $\lambda \models \varphi_2$
- $\lambda \models \varphi$ iff $\lambda[0] \models \varphi$, if φ is a state formula
- $\lambda \models \langle\langle A \rangle\rangle \psi$ iff there exists a set of strategies, F_A one for each agent in A, such that $\forall \lambda \in out(q, F_A)$, we have $\lambda \models \psi$
- $\lambda \models \psi_1 \,\mathcal{U}\, \psi_2$ iff $\exists i \geq 0. \lambda[i, \infty] \models \psi_2$ and $\forall 0 \leq j < i \lambda[j, \infty] \models \psi_1$.
- $\lambda \models \psi_1 \,\mathcal{R}\, \psi_2$ iff $\forall i \geq 0$, we have $\lambda[i, \infty] \models \psi_2$ unless there exists a position $0 \leq j < i$ such that $\lambda[j, \infty] \models \psi_1$.

3 Equivalences

These exact transformations are applied at the first stage of re-writing, to eliminate redundancy. In some cases, it is possible to perform the entire translation at this exact level. Discussion of how the rules are applied is deferred until Section 5.

We shall consider both $\wedge$ and $\vee$ as part of the basic language for our rule-set. The temporal operators we shall use are Until $\mathcal{U}$, Release $\mathcal{R}$. MOCHA accepts $\mathcal{U}$ but not $\mathcal{R}$. However, it does accept Weak Until (While). $\mathcal{W}$ and Release are related as follows:

$$\psi_1 \,\mathcal{R}\, \psi_2 \equiv \psi_2 \,\mathcal{W}\, (\psi_1 \wedge \psi_2) \qquad\qquad \psi_1 \,\mathcal{W}\, \psi_2 \equiv \psi_2 \,\mathcal{R}\, (\psi_2 \vee \psi_1) \tag{3.1}$$

Release is used because it is more natural to use the dual of Until and it can still be translated into acceptable input for MOCHA.

We assume that the input formula is in negation normal form, and this be easily achieved with known LTL and ATL identities.

3.1 LTL Equivalences

LTL equivalences can be used to replace parts of ATL* sub-formulae and also serve as inspiration for some native ATL* rules. Each rule is applied left to right and reduces the number of nested temporal operators. Some of the equivalences below are from [9], others extend or generalise them. Where a rule requires knowing that $\varphi_1 \Rightarrow \varphi_2$, this is established using the heuristic method described in [9].

Future and Global Equations 3.2 to 3.8 are generalised by 3.9 to 3.15, below. The F and G abbreviations are given to aid the intuition behind their generalisations. The duals are also used in practice, but omitted here.

$$\mathrm{FF}\varphi \equiv \mathrm{F}\varphi \tag{3.2}$$

$$\mathrm{FGF}\varphi \equiv \mathrm{GF}\varphi \tag{3.3}$$

$$\mathrm{F}(\varphi_1 \vee \mathrm{F}\varphi_2) \equiv \mathrm{F}(\varphi_1 \vee \varphi_2) \tag{3.4}$$

$$\mathrm{F}(\varphi_1 \vee \mathrm{GF}\varphi_2) \equiv \mathrm{F}\varphi_1 \vee \mathrm{GF}\varphi_2 \tag{3.5}$$

$$\mathrm{F}(\varphi_1 \wedge \mathrm{FG}\varphi_2) \equiv \mathrm{F}\varphi_1 \wedge \mathrm{FG}\varphi_2 \tag{3.6}$$

$$\mathrm{F}(\varphi_1 \wedge \mathrm{GF}\varphi_2) \equiv \mathrm{F}\varphi_1 \wedge \mathrm{GF}\varphi_2 \tag{3.7}$$

$$\mathrm{FG}(\varphi_1 \wedge \mathrm{F}\varphi_2) \equiv \mathrm{FG}\varphi_1 \wedge \mathrm{GF}\varphi_2 \tag{3.8}$$

Until and Release

$$\varphi_1 \Rightarrow \varphi_2 \vdash \varphi_1 \,\mathcal{U}\, (\varphi_2 \,\mathcal{U}\, \varphi_3) \equiv \varphi_2 \,\mathcal{U}\, \varphi_3 \tag{3.9}$$

$$\varphi_1 \,\mathcal{U}\, (\varphi_2 \,\mathcal{R}\, (\varphi_1 \,\mathcal{U}\, \varphi_3)) \equiv \varphi_2 \,\mathcal{R}\, (\varphi_1 \,\mathcal{U}\, \varphi_3) \tag{3.10}$$

$$\varphi_1 \,\mathcal{U}\, (\varphi_2 \vee \varphi_1 \,\mathcal{U}\, \varphi_3) \equiv \varphi_1 \,\mathcal{U}\, (\varphi_2 \vee \varphi_3) \tag{3.11}$$

$$\varphi_1 \,\mathcal{U}\, (\varphi_2 \vee \varphi_3 \,\mathcal{R}\, (\varphi_1 \,\mathcal{U}\, \varphi_4)) \equiv \varphi_1 \,\mathcal{U}\, \varphi_2 \vee \varphi_3 \,\mathcal{R}\, (\varphi_1 \,\mathcal{U}\, \varphi_4) \tag{3.12}$$

$$\varphi_1 \Rightarrow \neg\varphi_3 \vdash \varphi_1 \,\mathcal{U}\, (\varphi_2 \wedge (\varphi_1 \,\mathcal{U}\, (\varphi_3 \,\mathcal{R}\, \varphi_4))) \equiv (\varphi_1 \,\mathcal{U}\, \varphi_2) \wedge (\varphi_1 \,\mathcal{U}\, (\varphi_3 \,\mathcal{R}\, \varphi_4) \tag{3.13}$$

$$\begin{aligned} &\varphi_1 \Rightarrow (\varphi_4 \vee \varphi_5), \varphi_1 \Rightarrow \neg\varphi_3 \vdash \\ &\qquad \varphi_1 \,\mathcal{U}\, (\varphi_2 \wedge \varphi_3 \,\mathcal{R}\, (\varphi_4 \,\mathcal{U}\, \varphi_5)) \equiv (\varphi_1 \,\mathcal{U}\, \varphi_2) \wedge (\varphi_3 \,\mathcal{R}\, (\varphi_4 \,\mathcal{U}\, \varphi_5)) \end{aligned} \tag{3.14}$$

$$\varphi_1 \Rightarrow \neg\varphi_2 \vdash \varphi_1 \,\mathcal{U}\, (\varphi_2 \,\mathcal{R}\, (\varphi_3 \wedge \varphi_1 \,\mathcal{U}\, \varphi_4)) \equiv \varphi_1 \,\mathcal{U}\, (\varphi_2 \,\mathcal{R}\, (\varphi_3 \wedge \varphi_4)) \tag{3.15}$$

$$(\varphi_1 \,\mathcal{U}\, \psi) \wedge (\varphi_2 \,\mathcal{U}\, \psi) \equiv (\varphi_1 \wedge \varphi_2) \,\mathcal{U}\, \psi \tag{3.16}$$

$$\varphi \Rightarrow \psi \vdash \varphi \,\mathcal{U}\, \psi \equiv \psi \tag{3.17}$$

3.2 ATL* Equivalences

If ψ_1 and ψ_2 are ATL path formulae, then neither $\langle\!\langle A \rangle\!\rangle(\psi_1 \wedge \psi_2)$ nor $\langle\!\langle A \rangle\!\rangle(\psi_1 \vee \psi_2)$ are well-formed ATL formulae. However, just as there is an extension of CTL to allow boolean combinations of path formulae, we can similarly extend ATL. In CTL, the extension is called CTL$^+$ so we shall define an ATL$^+$ formula φ as:

$$\begin{aligned} \varphi &::= p \mid \top \mid \neg\varphi \mid \varphi_1 \vee \varphi_2 \mid \langle\!\langle A \rangle\!\rangle(\psi) \\ \psi &::= \varphi \mid \neg\psi \mid \psi_1 \vee \psi_2 \mid \varphi_1 \,\mathcal{U}\, \varphi_2 \mid \varphi_1 \,\mathcal{R}\, \varphi_2 \end{aligned}$$

It has been proved that CTL$^+$ is no more expressive than CTL [5], we show that this extends to ATL$^+$ and ATL by providing a translation procedure.

State Formulae A state formula occurring directly under a path quantifier is equivalent to the same formula outside the path quantifier e.g. $\langle\!\langle A \rangle\!\rangle p \Leftrightarrow p$. This is clear from the semantics of $\langle\!\langle A \rangle\!\rangle\psi$.

More generally, we can pull state formulae out from any boolean combination of path and state formulae by rewriting to disjunctive normal form and applying the following rule:

$$\langle\!\langle A \rangle\!\rangle((\varphi_1 \wedge \psi_1) \vee \ldots \vee (\varphi_n \wedge \psi_n)) \equiv \bigvee_{\emptyset \neq T \subseteq [1,n]} \left(\bigwedge_{k \in T} \varphi_k \wedge \langle\!\langle A \rangle\!\rangle \bigvee_{k \in T} \psi_k \right) \tag{3.18}$$

Where the φs are state formulae and the ψs are "pure" path formulae i.e. path formulae which are not state formulae and have no state formulae joined to them with boolean operators. Although putting something in DNF can produce an exponential increase in its size, we are only concerned about whether elements are state formulae or path formulae. Thus, $(p_1 \wedge p_2 \wedge \mathrm{F}p_3 \wedge \mathrm{G}p_4) \vee (q_1 \wedge Fq_2)$ is acceptable because $p_1 \wedge p_2$ is a state formula and $\mathrm{F}p_3 \wedge \mathrm{G}p_4$ is a path formula.

To see why 3.18 is valid, suppose $q \models \langle\!\langle A \rangle\!\rangle((\varphi_1 \wedge \psi_1) \vee \ldots \vee (\varphi_n \wedge \psi_n))$. There exists $n \geq i \geq 0$ such that $q \models \varphi_i$. We can say that $q \models \bigvee_{\emptyset \neq T \subseteq [1,n]} \bigwedge_{k \in T} \varphi_k$ i.e. At least one of the state formulae is true. Intuitively, if only one is is true, then A can enforce its paired path formula. If a subset T, are true then A can enforce at least one of the paired path formulae. This is exactly what the right hand side of the equivalence states.

Path Formulae Let ψ be a path formula made from boolean combinations of $\mathcal{U}$s and $\mathcal{R}$s. Let E be a function that retuns the set of $\mathcal{U}$ and $\mathcal{R}$ expressions in a path formula like ψ e.g. If $\psi = (\varphi_1 \, \mathcal{U} \, \varphi_2 \wedge \varphi_3 \, \mathcal{U} \, \varphi_4 \wedge (\varphi_5 \, \mathcal{U} \, \varphi_6 \vee \varphi_7 \, \mathcal{U} \, \varphi_8))$ then $E(\psi) = \{\varphi_1 \, \mathcal{U} \, \varphi_2, \varphi_3 \, \mathcal{U} \, \varphi_4, \varphi_5 \, \mathcal{U} \, \varphi_6, \varphi_7 \, \mathcal{U} \, \varphi_8\}$. To deal uniformly with $\mathcal{U}$ and $\mathcal{R}$ we define auxiliary functions on temporal formulae:

$sat(\varphi)$ is, intuitively, the formula that ensures definitive satisfaction of a temporal formula, φ:

$$sat(\varphi_1 \, \mathcal{U} \, \varphi_2) = \varphi_2$$
$$sat(\varphi_1 \, \mathcal{R} \, \varphi_2) = \varphi_1 \wedge \varphi_2$$

$wait(\varphi)$ is the formula that allows satisfaction to be postponed:

$$wait(\varphi_1 \, \mathcal{U} \, \varphi_2) = \varphi_1$$
$$wait(\varphi_1 \, \mathcal{R} \, \varphi_2) = \varphi_2$$

We say that a formula is *eventual*, intuitively, if it implies an eventual satisfaction:

$$ev(\varphi_1 \, \mathcal{U} \, \varphi_2) = \top$$
$$ev(\varphi_1 \, \mathcal{R} \, \varphi_2) = \bot$$
$$ev(\varphi_1 \wedge \varphi_2) = ev(\varphi_1) \vee ev(\varphi_2)$$
$$ev(\varphi_1 \vee \varphi_2) = ev(\varphi_1) \wedge ev(\varphi_2)$$

If φ is eventual, we translate towards ATL as follows:

$$\langle\!\langle A \rangle\!\rangle\psi \equiv \langle\!\langle A \rangle\!\rangle((\bigwedge_{e \in E(\psi)} wait(e)) \, \mathcal{U} \, (\bigvee_{e \in E(\psi)} (\langle\!\langle A \rangle\!\rangle(\psi[e := \bot])) \vee \bigvee_{e \in E(\psi)} (sat(e) \wedge \langle\!\langle A \rangle\!\rangle(\psi[e := \top])))) \quad (3.19)$$

Where $\psi[e := \bot]$ is ψ with the occurence of e substituted for $\bot$. If φ is not eventual, we simply replace the "until" by a "weak until" that does not entail eventuality:

$$\langle\!\langle A \rangle\!\rangle\varphi \equiv \langle\!\langle A \rangle\!\rangle((\bigwedge_{e \in E(\psi)} wait(e)) \, \mathcal{W} \, (\bigvee_{e \in E(\psi)} (\langle\!\langle A \rangle\!\rangle(\psi[e := \bot])) \vee \bigvee_{e \in E(\psi)} (sat(e) \wedge \langle\!\langle A \rangle\!\rangle(\psi[e := \top])))) \quad (3.20)$$

This pattern must then be called recursively for each cooperation sub-formula. Note that this recursion will generate several occurrences of a same formula, for instance $\varphi[e_1 := \top][e_2 := \top][e_3 := \top]$ will occurs 3! times, according to the possible orders in which e_1, e_2, e_3 can be satisfied. In an implementation, re-computing the translation for the identical subtrees can be avoided by memoisation.

Proof. (3.19) Suppose $q \models \langle\langle A\rangle\rangle\psi$ where ψ is of the form described above. Then there exists a set of strategies, F_A one for each agent in A, such that $\forall\lambda \in out(q, F_A)\ \lambda \models \psi$. Assume ψ is eventual (otherwise, we use 3.20). Let $\lambda[i]$ be the first point such that there exists some $e \in E(\psi)$ where $\lambda[i] \models sat(e) \vee (\neg wait(e) \wedge \neg sat(e))$ i.e. e is satisfied or eliminated. Since ψ is eventual, this point exists. We can say that $\forall j.i > j \geq 0 \forall e_i \in E(\psi)\ \lambda[j] \models wait(e_i)$ because $\lambda \models \psi$ and i is the *first* point such that $\lambda[i] \models sat(e) \vee (\neg wait(e) \wedge \neg sat(e))$.

- If $\lambda[i] \models sat(e)$, we prove that $\lambda \models \bigwedge_{e_i \in E(\psi)} wait(e_i)\,\mathcal{U}\,(sat(e) \wedge \langle\langle A\rangle\rangle(\psi[e := \top]))$. There exists a point $k \geq 0$ such that $\lambda[k] \models sat(e) \wedge \langle\langle A\rangle\rangle(\psi[e := \top])$. In fact, $k = i$ because $\lambda[i] \models sat(e)$ and we can construct a set of strategies G_A such that $\forall\mu \in out(\lambda[i], G_A)\ \mu \models \psi[e := \top]$. For all agents $a \in A$, we define $g_a(\lambda[i, n]) = f_a(\lambda[0, n])$. Even after e has been satisfied, F_A must ensure any other obligations of ψ are met. G_A can use this to ensure that all μs satisfy $\psi[e := \top]$. We have already seen that $\forall j.i > j \geq 0,\ \lambda[j] \models \bigwedge_{e_i \in E(\psi)} wait(e_i)$.
- If $\lambda[i] \models \neg wait(e) \wedge \neg sat(e)$, we prove that $\lambda \models \bigwedge_{e_i \in E(\psi)} wait(e_i)\,\mathcal{U}\,(\langle\langle A\rangle\rangle\psi[e := \bot])$. There exists a point $k \geq 0$ such that $\lambda[k] \models \langle\langle A\rangle\rangle\psi[e := \bot]$. Again, $k = i$ because we can construct a set of strategies G_A such that $\forall\mu \in out(\lambda[i], G_A)\ \mu \models \psi[e := \bot]$. For all agents $a \in A$, we define $g_a(\lambda[i, n]) = f_a(\lambda[0, n])$. e must not have been a requirement of ψ and once it has been seen to be false, F_A must still be able to enforce its other obligations. Again, we have already seen that $\forall i > j \geq 0,\ \lambda[j] \models \bigwedge_{e_i \in E(\psi)} wait(e_i)$.

Now we show the converse: For brevity, call the right hand side of Equation 3.19 $\langle\langle A\rangle\rangle\Phi$. Suppose $q \models q \models \langle\langle A\rangle\rangle\Phi$. Then there exists a set of strategies, F_A one for each agent in A, such that $\forall\lambda \in out(q, F_A)\ \ \lambda \models \Phi$. Let $\lambda[i]$ be the first point on λ such that there exists $e \in E(\psi)$ where $\lambda[i] \models \langle\langle A\rangle\rangle(\psi[e := \bot])$ or $\lambda[i] \models sat(e) \wedge \langle\langle A\rangle\rangle(\psi[e := \top])$.

- Suppose $\lambda[i] \models \langle\langle A\rangle\rangle(\psi[e := \bot])$, let $G_{A\lambda[i]}$ be the set of strategies to enforce $\psi[e := \bot]$ from $\lambda[i]$. We show that there exists a set of strategies H_A such that $\forall\mu \in out(q, H_A)\ \mu \models \psi$. Since $\psi[e := \bot] \Rightarrow \psi$, then $\lambda[i] \models \langle\langle A\rangle\rangle\psi$. Thus we can define H_A as the concatenation of F_A with a suitable $G_{a\lambda[i]}$. The wait conditions for all $e_i \in E(\psi)$ will hold up to $\lambda[i]$ and then $G_{A\lambda[i]}$ gives the strategy to ensure ψ from there.
- Suppose $\lambda[i] \models sat(e) \wedge \langle\langle A\rangle\rangle(\psi[e := \top])$, let $G_{A\lambda[i]}$ be the set of strategies to enforce $\psi[e := \top]$ from $\lambda[i]$. We show that there exists a set of strategies H_A such that $\forall\mu \in out(q, H_A)\ \mu \models \psi$. For this case, $sat(e) \wedge \langle\langle A\rangle\rangle(\psi[e := \top]) \Rightarrow \langle\langle A\rangle\rangle\psi$. We can create H_A by concatenating sets of strategies, as before.

□

4 Approximations

These approximations are applied when no more equivalences can be used on a formula. Again, they are applied left to right and match temporal operators with path quantifiers. The ψs in each rule represent ATL* path formulae. Each approximation produces a strong or a weak bound, which is closer to being in ATL than the original (one nested temporal operator is paired with a path quantifier). Details on how these are used follow in Section 5.

$$\langle\langle A\rangle\rangle(\psi_1\,\mathcal{U}\,\psi_2) \Rightarrow \langle\langle A\rangle\rangle(\langle\langle A\rangle\rangle\psi_1\,\mathcal{U}\,\exists\psi_2) \qquad \langle\langle A\rangle\rangle(\psi_1\,\mathcal{R}\,\psi_2) \Leftarrow \langle\langle A\rangle\rangle(\langle\langle A\rangle\rangle\psi_1\,\mathcal{R}\,\forall\psi_2) \quad (4.1)$$

$$\langle\langle A\rangle\rangle(\psi_1\,\mathcal{U}\,\psi_2) \Leftarrow \langle\langle A\rangle\rangle(\forall\psi_1\,\mathcal{U}\,\langle\langle A\rangle\rangle\psi_2) \qquad \langle\langle A\rangle\rangle(\psi_1\,\mathcal{R}\,\psi_2) \Rightarrow \langle\langle A\rangle\rangle(\exists\psi_1\,\mathcal{R}\,\langle\langle A\rangle\rangle\psi_2) \quad (4.2)$$

$$\psi_3 \Rightarrow \psi_1 \vdash \langle\langle A\rangle\rangle(\psi_1\,\mathcal{U}\,(\psi_2\,\mathcal{R}\,\psi_3)) \Rightarrow \exists(\langle\langle A\rangle\rangle\psi_1\,\mathcal{U}\,\langle\langle A\rangle\rangle(\psi_2\,\mathcal{R}\,\psi_3)) \wedge \langle\langle A\rangle\rangle(\langle\langle A\rangle\rangle\psi_1\,\mathcal{U}\,\exists(\psi_2\,\mathcal{R}\,\psi_3)) \quad (4.3)$$

$$\psi_1 \Rightarrow \psi_3 \vdash \langle\langle A\rangle\rangle(\psi_1\,\mathcal{R}\,(\psi_2\,\mathcal{U}\,\psi_3)) \Leftarrow \forall(\langle\langle A\rangle\rangle\psi_1\,\mathcal{R}\,\langle\langle A\rangle\rangle(\psi_2\,\mathcal{U}\,\psi_3)) \vee \langle\langle A\rangle\rangle(\langle\langle A\rangle\rangle\psi_1\,\mathcal{R}\,\forall(\psi_2\,\mathcal{U}\,\psi_3)) \quad (4.4)$$

Proof. (4.4) We only deal with one side of the disjunction because the other is an application of 4.2. Suppose $q \vDash \forall(\langle\langle A\rangle\rangle\psi_1\,\mathcal{R}\,\langle\langle A\rangle\rangle(\psi_2\,\mathcal{U}\,\psi_3))$. Then, for all computation paths λ, beginning at q, $\forall i \geq 0\ \lambda[i] \vDash \langle\langle A\rangle\rangle(\psi_2\,\mathcal{U}\,\psi_3)$ unless $\exists 0 \leq j < i.\lambda[j] \vDash \langle\langle A\rangle\rangle\psi_1$. Let $F_{A\,s}$ be the set of strategies for the agents in A to enforce $(\psi_2\,\mathcal{U}\,\psi_3)$ from a state $s \vDash \langle\langle A\rangle\rangle\psi_2\,\mathcal{U}\,\psi_3$. Let $G_{A\,s}$ be the set of strategies for the agents in A to enforce ψ_1 from a state $s \vDash \psi_1$. We can construct a set of strategies, $H_A = \{h_a \mid a \in A\}$ such that $\forall\mu \in out(q, H_A)\ \mu \vDash \psi_1\,\mathcal{R}\,(\psi_2\,\mathcal{U}\,\psi_3)$ as follows:

$$h_a(q_0,\ldots,q_n) = \begin{cases} \textbf{if } \exists i \leq n.q_i \vDash \langle\langle A\rangle\rangle\psi_1 \\ \quad \textbf{then } g_{a\,q_i}(q_i,\ldots,q_n) \\ \textbf{else } f_{a\,q_n}(q_n) \end{cases}$$

Intuitively, we use F_A until it becomes possible to use G_A. By repeatedly applying F_A, every path starting from the states up to $q_i \vDash \langle\langle A\rangle\rangle\psi_1$ satisfies $\psi_2 \vee \psi_3$. As long as this path ends with ψ_3, then it satisfies $\psi_2\,\mathcal{U}\,\psi_3$. The pre-condition that $\psi_1 \Rightarrow \psi_3$ ensures that this is so when G_A takes over. □

5 Termination and Complexity

The rewrite rules given above provide a framework for translating formulae from ATL* into ATL. The general pattern is to use equivalences as far as possible; then approximate to a strong and a weak bound. The process continues by repeating this for each bound until they are well-formed ATL.

Termination The process always terminates. To prove this, consider each group of rules:

1. LTL equivalences - Every rule reduces the number of nested temporal operators. There can only be finitely many of them, so the process terminates.
2. ATL* equivalences - The state formulae part is performed in one step. The path formulae part is called recursively but it will terminate since the number of path formulae joined with boolean operators is reduced by one at each call. Neither of these increase the number of nested temporal operators, so they do not interact with the other rules to create a loop.
3. ATL* approximations - Every rule reduces the number of nested temporal operators.

Completeness It is clear that the set of rules given will allow any ATL* formula to be translated into two ATL approximations. Any ATL^+ part can be removed, to leave only nested temporal operators. These operators can be dealt with using rules 4.1 and 4.2. The addition of extra rules for special cases serve to make the approximations more accurate.

Complexity The size of the resulting formula may be exponentially larger than the original. This is unavoidable in translating from ATL^+ to ATL. Wilke [12] showed that the lower bound for a CTL^+ formula being written into CTL is exponential. Clearly, rewriting ATL^+ and ATL will be at least as hard.

The exponential increase occurs due to sub-formulae being replicated in the translation process. In practice, these duplicate subtrees can be translated just once by using memoisation. This reduces the time needed for translation, and the isomorphic subtrees can be dealt with quickly in the symbolic model checking algorithm used by MOCHA.

6 Examples

To adequately measure our technique, it is not enough to just translate some formulae and look at the results. The real use or lack thereof comes from the result of model-checking translated properties against models.

An existing project[2] [4] has tried to ease the difficulty of writing temporal logic specifications. They identify a number of common patterns drawn from a range of application domains and provide these as templates. For example, the property *"p becomes true between q and r"* can be written in LTL as $\mathrm{G}(q \wedge \neg r \rightarrow (\neg r\ \mathcal{W}\ (p \wedge \neg r)))$. These patterns provide a level of complexity which is as deep as hand-written specifications are likely to be, thus provide a realistic setting to test our technique.

Although we have applied the technique to three systems, one has been chosen for inclusion here. Aside from the telephone system below, we also worked with a

[2] `http://www.cis.ksu.edu/santos/spec-patterns/`

mutual exclusion algorithm and a distributed consensus protocol. The telephone system was chosen because it had already been coded before this work (making it a more realistic test) and because it has interesting results.

6.1 Feature Interaction in a Telephone System

The model for this case study is one developed for a paper on proving Feature Non-Interaction in ATL [3] and as such, had a pre-written MOCHA model. Some of the specifications given in the paper were in ATL*, so they could not be checked at the time. Here, we translate the properties with our method and comment on the results.

The basic system was the Plain Old Telephone System (POTS) – Four phones and an exchange can interact to make calls in the familiar way. Then features were added with a construct described in the paper. For POTS itself, there are some basic properties to check; for the featured system, we examine the Call Forward on Busy feature. The results are summarised in Table 2.

To illustrate the translation process, the derivation of one property is given below. "*The user cannot change the callee without replacing the handset.*" Although the original property was successfully checked with our method, a variant given below gives a better illustration of how the translation works. Instead of using a $\mathcal{W}$ operator, we follow a specification pattern from [4] "Existence between p and r".

$p \equiv$ `i.callee=j` $q \equiv$ `i.trying` $r \equiv$ `i.idle`	} Renaming
$[[i]]\mathrm{G}(p \wedge q \rightarrow (p \,\mathcal{W}\, r))$	Original property from [3]
$[[i]]\mathrm{G}(p \wedge q \wedge \mathrm{F}r \rightarrow (p \,\mathcal{U}\, r))$	Same property, expressed using pattern from [4]
$[[i]]\mathrm{G}(\neg p \vee \neg q \vee \mathrm{G}\neg r \vee (p \,\mathcal{U}\, r))$	Negation Normal Form
$[[i]]\mathrm{G}\forall(\neg p \vee \neg q \vee \mathrm{G}\neg r \vee (p \,\mathcal{U}\, r))$	Approximation using Eq 4.1
$[[i]]\mathrm{G}(\neg p \vee \neg q \vee \forall(\mathrm{G}\neg r \vee (p \,\mathcal{U}\, r)))$	Equivalence using Eq 3.18
$[[i]]\mathrm{G}(\neg p \vee \neg q \vee \forall((p \wedge \neg r) \,\mathcal{W}\, (([[i]](p \,\mathcal{U}\, r)) \vee [[i]]\mathrm{G}\neg r)))$	Equivalence using Eq 3.20

The unknown result for the third property is a little disappointing, but this is actually an inaccurate specification. It doesn't allow for j putting the phone down whilst the call-forwarding is being resolved. If we add this to the formula, and check a new strong bound:

$\langle\langle i\rangle\rangle$`F`$\langle\langle i\rangle\rangle$`G(j.trying & j.callee=i & !i.idle`

```
        -> A (j.trying U ((j.trying & j.callee=k) | !j.offhook))
```

We find that the property is **true** – Call Forward on Busy has been implemented correctly. The translation method did not help in coming to this conclusion, other than by forcing consideration on why the original strong bound was false.

Table 2. Results of Translating and Model Checking for POTS and POTS+CFB

<table>
<tr><td colspan="3">Any phone may call any other phone (POTS)</td></tr>
<tr><td>Original</td><td><code>⟨⟨i, j⟩⟩ G F (i.talking & i.callee=j)</code></td><td>n/a</td></tr>
<tr><td>Strong</td><td><code>∀ G ⟨⟨i, j⟩⟩ F (i.talking & i.callee=j)</code></td><td>T</td></tr>
<tr><td>Conclusion</td><td>Original is true</td><td></td></tr>
<tr><td colspan="3">The user cannot change the callee without replacing the handset (POTS)</td></tr>
<tr><td>Original</td><td><code>[[i]] G (i.callee=j & i.trying & F i.idle
-> (i.callee=j U i.idle))</code></td><td>n/a</td></tr>
<tr><td>Strong</td><td><code>[[i]] G (!i.callee=j | !i.trying
| A ((i.callee=j & !i.idle) W
(([[i]] (i.callee=j U i.idle)) | ([[i]] G !i.idle)))</code></td><td>T</td></tr>
<tr><td>Conclusion</td><td>Original is true</td><td></td></tr>
<tr><td colspan="3">If user[i] is busy, they can force a call from j to be forwarded to k (POTS+CFB)</td></tr>
<tr><td>Original</td><td><code>⟨⟨i⟩⟩F G (j.trying & j.callee=i & !i.idle
-> j.trying U (j.trying & j.callee=k))</code></td><td>n/a</td></tr>
<tr><td>Strong</td><td><code>⟨⟨i⟩⟩F ⟨⟨i⟩⟩ G (j.trying & j.callee=i & !i.idle
-> ∀ (j.trying U (j.trying & j.callee=k)))</code></td><td>F</td></tr>
<tr><td>Weak</td><td><code>⟨⟨i⟩⟩F E G (j.trying & j.callee=i & !i.idle
-> ⟨⟨i⟩⟩ (j.trying U (j.trying & j.callee=k)))</code></td><td>T</td></tr>
<tr><td>Conclusion</td><td>No result</td><td></td></tr>
</table>

7 Conclusions and Related Work

Given a specification in ATL*, our method produces bounds in ATL which are guaranteed to be correct (i.e. the strong bound implies the original and the weak bound is implied by it). Although it is current practice for professionals using model-checking to perform mentally an approximation process similar to ours, and to write only a (weakened) CTL formula, we believe that is a better practice to write the simpler, more readable ATL* formula and, due to the risk of errors in the translation, perform the approximation automatically. Since ATL* contains CTL*, our algorithm can also be applied to CTL* formulae, and will then yield CTL formulae.

In Cadence SMV [11], specifications are written in LTL and then translated to CTL in order to perform symbolic model checking. Direct conversions are used where possible, otherwise new variables are introduced into the model to characterise the parts which cannot be translated. We intend to investigate this idea in the context of ATL.

References

[1] R. Alur, T. A. Henzinger, S. C. Krishnan, et al. *Mocha User Manual.* Computer and Information Science Department, University of Pennsylvania and Electrical

Engineering and Computer Sciences Department, University of California, Nov. 1999.

[2] R. Alur, T. A. Henzinger, and O. Kupferman. Alternating-time temporal logic. In *Proceedings of the 38th Annual Symposium on Foundations of Computer Science*, pages 100–109. IEEE Computer Society Press, 1997.

[3] F. Cassez, M. D. Ryan, and P.-Y. Schobbens. Proving feature non-interaction with alternating-time temporal logic. In S. Gilmore and M. D. Ryan, editors, *Language Constructs for Describing Features*. Springer-Verlag, 2000.

[4] M. B. Dwyer, G. S. Avrunin, and J. C. Corbett. Patterns in property specifications for finite-state verification. In *Proceedings of the 21st International Conference on Software Engineering*, May 1999.

[5] E. A. Emerson and J. Y. Halpern. Decision procedures and expressiveness in the temporal logic of branching time. *Journal of Computer and System Sciences*, 30(1):1–25, Feb. 1985.

[6] L. Lamport. "Sometimes" is sometimes "not never" - on the temporal logic of programs. In *Proc. 7th ACM Symposium on Principles of Programming Languages*, pages 174–185, Jan. 1980.

[7] L. Lamport. What good is temporal logic? In R. E. A. Mason, editor, *Proceedings of the IFIP Congress on Information Processing*, pages 657–667. North-Holland, 1983.

[8] T. Laureys. From event based semantics to linear temporal logic. Master's thesis, School of Cognitive Science - University of Edinburgh, 2 Buccleuch Place, Edinburgh, UK, 1999.

[9] F. Somenzi and R. Bloem. Efficient Büchi automata from LTL formulae. In *Proceedings of 10th International Conference on Computer Aided Verification*, pages 248–263. Springer-Verlag, 2000.

[10] Mocha. `http://www-cad.eecs.berkeley.edu/~tah/mocha/`.

[11] SMV. `http://www-cad.eecs.berkeley.edu/~kenmcmil/smv/`.

[12] T. Wilke. CTL^+ is exponentially more succinct than CTL. In C. P. R. et al., editor, *Foundations of Software Technology and Theoretical Computer Science (FSTTCS)*, volume 1738 of *Lecture Notes in Computer Science*, pages 110–121. Springer Verlag, 1999.

Model Checking Modal Transition Systems Using Kripke Structures

Michael Huth

Department of Computing, Imperial College of Science, Technology and Medicine
mrh@doc.ic.ac.uk

Abstract. We reduce the modal mu-calculus model-checking problem for Kripke modal transition systems to the modal mu-calculus model-checking problem for Kripke structures. This reduction is sound, preserves the alternation-depth fragments of the modal mu-calculus, is linear in the size of formulas and models, and extends the reach of modal mu-calculus model checkers to sound abstraction for the full logic. These results specialize to CTL* model-checking and CTL model checking.

1 Introduction

Model-based property verification of software inescapably has to mitigate computational complexities whose roots are the concurrent interaction of communicating programs and the size and structure of data types. Abstraction is widely recognized as a key technology in containing these complexities (e.g. [2,10,12,15,18,22,31,32]). Since todays software depends on a high degree of communication and reactiveness, property verification can only succeed if reasonable assumptions are being made about thread scheduling, the access policies to resources, progress conditions on communication, etc. Filter-based refinement [19] and fairness conditions [21] are well established and widely practiced approaches of formalizing and enforcing such additional assumptions about the interaction of software systems. The model checker SMV [26], for example, supports simple fairness constraints [8,9] that reduce state-space exploration to those paths on which a finite number of CTL formulas hold infinitely often. The modal mu-calculus of alternation depth 2 serves as a target specification language that can express (branching-time) filter-based refinement, CTL, CTL*, CTL with simple fairness constraints, and many other properties that need to be expressible in the verification of reactive software, such as "event p occurs at every other state" [20]. Although that fragment ($k = 2$) delineates, for most practitioners, the realm of property-verification applications, we present our technical work on the abstraction-based verification of concurrent, reactive software for arbitrary alternation-depth fragments ($k \geq 0$) of the modal mu-calculus. In [16], it has been recognized that the sound use of fairness assumptions for abstraction-based reasoning has to be exercised with some care and a sound three-valued solution for fair CTL* has been given. Although universal and existential properties can each be soundly abstracted with a corresponding notion of simulation

A. Cortesi (Ed.): VMCAI 2002, LNCS 2294, pp. 302–316, 2002.
© Springer-Verlag Berlin Heidelberg 2002

[29,33], more complex notions of refinement are required for the sound abstraction of their combinations [14,31,13] — examples being the symbolic encoding of CTL model checking with simple fairness constraints [8], and the use of logical implication for filter-based refinement in a branching-time logic.

In this paper, we re-examine this delicate but important combination of abstraction techniques and property verification for the modal mu-calculus and its alternation depth fragments in general. We use Kripke modal transition systems [23] (Kripke MTSs) as our designated models for abstraction-based model checking [22] which — being three-valued versions of doubly-labeled transition systems [17] — are expressive models for under-specified, or under-determined systems. The intent of our work is predominantly pragmatic in nature in that we mean to reduce the model-checking problem for Kripke MTSs to existing ones (Kripke structures), allowing the instrumented re-use of tools. Kripke MTSs are designed to guarantee soundness for abstraction-based model checking of arbitrary formulas of the modal mu-calculus [23].[1] This class of models encompasses important classes of qualitative models that have three-valued specifications — be they on transitions [27], state propositions [6] or expressed through divergence [30]. Consequently, a model checking reduction for Kripke MTSs applies to these models as well; see Figure 1.[2] The Kripke structures computed in our model-checking reduction can be described and checked (for CTL) in tools such as SMV [26] and extensions of Spin, e.g. tools that implement non-emptiness checking for hesitant alternating automata [36].

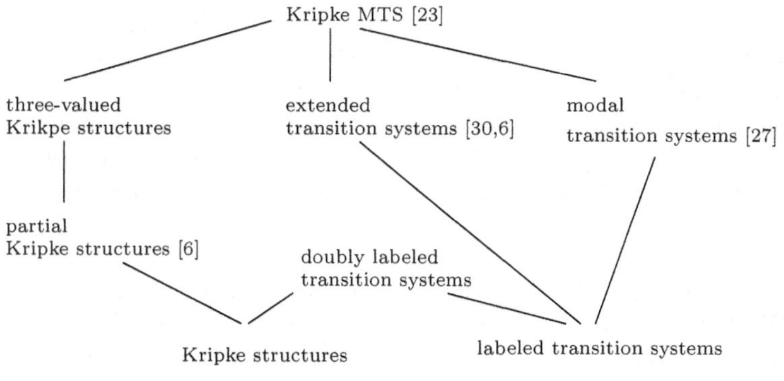

Fig. 1. A Hasse diagram of classes of two-valued (doubly labeled transition systems, Kripke structures, and labeled transition systems) and three-valued (all other classes) models, where the order represents class inclusion up to isomorphism.

[1] Similar guarantees have already been established for quantified logics with negation, e.g [6,13,31].

[2] Three valued Kripke structures are Kripke MTS with a sole action type.

Main results. The principal contributions of this paper are that we reduce the model-checking problem of the modal mu-calculus for Kripke MTSs to a model-checking problem of the modal mu-calculus for Kripke structures with an extended/collapsed signature. This reduction is linear in the size of models and formulas. For formulas, it leaves their entire recursion structure, and therefore their alternation depth, invariant. In particular, a model check of a Kripke MTS turns out to be no more complex than a model check of the resulting Kripke structure. Although our results apply to all fragments of the modal mu-calculus, the fragments of alternation depth 1 and 2 have practical importance. For example, for alternation depth 1, we get a reduction of model checking CTL over Kripke MTSs to model checking CTL over Kripke structures, at no additional cost.

Related work. In [7], Bruns & Godefroid pioneered such a programme for partial Kripke structures [6] (see Figure 1), which are three-valued versions of Kripke structures in that atomic propositions at states are either false, true, or undetermined. They transform such a structure into two Kripke structures and a model mu-calculus formula into one in positive normal form. Their model-checking reduction is sound and complete and does not increase the size of the models, nor the cost of the model check. We merely generalize such a result to the class of Kripke MTSs, which subsumes the class of partial Kripke structures and other three-valued classes of models (see Figure 1). Although it is possible that there is a direct translation from Kripke MTSs into partial Kripke structures, we do not know of any one in the literature. Even if such a translation exists, it is of interest to study the explicit nature of alternative translations, notably with respect to their capacity of preserving the "modalities" of paths (must-paths and may-paths [34]) — which would allow for the algorithmic separation of fairness constraints — and their ability of providing useful debugging information. Our reduction proceeds in two stages, one of which is a straightforward adaptation of a reduction of model-checking modal transition systems to model-checking labeled transition systems [22].

Outline of paper. In Section 2, we define doubly labeled transition systems (DLTSs) and Kripke MTSs, and two, mutually recursive, property semantics for Kripke MTSs — one for assertion checks and one for consistency checks. We mention that assertion checks on abstract Kripke MTSs are sound for all formulas of the underlying logic and that both semantics preserve the usual DeMorgan laws. Section 3 presents, for sake of illustration, the usual encoding of CTL with simple fairness constraints in the modal mu-calculus of alternation depth 2, and notes that its conversion into positive normal form won't change its meaning over Kripke MTSs. In Section 4, we first present two corresponding linear transformations of models and formulas: a transformation of a Kripke MTS into two DLTSs, and a transformation of a modal mu-calculus formula ϕ into a modal mu-calculus formula $T(\phi^+)$; both transformations extend the signature. Second, we describe a linear transformation that turns a DLTS into a Kripke structure with extended/collapsed signature and a modal mu-calculus formula ϕ into a modal mu-calculus formula $K(\phi)$. We prove that these transformations, and therefore their compositions, preserve meaning. In Section 5, we analyze the time complexity of model checking the Kripke structures constructed in this manner; it is no greater than the time complexity of model checking Kripke structures whose size equals that of the original Kripke MTS. Section 6 discusses, for sake of illustration, how one can or cannot separate fairness from the actual model check. Section 7 discusses related work and Section 8 concludes.

2 Abstraction-Based Model-Checking Using Kripke MTSs

We begin with defining the models of interest.

Definition 1 (Doubly labeled transition systems and Kripke MTSs).

1. *A* doubly labeled transition system *[17] (DLTS) $\mathcal{L}$ with signature* $(\mathtt{Act}, \mathtt{AP})$ *is a tuple (Σ, R, L), where Σ is a set of states,* $\mathtt{Act}$ *is a (countable) set of action symbols,* $\mathtt{AP}$ *is a (countable) set of atomic propositions, R is a transition relation with $R \subseteq \Sigma \times \mathtt{Act} \times \Sigma$, and L is a labeling function $L\colon \Sigma \to \mathcal{P}(\mathtt{AP})$.*
2. *A* Kripke modal transition system *[23] (Kripke MTS) with signature* $(\mathtt{Act}, \mathtt{AP})$ *is a pair $(\mathcal{M}^{\mathrm{a}}, \mathcal{M}^{\mathrm{c}})$ of DLTSs $\mathcal{M}^{\mathrm{a}} = (\Sigma, R^{\mathrm{a}}, L^{\mathrm{a}})$ and $\mathcal{M}^{\mathrm{c}} = (\Sigma, R^{\mathrm{c}}, L^{\mathrm{c}})$ with signature* $(\mathtt{Act}, \mathtt{AP})$ *such that $R^{\mathrm{a}} \subseteq R^{\mathrm{c}}$ and $L^{\mathrm{a}}(s) \subseteq L^{\mathrm{c}}(s)$ for all $s \in \Sigma$.*

It is useful to think of $\mathcal{M}^{\mathrm{a}}$ as the part of a specification that *asserts* state properties and behavior as necessary aspects of a modeled artifact, whereas $\mathcal{M}^{\mathrm{c}}$ expresses which state properties and what behavior are *consistent* (i.e. possible) with respect to the modeled artifact. E.g. in [23] Kripke MTSs are natural abstractions of a program's heap structure and in [22] they serve as abstractions of program statements as predicate transformers. As property logic for Kripke MTSs we choose, parametric in a signature $(\mathtt{Act}, \mathtt{AP})$,

$$\phi ::= \bot \mid p \mid Z \mid \neg\phi \mid \phi \wedge \phi \mid (\exists\alpha)\phi \mid \mu Z.\phi, \tag{1}$$

where $p \in \mathtt{AP}$, $\alpha \in \mathtt{Act}$, $Z \in \mathrm{var}$ for a countable set of recursion variables var, and all ϕ are formally monotone in $\mu Z.\phi$. We assume the standard embedding of $\mathtt{Act}$-CTL into (1), e.g. $\mathrm{EF}_\alpha\, p$ ("there is an α-path on which p holds eventually") translates into $\mu Z.p \vee (\exists\alpha)Z$ [4], and make liberal use of $\mathtt{Act}$-CTL connectives as abbreviations of their corresponding syntactic equivalents in (1). For $\rho = (\rho^{\mathrm{a}}, \rho^{\mathrm{c}})$ with $\rho^{\mathrm{m}}\colon \mathrm{var} \to \Sigma$ for $\mathrm{m} \in \{\mathrm{a}, \mathrm{c}\}$, we write $(\mathcal{M}, s) \models^{\mathrm{a}}_{\rho} \phi$ and $(\mathcal{M}, s) \models^{\mathrm{c}}_{\rho} \phi$ iff $s \in [\![\phi]\!]^{\mathrm{a}}_{\rho}$ and $s \in [\![\phi]\!]^{\mathrm{c}}_{\rho}$ (respectively). The denotational semantics $[\![\cdot]\!]^{\mathrm{m}}$ is defined in Figure 2, where $\neg\mathrm{a} \stackrel{\mathrm{def}}{=} \mathrm{c}$, $\neg\mathrm{c} \stackrel{\mathrm{def}}{=} \mathrm{a}$, and $\mathrm{pre}^{\mathrm{m}}_{\alpha}(A) \stackrel{\mathrm{def}}{=} \{s \in \Sigma \mid \exists s' \in \Sigma\colon (s, \alpha, s') \in R^{\mathrm{m}},\ s' \in A\}$. We refer to $\mathrm{m} \in \{\mathrm{a}, \mathrm{c}\}$ as the *mode of analysis*. The semantics in Figure 2 is the standard one for DLTSs, *except* for the treatment of negation: to evaluate $\neg\phi$ in mode m, first evaluate ϕ in mode $\neg$m and then negate that result [25].

$$
\begin{aligned}
\| \bot \|^{\mathrm{m}}_{\rho}\, s &\stackrel{\mathrm{def}}{=} \{\} \\
\| p \|^{\mathrm{m}}_{\rho} &\stackrel{\mathrm{def}}{=} \{s \in \Sigma \mid p \in L^{\mathrm{m}}(s)\} \\
\| Z \|^{\mathrm{m}}_{\rho} &\stackrel{\mathrm{def}}{=} \rho^{\mathrm{m}}(Z) \\
\| \neg\phi \|^{\mathrm{m}}_{\rho} &\stackrel{\mathrm{def}}{=} \Sigma \setminus \| \phi \|^{\neg\mathrm{m}}_{\rho} \\
\| \phi_1 \wedge \phi_2 \|^{\mathrm{m}}_{\rho} &\stackrel{\mathrm{def}}{=} \| \phi_1 \|^{\mathrm{m}}_{\rho} \cap \| \phi_2 \|^{\mathrm{m}}_{\rho} \\
\| (\exists\alpha)\, \phi \|^{\mathrm{m}}_{\rho} &\stackrel{\mathrm{def}}{=} \mathrm{pre}^{\mathrm{m}}_{\alpha}(\| \phi \|^{\mathrm{m}}_{\rho}) \\
\| \mu Z.\phi \|^{\mathrm{m}}_{\rho}\, s &\stackrel{\mathrm{def}}{=} \mathrm{lfp}\, F^{\mathrm{m}};\ \text{where } F^{\mathrm{m}}(A) \stackrel{\mathrm{def}}{=} \| \phi \|^{\mathrm{m}}_{\rho^{\mathrm{m}}[Z \mapsto A]}.
\end{aligned}
$$

Fig. 2. Property semantics over Kripke MTSs [23] for mode $\mathrm{m} \in \{\mathrm{a}, \mathrm{c}\}$.

Example 1 (Laptop modes). Figure 3 shows a Kripke MTS with $\mathtt{Act} = \{*\}$ that models the modes of a laptop, where x, y, and z denote "AC powered", "battery powered", and "in suspend mode" (respectively). The labeling in the Figure means $x \in L^{\mathrm{a}}(s_0) \cap L^{\mathrm{c}}(s_0)$, $y \in L^{\mathrm{c}}(s_2) \setminus L^{\mathrm{a}}(s_2)$, and $z \in L^{\mathrm{c}}(s_1) \setminus L^{\mathrm{a}}(s_1)$. Dashed lines represent transitions in $R^{\mathrm{c}} \setminus R^{\mathrm{a}}$; solid lines denote transitions in $R^{\mathrm{a}} \cap R^{\mathrm{c}}$. The mandatory part of that model specifies the state and behavior of the laptop's AC power supply. The possible part specifies an additional power source (a battery) and a suspend mode for the machine. The property $\mathrm{AG}\,\mathrm{EF}\, z$ — "all reachable states can reach a state in suspend mode" — is expressible in (1) as $\neg\mu Y.\neg(\mu W.z \vee ((\exists *)\,(W) \wedge (\exists *)\,\neg\bot)) \vee (\exists *)\,(Y)$. This formula is an invalid assertion[3] (we don't have $(\mathcal{M}, i) \models^{\mathrm{a}} \mathrm{AG}\,\mathrm{EF}\, z$), but a consistent condition (we do have $(\mathcal{M}, i) \models^{\mathrm{c}} \mathrm{AG}\,\mathrm{EF}\, z$). The evaluation of $(\mathcal{M}, i) \models^{\mathrm{a}} \mathrm{AG}\,\mathrm{EF}\, z$ effectively checks whether all R^{c}-reachable states contain a R^{a}-path to a state s, where $z \in L^{\mathrm{a}}(s)$. The evaluation of $(\mathcal{M}, i) \models^{\mathrm{c}} \mathrm{AG}\,\mathrm{EF}\, z$ conducts the same analysis, except that the modalities of paths are swapped.

Similarly to mixed transition systems [14,15], the usual DeMorgan dualities are preserved by each $\| \cdot \|^{\mathrm{m}}_{\cdot}$ and $\phi \vee \neg\phi$ does not hold for $\| \cdot \|^{\mathrm{a}}_{\cdot}$ in general. However, Kripke MTSs *do* satisfy $\phi \vee \neg\phi$ for $\| \cdot \|^{\mathrm{c}}_{\cdot}$ and, equivalently, *don't* satisfy $\phi \wedge \neg\phi$ for $\| \cdot \|^{\mathrm{a}}_{\cdot}$. Although these differences seem small, our semantic approach can be transferred to interpret under-specified models $\mathcal{M}$ of software specifications and requirements, where *explicit* consistency checks ($\mathcal{M} \models^{\mathrm{c}} \phi$) and assertion checks ($\mathcal{M} \models^{\mathrm{a}} \phi$), e.g. as found in the object-modeling language Alloy [24], are vital. The soundness of abstraction-based model checking using Kripke MTSs has been shown in [23], where a co-inductive notion of refinement $(\mathcal{M}, s) \prec (\mathcal{N}, t)$ between (pointed) Kripke MTSs of the same signature is defined and proved that, for all $(\mathcal{M}, s) \prec (\mathcal{N}, t)$ and ϕ of (1) with matching signature,

$$
\begin{aligned}
(\mathcal{N}, t) \models^{\mathrm{a}}_{\rho} \phi \quad &\Rightarrow \quad (\mathcal{M}, s) \models^{\mathrm{a}}_{\rho} \phi \\
(\mathcal{M}, s) \models^{\mathrm{c}}_{\rho} \phi \quad &\Rightarrow \quad (\mathcal{N}, t) \models^{\mathrm{c}}_{\rho} \phi.
\end{aligned} \tag{2}
$$

[3] If convenient, we identify models $\mathcal{M}$ with pointed ones [33] $(\mathcal{M}, i)$.

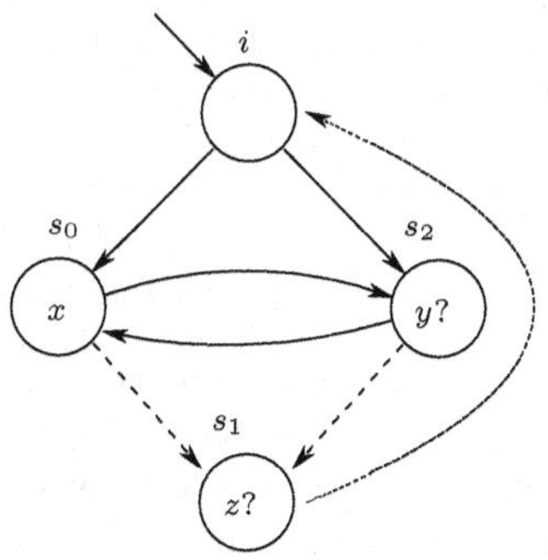

Fig. 3. A Kripke MTS modeling laptop modes.

3 Example: Fair Abstraction Using Kripke MTSs

Given an Act-CTL formula ϕ and a set of fairness constraints $C = \{\psi_1, \psi_2, \ldots, \psi_n\}$ written in Act-CTL, one can express the fair semantics of ϕ with respect to C in the modal mu-calculus of alternation depth 2 [20]. Specifically, all occurrences of EX_α, EG_α, and $\mathrm{E}[\cdot\,\mathrm{U}_\alpha\,\cdot]$ are replaced by their fair versions $\mathrm{E}_C\mathrm{X}_\alpha$, $\mathrm{E}_C\mathrm{G}_\alpha$, and $\mathrm{E}_C[\cdot\,\mathrm{U}_\alpha\,\cdot]$:

$$\mathrm{E}_C\mathrm{G}_\alpha\,\phi \stackrel{\mathrm{def}}{=} \neg(\mu Z.\neg(\phi \wedge \bigwedge_{i=1}^{n} \mathrm{EX}_\alpha\,\mathrm{E}[f\,\mathrm{U}_\alpha\,\neg Z \wedge \psi_i])) \tag{3}$$

$$\mathrm{E}_C\mathrm{X}_\alpha\,\phi \stackrel{\mathrm{def}}{=} \mathrm{EX}_\alpha\,(\phi \wedge \mathrm{E}_C\mathrm{G}\neg\bot) \tag{4}$$

$$\mathrm{E}_\alpha[\phi\,\mathrm{U}_C\,\eta] \stackrel{\mathrm{def}}{=} \mathrm{E}[\phi\,\mathrm{U}_\alpha\,\eta \wedge \mathrm{E}_C\mathrm{G}\,\neg\bot]. \tag{5}$$

In that manner, ϕ is translated into a formula of the modal mu-calculus of alternation depth 2. Note that alternation depths are defined through the positive normal form of formulas [20], so changing a formula into its positive normal form will not change its alternation depth, nor its meaning over Kripke MTSs. Finally, and crucially, the implications in (2) guarantee that model checking such encodings on abstract Kripke MTSs is sound. This is needed since the normal form of (3) is $\nu Z.\phi \wedge \bigwedge_{i=1}^{n} \mathrm{EX}_\alpha\,\mathrm{E}[f\,\mathrm{U}_\alpha\,Z \wedge \psi_i])$ which combines existential (the least fixed point for $\mathrm{E}[\cdot\,\mathrm{U}.\,\cdot]$) and universal (the greatest fixed point for νZ) aspects in one property.

4 Sound Abstraction Using Kripke Structures

For each $k \geq 0$, we transform the abstraction-based model checking problem of the alternation-depth k modal mu-calculus for Kripke MTSs with signature (Act, AP) to an alternation-depth k model-checking problem of the modal mu-calculus for Kripke structures with signature[4] $\mathtt{Act} + \mathtt{Act} + \mathtt{AP}$, where the transformations are linear in the size of models and formulas.

Definition 2 (Kripke structures). *A* Kripke structure $\mathcal{K}$ *with signature* $\mathtt{AP}$ *is a tuple* (Σ, R, L)*, where* Σ *is a set of states,* $\mathtt{AP}$ *is a (countable) set of atomic propositions,* $R \subseteq \Sigma \times \Sigma$*, and* L *is a labeling function* $L\colon \Sigma \to \mathcal{P}(\mathtt{AP})$*.*

We achieve this reduction by first reducing the model-checking problem for Kripke MTSs to two model-checking problems for DLTSs. As a property logic for DLTSs, parametric in a signature $(\mathtt{Act}, \mathtt{AP})$, we use the modal mu-calculus augmented with the duals of the clauses in (1):

$$\phi ::= \bot \mid \top \mid Z \mid p \mid \neg\phi \mid \phi \wedge \phi \mid \phi \vee \phi \mid (\exists\alpha)\phi \mid (\forall\alpha)\phi \mid \mu Z.\phi \mid \nu Z.\phi, \tag{6}$$

where $p \in \mathtt{AP}$, $\alpha \in \mathtt{Act}$, $Z \in \text{var}$, and ϕ is formally monotone in $\mu Z.\phi$ and $\nu Z.\phi$. The semantics $\| \phi \|_\rho$ over DLTS is the standard one, e.g. see [4], and we write $(\mathcal{L}, s) \models_\rho \phi$ for $s \in \| \phi \|_\rho$. There is a fairly rich literature on conversions of one kind of non-deterministic model into another, e.g. transforming Moore machines into Kripke structures [28], and Kripke structures into Büchi automata (see e.g. [36]) or DLTSs [17]. The significance of the latter transformation is that it maps one kind of observational equivalence (e.g. stuttering equivalence [5]) into another (e.g. branching bisimulation [35]). These equivalences have logical characterizations, but our intent of such transformations is more specific in that we seek to preserve meanings for all model checks $\mathcal{M} \models \phi$ of one logic and class of models by transforming formulas and models, $\mathcal{M} \mapsto \mathcal{M}'$ and $\phi \mapsto \phi'$, such that the model check $\mathcal{M} \models \phi$ is equivalent to the check $\mathcal{M}' \models \phi'$, for all $\mathcal{M}$ and ϕ. We proceed in two stages.

Stage #1. In a straightforward adaptation of a transformation of modal transition systems [22], we transform a Kripke MTS $\mathcal{M}$ with signature $(\mathtt{Act}, \mathtt{AP})$ into two DLTSs $\mathcal{M}^{\mathrm{p}}$ and $\mathcal{M}^{\mathrm{o}}$ of an extended signature $(\overline{\mathtt{Act}}, \mathtt{AP})$. By construction, checking ϕ in mode a and c on the Kripke MTS $\mathcal{M}$ is equivalent to checking a transformed formula $T(\phi^+)$ on the DLTSs $\mathcal{M}^{\mathrm{p}}$ and $\mathcal{M}^{\mathrm{o}}$ (respectively). This had already been done for MTSs and LTSs in [22]. Given a Kripke MTS $\mathcal{M} = ((\Sigma, R^{\mathrm{a}}, L^{\mathrm{a}}), (\Sigma, R^{\mathrm{c}}, L^{\mathrm{c}}))$, with signature $(\mathtt{Act}, \mathtt{AP})$, we define two DLTSs $\mathcal{M}^{\mathrm{p}} \stackrel{\text{def}}{=} (\Sigma, R^{\mathrm{p}}, L^{\mathrm{a}})$ and $\mathcal{M}^{\mathrm{o}} \stackrel{\text{def}}{=} (\Sigma, R^{\mathrm{o}}, L^{\mathrm{c}})$ with signature $(\overline{\mathtt{Act}}, \mathtt{AP})$ — representing the *pessimistic* and *optimistic* interpretations [7] of $\mathcal{M}$ (respectively):

$$\overline{\mathtt{Act}} \stackrel{\text{def}}{=} \{\alpha_\forall \mid \alpha \in \mathtt{Act}\} \cup \{\alpha_\exists \mid \alpha \in \mathtt{Act}\} \tag{7}$$

$$\begin{aligned} R^{\mathrm{p}} &\stackrel{\text{def}}{=} \{(s, \alpha_\forall, s') \mid (s, \alpha, s') \in R^{\mathrm{c}}\} \cup \{(s, \alpha_\exists, s') \mid (s, \alpha, s') \in R^{\mathrm{a}}\} \\ R^{\mathrm{o}} &\stackrel{\text{def}}{=} \{(s, \alpha_\forall, s') \mid (s, \alpha, s') \in R^{\mathrm{a}}\} \cup \{(s, \alpha_\exists, s') \mid (s, \alpha, s') \in R^{\mathrm{c}}\}. \end{aligned} \tag{8}$$

[4] We write + to denote disjoint union of sets.

We transform all formulas ϕ of (1) with signature $(\texttt{Act}, \texttt{AP})$ to formulas ϕ^+ of (6) with the same signature by applying the classical rewrite rules

$$\neg\neg\phi \rightsquigarrow \phi \qquad \neg(\phi_1 \wedge \phi_2) \rightsquigarrow (\neg\phi_1) \vee (\neg\phi_2)$$
$$\neg((\exists\alpha)\phi) \rightsquigarrow (\forall\alpha)(\neg\phi) \qquad \neg(\mu Z.\phi) \rightsquigarrow \nu Z.(\neg\phi).$$

Finally, $T(\phi^+)$ is a formulas of (6) with signature $(\overline{\texttt{Act}}, \texttt{AP})$ and is computed from ϕ^+ as follows: for all $\alpha \in \texttt{Act}$, we replace all occurrences of $(\forall\alpha)$ in ϕ^+ by $(\forall\alpha_\forall)$ and all occurrences of $(\exists\alpha)$ in ϕ^+ by $(\exists\alpha_\exists)$.

Theorem 1 (Correctness of first reduction [22]). *Given a Kripke MTS $\mathcal{M}$ with signature $(\texttt{Act}, \texttt{AP})$ and any ϕ of (1) with matching signature, let $T(\phi^+)$, $\mathcal{M}^{\mathrm{p}}$, and $\mathcal{M}^{\mathrm{o}}$ be the formula and the two DLTSs (respectively) as defined above. For any state $s \in \Sigma$, we then have*

$$(\mathcal{M}, s) \models^{\mathrm{a}}_{\rho} \phi \quad \textit{iff} \quad (\mathcal{M}^{\mathrm{p}}, s) \models_{\rho} T(\phi^+) \tag{9}$$
$$(\mathcal{M}, s) \models^{\mathrm{c}}_{\rho} \phi \quad \textit{iff} \quad (\mathcal{M}^{\mathrm{o}}, s) \models_{\rho} T(\phi^+). \tag{10}$$

Stage #2. We parametrically define a transformation $\phi \mapsto K(\phi)$ of formulas ϕ in (6) with signature $(\texttt{Act}, \texttt{AP})$ into formulas of

$$\phi ::= \bot \mid \top \mid Z \mid p \mid \neg\phi \mid \phi \wedge \phi \mid \phi \vee \phi \mid \mathrm{EX}\,\phi \mid \mathrm{AX}\,\phi \mid \mu Z.\phi \mid \nu Z.\phi, \tag{11}$$

with signature $\texttt{Act} \cup \texttt{AP}$, the range of p:

$$K(\bot) \stackrel{\mathrm{def}}{=} \bot \qquad K(\top) \stackrel{\mathrm{def}}{=} \top$$
$$K(Z) \stackrel{\mathrm{def}}{=} Z \qquad K(p) \stackrel{\mathrm{def}}{=} p$$
$$K(\neg\phi) \stackrel{\mathrm{def}}{=} \neg K(\phi)$$
$$K(\phi_1 \wedge \phi_2) \stackrel{\mathrm{def}}{=} K(\phi_1) \wedge K(\phi_2) \qquad K(\phi_1 \vee \phi_2) \stackrel{\mathrm{def}}{=} K(\phi_1) \vee K(\phi_2)$$
$$K((\exists\alpha)\phi) \stackrel{\mathrm{def}}{=} \mathrm{EX}\,(K(\phi) \wedge \alpha) \qquad K((\forall\alpha)\phi) \stackrel{\mathrm{def}}{=} \mathrm{AX}\,(\neg\alpha \vee K(\phi))$$
$$K(\mu Z.\phi) \stackrel{\mathrm{def}}{=} \mu Z.K(\phi) \qquad K(\nu Z.\phi) \stackrel{\mathrm{def}}{=} \nu Z.K(\phi).$$

Note that the transformations for $(\exists\alpha)\phi$ and $(\forall\alpha)\phi$ are the only clauses that change subformulas and cause the signature extension/collapse to $\texttt{Act} \cup \texttt{AP}$. In particular, $\phi \mapsto K(\phi)$ does not change ϕ's recursive structure, so ϕ and $K(\phi)$ have the same alternation depth. Next, we transform DLTSs into Kripke structures.

Definition 3 (Induced Kripke structure). *Given a DLTS $\mathcal{L} = (\Sigma, R, L)$ with signature $(\texttt{Act}, \texttt{AP})$, we define a Kripke structure $\mathrm{K}[\mathcal{L}] = (\Sigma \times \texttt{Act}, \bar{R}, \bar{L})$ with signature $\texttt{Act} \cup \texttt{AP}$ where*

$$\bar{R} \stackrel{\mathrm{def}}{=} \{((s,\alpha),(s',\beta)) \mid \alpha \in \texttt{Act},\ (s,\beta,s') \in R\} \tag{12}$$
$$\bar{L}(s,\alpha) \stackrel{\mathrm{def}}{=} L(s) \cup \{\alpha\}. \tag{13}$$

The semantics of (11) over Kripke structures with signature $\mathtt{AP} \cup \mathtt{Act}$ is the standard one — e.g. see [4] — and we also denote it with $\| \phi \|_\rho$ since the context will determine the logic and model. As usual, we write $(\mathcal{K}, s) \models_\rho \phi$ for $s \in \| \phi \|_\rho$. Finally, we prove that the original model check of ϕ in the DTLS $\mathcal{L}$ is captured by the model check of $K(\phi)$ in the induced Kripke structure $\mathrm{K}[\mathcal{L}]$.

Theorem 2 (Correctness of second reduction). *Let $\mathcal{L}$ be a DLTS with signature $(\mathtt{Act}, \mathtt{AP})$ such that $\mathtt{AP} \cap \mathtt{Act} = \{\}$. For any ρ: var $\rightarrow \mathcal{P}(\Sigma)$ define $\rho_{\mathcal{K}}$: var $\rightarrow \mathcal{P}(\Sigma \times \mathtt{Act})$ by $\rho_{\mathcal{K}}(Z) \stackrel{\mathrm{def}}{=} \rho(Z) \times \mathtt{Act}$. For any ϕ from (6) with signature $(\mathtt{Act}, \mathtt{AP})$, any $s \in \Sigma$, and any ρ as above, we have*

$$\| \phi \|_\rho \times \mathtt{Act} = \| K(\phi) \|_{\rho_{\mathcal{K}}}. \tag{14}$$

Proof. The cases $\bot$, $\top$ are immediate and $\wedge$ and $\vee$ follow by induction. The case Z follows from the definition of $\rho_{\mathcal{K}}$. The case p holds due to $\mathtt{Act} \cap \mathtt{AP} = \{\}$.

- We have $\| \neg\phi \|_\rho \times \mathtt{Act} = (\Sigma \setminus \| \phi \|_\rho) \times \mathtt{Act} = (\Sigma \times \mathtt{Act}) \setminus (\| \phi \|_{\rho_{\mathcal{K}}} \times \mathtt{Act}) = (\Sigma \times \mathtt{Act}) \setminus \| K(\phi) \|_{\rho_{\mathcal{K}}} = \| \neg K(\phi) \|_{\rho_{\mathcal{K}}} = \| K(\neg\phi) \|_{\rho_{\mathcal{K}}}$.
- Let $\alpha \in \mathtt{Act}$. Given $s \in \| (\exists\beta)\phi \|_\rho$, there exists some $s' \in \Sigma$ with $(s, \beta, s') \in R$ and $s' \in \| \phi \|_\rho$. By induction, $(s', \beta) \in \| K(\phi) \|_{\rho_{\mathcal{K}}}$. By definition, $(s', \beta) \in \| \beta \|_{\rho_{\mathcal{K}}}$. Thus, $(s', \beta) \in \| K(\phi) \wedge \beta \|_{\rho_{\mathcal{K}}}$. But $(s, \beta, s') \in R$ implies that the pair $((s, \alpha), (s', \beta))$ is in R and so $(s, \alpha) \in \| \mathrm{EX}\,(K(\phi) \wedge \beta) \|_{\rho_{\mathcal{K}}}$ which equals $\| K((\exists\beta)\phi) \|_{\rho_{\mathcal{K}}}$. Conversely, let $(s, \alpha) \in \| K((\exists\beta)\phi) \|_{\rho_{\mathcal{K}}}$. Then (s, α) is contained in $\| \mathrm{EX}\,(K(\phi) \wedge \beta) \|_{\rho_{\mathcal{K}}}$, so there exists some $((s, \alpha), (s', \gamma)) \in \bar{R}$ with $(s', \gamma) \in \| K(\phi) \wedge \beta \|_{\rho_{\mathcal{K}}}$. In particular, $(s', \gamma) \in \| \beta \|_{\rho_{\mathcal{K}}}$, which implies $\gamma = \beta$. But then $(s, \beta, s') \in R$ follows. By induction, $s' \in \| \phi \|_\rho$. Therefore, $s \in \| (\exists\beta)\phi \|_\rho$.
- Let $\alpha \in \mathtt{Act}$. We have $s \in \| (\forall\beta)\phi \|_\rho$ iff for all $s' \in \Sigma$, $(s, \beta, s') \in R \Rightarrow s' \in \| \phi \|_\rho$ iff for all $s' \in \Sigma$, $((s, \alpha), (s', \beta)) \in \bar{R} \Rightarrow (s', \beta) \in \| K(\phi) \|_{\rho_{\mathcal{K}}}$ iff for all $s' \in \Sigma$ and for all $\gamma \in \mathtt{Act}$, $((s, \alpha), (s', \gamma)) \in \bar{R}$ & $\gamma = \beta \Rightarrow (s', \beta) \in \| K(\phi) \|_{\rho_{\mathcal{K}}}$ iff for all $s' \in \Sigma$ and for all $\gamma \in \mathtt{Act}$, $((s, \alpha), (s', \gamma)) \in \bar{R} \Rightarrow (s', \gamma) \in \| \neg\beta \vee K(\phi) \|_{\rho_{\mathcal{K}}}$ iff $(s, \alpha) \in \| \mathrm{AX}\,(\neg\beta \vee K(\phi)) \|_{\rho_{\mathcal{K}}} = \| K((\forall\beta)\phi) \|_{\rho_{\mathcal{K}}}$.
- As for μZ and νZ, consider

$$F\colon \mathcal{P}(\Sigma) \to \mathcal{P}(\Sigma) \qquad F(A) \stackrel{\mathrm{def}}{=} \| \phi \|_{\rho[Z \mapsto A]}$$
$$G\colon \mathcal{P}(\Sigma \times \mathtt{Act}) \to \mathcal{P}(\Sigma \times \mathtt{Act}) \qquad G(B) \stackrel{\mathrm{def}}{=} \| K(\phi) \|_{\rho_{\mathcal{K}}[Z \mapsto B]}.$$

By induction, $F(A) \times \mathtt{Act} = G(A \times \mathtt{Act})$ for all $A \subseteq \Sigma$, since the environments $(\rho[Z \mapsto A])_{\mathcal{K}}$ and $\rho_{\mathcal{K}}[Z \mapsto A \times \mathtt{Act}]$ are equal. But $\mu Z.\phi/\nu Z.\phi$ and $\mu Z.K(\phi)/\nu Z.K(\phi)$ are the least/greatest fixed points of F and G (respectively), the function $A \mapsto A \times \mathtt{Act}\colon \mathcal{P}(\Sigma) \to \mathcal{P}(\Sigma \times \mathtt{Act})$ preserves all unions and intersections, and all fixed-point approximations for G are of the form $A \times \mathtt{Act}$ for some $A \subseteq \Sigma$. □

Of course, the model check on the right-hand side of (14) is performed over a Kripke structure of signature $\mathtt{Act} \cup \mathtt{AP}$. We can combine our two constructions to reduce model-checking a Kripke MTS $\mathcal{M} = (\mathcal{M}^{\mathrm{a}}, \mathcal{M}^{\mathrm{c}})$ with signature $(\mathtt{Act}, \mathtt{AP})$ to model-checking a Kripke structure with signature $\overline{\mathtt{Act}} \cup \mathtt{AP}$. For $\models^{\mathrm{a}}$, we model check $\mathrm{K}[\mathcal{M}^{\mathrm{o}}]$, for $\models^{\mathrm{c}}$, we model check $\mathrm{K}[\mathcal{M}^{\mathrm{p}}]$.

Corollary 1 (Composite model-checking reduction). *Let $\mathcal{M} = (\mathcal{M}^{\mathrm{a}}, \mathcal{M}^{\mathrm{c}})$ be a Kripke MTS with signature $(\mathtt{Act}, \mathtt{AP})$. For $\mathcal{M}^{\mathrm{p}}$ and $\mathcal{M}^{\mathrm{o}}$ as above, we have*

$$(\mathcal{M}, s) \models^{\mathrm{a}}_{\rho} \phi \quad \textit{iff} \quad (\mathrm{K}[\mathcal{M}^{\mathrm{p}}], (s, \alpha)) \models_{\rho_{\mathcal{K}}} K(T(\phi^{+})) \tag{15}$$

$$(\mathcal{M}, s) \models^{\mathrm{c}}_{\rho} \phi \quad \textit{iff} \quad (\mathrm{K}[\mathcal{M}^{\mathrm{o}}], (s, \alpha)) \models_{\rho_{\mathcal{K}}} K(T(\phi^{+})) \tag{16}$$

for all ϕ of (1), $\rho\colon \mathrm{var} \to \mathcal{P}(\Sigma)$, $s \in \Sigma$, and $\alpha \in \mathtt{Act}$.

Example 2 (Computing $K(T(\phi^{+}))$). Consider $\mathtt{Act} = \{*\}$ and the $\mathtt{Act}$-CTL formula $\mathrm{AF}_{*}\, p$ under a sole simple fairness constraint $C = \{q\}$.

1. We can express $\mathrm{AF}_{*}\, p$ in (1) as $\neg \mathrm{EG}_{*} \neg p$.
2. We convert the EG_{*} sub-formula to its fair version: $\phi \stackrel{\mathrm{def}}{=} \neg \mathrm{E}_C \mathrm{G}_{*} \neg p = \neg(\nu Z. \neg p \wedge \mathrm{EX}_{*}\, (\mathrm{E}[\neg p \, \mathrm{U}_{*}\, Z \wedge q]))$.
3. We compute the positive normal form

$$\phi^{+} \;=\; \mu Z. p \vee \mathrm{AX}_{*}\, (\nu Y. (Z \vee \neg q) \wedge (p \vee \mathrm{AX}_{*}\, Y)). \tag{17}$$

4. We change the actions $*$ attached to quantifiers to compute

$$T(\phi^{+}) \;=\; \mu Z. p \vee \mathrm{AX}_{*_{\forall}}\, (\nu Y. (Z \vee \neg q) \wedge (p \vee \mathrm{AX}_{*_{\forall}}\, Y)). \tag{18}$$

5. Applying K to $T(\phi^{+})$ does not do anything material in this example as its input formula mentions one action only. Note that this is not so in general, even for $\mathtt{Act} = \{*\}$.

5 Complexity of Model-Checking Reduction

We measure the size of the Kripke structures $\mathrm{K}[\mathcal{M}^{\mathrm{p}}]$ and $\mathrm{K}[\mathcal{M}^{\mathrm{o}}]$ in terms of the size of the Kripke MTS $\mathcal{M}$, showing the there is no significant increase in the size of models. Similarly, the transformation of formulas ϕ into $K(T(\phi^{+}))$ is linear.

Definition 4 (Model complexity). *Let $\mathcal{L} = (\Sigma, R, L)$ be a DLTS with signature $(\mathtt{Act}, \mathtt{AP})$. The* model complexity *[20] of $\mathcal{L}$ is $|\mathcal{L}| \stackrel{\mathrm{def}}{=} |\Sigma| + |R|$, where $|R| \stackrel{\mathrm{def}}{=} \sum_{\alpha \in \mathtt{Act}} |\{(s, s') \mid (s, \alpha, s') \in R\}|$. For a Kripke MTS $\mathcal{M} = (\mathcal{M}^{\mathrm{a}}, \mathcal{M}^{\mathrm{c}})$ we define its model complexity as $|\mathcal{M}| \stackrel{\mathrm{def}}{=} |\mathcal{M}^{\mathrm{a}}| + |\mathcal{M}^{\mathrm{c}}|$.*

Theorem 3 (Model-checking complexity). *Let $\mathcal{M} = (\mathcal{M}^{\mathrm{a}}, \mathcal{M}^{\mathrm{c}})$ be a Kripke MTS with finite signature $(\mathtt{Act}, \mathtt{AP})$.*

1. *Let $\mathcal{L}$ be either* $\mathrm{K}[\mathcal{M}^{\mathrm{p}}]$ *or* $\mathrm{K}[\mathcal{M}^{\mathrm{o}}]$. *Then*

$$|\mathcal{L}| = |\texttt{Act}| \cdot (|\Sigma| + 2 \cdot (|R^{\mathrm{a}}| + |R^{\mathrm{c}}|)) \leq 2 \cdot |\texttt{Act}| \cdot |\mathcal{M}|. \tag{19}$$

If ϕ of (1) has alternation depth k, then the time complexity for model checking $K(T(\phi^+))$ over $\mathcal{L}$ is in $O(|\phi| \cdot |\texttt{Act}|^{k+1} \cdot |\mathcal{M}|^{k+1})$.[5]

2. *If the Kripke MTS $\mathcal{M}$ has only one action type, then*

$$|\mathcal{L}| = |\Sigma| + 2 \cdot (|R^{\mathrm{a}}| + |R^{\mathrm{c}}|) \leq 2 \cdot |\mathcal{M}| \tag{20}$$

and the time complexity for model checking such a ϕ over $\mathcal{L}$ is in $O(|\phi| \cdot |\mathcal{M}|^{k+1})$.

Proof. The computation of model complexities is straightforward. As for the time complexities, they follow from the model complexities, the complexity bound given in [20], and the fact that $\phi \mapsto T(\phi^+) \mapsto K(T(\phi^+))$ is a sequence of linear transformations that each preserve the alternation depth of formulas. □

We emphasize that the time complexity in item 2 is identical to the one obtained if $\mathcal{M}$ were a Kripke structure already, i.e. if $\mathcal{M}^{\mathrm{a}}$ were equal to $\mathcal{M}^{\mathrm{c}}$ in that case [20]. Of course, our model-checking reduction allows the use of *any* efficient model checking algorithms for Kripke structures — be they established tableau methods [4] or more recent advances in automata-theoretic approaches to model checking, such as hesitant alternating automata [36] for the CTL* fragment of (11).

6 Example: Separating Fairness Algorithmically

The modal mu-calculus encoding for model-checking fair CTL has more efficient algorithms that separate the fairness constraints from the CTL formula ϕ to be checked [8,9]. These techniques can be applied to a Kripke MTS $\mathcal{M}$ of signature $(\{*\}, \texttt{AP})$: compute the fair maximal connected components of $\mathcal{M}^{\mathrm{a}}$ and $\mathcal{M}^{\mathrm{c}}$, or adapt the more space efficient methods of [11], and then restrict the semantics $\models^{\mathrm{a}}$ and $\models^{\mathrm{c}}$ to those states that lead into a fair maximally connected component. Unfortunately, these two model checks are mutually dependent and can therefore not be emulated in standard tools per se. It would be of interest to see whether our model-checking reduction can achieve a similar separation of concerns. Alas, the definitions in (8) "mix" state transitions of $\mathcal{M}^{\mathrm{a}}$ with state transitions of $\mathcal{M}^{\mathrm{c}}$, preventing a direct detection of fair "assertion-paths" and "consistency-paths" in the model $\mathrm{K}[\mathcal{M}^{\mathrm{a}}]$ or $\mathrm{K}[\mathcal{M}^{\mathrm{c}}]$ in isolation. Thus, the reduction of three-valued to two-valued model checking not only results in a loss of precision in the interpretation of conjunction, as discussed in [7], it may also require new tools to maintain the expressiveness needed in practice, e.g. for property verification under fairness assumptions.

---

[5] Or $O(|\phi| \cdot |\mathcal{M}|^{k+1})$ is we consider $|\texttt{Act}|$ to be constant.

Although our use of alternation-depth 2 model-checking introduces a computational penalty, there are good reasons beyond fairness for wanting to use properties of that fragment, an example being "for all paths, if the device is reset then there is some path on which it is eventually in its initial mode" which is not expressible as an alternation-depth 1 formula [20]. At the same time, it is unclear how severe that penalty really is, considering the progress made in automata-theoretic approaches to model checking modal mu-calculus formulas with hesitant alternating automata; e.g. for the alternation depth 1 fragment [3] and CTL* [36]. Since these approaches take a Kripke structure and a formula as input, our reduction enables the sound use of these tools for abstraction-based model checking of Kripke MTSs.

7 Related Work

Bruns & Godefroid [7] pioneered the reduction of three-valued model-checking problems to two-valued ones for partial Kripke structures [6], which are three-valued versions of Kripke structures $\mathcal{K} = (\Sigma, R, L)$, where the labeling function L has type $L\colon \Sigma \times \mathtt{AP} \to \{\text{false}, \text{true}, \bot\}$. Thus, atomic propositions at states are either false, true, or $\bot$ (undetermined). They also transform such a structure into two Kripke structures and a modal mu-calculus formula into one in positive normal form. Their model-checking reduction is also sound and complete and does not increase the size of the models, nor the cost of the model check.

Our reduction proceeds in two stages, one of which is an adaptation of a reduction of model-checking modal transition systems to model-checking labeled transition systems [22]. In that paper it was shown that abstraction-based model checking using modal transition systems incurs no additional cost or complexity over abstraction-based model checking of labeled transition systems.

Dams et al. [16] study fair CTL* over mixed transition systems [14,15], where transitions and propositions came in two flavors: free and constrained ones. Their fairness assumptions are boolean combinations of "infinitely often L", where L is a literal. To gain efficiency offered by some model-checking tools, they separate the fairness assumptions from the CTL formula ϕ to be checked. They convert ϕ into positive normal form and annotate ϕ on path quantifiers and atomic propositions. These annotations guide the satisfaction relation in its choice of free or constrained fair paths. The soundness of that approach for fair CTL* over mixed transition systems is then proved.

The semantics of $\vee$ for $\models^{\mathrm{a}}$ is an under-approximation, as the model check $s\models^{\mathrm{a}} p \vee \neg p$ with $p \in L^{\mathrm{c}}(s) \setminus L^{\mathrm{a}}(s)$ shows. Dually, the semantics of $\wedge$ for $\models c$ is an over-approximation, considering the model check $s\models^{\mathrm{c}} p \wedge \neg p$ with $p \in L^{\mathrm{c}}(s) \setminus L^{\mathrm{a}}(s)$. Generalized model checking [7] eliminates such imprecision for partial Kripke structures [6] — a special class of Kripke MTSs (see Figure 1) — but increases the model-checking complexity.[6]

[6] If it turns out that Kripke MTSs can be translated to partial Kripke structures such that refinements are preserved and reflected, then the generalized model checking of [7] can be applied to Kripke MTSs as well.

There exist linear-time temporal logics whose expressiveness exceeds that of LTL. For example, Intel developed a model checker for a linear-time temporal logic FTL [1] whose expressiveness supports a limited form of past tense modalities, subsumes ω-regular expressions (achieved through several redundant mechanisms), and contains a variety of syntactic support for hardware verification (e.g. multiple clocks, reset signals, and temporal connectives over time windows).

8 Conclusion

In [23], a model-checking framework based on Kripke modal transition systems was presented and shown that it allows sound abstraction-based model checking for the entire modal mu-calculus. In [22], it was demonstrated that abstract Kripke modal transition systems can be computed with a cost no greater than the computation of standard abstract doubly labeled transition systems. In this paper, we presented a transformation of modal mu-calculus formulas and Kripke modal transition systems into modal mu-calculus formulas and Kripke structures of an extended/collapsed signature such that this transformation is linear in the size of formulas and models and that it preserves the meaning of model checks. Specifically, for each mode of analysis $\mathrm{m} \in \{\mathrm{a}, \mathrm{c}\}$ a different Kripke structure is computed, whereas the transformed formula is the same in each mode. Since these transformations preserve the alternation depth of formulas, as well as the CTL and CTL* fragments, this model-checking reduction allows the instrumented use of efficient Kripke structure model checkers for the model checking of Kripke modal transition systems.

Acknowledgements

We wish to thank Patrice Godefroid and Radha Jagadeesan for inspiring discussions and most helpful comments. The anonymous referees are thanked for their constructive feedback.

References

1. R. Armoni, L. Fix, R. Gerth, B. Ginsburg, T. Kanza, A. Landver, S. Mador-Haim, A. Tiemeyer, E. Singerman, and M. Y. Vardi. The ForSpec temporal language: A new temporal property-specification language. Submitted, 2001.
2. T. Ball, A. Podelski, and S. K. Rajamani. Boolean and Cartesian Abstraction for Model Checking C Programs. In T. Margaria and W. Yi, editors, *Proceedings of TACAS'2001*, volume 2031 of *LNCS*, pages 268–283, Genova, Italy, April 2001. Springer Verlag.
3. O. Bernholtz, M. Vardi, and P. Wolper. An Automata-Theoretic Approach to Branching-Time Model-Checking. In *6th Int'l Conference on Computer Aided Verification (CAV'94)*, volume 818 of *Lecture Notes in Computer Science*, pages 142–155. Springer Verlag, 1994.

4. J. C. Bradfield. *Verifying Temporal Properties Of Systems.* Birkhäuser, Boston, Mass., 1991.
5. M. C. Browne, E. M. Clarke, and O. Grumberg. Characterizing finite Kripke structures in propositional temporal logic. *Theoretical Computer Science*, 59(1–2):115–131, 1988.
6. G. Bruns and P. Godefroid. Model Checking Partial State Spaces with 3-Valued Temporal Logics. In *Proceedings of the 11th Conference on Computer Aided Verification*, volume 1633 of *Lecture Notes in Computer Science*, pages 274–287. Springer Verlag, July 1999.
7. G. Bruns and P. Godefroid. Generalized Model Checking: Reasoning about Partial State Spaces. In *Proceedings of CONCUR'2000 (11th International Conference on Concurrency Theory)*, volume 1877 of *Lecture Notes in Computer Science*, pages 168–182. Springer Verlag, August 2000.
8. J. R. Burch, E. M. Clarke, D. L. Dill K. L. McMillan, and J. Hwang. Symbolic model checking: 10^{20} states and beyond. Proceedings of the Fifth Annual Symposium on Logic in Computer Science, June 1990.
9. E. M. Clarke, O. Grumberg, and D. A. Peled. *Model Checking.* The MIT Press, January 2000.
10. E.M. Clarke, O. Grumberg, and D.E. Long. Model checking and abstraction. *ACM Transactions on Programming Languages and Systems*, 16(5):1512–1542, 1994.
11. C. Courcoubetis, M. Vardi, P. Wolper, and M. Yannakakis. Memory-efficient Algorithms for the Verification of Temporal Properties. *Formal Methods in System Design*, 1(275–288), 1992.
12. P. Cousot and R. Cousot. Abstract interpretation: a unified lattice model for static analysis of programs. In *Proc. 4th ACM Symp. on Principles of Programming Languages*, pages 238–252. ACM Press, 1977.
13. P. Cousot and R. Cousot. Temporal abstract interpretation. In *Conference Record of the 27th Annual ACM SIGPLAN-SIGACT Symposium on Principles of Programming Languages*, pages 12–25, Boston, Mass., January 2000. ACM Press, New York, NY.
14. D. Dams. *Abstract interpretation and partition refinement for model checking.* PhD thesis, Technische Universiteit Eindhoven, The Netherlands, 1996.
15. D. Dams, R. Gerth, and O. Grumberg. Abstract interpretation of reactive systems. *ACM Transactions on Programming Languages and Systems*, 19(2):253–291, 1997.
16. D. Dams, R. Gerth, and O. Grumberg. Fair Model Checking Of Abstractions. In M. Leuschel, A. Podelski, C.R. Ramakrishnan, and U. Ultes-Nitsche, editors, *Proceedings of the Workshop on Verification and Computational Logic (VCL'2000)*, DSSE-TR-2000-6. University of Southhampton, July 2000.
17. R. de Nicola and F. Vaandrager. Three Logics for Branching Bisimulation. *Journal of the Association of Computing Machinery*, 42(2):458–487, March 1995.
18. M. B. Dwyer, J. Hatcliff, R. Joehanes, S. Laubach, C. S. Pasareanu, Robby, W. Visser, and H. Zheng. Tool-supported Program Abstraction for Finite-state Verification. In *Proceedings of the 23nd Intl' Conference on Software Engineering*, pages 177–187. ACM Press, May 2001.
19. M. B. Dwyer and D. A. Schmidt. Limiting State Explosion with Filter-Based Refinement. In *Proceedings of the ILPS'97 Workshop on Verification, Model Checking, and Abstraction*, 1997.
20. E. A. Emerson and C. L. Lei. Efficient Model Checking in Fragments of the Mucalculus. In *Proc. of the First Int'l IEEE Symposium on Logic in Computer Science (LICS'86)*, pages 267–278, Cambridge, Mass., June 1986. IEEE Press.

21. N. Francez. *Fairness.* Texts and Monographs in Computer Science. Springer Verlag, 1986.
22. P. Godefroid, M. Huth, and R. Jagadeesan. Abstraction-based Model Checking using Modal Transition Systems. In *Proceedings of the International Conference on Theory and Practice of Concurrency*, Lecture Notes in Computer Science, pages 426–440. Springer Verlag, August 2001.
23. M. Huth, R. Jagadeesan, and D. Schmidt. Modal transition systems: a foundation for three-valued program analysis. In Sands D., editor, *Proceedings of the European Symposium on Programming (ESOP'2001)*, pages 155–169. Springer Verlag, April 2001.
24. D. Jackson. Alloy: A Lightweight Object Modelling Language. Technical Report TR-797, Laboratory of Computer Science, Massachusetts Institute of Technology, 28 July 2000.
25. P. Kelb. Model checking and abstraction: a framework preserving both truth and failure information. Technical Report OFFIS, University of Oldenburg, Germany, 1994.
26. K.L. McMillan. *Symbolic Model Checking.* Kluwer Academic Publishers, 1993.
27. K. G. Larsen and B. Thomsen. A Modal Process Logic. In *Third Annual Symposium on Logic in Computer Science*, pages 203–210. IEEE Computer Society Press, 1988.
28. D. E. Long. *Model Checking, Abstraction, and Compositional Verification.* PhD thesis, Carnegie Mellon University, School of Computer Science, July 1993.
29. R. Milner. An algebraic definition of simulation between programs. In *2nd International Joint Conference on Artificial Intelligence*, pages 481–489, London, United Kingdom, 1971. British Computer Society.
30. R. Milner. A modal characterisation of observable machine behaviours. In G. Astesiano and C. Böhm, editors, *CAAP '81*, volume 112 of *Lecture Notes in Computer Science*, pages 25–34. Springer Verlag, 1981.
31. M. Sagiv, T. Reps, and R. Wilhelm. Parametric Shape Analysis via 3-Valued Logic. In *Proceedings of the 26th ACM SIGPLAN-SIGACT Symposium on Principles of programming languages*, pages 105–118, January 20-22, San Antonio, Texas 1999.
32. H. Saidi and N. Shankar. Abstract and model check while you prove. In *Proc. of the 11th Conference on Computer-Aided Verification*, number 1633 in Lecture Notes in Computer Science, pages 443–454. Springer, 1999.
33. D. A. Schmidt. Binary relations for abstraction and refinement. *Elsevier Electronic Notes in Computer Science*, November 1999. Workshop on Refinement and Abstraction, Osaka, Japan. To appear.
34. David A. Schmidt. From Trace Sets to Modal Transition Systems. Submitted for publication, July 2001.
35. R. J. van Glabbeek and W. P. Weijland. Branching Time and Abstraction in Bisimulation Semantics. *Journal of the ACM*, 43(3):555–600, May 1996.
36. W. Visser and H. Barringer. Practical CTL* Model Checking — Should SPIN be Extended? *Software Tools for Technology Transfer*, 2(4), 2000.

Parameterized Verification of a Cache Coherence Protocol: Safety and Liveness

Kai Baukus[1], Yassine Lakhnech[2], and Karsten Stahl[1]*

[1] Institute of Computer Science and Applied Mathematics
CAU Kiel, Preusserstr. 1–9, D-24105 Kiel, Germany.
{kba,kst}@informatik.uni-kiel.de
[2] VERIMAG, Centre Equation, 2 Av. de Vignate,
38610 Gières, France.
lakhnech@imag.fr

Abstract. In a previous paper we presented a method which allows to compute abstractions for parameterized systems modeled in the decidable logic WS1S. These WS1S systems provide an intuitive way to describe parameterized systems of finite state processes. The abstractions can be used to establish properties of the parameterized network. To be able to prove liveness properties, an algorithm is used which enriches the abstract system with fairness constraints. We summarize this verification method and present its application by the verification of both safety and liveness properties of a non-trivial example of a cache coherence protocol, provided by Steve German.

1 Introduction

There has been much interest in the automatic and semi-automatic verification of parameterized systems recently. Although the problem is known to be undecidable in general [AK86], automated methods for restricted decidable classes and semi-automatic methods have been developed.

Deductive methods presented in [KM89, WL89, BCG89, SG89, HLR92], [LHR97] are based on induction on the number of processes. A suitable network invariant has to be found during the verification process that abstracts an arbitrary number of processes.

Algorithmic methods presented in [GS92, EN95, EN96, EK00] show that for restricted classes of ring networks of arbitrary size, the verification can be reduced to the verification of networks of sizes up to a computable limit k.

In [KMM+97], regular languages are used in a semi-automatic method to represent sets of states of parameterized networks, where additionally finite-state transducers are used to compute predecessors. In [ABJN99, JN00] acceleration techniques are applied to consider the effect of taking infinitely often a transition.

An incomplete but fully automatic method for proving invariance properties is presented in [PRZ01]. Model-checking techniques on small instances are used

* Contact Author.

A. Cortesi (Ed.): VMCAI 2002, LNCS 2294, pp. 317–330, 2002.
© Springer-Verlag Berlin Heidelberg 2002

to compute candidates for invariant assertions. Deductive methods are used to check whether they are inductive and usable to prove the property.

In [BBLS00] we showed how to model parameterized systems in the decidable logic WS1S. The current state of each instance of the system is a fixed number of finite subsets of the natural numbers and the transitions of the processes in the network are described in WS1S. Given a boolean abstraction relation in WS1S, this allows to compute the abstract system automatically. This constructed system then abstracts every instance of the parameterized system and can therefore be used to verify properties of the whole parameterized network. With an additional marking algorithm and the lifting of fairness conditions presented in [BLS00] we were able to establish liveness properties for these protocols as well.

The method is implemented in a tool called PAX[1], that uses the decision procedures of MONA [HJJ+96] to check the satisfiability of WS1S formulae.

In this paper we apply our verification method for parameterized systems to a non-trivial example, a cache coherence protocol [PRZ01], and prove both safety and liveness properties. To our knowledge, it is the first time that liveness properties of this protocol are verified.

2 Protocol Description

Our goal is to verify a cache coherence protocol by Steve German which firstly appeared in an SPL notation in [PRZ01]. We give it in a slightly different notation using a guarded command language.[2]

The protocol consists of a central controlling component, called *home*, and a parameterized number of *client* processes. Messages are sent via three channels from *home* to a *client* c and vice versa:

- `chan1`[c]: The client sends requests for *shared* or *exclusive* access to the cache line to home via this channel.
- `chan2`[c]: Used by the home process to send *grants* to client c or the *invalidate* command enforcing the client to invalidate its cache status.
- `chan3`[c]: The client c uses this channel to send acknowledgments about invalidating its cache status to home.

Each client has a variable `cache`, which holds the actual state of its cache line with possible values `invalid`, `shared`, and `exclusive`.

The home process has several variables. Among them are variables `command` and `current_client` for the current job it has to process. If home receives a request from a client process c, then this request will be stored in `command` and c in `current_client` until the request is processed.

Moreover, there is a boolean variable `excl_granted` which is set to *tt* whenever an exclusive grant was given to a client.

[1] `http://www.informatik.uni-kiel.de/~kba/pax`

[2] Compared to [PRZ01] we consider some of the client transitions as home transitions, since these transitions modify only home variables.

Furthermore, the *home* process uses two boolean arrays, `sharer_list` which stores all processes to which a grant has been given, and `invalidate_list` which is used during the invalidation process. If the home process has to invalidate some clients, e.g., because they have shared access and some other process requests for exclusive access, then all processes which must be invalidated are stored in `invalidate_list`.

The transitions of the *home* process and one *client* c are given in Table 1 and Table 2 in a guarded command style language.

The protocol should ensure *coherence* between the clients, that is, whenever there is a client in `exclusive` state, then all the other clients are in state `invalid`.

The second kind of properties we are interested in are liveness (response) properties, namely, that requests of a process will be eventually granted. These liveness properties are only valid under further fairness assumptions, e.g., that the home process will eventually read the channel content of each process.

h_0 : ($\mathtt{command} = \mathtt{req\_shared} \wedge \neg\mathtt{excl\_granted}$ $\wedge\ \mathtt{chan2}[\mathtt{current\_client}] = \mathtt{empty}$) $\rightarrow \mathtt{sharer\_list}[\mathtt{current\_client}] := tt$; $\mathtt{command} := \mathtt{empty}$; $\mathtt{chan2}[\mathtt{current\_client}] := \mathtt{grant\_shared}$
h_1 : ($\mathtt{command} = \mathtt{req\_exclusive} \wedge \mathtt{chan2}[\mathtt{current\_client}] = \mathtt{empty}$ $\wedge\ \forall i : [1..N].\neg\mathtt{sharer\_list}[i]$) $\rightarrow \mathtt{sharer\_list}[\mathtt{current\_client}] := tt$; $\mathtt{command} := \mathtt{empty}$; $\mathtt{chan2}[\mathtt{current\_client}] := \mathtt{grant\_exclusive}$; $\mathtt{excl\_granted} := tt$
h_2 : ($\mathtt{command} = \mathtt{empty} \wedge \mathtt{chan1}[c] \neq \mathtt{empty}$) $\rightarrow \mathtt{command} := \mathtt{chan1}[c]$; $\mathtt{chan1}[c] := \mathtt{empty}$; $\mathtt{invalidate\_list} := \mathtt{sharer\_list}$; $\mathtt{current\_client} := c$
h_3 : ((($\mathtt{command} = \mathtt{req\_shared} \wedge \mathtt{excl\_granted}$) $\vee\ \mathtt{command} = \mathtt{req\_exclusive}$) $\wedge\ \mathtt{invalidate\_list}[c] \wedge \mathtt{chan2}[c] = \mathtt{empty}$) $\rightarrow \mathtt{chan2}[c] := \mathtt{invalidate}$; $\mathtt{invalidate\_list}[c] := ff$
h_4 : ($\mathtt{command} \neq \mathtt{empty} \wedge \mathtt{chan3}[c] = \mathtt{invalidate\_ack}$) $\rightarrow \mathtt{sharer\_list}[c] := ff$; $\mathtt{excl\_granted} := ff$; $\mathtt{chan3}[c] := \mathtt{empty}$

Table 1. Transitions of the *home* process

3 Verification Approach

We now explain in detail our verification method for parameterized systems. The extensions to prove also liveness properties will be presented in Section 5. We model parameterized systems as higher order transition systems in the logic WS1S. Given an abstraction relation, we then make use of the decidability of WS1S to construct automatically an abstraction for the whole parameterized network.

c_0 : skip
c_1 : (cache[c] $=$ invalid $\wedge$ chan1[c] $=$ empty) $\rightarrow$ chan1[c] $:=$ req_shared
c_2 : ((cache[c] $=$ invalid $\vee$ cache[c] $=$ shared) $\wedge$ chan1[c] $=$ empty) $\rightarrow$ chan1[c] $:=$ req_exclusive
c_3 : (chan2[c] $=$ invalidate $\wedge$ chan3[c] $=$ empty) $\rightarrow$ chan2[c] $:=$ empty ; chan3[c] $:=$ invalidate_ack ; cache[c] $:=$ invalid
c_4 : chan2[c] $=$ grant_shared $\rightarrow$ cache[c] $:=$ shared ; chan2[c] $:=$ empty
c_5 : chan2[c] $=$ grant_exclusive $\rightarrow$ cache[c] $:=$ exclusive ; chan2[c] $:=$ empty

Table 2. Transitions of a *client* c

Verification by abstraction. We first recall some definitions and the idea of proving properties of systems by abstraction. Given a deadlock-free transition system $\mathcal{S} = (\mathcal{V}, \Theta, \mathcal{T})$ consisting of a set of variables $\mathcal{V}$, initial states Θ, and a set of transitions $\mathcal{T}$, and a total abstraction relation $\alpha \subseteq \Sigma \times \Sigma_A$, we say that $\mathcal{S}_A = (\mathcal{V}_A, \Theta_A, \mathcal{T}_A)$ is an *abstraction* of $\mathcal{S}$ w.r.t. α, denoted by $\mathcal{S} \sqsubseteq_\alpha \mathcal{S}_A$, if the following conditions are satisfied: (1) $\Theta \subseteq \alpha^{-1}(\Theta_A)$ and (2) $\alpha \circ \tau \circ \alpha^{-1} \subseteq \tau_A$ for corresponding $\tau \in \mathcal{T}$, $\tau_A \in \mathcal{T}_A$.

In case Σ_A is finite, we call α finite abstraction relation. Let φ, φ_A be LTL formulae and let $[\![\varphi]\!]$ (resp. $[\![\varphi_A]\!]$) denote the set of models of φ (resp. φ_A). Then, from $\mathcal{S} \sqsubseteq_\alpha \mathcal{S}_A$, $\alpha^{-1}([\![\varphi_A]\!]) \subseteq [\![\varphi]\!]$, and $\mathcal{S}_A \models \varphi_A$ we can conclude $\mathcal{S} \models \varphi$. This statement, which is called preservation result, shows the interest of verification by abstraction: since if $\mathcal{S}_A$ is finite, it can automatically be checked whether $\mathcal{S}_A \models \varphi_A$. In fact, a similar preservation result holds for any temporal logic without existential quantification over paths, e.g., $\forall CTL^\star$, LTL, or $\mu_\Box$ [CGL94, DGG94, LGS+95].

If we have already proven some state property ψ to be invariant in $\mathcal{S}$, i.e., $\mathcal{S} \models \Box\psi$, we can strengthen condition (2) to (2′)

$$\alpha \circ (\tau \cap \{(s_0, s_1) \mid s_0 \models \psi, s_1 \models \psi\}) \circ \alpha^{-1} \subseteq \tau_A \ .$$

This allows to establish the abstraction relation for smaller abstract systems $\mathcal{S}_A$ (better approximations), for which usually more properties can be verified. We denote this type of abstraction by $\mathcal{S} \sqsubseteq_\alpha^\psi \mathcal{S}_A$.

In fact, in our verification approach, we will compute the abstract systems, and strengthening will immediately result in better abstractions.

WS1S logic. Terms of weak second order theory of one successor (WS1S for short) [Büc60, Tho90] are built up from the constant 0 and 1st-order variables by applying the successor function *succ*(t) (“$t+1$”). *Atomic formulae* are of the form b, $t = t'$, $t < t'$, $t \in X$, where b is a boolean variable, t and t' are terms, and X is a set variable (2nd-order variable). WS1S formulae are built up from atomic formulae by applying the boolean connectives as well as quantification over both 1st-order and 2nd-order variables.

WS1S formulae are interpreted in models that assign finite sub-sets of ω to 2nd-order variables and elements of ω to 1st-order variables. The interpretation is defined in the usual way.

Given a WS1S formula f, we denote by $[\![f]\!]$ the set of models of f. The set of free variables in f is denoted by *free*(f).

Finally, we recall that by Büchi [Büc60] and Elgot [Elg61] the satisfiability problem for WS1S is decidable. Indeed, the set of all models of a WS1S formula is representable by a finite automaton (see, e.g., [Tho90]).

WS1S systems. Now, we introduce WS1S transition systems which are transition systems with variables ranging over finite sub-sets of ω and show how they can be used to represent the parameterized system.

Definition 1 (WS1S Transition Systems). *A* WS1S transition system $cS = (\mathcal{V}, \Theta, \mathcal{T})$ *is given by the following components:*

- $\mathcal{V} = \{X_1, \ldots, X_k\}$*: A finite set of second order variables where each variable is interpreted as a finite set of natural numbers.*
- Θ*: A WS1S formula with free*$(\Theta) \subseteq \mathcal{V}$ *describing the initial states.*
- $\mathcal{T}$*: A finite set of transitions where each* $\tau \in \mathcal{T}$ *is represented as a WS1S formula* $\rho_\tau(\mathcal{V}, \mathcal{V}')$*, where primed variables refer to the post-state.*

The computations of $\mathcal{S}$ *are defined as usual. Moreover, let* $[\![\mathcal{S}]\!]$ *denote the set of computations of* $\mathcal{S}$. □

Example 1. We give transition c_1 as example. Since there are three different values for `cache`[c], we encode this variable with two sets, `cache_a` and `cache_b`. For example, $c \notin$ `cache_a` $\cup$ `cache_b` corresponds to `cache`[c] $=$ `invalid`. The different values for the channels are similar encoded.

```
# guard: cache[c] = invalid, chan1[c] = empty
c notin cache_a union cache_b & c notin chan1_a union chan1_b
# effect: chan1[c] := req_shared
& chan1_a' = chan1_a union {c} & chan1_b' = chan1_b \ {c}
# the other variables are unchanged
& (excl_granted' <=> excl_granted)
& ...
```

Abstracting WS1S systems. We now want to verify WS1S systems by abstraction, using the methods presented in [BBLS00, BLS00]. Let $\mathcal{S} = (\mathcal{V}, \Theta, \mathcal{T})$ be a WS1S system and let α be a boolean abstraction relation given by a WS1S formula $\widehat{\alpha}(\mathcal{V}, \mathcal{V}_A)$, where $\mathcal{V}_A$ are all the abstract boolean variables. Since the abstract variables are booleans, the constructed abstract system is finite and can be model-checked. Moreover, we make use of the fact that both $\widehat{\alpha}(\mathcal{V}, \mathcal{V}_A)$ and the transitions in $\mathcal{T}$ are expressed in WS1S to give an effective construction of the abstract system.

The initial states of the abstract system can be described by the formula

$$\Theta_A \stackrel{\text{def}}{=} \exists \mathcal{V} : \widehat{\alpha}(\mathcal{V}, \mathcal{V}_A) \ .$$

For each concrete transition τ there is one abstract transition τ_A in the set of abstract transitions $\mathcal{T}_A$, and it is characterized by the formula

$$\rho_{\tau_A} \stackrel{\text{def}}{=} \exists \mathcal{V}, \mathcal{V}' : \widehat{\alpha}(\mathcal{V}, \mathcal{V}_A) \wedge \rho_\tau(\mathcal{V}, \mathcal{V}') \wedge \widehat{\alpha}(\mathcal{V}', \mathcal{V}'_A)$$

with free variables $\mathcal{V}_A$ and $\mathcal{V}'_A$. The system $(\mathcal{V}_A, \Theta_A, \mathcal{T}_A)$ consisting of this initial state predicate and these transitions is clearly an abstraction of $\mathcal{S}$.

If we have already proven some invariance property ψ about $\mathcal{S}$, we can choose the following abstract transitions

$$\rho_{\tau_A} \stackrel{\text{def}}{=} \exists \mathcal{V}, \mathcal{V}' : \psi(\mathcal{V}) \wedge \widehat{\alpha}(\mathcal{V}, \mathcal{V}_A) \wedge \rho_\tau(\mathcal{V}, \mathcal{V}') \wedge \widehat{\alpha}(\mathcal{V}', \mathcal{V}'_A) \wedge \psi(\mathcal{V}') \ .$$

We say that we *strengthen* $\mathcal{S}$ with invariant ψ. The abstract initial states are similarly computed.

To compute the abstract system, one has to find all states fulfilling these formulae, which is possible since they are WS1S formulae. This means, choosing some formulae $\varphi_i(\mathcal{V})$ (we call them *abstraction predicates*) about the concrete system, we can automatically compute an abstract system with boolean variables $\mathcal{V}_A = \{a_1, \ldots, a_n\}$ according to the boolean abstraction relation

$$\widehat{\alpha} \stackrel{\text{def}}{=} \bigwedge_{i=1}^{n} (a_i \Leftrightarrow \varphi_i(\mathcal{V})) \ .$$

In Sections 4 and 5, where we will apply this verification methodology, for each used abstraction relation $\widehat{\alpha}$, we will solely give the abstraction predicates φ_i in natural language.

Universal properties. For the class of so-called *universal* progress or response properties, we use a slightly different type of abstraction relation. These properties guarantee that each single process i eventually makes some progress, or each request by i to j eventually is responded to by j. To prove those properties by abstraction the abstraction relation has to focus on processes, i.e., the abstraction relation contains i or i, j as free variables ($\widehat{\alpha}(\mathcal{V}, \mathcal{V}_A, i)$ or $\widehat{\alpha}(\mathcal{V}, \mathcal{V}_A, i, j)$).

Then, the abstract system contains as abstract transitions

$$\rho_{\tau_A} \stackrel{\text{def}}{=} \exists \mathcal{V}, \mathcal{V}' : \exists i, j : \widehat{\alpha}(\mathcal{V}, \mathcal{V}_A, i, j) \wedge \rho_\tau(\mathcal{V}, \mathcal{V}') \wedge \widehat{\alpha}(\mathcal{V}', \mathcal{V}'_A, i, j)$$

(or those with invariance constraints) and starts in initial state

$$\Theta_A \stackrel{\text{def}}{=} \exists \mathcal{V} : \exists i, j : \widehat{\alpha}(\mathcal{V}, \mathcal{V}_A, i, j) \ .$$

4 Coherence Property

We apply an incremental verification process to verify the coherence property that whenever there is a process in exclusive mode, then there is no other process having any access. Successively, we prove invariants of the system, which are then used to strengthen the system to establish further invariants, as explained in Section 3.

4.1 Step 1

In a first step, we want to show that the property

$$\begin{aligned}&\texttt{excl\_granted} \Rightarrow \\ &(\forall i : \neg\texttt{sharer\_list}[i] \\ &\vee (\exists i : \texttt{sharer\_list}[i] \wedge \forall j : j \neq i \Rightarrow \neg\texttt{sharer\_list}[j]))\end{aligned} \tag{1}$$

which states that whenever variable `excl_granted` is set, then there is at most one process in `sharer_list`, is an invariant for the protocol.

In order to verify the property using our approach, we have to define an abstraction relation to be able to compute an abstraction. We use an abstraction relation, which is defined by a set of abstraction predicates φ_i as described in Section 3. Each of the following items corresponds to one (or more, depending on the encoding of the protocol into WS1S logic) of these abstraction predicates φ_i:

- the truth value of Formula 1,
- `excl_granted`,
- whether the size of the `sharer_list` is empty, one, or greater one,
- whether there are zero, one, or more then one processes which have a message `grant_exclusive` or `invalidate` message in their input channel, and
- whether there are zero, one, or more processes with cache set to `invalid` or `exclusive`.

Using this abstraction relation, we computed the abstract system automatically and verified Formula 1 to be invariant using model-checking techniques or a simple state exploration.

4.2 Step 2

Invariant 1 can now be used to strengthen the concrete system. This enables us to establish simultaneously seven new invariants.

Together, these properties further determine the behavior of the system, e.g., Formula 2 and 3 state that during the invalidation process, processes are not in `invalidate_list`. Formula 4 describes that the home process does not give grants to a client which it wants to invalidate. Formula 5 states that the `sharer_list` contains at least all processes which have shared or exclusive access, or have such a grant in their input channel, together with all processes which are not fully invalidated. Formula 6 specifies that no process is invalidated without a request which enforces invalidation. Formula 7 is similar to Invariant 1, and specifies the same property for `invalidate_list` instead of `sharer_list`. The last formula states that every `invalidate_ack` received by the home process is correct because the corresponding cache is indeed invalid.

$$\forall i : \neg(\texttt{invalidate\_list}[i] \wedge \texttt{chan2}[i] = \texttt{invalidate}) \tag{2}$$

$$\forall i : \neg(\texttt{invalidate\_list}[i] \wedge \texttt{chan3}[i] = \texttt{invalidate\_ack}) \tag{3}$$

$$\forall i : \neg(\texttt{chan2}[i] \neq \texttt{empty} \wedge \texttt{chan3}[i] = \texttt{invalidate\_ack}) \tag{4}$$

$$\begin{aligned} &\forall i : (\texttt{invalidate\_list}[i] \vee \texttt{chan2}[i] \neq \texttt{empty} \\ &\vee \texttt{chan3}[i] = \texttt{invalidate\_ack} \vee \texttt{cache}[i] \neq \texttt{invalid}) \\ &\Rightarrow \texttt{sharer\_list}[i] \end{aligned} \tag{5}$$

$$\begin{aligned} &(\exists i : \texttt{chan2}[i] = \texttt{invalidate} \vee \texttt{chan3}[i] = \texttt{invalidate\_ack}) \Rightarrow \\ &(\exists i : \texttt{sharer\_list}[i] \wedge \\ &((\texttt{command} = \texttt{req\_shared} \wedge \texttt{excl\_granted}) \\ &\vee \texttt{command} = \texttt{req\_exclusive})) \end{aligned} \tag{6}$$

$$\begin{aligned} &\texttt{excl\_granted} \Rightarrow \\ &(\forall i : \neg\texttt{invalidate\_list}[i] \\ &\vee \exists i : \texttt{invalidate\_list}[i] \\ &\wedge (\forall j : j \neq i \Rightarrow \neg\texttt{invalidate\_list}[j])) \end{aligned} \tag{7}$$

$$\forall i : \neg(\texttt{chan3}[i] = \texttt{invalidate\_ack} \wedge \texttt{cache}[i] \neq \texttt{invalid}) \tag{8}$$

Here, we use in this step an abstraction relation built as described in Section 3 using abstraction predicates φ_i

- for the truth value of each of Formulae 2-8,
- which encode the values of the home process variables `command`,
- and the values of variable `excl_granted`.

Using the constructed abstract system, the invariants are easily established by model-checking.

Most of these invariants were found during the verification process by examining *counter examples.* Whenever the abstraction was too weak to show the properties so far, the analysis of the counter example led to a new property which was hurt by the example, but seemed to be an invariant of the system. Therefore, we added a new formula φ_i to the abstraction relation and recomputed the abstraction. Since the construction of the abstract system is fully automatically, there is very little user interaction necessary for the reconstruction.

4.3 Step 3

In a third step we strengthen the system with all properties verified so far. We are now able to prove simultaneously two more invariance properties, the second being the coherence property.

We want to show invariance of the following properties *for each arbitrary process p.* The first one specifies that the home process is always aware of processes having exclusive access, the second one is the coherence property.

$$\texttt{cache}[p] = \texttt{exclusive} \Rightarrow \texttt{excl\_granted} \tag{9}$$

$$\texttt{cache}[p] = \texttt{exclusive} \Rightarrow (\forall j : j \neq i \Rightarrow \texttt{cache} \neq \texttt{shared}) \tag{10}$$

Since these properties are *universal properties* as explained in Section 3, we now use an abstraction relation which *focuses* on one arbitrary but fixed process p. This allows us to generalize the property to an invariant for all processes. The abstraction is based on abstraction predicates φ_i describing

- the truth value of the Formula 9 and 10,
- the value of the home variable `excl_granted`,
- the content of p's input channel `chan2`$[p]$,
- whether p is in the sharer list (`sharer_list`$[p]$), and
- p's cache status.

Computing the abstract system corresponding to this abstraction relation, it can easily be used to establish the Properties 9 and 10.

5 Liveness Properties

It is well known that an obstacle to the verification of liveness properties using abstraction, is that often the abstract system contains cycles that do not correspond to fair computations of the concrete system. A way to overcome this difficulty is to enrich the abstract system with fairness conditions or more generally ranking functions over well-founded sets that eliminate undesirable computations. We present a marking algorithm that given a concrete system, an abstraction relation, and the abstract system, enriches the abstraction with strong fairness conditions while preserving the property that to each concrete computation corresponds an abstract *fair* one. The enriched abstract system is used to prove liveness properties of the WS1S systems, and consequently, of the parameterized network.

Throughout this section, we fix a WS1S system $\mathcal{S} = (\mathcal{V}, \Theta, \mathcal{T})$ and an abstraction relation α given by a predicate $\widehat{\alpha}$. Then, let $\mathcal{S}_A = (\mathcal{V}_A, \Theta_A, \mathcal{T}_A)$ be the finite abstract system obtained by the method introduced in Section 3. We show how to add fairness conditions to $\mathcal{S}_A$ leading to a fair abstract system $\mathcal{S}_A^F$ which remains to be an abstraction of $\mathcal{S}$.

5.1 Marking Algorithm

We use WS1S formulae to express ranking functions. Let $\chi(i, X_1, \cdots, X_k)$ be a predicate with i as free 1st-order variable and $X_1, \cdots, X_k \in \mathcal{V}$ as free 2nd-order variables; we call such predicates *ranking predicate*. Given a state s of $\mathcal{S}$, i.e., a valuation of the variables in $\mathcal{V}$, the ranking value $\zeta(s)$ associated to s by ζ is the cardinality of $\{i \in \omega \mid \chi(i, s(X_1), \ldots, s(X_k))\}$.

The marking algorithm we present labels some of the abstract transitions with the symbols $+_\chi$ and $-_\chi$. Intuitively, an abstract transition τ_A is labeled by $-_\chi$, if it is guaranteed that the concrete transition τ associated with τ_A decreases the ranking value, i.e., $(s, s') \in \tau$ implies $\zeta(s) > \zeta(s')$. The label $+_\chi$ denotes that the τ *potentially increases* the ranking value. Otherwise, the transition is not marked.

Input: WS1S system $\mathcal{S} = (\mathcal{V}, \Theta, \mathcal{T})$, abstraction relation $\widehat{\alpha}$, abstraction $\mathcal{S}_A = (\mathcal{V}_A, \Theta_A, \mathcal{T}_A)$, set of ranking predicates $\chi(i, X_1, \cdots, X_k)$
Output: Labeling of $\mathcal{T}_A$
Description: For each $\chi(i, X_1, \cdots, X_k)$, for each edge $\tau_A \in \mathcal{T}_A$, let τ be the concrete transition in $\mathcal{T}$ corresponding to τ_A. Moreover, let $\Delta(\chi, \tau, \prec)$, with $\prec \in \{\subset, \subseteq\}$, denote the WS1S formula:

$$\widehat{\alpha}(\mathcal{V}, \mathcal{V}_A) \wedge \rho_\tau(\mathcal{V}, \mathcal{V}') \wedge \widehat{\alpha}(\mathcal{V}', \mathcal{V}'_A) \Rightarrow \{i \mid \chi'(i)\} \prec \{i \mid \chi(i)\} \ .$$

Then, mark τ_A with $-_\chi$, if $\Delta(X, \tau, \subset)$ is valid, and mark τ_A with $+_\chi$, if $\neg\Delta(X, \tau, \subseteq)$ is valid.

Then, since we have only finite sets, it is safe to add the fairness constraint that a transition labeled with $-_\chi$ can only be taken infinitely often, if also one of the transitions labeled with $+_\chi$ is taken infinitely often.

Now, for each ranking predicate χ we denote with I_χ (D_χ) the set of edges labeled with $+_\chi$ ($-_\chi$). Then, we add for each such χ the fairness condition (D_χ, I_χ) which states that a transition $\tau_A \in D_\chi$ can only be taken infinitely often if one of the transitions in I_χ is taken infinitely often.

Assume that we have a ranking predicate χ and the marking algorithm marks exactly one transition τ_1 with $-_\chi$, and two transitions τ_2 and τ_3 with $+_\chi$. Moreover, assume that we know that τ_2 definitely increases the ranking value of χ. Transition τ_3 may increase the value for some pre states, for other the ranking value decreases or is the same. If we would add the fairness constraint, that τ_1 can only be taken infinitely often, if also τ_2 is taken infinitely often, we may remove behavior for the abstract system, which has a concrete counter part, namely computations where τ_3 is taken infinitely often in the right pre state, where the ranking value increases.

We will now apply this theory to prove two liveness properties of the cache coherence protocol, namely, that process requests for exclusive (resp. shared) access will be granted eventually.

Abstractions and fairness constraints. To be able to express the fairness constraints derived by the marking algorithm, it is required to be able to express which transition was taken in the last step. Therefore, all abstraction relations used in this section observe which transition τ was taken in the last step by abstract boolean variables $taken_\tau$.

This can be done syntactically, since one can denote, for each computed abstract transition, which is the corresponding concrete transition. After computing the abstract system, one can now simply add an assignment to the new abstract variables assigning adequate values to them, encoding which transition was taken.

5.2 Liveness: Exclusive Access Response

Our goal is to verify that for each process p, whenever p requests for an exclusive access, then this access will eventually be granted by the home process. This is again a *universal property*, so we use again an abstraction relation which focuses on one arbitrary but fixed process p, built on abstraction predicates observing

- cache[p],
- chan1[p]-chan3[p],
- whether sharer_list[p] is set,
- whether p = current_client,
- the values of the home process variables command and excl_granted.

Moreover, we add to the abstract system boolean variables $taken_\tau$ encoding which transition was taken in the last step, as described in the previous section.

As presented in Section 5.1 we use the following ranking predicates:

$$\chi_1(i) \stackrel{\text{def}}{=} \texttt{invalidate\_list}[i] \qquad \chi_4(i) \stackrel{\text{def}}{=} \texttt{chan2}[i] \neq \texttt{empty}$$
$$\chi_2(i) \stackrel{\text{def}}{=} \texttt{sharer\_list}[i] \qquad \chi_5(i) \stackrel{\text{def}}{=} \texttt{chan3}[i] = \texttt{empty}$$
$$\chi_3(i) \stackrel{\text{def}}{=} \texttt{chan1}[i] = \texttt{empty}$$

Our tool computes for each transition τ and predicate χ_j, whether τ will definitely decrease the set of processes i for which $\chi_j(i)$ holds, or potentially increase this set. Thus, for each predicate χ_j we build two sets of transitions D_j and I_j. Since all the sets appearing in the formulae describing the system are finite for each instance of the parameterized network, no such instance can have a computation containing infinitely many transitions from D_j and only finitely many transitions from I_j.

Choosing ranking predicates. These predicates were easily found, since it is sufficient to examine each transition locally, searching for a predicate which decreases for this transition without knowing the behavior of the overall system! This can easily be done, because all the behavior of the system is encoded in the manipulation of sets, and usually it is fairly easy to find one of these sets M which decreases (so one can choose the ranking predicate $\chi(i) \stackrel{\text{def}}{=} i \in M$) or which increases (one can use $\chi(i) \stackrel{\text{def}}{=} i \in P \wedge i \notin M$, where P is a set containing all process indices) when the transition is taken.

One could also try to choose arbitrary sub-formulae appearing in the system description, and calculate their ranking behavior. If the result of such a formula is a useful fairness constraint, one can add it to the system. It is guaranteed, that the computed fairness constraint will be satisfied by every instance of the parameterized network, so it is safe to add the constraint to the abstraction. In the worst case, the fairness constraint does not rule out any behavior.

In our case we get the following results:

$$\begin{array}{ll} D_1 = \{h_3\} & I_1 = \{h_2\} \\ D_2 = \{h_4\} & I_2 = \{h_0, h_1\} \\ D_3 = \{c_1, c_2\} & I_3 = \{h_2\} \\ D_4 = \{c_3, c_4, c_5\} & I_4 = \{h_0, h_1, h_3\} \\ D_5 = \{c_3\} & I_5 = \{h_4\} \end{array} \qquad (11)$$

For example, we derived from D_4 and I_4 the following fairness constraint:

$$\psi_4 \stackrel{\text{def}}{=} GF(taken_{c_3} \vee taken_{c_4} \vee taken_{c_5}) \Rightarrow GF(taken_{h_0} \vee taken_{h_1} \vee taken_{h_3})$$

Obviously, we also have to rule out taking transition c_0 forever, this can be done with another simple fairness constraint.

It turns out that the computed fairness constraints are too weak to show the liveness property, since it is possible that the home process just never reads the request of a single client, only processing requests of the other clients. Therefore, we have to assume chan1[p] to be fair, so that if home has infinitely often the possibility to read the request of process p, then eventually this will be done.

Assuming these fairness constraints, we can easily prove the exclusive response property.

5.3 Liveness: Shared Access Response

We now prove that also requests for *shared* access will eventually be granted. The same abstraction relation as in Section 5.2 can be used. It turns out, that even with all fairness constraints given in Section 5.2, the property cannot be proven. Examining a counter example, we found a further ranking predicate missing, namely

$$\chi_6(i) \stackrel{\text{def}}{=} \texttt{chan2}[i] = \texttt{empty} \ .$$

The fairness constraint derived from this predicate allows to rule out some traces where h_0, h_1, or h_3 are taken infinitely often and neither c_3, c_4, nor c_5 are.

Even this is not sufficient: assuming this fairness constraint enables us to show that eventually a shared grant will be sent from home, but it is possible that this grant will never be read from process p. But if we also assume chan2[p] to be fair (or we assume that each process will eventually make a step), then shared access response can be established.

6 Conclusions

We have presented a verification method for parameterized networks. Our approach is based on modeling the infinite family of finite state systems as one single higher order WS1S transition system. This system is then automatically finitely abstracted and model-checked. To verify also liveness properties, we presented an algorithm to enrich the abstract system with fairness conditions which are guaranteed to be valid in the concrete system. This method is implemented in an experimental tool called PAX, which uses MONA to decide WS1S formulae. We have applied the method to a non-trivial example of a cache coherence protocol and proved both safety and liveness properties. The results are very encouraging.

References

[ABJN99] P.A. Abdulla, A. Bouajjani, B. Jonsson, and M. Nilsson. Handling Global Conditions in Parameterized System Verification. In N. Halbwachs and D. Peled, editors, *CAV '99*, volume 1633 of *LNCS*, pages 134–145. Springer, 1999.

[AK86] K. Apt and D. Kozen. Limits for Automatic Verification of Finit-State Concurrent Systems. *Information Processing Letters*, 22(6):307–309, 1986.

[BBLS00] K. Baukus, S. Bensalem, Y. Lakhnech, and K. Stahl. Abstracting WS1S Systems to Verify Parameterized Networks. In S. Graf and M. Schwartzbach, editors, *TACAS'00*, volume 1785, pages 188 – 203. Springer, 2000.

[BCG89] M.C. Browne, E.M. Clarke, and O. Grumberg. Reasoning about networks with many identical finite state processes. *Information and Computation*, 1989.

[BLS00] K. Baukus, Y. Lakhnech, and K. Stahl. Verifying Universal Properties of Parameterized Networks. In M. Joseph, editor, *FTRTFT'00*, volume 1926, pages 291 – 304. Springer, 2000.

[Büc60] J.R. Büchi. Weak Second-Order Arithmetic and Finite Automata. *Z. Math. Logik Grundl. Math.*, 6:66–92, 1960.

[CGL94] E. M. Clarke, O. Grumberg, and D. E. Long. Model checking and abstraction. *ACM Transactions on Programming Languages and Systems*, 16(5), 1994.

[DGG94] D. Dams, R. Gerth, and O. Grumberg. Abstract interpretation of reactive systems: Abstractions preserving ACTL*, ECTL* and CTL*. In E.-R. Olderog, editor, *Proceedings of PROCOMET '94*. North-Holland, 1994.

[EK00] E. Allen Emerson and Vineet Kahlon. Reducing model checking of the many to the few. In *CADE 2000*, pages 236–254, 2000.

[Elg61] C.C. Elgot. Decision problems of finite automata design and related arithmetics. *Trans. Amer. Math. Soc.*, 98:21–52, 1961.

[EN95] E. A. Emerson and K. S. Namjoshi. Reasoning about rings. In *22nd ACM Symposium on Principles of Programming Languages*, pages 85–94, 1995.

[EN96] E. A. Emerson and K. S. Namjoshi. Automatic verification of parameterized synchronous systems. In *8th Conference on Computer Aided Verification*, LNCS 1102, pages 87–98, 1996.

[GS92] S.M. German and A.P. Sistla. Reasoning about systems with many processes. *Journal of the ACM*, 39(3):675–735, 1992.

[HJJ+96] J.G. Henriksen, J. Jensen, M. Jørgensen, N. Klarlund, B. Paige, T. Rauhe, and A. Sandholm. Mona: Monadic Second-Order Logic in Practice. In *TACAS '95*, volume 1019 of *LNCS*. Springer, 1996.

[HLR92] N. Halbwachs, F. Lagnier, and C. Ratel. An experience in proving regular networks of processes by modular model checking. *Acta Informatica*, 22(6/7), 1992.

[JN00] B. Jonsson and M. Nilsson. Transitive closures of regular relations for verifying infinite-state systems. In S. Graf and M. Schwartzbach, editors, *TACAS'00*, volume 1785. Lecture Notes in Computer Science, 2000.

[KM89] R.P. Kurshan and K. McMillan. A structural induction theorem for processes. In *ACM Symp. on Principles of Distributed Computing, Canada*, pages 239–247, Edmonton, Alberta, 1989.

[KMM+97] Y. Kesten, O. Maler, M. Marcus, A. Pnueli, and E. Shahar. Symbolic Model Checking with Rich Assertional Languages. In O. Grumberg, editor, *Proceedings of CAV '97*, volume 1256 of *LNCS*, pages 424–435. Springer, 1997.

[LGS+95] C. Loiseaux, S. Graf, J. Sifakis, A. Bouajjani, and S. Bensalem. Property preserving abstractions for the verification of concurrent systems. *Formal Methods in System Design*, 6(1), 1995.

[LHR97] D. Lesens, N. Halbwachs, and P. Raymond. Automatic verification of parameterized linear networks of processes. In *POPL '97*, Paris, 1997.

[PRZ01] Pnueli, Ruah, and Zuck. Automatic deductive verification with invisible invariants. In *TACAS: International Workshop on Tools and Algorithms for the Construction and Analysis of Systems, LNCS*, 2001.

[SG89] Z. Stadler and O. Grumberg. Network grammars, communication behaviours and automatic verification. In *Proc. Workshop on Automatic Verification Methods for Finite State Systems*, Lecture Notes in Computer Science, pages 151–165, Grenoble, France, 1989. Springer Verlag.

[Tho90] W. Thomas. Automata on infinite objects. In *Handbook of Theoretical Computer Science, Volume B: Formal Methods and Semantics*, pages 134–191. Elsevier Science Publishers B. V., 1990.

[WL89] P. Wolper and V. Lovinfosse. Verifying properties of large sets of processes with network invariants (extended abstract). In Sifakis, editor, *Workshop on Computer Aided Verification*, LNCS 407, pages 68–80, 1989.

Author Index

Barthe, Gilles, 32
Baukus, Kai, 317
Bernardeschi, Cinzia, 1
Bruynooghe, Maurice, 167

Catthoor, Francky, 167
Charatonik, Witold, 109
Cimatti, Alessandro, 196
Codish, Michael, 126
Coppo, Mario, 255

Dezani-Ciancaglini, Mariangiola, 255
Dufay, Guillaume, 32

Faella, Marco, 94
Focardi, Riccardo, 16
Francesco, Nicoletta De, 1

Gallagher, John, 126
Genaim, Samir, 126
Gori, Roberta, 225

Harding, Aidan, 289
Hill, Patricia M., 154
Huth, Michael, 302

Jakubiec, Line, 32
Janssens, Gerda, 167

Kesten, Yonit, 208
Krstić, Sava, 182

Lagoon, Vitaly, 126
Lakhnech, Yassine, 317
Levi, Giorgio, 225

Matthews, John, 182
Melo de Sousa, Simão, 32
Mukhopadhyay, Supratik, 109
Murano, Aniello, 94, 240
Murawski, Andrzej S., 139

Napoli, Margherita, 240

Piazza, Carla, 16
Pistore, Marco, 196
Pnueli, Amir, 208
Podelski, Andreas, 109

Rossi, Sabina, 16
Roveri, Marco, 196
Ryan, Mark, 289

Schobbens, Pierre-Yves, 289
Sebastiani, Roberto, 196
Shyamasundar, R.K., 46
Sidorova, Natalia, 79
Spoto, Fausto, 154
Stahl, Karsten, 317
Steffen, Martin, 79

Tan, Li, 65
Ţiplea, Aurora, 272
Ţiplea, Ferucio Laurenţiu, 272
Torre, Salvatore La, 94, 240
Tronçon, Remko, 167

Yi, Kwangkeun, 139

Zuck, Lenore, 208

Lecture Notes in Computer Science

For information about Vols. 1–2248
please contact your bookseller or Springer-Verlag

Vol. 2248: C. Boyd (Ed.), Advances in Cryptology – ASIACRYPT 2001. Proceedings, 2001. XI, 603 pages. 2001.

Vol. 2249: K. Nagi, Transactional Agents. XVI, 205 pages. 2001.

Vol. 2250: R. Nieuwenhuis, A. Voronkov (Eds.), Logic for Programming, Artificial Intelligence, and Reasoning. Proceedings, 2001. XV, 738 pages. 2001. (Subseries LNAI).

Vol. 2251: Y.Y. Tang, V. Wickerhauser, P.C. Yuen, C.Li (Eds.), Wavelet Analysis and Its Applications. Proceedings, 2001. XIII, 450 pages. 2001.

Vol. 2252: J. Liu, P.C. Yuen, C. Li, J. Ng, T. Ishida (Eds.), Active Media Technology. Proceedings, 2001. XII, 402 pages. 2001.

Vol. 2253: T. Terano, T. Nishida, A. Namatame, S. Tsumoto, Y. Ohsawa, T. Washio (Eds.), New Frontiers in Artificial Intelligence. Proceedings, 2001. XXVII, 553 pages. 2001. (Subseries LNAI).

Vol. 2254: M.R. Little, L. Nigay (Eds.), Engineering for Human-Computer Interaction. Proceedings, 2001. XI, 359 pages. 2001.

Vol. 2255: J. Dean, A. Gravel (Eds.), COTS-Based Software Systems. Proceedings, 2002. XIV, 257 pages. 2002.

Vol. 2256: M. Stumptner, D. Corbett, M. Brooks (Eds.), AI 2001: Advances in Artificial Intelligence. Proceedings, 2001. XII, 666 pages. 2001. (Subseries LNAI).

Vol. 2257: S. Krishnamurthi, C.R. Ramakrishnan (Eds.), Practical Aspects of Declarative Languages. Proceedings, 2002. VIII, 351 pages. 2002.

Vol. 2258: P. Brazdil, A. Jorge (Eds.), Progress in Artificial Intelligence. Proceedings, 2001. XII, 418 pages. 2001. (Subseries LNAI).

Vol. 2259: S. Vaudenay, A.M. Youssef (Eds.), Selected Areas in Cryptography. Proceedings, 2001. XI, 359 pages. 2001.

Vol. 2260: B. Honary (Ed.), Cryptography and Coding. Proceedings, 2001. IX, 416 pages. 2001.

Vol. 2261: F. Naumann, Quality-Driven Query Answering for Integrated Information Systems. X, 166 pages. 2002.

Vol. 2262: P. Müller, Modular Specification and Verification of Object-Oriented Programs. XIV, 292 pages. 2002.

Vol. 2263: T. Clark, J. Warmer (Eds.), Object Modeling with the OCL. VIII, 281 pages. 2002.

Vol. 2264: K. Steinhöfel (Ed.), Stochastic Algorithms: Foundations and Applications. Proceedings, 2001. VIII, 203 pages. 2001.

Vol. 2265: P. Mutzel, M. Jünger, S. Leipert (Eds.), Graph Drawing. Proceedings, 2001. XV, 524 pages. 2002.

Vol. 2266: S. Reich, M.T. Tzagarakis, P.M.E. De Bra (Eds.), Hypermedia: Openness, Structural Awareness, and Adaptivity. Proceedings, 2001. X, 335 pages. 2002.

Vol. 2267: M. Cerioli, G. Reggio (Eds.), Recent Trends in Algebraic Development Techniques. Proceedings, 2001. X, 345 pages. 2001.

Vol. 2268: E.F. Deprettere, J. Teich, S. Vassiliadis (Eds.), Embedded Processor Design Challenges. VIII, 327 pages. 2002.

Vol. 2269: S. Diehl (Ed.), Software Visualization. Proceedings, 2001. VIII, 405 pages. 2002.

Vol. 2270: M. Pflanz, On-line Error Detection and Fast Recover Techniques for Dependable Embedded Processors. XII, 126 pages. 2002.

Vol. 2271: B. Preneel (Ed.), Topics in Cryptology – CT-RSA 2002. Proceedings, 2002. X, 311 pages. 2002.

Vol. 2272: D. Bert, J.P. Bowen, M.C. Henson, K. Robinson (Eds.), ZB 2002: Formal Specification and Development in Z and B. Proceedings, 2002. XII, 535 pages. 2002.

Vol. 2273: A.R. Coden, E.W. Brown, S. Srinivasan (Eds.), Information Retrieval Techniques for Speech Applications. XI, 109 pages. 2002.

Vol. 2274: D. Naccache, P. Paillier (Eds.), Public Key Cryptography. Proceedings, 2002. XI, 385 pages. 2002.

Vol. 2275: N.R. Pal, M. Sugeno (Eds.), Advances in Soft Computing – AFSS 2002. Proceedings, 2002. XVI, 536 pages. 2002. (Subseries LNAI).

Vol. 2276: A. Gelbukh (Ed.), Computational Linguistics and Intelligent Text Processing. Proceedings, 2002. XIII, 444 pages. 2002.

Vol. 2277: P. Callaghan, Z. Luo, J. McKinna, R. Pollack (Eds.), Types for Proofs and Programs. Proceedings, 2000. VIII, 243 pages. 2002.

Vol. 2278: J.A. Foster, E. Lutton, J. Miller, C. Ryan, A.G.B. Tettamanzi (Eds.), Genetic Programming. Proceedings, 2002. XI, 337 pages. 2002.

Vol. 2279: S. Cagnoni, J. Gottlieb, E. Hart, M. Middendorf, G.R. Raidl (Eds.), Applications of Evolutionary Computing. Proceedings, 2002. XIII, 344 pages. 2002.

Vol. 2280: J.P. Katoen, P. Stevens (Eds.), Tools and Algorithms for the Construction and Analysis of Systems. Proceedings, 2002. XIII, 482 pages. 2002.

Vol. 2281: S. Arikawa, A. Shinohara (Eds.), Progress in Discovery Science. XIV, 684 pages. 2002. (Subseries LNAI).

Vol. 2282: D. Ursino, Extraction and Exploitation of Intensional Knowledge from Heterogeneous Information Sources. XXVI, 289 pages. 2002.

Vol. 2283: T. Nipkow, L.C. Paulson, M. Wenzel, Isabelle/HOL. XIII, 218 pages. 2002.

Vol. 2284: T. Eiter, K.-D. Schewe (Eds.), Foundations of Information and Knowledge Systems. Proceedings, 2002. X, 289 pages. 2002.

Vol. 2285: H. Alt, A. Ferreira (Eds.), STACS 2002. Proceedings, 2002. XIV, 660 pages. 2002.

Vol. 2286: S. Rajsbaum (Ed.), LATIN 2002: Theoretical Informatics. Proceedings, 2002. XIII, 630 pages. 2002.

Vol. 2287: C.S. Jensen, K.G. Jeffery, J. Pokorny, Saltenis, E. Bertino, K. Böhm, M. Jarke (Eds.), Advances in Database Technology – EDBT 2002. Proceedings, 2002. XVI, 776 pages. 2002.

Vol. 2288: K. Kim (Ed.), Information Security and Cryptology – ICISC 2001. Proceedings, 2001. XIII, 457 pages. 2002.

Vol. 2289: C.J. Tomlin, M.R. Greenstreet (Eds.), Hybrid Systems: Computation and Control. Proceedings, 2002. XIII, 480 pages. 2002.

Vol. 2291: F. Crestani, M. Girolami, C.J. van Rijsbergen (Eds.), Advances in Information Retrieval. Proceedings, 2002. XIII, 363 pages. 2002.

Vol. 2292: G.B. Khosrovshahi, A. Shokoufandeh, A. Shokrollahi (Eds.), Theoretical Aspects of Computer Science. IX, 221 pages. 2002.

Vol. 2293: J. Renz, Qualitative Spatial Reasoning with Topological Information. XVI, 207 pages. 2002. (Subseries LNAI).

Vol. 2294: A. Cortesi (Ed.), Verification, Model Checking, and Abstract Interpretation. Proceedings, 2002. VIII, 331 pages. 2002.

Vol. 2295: W. Kuich, G. Rozenberg, A. Salomaa (Eds.), Developments in Language Theory. Proceedings, 2001. IX, 389 pages. 2002.

Vol. 2296: B. Dunin-Kęplicz, E. Nawarecki (Eds.), From Theory to Practice in Multi-Agent Systems. Proceedings, 2001. IX, 341 pages. 2002. (Subseries LNAI).

Vol. 2297: R. Backhouse, R. Crole, J. Gibbons (Eds.), Algebraic and Coalgebraic Methods in the Mathematics of Program Construction. Proceedings, 2000. XIV, 387 pages. 2002.

Vol. 2299: H. Schmeck, T. Ungerer, L. Wolf (Eds.), Trends in Network and Pervasive Computing – ARCS 2002. Proceedings, 2002. XIV, 287 pages. 2002.

Vol. 2300: W. Brauer, H. Ehrig, J. Karhumäki, A. Salomaa (Eds.), Formal and Natural Computing. XXXVI, 431 pages. 2002.

Vol. 2301: A. Braquelaire, J.-O. Lachaud, A. Vialard (Eds.), Discrete Geometry for Computer Imagery. Proceedings, 2002. XI, 439 pages. 2002.

Vol. 2302: C. Schulte, Programming Constraint Services. XII, 176 pages. 2002. (Subseries LNAI).

Vol. 2303: M. Nielsen, U. Engberg (Eds.), Foundations of Software Science and Computation Structures. Proceedings, 2002. XIII, 435 pages. 2002.

Vol. 2304: R.N. Horspool (Ed.), Compiler Construction. Proceedings, 2002. XI, 343 pages. 2002.

Vol. 2305: D. Le Métayer (Ed.), Programming Languages and Systems. Proceedings, 2002. XII, 331 pages. 2002.

Vol. 2306: R.-D. Kutsche, H. Weber (Eds.), Fundamental Approaches to Software Engineering. Proceedings, 2002. XIII, 341 pages. 2002.

Vol. 2307: C. Zhang, S. Zhang, Association Rule Mining. XII, 238 pages. 2002. (Subseries LNAI).

Vol. 2308: I.P. Vlahavas, C.D. Spyropoulos (Eds.), Methods and Applications of Artificial Intelligence. Proceedings, 2002. XIV, 514 pages. 2002. (Subseries LNAI).

Vol. 2309: A. Armando (Ed.), Frontiers of Combining Systems. Proceedings, 2002. VIII, 255 pages. 2002. (Subseries LNAI).

Vol. 2310: P. Collet, C. Fonlupt, J.-K. Hao, E. Lutton, M. Schoenauer (Eds.), Artificial Evolution. Proceedings, 2001. XI, 375 pages. 2002.

Vol. 2311: D. Bustard, W. Liu, R. Sterritt (Eds.), SoftWare 2002: Computing in an Imperfect World. Proceedings, 2002. XI, 359 pages. 2002.

Vol. 2312: T. Arts, M. Mohnen (Eds.), Implementation of Functional Languages. Proceedings, 2001. VII, 187 pages. 2002.

Vol. 2313: C.A. Coello Coello, A. de Albornoz, L.E. Sucar, O.Cairó Battistutti (Eds.), MICAI 2002: Advances in Artificial Intelligence. Proceedings, 2002. XIII, 548 pages. 2002. (Subseries LNAI).

Vol. 2314: S.-K. Chang, Z. Chen, S.-Y. Lee (Eds.), Recent Advances in Visual Information Systems. Proceedings, 2002. XI, 323 pages. 2002.

Vol. 2315: F. Arhab, C. Talcott (Eds.), Coordination Models and Languages. Proceedings, 2002. XI, 406 pages. 2002.

Vol. 2316: J. Domingo-Ferrer (Ed.), Inference Control in Statistical Databases. VIII, 231 pages. 2002.

Vol. 2317: M. Hegarty, B. Meyer, N. Hari Narayanan (Eds.), Diagrammatic Representation and Inference. Proceedings, 2002. XIV, 362 pages. 2002. (Subseries LNAI).

Vol. 2318: D. Bošnački, S. Leue (Eds.), Model Checking Software. Proceedings, 2002. X, 259 pages. 2002.

Vol. 2319: C. Gacek (Ed.), Software Reuse: Methods, Techniques, and Tools. Proceedings, 2002. XI, 353 pages. 2002.

Vol. 2322: V. Mařík, O. Stěpánková, H. Krautwurmová, M. Luck (Eds.), Multi-Agent Systems and Applications II. Proceedings, 2001. XII, 377 pages. 2002. (Subseries LNAI).

Vol. 2324: T. Field, P.G. Harrison, J. Bradley, U. Harder (Eds.), Computer Performance Evaluation. Proceedings, 2002. XI, 349 pages. 2002.

Vol. 2329: P.M.A. Sloot, C.J.K. Tan, J.J. Dongarra, A.G. Hoekstra (Eds.), Computational Science – ICCS 2002. Proceedings, Part I. XLI, 1095 pages. 2002.

Vol. 2330: P.M.A. Sloot, C.J.K. Tan, J.J. Dongarra, A.G. Hoekstra (Eds.), Computational Science – ICCS 2002. Proceedings, Part II. XLI, 1115 pages. 2002.

Vol. 2331: P.M.A. Sloot, C.J.K. Tan, J.J. Dongarra, A.G. Hoekstra (Eds.), Computational Science – ICCS 2002. Proceedings, Part III. XLI, 1227 pages. 2002.

Vol. 2332: L. Knudsen (Ed.), Advances in Cryptology – EUROCRYPT 2002. Proceedings, 2002. XII, 547 pages. 2002.

Vol. 2334: G. Carle, M. Zitterbart (Eds.), Protocols for High Speed Networks. Proceedings, 2002. X, 267 pages. 2002.